A FIGHTING
WITHDRAWAL

A FIGHTING WITHDRAWAL

The Life of Dan Davin

WRITER, SOLDIER, PUBLISHER

KEITH OVENDEN

Oxford   New York

OXFORD UNIVERSITY PRESS

1996

Oxford University Press, Walton Street, Oxford OX2 6DP

Oxford New York
Athens Auckland Bangkok Bombay
Calcutta Cape Town Dar es Salaam Delhi
Florence Hong Kong Istanbul Karachi
Kuala Lumpur Madras Madrid Melbourne
Mexico City Nairobi Paris Singapore
Taipei Tokyo Toronto
and associated companies in
Berlin Ibadon

Oxford is a trade mark of Oxford University Press

British Library Cataloguing in Publication Data
Data available

Library of Congress Cataloging in Publication Data
Ovenden, Keith.
A fighting withdrawal : the life of Dan Davin, writer,
soldier, publisher / Keith Ovenden.
Includes bibliographical references and index.
1. Davin, Dan, 1913–1990—Biography.
2. Novelists, New Zealand—20th century—Biography.
3. Publishers and publishing—Great Britain—Biography.
4. Oxford University Press—Employees—Biography.
5. World War, 1939–1945—New Zealand.
6. Soldiers—New Zealand—Biography. I. Title.
PR9639.3.D35Z8 1996 823—dc20 95-38093
ISBN 0-19-212335-1

1 3 5 7 9 10 8 6 4 2

Typeset by Pure Tech India Limited, Pondicherry
Printed in Great Britain
on acid-free paper by
Biddles Ltd.
Guildford and King's Lynn

for Helen

'Madonna, mia bisogna
voi conoscete, e ciò ch'ad essa è buono.'

Ed ella a me: 'Da tema e da vergogna
voglio che tu omai ti disviluppe,
Sì che non parli più com' uom che sogna.'

(Dante, *Purgatorio*, xxxiii. 29–33)

In my arrogant youth I had wanted to be a 'universal' writer-poet, historian, novelist. It was only gradually that I realised that, after one's twenties, life is a fighting withdrawal . . .

(Dan Davin, 'My Language and Myself', *Round Table*, no. 261 (1976), 22)

One hears about life, all the time, from different people, with very different narrative gifts. Accordingly, not only are many episodes, in which you may even have played a part yourself, hard enough to assess; a lot more must be judged from haphazard accounts given by others. Even if reported in good faith, some choose one aspect on which to concentrate, some another.

(Anthony Powell, *Temporary Kings*, 256–7)

PREFACE

Dan Davin was born eleven months before the start of the First World War and died eleven months after the breaching of the Berlin Wall. His life thus conforms exactly to what Hobsbawn has recently called 'The Short Twentieth Century'. Since I subscribe to Ulick O'Connor's view that biography is akin to portraiture, this biography of Davin may be read as, so to speak, a detailed portrait to set alongside the broad brush canvas of Hobsbawm's *The Age of Extremes* (1994).

This may seem a large claim for a relatively obscure man. It is true that outside his native New Zealand Davin was never a famous or even a particularly public figure. His success as a writer, though considerable in New Zealand, was limited to progressive, bohemian, and academic literary circles in Britain. His life as a soldier, though he saw plenty of action, was important not in the annals of heroism or daring, but for its impact on him, and what he was then able to tell us about war and the men who make it. His influence as a publisher on both scholarship and scholarly publishing was immense, but outside the small circles preoccupied with such matters, not more widely known. Yet in each of these quite different fields of endeavour, and in all of them when fused together in the singular character of his own world of friendship, his life was an expression of the age. The *Zeitgeist* burns in him. To follow his life is to relive the century of its living.

I should say that in some measure this proposal is *post hoc. A Fighting Withdrawal* was in an advanced stage of composition when Hobsbawm's book was published, and I did not read it until my own work was finished. Even so, perhaps especially so, the fit is striking. I might well have divided the text of Davin's life into the three parts Hobsbawm calls 'The Age of Catastrophe', 'The Golden Age', and 'The Landslide', so well do the divisions apply to the individual as well as his times.

The perception reinforces what we ought, from time to time, to remind ourselves of: that biography is a branch of history, the master, or indeed mistress, of all knowledge. In recent years the popularity of biography has led to the laying of large and diverse claims and counter-claims about the nature of biographical truth, the intentions, purposes, even silent or secret agendas, of biographers, and the underlying significance of the biographical text as cultural signifier. In this, as in other areas of contemporary letters, the arguments of cultural critics enfold each other like Russian dolls. Among practitioners, the debate has tended to be more practical, if only because all biographers know that art requires discipline as well as inspiration, and that in the historical arts the requirements of historical truth, the accumulation and assessment of factual evidence, and a strategy of design in composition must take precedence over other considerations. None the less, it is surely true to say that there is currently widespread sympathy for, if not agreement with, the proposition advanced by Richard Holmes in a memorable passage, that biography is concerned with 'the kind of human truth, poised between fact and fiction, which a biographer can obtain as he tells the story of another's life, and thereby makes it both his own (like a friendship) and the public's (like a betrayal). It asks what we can know, and what we can believe, and finally what we can love.'[1]

I have puzzled over this penetrating insight, sometimes in partial agreement with it, sometimes loath to adopt its more troublesome implications, particularly in the matter of friendship and betrayal. The moral implications of one's actions apply to one's contemporaries. We cannot be responsible for those who went before us (though we may have some moral obligation to alleviate the consequences of wrongs that they perpetrated) and such merit as any past life may have for us now is exemplary. Perhaps as key to what he means, Holmes also writes that the central tenet of biography is empathy, making it 'essentially a Romantic form'.[2]

This argument is troubling. Empathy is surely a quintessentially twentieth-century notion drawn from the lexicon of German psychology, and proposing the possibility of projecting one's own personality into an object of contemplation in order fully to understand it. It may well be that this doctrine now dominates the writing—and perhaps the reading too—of biography, and if so it can only be helpful to any reader approaching *A Fighting Withdrawal* to say at the outset that I do not adhere to it. Like Anthony Powell, and Davin himself, I accept that insight acquired through attempts at empathy are at best self-deception, at worst delusion. The best that we can hope to achieve by a steady focus on the facts and constantly shifting evidence of a life is a sympathetic understanding of others and their circumstances. The great majority of terms and analytical devices that we habitually employ to define character and explain motivation, though they are certainly projections, seem to me to be pegs on which to hang our own prejudices, themselves born of ignorance or partial (mis)understanding. 'One passes through the world,' as Powell so

[1] Richard Holmes, *Dr. Johnson and Mr. Savage* (1993), 4–5.   [2] Ibid. 230.

succinctly puts it, 'knowing few, if any, of the important things about even the people with whom one has been from time to time in the closest intimacy.'[3]

From first to last in writing this book I have been able to remind myself of this truth by introspection. I knew Dan Davin, though far from intimately, for the last twenty-two years of his life. Though I was often abroad and he travelled less and less, we met fairly frequently and corresponded a little. I believed I knew him well, and it was my admiration for what I believed I knew that first led me to want to write his biography. In nearly four years of enjoyable research I discovered that I had not really known him at all, and that the figure whose life I can now document and describe in great detail remains bafflingly remote. I set this down at the start more as warning than disclaimer. I could not claim to catch his character, or grasp his motivation, because the closer one gets the more slippery these matters become. And in the large issues of his life, places of deception and privacy, the regions of friendship, love, and happiness, areas of depressive illness and preoccupation with death, the urgency of sexual desire, the determined, indeed heroic, resistance to systems of thought pretending to offer salvation whether temporal or spiritual, in all these matters the possibility of explanation seems even more remote at the end than it did at the beginning.

I have attempted to deal with this impediment by a method that, since I intend it to be innovative, may require guidance. In the construction of the book—which has similarities in my view to architecture—I have tried not only to lay foundations on which to erect the structure of the life, but also to meet the challenge of explanation which life poses with what I believe to be the two principal devices at the disposal of the biographer: sympathy and syntax. In syntax each phase of Davin's life is treated slightly differently, meeting in the flow of language the state of his mind and circumstances in so far as I have apprehended them myself. If I have done this as well as I dare to hope, the reader may discover for herself or himself some underlying, though unarticulated, awareness of the subject's own state of mind even in the absence of any other guidance from me. As James Joyce, one of Davin's earliest enthusiasms, demonstrated, there is far more to be exploited in language than just the meaning of words.

K.O.

8 April 1995

---

[3] Anthony Powell, *The Kindly Ones* (1962), 218.

ACKNOWLEDGEMENTS

I am principally indebted to Mrs W. K. (Winnie) Davin, who agreed that I should write a biography of her husband, allowed me access to his papers at her home in Oxford, and invited me to stay as a guest so that I might work in his study and eat at their table. She lent me innumerable documents from her own papers, and entrusted me with the recollections of a lifetime. The work would not have been possible without her. When the book was in final draft she read and commented on it both as participant and as experienced editor. It was immeasurably improved as a result. Her death on 26 March 1995, only a few days after the completion of this work, deprived her of the pleasure of its publication, to which she had long looked forward. I shall remember her friendship and intellectual companionship with pleasure and gratitude for the rest of my life.

I owe another debt to Davin's literary executor, his youngest daughter, Mrs Brigid Sandford Smith. She encouraged me from the start, and was a steady support throughout the sometimes difficult process of reading and interpreting her father's papers. Anna Davin, the oldest of the Davin daughters, and herself a historian, was the first in the family to encourage me to take up the project, and her support, like that of her sister Delia, I greatly value. Delia Davin was particularly helpful in bringing me together with Elizabeth Tylecote and in solving various problems. Each of the sisters also talked to me with generosity, humour, and insight about growing up with Dan and Winnie, and about their own adult lives as background to Dan's. Such difficulties as they may have encountered in this they concealed from me admirably.

The first suggestion that I should write Davin's life came from the New Zealand writer James McNeish, whom I have counted myself fortunate to have as a friend for many years. He found a willing ally in my wife Helen Sutch, who supported me with grace, sympathy, and enthusiasm (as the occasion demanded) through long research and arduous composition. She and our old friend John Ridge in Lancashire were resourceful in criticism and prodigal in tolerance.

In a less personal context I owe a debt of gratitude to the Queen Elizabeth II Arts Council of New Zealand which made its Non-Fiction Writing Bursary available to me in 1992. Without this support, which paid research expenses at a critical time, progress with the work would have been impeded. In particular I wish to thank Professor Terry Sturm

of Auckland University, and Ms Rosemary Wildblood, Manager of the Arts Council's Literature Programme, both of whom gave steady support to the project. I was also fortunate to receive financial assistance from the New Zealand History Research Trust Fund, which helped to defray expenses in 1993. I am glad of this opportunity to express both to the trustees, and to their advisers under Dr Jock Phillips in the Historical Branch of the Department of Internal Affairs, my sincere thanks.

In Dunedin I received help and advice from the staff of the Hocken Library, and the Library of the University of Otago, and hospitality from the then Registrar, Douglas Girvan, and also from the staff of St Margaret's College. George Griffiths at Otago Heritage Books, himself a historian of Otago and Southland, gave me guidance at an early stage. Dr Janet Wilson, of the English Department at the University of Otago, and her assistant in the New Zealand Cultural Studies Research Centre there, Candi Young, gave assistance on a number of occasions. The curators of the museums in Balclutha and Gore made me welcome.

In Wellington I have a debt to the librarian and staff of the Alexander Turnbull Library, and in particular the Curator of Manuscripts and Archives, David Colquhoun, and the Research Services Librarian of the Archives and Manuscripts Section, David Retter. I am grateful to Graeme Lay and the Sargeson Trust for permission to read the Sargeson papers; and to Bill Pearson and Maurice Shadbolt for permission to read their own personal papers, all of which are held in the Turnbull Library. Professor Vincent O'Sullivan of Victoria University drew my attention to Ian Milner's papers, which came to the Turnbull Library while my research was in progress. The staff of the New Zealand National Archives were helpful on all the occasions when I went to them for assistance. I am grateful to the New Zealand Vice-Chancellors Committee, Lindsay Taiaroa, the Executive Officer, and Ruth Edghill, the Special Projects Officer, for permission to read the minutes of the Rhodes Scholarship Selection Committee for 1934 and 1935. Hugh Templeton of the New Zealand Rhodes Scholarship Society was counsel, guide, and friend.

In Auckland, I am grateful to the Principal and staff of Sacred Heart College for permission to visit. Father Maurice Russell, Brother Gerard Hogg, and Brother Lawrence Bennett of the New Zealand Marist Brothers gave invaluable assistance.

In California, Professor Gordon Craig was most helpful, and I am grateful both to him and to Margaret J. Kimball, Head of Special Collections at the Cecil H. Green Library of Stanford University. In Washington, DC, William Sittig and Elizabeth Jenkins-Joffe of the staff of the Library of Congress were generous with their time and professional skill, which I greatly appreciated.

In London, Bruce Hunter of Higham Associates was a friend to this project from the beginning, and generously made the firm's private records available to me. I am also grateful to my literary agent, Michael Shaw, a friend of many years who knows what this work has cost as well as what it is worth.

In Oxford I am grateful for the generous assistance of Dr John Jones, Fellow-Archivist of Balliol College, and Ms Penelope Bullock and the staff of Balliol College Library; the Trustees of The Rhodes Trust, and Sir Anthony Kenny, Secretary, for permission to read in the Rhodes Trust Archives; Dr John Gurney of Wadham College for advice on the Bowra papers; and the Librarian and staff of the Bodleian Library. Oxford University Press did not commission this work, which went forward to publication in the customary way after an expert reader's review and ordeal by Delegates' Meeting. Davin liked to quote the historian G. M. Young: 'Being published by Oxford University Press is like being married to a duchess. The honour is rather greater than the pleasure.' I have no experience of duchesses, but the pleasure of work on the biography was greatly increased when Mr James Arnold-Baker, Secretary and Chief Executive of OUP, afforded me the privilege of unrestricted access to the Press archives. The book would not have been possible in anything like its present form without this unique opportunity. As an additional blessing of his generosity, I now count among my friends Mr Peter Foden, OUP's diligent, meticulous, and considerate archivist. The OUP librarian, Mrs Celia Clothier, welcomed me to her well-regulated domain with benevolent tolerance. It may not be necessary, but I think it appropriate, to state that at no time did any employee of OUP, past or present, exert any pressure on me to adapt my interpretation of Press affairs to suit objectives other than the scholarly.

Many people kindly agreed to talk to me about their experineces with Davin, many others wrote to me—sometimes at length and at some personal cost to themselves—and many also lent me correspondence, photographs, and other documents. I am particularly grateful in this regard to Mr Alan Bell, Sir Geoffrey Cox, Professor Gordon Craig, Mr Geoffrey Flavell, and Mrs Mollie Joseph, all of whom welcomed me to their homes as well as their confidence. The others to whom I have particular debts of gratitude are: Dave Arthur, Richard and Pauline Austin, Mollie Baird, Stephen and Margaret Baird, Denise Beerkens, Eric W. Belcher, John Bell, James Bertram, Margaret Black, Camilla

Boodle, Monsignor John Broadbent, Eric Buckley, Harriett Hawkins Buckley, Robert Burchfield, Laura Buxton, Richard Charkin, Mr Justice Cook, Bella Costello, Bob Cotterall, Antonia Davin, Martin Davin, Patrick Davin, Rachael Davin, Brian Easton, Noel (Wig) Gardiner, Helen Garrett, Gerard Hall-Jones, Bernard Hickey, Liz Hodgkin, Alan and Dorothea Horsman, Trevor James, Lawrence Jones, Philip Kaiser, Fred Kersh, Dr Tim Kidger, Elizabeth Knight, Janet Maconie, Michael King, Judith Lawrence, Hugh Lee, Peter Leech, Caroline Lewis, Godfrey Lienhardt, Ida Logan, Len Logan, Eric McCormick, Edward (Teddy) McCullough, James and Helen McNeish, Philip Manger, Elizabeth Mason, Hart Massey, O. E. (Ted) Middleton, David Mitchell, W. E. Murphy, Nuala O'Faolain, Vincent O'Sullivan, Janet Paul, Bill Pearson, Jock Phillips, David Pocock, Father Pound, Leonard Prager, Donald and Pat Prater, Bruce Purchase, Arthur Pyper, Michael J. Rabbitt, Vince Rabbitt, James Raeside, Ian Richards, George Richardson, Elspeth Sandys, Sally Savage, Maurice Shadbolt, J. M. (Murray) Sidey, Celia Sisam, Harry Smith, Raewyn Smith, Shirley Smith, Jon Stallworthy, Marion Steven, Tony Stones, Peter Sutcliffe, Rory Sweetman, Hugh Templeton, Malcolm Templeton, Lt.-Gen. Sir Leonard Thornton, Kathleen Tillotson, Brian Turner, Elizabeth Tylecote, Merle Van de Klundert, John Wain, Sir John White, John and Anne Willett, Sir Edgar (Bill) Williams, Janet Wilson, Michael Wolfers, Charles Zambucka.

In Paris Chris and Joy Beeby, old friends, facilitated my research with hospitality. Alistair Bisley and Lydia Wevers did the same for me in Geneva, and Donald and Pat Prater at Gingins. Denis McLean at the New Zealand Embassy in Washington was a source of practical help as well as intellectual encouragement. I am particularly grateful to my friends Dave Galler and Ema Aitken, and Gerald and Rina Kember in Auckland; Rob and Colleen Laking in Wellington; Jimmy and Eve Wallace in South Canterbury; Patrick Ensor and Judith Thomas, and Austin Mitchell and Linda MacDougall in London; Gerry and Edith Holtham in London, Oxford, and Nantymoel—all of whom generously supported me with tolerant good humour.

Parts of the manuscript were read in draft by Sir Geoffrey Cox, Dr Tim Kidger, David Mitchell, George Richardson, and Professor David Pocock. The whole manuscript was read by Alan Bell, Professor Gordon Craig, John Ridge, Kendrick Smithyman, Professor Jon Stallworthy, and Helen Sutch. Their corrections and suggestions have improved the work greatly. Such errors and omissions as remain are mine. The manuscript was read at the last by Anna Davin, Delia Davin, and Brigid Sandford

Smith. They know the extent of my gratitude without wanting it published—a view summed by one of Dan's early loves, Sir Walter Scott: 'Under all speech that is good for anything there lies a silence that is better.'

For permission to quote extracts from Anthony Powell's sequence of novels, *A Dance to the Music of Time*, the author and publisher are grateful to Anthony Powell and to Heinemann: *A Question of Upbringing*, pp. 54, 70, and 105; *A Buyer's Market*, p. 261; *The Acceptance World*, pp. 70, and 178; *At Lady Molly's*, p. 194; Casanova's *Chinese Restaurant*, p. 96; *The Kindly Ones*, pp. 11 and 13; *The Valley of Bones*, pp. 206 and 244; *The Soldier's Art*, p. 93; *The Military Philosophers*, p. 173; *Books Do Furnish a Room*, p. 19; *Temporary Kings*, pp. 229, and 256–7; *Hearing Secret Harmonies*, p. 76. Reprinted by permission of David Higham Associates.

Author and publisher are also grateful to the following for permission to quote from private correspondence: the estate of Brigid Brophy, letter to DMD of 1 November 1983; Arthur Crook, letter to DMD of 11 July 1968; Keving Ireland, letter to Maurice Shadbolt of 14 December 1978; Professor J. G. G. Ledingham, letter to Delia Davin of 3 June 1991; Maurice Shadbolt, letter to Eric McCormick of 19 December 1979; Tony Stones, letter to Noel ('Wig') Gardiner of 3 October 1990; the estate of Patty Watson, letter to DMD of 17 March 1988; and John Willett, letter to DMD of 30 August 1973.

CONTENTS

CONTENTS

LIST OF ILLUSTRATIONS

Between pages 234 and 235

Daniel and Nora Sullivan, Dan's grandparents, *c.*1916
DMDP

Patrick Davin and Mary Sullivan on their wedding day, 28 January 1907
DMDP

Five Davin children, Dan, Martin, Molly, Evelyn, and Tom, *c.*1917
Delia Davin

Marist Brothers' High School, Invercargill, 'examination successes' 1929
Father Pound

Otago University Latin picnic 1932
Photo: Norman Davis, contributed by Ida Logan

Winnie Gonley as provincial schoolteacher, *c.*1936
WKDP

Dan as he left New Zealand, 1936
Photo: Eileen Deste

Peggy Spence-Sales, *c.*1934
DMDP

Dan in Balliol, 1937
Photo: Gordon Craig

Arthur Pyper and Hart Massey, *c.*1938
Estate of Arthur Pyper

Americans of 'the short twentieth century': Rhodes Scholars Walt Rostow, Philip Kaiser, and Gordon Craig, Balliol, 1937
Gordon Craig

In the hills above Florence, July 1937
Photo: Winnie Davin, contributed by Helen Garrett

Winnie in the Rue Delambre, summer 1938
DMDP

Winnie with Delia, Brigid, and Anna, summer 1946
Photo: Teddy McCullough, contributed by Delia Davin

Dressed in the nick of time. Wedding day, Balliol quad., July 1939
DMDP

Paddy Costello, intelligence officer, 8 April 1943
Photo: Sir John White

Between pages 266 and 267

ABBREVIATIONS

AA	Anti-aircraft
ACV	Armoured Command Vehicle
ADS	Advanced Dressing Station
ATL	Alexander Turnbull Library, Wellington, New Zealand
BEF	British Expeditionary Force
BP	Dan Davin, *Brides of Price*, London: Hale, 1972
BS	Dan Davin, *Breathing Spaces*, London: Hale, 1975
CoF	Dan Davin, *Cliffs of Fall*, London: Nicholson & Watson, 1945
Coy HQ	Company headquarters
CP	Clarendon Press
Crete	Dan Davin, *Crete*, Official History of New Zealand in the Second World War 1939–1945, Wellington: War History Branch, Department of Internal Affairs, 1953
CT	Dan Davin, *Closing Times*, London: OUP, 1975
DMD	Dan Davin
DMDP	The Davin Papers, Alexander Turnbull Library
DNB	*Dictionary of National Biography*
FTROOL	Dan Davin, *For The Rest Of Our Lives*, London: Nicholson & Watson, 1947
GBP	Dan Davin, *The Gorse Blooms Pale*, London: Nicholson & Watson, 1947
GOC	General Officer Commanding
GSO 3 (I)	General Staff Officer, Grade 3, Intelligence
Hocken	The Hocken Library, Dunedin, New Zealand
IO	Intelligence Officer
LCV	Light Command Vehicle
MP	Military Police
NHNN	Dan Davin, *Not Here, Not Now*, London: Hale, 1970
NR	Dan Davin, *No Remittance*, London: Michael Joseph, 1959
OCTU	Officer Cadet Training Unit
ODT	*Otago Daily Times*
OED	*Oxford English Dictionary*
OUP	Oxford University Press
OUPA	Oxford University Press archives
POW	Prisoner of War

RAMC	Royal Army Medical Corps
RAP	Regimental Aid Post
RFH	Dan Davin, *Roads From Home*, London: Michael Joseph, 1949
RMT	Reserve Mechanical Transport
RSA	Returned Servicemen's Association
RTA	Rhodes Trust Archives
SHC	Sacred Heart College, Auckland, New Zealand
SOED	Shorter Oxford English Dictionary
SS	Dan Davin, *Selected Stories*, London: Hale, 1981
TEWT	Tactical Exercise Without Troops
The Div.	2 NZ Division, the main fighting component of 2NZEF
TLS	*Times Literary Supplement*
TSB	Dan Davin, *The Sullen Bell*, London: Michael Joseph, 1956
TSF	Dan Davin, *The Salamander and the Fire*, Auckland: OUP, 1986
2NZEF	2nd New Zealand Expeditionary Force
UCL	University College London
WKD	Winnie Davin
WKDP	The Winnie Davin Papers, private collection

PART I

FAMILY AND CHILDHOOD,
SCHOOL-DAYS AND STUDENT LIFE
1913–1936

1

ORIGINS

All family trees are shady.
(From a speech by DMD to the American Association of
Academic Publishers, Baltimore, 12 June 1978)

Clearly some complicated process of sorting-out was in progress
among those who surrounded me: though only years later did I
become aware how early such voluntary segregations begin to
develop; and of how they continue throughout life.
(Anthony Powell, *A Question of Upbringing*, 70)

At the beginning was his name: Daniel Marcus Davin. He was to be
known variously as Dan, Daniel, Davin, DMD; but never Marcus. The
classical allusion of the silent middle name is suggestive of Marcus
Aurelius, the Roman author of the Greek *Meditations*, gloomy memo-
randa of stoic resistance to the fear of death. This reference would echo
to the end, but it was not intended. He was simply named after his
great-uncle Marcus, Marcus Davin of Ireland.

The Davins were Irish Catholic small-holders in Galway. The name
Davin comes from Gaelic, either from *damh*, meaning an ox or stag, or
from *dámh*, meaning a poet.[1] It originated in Co. Tipperary, and until the
late Middle Ages was the name of the Lords of Fermanagh, an aristocratic family that migrated south in the first half of the fifteenth century.
Of this noble line of descent only heraldic devices survived into the
nineteenth century, but both these and the family motto, *Fortiter et
Fideliter* (Strongly and Faithfully), were known to the Davin family in
New Zealand.

Dan's father Patrick was born at Tonegurrane, a tiny townland in the
parish of Corrandulla, Co. Galway, on 23 November 1877, one of the six
sons and five daughters of Thomas and Sarah Davin. Two of his siblings
died in infancy, two others migrated to the United States. His father died
when he was about 12. Patrick himself fled the poverty and superstition
of the 'old country' at the turn of the century, a solo migrant manual
labourer, more or less illiterate, though bilingual in Gaelic and English.
Later, a much younger brother Tom followed him, and kept a public

3

house at Opunake, on the sea at the foot of Mount Taranaki in the North Island of New Zealand. Apart from him, Patrick never saw any of his immediate family again.

The solitary character of this migration is suggestive, possibly of intense independence of spirit, possibly of some element of compulsion. 'Old Tom'—a childhood friend of Patrick—told Dan many years later that Patrick and his brother Mark had rebelled at school in Galway one day, refusing to be beaten by the expedient of knocking down the boy on whose back they were to have been flogged, and then assaulting the monk, their schoolteacher, before fleeing through the open window of the schoolhouse 'to defer their subsequent studies until after they'd emigrated.'[2] The tale rings true. Patrick was a tough enough character, remembered for a hard fist, an inflexible will, and a robust capacity for strong drink. But if, as a young man, he played the larrikin, New Zealand soon made him a fair though hard man, still tough, but more disciplined. In time he acquired a considerable reputation for Cumberland wrestling, the peculiarly courtly form of violent sport in which a formal embrace leads to a throw, and in which balance as well as great strength are required.

Patrick landed at Bluff, a deep-water port and fishing town, famous for its oyster beds, at the very southern tip of the South Island of New Zealand, and eighteen miles from Invercargill, the principal town of the province of Southland. It is hardly possible to go further from Galway, and there are few places on earth closer than this green isolation to the frozen continent of Antarctica, 1,500 miles away across the Southern Ocean. To this day visitors from Europe still feel, when they stand on the wharf at Bluff, that they have come as far as it is possible to go, that they are at the end of the world. It can be bitterly cold here. Sometimes you may feel that the drenching wind-swept rain will fall for ever. And then there are days when the air is still and warm, the sky a vast heavenly blue, and the light and horizon so clean and clear that they link you to the infinite, in grace as well as space.

Patrick's journey may have been solo, but it was not random. Like most migrants of the great Irish diaspora of the last quarter of the nineteenth century, he was following lines of escape laid down by the preceding generation. His father's oldest brother, John Davin, had been the first to come. He settled in East Gore, forty miles north-east of Invercargill, where he married Winnie Scully and they raised two daughters and a son. John's sister Julia followed, married to an O'Sullivan, and they too settled in East Gore, and also brought up two daughters and a son. Yet another of Patrick's aunts, Nora Davin, married to John Wyatt, also migrated to New Zealand where she and her husband settled in Greenhills, a small community on the track from Bluff to Invercargill. Dan remembered his father's account of how it was Aunty Wyatt who sent him the five sovereigns that paid for his voyage out.[3]

Patrick Davin, young and single as he was, came to a land of uncles and aunts, cousins and connections. The connections, like the extended family, were all provincial Catholic Irish, scattered over the small towns and rising hills of Southland and south Otago—the province to the north—not so much a community as a tribe, one that has been characterized as 'bound together by their fierce loyalty, rigid faith and common struggle against adversity'.[4] True to a point, but short of the full truth because these people also shared their wit and laughter, their love of story-telling from a common storehouse of legend and myth, and an unselfconscious pleasure in song and conversation. It is true that they brought with them their folk-grudge, Catholic against Protestant, and that old animosities, stirred by bigots on both sides, helped cement tribal loyalties. But these loyalties also had other, and more lasting roots:

migration . . . its pressures and exigencies, drove emigrant family members together, not apart; for society, for money, for protection, for chain migration schemes, for companionship in a common, large enterprise. Emigration welded them together, and also demanded they come out of themselves to face the new environment, itself diverting, outward-going.[5]

Irish Catholic community and family life was more cohesive, more practical, more secure in its affections in the new world of migrant endeavour than ever it had been at home in Ireland. One result was that first- and second-generation Irish New Zealanders grew up with an idea of 'home' distorted through the prism of romance, modern myths grown warm in the telling in a better environment.[6]

This was the new frontier, 'half the world from home',[7] to which Patrick Davin came. Like others of his tribe he was not long in bettering himself, seizing the opportunities that had been denied to him in Ireland. At first he worked as an itinerant labourer, doing everything from ditch-digging to rough carpentry, but by 1904, when he appears in the employment records of New Zealand Railways, hired as a labourer to work at Bluff, he had learned to read and write.[8] A Davin family story records that he returned to school when he must have been 26 or so, a grown man among the primers to learn his letters. Employment by the railways required not just literacy, but adjustments in ambition. The job brought security, but it meant abandoning whatever hopes Patrick may once have had for a farm, a dream that survived in his passion for gardening, and the smallholding that he later contrived to establish in his spare time from work.

In exchange, security opened up the possibility of marriage. Patrick Davin was a short man, but handsome, slim at the waist, muscular. As a young man he wore a smartly trimmed moustache, which with his clear eyes and open countenance made him a handsome match. In the bar of the Golden Eagle pub in Bluff he met Mary Sullivan, a Southland-born woman and, like himself, of Irish Catholic extraction.[9] They were married on 28 January 1907 in the Sacred Heart Church in Wellington.

Mary Magdalene Sullivan was born in the Georgetown district of Invercargill at the end of July 1878, the fourth child of Daniel and Nora Sullivan who had migrated four years earlier from Cork aboard the *Cory Castle*.[10] Though Daniel Sullivan was a tailor by trade, he would work at anything. At one time he was a navvy on the construction of the Kingston railway line, which took him away for months at a time. Eventually, under a land development scheme, the family established themselves as small farmers at Makarewa, an unpromising little place about twelve miles north-west of Invercargill on the road to Winton: 'Under enormous skies, the hills far off.'[11] Poor Catholics tended to settle on this side of Invercargill, which was a predominantly Scottish Presbyterian town, its streets named Tay, Spey, Esk, and Dee. The land was poorer here, so less sought-after, and there was still dense bush to clear, swamp to drain. This was subsistence farming of the most primitive kind, mixing poor housing with seven young children, and pioneer physical labour. Mary Sullivan's family circumstances and upbringing might suggest to a modern age little but hardship and suffering. Certainly there is a dour intensity apparent in the figures of her parents as they appear in one surviving photograph, 'the hard nose and the hard undoubting eyes'.[12]

Doubts or not, Mary's mother Nora was 'a tough old hen'[13] who spoke Gaelic as well as English, so that Mary grew up with the musical rhythms of Gaelic in her ears. And although her father Daniel could not speak Gaelic, and had no background as a farmer in Ireland, he appears to have been a strong, hard-working toiler. Furthermore the Sullivans, like Patrick Davin and his uncle and aunts, were escaping far greater privations at 'home' in Cork and Galway. Makarewa, with its glimpse of the distant Southern Alps on a crisp autumn morning, the cow or two to milk with raw hands in winter, the field of turnips for the stock and the vegetable garden for the family table, the few ewes to lamb amid the snow and mud of a September spring: for all its toil and difference, Makarewa represented improvement. The children were fed and clothed, the family and connections supportive. The ragged, malnourished, illiterate childhood of poor, exploited Catholic peasant life in Ireland, had been escaped. Nora Sullivan bore seven children: Jack, her oldest, in Ireland before migration; Ellen aboard the boat *en route* for Bluff; then Johanna, known as Annie, in 1876. After Mary came a son, christened Dan after his father; Honora, known as Nora, like her mother; and Margaret, known as Maggie. There was no still-born, and none died in infancy. They were not tall, but they were sturdy and healthy. As one impressionistic account puts it: 'food is plentiful, money is scarce, and everybody has to be careful.'[14]

Mary Sullivan, a child of her times, was educated only a little beyond literacy. Dan believed that his mother and her older sister Annie were the best pupils then attending the village school in Makarewa,[15] but at the age of 13 they had to leave. For girls of their class and Irish background in the 1890s life meant labour, and labour meant service. Ten years later, working as a parlour maid at a hotel, she first met Patrick Davin. We do not know how he courted her, or when it was she accepted his proposal of marriage. The implication of his quest for literacy and his subsequent employment by the Railways, is that there may have been terms and conditions. If so, he was a determined suitor, earning his reward. Nor do we know why it was that they were married in Wellington, 500 miles away to the north. The location suggests a possible family breach. Why else were they not married in Invercargill, where the Sullivan and Davin families from Gore, Makarewa, and Greenhills could easily have attended? A photograph of the occasion, staged and formal, shows Patrick and Mary, with her sister Annie, and his cousin John Wyatt, who was then working as a railway shunter driver in Wellington. The other celebrants in the picture are believed to be the Wellington publican Ryan, and his wife and daughter. The photograph captures the 'lace curtain Irish' aspirations of the colonial working class.

The idea of family antagonism seems hardly plausible in the context of Patrick's earnest commitment and Mary's devotion, both to her family and to her religion. Her church was St Mary's in Clyde Street—the only Catholic church in Invercargill until the Basilica was consecrated in 1905—and her faith the simple stern Jansenism that the New Zealand Catholic Church had imported with its peasant priesthood from Ireland. She seems to have been a superstitious young woman, easily worried, often anxious. Her rosary was a constant companion. She decorated the walls of the matrimonial bedroom with sacred hearts, and sprinkled her everyday conversation with reference to the holy family, the prospect of salvation, and a mortal terror of the fires of damnation.

Was this more style than content? Again, their wedding photograph suggests a gentle and straightforward affection, posed in the manner of the times, various ostriches stripped to decorate celebratory hats. And what money they spent, these working-class Edwardians, on the business of matrimony! Patrick Davin, the bridegroom, who proved 'a good husband' in the traditional sense—loyal, a hard-working breadwinner—though religious in his way, was never devout in the narrow-minded sense. Dan grew up to believe that Irish men were reticent about their feelings, while women had a duty to express them. He recalled that his father went to Mass every week, but to Communion, preceded by Confession, probably only once a year. 'He wasn't a very devout Catholic by any means, but on the other hand he'd probably have knocked anyone down who insulted the Pope.'[16] Reticent in word but demonstrative in action. In any event, the recollection may be faulty. Another schoolboy witness recalls visiting the family home and hearing 'the old man laying down the law'.[17]

What does seem incontestable is Patrick's compartmentalized world, a world of spheres: a woman's sphere at home, child-rearing, keeping the hearth; a man's sphere at work and in the garden; the priest's sphere in church, on Sundays and holy days, a place where children learned their morals, and a man might occasionally admit to himself that he had made a mistake, or been in the wrong. Mary accepted these spheres too, though her view of the Church was founded in superstition, etched with the fear of death and dread of judgement. Her religion was not a Sunday affair, but a daily companion, waking and sleeping. With its concentration on sin, the blood of the martyrs, and the uncertainty as well as difficulty of redemption, it is hard to believe that it brought her much comfort.

After marriage in Wellington Patrick and Mary returned to Southland, where Patrick still worked for the Railways at Bluff. They settled in the village of Makarewa, close to her parents and not far from her married sisters Ellen and Annie. Ellen had married Michael Concannon in February 1895, and they now had a farm at Woodlands, twelve miles to the north of Invercargill. By the time Mary and her bridegroom settled back in Southland in 1907 Ellen already had seven children, and was to have two more. Sister Annie, married to Harry Doley, had four children of her own. Here was a tribe of cousins to which the Davins quickly made addition. A first child, Evelyn, was born on 2 March 1908. Another daughter, Mary, known as Molly, followed on 2 May 1910. A year later, on 7 May 1911, came a first son, christened Thomas Patrick.

Daniel Marcus, fourth in line, second son, was born in his parents' bed at Makarewa on Monday, 1 September 1913.

Makarewa was not his home for long. When Dan was a year old his father was posted by the Railways to Gore, forty miles to the north-east, and the family moved there in the spring. Gore was a small town, first settled in 1862, and owing its subsequent existence to the railway, which bridged the Mataura River there in 1875.[18] By 1880 its population was 600. It became a borough in 1885—so it must have had at least 250 house-holders—and a road traffic bridge was erected beside the rail bridge in 1896, thereby safely linking the higher ground of East Gore, including, no doubt, Patrick's uncles and aunts, with the commerce of the town. Gore grew into a trading centre for the increasingly profitable farms of the Mataura Plain, with a Main Street of stock and station agents, banks, tradesmen and suppliers, and the railway station at its centre. Gore's biggest business was the Creamoata Mill, which began by making por-ridge oats and flour for the Scots of Southland and Otago, and became a major exporter. But even so, by the spring of 1914 when the Davin family arrived, it was still a small community, owing its prosperity to its position on the railway that linked it to the larger centres of commerce, south and north, in Invercargill and Dunedin.

Gore does not appear to have been a particularly safe place in which to live. In the first decade of the century it became known as 'the city of blazes' for the frequency and ferocity of its fires. Blocks of shops, stables, hotels, even the railway station itself in 1904, none was safe from the destruction. After the plague of fires came the floods. The Mataura River inundated the town to a depth of five feet on 29 and 30 March 1913, and did it again, though with somewhat less depth, a year later just as the citizens had begun debating the engineer's report on the first flood. It can have been little comfort to Mary Davin to find, on arrival, that their railwayman's cottage lay behind the railyards, close to the river.

Dan's father was now a guard, and rode the trains back and forth to Invercargill. The new work meant he came to live by the clock, his waistcoat watch a feature the children never forgot. He developed an instinct for the exact time of day, and, like railwaymen all over the world, could always tell what time it ought to be by the timbre of a whistle or hooter announcing the passage of a distant train. Dan grew up with the same instincts. Even as a boy he always knew the exact time, was a stickler for punctuality, and was easily lulled by the rumble and whistle of passing night-time trains. Life on the railways also meant that Dan's father worked irregular hours, with night shifts, and frequent periods away from home. The image of the father was passed down to the children. He did physically demanding and responsible work. He wore a uniform, which brought with it authority of the whistle-blowing, flag-waving kind. Often he was up and away early, home late. At the end of the week he turned over his wages to his wife, yet always had a bit of silver to jingle in his pocket. Punctuality; loyalty with independence; a willingness to accept responsibility; the importance of money. Dan absorbed these things as aspects of his own character, perhaps never seeing them explicitly as his father's legacy.

Away from work and religion, Patrick Davin's life was unexceptionable for a working man of the times. He liked a drink, but it was impossible to get one legally in Gore, which had been 'dry' since the Mataura electorate—in which it was located—voted for prohibition in 1902. As a result 'sly grog shops', where you could drink illegally, and the 'Hokunui hooch' and other illegally distilled or brewed liquors that found their way to the palates of thirsty topers, were a common or garden part of a small boy's expanding knowledge of his father's world. The *frisson* of excitement at breaking a law became entangled with the concept of authority in the mind of the growing child whose father occasionally slipped away for a drink, and, when the opportunity arose, one too many. Drink was a subject of interest.

So too were the events of the annual calendar of small town life. The Caledonian Society's annual sports meeting would offer Patrick his opportunity at Cumberland wrestling,[19] and his children the chance to see him excel. Gore was a noted centre of wrestling, and the contests on the Caledonian grounds 'attracted good crowds, and athletes from far and wide.'[20] Similarly, though for different reasons, the Agricultural and Pastoral Society's Annual Show drew crowds in a holiday atmosphere, and, like the annual race meetings at the Gore Racecourse, provided young eyes and minds with spectacle as well as a sense of community.[21]

All these experiences, the common fare of country life, were diminished for the young Davin children, however, by the supreme event of Dan's infant years: the First World War. Its course dominated domestic affairs for the four years from August 1914 to November 1918. Gore, with a small population, none the less lost scores of men to the slaughter. Its war memorial, like hundreds similar the length and breadth of the country, speaks eloquently of the distant carnage, and the weight of sorrow and loss that it returned to bereaved families. The little boy wrapped in the cocoon of a Catholic family and community, with several of his own extended family away at the war, and with the prayers and requiems offered for the living and the dead, grew up among the semi-tones of misunderstanding, mystery, and dread that war brings home to children. Warfare, distant and menacing, posed a threat, but not one that a 5-year-old could understand in anything other than vague forms: colours perhaps, sensations of exhilaration or dread. Reflections about this raise questions about how news of any kind might have reached him. Dan's family world was, by other standards, rather closed. The family subscribed to the Catholic weekly *The Tablet*, which circulated widely among Catholics. Despite its rabid Irish nationalism and bigoted Catholic opinion, it was a serious, even highbrow journal, raising doubts about the thoroughness with which it may have been read in working-class homes. In any event, it contained mainly commentary, and very little news. No doubt Patrick saw other papers as he plied back and forth on the main line, but for the rest of the family there were few sources of news other than word of mouth, rumour and gossip. These were to become of increasing interest to young Dan.

Most of the time, however, the outside world barely intruded. The Davin family, six young children and their hard-working parents, needed little encouragement to cultivate their own garden, either figuratively or in practical terms. Patrick Davin's interest in gardening was nothing out of the ordinary. To grow your own vegetables and raise a flower garden alongside was almost universal in the Southland working-class culture of the time. What set Patrick apart was his skill at it, a natural instinct for horticulture coupled with a deep knowledge of technique and seasonal tasks. He was a tireless provider, and the family rarely, if ever, ate a vegetable that he had not grown. Three square meals a day, plenty of tucker, a good feed, the Davin children always remembered the home table, and how they never went hungry.

From his earliest days Dan attached value to plants. As a toddler he imagined he had found a huge diamond among the carnations. Reaching to pick it up he slipped, and the shard of broken glass slit the skin of his right hand, between thumb and forefinger. The scar bothered him for years, so that when he learned to write he could never hold the pencil as others did, and so evolved a method of writing, and hence a script, that was strangely personal, sometimes hard to read.

On another occasion, as a boy of 5, he was so delighted with the profusion and beauty of the nasturtiums that he raided his mother's purse, and scattered the coins under the flowers, payment for looking so nice—just as his mother might give him a penny on Sundays for being well turned out himself. Beauty was to be rewarded.[22]

Perhaps here too, among the plants, there may have been some competition for his mother's attention. A younger brother, Martin, was born on 8 September 1914, when Dan was just one year and one week old. The new child, premature and frail, was not expected to live, and his mother was preoccupied with him. Matt, or Mutt, as he was known in the family, did survive, but his arrival, whether or not Dan was now weaned to make way for him, drastically altered his relationship with his mother. Three years later, on 15 September 1917, another brother, Patrick, arrived. Dan was now a 4 year-old, one of a crowd of six children in a small house, two of the others babies with first call on their mother's attention. As with large working-class familes everywhere, newcomers displaced predecessors into the company of older siblings, or into the solitude of their own devices.

Dan's older sisters, Evelyn and Molly, were 9 and 7 years old respectively by the time their youngest brother Pat was born. With their 6-year-old brother Thomas they were pupils at St Mary's Convent School on Ardwick Street. The school was run by the Sisters of Mercy. It had originally opened in East Gore—where most of the Gore Catholics then lived—in 1890, after a visit by the Catholic Bishop of Dunedin, Patrick Moran. It moved to its location in Ardwick Street in 1907, where a new Catholic church was opened on an adjacent site in 1913, and a nearby house purchased in 1917 to serve as a presbytery. By the 1920s there were three resident priests, as well as the nuns in charge of the school. This suggests a confident local Catholic community, expanding its range. The school had about a hundred and fifty pupils during the First World War. The three older Davin children all acquired there the sort of childish piety that made their younger brothers grimace with distaste long into adult life.

Their mother, on the other hand, superstitious, pious, protective of her brood, encouraged them in their 'goodness', their wish to become nuns or priest, or to seek martyrdom in the cause of the Virgin. A barrier grew up between the three little boys and the three older children. Their mother, with her flourbag apron, her coarse hands, her down-at-heel shoes, ever available, up and cooking before dawn, her arms and hands chapped raw from the winter-cold hard water of the weekly washing, certainly wanted her offspring, especially her daughters, to be different. The religious life represented an ideal: an enclave of purity, social standing, and safety in a world of dirt, hard work, and trouble. It was natural enough for her to harbour the dream that God might have given her some pure souls to nurture and give back to Him in life.

Her younger sons grew up unable to cherish this dream on behalf of their older siblings. Divisions grew. The two older girls lived one life, monitored by their mother. Thomas, the oldest boy, lived another, much directed and controlled by his father, but under the spell of his mother's religion. Dan, Martin, and Pat had a third: liberated, free, relatively unburdened, and with Dan and Matt a pair. Pat, four years younger than Dan, was a mischievous boy, a little resented by the other two for being their mother's favourite. Most of this lay in the future, but the foundations of these alignments were laid at Gore, when the children were still very young.

Dan's independence of spirit, and the first noticeable stirrings of a keen natural intelligence, can be traced to this time in his infancy, when he was 4 or 5 years old. He expressed it by teaching himself to read. The method to hand lay in two cheap Zane Grey cowboy novels, which a neighbour— Dan believed the wife of the manager of the flour mill—lent to the Davins when they were ill with the flu: *The Lone Star Ranger* and *The Rainbow Trail*.[23] The older man may have romanticized a childhood connection here. Zane Grey was hugely popular at the time, the westerns readily available in lending libraries. But whatever the origins of the opportunity, Dan mastered reading simply by concentration, and the application of a certain internal logic. The skill, which his parents for a while did not realize he had acquired, brought him a new life of the mind and the imagination.

The impetus for this development lay in the preoccupation of the rest of the family with events elsewhere. Just three weeks after Pat was born in 1917, Mary Davin's oldest sister, Ellen Concannon, died suddenly of pneumonia. Her widower, Michael Concannon, originally also from Galway, was a hard man, quick to anger, violent in his moods, and the family home at Woodlands was a 'house devoid of affection'.[24] This death and the anxiety it brought for the welfare of her nephews and nieces deeply distressed Mary Davin. The youngest of Ellen's children, Peter and Pat, were only 5 years and 3 weeks old respectively, when she died. Their welfare, and problems of supplying practical help, were to preoccupy her for much of the next twelve years.

Nine months later, on Tuesday, 25 June 1918, the Mataura River flooded again. Once more Gore was under several feet of water. The Davins were forced to evacuate their home, and were accommodated elsewhere as temporary refugees—possibly on the safe slopes of East Gore with the Davin or O'Sullivan connections. When the water receded and the woodwork had dried out, the Railways jacked the house up and moved it to slightly higher ground, across the railway tracks and fronting on to Main Street. This may have seemed like a step in the right social direction, but the events themselves were a nightmare of terror and distraction. One of Dan's little classmates in the kindergarten was drowned. The obstacles for Dan's mother, with six children, three of them under 5, one a babe in arms, were frightful. Dan may have seen it all as adventure, a little Zane Grey intruding into his own life. In all probability, however, once the waters had subsided and survival gave way to clearing up, it meant that he had more time to himself, less supervision from grown-ups and older sisters burdened by events. One immediate effect of this was that when it came time to start at the primary school, in September of 1918, he was advanced into a class with older children, amongst whom even so he could easily hold his own.

Another benefit brought by the flood was that the new location of the house meant a clear view of the railway lines at the bottom of the garden. The boys would clamber on to the tin roof of the lean-to shed where their father kept his garden tools, and wave to the passing trains. Within months these were packed with soldiers returning from the war, balloons and streamers flying from the windows and door-handles. With them the soldiers brought the great flu epidemic that was sweeping the world. Gore was relatively isolated from this, but even so the illness did the rounds. The entire Davin family fell ill, one by one, each recovering in turn, Dan recalling that his mother succumbed last, only when she was sure the others had been successfully nursed through.[25] They all recovered. Not so Mary's younger sister Nora, however. She died of pneumonia early in 1919 in Waitara, near New Plymouth where—a single woman—she had gone to work. Dan recalled for the rest of his life his mother's grief for this second lost sister, her rough apron held up to the tears on her face, her body rocking back and forth on the stool where she knelt, her fingers working the rosary beads as she prayed.[26]

These tragic events touched Dan more by their mystery than their grief. He had known neither of his dead aunts; the war brought death to other families, but, miraculously, not his own; floods were adventures: grown-ups could be very strange. At school he was learning to write, the pencil gripped oddly because he could not bend his right thumb. At night the 6-year-old boy, dreaming of cowboys and adventure, fell asleep to the sound of slow-moving trains on the tracks outside his window. He was small but sturdy, with large deep blue eyes, a broad forehead, a head of dark hair. He was quick at his schoolwork, fast of tongue, not slow to defend himself in schoolboy scraps, generally bright and cheerful. Yet there was something else too: a reserve, a distance, a touch of shy sadness about nothing in particular.

Then his father was moved again. In the spring of 1920, after six years in Gore, the family travelled the forty miles back south to Invercargill. Dan was 7, and a stage in life, though he did not know it, had come to an end.

2

A CATHOLIC CHILDHOOD

The back gate leading to the garden was open and Mick sat there to keep the hens from getting in. He had the Catholic weekly and . . . there was a lot of stuff about a writer on the literary page. He must be pretty bad because the editor kept talking about Liffey mud and the disgrace to the glorious literary tradition of Ireland. But it was hard to tell what it was all about. Some day when he grew up he would read all the books in the world and know all about everything, even about this writer.

(DMD, 'The Vigil', *GBP*, p. 16)

Here, among these woods and clearings, sand and fern, silence and the smell of pine brought a kind of release to the heart, together with a deep-down wish for something, something more than battles, perhaps not battles at all; something realised, even then, as nebulous, blissful, all but unattainable: a feeling of uneasiness, profound and oppressive, yet oddly pleasurable at times, at other times so painful as to be almost impossible to bear.

(Anthony Powell, *The Kindly Ones*, 13)

Back in Invercargill, Patrick got a loan from the Southland Investment Society, bought a section and built a house at 36 Morton Road, in the Georgetown district, south of the railway line. This was then almost on the edge of town, so that the house stood in the borough, while the back fence, facing east, gave on to the sections of Conyers Road, where the boundary ran. Beyond this, and outside the limits of town planning restrictions, were open paddocks.

The house, a typical New Zealand bungalow of the period, had three bedrooms. The girls had a bedroom at the front of the house, and there were two others for the boys. Dan shared a double bed, first with his older brother Tom, later with Matt. Their parents slept in a small room off the kitchen. There was little insulation, so almost no privacy. Lighting was by gas. A small room that doubled as dining- and sitting-room had a piano, and a table for homework, but the family rarely either ate or sat there. Family life was lived in the kitchen, where the range, fed on wood and coal, provided warmth in winter, hot water the year round, and heat for cooking. The oven had no heat gauge, and Mary would put her elbow in to judge the temperature for baking and roasting.[1] A big table was for food preparation, meals, conversation, and games. Their father, especially when working awkward shifts, would eat at a separate table, off to one side. A small washhouse was for washing-up and laundry. Dan's mother's world had its hub in this small compass. In her fourteenth year of marriage she was now a large woman, ever more matronly as the years passed, worried about goitre, increasingly troubled by rheumatism.[2]

In the yard behind the house Patrick Davin planted his vegetable and flower garden, 'a disciplined jungle'[3] of beans and cabbages, carrots and beetroot, parsnips, rhubarb, and tomatoes. Facing east, but with no obstruction to the north, it took the sun for almost as long as there was sun in the sky. Beyond a small lawn, and at the bottom of this kitchen garden, a gate led through the fence to an area of outhouses: a shed for potatoes, another for the cows, and a hen coop for chickens.[4] On the other side of a thick gorse hedge that blazed golden in the spring was a compost heap, warm and fecund, and then the paddocks. Patrick Davin believed that they were owned in separate lots by investors who, years before, had been sold the belief that Invercargill might eventually become the capital of New Zealand. By 1920 such unworldly optimism was long since disappointed, its victims dispersed with their dreams. The sections remained, unclaimed. Here it was that, free of the town's objections, Patrick Davin grazed his cows and planted his potatoes and turnips. For a few years he kept pigs as well, hanging rolls of bacon from the kitchen ceiling. Pat Davin remembered his father as 'a frustrated farmer'.[5]

Beyond these fields was open country, a land of distant hills, streams and rivers, macrocarpas and bush.[6] In the quarries and sandpits were frog spawn to watch turn to frogs, crawlies to catch on hooks with bits of bacon, and pirate adventures on badly cobbled rafts.[7] The surrounding fields teemed with rabbits. Nearby orchards offered the enticement of stolen fruit in the autumn. This was the physical world of Dan's childhood as he was to recall it ever afterwards. It was a world of animals. They always had a dog, a cat, rabbits, ducks as well as hens, later ferrets. And a world of the outdoors, where games of adventure coincided with nature.

Every day he had his chores: the two older boys were responsible for milking the cows morning and evening, then putting the milk through the separator. At one time there were perhaps as many as four cows, one of them, Rosy, an awkward and occasionally malicious beast adept at getting a hoof in the milk bucket if your attention strayed. However, they 'always credited Rosy with super-bovine sagacity', and Dan called her 'one of the few wise cows I have met'.[8] Oyster shells were crushed with a mallet on the boot-last to make grit for the hens. In winter the boys dug turnips for winter feed. All year round there was the skim milk to feed to the pigs, kindling to cut, coal to haul, eggs to be collected, produce to deliver to neighbours, friends, and family.

The chores were onerous. During term-time they meant an early rise at 6.30 because jobs had to be done before school began at 9.00. In the evening they meant no school sports like other boys, but home by 4.00 to finish the chores by 6.00. Then tea and homework before bed, to be ready for the next early morning. But at weekends, and during the school holidays, especially in the long weeks of the summer, household tasks were prelude to other seemingly limitless possibilities. Dan's partner for domestic jobs was Tom, but his particular companion in play was his brother Matt. All the boys gave Dan the nickname McCabe, and McCabe he was until he left home. Matt was an argumentative boy, opinionated, sometimes cantankerous, but Dan was full of guile, 'a smooth operator',[9] so able to keep Matt in check. On a summer's morning, the chores finished, they would bolt their breakfast of fried eggs and bacon, bread and milk, and rush out to the sun, the pet collie Glen at their heels, a long day of rabbiting and fishing, foraging and adventure ahead of them. One night Dan and Matt dared each other to walk through the Eastern cemetery at midnight. Secretly they crawled back through the bedroom window afterwards, their terror ebbing. During the day, more conventionally, they climbed trees, sometimes hanging a swing from the branches. Mysteriously this would generally collapse just when their brother Tom climbed on, and they would run from his anger. Their contemporaries at school were jealous of the freedom the Davin boys had, one of them remembering that 'they never had to ask permission to do anything. Not like my family.'[10]

There is no better evidence of this than the ferrets. One Saturday morning Dan and Matt borrowed ten shillings, a princely sum, from their mother, and went to Todd's auction rooms to buy a ferret. They came home with a lively black specimen that announced its intentions early by biting Matt on the finger and attempting to escape. The next day, after Mass, they took it to a nearby warren, spread their nets, and released it down a burrow. One by one eight handsome rabbits flew from the holes into the boys' eager hands. No sign, however, of the ferret. It came on to rain. Dan and Matt broke into burrow after burrow, drenched to the skin by now, sand and dirt in every crevice of their clothes. No ferret. They trudged home disconsolate, though the day proved profitable enough when the skins were sold, and their mother cooked two of the rabbits for tea—a man's contribution to the household economy. Eventually, with another ferret, they were able to repay the loan.

Dan and Matt set up a fund to buy themselves BSA bicycles, a project they accomplished in due course. Later still they bought a rifle. These projects required patience, if not parsimony. Rabbits, though you might get 1s. 9d. for 'a good winter buck skin',[11] generally brought in only 'a few coppers'.[12] By the end of 1929 they were getting more—at 25s. a time—for the ferrets they bred. Mysterious diminutions in the quantity of their savings, kept in a bedroom drawer, were traced to their sisters, who relied on the fund to augment their church donations. In this way, though only for a while (the savings were transferred to a more secure location) Dan supported the priesthood.

What other boys noticed was the air of country competence. The rabbits rushed into the nets, were grabbed, necks snapped, skins removed. It seemed over in a trice. Dan carried a sharp sheath knife along with his shanghai,[13] and always knew where to get the best materials—a fork off a branch with the most spring; the toughest elastic; the best whetstone for a sharp edge.

What Dan and Matt could not teach each other about such things must surely have been learned from their father, but the rest of Dan's immediate family, though of, were somehow not in, this side of his life. His sisters had showed small aptitude for school work, and were set to acquire refinements: piano playing and singing. The piety and solemnity of the sisters' devotion to their various enthusiasms—saints' day observance, music, singing (there was widespread agreement that they had good voices)—brought Evelyn the younger boys' sobriquet 'Bane'. Girls were a nuisance, a menace in coalition with Mum, to whom Evelyn and Molly would frequently appeal. In retaliation McCabe and Matt put carbide down the lavatory. They knew to expect a stink as well as a satisfying though disturbing froth, and they were not disappointed.[14]

Dan's older brother Tom, 12 in 1923, shortly to start at Southland Boys' High School, was serious and solemn, devout in his Catholicism, already showing signs of the earnest pursuit of first one enthusiasm, and then another, that may be a feature of oldest sons on whom parental expectations for success weigh heaviest. He was 'a good boy' in a way that his younger brothers could not emulate. Nor were they expected to. He was becoming a rather pompous authority, the expert on milking technique, wood cutting, turnip digging, even igloo building in the winter snow.[15] He took his pre-eminence in these weighty matters seriously, bringing a dogged determination to bear as well as firm instruction for his brothers. The bonds that developed in this setting were strong, but it was love mediated by irritation. The younger boys were bound to Tom, but their affection grew over the years into a sort of sorrowful regret: he was so tight, so earnest, so humourless.

Tom, of course, could not displace the father, still the bench-mark of manliness. He was middle-aged now, turning 50 in 1927, but a life of hard physical work and a robust constitution had kept him phenomenally fit. He took a 17-inch collar, had biceps like 'red pine',[16] and when not at work would be hard to coax in from his garden before dark. To and from work he rode an enormous, iron-framed bicycle, too heavy for the boys to lift, and to which he had fitted a broad motor-cycle seat. He still liked a drink, but it was no easier to get one here in 'dry' Invercargill than it had been in Gore. However, prohibition was not in force in the surrounding county, and the White House on Bay Road, just across the boundary, was close enough to the railway station and goods yards to offer temptation. And there was always the local custom of kegging, to which the police might turn a blind eye.[17] Patrick Davin's authority in the family was unquestioned. He was never heard to swear: 'by crikey' or 'beggar it' were as close as he came. He backed up his discipline by his physical presence. For the boys, this was the law. He laid it down, and he enforced it. Its sphere was the garden and the animals. He neither needed nor sought to make his writ for discipline run much further than this. 'Do as your mother tells you', was the stock-in-trade of his brand of authority. As children, the boys learned never to question it.

Within these limits of paternal authority Patrick exerted an opaque, implacable will. Two events brought this phenomenon home to Dan so forcefully that he wrote and talked about them for the rest of his life. One concerned Rosy the cow, so called because of her red colouring. Rosy was a Shorthorn. Every year she was put to the bull, and every year she calved, but hope against hope every year she gave birth to a bull calf. The male offspring meant only trouble to a smallholder interested in milk and butter, so had to be slaughtered. Every year Patrick did the deed himself. Dan recalled going with him to the paddock to find the cow and calf, his father carrying the infant home across his shoulders, shutting Rosy away in her shed, and then smashing the little bullock's skull with his sledgehammer. Rosy, bereft, bellowed and moaned till the days and the memory passed.[18]

This was an annual event, melancholy and violent, but in rhythm with the seasons. A man did what was necessary. Nature was cruel. With Glen, the boys' pet collie, loss, innocence, and will were all far more intensely focused. The dog was an extension of the younger boys, especially Dan and Matt. Apart from school, they never went out without him.[19] The boys talked to Glen like another brother, shared their food and adventures with him. His loves were theirs: rabbiting, running, swimming in the creeks. He would waste his half of the apple once he had it, but the offer had to be made.[20] As he got older, Glen could nip, especially if interfered with over a bone. One day he nipped one of the girls. Weeping and wailing she went to her mother. Mary made up her mind that the dog was a menace and had to be destroyed. The boys argued, begged, and pleaded. Mary made the issue one of parental solidarity, and appealed for her husband's support. ' "Your mother's right", he said.'[21] The boys conspired to hide the dog, finding as they thought a remote spot, concealing him there, taking him food secretly reserved from the breakfast table. The plot was utterly transparent to Patrick. He found Glen and shot him. The grief of this was a first taste of despair, the emotion born at the death of happiness. It also led to stubbornness, to a distaste for authority, and a mistrust of any love so willing to inflict pain.

There was little here to hearten 10- and 12-year-old boys. Though life apparently continued as before—they got a new dog, the busy daily round continued—barriers had been built. The breach with their sisters was wider; their mother's unquestioned love now questioned; the justice of fathers discredited. Dan's tendency to occasional loneliness, a melancholy without apparent reason, grew more marked. The countryside, wild and empty, gave space for it, and he became more solitary. His contemporaries thought him a loner.[22] In a manuscript fragment, written late in life but never published, Dan wrote what may be an addition to his story about this incident, 'Death of a Dog'.

I didn't tell Ned but ever since Dad had shot Jack for biting my sister I had had an imaginary place I called 'Vale of Dreams' because of the way the priest and my mother at the end of the Rosary talked about this world being a Vale of Tears.
'What are you whistling at?' Ned asked.
'Oh, just nothing.'[23]

Alone in the fields, trudging home under the 'glowing sky'[24] of a January sunset, Dan experienced the oppression of circumstance, the almost joyful pain to be found in the sense of isolation, the solitary individual confronted with a meaningless universe, alone, and on the edge of nothingness. Not a bad image for the whole of Southland.

All this lay slightly in the future. For the time being, the big family change that the move to Invercargill brought was the return to a world of uncles and aunts and cousins. The Concannon children from Woodlands became regular visitors, and the two little Concannon boys, contemporaries of Dan and his youngest brother Pat, became their playmates. Esmond Doley, the youngest of Aunty Annie's brood of four on their farm at Oteramika, stayed with the Davins from Monday night to Friday morning during the school year so that he could attend the Marist Brothers' School. As he grew up he became a close friend of Pat Davin, while Florence, his sister, became a particular favourite of Dan's. The wider world of family, its intensities as well as its freedoms, was also brought home to Dan by absence and by death. Mary's younger sister Maggie had married someone called Jack Gunn, and gone to live in Auckland, a thousand miles away. Auckland, for 10-year-old Dan, was impossibly remote. Mary and her sister more or less lost contact.

Then the virus that had brought the 'big flu' in 1919, and which lingered on for some years afterwards, caused the death of his grandparents, Daniel and Nora Sullivan, who died within four days of each other in October 1923. They were 73 years old, had been in New Zealand 'about 48 years' (as their death certificates put it), and lived till the end on the old property at Makarewa. Dan was never close to his grandparents. He had barely seen them till he was 7. To visit them from Invercargill meant a journey on the Wairo branch railway line. To them Dan was one of many, for they had twenty grandchildren. To him they were remote, rather forbidding, 'old' in a definitive though impenetrable way. When they died it was not so much his own loss that he felt, as his mother's. Mary Davin now drew even closer to her sister Annie.

To the sisters, these funerals must have seemed ominous. There was so much suffering. Two sisters and both parents all dead within the space of six short years. And an older brother who was a source of worry and dismay. This was Jack, the oldest of them, almost 48 when his parents died. He had had a chequered career. As a young man a pregnant woman accused him, wrongly as it eventually transpired, of being the father of her illegitimate child. Old Nora Sullivan, 'with grim Irish puritanism',[25] denounced him, her own son, and said he had to marry the girl. Rather than submit, he disappeared to the West Coast, where he got a job in a sawmill. Here he suffered a serious head injury in an accident, and was unconscious for days. When he eventually revived, one of his eyes was askew, and ever after he suffered from periods of inattention, forgetfulness, and eccentricity. He believed the fairies responsible for smoking his pipe tobacco at night. Occasionally he would get up and walk in his sleep, coming to in his nightshirt miles from home. This behaviour was a source of great worry both to him and to his sister Mary, of whom he was very fond. Dan remembered him being a frequent visitor to the house, when he would give the children 'lollies' and play *The Three Little Blackberries* on his violin. Eventually he was so depressed by his own deviant behaviour that he became a voluntary patient at Seacliff, a psychiatric hospital on the coast north of Dunedin. In this way he passed out of Dan's life, but not out of the circle of family lore. Seacliff was the most menacing institution in the South Island, the condition of its inmates notorious, the character of its medical ministrations deeply feared. It had difficulty securing staff, and the shame of ever being sent to Seacliff was coupled with fear in the minds of even educated people.[26] To Mary Davin and her sister Annie it was a place of dread.

And Jack was not the only worry. Annie's husband, Harry Doley, was a man becalmed. English and Protestant by origin, so an oddity in the family, he seemed devoid of ambition, drifting along on the small farm at Oteramika, barely managing to keep the family fed and clothed on his herd of twenty dairy cows, incompetent at farm maintenance, never happier than when lifting a glass and yarning on the crumbling verandah.[27] Could nothing stir him into activity? And then there was 'Aunty Sullivan', Julia Davin, Dan's father's aunt, who had migrated to East Gore. By this time she was very old and living at Clifton, a few miles from Invercargill, with her cousins the Dales. Driven by demented fantasies, she would get up in the night to drive the cows, and have to be hunted down at daylight by her distracted relatives. On one occasion her nocturnal cattle drive was in the general direction of Morton Road, and the Dales brought her into the house after her recapture. She was very tiny and shrunken. Seeing Dan, she broke into a stream of Gaelic. Dan's father said to the perplexed boy: 'She thinks that you're me, and that we're back in Galway.'[28]

These eccentricities of family life were not recounted outside the Irish Catholic community. Neighbours recall that the Davin home was an open house, always full of people, the grown-ups talking round the table, the girls playing the piano and singing, the children outside playing in the garden or the fields, or up on the roof. The kitchen smelt of freshly baked bread, and there was always a meal just about to be served or only just cleared away. It seemed a romantic spot to neighbours and visitors from less expressive homes.[29] After Mass on Sundays, Patrick would invite to dinner more or less anyone who wanted to come. With an eye to his daughters' futures, young, single Irishmen, recent migrants in particular, were always welcome. Dan grew up to think of home as a place where people came, where there was always somehow a spare bed if you were stuck, and where hospitality meant a feed, and a story or a performance, like Uncle Jack playing his violin.

Home was really where everything happened. The family never took a holiday away. The closest to such a thing was to go out to the Concannon farm at Woodlands for a long weekend or so in the summer, or during the May holiday from school. Even then the boys would go in rotation. There were still cows to milk, after all. Once a year there would be the Railways picnic excursion to Bluff, a special train hauling employees and their families down to the coast. Old Aunty Wyatt, still living at Green-hills, came out of her house to wave at the train as it steamed by.[30] Christmas was special, with Mass on the day and not just if it was Sunday, and then a roast goose. But there were no presents. They were not a part of the family tradition. The most memorable day of all came at the New Year 1926, when Patrick and Mary took the entire family on a day trip to the New Zealand and South Seas International Exhibition, 140 miles away in Dunedin: the first time the children had been there.[31] They travelled on the train at a railwayman's concessionary rates, going up early in the morning and returning exhausted at night. The exhibition grounds, on the newly drained Logan Park, were close to the university, but the proximity meant nothing to 12-year-old Dan. He and Matt distinguished themselves by slipping away for a while in the afternoon, much to their mother's alarm. No doubt the amusement park, 'the chief memory of the Exhibition for thousands of young people',[32] played some part in this.

At home again, once in a while there would be a visit from Larry Hynes, an itinerant story-teller, with his tales of the old country, of myths and fairies, poteen and Finn McCoul, scandal, poetry, revolt, and love. Sometimes the stories were in Gaelic. The children, sent to bed eventually, would pretend to go, and then hide behind the chairs to listen, holding their breath with the excitement. The grown-ups, pretending not to see, would wink and smile, and ask for another tale. Old Hynes had a regular circuit which he made on his bike, so he could be expected to turn up at any of the homes of the Davin or Sullivan families or their Irish connections in and around Invercargill—the Faheys, Hogans, and Concannons—ready to tell his stories for a meal, a bed to sleep in, and enough in his pocket to move on again, north-west to Otautau, Riverton, and Tuatapere, then on to the coal-mining townships of Ohai and Nightcaps, and so on up into Central Otago. The itinerant story-teller, and the homes that would make space for him and his talent, were powerful images in the mind of a young boy.[33]

But not all the talk of Ireland was of the past, or of established myth and legend. These were the years of Ireland's final victorious struggle for independence, and the birth of a new, Catholic state. Dan was too young in 1916 to know of the Easter uprising when it happened, but the aftermath, the trials and executions, the murderous calamity of the IRA and the Black and Tans, the peace negotiations, partition and independence, the creation of the Irish Free State, and civil war: these matters were the common fare of family and community discussion, led by the Catholic weekly *The Tablet*, still the family's main source of news, and then under the 'belligerently Irish' editor, Father James Kelly.[34] Dan grew up to know about these matters just as every Irish Catholic boy grew up to know about the famine of 1845–8, and about the Irish diaspora of the fifty years that followed. He was brought up a Republican, assumed to be green to the bottom of his moral and political being, but as with many Irish Catholic boys in New Zealand, the culture did not quite take as the parents' generation imagined that it would. The Davins, Sullivans, and Concannons were not Fenians, or men of the gun, but Irish Republicanism was their side, and they lined up with it, even on the far side of the world. The next generation accepted this, went through the motions of St Patrick's Day, but it was a different and lesser commitment. For them, Ireland was impossibly far away, an imaginary concept really. They thought their mother's talk of 'the black strangers' eccentric, even funny. Matt, when he was a little older and keen on dancing, went on Saturday nights to the Invercargill Orange Lodge because it had the best dance bands. Knowing that his parents would never forgive him if they found out, he never told them.[35]

The political and cultural tradition of home was oral, not literary. Dan recalled that there were only four books in the family home: a history of the Irish struggle, a book of Irish heraldry, 'an old bound copy of *Chambers' Journal* for some year at the turn of the century', and Harry Holland's *Armageddon*.[36] Holland's little book is a pointer. Dan's father was a loyal member of the Railwaymen's union, and, like the great majority of people of Irish Catholic extraction in both Australia and New Zealand, a supporter of the new Labour Party. In practical terms, however, his Irish cultural roots bound him to the Liberal Joseph Ward, for whom he voted. Dan's father reckoned Ward was 'a bit of a scoundrel', but Ward called him Paddy when they met on the train, and once gave him a cigar.[37] Dan may himself have felt humiliated at how easily his father was won over.[38] There were no illusions, however, about theirs being a working man's household. During the railway strike of 1923, a teacher at school, illustrating the concept of perspective by drawing converging railway lines on the board, suddenly turned to Dan to ask, in front of the whole class, whether 'you don't feel that the perspective of a railway line exists now that your father is out on strike?'[39] Dan portrayed this later as 'a teacher's clumsy sarcasm', but he was wounded by 'the obsequious laughter of the others'.[40] Late in life Dan said about this incident that 'from then on I believed that religion should not interfere with politics'.[41] What seems more likely is that the 10-year-old boy, hot with embarrassment, angered at public ridicule of his father's union loyalty, formed a stubborn intention not to let religion interfere with *his* politics. Whatever politics were . . .

The difficulty was that religion was in everything. On Sundays there was Mass at the Basilica on Tyne Street, almost astride the railway line. In this small world the two institutions belonged together. The Davins' neighbours, the Woods, had a car, in which Mary would be driven to church while the children came on foot. Young Sally Wood was in love with Dan, but never dared to tell.[42] Afterwards, on the steps of the Basilica, Irishness, Catholicism, Invercargill, the railways and school were all one, as the community lingered to talk. It was a seamless world. No one part of his life could be partitioned from any other. Even so, Dan never became an altar boy. His father imposed no pressure of this kind, and his mother was satisfied, no doubt, at the piety of her three oldest children. Tom became intensely religious in adolescence, attended Mass every day, and contemplated the priesthood. For Dan, however, belief was a matter of custom. You went to church, observed the holy days, prayed as required. Like Irishness and the railways, it was what you had, or were. It was a given, but it was given more loosely than the donors realized, not just as formal ideology, though there was plenty of that at school, but as customary practice. Perhaps it was precisely because it brooked no alternative that a questioning mind might find it out.

All this was further endorsed at school. From 7 February 1921 until the end of the decade, Dan was a pupil at the Marist Brothers' School, first of all in Clyde Street, a two-mile walk from home, and then after its transfer there in 1925, in Mary Street. At first he went on foot, jumping the Puni Creek on the way.[43] Later there was the BSA. The school had been founded in 1897 in response to enthusiastic encouragement by the parish priest, Dean Burke, and within months its three teachers had 110 pupils organized in primary and junior grades.[44] The school was quickly brought under the Public Schools' Inspectorate, and by the 1920s it had doubled in size, though its premises in the old church on Clyde Street were by then dilapidated. The shed which served as a gym had a mud floor, and the classrooms rotting woodwork.[45]

The education it offered sounds dour—even dire—today, at least in part because of the life of the teaching Brothers themselves. If strictly adhered to, their rules had them living by the clock under a blanket of prohibitions. Their day, which began at 5.25 a.m. and ended with prayers at 9.30 p.m., consisted of school (8.45 a.m. to 5.15 p.m.) and religious observance. They were required to maintain silence outside school time, except for one hour of community recreation after dinner. They were forbidden morning tea, supper, tobacco, wrist-watches, cinemas, boxing tournaments, football, bicycles, and Sunday, evening, or weekly secular newspapers.[46] A curious list, and if followed, pretty well certain to ensure that they remained ignorant of any topic likely to be of interest to the average schoolboy. In practice, the rules seem to have been honoured in the breach, at least in Invercargill by the 1920s.

On the academic side, religious instruction dominated the curriculum. Beyond that the purpose of the school seems to have been to provide a basic education—literally reading, writing, and arithmetic—to boys who were expected to find jobs as tradesmen and labourers. Even so, the task was not easy. Many of the boys were tough, and the Brothers ruled by stern discipline, with plenty of physical chastisement. Dan's knuckles were routinely rapped with a ruler for his failure to hold a pencil 'correctly'. Pupils who failed to make the grade in annual examinations would be kept down to repeat, so that smaller boys found themselves sharing classrooms with rather older, more truculent boys. Bullying and fighting were common. Dan was physically strong, so he and his younger brothers 'weren't punished for being bright'.[47] But in this way he learned to fight, and to relish victory. When Dan joined the school there was no Marist Brothers' high school to go on to. Most boys left to look for jobs after junior school, and only the lucky and able few, like Dan's older brother Tom, transferred to a secular public school, like Southland Boys' High, or went on to the Technical Institute for training in a trade. Educational standards were not improved by the fact that Superiors in the Marist

Brothers' order were 'distinctly cool, or even hostile'[48] to the idea that the Brothers should themselves secure higher education.

All the Davin boys survived and prospered not just by being good in a scrap, but by acquiring cunning, another skill likely to come in handy later. Given that Dan could read before he went to school, and had started to learn to write before he arrived in Invercargill, it is doubtful that, apart from arithmetic, he learned very much of a formal scholarly kind at all in his early years at the school. These years were obviously not wasted, since home and community gave an education of sorts, but a natural intelligence of his dimensions would have accomplished far more had it been offered a richer diet of intellectual matter. He certainly came to see this himself later, but the loss may also have been sensed by the boy. He effortlessly dominated his class at any test or examination, and was dux of the school in 1926.

The sense of expanding powers in a wider world was emphasized in a lucky discovery. Out playing at a flooded quarry one day, he found on the rubbish tip at one end of the artificial lake a cache of discarded books, thrown away by a retired schoolteacher. They included a collection of readings, *The Pageant of English Prose*, and a cheap limp edition of Coleridge's *Rime of the Ancient Mariner*. He brought the books home, and dried them on the rack above the kitchen range. The find was a turning-point of a sort. Later in life he would exploit it several times in different settings, in one of which he listened 'to the sombre tale of the mariner, not as the reluctant wedding-guest but as the creature of guilt relating his own crimes'.[49] What is perhaps more to the biographical point is that Coleridge's verse, with its irresistible rhythm and forward motion, and its story of death and mysterious punishment, captured Dan's mind. Here was true poetic force, simple but powerful. And the story it told, of terror and remorse in the context of celebration and order, endorsed his own maturing sense of the sombre, gloomy aspects of experience.

The story seemed to have personal point too. Out with brother Matt one day Dan had fired a stone from his shanghai at a handsome drake that belonged to a local carrier called Murray. Later he called the bird a seagull.[50] The truth is, if anything, more poignant. The stone, to their surprise and terror, found its mark, and dropped the bird stone dead. Cause and effect. The two boys buried the drake, and went in fear of Murray for days afterwards while he searched for his missing bird. The boys kept their secret, but the guilt was terrible. 'Instead of the cross, the Albatross | About my neck was hung.'

From the age of 13 or 14 every witness has Dan with his head in a book. This change coincided with changes at school. The new school buildings were opened in Mary Street, and the Brothers laid plans to extend teaching to the upper forms. The timing was propitious because besides Dan several other boys in his year showed aptitude as well. Dan was encouraged to sit an examination for a scholarship—only one was available—that would have taken him to Sacred Heart College in Auckland in 1928.[51] This was a Catholic boys' high school that was the one really reputable academic institution in the Marist Brothers' system at that time, and a transfer there would certainly have suited his talents. The Invercargill Marist Brothers were surprised and disappointed when he failed to obtain it.

However, in February 1927 the upper school in Invercargill was duly opened. It consisted of a single third form of about ten boys, one of them Dan. Much of the instruction continued as before, but now Latin, French, and Mathematics were added to the syllabus, in preparation for the Public Service and Matriculation examinations that the pupils would sit at the end of the fourth and fifth forms, when they were 15 or 16. How limited the instruction was is illustrated by the Latin class. For most of the first half of the century Marist Brothers were forbidden to learn Latin, which was interpreted by their Superiors as indicative of an intention to leave for the priesthood.[52] As a result, if Latin was taught at all in a Marist high school the teaching was generally done by a local priest. Not, however, in Invercargill, where Brother Tarcisius was responsible for introducing the boys to the classics. Dan quickly figured out that the teacher knew no more Latin than he did, and was coping only by keeping one lesson ahead in the textbook. He determined to do the same, and in this way 'acquired an astonishing reputation for scholarship'.[53]

The reputation expanded with the help of his Uncle Jim. Jim Walsh, a retired surfaceman on the railways, was some sort of second cousin to his mother. He kept a parrot on his shoulder which, like Merlin's owl, deposited droppings down his back when he came over the road for dinner in the evenings. Uncle Jim was a great frequenter of auctions, especially Todd's. Here he could be found locked in bidding battles with a retired cook, Sandy McNab, who lived in a hut on the fields behind Morton Road. Sandy was Chinese, but had taken a Scottish name thinking, correctly, it might improve his chances of securing employment as cook on a sheep station. Both great readers, he and Uncle Jim competed at Todd's 'for the most spectacular, fearful rubbish'.[54] This was how

Uncle Jim had a copy of an ancient edition of Lewis and Short's *Latin Dictionary* and Liddell and Scott's *Greek Lexicon*, both of which eventually found their way into Dan's hands. Lewis and Short was invaluable for preparing apparently innocent but deadly questions to torment Brother Tarcisius at school.

To be fair, the Brothers knew that they had an unusually talented child on their hands, and the school did have 'some excellent teachers'.[55] In 1927 Brother Herbert organized the third form boys to participate in the Southland Competition Society, where they performed the trial scene from *The Merchant of Venice*. Dan was the Duke, sitting in judgement. The performance was a triumph, and the Marist boys won the competition at their very first attempt.

The head of the junior school, and a prime mover in getting a senior school started, was Brother Egbert. 'Even to barbarian boys he was obviously good, kind, holy and good-humoured, and a good teacher. But his eccentricities were numerous and obvious . . . He was round and fat—"Eggy"—with a sonorous, mimic-inviting voice.'[56] He was easily recognizable around the town as he puffed along on his huge double-barred bicycle, its tyres like balloons. It would have been surprising if Brother Egbert had not taken a particular interest in Dan. The school had no library, and there were no free libraries in Invercargill, so he arranged a small scholarship which paid a subscription to the Public Library. Since Dan also had access to the Railway library, available for use by railway employees, he was launched on the habit that a few years later would become a passion. He read what children elsewhere were reading: *The Last of the Mohicans*, *Buffalo Bill* and *Magnet* comics, Charles Dickens, W. J. Locke, and *East Lynne*. The boys found a huge collection of *Buffalo Bill*s in a nearby house when its occupants moved, leaving them behind: an unaccountable dereliction. Pat Davin described how they would sit up against Rosy's stomach, keeping warm, reading the *Magnet*, accompanied by the cow's rumbles and gurgles.[57] More advanced than most, Dan also discovered and read the complete works of Sir Walter Scott. Several contemporaries remember him as stubborn, or 'very determined' once he'd made his mind up about something. His reading of the entire Walter Scott *œuvre*, itself not uncommon among clever literate youngsters, persuaded them the characteristic was evident at an early age. And there was a generous side to his determination too. Sally Wood recalled how, over a period of time, he helped her with Latin when she was preparing for Matriculation examinations in the hope of studying nursing.

There were good reasons for Dan's seriousness. The family was growing up. Tom left school when he turned 16 without sitting Matric., and got a job as a clerk in the railways. Evelyn turned 21 in March 1929. Dan was committed to staying at school for the examinations in November 1929, but the question of a job, of a future life, was now pressing. The transition from boy to adolescent to adult is never a matter of strict boundaries: episodes overlap, sometimes in a perplexing way. The boy, with his shanghai and rabbit skins, overlaps with the adolescent, conscious of girls, ready to experiment with beer and cigarettes in imitation of the adults. Dan formed a friendship with a classmate Cliff Murfitt, known as Muff, and together they would hang about on street corners to watch the girls, go to Saturday night dances in town, or dress up a bit to go to the cinema, or to the Brown Owl café on Esk Street, a favourite meeting-place for young people.[58]

Simultaneously, however, Dan could still be an urchin. One night, after a *Merchant of Venice* rehearsal, he paused in the street to demonstrate the efficacy of the new elastic on his shanghai. A couple of shots at street lamps drew the attention of a passing local policeman. McCabe was completely unperturbed by this figure of authority, handing over the delinquent weapon with a stubborn and unapologetic gravity. The bobby, thinking to teach a lesson, drew out a pocket knife to cut the elastic. Back and forth he sawed at it while the cluster of boys watched. It could not be cut. Disappointed and defeated, the dejected policeman pedalled away with the shanghai, leaving Dan perversely triumphant, somewhat taller still in his schoolmates' estimation.[59]

In 1929, with another boy from school, Pat O'Neill, he was caught stealing late summer fruit from the property at Lennel of G. F. Hall-Jones, a prominent Invercargill citizen and historian of Southland.[60] Dan was 15½ then, his voice long since broken. His mother had bought him a suit, and he could look quite grown up, but he was also still climbing trees, skinning his knees. He was nearly his full adult height of six feet now, and his body was filling out. Muscular and strong, he was a good runner and moderate swimmer. He had a head of dark, wavy hair above large, sensitive blue eyes. His jaw had gone square, the nose broadened and straightened, and his mouth had bloomed, the upper lip slim and tense, the lower full, some thought sensuous.

Sex was now a matter of interest, but the topic, like alcohol, was banned. The boys were given no sex education at home.[61] At school and church, of course, Dan received the routine awful warnings about sin and damnation, but even these were delivered in code. Instruction about contraception was impossible, being itself a sin. Abstinence from It, whatever it was, was best. Outside schoolboy circles, where jokes and ignorance mixed the usual brew of desire and trepidation, no one ever spoke to the boys about either the sexual organs, or sexual congress as one expression of love between two free people. It was a dark topic, its attractions no doubt much enhanced by its obscurity, though the medical encyclopaedias at the library were not amenable to censor, nor the sounds of parental coitus at home to suppression.

Later commentary occasionally referred to Southland Catholics as *puritan* about sexual matters,[62] but this seems hardly fair. If anything they were *prudish* about it. It was not discussed, taught, or even referred to outside matrimonial privacy—probably not much even there. But this is not puritanism. The history of Catholic settlement of Southland hardly suggests a people concerned to repress sex. There is no evidence to suggest that they practiced it less than others, enjoyed it less, or felt more guilt about it. In this, as in other matters, such as violent punishment and poor-quality teaching at school, there is little to suggest that the Catholic community was really any different from the rest of New Zealand society at the time. O'Farrell takes a slightly different line. 'I do not recollect that they [his parents and their generation on the West Coast] were gravely afflicted by the Jansenism in sexual matters allegedly typical of the Irish. They were not prudes.'[63] One does not have to be a Jansenist to be a prude, though perhaps it helps. Prudishness is simply an excessive primness about sexual matters, and that certainly seems true of Dan's family when he was growing up. In any event, such aspects of the religion as might have rubbed off on Dan in his social life—a morbid concern about sin and redemption, say, or a tendency to look for suffering or some sort of surrogate martyrdom in life— seem to have gone to the older children, his sisters and his brother Tom. Dan and his two younger brothers, beneficiaries of benign neglect, slipped the net.

There was however something—a dark side, a tendency to depression. Dan was already showing signs of it as he turned 16. There were days when he felt his nature to be melancholic, when he lacked energy or purpose. They passed soon enough, but they left a reminder of the rather younger schoolboy, foraging alone in the sandpits and the bush, suddenly struck by his loneliness, and of how the misery of his isolation was tinged with a perverse happiness, that 'feeling of uneasiness, profound and oppressive, yet oddly pleasurable'. The sensation came more frequently as he grew, an increasingly familiar companion.

The principal impression he left his contemporaries, however, was one of extreme cleverness. At the end of the fourth form, 1928, he sat the Public Service Examination and came top for the whole of Southland. A year later he took Matriculation. Again he was top in Southland, and also placed 15th in the whole of New Zealand, 'with special distinction in English, French and Latin'.[64] He was captain and dux of the school. Brother Egbert came to see Mary Davin. The boy who had won the scholarship to Sacred Heart College in Auckland two years previously was unable to continue into the sixth form. Brother Egbert had taken it on himself to write to the College, and had secured agreement that Dan could take the now vacant place.[65] Perhaps there was an element of atonement here, as well as ambition for Dan, because the Director had learned that Dan's arithmetic paper in that previous examination had gone astray, and never been marked. He should surely have been awarded the scholarship in the first place.[66]

For a moment, Dan's future may have hung in the balance. He was uncertain what he wanted. Muff was joining an insurance company. Tom, a Railways cadet, had been sent to Wellington for training, which was a major achievement for a boy of his background. Returned now to Invercargill, he was thinking of buying a motor bike. There were many temptations, especially in thoughts of girls. Mary Davin paled at the suggestion of Dan's going away. Sixteen was very young to go so far.

Brother Egbert was famously tenacious in advocating causes in which he believed, however, and most unlikely to give way in such a discussion. The scholarship would pay fees and board. This was an opportunity not to be thrown away. The boy had great talent, but there was nothing more they could do for him in Invercargill. If he went to Sacred Heart, then there was a real chance that, after two years, he might win a scholarship to university. The presumption of Catholic separatism was not necessary. Dan could have transferred to Southland Boys' High School, as Tom had done before him, and from there could have tried for a university scholarship without leaving home or having to pay fees. Brother Egbert's concern, presumably, was to keep him in the faith. Perhaps Patrick and Mary suspected that Dan might find the allure of the streets too compelling unless he went away to board.

Dan told the story that his mother turned to him for his opinion, and that 'without disclosing it, I changed my mind. You could say I began to negotiate for conditions.'[67] He did not know what the university was, but he guessed that it would be expensive, causing trouble in the family budget. He would, he said, agree to go to Sacred Heart College in Auckland, and try for the university, but only if his mother promised never to reproach him for the expense. She agreed, and the pact was sealed. And she never broke her word.

3

AUCKLAND INTERLUDE

perhaps my chief impression from childhood is either never
getting what I wanted, certainly never being *given* it, or else
finding it was valueless when I did get it.

(WKDP: DMD to WKD, 'Tuesday night' [26 Jan. 1932?])

Friendship, popularly represented as something simple and
straightforward—in contrast with love—is perhaps no less complicated, requiring equally mysterious nourishment; like love,
too, bearing also within its embryo inherent seeds of dissolution,
something more fundamentally destructive, perhaps, than the
mere passing of time . . .

(Anthony Powell, *The Soldier's Art*, 93)

Mary Davin took Dan to the railway station in Invercargill to see him off
to Auckland. He found a corner seat, and before the train had pulled out
he was reading *Little Dorrit*, and so forgot to wave goodbye. He needed
a long book for what was then, in the absence of aeroplanes, a long
journey. The train ride to Lyttelton, near Christchurch, took all day.
Then there was a ferry passage overnight from Lyttelton to Wellington:
'a place where I used to sleep for a day in the middle of a long journey.'[1]
After that the Limited Express departed for Auckland at 7.15 in the
evening, and arrived at Auckland 500 miles to the north at breakfast-time
the next morning. When he arrived it was 4 February 1930, first day of the
school year for new entrants. Dan was 16 years and 5 months old. He had
never been away on his own before. The furthest he had ever been was on
the family outing to Dunedin four years earlier.

The boarding-school that he arrived at, Sacred Heart College, was at
that time located in Richmond Road, in the Auckland inner city suburb
of Grey Lynn.[2] This neighbourhood, along with the adjacent suburb of
Ponsonby, 'was then a sort of Irish *quartier*, the heartland of Catholic
Auckland',[3] and there were five Catholic schools in this area of town.
Sacred Heart was a Marist Brothers' school for boys, established in 1903,
and occupying 'a position of dominance' in the Marist system.[4] In 1930 it
had 325 pupils, approximately a third of them boarders. The school was
accommodated in a cluster of buildings, the main one a large, rambling

35

grey mansion, gable-roofed, with long balconies on the ground and first floors front and back. Behind it, above two extensive playing-fields, were a series of wooden buildings that housed classrooms and dormitories. A gully divided one playing-field from the other. Down the hillside to the west were glimpses of harbour, and in late summer and springtime the boys would occasionally be taken down to Shelly Beach for a swim.

The school, though nominally a part of the same system from which Dan had come in Invercargill, had few similarities with it. Here, though the neighbourhood was notoriously Irish, there were also Catholics named Smith and Williams. School fees were £75 a year, including board, equivalent to about £2,000 or $NZ5,000 today: a price quite out of the Davin family class. Following the prices quoted by George Court & Sons Ltd., on Auckland's Karangahape Road, it would have cost about £32, getting on for two months of his father's salary, to equip Dan with the minimum requirements for school uniform and sports. The other boarders came from well-to-do homes, so that merely mixing with them was a new experience for Dan, who knew no one like that in Invercargill. He had little pocket money to spend, only the barest minimum of required uniform and other equipment, a background almost wholly Irish in style. What the other boys noted above all was that he came from Invercargill, the deep, cold south, a legendary place to them. In an end of year satirical review he was cast as Daviel, an Eskimo.[5] He surely felt as out of place as the role implies.

The school regime was 'spartan';[6] 'pretty rugged', as one contemporary described it.[7] The day began with a cold shower at 6.00 a.m. which was followed by Mass at 7.00, breakfast at 8.00, and school at 9.00. Food was uninspired, of the sausages and spotted dick variety, and some boys remembered being 'always starving'.[8] Brother Hyppolite's 'bickie parade' was popular with the boarders because they could trade the biscuits with other boys for cut sandwiches from outside. There were sports at the end of the normal school-day, prep. before and after tea, lights out at 8.30. Sixth-form boarders shared one long dormitory. Discipline was by corporal punishment, and was swift and unrelenting. One pupil recalled that Brother Hyppolite, known inevitably as 'Hippo', who was prefect of studies and in charge of discipline, always caned boys for being late, even if they arrived on the school bus, when their lateness could not conceivably have been their own fault.[9] 'Hippo' came from Alsace, and was much imitated by the boys for muddling his syntax. Another witness recalled 'one particular Maths master [who] was addicted to it [the stick], and ready, blue eyes madly blazing, to cane half the class for failing to solve their geometry problems'.[10] A former Director said that discipline at the school was tough, but the toughness lay in its repetitiveness and regularity: work, washing, chores, a Sunday walk, all imposed 'as a part of life'. He believed that it 'produced a bond between the boys because they lived and suffered through the same things', and that the pupils 'admired their teachers, rather than loved them, because they knew the teachers were following an even tougher discipline than they were'.[11] Such generalizations do not, however, capture the quality of individual experience.

For formal instruction some of the teachers were clearly good. The Director, Brother Benignus, 'Ben', was a steady enough administrator who eventually went on to be Provincial of the Order. One contemporary of Dan described him as 'a thin quietly spoken man who spoke with his piercing blue eyes as much as with his voice'.[12] He didn't appear to make much impression as a leader, and often seemed 'a bit peevish, a bit querulous'.[13] None of the boys then knew that 'Ben' had had serious surgery. Over sixty years later one of them wrote: 'Slight, greying, stooping, often in pain, he did his duty . . . When he paused, in a walk across the playground, and put his hand to his side, I thought: "What's up now with the silly old B?" Well, *now* I know: *mea culpa*.'[14] Unlike 'Ben', Brother Borgia, nick-named 'Pot' for his portly stature and suet-pudding complexion, did command respect. He taught Dan both Latin and French with a grammarian's emphasis on precision, illuminated by occasional shafts of 'a grim sense of humour'.[15] Moving briskly, his gown billowing around him, he was the sort of teacher who got instant silence from any classroom, and not all of it dependent on his willingness to use the cane.[16]

On the teaching side, however, Dan's particular piece of good fortune was that in the February that he arrived at the school, a new English teacher, Brother Stephen, also made his début. Stephen was 34 years old, had studied for a BA at Sydney University (where he won the Wentworth essay medal in his first year), and was an enthusiast for his subject, not just teaching the boys their set texts, but giving them a feeling for the subject as a whole through such disparate figures as Francis Thompson and Banjo Paterson—both of whom he could quote extensively. In addition to teaching the sixth-form boys English, he also took over responsibility for the College Library, and the annual SHC *Magazine*, which the senior boys wrote under his general and apparently benign editorship at the end of the year. Dan said later that it was 'under the guidance of Brother Stephen, [that] I came to have any ordered notion of literature'.[17]

Order was perhaps the best word to apply to the disciplines of study. In addition to Latin, French, English, and Maths, which all the University Entrance examination candidates had to study, Dan took as his two options History and Mechanics—Applied Maths, as it would be called today. The school offered eleven subjects in all, including Commerce, Woodwork, and Agriculture, but these latter topics were not for sixth formers contemplating university entrance.

The orderliness of it was enhanced by the fact that this was, after all, a Catholic school. The boys had regular instruction in Christian doctrine, Bible, and Church history. Prayers and worship were a part of everyday life. The Brothers believed that 'prayer was an adhesive',[18] and thought it responsible for the lifelong friendships the boys made. In addition to regular worship and the celebration of saints' days, the school also organized a retreat, which in 1930 was held from 22 to 25 April. The days were set aside for a period of intense devotion combining organized worship with private prayer, penance, and contemplation, and culminating in a sermon given by a redemptorist, a priest specializing in illustrating to young and suggestible minds the sure and certain consequences in the next life of moral transgressions in this one. The school *Magazine* refers almost gently to 'Father Cahill [promising] us a hot time'.[19] The reality was probably a little more robust, though not without its own amusing side. The school chapel was located above the kitchens where there was a large freezer that had a noisy motor with a particularly menacing tone. The redemptorist favoured by the school authorities for a number of years was one Father Duggan. He was particularly successful at arousing terror in his juvenile audience. Below him, in the hothouse of the kitchen, the defective freezer motor would invariably cut in at moments when the fear of hell fire among his congregation was at its most intense, terrifying the younger boys.[20] The redemptorist was still performing twenty-five years later, when the sermon 'was always followed by an immense, but spontaneous queue for Confession. And temporary cessation of all Pocket Billiards.'[21]

The Catholic thread also ran, though with less menace, through the literature the boys read for pleasure under Brother Stephen's guidance. His tastes, though they included Johnson, Shakespeare, and Milton, also ran to Belloc and Chesterton.

Whatever the influence of teachers and the Catholic faith, however, it was surely his contemporaries at the school who made the profoundest impact on Dan. The sixth form was small, with just thirteen boys organized in two classes, A and B, though in practice all thirteen boys spent most of their time together. Dan, who was expected to have the routine two years between Matriculation and university scholarship examinations, was put in VIB. For the first time in his life he found himself among students of similar intellectual calibre. Michael Joseph, nine months younger than Dan, became a particular friend. Tall, slim, quick-witted and imaginative, Mike was the son of a successful English businessman who had emigrated to New Zealand for health reasons in 1924, and established a citrus fruit orchard at Bethlehem, just outside Tauranga. Mike had been born in London, but lived from 1920 to 1924, between the ages of 6 and 10, in various places in Belgium and France, where he acquired some facility in French. His extended family included intelligent and eccentric people as well as resourceful businessmen. He was the acknowledged brain of his year at SHC, and was not to be dislodged.

Rupert Cuddon-Large was the acknowledged social leader, a skilled debater, keen on games, the student selected to speak for the pupils when the school was visited by the Catholic Bishop of Auckland, James Liston.[22] Fred Petricevich, 'Yugoslav by descent and temperament',[23] was a loner who found it hard to make friends. Dan secured his confidence, and perhaps in an alliance of outsiders, they became close. Fred's father had died when he was young, and his mother had remarried, with a second family. She was domineering and forceful, with high academic hopes for Fred which he was then clearly capable of realizing. He played the violin well, was devoted to Tchaikovsky, and was clever at maths, chemistry, and mechanics, at which Dan had no background, and which he found maddeningly difficult to master. Charles Zambucka, Zam, was of Lebanese extraction, with a marvellous Levantine face, a broad grin and quick sense of humour. He came from a large and hospitable family—he had six brothers—and his parents, who had migrated from Beirut and were in the garment trade, endowed him with remarkable powers of independence and survival. He was gifted in mimicry, giving particularly good imitations of the dreaded Father Duggan, which Dan enjoyed. 'Zam, do Father Duggan', he would say.[24] And he would. Bob Cotterall, like Zam, was a day boy at the school. His father, a pharmaceutical chemist, kept Cotterall's Chemist Shop in Ponsonby. Bob was a keen, devout Catholic who 'combined common sense, a good heart, and an acid wit'.[25] Thrown into close proximity with these amusing and intelligent young men, in no position to look anywhere else for company, Dan might here make friendships that could last a lifetime.

But this was not all that easy to do, at least initially. When Dan arrived at the school these boys were its established stars, and he an interloper. He was not appointed a school prefect, as he was an unknown quantity, with no track record. Some prowess in the school attached to the ability to play cricket and rugby football, but Dan had never played either, and now found himself little better than average at activities at which others thought it important to excel. Despite his strength, speed, and solidity, he was never selected to play for an A rugby team, and turned out in the third fifteen, where he was remembered for his ferocious tackling. The sports at which Dan could do reasonably well were solo games, like handball and running. Handball, a version of fives, and a tougher game than squash because played with the bare hand, was popular at the school, and Dan was a keen player. In running, he came fourth in the school half-mile championship, inches behind two boys who ran a dead heat for second behind the speedier Cotterall. Politely, the school recorded Dan as having come 'third'. He really did come third in the annual school 'steeplechase' event, a three and three-quarter mile run through Herne Bay, Westmere, and Richmond that was held on 7 October. His time of 23 minutes and 40 seconds was quite good for those days, especially given that the boys did no real training, but he was 1 minute and 32 seconds behind the winner, who smashed the previous record.

Coming third was a new, and one imagines not altogether comfortable, experience for Dan, and taught him the need to struggle if you were to do well and be noticed. The same applied to his studies. At academic work he was clearly good, far better than competent, but men like Joseph, Cuddon-Large, and Petricevich were not to be dislodged easily from their positions of eminence. No one was unkind to him, his contemporaries were friendly, but the easy dominance of his immediate Invercargill past now counted for little. To these confident, and in many cases well-heeled, young men, Invercargill was a village, very cold, somewhere a long way away, and he its only representative in this far more advanced northern city. Judging by the jokes made in the school *Magazine* about the sons of cow cockies from Taranaki, Dan would have done well to keep quiet about his former domestic chores. His friends in the sixth form nicknamed him *Dangle*, though whether in deliberate reference to Sheridan is not known.

Perhaps what was hardest for him was that he felt the school to be like a prison, from which the boys were allowed out of custody only very rarely. Such opportunities as there were to see the outside world were occasional, and rather formal. The school Corps, which conducted drill every morning from 8.45 to 9.00, and for an hour at lunchtime on Fridays, held its annual camp at Narrow Neck from 10 to 15 March. The days were filled with war games and manœuvres, shooting practice, and swimming in the sea, while at night there was camp food and sleeping under canvas. It must have seemed highly regimented to a boy used to the freedom of Southland's creeks and bush.

Other expeditions were equally carefully organized: on 17 March, St Patrick's Day, for the parade, and the evening concert in the Town Hall; on 25 April, Anzac Day, for a parade and wreath-laying ceremony; on 19 June for the Procession of the Blessed Sacrament at the Home of the Little Sisters of the Poor; and on 19 and 26 July to see rugby matches involving the touring English side at Eden Park. There was an annual dance at St Mary's Convent School, held that year on 12 August, and the Auckland Secondary Schools' Sports Day in the last week of October. Occasionally on a Saturday, especially in summer if cricket was rained off, the boys might be 'marched off to the movies'.[26] But these were all formal and chaperoned events, fun—at least in the case of trips to the cinema, and football matches where the English were soundly beaten—but completely lacking in the freedoms that had characterized life at home.

Weekends were oceans of boredom. On Saturdays there was sport or private reading. On Sundays worship, prep., letter-writing home, private reading, and a walk. But where would a 16-year-old schoolboy go on an Auckland Sunday in 1930, when everything except the churches was shut? On one day a term the boarders were given a half-day on which they could go out on their own, perhaps to a cinema, or to a milkbar, or to browse in the bookshops on Wellesley Street, and in the Strand Arcade.[27] But even then, where was he to go, what was he to do? He had little money, Auckland was a strange city. And in 1930 two of these half-days—23 March and 16 November—fell on Sundays. Only one, 27 June, fell usefully on a Friday. For Dan, literally a thousand miles from home, knowing almost nobody in Auckland, this must only have emphasized his isolation, not cured it. The melancholy in this was further emphasized by a coincidence. In 1930 Remarque's novel *All Quiet on the Western Front* arrived in translation in New Zealand. The boys read it, and also went to see *Journey's End*, the anti-war play by R. C. Sherriff, which was also just then published and enjoying theatrical success around the world. Mike Joseph wrote in his *Memoir*: 'already we were part of a generation that had no illusions about war.'[28]

Sacred Heart College represented such a complete change of life for the boy who had grown up with the outside world on his back doorstep, a ferret in his pocket, the animals, farmland, and bush of his childhood awaiting him, that he again turned in on himself. Later he said that he 'hated it'.[29] In practice the experience may have been rather less intense than this implies. Like many boys sent away to boarding-school for the first time, enduring the sudden disruption of their previous way of life, missing the comforts of a mother's cooking and a brother's companion-ship, no longer able to keep a pet, seemingly caged against nature itself, he was miserable. His ego was taking a few knocks too. And these things were added to by his own disposition to gloom, feelings magnified by the timing of his immersion in boarding-school. He had just started to get interested in girls, beer, and cigarettes. All three were now as far from his reach as it was possible to imagine. By way of substitute, Miss Daphne Knight gave dancing classes for the boys in College on a Saturday evening in the winter months, causing Rupert Cuddon-Large agonies of embar-rassment by calling him Mr Large.[30] She was host to a dance on 3 October when the girls from St Mary's Convent School joined together with the Sacred Heart College boys for mutual entertainment. The social pain of this occasion for all parties is readily imagined, and not disproved by the SHC *Magazine*'s hollow assurance that 'the evening passed all too quickly'. Miss Knight also gave the boys 'elocution' lessons, but Dan, arriving only in the sixth form, may have evaded this privilege.

Dan never wrote anything that draws even tangentially on the year he spent at Sacred Heart. Among his papers there are various pieces of autobiographical writing, but nothing dealing with 1930. Many years later, when he talked about his life to various interlocutors with a tape recorder running, he passed over 1930 as though it were barely there, merely a necessary preliminary to something far more important. It would be wrong to assume from any of this that Sacred Heart College was irrelevant to him. The truth may be rather that the exact nature of its importance is hard to detect from a record which is so thin. It is not even certain whether or not he went home for one of the school holidays in either May or August/September, though the balance of probabilities is that he did not.[31] His younger brothers had no recollection of his coming home, which surely they would have done, given his now extraordinary status in the household. Certainly for one vacation he went to Tauranga and stayed with Michael Joseph's family. They were hospitable and lively, their dinner table a place of laughter and intelligent, quick conversation. Dan remembered it as 'a shining spot' in the year.[32] Of course it would have been difficult to go home, and in any case it was not essential. He could have stayed on at the school, but in all probability he went in the other school holiday to stay with his Aunt Mag, Maggie Gunn, his mother's younger sister who had migrated to Auckland so many years before. She now kept a boarding-house in Parnell, a 'hilltop slum' as Dan recalled it over fifty years later. He would not have enjoyed it much. She was eventually 'driven out by bugs'.³³

The implications of this are indicative. It is as if young Dan felt himself to have disappeared when he went to Sacred Heart College, that *real* life had been suspended in favour of an artificial world whose only importance lay in teaching the virtues of self-preservation, patience, and escape. For all the prayer and meditation of its Catholic discipline, the lessons he carried away seem to have been instrumental and material rather than ideal, for he drew the conclusion that salvation lay in work, which might enable him to evade the further torment of this lonely and unreal existence. So he buckled down to it. Many people would note, over the years, his formidable capacity for work, and the speed with which he could dispatch it. The basis of this talent seems to have been laid down here in the earnest desire to escape by the only means open to him.³⁴

In the end of year school examinations he came top in aggregate in his VIB class, and was awarded the Gold Metal for Latin. Then the University of New Zealand Entrance Scholarships examinations began on 1 December and continued for a week. After that the sixth-form boys had eight days or so of relative freedom at school: 'We boarders were officially allowed to get lost, and we spent our time sunbathing and reading in the long grass of the gully.'³⁵ Then they said their farewells 'without great nostalgia, certainly with no regret',³⁶ and he set off on the long journey south, home for the summer.

When the examination results were published in January Dan surprised his school, though perhaps not himself. He had come third in the whole country in History, ninth equal in Latin, tenth in English, where he had done slightly better even than Mike Joseph. But for his lamentable performance in Mechanics—24 per cent—his overall position would have been much higher than his actual thirty-fifth place. Recognizing this, the examiners awarded him a special University National Scholarship. Out of twenty-eight Scholarships awarded that year Sacred Heart College had four, the others going to Mike Joseph, who came first on aggregate in the whole country, Fred Petricevich (tenth), and Rupert Cuddon-Large (fourteenth). Dan was only fourth among his peers in this high company, but he had done it in one year, when they had taken two.

From Uitenhage in South Africa, Brother Borgia, who had left SHC towards the end of November, wrote to Dan in February of the new year with his congratulations, but also to encourage him to return to Sacred Heart for his second year of sixth-form work.[37] The letter came too late to influence Dan's decision, but would have made no difference in any case. His mind had long since been made up. Nothing would have persuaded him to return to Richmond Road, from which success in the examinations was meant to secure release. He was free of school. Was he ready for the university?

4

LOVE AND BOOKS

my own private struggle is the struggle to keep myself out of the
bourgeois and the commonplace. You have seen the sentimental
in me and the rest too, no doubt. And it is pretty strong in me
too. It is a long jump out of the working class over the bourgeois
swamp. But I have a pair of running shoes.

(WKDP: DMD to WKD, 5 Sept. 1932)

I was impressed for the ten thousandth time by the fact that
literature illuminates life only for those to whom books are a
necessity. Books are unconvertible assets, to be passed on only to
those who possess them already.

(Anthony Powell, *The Valley of Bones*, 244)

The question of which university Dan should go to did not arise:
Otago University, in Dunedin, was the obvious choice. The formal
status of Otago University was as one college of the University of
New Zealand, which had three other constituent colleges in Auckland, Wellington, and Christchurch. But the University of New Zealand, which was born a 'child of discord',[1] was an examining body of
little or no importance to the teaching institutions, and among these
Otago University had a distinctive identity. At its foundation in
1869, under Scottish and Presbyterian influence, it had been the first
institution of higher education in the country. It surrendered its formal independence almost immediately,[2] but its status, as the retention
of its name implied, remained different from the other colleges. It was
the only one to have schools of medicine, dentistry, mining, home
science, and commerce, so that, unusually for the times, most of its
students were full-time. This gave to both the university and the town
the intellectual as well as the social air of a university city which the
other centres, where students generally lived at home, and higher education took place mainly in the evenings, certainly lacked. Dunedin was the
obvious place for Dan to go, not simply because it was nearest his home,
but because it was, *qua* university—in the full meaning of the term—the
best place to go. Students came to it from all over the country.

The city of Dunedin was really no more than a small town. Its population in 1931, when Dan arrived for the first day of term on 10 March, was little more than 80,000.[3] They lived in stone and wooden houses, built largely in imitation of Scottish architectural forms, on the hills overlooking Port Chalmers, a deep-water port that was the original basis of the city's commercial success. This natural harbour is sheltered by a long and beautiful peninsula of hills and woodland, a place of sheltered beaches, wild rocky coves, seal colonies, and, high upon its seaward cliffs, the breeding grounds of the albatross.

The university was housed in a cluster of stone buildings modelled according to Victorian mock-Gothic Baronial taste, beside a small stream that really is called the Water of Leith. The lawns that lead down to the steep gully of this stream, and the bridges that span it to link the university grounds with the town, are planted with shrubs and ornamental trees, providing space to linger and talk, or to read in the summer sun. A short walk to the north are the municipal botanical gardens, which lead to the suburb of Opoho and the secluded grounds of Knox College, a Presbyterian theological school that also functioned as a hall of residence for the university. To the east, and running almost to the banks of the harbour, was Logan Park, the site of the great Exhibition where Dan had come five years before, and which now served as playing-fields for the university, and the site of the Dunedin city art gallery.

The university, like the civic leaders, thought of itself in a Scottish context, heir to the tradition of Edinburgh and St Andrews rather than Oxford and Cambridge. The degree course was structured in imitation of the Scottish: three years leading to a BA, followed by one year of Honours work for a classified MA. This identity of origins and purpose at the university was mirrored in the town. Dunedin was administered by a small group of prosperous merchants, Scots and Presbyterians almost to a man. Their wives, the matrons of the city, combined with the wives of the professoriate to set its social tone. The university did not so much accept these local codes as adhere to them naturally. Theirs was an identity of interest as well as of style and manners.

As with other students both before and since, Dan's first experience of university life was in its living arrangements. He went straight into private lodgings, at first with a family called Clayton who lived close to the university. Here he had a room to himself and three meals a day for twenty-five shillings a week, and was required to keep the rules of the house: no female visitors, no drink, no late nights. The room was cold in winter, which often seems like most of the year in Dunedin, and a serious

young man, once the university library was shut, would go to bed to
continue his studies. The Claytons and their unmarried grown-up
daughter were friendly and decent people, the food better than at Sacred
Heart, but old Mr Clayton was mortally ill. Confined to bed, but concerned for his dignity in what he knew to be his last months of life, he got
his 17-year-old lodger to shave him every day. Mr Clayton died during
Dan's first year, leaving him in the slightly awkward position of man of
the house, doing the odd jobs that required—as it was then presumed—
masculine powers. The implied intimacy of his relationship with Mr
Clayton also left him feeling that he could not now just leave, if he should
want to. Somehow, the Clayton women had become an obligation.

In common with the city, the university Dan joined was small. There
were 1,123 students enrolled in 1931, the great majority of them concentrated in the Special Schools.[4] A single Faculty of Arts and Science
catered for the remainder, of whom 344 were studying Arts and Music.
The entire staff of this faculty consisted of eleven professors and eighteen
lecturers and tutors. Of the professors, only two had been there for less
than ten years. Six had been there since at least the middle of the First
World War. None was a woman. Of the eighteen other staff, five were
women, though four of them, all spinsters, were among the six longest
serving staff. Miss Turnbull, the lecturer in Classics, had held her post
since 1915, but her professor, Thomas Dagger Adams, who had held it
before her, had been at the university since 1907. Professor Findlay, a
brilliant young philosopher originally from South Africa, but trained at
Oxford and Graz, who arrived at Otago in 1934, was the only new
member of the Faculty of Arts and Science in the entire five years that
Dan spent there. Universities are always places of gossip. The intimacy
and stability of Otago University reinforced the characteristic.

The university library was housed in a single, long room, always silent.
There was a large lecture room for first-year lectures, and a small one for
the rest. The young men sat to one side, the young women to the other.
A photograph of the Latin class annual picnic, taken in the summer term
of 1932, shows Professor Adams and Miss Turnbull with their entire
student body: just eighteen in total, and still segregated. This was a small,
comfortable and conservative world where not much had changed in a
long time. Contemporaries recalled that learning was by instruction, not
by discussion or participation.[5] Lecturers told classes of students what
they were required to know. Examinations were structured for students
to regurgitate it. Dan enrolled in courses for four full units, French, Latin,
Greek, and English I: a fairly standard diet from a limited bill of fare.[6]

The course work was heavily weighted towards the history and grammar of language, and required numerous hours of compulsory attendance at lectures each week.

The students themselves were drawn almost entirely from the Anglican and Presbyterian middle classes. For one thing, university was expensive, and there were very few scholarships. And in any case, most of the scholarships were won by people from the middle classes. Student dress reflected these origins. The men wore suits, or blazers and slacks, with collars and ties. They smoked pipes, or Players Gold Leaf, and wore evening dress for dinners and dances. Many of them owned cars, or had access to their parents'—a great luxury at the time. The young women also dressed like their elders: frocks and stockings, sensible shoes, hats, gloves, and handbags in the daytime; party dresses, ball gowns, and long gloves for evening occasions.

Dan felt out of place here, but initially he seems to have done his best to fit in. His family ribbed him, at the end of his first term, about the Scottish accent he came home with, and which he promptly lost again.[7] He was careful about his dress, polite in his manners, studious in his approach. The good work habits that he had imposed on himself at Sacred Heart stood him in good stead in this new, but not wholly different, scholarly environment, where a good memory and powers of recall were still the keys to success. He was keen to prove himself, but the ambition was still unfocused, perhaps more a wish to justify the sacrifice that he knew his parents to be making, than to pursue any particular laurels.[8] From the start, he determined to come first in every course he took.

He was not long in discovering that few people stood in his way in this ambition, but that the ones who did were worthy of the competition. First among them were Winifred McQuilkan and G. F. Hall. Dan already knew the names: Frank Hall, from the Christian Brothers' school in Dunedin, had been placed sixth on the scholarship list in January, and Winnie McQuilkan fourteenth, both well ahead of D. M. Davin. These two could hardly have been less like each other. Frank was a Catholic from a wealthy family, and lived in a substantial house at 17 Granville Terrace, in the smart Dunedin suburb of Belleknowes, above the Town Belt. His father, a retired ear, nose, and throat specialist, was an eccentric who regarded the university as a sink of iniquity, and would occasionally propose donating the entire family fortune to charity. By contrast, Winnie McQuilkan was the daughter of an alcoholic father and a mother who kept a small dairy. They both died when she was young, but her mother had left her a little money, and with this she spent nine years as a boarder in Invercargill to attend junior school and subsequently Southland Girls' High School, spending her vacations with an aunt in Riverton. She and Dan came from different sides of the Invercargill religious tracks, and so had never met.

The three of them, Dan, Frank, and Winnie, all respected each other's intellectual powers, but whereas the acquaintance between Dan and Frank grew into a deep friendship over their years at Otago, Dan and Winnie remained merely rivals on good terms, though she was very fond of him, and used to knit him mufflers. In one way, however, Winnie McQuilkan was responsible for Dan's academic success. She was an excellent Latin scholar, and, year on year, he had his work cut out to beat her in the examinations. Frank, more diffident, uncertain about the course he wanted to pursue in life but shielded from any immediate necessity to make up his mind by the family fortune, never sought to compete with Dan, whom he regarded from early on as his intellectual superior.[9]

At first, like all beginning undergraduates living alone for the first time in a strange town, Dan was lonely. Both Rupert Cuddon—he dropped the Large when he got away from Miss Knight—and Fred Petricevich were also at Otago, but they were in the Medical School, keeping even longer academic hours, and in a slightly different part of town. Dan still spent some time with Fred, however. Before they began their first year Fred went down to Invercargill to spend a few days with him, and sent reports of the inadequacies of this hick town (as he portrayed it) home to their erstwhile colleagues in Auckland.[10] Together, on occasional after-noon forays in Dunedin, they began to explore the pubs.

Apart from this, Dan's first social activities at the university were concentrated on the Catholic Students' Association, which met on Friday evenings in St Joseph's Hall, next to the Catholic cathedral on the steep hillside of Rattray Street. Here he found the customary fruit cup of socials and dances; weekend walking expeditions; tea and cakes; earnest student discussion, and prayer. And here Dan first saw and fell in love with Winnie Gonley.

Winifred Kathleen Gonley was the daughter of Irish Catholic parents from the small town of Otautau in Southland, little more than a village really, situated at the confluence (Otautau is Maori for the meeting of the waters) of the Otautau Stream and the Aparima River, about thirty miles north-west of Invercargill. This is rolling hill-farming country with stands of bush, the town snuggled against the side of the elegant

49

Longwood Range of low mountains that folds away to the west, to Merivale and Tuatapere, and out to the sea. Winnie's father, Michael Gonley, was a merchant seaman, born and raised in Manor Hamilton, a suburb of Sligo. After working the Pacific routes south from San Francisco, he tried living for a while in Australia, where amongst other things he worked as a professional boxer and sparring partner. He came on to New Zealand at the turn of the century, met and married Winifred Crowe, ten years his junior, and settled in Otautau, where they opened and kept a village shop in the middle of the High Street, opposite the Otautau Hotel. They specialized in what were then known as 'fancy goods': pieces of china, table decorations, doilies and crochet work. They sold books and newspapers, and held various local service franchises. Michael also kept the village barber's shop and billiard saloon, and, under the counter, kept a book. Gonley's book was so honest that policemen laid their bets with him.[11] Michael and Winifred had five children, three boys and two girls, and Winnie, born on 27 July 1909, was the middle child.[12] She shared her birthday with Dan's mother.

Her own mother, after whom she was named, came from tough settler stock. She had been born in New Zealand, the only daughter of John and Ellen Crowe, and she and her eight brothers had been raised first at Temuka, in South Canterbury, and then in Southland. Her mother, Winnie's grandmother Ellen Crowe, born Ellen Silke, had migrated from Galway in 1866, when she must have been about 20 years old, to join John Crowe to whom she had been promised in matrimony.[13] In the years that followed, the Crowes then financed the migration of much of the rest of her family: first a sister, then her mother and three brothers, then another brother.[14] Her sister Mary married a James Kane and they also settled in Southland. Silkes, Crowes, and Kanes were to the Southland interior what Davins, Doleys, and Concannons were to the immediate environs of Invercargill. Even down to their origins in Galway, young Winnie Gonley's family connections were a kind of mirror image of Dan's. The families did not know each other personally, but they certainly knew *of* each other. Old Larry Hynes, pedalling his Irish tales across the Southland landscape, was a link between these two branches of the same immigrant tree.

At first Dan knew nothing of these connections, and was far too timid to find out. Winnie was four years older than he was, already something of a star in student circles, and just embarked on her MA year of study in English. She was short in stature, slim and sturdy together, with a quicksilver personality and a quick tongue. But there was a side to her that, studied in tranquillity, was both tender and passionate, with a serenity reminiscent of Vermeer's *Portrait of a Young Girl*, dark-eyed and calm, deep and a little mysterious. Her fame in university circles was partly literary. She had ambitions to be a writer, and was encouraged in them by both the Professor of English, Herbert Ramsay, and the lecturer, Gregor Cameron, a young man appointed in 1928 and, unusually for the time, on good first-name terms with many undergraduates.

Winnie's impact on Dan was, as in all adolescent love, both perfect and complete. Fifteen months later he recalled how, in church on Sunday, he would 'sit well forward for the quickening of pulses when I knew that you were present though I could not always see you. And with an absurd calmness that was really ecstasy I used to meet you. How queer that I could have been so calm when I was surging and seething.'[15] Their first contact of this sort was over the loan of her copy of Lewis and Short's *Latin Dictionary*, which she suggested he 'dart' over to her place at 103 Union Street to collect. By the end of term they had become friends, had exchanged first kisses, and endured their first row when jealousy overtook him at the Law Faculty Ball. These were no more than the first innocent exchanges of a mutual attraction, one which he felt far more deeply than she. Dan was quite inexperienced with girls. He had 'walked out' a couple of times with a friend called Win Heywood in Invercargill over the summer vacation, but in practical terms he was a beginner. Winnie Gonley filled his mind, his imagination, and all his potential imagined future.

By the end of his first term he was not only hopelessly in love, but gloomy about his propects, pessimistic about her feelings for him, jealous of her other friends. When he got home to 'Kegville, having to pretend I am having a good holiday', he wrote to her about his 'torturing doubts'.

I know that I may offend you terribly by this, Winnie, but viewed in the nearest approach to the cold light of reason I can muster, what does it amount to? I a tiresome fool and egoist am presuming to hope to inspire a liking that will endure, in the bosom of a Being like you. How can you the sought-after Winnie Gonley, the popular member of parties, the blasé, the clever and the gay, feel anything but a transitory pity for *me*?[16]

Good questions, but Winnie was having none of it. She replied from Dunedin, where she had stayed on in the vacation to work, refusing to categorize the feelings that they might have for each other. 'I refuse utterly to be swept into this maelstrom of anxiety grief and restlessness which is engulfing you. . . . It's a terrific and terrifying piece of egotism that, to imagine that my whole column of emotion topples because you are not looking at it.' None the less she offered enough encouragement to improve his mood: 'So, my silly child, my darling, mo vohileen bawn, of course I haven't changed overnight.'[17]

In Dan's state of mind these protestations probably made little difference. His love was as irrational as his fears were well grounded. Winnie had been in university life for four years already. She was popular, and had a large circle of friends. She knew Dr John Stallworthy a little, a senior medical student, then in his second year as President of the Student's Association, and about to leave for Britain and postgraduate work. And she also knew Andrew Sharp, already a Rhodes Scholar when Dan arrived at Otago, and Geoffrey Cox, a final year law and history student, who was, like her, associate editor of the Otago *Review*, the annual university journal which was a combination of literary magazine and year-book. Cox won his Rhodes Scholarship in 1931, when Dan was a freshman. Gregor Cameron, the shy English lecturer, was in love with her. Some of her friends were intimates of some years standing. Before university she had been a pupil at St Dominic's Catholic boarding-school for Girls in Dunedin with a group that included Mary Hussey, Marge Thompson, and Antonietta McGrath. Toni McGrath was her particular friend, and they flatted together as university students in Upper Albany Street. Both had been well educated in Latin and French, and they shared a wide-ranging curiosity, about both life and literature, though they had been far better educated in the latter than the former.[18]

These young women thought themselves, probably rightly, to be a part of the very first generation of young New Zealanders to discover and to read not only contemporary English, American, and European literature, but also Katherine Mansfield. Mansfield they worshipped not only for what she had written, but also for how she had lived: the romantic determination, undeterred, as they saw it, by fate. They called her, and thought of her, on first-name terms. It was Katherine who inspired them to read more widely in authors who lay, at that time, outside the boundaries of bourgeois New Zealand culture: D. H. Lawrence and Aldous Huxley; James Joyce and Oscar Wilde; Dostoevsky and Chekhov. More important even than this, through her *Journal* and *Letters* Katherine inspired them to think of the possibility of themselves becoming writers. They could conceive of nothing more important, more exciting, more fully alive, than to live the life of travel, experiment, and love, while devoting themselves to literature. Ambition conceived in romantic illusion, perhaps even folly, but one on which they had fixed. They seemed to Dan free spirits.

Toni McGrath had two sisters, Adelina older, and Joan younger. All three were convent educated, but their mother had died when Toni was about 15. The youngest, 'Wee Joan' as Winnie called her, also went to Otago University where she was a contemporary of Dan's, and became a part of Winnie's circle. Another friend was Hypatia Johnson, known as Paish. She was the daughter of a Danish seaman who kept a fish shop in North Dunedin, painted seascapes, and named his children after free-thinkers.[19] But the two strongest of all these characters may have been Dick Purves and Mabel McIndoe. Mabel lived in the South Dunedin suburb of St Clair with her mother, who was an artist, a contemporary of Frances Hodgkins. She would disappear from time to time to Tahiti and Nice on painting expeditions. One of Mabel's older brothers, Archie, was a remarkable physician, and became a truly great man as the pioneer of plastic surgery. Like him Mabel was determined to study science. She was witty and outspoken, drove her mother's enormous Humber, which she called the 'Struggle Buggy', and affected the manners (or lack of them) of the English flappers of the 1920s, thumbing her nose at convention and throwing herself into 'What ho', 'corker', and 'amusing' activities. A tireless talker and hedonist, she was the sort who might upend a bowl of sugar on the head of a hapless dance companion.[20] Intoxicatingly witty, such people are the life of the party and the source of the hangover. Dick Purves could hardly have been more different. He was a young research scientist with a degree in physics who moved into the fledgling field of biochemistry.[21] An early girlfriend would greet every suggestion he made to her, however innocent, with the words 'Not here, not now'.

Friendship with the unconventional was emphasized by Winnie's attachment to a young man called Harry Aitken. She called him Alpha. He was a bohemian figure, tall and thin, with a white complexion, and would wear a long dark overcoat, a broad-brimmed black hat, and carry a cane. Over a number of years they had become close friends. Habitually, she visited him on a Sunday. Harry was an enigma, a brilliant biochemist with what many people thought a difficult temperament. Somehow he got on the wrong side of his professor in the Chemistry Department and was awarded only a second-class degree, but the Medical School snapped him up with an offer of a research post, and he had ambitions to travel to Britain for postgraduate work. His rather older and equally brilliant brother A. C. Aitken was already Professor of Mathematics at Edinburgh University, where he was acquiring a slightly odd reputation, among other things, as a genius at mental calculation.[22] Alpha was that engaging rarity, the scientist with a literary intellectual background. He knew the classics, spoke French, and was a witty though sometimes threatening conversationalist. He suffered from terrible headaches, and could be morose, cutting, sarcastic, and nihilistic. But he offered a glimpse into the world of the mind that was at once exciting and terrifying in pedestrian and provincial Dunedin: a gothic world where all the emotions—love and hate, terror and exhilaration—were magnified.

Young Dan, only 17 years old, a freshman dazzled by his new connections, knew barely any of this. He was aware of Alpha's importance, of which he was jealous, but he was still innocently lacking in self-confidence. What drew Winnie to Dan was his academic brilliance, his air of innocent promise, still unshaped and unformed. In return he began to confide in her, to tell her about his family and his schooldays, and in doing so felt the cool breeze of a fresh consciousness lifting and brushing aside the melancholia that loneliness induced. 'There was something clogged about my affections . . . A dog was all I ever really loved. But since we met I seem to have softened.'[23] From his tales of home and school she detected a parallel with James Joyce's hero Stephen Dedalus, perhaps particularly in Dan's passage through Sacred Heart College, with its violent punishments and endless devotions, its annual retreat and redemptorist hell-fire preacher. At the end of his first term she lent him her copy of *A Portrait of the Artist as a Young Man*.[24]

Furthermore, Dan was handsome, with his strong bones and dark features, and it was the combination of this with his freshness and innocence, and the power of his intellect, that appealed to Winnie. She calls him 'my child' in her early letters, takes him under her intellectual wing, starts to tell him what he ought to read, and how he should behave. 'I reckon you're a naughty boy, for being sentimentally sensual in letters—It's not *comme il faut*. I thought I'd sophisticated you', she wrote in one letter.[25] 'Please don't expect too much of me. Don't grieve when I don't write. Trust yourself more', she said in another.[26]

From the beginning she was ambitious for him. Geoffrey Cox recalled that at his only meeting with Dan at Otago, in 1931 or 1932, Winnie introduced the freshman as someone 'who is going to do great things'. Cox remembered the moment: he was descending the stairs in Allen Hall, coming down from the Students' Association executive office, and saw Winnie with this young man below. It was an epiphany, and he always carried it with him.[27] Feeling callow and immature, Dan was profoundly grateful for the guidance he got from Winnie, and continually sought ways of doing things for her. Winnie was hopeless at getting up in the morning, and would lie abed till lunchtime despite alarm clocks. Dan would get her out of bed by throwing pebbles at her windows, so that she would get to her morning lectures. One sunny early spring afternoon at the end of the second term they went walking on the hill in the botanical gardens, the upper gardens as they were known. They were happy talking, and he broke rhododendron blossom from the shrubs to give to her. Her friendship brought him the full range of emotional response, from intense happiness to jealous misery, romantic longing to nihilism, misanthropy, and despair. But it also had another, and in many ways more important, social effect. In his first year at university, Winnie Gonley lifted him out of the company of his own contemporaries, and propelled him into a world of MA students, far more mature and well read. Here, with only the occasional exception, he was welcomed, and well liked. They gave him presents on his birthday: a new experience. Because he had admired it so much, Marge Thompson gave him a revolver that she owned. The weapon was at least forty years old, but in perfect working order. Marge told him that it had belonged to her grandfather, who had himself obtained it from a character known as 'the King of the Goldfields'. Generosity was simply a part of friendship. In the early summer of his third term they went for long walks at weekends on the peninsula, stopping for a beer at a pub, talking poetry and religion. Winnie's circle were unusual people, too bright to be a part of the conventional undergraduate world. When all the talk among female undergraduates was about slimming, they formed 'the ten stone club', a hypothetical society with a minimum weight for membership sufficiently high to exclude bores.[28] They drank and smoked. They had the reputation for being a bit fast. But above all, they took the study of literature seriously without allowing their relish for the subject to be diminished in academic drudgery. Dan, with his dogged work habits, and his gloomy and pessimistic view of the world, needed such a stimulant.

Not that Winnie's was a carefree world. She had been deeply touched by her grandmother's death, and this was closely followed by a deterioration in her mother's health. Sick, often unable to eat, Mrs Gonley had periods of relapse at home when she was confined to bed, then periods of treatment in hospital in Invercargill. Winnie and her older sister Mollie, who was 26 in 1931 and a home science teacher at the Southland Girls' High School in Invercargill, had to fill in for their mother in the Otautau shop during their vacations from university and school. Managing their father, himself distracted with worry about his sick wife, and frequently of uncertain temper, was an additional burden. The young women, though they were free to do whatever they liked while away in Dunedin or Invercargill, knew that at home the old rules of their childhood still applied. There was no going out without permission, and boyfriends were a sticky topic. They could never be quite sure how their parents would react.

This preoccupied Dan and Winnie as the end of the 1931 academic year approached. Theirs was the fragile love-affair of two young Catholics, still at a kissing and hand-holding stage. For Dan, romantically engaged, committed by yearning as well as by habitual determination, three months of vacation was a menacing desert of loneliness. After examinations he went down to Invercargill on 21 November, leaving Winnie behind in Dunedin to begin work on her thesis—'New Zealand Life in Contemporary Literature'. Ten days later she followed him, staying overnight with Mollie at her lodgings in Robertson Street, Invercargill, and contriving to spend the whole of the next day with Dan before going home to Otautau in the late afternoon. The following evening she scribbled him a happy letter, not knowing 'whether it's love or not', but calling their afternoon a 'splendid shining everything'. In her state of animated excitement she had picked up and taken with her the wrong suitcase from the ladies' waiting-room at Invercargill station.[29]

Two weeks later, after carefully orchestrated preparations between them, Dan visited the Gonleys in Otautau on his bicycle, arriving as if by chance, knocking at the door in the guise of an acquaintance who just happened to be passing. Winnie had deliberately worn an old frock so that her sister would suspect nothing. Thoughtlessly, Dan arrived at one o'clock, just as the family was sitting down to lunch. The housekeeper, whom Winnie detested, came to the lunch table with the news that 'There's a young gentleman asking for Miss Winnie', at which Winnie blushed disastrously. Her father was equable, however, an extra place was laid, the meal went off serenely enough. Mrs Gonley was too ill to get up, Mr Gonley busy in the shop. Dan and Winnie spent a summer afternoon talking and walking on the hills above the little town. He was invited to stay the night. In the morning she woke him with a kiss.[30]

Dan fed on the memories of this experience through the wastes of Christmas and the new year. He sent the Gonleys a box of gooseberries from his father's garden, and bought Winnie a pocket edition, bound in soft brown leather, of Dostoevsky's *Poor People* as a Christmas present. This was Dostoevsky's first novel, completed when he was 24 'If I do not find a publisher for it,' he had written to his older brother, 'I shall probably hang myself.'

This world of emotional intensity was clandestine. On the surface, Dan's home life continued much as before, with visits to Woodlands, hunting expeditions with Matt, days spent reading in the library, or with his legs tucked up to his chin on the bed at home. The university examination results arrived. He had first-class marks in Greek, Latin, and English; was first equal—that dratted McQuilkan—in Latin; and first in English. He was awarded the Gilray Memorial Prize in English: two guineas for buying books. On New Year's eve he was in the Brown Owl with Rex Railton, an acquaintance at university, where Janet MacBride, another student from his own year, found them by coincidence, and they saw in the new year together.[31] Even in Invercargill there was an expanding social horizon brought by university life.

Winnie set him a reading list that included Proust, Giraudoux's *Siegfried et le Limousin*, and *Le Grand Meaulnes* by Alain-Fournier.[32] He read Apuleius' *The Golden Ass*, Compton Mackenzie's *Three Couriers*, *Vanity Girl*, and *Vestal Fire*, which he thought 'a masterpiece',[33] and D. H. Lawrence's *The White Peacock*.[34] By the new year he had read Balzac's *César Birotteau*, Compton Mackenzie's *Carnival*, and Volume II of *Sinister Street*. Then he worked on Martial's *Epigrams*, and started to read Anatole France's *Les Dieux ont soif*.[35] Later in the month he read D. H. Lawrence's *The Plumed Serpent*, George Moore, Casanova: 'he must have possessed a diabolical resolution.'[36] After that Walter Pater's *Marius the Epicurean*, and then Proust's *Du côté de chez Swann*, which he declared 'an extremely sympathetic and faithful record of a love affair in its rise and decline'.[37] In February, Martial, translating with detailed care, then Aldous Huxley's *Antic Hay*. Huxley 'has a knack of making you feel gallingly provincial', but '[h]e doesn't come up to D. H. or Comp.'[38]

Over this summer books became a passion that was to last almost to the end of his life. Here it was that he learned to read rapidly, and without loss of substance. And here it was too that he came to love the texture of books: how they had been made, printed, bound. How well they held together, and how well they would last. Even how they smelt. The book as artefact is a more powerful component of literary culture than is commonly supposed. Dan learned this lesson early: it is a part of the heritage of publishing.

Yet despite this world of the literary imagination, Dan was desperately lonely. He and Winnie attempted to engineer a meeting at the Tuatapere races on New Year's Day, but it fell through, leaving him depressed. Out walking with Muff one evening he 'felt all the want of you that I had smothered in books through the day'[39] but she told him not to be 'Rachelish'.[40] He managed another day-long visit to Otautau on 13 January, and, rather more daring, Winnie paid him a visit at his home in Invercargill on 21 January. Afterwards Mary Davin told her son that it was good for a man to have a girl a few years older: 'it lends him steadyness.'[41]

Winnie was actually going through a phase of profound turmoil. Her mother's health was still deteriorating. She was making little progress on her MA thesis. Worried about her future, she had decided to return to Dunedin for another year to go to Teachers' Training College, but she had little interest in the coursework, and viewed the prospect as little better than a necessary bore. Her friend Toni McGrath, more determined than ever to seek her romantic fortune *à la* Mansfield, left for Sydney *en route* for Britain on 15 January. At the end of the month Alpha also left, setting off to pursue his brilliant scientific career in Edinburgh and London. Winnie felt his going like a bereavement. In this state, on 24 January, she wrote Dan a tender, intense, dramatic letter, declaring her love for him, retracting it, wishing, modifying, projecting.

There is only one certainty for me; in my relations with you there is no certainty. Even as I wrote that, despairingly, I was aware that that is not true. I just don't know. But I shall know, Dan. Now, during the last few months I am filled with the desire to love you, so urgent sometimes, that the desire is almost fulfilled, but no. There is no completeness about my love for you, no steadfastness—A steadfast affection, yes—And frequently, many many times I want you to be with me . . . Pray for me, and pray for Alpha, Dan. I pray for you both always now . . . and for Toni—Toni sailed from Sydney on Friday: I think I shall never see her again. It is such agony, Dan, to think that. And it foreshadows agony I *cannot* endure. Dan, how is it to be borne? Alpha. It is as though the sun were going to shine on Mars, as though the sun were departing, as though we should never again know the sun's light and warmth. Dan, Dan . . . Dan write to Winnie.[42]

He did, two days later, touched and humbled, a little bitter perhaps at the strength of her enduring affection for his departing competitor, but feeling for her in her loss. 'I sometimes torture myself with the thought that it may become a fellow feeling.'[43] This exchange of letters marked the beginning of a change in the balance of their relationship. Until now Winnie had been the leader, Dan her acolyte. She was moulding him, and, still unformed, shy, and inexperienced, he responded to her lead. With the fracture of her world in the early new year of 1932, however, she began to show a need for his support.

The change was subtle, unnoticed at the time. In late February he still saw himself as the supplicant, though ambitious for equality: 'something within me pipes up and says, "What right have you to be near Her? Haven't you got a cheek?" . . . I feel as if I ought not to be surprised if you turned and sent me about my business. But that's rot and I'll get up to you yet . . .'.[44] The changing balance of their relationship, and the sense in Dan of his own growing competence, now coincided with a piece of good luck. Miss Clayton wrote to tell him that her mother had had to go into hospital, and that under the circumstances she was not able to have him to board for the new academic year.[45]

In the middle of February he went up to Dunedin for the day to find new lodgings, and eventually found them with the McDowells at 568 King Street, a house which is still there. Here, a five-minute walk from the university, he had an upstairs room with broad windows looking out over the rugby pitch of North Grounds to the back of the Anglican hall of residence, Selwyn College. The McDowells, 'a pair of fairly ancient birds and very decent sorts',[46] wanted 27s. 6d. a week, but they had no objection to female visitors. Winnie went up to Dunedin herself a day later to start work at the Training College. She had trouble finding somewhere to live, but eventually moved into 'a tiny, tiny room' at Scurr's, a boarding-house at 81 York Place.[47]

The new academic year began on 7 March. As before, Dan registered for four full units: Latin II, Greek II, and English II, plus History I, though he dropped Greek before the end of the year. English was mainly the history, structure, philology, and etymology of the language, including Old English grammar, where they studied Sweet's *Anglo-Saxon Reader*, Sisam's *Fourteenth-Century Verse and Prose*, and Chaucer's *Canterbury Tales*. Latin followed a similar development, with emphasis on unseen translations both from and into Latin. Set texts were Tacitus' *Annals* and Horace's *Odes*, and this year he was expected to master the general literature and history of the Roman world from the death of Sulla to the death of Nero.[48] In History he studied the main developments of Europe, America, and Japan from 1815 to 1914.

The young man who came back to Dunedin for his second year was rather different from the boarding-school adolescent of the year before. He was still a Catholic, still going to Mass every Sunday, confession from time to time. He still went, though with less regularity, to the Catholic Students' Association on Friday evenings. The ties, however, were loosening. Most of what he was reading, unknown to his family, was hardly conducive to an unquestioning obedience either to social convention or to the Catholic faith as it was then constituted in New Zealand. It is not hard to imagine what his parents, for instance, would have thought of the sexual satires of Compton Mackenzie, or the explicit emotional and sexual passion of D. H. Lawrence. Odette de Crécy and Mémé would hardly have been thought appropriate companions at that time for any citizen of Invercargill, any more than the company of Stephen Dedalus would be thought, in Catholic circles, appropriate preparation for Communion. That he should have been reading these books in the company, and at the instigation of, a young woman, would certainly have shocked them. Like most intelligent young people from such backgrounds both before and since, he coped with this situation by keeping quiet.

The necessary domestic silences of his intellectual apprenticeship helped to accelerate the growth of the distance that divided him from the rest of his family. He described himself 'horribly afraid of seeming like "the man from Varsity" '[49] but as other working-class young men and women discovered, he really had no choice. As his academic and intellectual development went ahead, he simply grew away from his relations. Partly it was boredom. He detested the small talk and the petty quarrels of home. Partly it was conviction. He came to despise opinions founded on prejudice rather than knowledge or thought. Partly it was aesthetic. He became a partisan of the beautiful, especially in literature, so that the ugly or the inept jarred. And partly it was temperament. He parted company with his older brother's solemnity and bigotry; his sisters' spite and malice; his youngest brother's insolence and his mother's favouritism towards him; the fact of his father's being stuck in a rut from which he neither would nor could escape. These are the normal enough frustrations of an intelligent adolescent in a non-intellectual household. They were possibly given additional edge by Dan's own inclinations: he became a stickler for grammatical precision, took pleasure in the correct use of words, was in short a true lover of language. On these matters he found most of his family out of sympathy, and no doubt they thought him a pedant.[50] Matters could not have been helped by his astonishing powers of memory: few situations can have occurred that did not bring to mind a Latin tag, a quotation from Shakespeare or Dryden, or a scene from D. H. Lawrence. In circles where books are not read there is nothing more likely than the mention of such things to terminate a conversation, or less likely to improve relations. Barriers went up. Dan's family was proud of his achievements, but their pride was spiked with gall. To grow away from the simple ordinariness of obscure family life, especially one embedded in the rituals and certainties of a tribal culture, is to commit the sin of success, for which there is rarely forgiveness.

The growing distance was emphasized in his second year at Otago by events at the University. Exuberant undergraduate excess during Capping Week[51] in 1931 had provoked a response from the authorities. The University Council, a body composed of representatives of the professoriate and the local community, stepped in with punishments. Celebrations in 1932 were curtailed: there was to be no Procession and no Capping Ball. As so often with university authorities big sticks were employed to swat gadflies. The prohibitions on Ball and Procession were particularly ill-chosen because they were popular in the town. Some students made earnest representations to the Chancellor of the University, Sir Thomas Sidey, a prominent local businessman and former MP. Undergraduate discontent with the prohibitions was vented in the student paper *The Critic*.[52] An amusing article written under the pseudonym 'Cunctator'[53] by the paper's editor H. A. Small, a fifth-year medical student, attacked the entire university: Council, professors, teaching methods, examinations, students, and tradition.[54] The article was unfair and ill-judged, but it captured the sense of frustration felt by the better sorts of students. Meanwhile, Sir Thomas and Lady Sidey had come to the view that it was a pity to deprive graduates of their Ball, and offered to sponsor it privately themselves: which they did.[55] Civic and university tempers were short, however, and Sir Thomas's sense of proportion not widely shared. Mr Small was summarily called before the university disciplinary committee and sent down. The punishment, which would have meant the termination of his medical career, was so disproportionate that it produced something of a crisis in relations between the university authorities and the student representative bodies.[56]

Matters such as these loom large in the minds of students, and of senior university and civic figures too long accustomed to taking themselves over-seriously. To anyone else they risk appearing inconsequential when not incomprehensible—even more so in the light of events elsewhere in New Zealand in 1932, when unemployment riots put issues of academic freedom, freedom of speech, and censorship at both Auckland and Canterbury University Colleges in a far more serious and urgent context. In Dan's life these developments served further to separate him from his home and his past. The university, with its squabbles and its internal rifts, was a world apart, mysterious and impenetrable to his parents, of no particular interest to his siblings, but all-absorbing to its initiates, of whom Dan was now one. The lesson that he took from the university excitements of April to June was that the city fathers and their allies in the University were dangerous opponents in a brawl, and that if you were to win you would need allies.

During his first term of this second year Dan suffered from serious headaches that lasted for two or three days together, intensifying his feelings of gloom. On 6 June, in the middle of the university vacation, he went into the Cairnsmore Clinic in Invercargill for an operation to clear his sinuses. He was in the clinic for only a few days, but they coincided with Winnie's learning the news that her mother was dying of cancer. She wrote to him in hospital, partly in French, but then abruptly switching to English, linking him to the tragedy in her family: 'Every word of the French is true, but it is only a shadow of the truth. I mean more than that far more. For I know now what love is. And it is from my parents that I have learnt it. . . . It is . . . deeper than consciousness: so that my mother's death will be in some sort the destruction of my father's life . . . it seems that this is the only worthwhile thing I have learnt in my life.'[57] Winnie went to see him in the clinic with his mother, taking fruit and flowers, but the visit was terrible, and she fled.

Back in Dunedin in mid-June for the second term they were happy and miserable by turns. She was edgy and irritable, her mother dying in hospital in Invercargill. He was pressing and ardent. The conflicts between them were lovers' sharp quarrels, mended as soon as begun, but they pushed Dan into depressions from which he was not easily revived. He went to pubs more often, and was quick to anger, getting into fights, sometimes going looking for them. His old friend Zam from Sacred Heart had come down to Otago as a freshman this year, and with Fred the three of them argued about religion. Fred and Zam were going through a period of intense doubt, while Dan played the role of defender of the faith. 'The trouble with you two', he would say, 'is you're too bloody religious.'[58] He gives every impression, at this stage, of being a muddled young man, full of passionate energy, but frustrated and undirected.

Winnie's mother died at the end of June. Winnie was preoccupied, with her own grief, with her father, with her sister and brothers. When not away from Dunedin she was heavily committed either at the Training College or in trying to finish her MA thesis. '[It] is only fifth rate literary criticism of tenth-rate novelists for the most part, except when I talk about Katherine and there it is an impertinence.'[59] In August she was away from Dunedin to do teaching practice in Invercargill.

In the vacuum of these circumstances, Dan's way of life altered. He changed lodgings, moving into a room at 598 George Street, where Fred Petricevich was living. At about this time Winnie also moved, leaving her tiny room at Scurr's in York Place, and taking a room at 589 Castle Street where the landlady was a Mrs Pullar. This house—it is still there—is almost in the university grounds, near Dundas Street and close to Selwyn College. Mrs Pullar allowed her to keep her room on when she was away teaching, and it became the base to which she returned at weekends. Dan's circle of friends expanded and changed. He met and became friends with Geoffrey Flavell, a clever young medical student with powers of expression greater even than his own. Geoffrey was funny and exuberant, very quick witted, a *poseur* adept at self-satire. He sometimes wore spats and plus-fours, and carried a cane, and he wrote wickedly funny letters. He in turn was friends with a young man called Bill Macdonald, whose father was a lecturer in the Medical Faculty, and mother one of the city matrons, prominent in good works. Bill wanted to study Law, but his parents were opposed, and in the course of conflict with them he became a drifter, dreaming of being a pilot, though he was surely overweight for this new and romantic career. Dan also got to know another medical student, 'Teddy' McCullough, a university personality. Like Flavell, Teddy was also an impeccably snappy dresser, and affected in his mannerisms, but whereas Flavell was in the tradition of Swift, McCullough seemed to be courting disaster in the manner of Wilde or Charlus. Flavell's attraction to Dan lay in the fact that behind the posture there was substance. He was extremely clever, good at medicine, and with time left over to devote to aesthetic interests. He read widely, and was keenly interested in painting, about which he had somehow become authoritative at an early age. One day, at the age of 14 or 15, coming out of the Dunedin City Art Gallery with his father, a wealthy businessman, they bumped into Sir Lindo Ferguson, Chairman of the Gallery Trustees.[60] 'Well, my lad,' said Sir Lindo, 'what do you think of our beautiful gallery?' 'Very fine, sir,' he replied, 'but it would be nice if we had a Cézanne or two.' Sir Lindo's 'face swelled like a turkeycocks's . . . "Cézanne! If any of that filthy stuff ever enters here it will be over my dead body!" '[61]

By the time Dan went home for the vacation (25 August to 12 September) after the winter term, his horizons and ambitions had expanded. He worked on Lucretius and Horace, read more D. H. Lawrence, and then Robert Graves's *Goodbye To All That*. He went hunting with Muff, who nearly shot him by accident. '[T]he bullet buried itself in the ground beside me. Somehow it seemed terrible the thought that I could die and you not be conscious of it.'[62]

Home life, books, the countryside, everything was now subordinate to his preoccupation with Winnie. 'I have set my heart on having you. And I feel I am tempting Providence in resolving . . . that I *will* have you . . . I think sometimes that I am loving you to the very utmost of my capacity for love. And then at distant intervals there comes a depth and a power to my feelings that makes me feel all else was shallowness . . . At such moments you would not accuse my love of evanescence in words that wounds me and pain long after they are spoken.'[63]

A day or so later, his nineteenth birthday, she came in to Invercargill. They were lovers now. The next day, Friday, 2 September, she wrote to him:

Yesterday was a dream. I could hardly walk when we came back through the pine avenue because my legs had lost their solidity. I think you have broken my bones and taken the marrow. Have you, dark head? How I love your black hair. Come here. Your shoulders and thighs, strong; you: the touch of you, smell of you. Your voice . . . Your voice is like smoke, soft and rather hurting, and it goes straight through my skin. . . . There are such millions of things I know about us, that I forget to tell you, I'm frightened I won't have time to: because we're hurling through time—I hope it's to eternity, Dan, because otherwise I'll never be able to love you enough. Not in sixty beggarly short little years.[64]

Dan was so touched by the force of this letter that he was unable to find an adequate response: 'you wrote me such a lovely letter. . . . It was corker and it is the proud man I am too.'[65]

After this consummation, Winnie's letters to Dan, whether of love or discord, whether written in happiness, misery, or anger, seem composed with an effortless facility: of love, of guidance and wisdom, and with an occasional poem, like this undated 'litany':

Dark head	love me
Wine mouth	love me
Stern youth	smile on me
Stricken heart	come to me
Olive tree	shelter me
Fire-limbed	love me
Strong river	bear me
Love, love	love me.[66]

The higher plateau of passion and physical intimacy to which they had climbed was a place at once more deeply loving and more stormy. The four years' difference in their ages had never seemed either more or less important. She was a mature woman. By Christmas she would have completed her teacher training and be looking for a job. She had 'graduated' from her difficult relationship with the mysterious and dangerous Harry Aitken and embarked, initially with deep misgivings, on a passionate affair with a man who, in comparison with her other friends, was young and still immature. Dan, still unformed, though deeply in love, did not fully understand what he was doing. He was bitter about being so young: 'Why in God's name was I born a few years too late[?]'⁶⁷ He was passionately, sometimes wildly, jealous, especially of her past—about which, of course, he could do nothing—and he was deeply apprehensive about the future, which he thought would rob him of her, carry her away to teach in a strange town where other men could not fail to pursue her.

The passion of her love for him made it worse in his imagination. In strait-laced Otago and Southland a woman who loved out of wedlock had 'fallen' and would be prey for other hunters on the sexual savannah. Though Dan knew that she loved him, he was tormented by this improbable possibility. His rages, like all jealousy, carried their relationship into a sea of constant self-examination, some of it written down in their exchanges of notes and letters. This was a correspondence within a correspondence, and the letters were often undated. Others, written, were not sent. Still others, sent, were burned in anger. These were young and highly intelligent people, capable of depths of feeling that were unusually profound, and their chosen field of literature, in which Winnie was widely read and Dan was racing to catch up, gave them an ideal space in which to locate the energy of the emotional fire that, turn and turn about with the harmony and the fusion that came from sexual happiness, now seemed to consume them.⁶⁸

The main influence here was unquestionably D. H. Lawrence. Winnie introduced Dan to his work, and he adopted it, uncritically at first, in response to her enthusiasm. Lawrence's view of human relations, the emotional struggle that necessarily (in his view) accompanies all *true* passion, and his conviction that sexual and emotional love necessarily entail a struggle for mastery of one partner by the other, coloured Dan's understanding of his own circumstances. Winnie, whom he now called Winushka or Nushka, was the dominant force. In years, experience, knowledge, and physical dominion, control lay with her. He imagined she wanted not simply to help liberate him from his past, to help him become a writer and a scholar—which she certainly thought him capable of—but that in moulding him she sought also for control; that he would lose his freedom in the very liberty that she was bringing to their con-gress. He thought it not just necessary but inevitable that he should struggle against this, to free himself from her bondage by establishing his own mastery over her. Behind the apparently calm exteriors of two young Southland Catholics a struggle of truly Lawrentian properties and dimensions now began to work itself out.

This was, perhaps, the dark side of Lawrence's influence. But there was another, equally important, and at least to some, more benign. Lawrence was, for the new generations of young people that spanned the First World War and the inter-war years, the apostle of revolt against the 'Old Men', and the way of life that, as they saw it, had brought and sustained the catastrophe of the trenches. Personally brave, fearlessly arrogant by some standards, Lawrence stood for resistance to the dual tyrannies of convention and petty-mindedness. And he offered not just conviction and insight, but an alternative way of life. This was clear fresh spring water to young palates raised by the muddy well of prudishness.[69]

Throughout all the turmoil of the emotions aroused by these forces, Winnie was by far the more expressive and positive force. She called him Danilla, sometimes 'Dark Head' or 'Ram Lamb', and later, after reading Synge, 'Mister Honey':

As for what you'll do next year, don't worry. You'll love me, and you'll work, and you'll laugh. It'll be alright, I know now. I'll go away to a strange town, where I know no one, and where I don't like the work; and I'll leave you a heritage here. My friends and my work that I like. So you be brave, because it's worse for me, and I'm not unhappy; there's nothing to be unhappy about, so long as we trust each other and feel alright about each other. We're potentially happier than anyone I know—probably, than anyone in the world.[70]

And a few months later:

Do you feel, even when we struggle, even as our anger flashes like a sword between us, that it cannot separate us[?] Even at a moment of despair, when I hate you, hate to be yours, I know I feel you are my ineluctable destiny. I never feel this with anyone else. I never felt it with Harry, whom I loved. I love Harry still, as I love Shakespeare and D. H. But you, I love and hate you as I do myself.[71]

Dan left Dunedin for Invercargill for the summer vacation on Monday, 21 November. They had spent Sunday together at the beach, and he departed with the scent of lupins in his clothes, reading Katherine Mansfield's *Journal* on the train ride south. He wrote to Winnie the next day, for the first time in green ink, which became a feature of the next few

years. He was unhappy at having to share a bedroom again—'embarrass-
ing for a fellow of my erotic temperament', and complained about
his family: 'my sister's girth, Pat's insolence, Tom's piety.'⁷² He read
Katherine Mansfield's *Letters*, then *Sappho*.

Whatever changes may have been wrought in him by the year past he
concealed them well enough from his family, perhaps behind his habitual
determination. He took Meissner's German language textbook home,
and at the rate of a lesson a day began to teach himself a new language.
Confined to bed with bronchitis for a few days, he read Osbert Sitwell's
Man Who Lost Himself, then wrote to Winnie for advice on what he
should read next. She suggested Eugene O'Neill, Noel Coward,
Clemence Dane, Willa Cather, Robert Graves, Sacheverell and Edith
Sitwell, Virginia Woolf, and Catherine Carswell. Then also Dostoevsky,
Tolstoy, Turgenev, Pushkin, Gorky, and Sigrid Undset's trilogy *Kristin
Lavransdatter*.

In mid-December the examination results were published. He had
first-class marks in every subject, coming first equal in English, first in
History, and first in Latin not just at Otago, but throughout the University of New Zealand. This was welcome news, that he could compete at
the national level. Winnie had already been urging him to think of
applying for a Rhodes Scholarship. This success in Latin made the
ambition firmer.

The summer also brought a new opportunity. His father had been
promoted from guard to railway foreman at the port of Bluff, which put
him in a position to know when ships would be arriving to load or offload
cargo. He exploited this information on Dan's behalf, tipping him off in
advance, so that henceforth in his vacations, and despite the Depression,
he stood a fair chance of getting casual labour, hired from day to day, as
a wharfie. He started on Thursday, 22 December, working all day until 10
o'clock at night, and earning twenty-six shillings. From it came his first
piece of imaginative prose, written in a letter to Winnie late at night,
squatting in his bed at 'Gravey's' in Bluff.

It is hard to say whether the wharf looks better on a fine day or a fine night.
On a fine day there are sweating heaving men spattering obscenities, and a
blue sky and a blue sea and whirling gluttonous gulls; but at night the gulls
are gone, and the same men swearing the same obscenities sweat less and are
more weary. The entanglement of derricks and tackle and spars and rigging
has all become black against the sky now a darker blue and the whole drama
of men in action takes a more elemental hue such is the force of silhouette
and stars. And the ragged clouds float past a dreary moon.

But the men themselves provide the interest to which all else is background. Ragged obscene wasters for the most part, the toughest lowest dregs of life, compound of failures past and failures to come, taciturn and garrulous with a queer crazy crude humour and a fishwife's appetite for gossip they are the most motley most unsavoury and most absorbing mass of humanity to be met. With them you are nearer the surface. Greedy, filthy, inquisitive, full of foulness which ceases as though magically when the cry comes that 'women' are about, their ranks are recruited from the duffers of school and the duffers of life. . . . There are hunchbacks and cripples and war cases to spare, boozers buggered by booze the rule rather than the exception and exboxers are plentiful. . . . But you cannot but admire the mad folly with which they make money and throw it to the publicans and whores who grow white-faced and fat like wharf fed cash bloated parasites existing on sweat.[73]

He was at work there again the next day, surprised, for the first time, to hear his father swear (which he had never heard before) and then he was at home for Christmas. For a present he gave Winnie Chekhov's *Roths-child's Fiddle and Other Stories*, then till the new year he read Hudson's *The Purple Land*, and made a start on Winnie's reading list with Virginia Woolf's *To The Lighthouse*.

The summer went past in this way. There were occasional meetings with Winnie, but they were hard to organize, and Dan felt the presence of her older sister Mollie, who perhaps now saw herself as guardian of her younger sister's welfare in the absence of their mother. Dan was certainly intermittently hostile towards her at this time, presumably because she got in the way, and made the physical intimacy of life in Dunedin impossible to duplicate in Invercargill or Otautau. He went on a brief camping trip with Muff. He worked on his Latin and his German; went out to Woodlands; ran shop errands for Winnie in town. He read *Wandering Stars* by Clemence Dane, Hardy's *Under the Greenwood Tree*, and Aldous Huxley's *Brave New World*, which Winnie lent him.[74] His brother Matt, too taken with ballroom dancing at the Orange Lodge perhaps, had failed Matriculation ('Confound relations—it's bad enough to have to be sorry for yourself without feeling that way for other people') and gone off to Woodlands, leaving Dan with the bed to himself.[75] He had a Sunday at the beach with Muff—'shoals of sweating fleshy obscenely-leg-waving humanity make me sick'.[76]—and spent a lot of time waiting for the postman. He was lonely and frustrated, spent many hours composing love-letters, and longed for the end of the vacation so that he could return to Dunedin, and a life of freedom. 'I long for the day when I will have my waiting over, in the palm of my hand and will be in realisable distance of getting what I want, you and freedom from the dead weight of fretting convention, and useless time loss that hangs on me like a three-month millstone.'[77] He read the poetry of D. H. Lawrence, James Stephens, Francis Thompson, and Robert Graves. His Uncle Tom, who kept a pub at Opunake in Taranaki, arrived for a visit, and took his wife her breakfast on a tray every morning. Observing him, Dan wished he could be doing the same for Winnie.[78] They both spent time daydreaming.

Whether they would actually be together or not in the new academic year of 1933 remained uncertain. Winnie had qualified as a teacher, and spent the summer applying for jobs, some of them in the North Island, though without success. Her MA examination results had been less than she hoped, though much as she feared, a second-class degree. She was trying to write, and reworked a short story called 'The Letter' which she had written the previous spring. She was trying to plan a novel, and starting a new short story. But her progress was slow, and she was worried about being unemployed, having no money to enable her to live away from home. Eventually, still without a job offer, she decided to return to Dunedin where she once again lived at 589 Castle Street, and set about finding private pupils to tutor. When the new university year began on 6 March, Dan was also back in town, still in the flat at 598 George Street which he shared with Fred Petricevich.

This year he enrolled in the Stage III units in English and Latin, which consisted of the inexorable surveys of literature, and forced diet of language and translation. He was now committed to the idea of a Rhodes Scholarship, and set about the business of acquiring the right qualifications. Rhodes's will, in which he set out the conditions, put emphasis on sporting and all-round ability as well as scholarly attainment, and Dan had made few efforts in these directions at all. He began to write for the undergraduate paper, *The Critic*,[79] and on 7 April was appointed associate editor of the Otago *Review*.[80] He became active in the Arts Faculty student clubs, was elected Secretary of the Literary and Dramatic Society, and played a prominent part in the creation of a Faculty Debating Society, of which he was elected first President. These were not sinecures. He was an active secretary of the Literary and Dramatic Society, which held frequent meetings at which papers were read and play readings performed.

The Critic developed into a major focus of his activities, and in 1933 it played a prominent part in university life. Under the editorship of Frank Guest, a senior Law student, and within the limits of what was possible given the conditions of university and town, *The Critic* blossomed into an intelligent, often witty, and always well-written paper. Geoffrey Flavell wrote about modern art,[81] and Zam—now active in student theatrical production—about the cinema;[82] Winnie McQuilkan made her entry as the satirical Susan Schnozzletippet;[83] Ralph Park contributed his brilliant, witty poetry in the manner of Ogden Nash; and Dan began to contribute an occasional series of pieces of social satire under the Swiftian pseudonym of Jonathan Sloe.

Three of these pieces appeared in the first half of the year.[84] The first—'A Modest Proposal'—seems to us now just that, since it suggests that the Otago University Students' Association should itself run a bar, thereby bringing numerous benefits—which he enumerates—to the university. The piece is best seen today as illustrative of the social climate of the 1930s, where such a proposal might be thought scandalous. Even so, it is hard to believe that it merited its title.[85] Perhaps he was only getting into his stride, for the next two pieces are stronger: 'A Serious and Useful Scheme for the Benefit of Scholars' being a well-turned attack on the weekly paper *Truth*—'a paper . . . whose every guiding principle is implicit in its title', and 'The Aposanctosis', a skilful little satire on contemporaries in student politics that, in pretending to be the translation of a fragment of a newly discovered antique document, draws on both *The Satyricon* and Apuleius' *The Golden Ass*. With these pieces Dan made his first serious entries into print. He was still not quite 20 years old, but they are strong enough to avoid dismissal as juvenilia, and their purpose in a student publication, to entertain and to score points, was surely realized.

Like his friend in the Medical School, Geoff Flavell, Davin now seemed to be everywhere, at debates, at literary discussions, at Bob Hop dances in Allen Hall, even on the rugby field, where he turned out in the scrum for the University D (i.e. fourth) fifteen.[86] Laughter from *The Critic* office is still almost audible as he and Cuddon, in the pack, are described as sometimes showing 'astounding pace',[87] though he may have regretted this only a week or so later when, in a match against Kaikorai, his nose was broken. The look of a handsome but unsuccessful pugilist remained his for the rest of his life.

This was a far fuller and more active university life than Dan had led before. It brought him a wider circle of friends, and marked a decline in the importance of some others. Fred Petricevich, with whom he was flatting in George Street, had fallen into a state of deep despondency. He was dropping out of Medical School, unable to work, tormented by his interfering mother in Auckland. He brought his problems to Dan, who found them hard to understand. He knew that Fred was very clever, and could not see why he failed to employ his powers to work hard, and so free himself from his family problems. Little by little he lost Dan's sympathy, and ultimately his confidence.[88]

Dan stayed with him at 598 George Street until the May vacation, when he again went to work on the wharf at Bluff, but on his return in June he moved into a room at 129 London Street, 'the street of doctors'.[89] This was a house on a back section, nicely secluded, and high on the third rise of the hill, just below Otago Boys' High School. On a winter's morning, the ground frosty and cold, the sky densely blue above, he would come out to be greeted by breath-taking views of town, university, and harbour, the smoke from a thousand chimneys curling at his feet. It was during his life here on the hill that he met Marion Steven and became firm friends with James Raeside. Marion was yet another medical student, a scholarship winner like himself, and already being thought of by the Medical Faculty as a future academic. James was a soil scientist with a mind at once logical and imaginative. He was a keen fencer, a shrewd chess player, and a better than competent violinist. He played in the Dunedin Symphony Orchestra, and tried to stimulate Dan into some appreciation of classical music by taking him to concerts, though later he felt the performances 'ill chosen'.[90] James and Dan shared lodgings off and on over the next three years, often playing chess late into the night. With Gregor Cameron and Frank Guest these young people came to form the inner circle of Dan's Dunedin companions during his last years at the university.[91]

By contrast with Fred, Dan himself was completely on top of his work, reading widely, hugely enjoying life. There were still periods of depression, but the headaches of the previous year were gone, he still had Winnie beside him as lover and intellectual companion,[92] and he was feeling the full expansion of his powers. In this climate of what amounted to self-liberation his way of life became, by the standards of the time, increasingly bohemian. His relationship with Winnie, though they were as prudent as they could be, was well known. The possibility of pregnancy was a constant anxiety, and the menace of gossip in a Presbyterian citadel an ever-present reality. By the standards of the 1930s he was living dangerously. He drank more, spent more time in pubs, and experimented with brandy and liqueurs.[93] He was attracted to the drawings of Aubrey Beardsley, began to read in the literature of the 1890s, the age of the *Yellow Book*, of the sexual underground, of deliberate fracturing of convention in decadence. He pretended to a sort of diabolism, meant as a joke, but, from a young man of Catholic upbringing, likely to be mis-interpreted. His bedroom had black wallpaper (though with a flower pattern on it), and he hung a Beardsley *Woman with Black Cat* on the wall above a bureau on which he set two long brass candlesticks, Marge Thompson's revolver between them. At the end of the winter term *The Critic* 'Personalities' column reported 'that the last meeting of *The Critic* staff took the form of a tea party somewhere or the other. We asked "Jonathan Sloe" about it, but he just smiled satanically.'[94]

Was this prudent behaviour for a young man fixing his ambitions on a Rhodes Scholarship? He had freed himself from so many taboos and conventions by this time, come to live in a way that he had invented for himself, and which pleased him so much, that it seems possible that the question never even occurred to him. That the ambition was there is certain. At the end of July he wrote to his former head teachers, Brother Egbert and Brother Benignus, to canvass their views, and they both replied with enthusiastic support.[95] The young man who went home to Invercargill at the end of term on 24 August saw himself as two-thirds of the way through his Otago University career, and believed himself within sight of his goal. 'They say I have never come home looking so well. Nor have I ever come home from a happier term so it seems.'[96]

5

DOMINANCE AND ESCAPE

There is no liberty in love. Noone knows that better than me. Yet I am silly enough to value the appearance of liberty and these little gambits are a sort of evidence to myself that I am still my own. . . . Trust me as I trust you. Remember what a good and solid thing is between us. Think of the days nights and long hours we have had together and what a bond even our quarrels constitute. Remember the power our bodies have over each other, and remember that my mind's rebellion against the domination of yours is a sign that our relations are vital and living.

(WKDP: DMD to WKD, 28 Aug. 1934)

Being in love is a complicated matter; although anyone who is prepared to pretend that love is a simple, straightforward business is always in a strong position for making conquests. In general, things are apt to turn out unsatisfactorily for at least one of the parties concerned; and in due course only its most determined devotees remain unwilling to admit that an intimate and affectionate relationship is not necessarily a simple one: while such persistent enthusiasts have usually brought their own meaning of the word to something far different from what it conveys to most people in early life.

(Anthony Powell, *A Question of Upbringing*, 105)

William Murn Macdonald, 19 years old, 'rather stoutly built', walked into the Union Bank of Australia on the Square in Palmerston North at 11.00 a.m. on Friday, 11 August 1933, and told a teller to give him £200 in used notes.[1] To encourage compliance he produced a cocked revolver and handed over a note that read 'I have you covered. If you attempt to give the alarm I will shoot you. I'm desperate. Don't hesitate.'[2] The teller, William Loudon, a smart young man in a clerk's suit, paused only briefly. Something about young Macdonald, his polite middle-class accent perhaps, told him he could chance his arm. Instead of producing money he dived to the floor, where he kept a revolver of his own. He fired three shots, one of which broke a pane of glass in a swing door. Macdonald fled, the police arrived, and fifteen minutes later Bill Macdonald was arrested, still on the Square, still carrying the cocked revolver. On examination it proved to be loaded.

A UPA report of this incident was in the *Otago Daily Times* the next morning under the headline 'Bank Sensation', and so it was in Dunedin. Bill Macdonald's father had been a prominent Dunedin medical practitioner, a stalwart of the Dunedin Public Hospital, a lecturer at the Otago University Medical School, and a man who had only narrowly been passed over in 1919 for appointment as Mary Glendining Professor of Systematic Medicine.[3] His wife, Bill's mother, had been prominent among the matrons of Dunedin for her energetic charity work, which included the provision of a summer camp for First World War orphans. His friends recalled that she would put Bill to board in Otago Boys' High School when she was busy with good works.

Even as the citizens of Dunedin were digesting this information with their breakfast porridge, Bill Macdonald was appearing before Mr J. L. Stout, SM, in the Palmerston North Magistrates' Court, where he was granted suppression of name: 'He may not be altogether responsible. Perhaps in the circumstances his name should be suppressed until the full facts have come out.'[4] But it was too late. For poor Mrs Macdonald the eddies and quicksands of gossip were already pulling her under: a woman caring for delinquent boys while allowing her own son to go wrong being the chief line of tea-table innuendo. 'She was made to look ridiculous.'[5] As far as the young man was concerned, it was 'a fair cop'. In court the following Friday he pleaded guilty to one charge of armed robbery, and four other charges of breaking and entering, stealing, and passing stolen cheques, offences all committed in the Masterton and Palmerston North localities over the previous several weeks.[6] On 15 September the Chief Justice, Sir Michael Myers, sentenced him to four years in Borstal.[7]

Mrs Macdonald, though distressed, was not a woman who easily tolerated humiliation, and she was blessed with remarkable organizational powers. She ransacked her unfortunate son's bedroom, and there discovered a cache of letters that had been written to him by his old friend from school-days, Geoffrey Flavell. 'We used to write to each other frequently, and, purely for his amusement and entertainment, I would give him highly coloured accounts of undergraduate excess: drinking, heterosexual "orgies" (two used condoms) in Jubilee Park, tours of the Dunedin Hospital public wards with eye-witness accounts of the blood-soaked gauze being removed from an old man's prostate operation. That sort of thing. Harmless fun really, though Dan always referred to my letters as "New Zealand's only serious contribution to literature." '[8]

Outraged by what she had discovered, convinced that her son had been led astray by pernicious influences, Mrs Macdonald made up her mind that the real culprits would be punished one way or another. The letters were copied and circulated among senior people in the Dunedin medical establishment. Was Flavell the sort of person who should be walking the wards of the Dunedin Public Hospital? The Medical Superintendent of the hospital thought not, and Sir Lindo Ferguson, Dean of the Medical School, agreed with him. After an interview with the Dean, Flavell went to his father, hoping to appoint a lawyer and fight the case, but his father thought the cause hopeless. Mrs Macdonald found allies among the students too. When Flavell was nominated to the publications committee of the Students' Association executive, a counter-resolution was successfully moved by Joel and Dunne.[9]

The Medical School was effectively expelling Flavell, since if he was excluded from the wards of the hospital, he could not complete his training. And the Students' Association, peopled by the offspring of the town worthies, was signalling that it would not support him. Realizing that he was about to be sent down, Flavell got in first and withdrew. He left the university at the end of term and sailed for England in the New Year of 1934, and completed his medical studies at Bart's.

These developments were ominous for Dan. Everywhere that gossip of the Flavell letters surfaced Davin's name was likely to be mentioned. At least one of the letters described, in Flavell's amusing hyperbole, the conduct of a Black Mass in Davin's lodgings. Such an image, drawn from the undergraduate life of a presumably lapsed Catholic, could send a *frisson* of horror through Presbyterian Dunedin. And some parts of the ground in which this innuendo was planted were already fertile. Among faculty and students who knew him only by reputation he was not always popular. His distaste for bourgeois morals and style was real, and he was known to be in revolt against convention and the restraints of 'polite' society. He could be quick to take offence. Outside the lecture room he could affect a working-class Irish style. He wrote in green ink, wore a green tie, even green pyjamas,[10] One woman in the same year as Dan remembered him as 'a lout',[10] and she was not alone in her view. He did not, of course, make things easier for himself by cleverness and hard work, which together produced the appearance of effortless brilliance. There are always narrow minds that wish to see success punished. It was the Depression, and feelings—inchoate for the most part—about class and class divisions ran fairly strong through the university, where there were almost no students with genuine working-class backgrounds. There is no doubt that Dan played on this fact. He was on good terms with a student communist called McClure, whom he admired for the tenacity of his beliefs, and with whom he sympathized in his status as an outsider in undergraduate circles. Dan was a working-class young man, and in some quarters his academic triumphs were resented as reverse discrimination on the part of the academic authorities. The sneer is not a recent invention.

These were danger signals for someone planning to apply for a Rhodes Scholarship. The ideal candidate was expected to be an all-round man, a future leader, the sort who inspired confidence. The sorting process for the award each year involved a written application in August. In September and after interview, each constituent college of the University of New Zealand nominated its candidates: never more than two, sometimes only one, or none at all. The nominees were then interviewed in Wellington in early December by a committee of Establishment figures chaired by the Governor-General. As part of the college nomination process, the Students' Association at Otago ranked the applicants according to its own assessment of their comparative worth, and this ranking was held to carry weight with the Professorial Board.[11] Flavell's treatment, and the spreading stain of gossip about Davin's part in the supposed corruption of Bill Macdonald, did not augur well for his ambitions.

When Dan returned to Dunedin in early September for the final term of his third year there were other clouds in the sky. Winnie's spell of teaching at the Technical Institute had come to an end, and she had been appointed to a relieving post at the school in Palmerston, a small town forty miles north of Dunedin. Palmerston was on the main road, so she kept her room at 589 Castle Street, and commuted back and forth for weekends by bus. Dan would let himself into her room on a Friday evening, and hide behind the door to surprise her when she arrived.[12] Their happiness was edged with distress, however. Winnie's father was ill in the winter, and went into Riverton hospital at the end of August, irascible and cruel to her when she visited him, which she did every day while the school holidays lasted.[13] Her anxiety was acute and not misplaced. He had cancer, and was already in terminal decline. He died at the end of the first week in September, just fourteen months after his wife, and thus appeared to bring true Winnie's prediction that her mother's death would be his as well. He was buried in a grave beside his wife in Otautau on Monday, 11 September.

The burden of his death was not just emotional, but financial. The family business in Otautau had somehow to be sustained. Ideally, the two brothers and two sisters would have sold it, but it was still the Depression, and businesses, even reasonably successful small ones like Gonley's Otautau store and billiard rooms, were hard to sell. Winnie's younger brother Mick took on much of the responsibility, while Mollie and Winnie tried to do as much as they could in the school vacations. Their older brother Jack was away working in Timaru.

Under these clouds Dan worked as usual, busy with Arts Faculty debating, the Literary Society, and *The Critic*, where Jonathan Sloe had 'A simple and ready scheme for the alleviation' of unemployment. Here he proposed, *à la* Swift, that since the root cause of unemployment was the existence of unemployed people, they should all be disposed of. Unemployment relief should be stopped immediately. The great majority of people would be in favour of such a move, and opposition would come only from the unemployed, who were biased by their dependence. Many would then die of starvation, while those who, 'out of a desire to thwart the good of the better sort', did not, could be dealt with by the reintroduction of the death penalty 'for all crimes from petty stealing to cursing their better-fed neighbours'. '[T]he wretches thus humanely despatched would derive the utmost satisfaction from the reflection that they were departing this life in strict conformity with the laws and that they were in a manner giving their lives for the sacred cause of justice.'

The parody is well done, and its target—comfortable middle-class opinion—effectively struck. Since it wittily deprecated the charitable instincts of conservatives, however, it was unlikely to find popularity among them. And these people were now taking control of the Otago University Students' Association. The new executive for 1933–4 was dominated by the Medical School, with a man called Hawksworth elected unopposed as President.[14] The Vice-President and Lady Vice-President were also medical students. Dan stood for the post of Social Representative on the Executive, but the election, unlike all the others, was heavily contested, with candidates from Medicine, Law, and Commerce, as well as Davin and Angus Ross, a young historian and prominent member of the Student Christian Movement. Election might have strengthened Dan's candidacy for a Rhodes among his peers, but his candidacy was not advanced with sufficient gravity: 'A propos of his candidature, we asked him if he was a sociable animal. "If you ask me to come and have a drink, I am," said Mr. Davin.'[15]

He was not elected, but though he missed the larger stage he did do better in the smaller arena of the Arts Faculty, where he was elected Vice-President, and in this role became a member of the Otago

University Students' Council when it held its AGM in Allen Hall on 27 September. It would be wrong to imagine from these events that Dan took student politics seriously. He was involved because his advisers and mentors, Winnie of course, but also Professor Ramsay and Gregor Cameron, Frank Hall, and Frank Guest, assured him that it could only help in the quest for a Rhodes. In truth, he was not particularly interested in politics, and found its student version trite, and its protagonists shallow and representative of precisely those bourgeois traits that he detested. His private correspondence of the time has almost nothing to say about public affairs, and such passing references to student politics as exist consist largely of splenetic outbursts against people whose motives he distrusted and whose values he abhorred.[16] Many responded in kind. He made particular enemies of Hawksworth, the Student President, and a friend of his called Kempthorne, who beat Dan for the post of Social Rep. Hawksworth and Kempthorne, young gentlemen to the tips of their evening-dress tails, were shocked by the Flavell correspondence, and sharp antagonists of the bohemian that they detected in Davin.

And his bohemianism was nowhere more clearly illustrated than in his relationship with Winnie. With her appointment as a relieving teacher at Palmerston she embarked on what was to be almost four years of itinerant life in New Zealand, moving from one small town in Otago or Southland to another for a term at a time. During these years her life with Dan, in so far as it had a pattern, consisted of lonely weeks apart interspersed with hurried weekends together. To the personal strain of living in such a way had to be added another: that by the standards and expectations of the age they were living scandalously. At first, and from their families especially, they sought concealment by subterfuge, but as the years passed, and with the natural casualness of the familiar, the disguise was barely sustained. Their intimacy was common knowledge. The effect, in a culturally conservative, not to say repressive, environment, with the parallel miniature world of Catholic prohibitions, was to make people partisan, for and against. For a young woman the difficulties of living in this way were made worse by repression disguised as civility. Most career avenues were closed to her because she was a woman. The one that was open—teaching—was watched over by the guardians of public morals. Matters were made worse by the Depression, when the Education Department appointed few teachers to permanent positions, and made mainly short-term appointments, all at the same low pay irrespective of class size or hours worked. Winnie's numerous applications for permanent jobs were all unsuccessful. A less sanguine temperament might have suspected discrimination.[17]

Dan's own prospects seemed, if anything, rather worse. He was brilliant at academic work, but his subjects led in no particular career direction. There were effectively no jobs in university teaching or research, certainly not without the tenure of an overseas scholarship first. New Zealand had only a very small publishing industry. The broadcasting industry was small and provincial in focus.[18] Apart from occasional visits by foreign companies, usually British or Australian, there was no professional theatre, orchestra, opera, or dance, and no film industry either. His talents for languages, literature, and criticism were not then valued in his own country. And all of this was made worse by the Depression, in which scarce work was made even scarcer by economic orthodoxy. These facts of life, coupled with their growing sense of being outsiders, led them to conceive of their futures in terms of escape: by writing, by the life of the mind, and by academic preferment. These were not new ambitions. Winnie wanted to be a writer even before she knew Dan. The notion of escape grew as the bonds between them strengthened. At first it nourished their relationship with dreams. Dan used to write to her at one time of their having a caravan, simply wandering away. She wrote to him of going to India, or to China, of spending Easter in Paris. These were almost unimaginable dreams for two young people from the restrictive backgrounds in which they had grown up, but by 1933 they had taken clearer and harder shape, and in Dan's case the Rhodes came to stand not just for his meal ticket, or for liberation from dependence on his parents, but for escape from the toils and constrictions of a reactionary and culturally barren society.

This objective was all the more daring because it openly opposed the unconventional and scandalous nature of his own way of life to the full stuffiness of Establishment conventions. The Rhodes was more than simply a scholarship awarded for academic and/or sporting eminence: it was a judgement, formed by the Establishment, on the manners and morals of the young. In New Zealand it was also an exclusive club, in which the members, once admitted, stood as guardians of the gate for new initiates. In this way, Dan was to become, privately at first, more publicly later, the candidate of the opposition to all that was correct and polite.

One incident illustrates well the difference between Dan and his friends and those of, say, Hawksworth. An Otago friend of Dan and Winnie, Annette, had formed an unhappy and ill-considered liaison with a young man, Ronnie Maxwell, as a result of which she was pregnant. Dunedin, with its Medical School, was at the time perhaps the only place in New Zealand where it was possible to get a reasonably safe, though of course illegal, abortion. Annette, a Catholic, refused to contemplate this option, but hesitated between the alternatives: marriage and keeping the baby, or having the baby outside wedlock which, at the time, meant its going for adoption. There were almost no exceptions to this inflexible rule. Eventually she chose marriage, and very late in her term, she and Ronnie went through a Catholic ceremony with a few friends in attendance. Winnie could not get there from Southland, but Dan was the best man.

Annette's timing was nothing if not close. She went into labour during the ceremony, and immediately afterwards was hurried away in a taxi to the clinic where a bed was already reserved. Dan accompanied Ronnie, whom he barely knew, to a restaurant, where they had a celebration of sorts. After that he saw him home, a little the worse for drink, to Annette's rooms where he was now to live. The delivery of Annette's child was difficult, and eventually it was stillborn. Ronnie, when messengers went to find him, had taken all of her money and savings bonds, and disappeared. He was never seen again. Annette's distress was acute, though mitigated in due course by the sense of having been saved by fate from a lifetime of misery. What she wanted, when she recovered from the loss of child, husband, and money, was not just a divorce, but an annulment, so that she might remain a Catholic. Winnie, who had baked a cake, arrived a few days after the wedding-day events. They dubbed it an annulment cake, and ate it with relish. Divorce was simple enough to arrange since Ronnie, presumed to have fled to Australia, had clearly deserted Annette. An annulment before the Church was more difficult since it required evidence that the marriage had never been consummated.[19] Who better to give it than the best man at the wedding? He could assert in all truthfulness that he had, so to speak, held hands with the groom from the moment the ceremony began, to the moment when he went to his cold bed, the object of his passion secluded in a private clinic where husbands were not permitted until well after delivery, and that at no time during this interval had sexual congress occurred.

Off and on over the next two years Dan was called on either to prepare himself for, or actually to give evidence at, the ecclesiastical hearings on this matter in Dunedin. It might be said that the incident, kept obscure enough, illustrated much that was incongruous in his own circumstances: the constant threat of conception, the difficult decision about what to do if it happened, the role of the Church and other institutions in judging the consequences. Under the surface of everyday life, these were constant nagging anxieties that fed on the fringes of a bohemian existence.

Whatever his social transgressions, Dan's academic progress was beyond reproach. In the end-of-year exams he was again top in English, and top throughout New Zealand in Latin. The University of New Zealand awarded him the George Young Scholarship for 1934. These triumphs could not still the disquiet, however. A Catholic priest 'well-wisher' was in touch just before he left Dunedin, 'solicitous for my welfare'.[20] It was indicative of how gossip might spread. He reread *A Portrait of the Artist as a Young Man*, finding it 'the same great book', and left Dunedin 'in a rage of contemptuous misanthropy, though cheerful enough withal'.[21]

The long summer vacation resolved itself into the familiar pattern of reading, work on the wharf and in the woolsheds at Bluff, a camping trip with Muff, increasing alienation from home life, and lonely love-letters to Winnie. In one important regard, however, things were different. Michael Gonley's death meant that the Gonley home at Otautau was no longer presided over by the older generation, and Dan could now visit whenever Winnie would have him. In 1933 he went for Christmas, joining Winnie and Mollie and their brother Mick and Joan McGrath for the three days from Christmas Eve to Boxing Day, before going back to work at the Bluff. He wrote to Winnie at the end of the year: 'If we were together now we would drink to 1934. May its Xmas see us as united and loving as this.'[22]

While Dan read *Kristin Lavransdatter*,[23] continued to work at his German, and went back to the Bluff for a week in February, Winnie returned to Dunedin, still uncertain of her immediate future. On 17 February she read in the newspaper that her friend Toni McGrath had committed suicide in London. A week later she had a letter containing bad news of Alpha, who was ill in a hospital in Surrey, apparently suffering from a nervous breakdown. And then the very next day came news of her appointment as relieving teacher at the secondary school in Balclutha, fifty-five miles south of Dunedin.[24] Once again they would have to be apart. Dan went at once to Balclutha to be with her for one last weekend before the beginning of his term, and they stayed at the Crown Hotel, before she then moved into lodgings with a Mrs Carter in Clyde Street—'a respectable establishment'.[25]

Back in Dunedin, Dan found new lodgings at 11 Park Street, almost at the junction with George Street, close to the university but closer to the pubs. He hated these digs: 'the faded walls, the cold untidy fireplace, the hideous wardrobe, the ragged dirty mat and the repulsive frigid squeaking linoleum.'26 When term started on 5 March, he was enrolled for Single Honours English, falling back into the pattern of his former life, writing for *The Critic*, working hard, playing chess with Raeside. He was lonely and easily depressed, and sought the compensations of university activities: the Arts Faculty dinner,27 debating, the Literary and Dramatic Society.28 He wanted company to keep him distracted from his own gloom, but there were still days, sometimes days on end, when he was immobilized by melancholia. Winnie was able to travel to see him in Dunedin for only one weekend in mid-March because her work was too demanding, and she had begun to study for an MA in French. He cursed his present discontents, and viewed the prospect of his possible success in the Rhodes scholarship competition with even deeper gloom. It would enable him to escape, but into what? And at what cost? In his *Critic* leading article on the graduation ceremony of 15 May he wrote: 'New Zealand resembles a prison both in the treatment of its inmates, and in the surprise and resentment it expresses when they desire to escape.'29

Such revulsion, though grounded in his experience, was abstract. Winnie's was all too real. Two weeks after her visit to Dunedin in mid-March, her brother Jack, on his way from Timaru to Invercargill, stayed with her in Balclutha. Early in the morning she had a terrible dream that Alpha was dead. Frightened, and freezing cold, she went to her brother, who had her crawl into bed with him to warm up. Later she learned that this happened exactly at the time when Marge Thompson, catching an early train in Dunedin, read in the morning paper that Harry Aitken had indeed died, alone, in a Surrey clinic, of a brain tumour. Winnie was devastated by this news, which, coming so soon after Toni McGrath's suicide, seemed to seal her off from her own past. The two deaths together appeared to justify the terrible feelings of foreboding that she had experienced two years before, and which she had confided to Dan.

Dan can have been of no help to her here. On 28 March, when he heard the news of Harry Aitken's death from Frank Hall, he wrote Winnie a letter of little comfort, which he long regretted. In it he writes almost nothing of Harry, and of what he meant to Winnie, but passes quickly to talk of himself, and his numerous activities, trivial in the context of her suffering. The tone is vain and self-assertive, and leads one naturally to wonder whether he viewed this development as the final clearing of whatever impediments he may have imagined still lay in the way of his complete mastery of her. He concludes by saying that he is considering starting a diary: it 'might act as a mental sieve'.30

He bought his first diary notebook in the middle of April, at about the same time that he made friends with a man called Torrance Doig, a year older than himself, who had arrived at Otago after studying agricultural economics in Canterbury, and was a lively source of stories and amusing activities. He began writing in it at the end of June, but stopped as soon as he had begun.[31] His correspondence, however, suggests a man drifting further and further away from his own society. After a visit to Cargill's Castle one Saturday evening with Earl Murfitt,[32] where he had had the company of a young Catholic girl from South Dunedin, he fell into a diatribe against the pettiness of society: 'A solid block of malice and ignorance and malevolence towards people who dare to preserve themselves in themselves. They are a menace. New Zealand is not safe for us and people like us. Perhaps no place is safe. What a relief to read Lawrence's *Letters*. My God, the man was brave. And he knew what he was up against.' Dan comments to Winnie, as if in reverie to himself: 'May I never be fool enough to lose you.'[33]

The comment is pregnant in the context of Winnie's now fragile state of mind. She travelled up to Dunedin for the last week of the university autumn term on Saturday, 12 May. Dan and she went to the Capping Ball where she danced exclusively with him. A week later they travelled south on the same train, Winnie getting out at Balclutha, Dan keeping on to Invercargill. Here he settled back into a regime of hard work at English. He read Boswell's *Life of Johnson*, a dip into the sanity of the Augustan age that may have helped adjust the focus on D. H. Lawrence. After further reading in the *Letters* he wrote to Winnie: 'It is amusing to notice how furiously Lawrence condemns his friends as malignant obstinates merely because they attempt to do what he does—cling to their own convictions. His philosophy I cannot understand and for the most part cannot accept.'[34] This is an intellectual and not a social rejection, however, and he still compares their own relationship with those of Lawrence and Frieda, Murry and Katherine—'there is a solid bond like theirs between us.' Still, the reverence is gone. One is reminded that Winnie loved Harry as she loved 'Shakespeare and D.H.'. Dan's rejection of an uncritical view of Lawrence seems to mark the end of something more than a literary passion.

It is tempting to assume that this development coincided with the need to cope with the force of gossip. The Flavell scandal lingered on in Dunedin, evidence of the fact, always a painful discovery of early adult life, that reputation may have little to do with truth. And Dan now detected the phenomenon at home in the parish pump gossip of

Invercargill: 'the vicarious and furtive thrill these parish women get out of discussing who is married and who is born and who is dead. Invercargill is South Dunedin over again. It stinks with conventional respectability and conventional morality.'³⁵

Winnie replied to this letter from Gray's Hotel, Milton. She had been transferred from Balclutha, and was settling in to a new school, though not unhappily as it brought her 20 miles closer to Dunedin. He wrote to her there, saying how he detested 'respectability',³⁶ to which she replied that they would never be respectable, but 'a trifle eccentric, dangerously liberal, nay more, rogues and vagabonds. Much as I have desired Respectability, just like good clothes, I have not been able to attain it. Pour toi, mon ami très-très-cher, never have you had the least desire—Respectability is as repugnant to you as immorality.' She jokes about coming to see him at the railway station—Milton was a refreshment stop for the Invercargill to Dunedin express—'I don't think the headmaster would mind if I explained it was my lover.'³⁷ Dan thought this letter 'the very essence of all I love in you.'³⁸

After a few days of holiday at Te Anau in the Southern Alps with Muff,³⁹ Dan returned to Dunedin for the winter term. On Wednesday, 26 June he read a paper to the Literary Society—of which he was now Vice-President—titled 'The English Decadents of the 1890s'.⁴⁰ It is a summary of his state of mind and intellectual convictions. Decadence he defines as 'a baffled romanticism' in which the poets Wilde, Dawson, Beardsley, Johnson, and Davidson turned to 'the cult of the grotesque, of the perverse and of the erotic'. Theirs was not 'an exhaustion of vitality but an exhaustion of legitimate fields in subject matter'. The 'pleasure taken in baiting the bourgeoisie' was clearly a centre-piece of their appeal for him, but '[i]f they found beauty it was the beauty of evil, the condition of whose acceptance is desolation'. The force of this art is interpreted entirely in personal terms.

Had these men babbled of beauty, of evil, and of exotic vices and not reflected their confessed feelings and convictions in their lives, then they would have been fit subjects for ridicule. But the poseur who lives and suffers his pose is not a ludicrous spectacle; and when he dies in it as these men did we suspect there was less pose and more sincerity than our bourgeois vanity defending us against satire would have us believe.

They helped to free English poetry from 'the interfering ethical element', but their betrayal lay in their assuming the role of amateurs of literature. '[T]he amateur status is as fatal to true art as the professional is fatal to true love.' And in pursuing sensation to its limits they were condemned to discover that '[w]hen the last confines of sensational experience are reached there is nothing left but the essential disappointment of sophistication, ashes in the mouth'. The personal truth to be taken from this is 'that it is impossible to dally with gloom and black melancholy and perverse egotism and return at will to oneself . . . [for] the basilisk fascination of the morbid never lets its votaries free'. And each was destroyed by society 'which is compact of the brutal, property-loving, conservative elements . . . whose only ideal is the average'.

The importance of this paper to Dan must have seemed short-lived. Winnie rang him in the early hours of the morning some thirty hours later in deep distress. Her young brother Mick had been killed in a motor accident, she was going home from Milton to Otautau, her sister Mollie was unable to help because she was in bed with pneumonia. She needed him. Dan travelled south the next day in time to witness a grotesque disturbance in the little Roman Catholic church of St Joseph's in Otautau. Jack Gonley, Winnie's older brother, could not accept that Mick was really dead. He opened the coffin and claimed to see movement, breath from the lips. He clung to the corpse, protesting that the casket should not be closed again. Only Dan's presence, his size and strength, his calming influence, was sufficient to persuade Jack of the truth, and physically to bring him, broken down and weeping, away from the church. The funeral followed the next day, and Mick was buried beside his parents, and his little younger brother, in the same Otautau grave.[41]

These events marked a turning-point in the relationship between Dan and Winnie. Winnie was in deep distress. She became, *mutatis mutandis*, dependent on him, and he in his turn made a permanent commitment to her. She refers in a brief letter of 16 July to her hopes of selling the business 'so that I will have some money or income, so that we can marry all the sooner. It won't be very much. Perhaps enough to pay for one child . . . I don't think I ever loved you a quarter as much as I do these dazed days. It is a dream from which I shall escape to my reality, you. My life. My love.'[42]

There was both fantasy and truth in this. Fantasy because they both knew that Dan was applying for a Rhodes, and that the terms of the scholarship specified celibacy. Married men were ineligible. Scholars who married had to resign their scholarships. Truth in that, whereas until now each had maintained the earnest intention of preserving independence in their relationship, now they recognized that everything was changed. Their lives were indissolubly linked.

Under these onslaughts and transformations Winnie went into mental hibernation. She stayed on at Otautau, unable to return to teaching at Milton, and over the next seven weeks barely wrote even to Dan. Frank Hall drove him down to Milton one Sunday in July, and they collected her personal possessions from Gray's Hotel and took them back to her room in Castle Street. Dan sent her a necklace for her birthday, and he pined for her, but he was also deeply engaged at the university, and distracted by the demands upon his time.[43] His Rhodes Scholarship application, due on 15 August, was driving him 'crazy', though Frank Hall was helping him to prepare it.[44] He was bored, and hating his work,[45] and devoted time to trying to improve his image among senior Faculty and student reps., dancing with Ida Lawson at the Arts Faculty Ball on 6 July, and again at a Bob Hop on 28 July.[46] They got on well, and she said she would talk to the Lady Vice-President, Margaret Binks, about him. 'Good business', he commented, rather ruthlessly.[47] He even contemplated going with 'innocent but determined candour' to discuss his prospects with Professor Carmalt Jones, but perhaps wisely refrained.

In these changed circumstances of Winnie's dependence on him, and their decision to marry, Dan now felt the onset of all those desires for freedom which previously he had only imagined in a literary context. Freedom within commitment: the dilemma posed by Lawrence. The problem was also one of sexual urgency, which Dan felt intensely. He never enjoyed solitude, partly because he feared the onset of depression, and he yearned particularly for female company. His letters to Winnie of this July are eloquent with sexual desire, unassuaged and frustrated. Until then his life with Winnie must have seemed the very expression of freedom with risk. A commitment to marriage and children seemed, on the other hand, however freely taken, a denial of both. Perhaps, in his own mind, he may also have sensed, however vague and unformed, an element of duress. Winnie's suffering was so extreme that his commitment, honest though it was, may have felt in some way compelled, not quite as freely chosen as he might have imagined previously that it would be.

This was the frame of mind in which he now met a young woman called Peggy Spence-Sales. She worked in Wellington, and had come down for a winter holiday. Shortly after she arrived she lost her job, and so stayed on for a month or so. She was attractive in a wide-mouthed sort of way, slim and slightly angular, full of vitality and sexual energy. She had connections with the university—where her two sisters studied Medicine—and ambitions of her own, realized eventually, to be a painter. She was quick at sketching, proficient at drawing, and Dan sat for her on numerous occasions. He took her out in early August, and wrote to Winnie about her.[48] He was very strongly attracted to her, and soon became her lover, infatuated with her. Winnie learned more of her when she dropped in to see Dan in the third week of August on her way to Wellington to spend a week's holiday with her brother and sister.

Dan went home for ten days from 25 August, already tense and confused. When the Students' Association ranked the candidates for the Rhodes, he had been placed fourth out of six, and he was bitter against Hawksworth and Kempthorne, his old enemies.[49] He and Winnie exchanged letters, Dan's distant and cold, hers generous and calm.[50] She was writing to him for his twenty-first birthday, and enclosing a book. 'You don't need to tell me to remember you and the bonds that bind us to each other. They hug me a little whenever I am away from you, and when I want to be free of you they hug me till they hurt me bitterly. I can't escape them.'[51]

He passed his twenty-first birthday in a state of great emotional tension, though his family remember it chiefly for the harvest of mail that came for him, and the gold wrist watch that his mother had somehow saved to buy as a present. Rosy calved on the day too: another calf that had to be slaughtered. He wrote about his feelings in the notebook he had bought in April: juvenile parody of a Lawrentian type (he was reading *Women in Love*): not at all the mature critical insights of the paper on decadence in the 1890s, but a young man revelling in the simultaneous love of two different women, and deciding not to choose between them. 'In the event of a crisis my choice must be Winnie. And the devil of malignancy says bide your time and both will leave you or you will leave both.'[52]

In this mood he then engineered a crisis. Peggy wrote to him saying that she had to return to Wellington on 6 September, and would he come up early so that she could see him.[53] Winnie was to be in Dunedin at the same time, on her way south from Wellington. He travelled up from Invercargill and took them both out to supper together. The occasion was a disaster. Peggy was no intellectual, and her presence at dinner an affront to Winnie, who had important private matters that she wanted to discuss: her brother's state of mind, her relations with Dan, the future of the Otautau business.[54] Peggy, who knew of Winnie's importance to Dan, and had set her heart on winning him away from her, prattled to score points, looking for effect.[55] Afterwards, in Dan's dismal room, Winnie was in a fury of grief and bitterness. In the 'cold untidy fireplace' she set fire to letters of his which she had been carrying with her, and eventually, in a state of despair walked out on him.

There was a reconciliation of sorts by mail, but Dan's mind was now divided. On 11 September he copied two poems into his notebook, Lawrence's 'But let me finish what I have begun', about bondage and subjugation, and another about will and independence:

> I am separate still!
> I am I and not you!
> And my mind and my will
> As in secret they grew
> Still are secret: unreached and untouched
> And not subject to you.

Peggy returned to Dunedin from Wellington at the end of September and Dan's infatuation with her continued, though by the middle of November she was back in Wellington, perhaps driven away by his determination to work. This was now more intense than ever. The Professorial Board took a different view of Rhodes candidates from the Students' Association. On 13 September, after interview, they nominated him as one of their two candidates for a Rhodes Scholarship.[56] Dan immersed himself in work, finding the prospect of finals intimidating: 'It's like nibbling off bits of the sky. You don't know where to begin.'[57] His final examinations began on 9 November and went well enough, though he would not know the results for months, as the scripts were sent to England for marking.

After a week at home in Invercargill he made the long journey north to Wellington for his Rhodes interview, which was held at Government House, the official residence of the Governor-General, on Friday, 30 November.[58] Lord Bledisloe, known colloquially as 'chattering Charley', was chairman of the committee, which also consisted of Sir Michael Myers, the Chief Justice, the Hon. J. A. Hanan, Pro-Chancellor of the University, Dr J. Hight, CMG, representing the Academic Board, and Mr S. M. Ziman and Professor F. F. Miles, both former Rhodes Scholars.[59] There were eight candidates. Bledisloe was a blimp, but Dan seems to have kept a straight face, dealt with his esoteric Latin pronunciation, and even managed to handle a question about cattle breeding, favouring a cross between Shorthorn and Jersey for New Zealand conditions. After the interviews there was an unusually long wait, and the candidates were fed sandwiches in an ante-room by the kitchens. Eventually it was announced that this year, exceptionally, there were to be three Rhodes Scholars. Those selected were E. P. Haslam, from Auckland, Moller, from Otago, and W. F. Monk, from Canterbury.

The selection committee minutes show only that Haslam and Moller were selected in a first round, after which all the other candidates except Monk and Davin were eliminated, and eventually Monk won the decision. What they do not show is the role played by J. A. Hanan, the Pro-Chancellor of the University. He knew Mrs Macdonald personally, had been shown the Flavell letters, and took the view that Davin was an inappropriate choice for a Rhodes. Bledisloe supported him, and other members of the committee, who had known nothing of this in advance, eventually found it easier to exclude Davin, though from the order of business not without a long discussion. Later, in a brief interview with the secretary to the committee, J. B. Calan, Dan learned, off the record, that there was some sort of a problem which had made his candidacy difficult to support.

Bitter is too weak a word to describe the mood in which Dan left Government House. Mistakenly, he had jumped to the conclusion that the Chief Justice, who had after all sentenced Macdonald, was the source of the discrimination. He already disliked both authority and the Establishment. Now his disappointment fuelled resentments long held. The repudiation was a crisis in his young life. He had no money or alternative prospects, and he had set his heart and mind on 'escape' from the prison of New Zealand pettiness. Now that very same small-mindedness was making it impossible for him to make good his escape. He was in a reckless frame of mind.

Peggy Spence-Sales was in town, staying in a bach[60] near Eastbourne, on the far side of the harbour, with her friend Eileen Deste, known as 'Dusty'.[61] Eastbourne was Katherine Mansfield territory. The weather was sunny and hot. For eight days Dan disappeared into another life. He was drunk much of the time, lay on the beach during the day, made love at night. Family and friends in the south didn't know where he was, or how to get in touch with him.[62] Eventually Winnie tracked him down by sending a telegram to her brother Jack, also then living in Wellington, who knew where he was, and Dan wrote to her on 8 December on notepaper from the Grand Hotel. It is the letter of a badly wounded ego. Rhodes Scholarships were big news. Candidates had their photographs and personal interviews in the newspapers. The winners were, at least briefly, national celebrities. Dan's connections may not have known where he was, but they knew what he had lost. Washed out and humiliated, he went south again: first to Dunedin, where he stayed for a few days with Frank Hall in the big house at Bellknowes, then on to Invercargill. On the weekend of 15 and 16 December Winnie came in to

Invercargill to see him. They rowed bitterly, and parted in anguish and despair.[63]

He went back to Bluff to work on the wharf and in the woolshed, then to Stewart Island on a camping trip with Muff. He sent Peggy a volume of Blake's poems for Christmas, though goodness knows what she made of them.[64] When he returned to Invercargill on 7 January he still believed that his life and everything that he had struggled for was in ruins. He wrote to Winnie: 'It is no good . . . there being any more talk of marriage', protesting that he still loved her, but that he loved Peggy too, and that it would be for the best if she, Winnie, were 'to cut me adrift for the sensual and selfish scoundrel that I have proved myself'. As for 'the ethics or morals of the issue. I feel they are irrelevant.'[65]

For a time she did as he suggested, and they were completely estranged. She wrote him a number of brilliant and angry letters breaking off their relationship. There was an incisive style to her letters which he could never match. At this time she wrote the poem *In his own image and likeness*—one of her few literary works to be published—that sums up her feelings with characteristic economy:

> A dream?
> Is your calm face the shadow of a dream?
> I look on your calm face and curse it.
> I wish you dead.
> Ah, hungry worm
> Consume this shadow,
> Give me back my wild dream.[66]

It would be easy to forget, in the details of this private calamity, the satisfaction doubtless then being felt by Mrs Macdonald, who must surely have been enjoying the taste of revenge. There is no evidence for this, but the thought could not have been lost on Dan either. Reflection on her satisfaction contributed to his emergence from the irrational and passionate self-pity and misanthropy into which he had descended. In the new year of 1935, as January turned to February, his old stubbornness and determination began to reassert itself. He *would not* be defeated.

Various possibilities for the immediate future had already been canvassed. Frank Hall's father had a scheme to finance both Frank and Dan privately to Cambridge. Another alternative, to attend Teachers' Training College, had already fallen through when his application was rejected.[67] A third was to activate a plan he had long held, to return to Otago for one more year to read Honours Latin. Late in the summer his confidence was boosted by learning that he had been awarded a first-class degree in English. By the end of February, with a little money in his pocket from working at Bluff, and with the bitterness of rejection beginning to fade, he made up his mind to return to Dunedin, to read an honours year in Latin, and to stand once more for the Rhodes.

By the start of term on 11 March he was in lodgings at 17 Elder Street, the last house on the south side, just below the steps up to Constitution Street. This was a great change from the previous year, a rather grand villa with a gravel drive leading to a portico, and high-ceilinged rooms inside. Torrance Doig also had a room here, and James Raeside, his old chess partner and music lover, was a frequent visitor. Dan was now a senior man, a slight oddity in the Arts Faculty, a fifth-year student. He was still associate editor of the *Review*, this time with Frank Guest, but junior men, Arthur Prior and Martyn Finlay,[68] were now assistant editors of *The Critic*.[69] Dan occupied an Olympian position in this company, a position that suited his state of mind. He gave a paper to the Literary Society, of which he was now President, on modern American poetry, mainly discussing Pound and Eliot, after which he and Guest engaged in a discussion on 'defeatism'.[70] In a letter to *The Critic* he castigated the university for its weakness of creative impulse. 'The communal genius as a productive agent does not exist, and the artistic life of the University is as faint and feeble as its pulse. The writers are mediocre and immature. It is because they are the spokesmen of the mediocrity and immaturity about them.'[71] One is reminded of Shelley finding in gloom and misanthropy 'the solace of a disappointment that unconsciously finds relief only in the wilful exaggeration of its own despair'.

He experienced no difficulties with Honours Latin, which he mastered easily, partly because his old work habits were still intact: they had survived despite his occasional bouts of self-destructive pessimism and (in the light of his own definition of it) his decadence. He had returned a hardened man, more ruthless than before, and now thought of the Rhodes Scholarship as an objective to be pursued through a campaign of intrigue, perhaps even manipulation. He once more became active in the Catholic Students' Club, and had himself elected Vice-President. He made a point of getting to know Dr Morkane, DD.[72] He played rugby again, and was made captain of the C fifteen. He developed his friendship with Professor John Findlay, the philosopher, who became a supporter, and encouraged him in his determination. He still cultivated Professor Ramsay, and added to him the newly appointed Dean of the Law Faculty, Professor Aubrey Stephens.[73] At the time of Capping in the third week of May he gave a drinks party at his rather splendid lodgings, and invited Stephens and his wife Elsie. The contact developed into admiration—on their side—and he was a guest at a dinner party at their home on 15 June. A week later they went to the theatre together, and then had supper afterwards. He may have found Mrs Stephens a bit of a handful, but apparently weathered the situation.[74]

By this time there had been a *rapprochement* with Winnie. In April his infatuation with Peggy Spence-Sales collapsed and expired as suddenly as it had come into existence, and he sought Winnie's company and forgiveness. These were readily given, and he was back in Otautau for Easter, but the relationship never returned to either the intensity or simplicity of its early form. Winnie taught for the first term of the year at Riverton, going from Otautau every day on the train, but after that she resigned, and tried to live at home in Otautau, supervising the shop, beginning a novel. She had given up her room in Dunedin, and never lived there again, and she was now too far away for weekend visits. She slipped into a state of slightly dazed isolation. In February, when his misery and loneliness were first exerting the pull of desire to return to her, Dan had given Winnie a cocker spaniel puppy which they called Cleopatra—more usually Cleo—but it was run over and killed in April: a bad omen. With all that had happened to her in such a short space of time, she had lost confidence, both in herself and in Dan. Despite a sort of robust Irish grittiness, intellectually she had become a waif. She suffered from violent erotic dreams, and fits of weeping. She became acutely conscious of, perhaps even obsessed by, how the balance of her relationship with Dan had changed. 'The fact is our relationship is just entirely reversed. I am to you now what you were to me in the first year. So you have your desire there, Uncle Daniel?'[75] She drank a lot, especially *crème de menthe*, went to the races; and had occasional exotic, though innocent encounters with travelling salesmen or men friends from the village, to whom her status was surely ambiguous. She became friendly with a local farmer called Roderick McKenzie, who was kind to her, and took her home to meet his mother, whom she liked very much. They were related to the Martin's Bay McKenzies, a famous pioneer family whose name was still one to conjure with in Southland and South Westland,[76] and a part of her was attracted to the idea of giving up the struggle of bohemian life, and settling back into a more traditional existence.[77] One day Roderick told her a story about four 10-year-old wild horses that had been captured on Walter Peak station. The men tied one of them up and set about breaking it in. 'It struggled and fought at every step; the men pitted their strength against it, tried to master it. You have to be cruel to a horse to tame it.

But its will wouldn't submit, and its struggle killed it. They let the other three horses go free again into the hills.'[78]

These developments may have caused Dan anxiety, but it seems unlikely. Winnie was done with the struggle of a tempestuous relationship. She wanted no more Lawrentian emotional heroics. She committed herself now to doing whatever he might want of her. 'Although I rebel against you and your moods and changes,' she wrote two weeks later, 'I don't forget how I couldn't leave you, even when you drove me away. I am a horse that you broke in, and no matter how I kick and leap and toss my head, if you touch me I remember.'[79]

With Winnie's submission came a new and different commitment from Dan. He had learned that mere sexual liaison was an indifferent form of human contact, one that leads rapidly, without intellectual nourishment or social congruence, to spite and mutual contempt, 'the condition of whose acceptance is desolation'—as he wrote of the decadent poets of the 1890s. What he needed from Winnie was her companionship, her insight, her wit, her lively and imaginative mind, as well as her physical warmth and the sexual harmony of which they were capable. What he brought to her was the renewed bond of a deep and enduring love, whose preservation he now saw was as much fundamental to his own stability and chances of happiness as it was to hers. It is easy to see that Winnie was now tied to Dan: what it may be too easy to lose sight of is that he was equally bound to her. What they had shared in four short years, both of happiness and misery, gain and loss, immeasurably outweighed anything that any third person might try to interpose between them. In its own way, the knowledge of this brought a kind of peace to Winnie. She always feared that her Dan would be unfaithful to her from time to time in a sexual way, and her fears were often enough realized, but she rarely underestimated the strength of her own hold over him, and, as the future was to show, he never underestimated the power of her mind or the subtlety of her judgement, on both of which he was dependent.

With this settlement between them, Dan's life was also lived at a somewhat lower level of intensity. Winnie joined him in Dunedin for Capping Week, when he received his own MA. After his successful drinks party and the Capping Ball, they went south together, and he spent much of the vacation at Otautau, working on his Latin, going for winter walks. Back in Dunedin for the winter term in June his circle of friends was small and more closed, the undergraduate world fading: Frank Guest and Frank Hall; James Raeside, Marion Steven, and

Torrance Doig. He made two new friends from the world of books: Eric McCormick and Archie Dunningham, who were both librarians and archivists of great curiosity and with scholarly instincts. Together with Professor Findlay they formed a triumvirate that was a breath of fresh intellectual air in the stuffy Dunedin world, and they all took to Dan, inviting him to their homes for meals, talking to him about his ambition to be a writer. They helped him to see, no doubt, that it was possible to be a scholar and a writer, and to be your own man as well. McCormick and Findlay, both of whom became internationally renowned scholars, remained lifelong friends.

At this time he also met and befriended a young first-year undergraduate called Peggy Peacock.[80] She was striking to look at, with copper coloured hair and strong features. Legend has it that he first met her when coming out of the gate of his Elder Street lodgings as she was coming down the steps from Constitution Street. 'My goodness,' he said, 'But you're so beautiful. Please come in and let me kiss you.' And she did. He introduced her to his circle, where she was not uniformly liked, and she rapidly fell in love with him. Occasionally he would take her out, and he may have made love with her, but all his young women now had to understand that they had no hope of disturbing his commitment to Winnie.[81]

For the most part, however, he worked, either at Latin or at the final editing of the *Review,* and otherwise concentrated relentlessly on improving his chances for a second Rhodes nomination. When applications closed on 15 August both Dr Morkane and Professor Stephens had agreed to act as his referees, and he had solid support among the professors in general. The gossip was still abroad, however. On Monday, 8 July he was asked to go to see Dr Bell, the Professor of Mathematics, a man of 'businesslike habits and conciliatory character',[82] who warned him that the rumours were still likely to be to his detriment. Bell promised him a fair deal from Otago, but said that some professors questioned the wisdom of sending him up to Wellington pointlessly. He thought Davin should consider seriously whether it was worth his while to stand, but also said that he would write to J. B. Calan, the secretary of the selection committee in Wellington, to take soundings.[83] Dan talked again to his supporters among the professors, and once again decided not to be budged. Perhaps now too there was, at least in student circles, a slight move in the tide of gossip back in his direction, suggesting that he had been unfairly maligned. In any event, the local competition was rather weaker on this occasion—only one other candidate—and the Students'

Association made Dan their first choice.[84] On 26 August the Professorial Board once again nominated him from Otago University.[85]

With half his project now accomplished he again went south for the vacation, spending most of his time at Otautau, and working at Suetonius and Martial. In his final term he was very hard up, and had little social life,[86] but once examinations were over in mid-November Winnie came to join him and they said goodbye to their friends together before going back to Southland. Once again he went to Wellington for the Rhodes Scholarship interview, this time held on Tuesday, 3 December. Perhaps only for curiosity's sake he had written to Dusty and to Peggy Spence-Sales to suggest seeing them, and to ask if he could sleep in the photographic studio when he was in Wellington. This was agreed to, but Peggy said it was 'impossible for it to be like it was'.[87] He did see her while he was there, and they had what he called a final break-up, though in reality this had come many months before.[88]

For the Rhodes interview there was a new Governor-General, Viscount Galway, who was thought to be more intelligent than his predecessor. Myers was there again, much to Dan's despair, as were Hanan, Hight, and Ziman. They were joined by Sir Andrew Russell, a representative of the business world, who had been absent the previous year because of illness in his family, and Dr A. L. (Alec) Haslam, a lawyer who had been a Rhodes Scholar in 1927.[89] The interviews proceeded much as they had done the year before, though Dan noticed that his own was rather shorter, a cause for dismay perhaps in the brief waiting period afterwards. Then it was announced that D. M. Davin from Otago and J. D. Lewis from Auckland had been selected.

The sense of victory, of disappointments vanquished, was understandably strong. It is perhaps vain to hope that Dan spared a moment's sympathetic thought for Mrs Macdonald, whose son was about to be released after two years and four months of his four-year sentence. The strain of revenge ran pretty deep in both Dan and Geoff Flavell. Dan was particularly bitter that the gossip had cost him, as he saw it, a full year marking time in Dunedin. What he did not know immediately, though he was to learn parts of the story afterwards from Calan, and was to piece together more of it over the years, was that the Macdonald vendetta had still been in play, and that once again Hanan had brought it up in the privacy of the selection committee. This time, however, Sir Michael Myers, the Chief Justice, spoke up. He had himself had a letter from Dunedin in which the story of the Flavell letters was depicted as hollow, a piece of Dunedin gossip of little importance and less truth. He explained that Mrs Macdonald had been pursuing an unjust vendetta out of malice; that Davin had already been improperly discriminated against once; and that Otago were renominating him in the full knowledge of these facts. Sir Michael accepted this account and explained to the selection committee that he thought they would be unwise to compound one injustice with another. In the circumstances they would do well to give the tenacious Davin his reward. No doubt Haslam's legal antennae would have made him agile in Myers's support. Hanan, feeling the wind turn, withdrew his objections.[90]

In the wake of this affair much else was anticlimax. Despite a hangover Dan wrote Winnie a happy letter on 5 December: 'I am in a very good humour because of my revenge and recapture of my self-respect. If I had any money I would buy you a ring on my way home and make you wear it. Actually I am down to 14/-.'[91] He travelled south again the next day, stopping to see Frank Hall for a day or two, and then home to Invercargill and Otautau.

He was a celebrity now, presumed to be an Establishment figure himself. In the new year he was offered interim teaching positions at both the Technical College in Dunedin and Sacred Heart College in Auckland, his old *alma mater*.[92] He went to the Tech. for the months of February and March, moving back into his room at 17 Elder Street, taking up once more with his old circle of friends. In April he was back in the south, sometimes living with Winnie at Otautau, sometimes at home in Morton Road with his parents. In May and June he went back to Dunedin for a round of university farewell events. This time he lived at 3 Queen Street, almost on the corner of Pitt Street, a house in which Winnie had herself lived in 1930, before Dan even came to the University. How she must have felt that her world had been turned on its head. 'We have in five years somehow in some incomprehensible manner changed places', she wrote. 'You now are confident and insouciant, I incredulous and inept.'[93] She went to join him for Capping, where he received his MA in Latin, once again first class, and where he was awarded the James Clarke Prize. At the Ball they danced to the New Collegians band.[94] Briefly now he was serene, if anything regretting that he was to go away. 'I shall never know this spring', he wrote in a winter letter, reflecting on the song of a blackbird.[95]

In a world of new certainties he had decided on one of his own. 'Give me a year or so in Oxford to find my way about,' he wrote to her, 'then if the business can be sold or you can escape come over to London and we will join forces again and erect a new fabric for ourselves in a new land of

Cockayne.'⁹⁶ Winnie agreed, but events had not done with her yet. On 28 June, the second anniversary of her brother's death, and when she was at home in Otautau, a fire broke out in the house, and most of it, along with part of the business premises, was destroyed. Winnie and her sister were unharmed in the blaze, from which, however, very few of their possessions were rescued. The calamity made what remained of the business even harder to sell, though in due course it did bring her some hundreds of pounds in insurance compensation, money which eventually enabled her to travel to Europe to be reunited with Dan.

His commitment was nothing if not categorical, but even so, in this last year in Dunedin, he was also seeing a young woman, Shirley Brightwell, who worked as an assistant in one of the city department stores. From the letters that she wrote him in the first year after his departure to Oxford it is clear that they were, at least occasionally, lovers.

In the winter Dan was guest of honour at a Marist Brothers' School reunion dinner in Invercargill. Then in the last week of July he left 'Kegville' for the last time, travelling north with his father and with Winnie. When he kissed his mother goodbye at the railway station it was also for the last time: he would never see her again. A woman of great anxieties, living 'a life of quiet desperation', she probably thought so herself at the time. There was another emotional farewell at Dunedin railway station a few days later, with a great crowd of his friends to see them off, both Peggy Peacock and Shirley Brightwell among them trying to conceal their tears. They paid a visit to Opunake to see Dan's Uncle Tom, who had earlier, on hearing that Dan had insufficient money to pay his fare to England, offered to pay it for him.⁹⁷ Dan was actually given a free passage by the NZ Shipping Line, one of whose executives was the father of Les Clark, a fellow student whom Dan had known when they both worked on the wharf at Bluff in the May vacation of 1933.⁹⁸ Clark offered to consult his father about the possibility of a job for Dan on a ship to England. Clark's father mentioned the situation to Sir Robert Anderson, the owner of the line, who said the company would be proud to shout him a first-class passage.⁹⁹ At Opunake, much to his father's relief, Dan and Winnie said that they were engaged. She gave him a copy of *Martin Arrowsmith* by Sinclair Lewis. Alpha had never liked Sinclair Lewis. It was a complicated gesture, and Dan treasured the book for the rest of his life.

In Auckland there was a dinner at Sacred Heart College where Patrick Davin made a speech. Later, at the Waverley Hotel, where they were staying, Dan set fire to his bed. Was he dreaming of Scott, and the

Invercargill public library, ten years before? Anyway, he damaged the bedclothes so badly that he got Mike Joseph to help smuggle him from the hotel unnoticed.[100] He sailed on the *RMS Akaroa* on 14 August, Winnie and his father waving farewell from the wharf. If, symbolically, he had burnt his beds behind him, he was not entirely free to remake them on the voyage. Also on board was a Catholic priest, Father Terry, who kept an eye on him all the way to Southampton.

PART II

SCHOLAR AND SOLDIER,
OXFORD AND THE WAR
1936–1945

6

RHODES SCHOLAR

It is the paradox of our generation that pessimism is accounted
youthful and optimism senile.

(WKDP: DMD to WKD, 28 Oct. 1936)

At the same time, a faint sense of disappointment superimposed
on an otherwise absorbing inner experience was in its way
suitably Proustian too: a reminder of the eternal failure of
human life to respond a hundred per cent; to rise to the greatest
heights without allowing at the same time some suggestion,
however slight, to take shape in indication that things could
have been even better.

(Anthony Powell, *The Military Philosopher*, 173)

The world that Dan sailed into was far more intense than the one he had
left. It was a world of ideological conflict, of divisions and mobilizations:
ominous terminology from the lexicon of war. He experienced it at first
hand almost immediately. Having linked up with Geoff Flavell in London, the two of them went to the East End on Sunday, 4 October 1936 to
watch a Fascist demonstration. This turned into the famous Cable Street
riot in which the London Left fought a barricade battle with the police to
prevent Mosley's British Union of Fascists holding their march, an
objective in which they succeeded. Caught up in this battle of loyalties,
Dan commented: 'We . . . thoroughly enjoyed ourselves. The Communist sympathies were very strong. I felt very partisan and incited my
neighbours to resistance of the police. But they were men of straw. So was
I. Then we had dinner at a Chinese restaurant . . . Flavell was very
charming and we talked well.'[1]

This was political tourism, but it may appear to make him more
detached than he was. The intensification of hostility between ideological
points of view was in the nature of the times, and its effect on Dan was
twofold. First, he soon grasped that the Spanish Civil War, then in full
spate, was a rehearsal of a more general conflict in which Nazi and Fascist
would seek to take control of the world. There would, inevitably, be
another war, and he would, by virtue of his age and character, just as
inevitably be involved in it. Being in some measure a romantic, and

gloomy by temperament, he expected to be killed in France in the first year of the conflict. This expectation necessarily gave to his years at Oxford the character of prelude, not by hindsight, but *at the time*. Oxford was, for him, not an experience in itself, or a preparation for a career, but a marking of time before the shooting started. And as his Oxford years passed, and the war became ever more certain, so the loss of that year to Mrs Macdonald's machinations irked him more.

Second, he was dismayed and alienated by the attitude towards the war in Spain that was taken by the Catholic Church. Unlike many others of his generation, Dan seems not to have believed that right and wrong in Spain were matters of white and black. He was a rebel, and a Republican sympathizer, but a Catholic upbringing had prepared him well for sniffing out dogma. His working-class origins, in which labour on the wharves had given him first-hand experience of the actual characters of real working men, left him largely immune (at least when away from the mob) to the temptations of middle-class Communism. But he believed that the Spanish Republic was falling victim to Fascist conspiracy, and that Fascism would, by its own lights, and in a larger context, have to be defeated on the battlefield. The Catholic Church's support for the Nationalist cause, with its anti-humanism and its atrocities, accelerated his already strong tendencies away from the Church. So too did the death of McClure. The young, committed communist of 1930s Dunedin had joined the International Brigade, and was killed in Spain in 1937. Dan did not believe that McClure's politics were right in 1935, but he admired the man's commitment to his beliefs, and always sympathized with the outsider. Now he also felt the pangs of guilt for a life given, as he thought in 1937, honourably—at least in comparison with what appeared to be his own life of futile intellectual luxury. In his short story 'The Hydra' a Davin character called Collins reflects on the time leading to the death in Spain of a McClure character called McGregor.

Two years, carrying McGregor to his bullet in Spain and him to this comfortable room in Oxford, silly parties, more literature, ease and malaise. Dead in Spain, dead in Oxford. Spain was a place you got killed in, for something. Oxford you just went on dying in, for nothing.[2]

To say that something as large as religious faith can be lost over specific events, or particular disagreements, is to beg more questions than are answered, questions about the deeper characteristics of personality and intellect, previous experience and predisposition. Perhaps even without the Spanish War Dan was ready for a breach with the Church.

But whether it was merely a precipitating factor or not, some time between the Septembers of 1936 and 1939 Dan lost his attachment to the Church, and then his faith as well. He never expected to get either of them back.

These developments did not dominate his time in Oxford, but they were the backdrop against which everything else occurred, and they made the nature of his experience there quite other than that imagined by his family and friends at home in New Zealand. They also had an important effect on his relations with these people. As far as family was concerned, the break with Catholicism meant a break with the tribal culture of his childhood and youth. The ties had been weakened already by his intellectual development, but a break with the Church meant a final severing of relations with his home. This introduced a new element of restraint into his family dealings. He never admitted to them, while his mother was alive, that he was no longer a Catholic. Communications already perfunctory now grew ever more elliptical as well. In his own mind, the break converted the childhood that he had lost into an arcadian world of the recollection, somewhere he had been perfectly happy not because always at ease, but because he had been at one with it—Rousseau's state of nature, in which the boy and his will lived in harmony with circumstance. He captured his fall, or expulsion from this arcadia, in the poem 'Knowledge', written in Oxford in the Michaelmas term of 1937, and published in the Otago University *Review* for 1938.[3] It is his best-known poem, perhaps the most successful of the handful of poems that he published. Its simplicity and melancholy capture well the loneliness of his first months in college, as well as the spiritual isolation of a new life to be lived without religious faith, and without even the consolation of being able to explain the changes:

> God blazed in every gorsebush
> When I was a child.
> Forbidden fruits were orchards,
> And flowers grew wild.
>
> God is a shadow now.
> The gorse blooms pale.
> Branches in the orchard bow
> With fruits grown stale.
>
> My father was a hero once.
> Now he is a man.
> The world shrinks from infinity
> To my fingers' span.

> Why has the mystery gone?
> Where is the spell?
> I live sadly now;
> Once I lived well.

The sense of exclusion was echoed in more mundane ways. While he was in Oxford, his family's world in New Zealand also changed by events in which, of necessity, he could not participate. His older sister Evelyn married a widowed fruit-grower from Roxburgh called Dunlay, and moved away to a different and more affluent way of life. Tom, Dan's serious older brother, having transferred to Wellington in October 1936, almost immediately met and became engaged to Adelina McGrath, Toni and Joan's sister. Joan wrote to Dan welcoming him to 'the bosom of the family'.[4] Dan must have felt that his brother was following him about.

As for his friends, while he moved away from the Church, they tended back towards it. Cliff Murfitt, from the domain of adolescent Invercargill, became devout. Marge Thompson went further, and became a nun. 'Please don't be angry with me', she wrote.[5] Paish Johnson converted to Catholicism. Four of Dan's classmates from the Marist Brothers' School in Invercargill became priests. Others of his friends from SHC, Michael Joseph in particular, were drawn back into the Catholic faith. By contrast, Dan's experience in Oxford led him to the view that there was little to choose between one set of dogmas and another, that Fascism, Catholicism, and Communism all offered much the same kinds of inducements and intimidations, balms to uneasy emotions, or convenient simplifications of the complex and the impenetrable. In this way, experience and conviction joined together at Oxford to cut him loose from his recent past. The development was not immediate or instantaneous, there was a lively correspondence at first between himself and his New Zealand friends. His own mind was still cautious in making its judgements. But the process was inexorable, and, by the end of the decade, complete.

At first, though, it was disguised. Mike Joseph, coming to study on private means at Merton College Oxford, arrived in England only twelve days after Dan. With him was Fred Petricevich, who had failed Medical School in New Zealand, and planned now to escape his mother by pretending to study in London. A year or so later Bob Cotterall came on a visit with his younger brother Richard, and Teddy McCullough, debonair and exotic as ever, arrived in 1937 for postgraduate medical work at Queen Charlotte's maternity hospital. Geoffrey Flavell, already installed in London, shared lodgings with other expatriate New Zealanders. Ida

Lawson, studying at Cambridge, came down to London to meet Dan on arrival, and invited him to visit friends of hers in Surrey. In Oxford, the Rhodes Scholars who had preceded him, Lester Moller and Norman Davis, formed a welcoming committee. Winnie McQuilkan, his old competitor from Otago, arrived at Somerville in October 1937 on a postgraduate scholarship. And behind all these contemporaries there stood other New Zealanders whom he would know in due course, like Shirley Smith, studying Mods. and Greats at St Hugh's, Helen Coates who came up to read English in 1937, and John Mulgan, then Assistant Secretary at Oxford University Press. Even in the 1930s a travelling New Zealander might find it hard to escape his compatriots.

Dan was not, however, trying to escape churchmen. He admired the rigour, and enjoyed the logic, and the liturgy of Catholicism, and, unlike many who lapse, he never turned against individual Catholics, especially not theologians. Within days of arriving in Oxford he made himself known at Campion Hall, the Jesuit college. He got on well with Father Blake, a New Zealander from Christchurch.[6] He had a letter of introduction from John Findlay to Father Gervase Mathew, a Dominican at Blackfriars, and a brilliant Byzantine scholar and medievalist, who showed Dan round Oxford, and became a lifelong friend. Like Dan, Mathew was a strong anti-Fascist. Dan went to dinner with Father 'Ronnie' Knox in his first term, and he enjoyed hearing sermons that were intellectually demanding and thoughtful. Dan's quarrel with the Church was political and philosophical, never social or personal. This attitude of tolerance and respect he repeated in other spheres of life.

There is a sense, too, in which his disaffection from Catholicism was part of a more general alienation during his first year at Oxford, and initially the causes of this lay more with Oxford than with its Catholics. On the advice of John Findlay, Dan had applied to Balliol as his first choice, and the college admitted him into residence on 7 October. He matriculated into the university to study in the Honours School of Literae Humaniores, known colloquially as Lit. Hum., where he read Greats: Greek and Roman History; Classical Literature; Philosophy; plus papers in unseen translation. This was an undergraduate degree, though Dan had senior status in the college, which meant the privileges of a graduate student. The privileges were few because the college and university stood *in loco parentis* to students, which meant strict hours, and few opportunities for travel away from the university during term.

Dan was 23 years old, five years older than the freshmen who came up to Balliol at the same time. These included Leonard Fletcher, Hugh

Fraser, Alex Giles, Charles Gordon, Thomas Harvey, and Denis Healey. Those starting their second year in October 1936 included Robertson Davies, Edward Heath, Nigel Nicolson, and Paul Rolo. Before he left, the college also housed Julian Amery, Ralph Davis, Richard Hare, James King, Peter Soskice, Manning Clark, Roy Jenkins, Alexander Kafka, Maurice Macmillan, Peter Self, and Francis Seton. The eminence of these names is, of course, retrospective. At the time, Dan did not take to the younger undergraduates who surrounded him. Their ambitions were, to his mind, juvenile, and he was a little too mature to share their interests. He felt himself an outsider, not just by nationality, but by his working-class origins, his religion, and his comparative maturity. When Edward Heath knocked on his door on the first day of term to invite him to join the Conservatives, Dan declined with a short lecture on the reasons why no sensible man would do such a thing.[7] He was 'dreadfully depressed that first term or two and hated Oxford and hated Balliol and hated everybody'.[8]

Part of his alienation, common to many in their first term or two at Oxford, lay in cultural difference. Dan first experienced this even before term began when, on 23 September, he went to visit Lester Moller, his contemporary at Otago, who had won a Rhodes Scholarship in 1934. Moller had stayed on in his college, Brasenose, to work over the summer. After a night in various pubs the two of them went back to his rooms, and, for want of spare accommodation, slept in the same bed, head to toe. Moller's scout (college servant), coming in to wake him with hot shaving water in the morning, believing he had disturbed a homosexual tryst, dropped his tray, perhaps in surprise. Moller placated him with a bottle of sherry. Dan fled back to London, wondering what he was getting himself into.[9]

Back in Balliol for the start of term, he had two rooms to himself, study and bedroom—a source of wonder to his friends in New Zealand—on the second floor of staircase VII, on the Summer Quad. From here he had a view on to the Martyrs' Memorial in St Giles'. Though he complained about his poverty, and was to go on doing so for many years to come, £400 a year was more than sufficient to live well, with plenty left over for books and clothes, now and increasingly his two biggest forms of expenditure. He discovered Blackwell's—'Circean' he called it[10]—and Hall's, the outfitters on the High Street. Both were to do good business with Dan for the next fifty years.

His tutors in Balliol were Duncan MacGregor and Donald Allan. MacGregor—'a wizened Scotchman'[11]—was an ancient historian, to whom Dan took immediately—'altogether rather likeable'.[12] MacGregor recognized both Dan's ability and his melancholy, and was concerned from the start for his welfare. He was also an extremely good tutor, enthusiastic for his subject, and with natural talents as a teacher. Unfortunately, MacGregor was himself a depressed man. A veteran of the First World War, in which he had been gassed, he drank heavily to forget. He also smoked incessantly. His wife, a nurse, struggled to free him from dependence, but neither she nor scholarship was sufficient inducement. MacGregor died while Dan was still a student in Balliol, leaving him with even greater feelings of isolation.

Donald Allan, a philosopher, was altogether different: he had a shy and awkward manner that, at first, made Dan feel diffident and incompetent. He was well known for this. It was popularly said of him that he was inaudible beyond three feet and unintelligible within them. With Allan, Dan had to cover the entire syllabus of philosophy from the sophists to Kant. 'A tutorial with Donald', he wrote to Winnie, 'is quite a strain, with each of us avoiding the other's eyes through long intervals of embarrassed silence.'[13] Dan's anxieties about the difficulties of the philosophy syllabus preyed on him, and were one more reason for his wishing Winnie would come to England to join him. He badly missed the intimate exchange of ideas.

Loneliness and remoteness from Winnie were the predominant, linked themes of his first year at Oxford. The mails were slow, six weeks for a letter to travel from England to New Zealand by sea, and two weeks by air, which was also extremely expensive. Cables were inadequate—though occasionally resorted to—and telephone links non-existent. Dan met few women he thought interesting during his first year, and suffered from sexual yearnings of great intensity, all of them now focused on Winnie, unattainable in New Zealand. Dejected in London near the beginning of term, he eyed the prostitutes with bitter distaste:

> With hungry eyes I walked in London
> And found there those who sold
> What my lost friends gave.[14]

The autumn and winter weather was cold and wet. Oxford was dull and boring. He was miserable. Once again, as three years before when Winnie first left Dunedin to go supply teaching, he sank into a state of melancholia and misanthropy which, with all its railings against the English and their society, now seems comic. The only friends he made early on were a young Australian couple, Bill and Joy Forsyth, whom he admired for their resistance, similar to his own, to English conditions. The food was bad, the cities filthy, the people intolerable, the culture shallow: modern opinion was vulgar, and traditional opinion broken on the wheel of history. Nothing survived the blunt knife of his condemnation.

During his first term he returned to keeping a diary notebook, briefly jotting down his comings and goings, and lists of the letters he wrote. He joined the Labour Club, and went to its meetings in both Balliol and the University. He heard the luminaries of the Left, like John Strachey, and listened to debates on motions supporting the Popular Front: 'Much sense and much nonsense.'[15] Early in Hilary Term 1937 he went to a Labour Club meeting after which there was a singsong in Kemp Hall:

There was an SCM atmosphere, song without beer. Pastoral proletarians singing modern eclogues of the worker. All very mistaken except the songs, the 17th century repeats itself in disguise. Strange to hear these intellectual, youthful, ingenuous, impractical, unblister-handed young rococo devotees of the new political religion chanting their hymns uneasily, most of the words set to tunes which have unfortunate associations with bawdy songs. They all suffer sadly from the frailties of the spirit and too few of them have found the strength of the flesh. . . . I was interested but being only a worker's son who happens to have done some work felt uneasily out of place.[16]

In resistance to this sort of theatrical politics he baptized himself a Davinist: an adherent of no known political party. The Davinist may have been neutral, but he was never a eunuch. He hated Fascism, detested Conservatism, was hostile to Liberalism, and in intellectual resistance to Communism. This did not mean political indifference, however. Dan may not have been confirmed, but he was a lay member of the congregation, however uncomfortable, in the broad church of the late 1930s Left.

At another Labour Party function he met Ian Milner, a New Zealand Rhodes Scholar ahead of him.[17] Milner had already established a reputation as a left-wing intellectual at Oxford. Milner wrote in his memoirs that he thought of offering Dan some advice, but,

As we shook hands Davin's face and bearing didn't betray need of counsel . . . I thought I'd begin with the Oxford blues. I elaborated ways of coping with the peak incidence of the malady in the after-lunch hours: a brisk walk, a jog trot, football two or three times a week . . . 'I find gin helps,' Dan broke in, knowing an innocent when he saw one. We chatted amiably, if a little stiffly on my part, on other matters.[18]

Dan felt ambivalent about Milner. On the one hand he could admire a man who was making a break with his past. On the other, that very past probably made him culpable by association. Milner came from the side of New Zealand that Dan believed populated by his enemies: the Presbyterian and Anglican middle classes of English and Scottish descent. Milner's father, a famous Empire jingoist,[19] was founder and headmaster of Waitaki Boys' High School, an imitation English public school in Oamaru. Ian was one of its products.[20] Dan had not escaped to Oxford to mix with these people, and having met one he certainly would not be upstaged into accepting his advice.

When he was not working, writing critical or gloomy letters to his friends in New Zealand, day-dreaming about Winnie, or finding Oxford unsatisfactory, Dan was thinking about writing. The project to be a writer, already formed at Otago,[21] and given expression in his contributions to *The Critic* and the *Review*, now took clearer shape. The stiff and awkward verse of his Otago years gave way to a still formal but slightly easier style of poetry. He mapped out various short stories. After going to a college concert on 1 November he noted that the music had been 'excellent for literary gestation', and jotted down in outline the four-part elements of a novel to be called *The Mills of God*. In this work a man discovers a murder, and joins in the hunt for the killer only to find himself: a discovery that leads to suicide. 'Too much melodrama and too rounded a plot?' he asked himself, and comments: 'Almost feel like writing it but better keep it and do it well.' He began work on it two weeks later, at the end of a weekend of deep depression, but in a letter to Winnie called it 'Rather chaotic still'.[22]

It seems likely that the decision to begin writing signalled that the worst of his isolation was now over. The night before, returning from an evening drinking with Mike Joseph, he climbed in through a window of the Junior Common Room, which was in a mess. He sat down on an upturned table and was found there by a big blond young man who asked him if he wanted to fight. They agreed to wrestle, and after Dan had thrown the man three times he gave up and went to bed. Later Dan discovered this was Bill Sitwell, a kinsman of the famous literary family whose work Dan had read as an earnest young student. Dan and Bill became good friends. Bill was in revolt against aesthetes, with whom his family was well stocked, and was a famous Oxford hearty, a drinker and sailor. In due course he introduced Dan to his friends, men who were not interested in promoting themselves in the Union, or the Tory or Labour Clubs. Two of these, Thomas Hodgkin and Arthur Pyper, became friends of Dan's.[23] Hodgkin was the son of an intellectual family, with roots in the same part of Northumberland as Bill Sitwell. Pyper, a quiet man and a keen oarsman, was a Northern Irish Protestant, tall with a soft rich voice and 'a comic turn of speech'.[24] A man of very great charm, Dan called him 'the Arthurian legend'.[25] Pyper remembered Dan for 'his striking appearance and his broad New Zealand accent'.[26]

Through Sitwell Dan also met another Irish Protestant, John Kennedy, whose family came from Cashelnagor, in Donegal. Over a year later, Dan, who had by this time been joined by Winnie, went to stay with John at his family's deserted country house, where they lit a big fire in the hall, and had dancing every evening to which the young people came from the surrounding villages. They brought fiddles, and the 'girls would sing, hiding their faces, and they all danced "The Bridge of Athlone," "The Siege of Derry," "The Waves of Tory"—beautiful folk dances—the last my favourite'.[27] There was a lake on this country estate, and a minstrel gallery above the hall. The winter weather was cold, and the house seemed frozen through, especially the hall, draughty from its seven doors, and the bathroom, still riddled with bullet-holes from The Troubles. But Dan and Winnie were happy reading Rimbaud's poetry and eating salt fish, which was almost the only food to be had in mid-winter in this poor countryside.

Pyper's boat-club connections also brought Dan together with a young Canadian, Hart Massey, whose father Vincent was then the Canadian High Commissioner in London, and a notable art collector. Hart's uncle, Raymond Massey, was a famous actor, then at the height of his powers. As a result of an operation on his pituitary gland at the age of 5, Hart had not then grown beyond the stature of a boy, though he had great personal toughness. These qualities made him an ideal cox, and he became the smallest man ever to steer in the Boat Race. He remembered Dan as having 'unusual intellectual distinction but with . . . kindness and a sense of humility'.[28] Hart had rather splendid rooms in Balliol, and, although he was only 18 when he came up, kept what amounted to a salon, with amusing conversation, and plenty to eat and drink. Two student societies, the Leonardo, devoted to serious discussion, and the Brackenbury, 'a play-reading and mulled-claret-drinking group', usually met in his rooms.[29] It was at a meeting of the Leonardo Society on 26 January 1938 that Dan debated the Special Powers Act and the Irish Question with Arthur Pyper before a substantial audience that included the young Denis Healey. Healey records in his memoirs that Pyper and the 'shaggy' Irish New Zealander taught him everything he 'ever needed to know about the insolubility of Ulster's problems'.[30] Another one of those present noted in his diary that 'Davin in a prepared answer and in discussion tore [Pyper] to pieces'.[31] Dan was a practised debater and a skilful public speaker, and the cut and thrust between him and 'the Arthurian legend' would have been worth hearing.[32]

Despite a naturally critical spirit, Dan formed his friendships easily. His own Irish Catholic and Republican background never made him exclusive, mainly because of the New Zealand influence, the ready acceptance of mixing and sharing, sleeping head to toe. Nor did friendship cloud his judgement. Dan accepted people for what they were, and never attempted to alter or improve them. Bill Sitwell was 'a good natured and stupid hearty' and he liked him for that.[33] Bill got a fourth-class degree, which is the polite Oxford way of saying he failed: the equivalent of coming 3rd in a Sacred Heart College race. When he found out that Dan had got a First he said: 'If I'd known you were a bloody intellectual I'd never have spoken to you.'[34] They were to be friends for twenty years, and Dan deeply regretted that they later lost touch.

Pyper had rooms on Dan's staircase, and on the same floor as an American Rhodes scholar from Princeton, Gordon Craig. Craig was writing a B.Litt. thesis on 'The Luxembourg Crisis of 1867 with Special Reference to British Foreign Policy', a topic that filled his contemporaries with mirth. But Craig and two other American Rhodes scholars in Balliol, Philip Kaiser and Walt Rostow, were, like Dan, older and more mature men, outsiders, people more to his temperament. 'Craig is a small white-haired American,' Dan wrote, 'with a good brain, sensibility, a rich deep voice and a richer humour. I am on better terms with him than anyone else here.'[35] This is testament to Craig's wonderful vitality. Their first meeting was late at night, and began in the quad where Dan, who appeared to be shickered,[36] asked Gordon: 'Are you sex-starved, Brother Craig?'[37] He said he was, so they agreed to find something more to drink to alleviate it. Near the top of staircase VII, Craig wrote later:

Davin gave a maniacal cackle and, lifting me up bodily, held me over the stairwell, which looked to me to be as deep as the Mendip Mine. 'What a loss to culture if I should let you go, Brother Craig!' he said in an unpleasantly gloating way. I admitted the truth of this proposition but pointed out that, with the world in its present state, which did not promise to improve, he and I, as responsible and reflective men, had no right to inflict this further blow upon it. It was clear that he had not considered this aspect of the question, for he released me, and we went on to wake up Walt and Phil, congratulating each other on our nobility and forbearance.[38]

Brother Craig, who was always known as Gordie in these days at Oxford, became the nucleus of Dan's circle of friends. This included a

number of other Americans, like Joel Carmichael,[39] a student at Wadham, and Guy Nunn, who came up a year after Dan, in 1937. Like Dan,
Guy was from a working-class background, though less fortunate in his
family, having spent some of his childhood in an orphanage, and some of
it wandering Mexico and California with his father looking for work. He
was a man of action, wonderfully articulate, quick and direct, prepared to
risk himself for his principles; a thoroughgoing anti-Nazi who, like
Gordie Craig, spoke fluent German, and never concealed his contempt
for Fascism. It was through Guy and Gordie, who gave him a copy of
Goethe's *Faust*, that Dan was encouraged to keep up his German. And
Guy, like both Gordie and Dan, was very attractive to women, as well as
winning the admiration and respect of his Oxford male contemporaries.[40]

All these young men were lonely for female company. There were few
women students in Oxford, and the peculiar institution of the college,
with its strange and to them alien rules, like not being permitted to go out
after 9.00 p.m., and having to be in by midnight if you *had* gone out
earlier, smacked more of the monastery than the university. Craig, who
was like Flavell in the speed of his wit and the pleasure he took in
language, wrote verse, and in Oxford took to writing lyrics to tunes which
Rostow would compose for the piano—though only in the key of C. The
songs dealt with the stuffiness of college life and the girls for whose
company they yearned. *Claustrophobia Blues* ends:

> If only this damned monastery
> Would burn to the ground or such;
> If only the porter had a fairly decent daughter
> Who'd be susceptible to the touch!
> But he hasn't. I'm hittin' the booze!
> I've got those Claustrophobia Blues!

This was written more or less exactly at the time Gordie and Dan first
met. A week later Craig wrote *Dancing Man Blues*, then *All Alone Blues*:

> There ain't no shine in the sun no more,
> No chowder in a clam,
> And even Niagara's lost its roar,
> Since she took it on the lam.[41]

Craig and Rostow became an Oxford phenomenon, invited to perform at
JCR functions all over town. Dan contributed verses to some of the later
songs, and was remembered by all these young men as a terrific social
asset, funny and talkative, a good listener; and a man with a prodigious
knowledge of Oxford pubs, and the capacity to go with it, who, as the

drink warmed him, became brilliant and impossibly inventive, his talk seeming to dance and flow in ways they'd never before heard or dreamed possible.[42]

To know Dan at his best you had to go to the pub, which in Oxford meant the Lamb and Flag, the Horse and Jockey, or the Gardeners Arms in Plantation Road,[43] and, late in the evening when the others had shut, the Clarendon. In London it invariably meant the Fitzroy on the corner of Fitzroy and Charlotte Streets, with dinner at Bertorelli's, just opposite, or the Plough in Museum Street. Here Dan and his friends would cluster for conversation and whatever else might develop. If there was a piano, and Gordie was in voice, they would sing. As often as not the conversation would turn fantastic. Celebrating the Coronation, on the night of 13 May 1937, Dan drank far too much, and was launched on a weird night odyssey involving a small man with an umbrella, a visit to outpatients with a cut lip, a hazardous climb into college at 12.30 a.m., and being discovered on Gordie's couch at 4.00 in the morning when 'the curtain was rung down on the coronation at last'. One night, in London during the Easter vacation of 1938, dinner at Bertorelli's turned into an impromptu party at Gordie's new digs off Tavistock Square. The morning after the tumultuous excesses of this occasion Gordie understandably approached the obligation of breakfast with his new landlady in some trepidation only to discover that 'the charming Dr. McCullough' had quite won her heart, so his friends could do no wrong in her eyes.[44]

From December 1937 Winnie became part of this life, at least during vacations, and at weekends in either Oxford or London.[45] Thus Dan had managed by his second year to reassemble many of the elements of his previous way of life in Dunedin: term-time weekdays of work and reading, with friends for the essential elixir of conversation, and the occasional comforts of more tender affections;[46] and his weekends of a rather different stamp, surprising, sometimes ridiculous, often exotic, and in the company of Winnie, his chosen companion.

The face that Dan presents in his notebook, in his letters to Winnie, and apparently in his dealings with his tutors, is rather different from the impression that he left on most of his Oxford contemporaries. In the former he is depressed, alone, embittered. To the latter, a convivial drinking companion, a great turner of epigrams, a tireless conversationalist, a writer of sparklingly funny letters, a man given to sudden and possibly dangerous practical jokes with a manic edge to them. The two impressions are widely different, though they are not incompatible.

Dan was what recent psychological analysis terms a cyclothymic personality, episodes of melancholy alternating with bursts of high spirits.[47] He discovered in his early twenties that he could keep depression at bay in congenial company, which he sought as a remedy, sometimes compelling himself to take part in social activities for which he felt little inclination. As time went by he turned the need into habit, going to places where he knew he could be assured of company, and so avoid the mental hazards of solitary reflection. Since he was adept at conversation, both as talker and listener, stimulator of others, his acquaintances found him a delightful companion. And as he always gave back in concern for others more than he took in food for his own ego, they generally formed the opinion of an easy friendship. Alone in his private correspondence with Winnie, in his diaries and notebooks, and in the solitary turning of his own ever-active mind, however, the world for Dan was a rather different and far more sombre place. At the end of Trinity Term 1937, C. K. Allen, the Warden of Rhodes House, reported him 'a very nice and able fellow . . . [but] Not a very easy man to read'.[48]

This Janus-like duality of temperament, of which he became aware himself in due course, was illustrated during his first vacation from Oxford when he went back to London, to Geoff Flavell's lodgings in Devonport Street.[49] Three other ex-Otago men also lived in this 'absolute madhouse'[50] presided over by a bisexual smuggler with a large collection of obscene photographs in which he himself featured prominently. Here Dan had a well-furnished room, and a good breakfast and dinner each day for two guineas a week, but the circumstances were bizarre.

Fortunately there is something unaccountably fantastic about the house which makes what ought to be disgusting comic, some Rabelaisian atmospheric condition which compels you to accept the most flamboyantly grotesque aberrations from normal morality as the normal manifestations of morality itself. The manageress is under the thumb of the maids, the maids are under the thumb of the owner who in some inexplicable manner is under the thumb of the sexual smuggler. The latter never pays any rent and keeps the whole house beating to the rhythmic pulse of his nocturnal activities.[51]

For a week Dan alternated between bouts of high spirits and drinking—'the urge to recklessness and self-escape'[52]—and bouts of depression, though Flavell was, as ever, a good companion, and took him on tours of the art galleries. After this, on 14 December Dan set off for his first visit to Ireland.

He went by train and boat via Holyhead and Kingstown (Dun Laoghaire), travelling with Father Blake, who was on his way to

Dublin. Then train again to Galway, and after a night in a cheap hotel, a twelve-mile walk in the rain to find Tonegurrane, his father's birthplace, and the home of his surviving uncle, Michael. Michael Davin, a widower with six children, he found living in the same thatched cottage where his own father had been born: two poor rooms, a peat fire, soda bread and turnips to eat. His uncle, 'a quiet good-tempered man about my build but thinner and bent with work',[53] first mistook him for his father, as his 'Aunty Sullivan' had done years before in Morton Road. Once correctly identified, he was made hugely welcome. They drank the Scotch that Dan had brought but spent a wretched night uncomfortably on chairs before the fire, because there was only one bed, and neither would go to it if the other could not. In the morning, Mary, the oldest daughter, 12 years old, produced a solitary egg and boiled it for the visitor. The others sat round and watched as he ate it.

This was hardly the Ireland of colonial memory, or the legend of the travelling story-teller, and Dan had adjustments to make. '[R]eality was no match for fond remembrance.'[54] After breakfast, in the rain and winter cold, they walked five miles to visit Michael's wife's people. In the evening some neighbours, the Lardners, with a rather larger cottage, gave a party for which Dan contributed the drink with his last few pounds. '[T]he whole village turned up at intervals to meet me. We had a real Irish evening, singing, reciting, step dancing, Irish reels etc. I wished all the time you [Winnie] were there, although . . . I was getting hell from fleas lice and vermin of all descriptions.'[55] The next day, broke, he made his way back by bus, train, and boat to London, promising to return in the summer.

This brief excursion into his family past made a deep impression on Dan. Back in London at the weekend he wrote the experiences down, and throughout his life went on tinkering with the manuscript. He was shocked by the poverty, and began sending his uncle Michael a little money, as he could afford it from time to time. He was also shocked by the local omnipotence of the Church, and the superstitions of the people, which together gave him the sense of not belonging where he had keenly expected to fit. In a poem written the following summer, he cast the strange land as 'Lost in my father's youth' where 'gentle Irish rain fell melancholy | On the son of a lost son.' 'Only the sad leprechauns remained | And they were lost to me.'[56]

Against this feeling of rejection and alienation was another, positive, and dense in possibilities.

I really liked Ireland and felt ever so much better after going there. I didn't hear an obscene word while I was there and the whole atmosphere was a relief from the overcharged sexual atmosphere of London and a houseful of medical students. These Irish peasants are very ignorant, very unhygienic and very simple, but they are most ascetic in their habits and really likeable as well. I think we will love it when we go over in summer.[57]

They did not go over in the summer, or for many summers to come, but the seeds of Dan's later deep affection for Ireland, already planted in New Zealand, germinated on this trip. They later bore rich fruit.

After Christmas and New Year with Flavell and his medical cronies, Dan went back to Oxford on 15 January. He was initally very depressed again, but now pulled himself together, drank rather less, and started to work hard and read widely. He read Evelyn Waugh, Sherwood Anderson, and, once again, James Joyce's *Ulysses*, 'which gets me more than ever'.[58] He played rugby regularly. His natural instinct for scholarship found an outlet in Greek, where he was studying Plato: 'a fanatical combination of logician, Fascist, Communist, idealist, theoretician, and an artistic masochist (that means he was a poet himself but argued them out of a share in his Republic). Writes beautiful Greek.'[59]

A pattern was now setting itself. Vacations away from Oxford, filled with travel and experience. Terms in Oxford filled with work, the fellowship of college life, reading and contemplation. Dan made a few new friends at this time, notably Mark McClung, a Canadian Rhodes Scholar in Oriel. A great drinker, he and Dan became sparring partners of pub conversation, the dialectic racing back and forth between them in orgies of inventive hyperbole. He also met Richard Cobb, a history student and ferocious talker from Merton; and a friend of Joel Carmichael's, Michael Sacher, the wealthy son of one of the owners of Marks and Spencer's. By and large, however, his circle was complete, and he was happy enough living in it. He went to the cinema with Sitwell or Mike Joseph, sat up late talking with Pyper and Massey, Craig and Kaiser, dined in Merton with Joseph, Carmichael, Cobb, and Nunn,[60] and joined in the singing when Craig and Rostow performed their songbook. Gordie Craig's rooms were where he would habitually end his day, talking till late into the night. Gordon, for whom he developed a deep, lifelong affection, became his intimate in these years, the man to whom he confided his secrets, and whose own fears and longings he heard and discussed. The affection was returned. 'A very good friend, my Daniel', Craig wrote in his diary.[61]

With a life more varied and balanced, Dan stopped writing in his notebook regularly, and such energy as he now devoted to rehearsal of his own misery he seems to have reserved for his tutors, who reported him working away 'rather gloomily', and wished he had 'a little more liveliness'.[62] Some of this was perhaps due to a trait of Winnie's that surfaced for the first time late in 1936. After five years of almost continuous and rich correspondence she lost interest in writing letters, finding it an increasingly unwelcome and burdensome task. Dan did not hear from her between 9 December 1936 and 26 February 1937, and filled his own correspondence with anxious queries about her health and steadfastness. Once she had at last replied, the focus of their letters shifted to plans for her coming to be with him, Dan giving her minute instructions about what she was to bring, how she was to travel, and what they might do on her arrival.

For the Easter vacation of 1937 Dan went to Venice, travelling with Joel Carmichael and Michael Sacher in Michael's car. These were the great days of European touring, and the drive down was beautiful. They arrived on 24 March and stayed in the Calle dei Fuseri in the Sestiere di San Marco, close to the Campo di San Luca, with a young anthropologist from Columbia, Hannah Kahn, a friend of Joel's. This is a central location, not far from the Piazza San Marco, and in the spring of 1937 very much quieter than it is today. Venice he found 'absolutely wonderful'.[63] It suited him perfectly, mood, temperament, climate. He wrote letters, worked on Herodotus, went to the cinema, read Dostoevsky's *The Possessed*—the first Dostoevsky in five years—talked to Hannah about Winnie, sat in and strolled about the city, drank at Harry's Bar.[64] On 14 April he had a cable from Winnie telling him that she was booked to sail on the *Ormonde* from Sydney, arriving at Toulon on 25 June.[65] Dan's affection for Italy, as also for its language, which he never studied but could understand and learned to speak during the war, started in these happy few weeks which were only disturbed by one coincidence. He ran into a Dunedin matron on the Piazza San Marco and extracted some small pleasure from trying to imagine the gossip she might take home with her.

Back in Oxford he spent much of the summer term in an agony of anticipation of Winnie's arrival. She left Otautau at the beginning of May, and travelled via her friends in Dunedin to Wellington and Sydney, where she joined the *Ormonde* that sailed for Europe on 20 May via Colombo, the Suez Canal, and Naples. By the time that Dan left Oxford to go to meet her in Toulon, his tutors had formed the view that his bouts of depression were a threat to his general well-being. MacGregor suggested that he should take a complete break, and do little work over the summer months.

Dan hardly needed encouragement now that Winnie was the focus of all his desires, but his dreams of an idyllic reunion on the Toulon quayside on 25 June were not realized. The *Ormonde* hove to outside the port, and passengers were put ashore by tender. Winnie was given wrong instructions about which tender to take, so that she was late ashore, and Dan had to suffer uncertainty. She found him beside himself with disappointment and recrimination. Many passengers on the ship had contracted a form of dysentery, an affliction to which Winnie fell victim on arrival at Toulon, which caused her a few days of misery.

Joy was established, however, and they spent ten days and nights lost together in Toulon, days and nights of which no record survives. Then they went by train to Rapallo on the Italian Riviera, where they lodged for two weeks in a *pensione* close to a villa rented by the Forsyths, Dan's Australian friends from Oxford. Here they spent their time idling in the sun, loving and reading, the first time they had been to the beach together since a November Sunday in 1932 when he had gone home still smelling of lupins. From there they went on to Florence, and found a *pensione* in the centre, near the Pitti Palace and the Boboli Gardens. They were close to the house, 21 Piazza Pitti, facing the *palazzo*, where Dostoevsky stayed in 1868 and wrote *The Idiot*. On the Ponte Vecchio, under the awnings of the jewellers' shops overhanging the Arno, Dan bought Winnie an engagement ring for her birthday, an emerald set among little pearls and sapphires, an antique, originally made in France. The weather in Florence was phenomenally hot, and mosquitos made life miserable. Eventually, in the last week of July, they retreated north to Paris.

This was Dan's first visit to Paris, and he took to it as to a second home. They rented a couple of rooms in a big block of apartments at 3 Square de Port-Royal, where they also had use of a kitchen, and settled down to a life of semi-domesticity. The Square de Port-Royal is in a rather dull area of the XIVth *arrondissement* dominated by the Santé prison.[66] However, it is a very short walk from Montparnasse and the historic *quartier* that runs from the Rue de Gaieté to the Seine, and which incorporates the bohemian area of the Left Bank. Here there are quiet gardens to sit in and read, historic churches and monuments to visit, all the bars and bistros of the Boulevard du Montparnasse, the Dôme and Coupole, and of the Boulevard Saint-Germain, the Deux Magots, the Brasserie Lipp, and the Flore. The social customs suited Dan. There were numerous little restaurants where they could eat well for what seemed unbelievably low prices. One of these, A L'Alsacienne, at 64 Boulevard de Port-Royal, just round the corner from their lodgings, became a favourite.[67] The life of the bistros was agreeable: good beer and cheap brandy, chess sets and people to play against, odd characters to talk to, and the pleasure of simply sitting and watching Parisians.

Montparnasse was full of refugees. They met and befriended a Dane called Torstein Hofaerdson, an ex-diplomat and would-be writer who looked like Hitler, and who never did write his novel 'because his first sentence was too good. The sentence was "Only the tame birds have a longing; the wild ones fly." '[68] Torstein introduced them to a Norwegian friend, a painter, who along with a German *émigré*, Fritz Oberender, 'not Jewish . . . but couldn't stand Goebbels', made up a triumvirate of sometimes infuriating but always diverting companions.[69] The Dôme was their regular haunt, often into the early hours after going dancing at La Boule Blanche, a Martinique night-club.

Dan was so happy here that he wanted others to share it. He wrote to Gordon Craig, urging him to come, but Gordie was working on his thesis in London, and proved immovable. Dan had more success with Flavell. He had been in Europe since the beginning of 1934, and already knew and liked Paris well. He arrived in the middle of August from Italy and Corsica, and took them on tours of the art galleries, the modern independent show at the Petit Palais, and the art exhibits at the international festival then running in Paris. He also introduced them to a painter, Judith Gluckman, the sister of a friend at Bart's. For a 40 franc fee, Dan modelled for her wearing a hat that he had bought in Paris. An 'apache hat' he called it, 'because of the sinister effect it produces on my otherwise ingenuous face.'[70]

There were the usual adventures to be expected when Geoffrey was about. One night he and Dan stole a churn of milk and smuggled it into their rooms. A day or so later, when both Geoffrey and the milk had gone off, its presence in the wardrobe became increasingly unwelcome. Flavell sent telegrams from London: 'Has it become cheese yet?' 'What sort of cheese?' Eventually Dan disposed of it down a lavatory, but the problem of what to do with the empty churn remained. One morning, very early, he and Winnie carried it from the lodgings in a trunk, and got it as far as the Montparnasse cemetery, a secluded and tranquil spot, now famous as the last resting-place of Jean-Paul Sartre. Here, after some playful embracing to deter further investigation by passing *flics*—'In Paris if you embrace somebody it shows that everything is normal'—they managed to abandon the churn and beat a retreat to their lodgings, where they were regarded with deep suspicion by the concierge. She had witnessed them leave with a far heavier trunk, and, being unaware that Monsieur Flavell had left to return to England, developed the deepest suspicions of the two resident *immoralistes* from New Zealand.[71]

Dan was happier in Paris than he was in England. He found it easier to write, composing his poem 'Galway, 1936', on 6 August. He started work on a short story about his Uncle Jack, and developed his ideas for *The Mills of God*. He took enormous pleasure in conversation, especially with Flavell, whose rhetorical powers were as sharp as ever. Geoffrey would pursue flights of fancy about the people and places around them, one night characterizing the clientele of the Dôme as figures from *A la recherche du temps perdu* who had escaped briefly from its pages. Dan surveyed the harlots of the pavement tables. 'Proustitutes', he said.

After Geoffrey's visit, Fred Petricevich came and stayed for two weeks. He was 'the same as ever silent and uncommunicative. He irritates me in lots of ways and it is practically impossible to work while he is about . . .'[72] On 1 September, out celebrating Dan's twenty-fourth birthday, there was 'a frightful quarrel and Winnie vanished' only to turn up later having spent some hours in Le Monocle, a famous lesbian night-club. This then became one of their favourite night-spots, though their tenure was abruptly terminated on a later visit after some sexually charged exchanges directed at Winnie by Jo, girlfriend of the boss, herself an elegant woman who always wore a dinner-jacket.

This was all far more interesting than anything that London or Oxford could offer, and its existence acquired magnetism. When Dan returned to Oxford at the end of September, Winnie stayed on in Paris. She registered for language courses at the *Alliance Française*, bought a typewriter with French keys, and hoped to live as a freelance writer. Even after she had left at the end of the year, and taken a job teaching at St Teresa's Convent school at Effingham in Surrey, they both dreamed of being able to return.[73] They laid plans to go to other countries, and also to visit Marseilles and Mandelieu, but these never matured because Paris exercised such a pull on them. In August 1938 they did pay a brief visit to Germany, but it ended abruptly in Munich, their first port of call, when they were nearly arrested, and deemed it prudent to depart. The offence was Winnie's attempt to light a cigarette from the Eternal (*sic*) Flame at the Nazi Martyrs' Memorial, a gesture considered insulting. Both Dan and Winnie liked to think that it was correctly interpreted.

Back in Paris, they lived in an apartment rented by Guy Nunn at 33 Rue Delambre, a narrow street of shops and apartments that runs from the Boulevard du Montparnasse to the Boulevard Edgar-Quinet. Here they were only a hundred yards from the Dôme. It is difficult to think of a better location from which to enjoy the pleasures of Paris, while remaining free to withdraw from them to write. It was here that Dan lived through the crisis of Munich during the last days of September, while working away at *The Mills of God*. By now he had evolved a method of composition that suited him. He would spend a long time in gestation, and then, in a foolscap bound notebook, leaving the reverse of each page empty for later additions and emendations, write rapidly, fluently, and in near to final draft.

They returned to Paris for Christmas and the New Year, and for the first half of January 1939. It snowed heavily and was particularly peaceful and beautiful, the snow settling on the capes of the police as they directed traffic in the streets. Mike Joseph and his friend Northrop (Norrie) Frye came to visit, whisking Winnie round the galleries, and sitting up late to talk to Dan on the *terrasse* of the Dôme. Frye was 'excellent company' but Dan did not exactly share his and Mike's approach. 'I had more of a taste for the wild side, one foot in Bohemia while they had their feet pretty firmly in the door of academia', he wrote later. 'At the time I fear I was faintly patronising towards their kind of book-gallery-museum culture.'[74]

At the time, Dan was not alone in holding the conviction that the end of the age was upon them. Winnie wrote to Marge Thompson from Paris: 'come over for the war. We'll weather it together. Isn't it hell? Everyone here just awaits it fatalistically.'[75] Dan had seven stories finished by this time, and about twenty poems.[76] Via the sister of an Oxford acquaintance the stories were read by John Hackney, a London literary agent,[77] and although nothing came of this, the warmth of Dan's ambition was not cooled. He wanted to write, but had to find a means of support. He was increasingly preoccupied with what to do after June, when he would finish at Oxford. Sometimes he thought of returning to New Zealand, sometimes of looking for a job in England, perhaps in publishing, sometimes of joining the British Council and living abroad, sometimes of trying to lead the life of a writer in London, eking out a living from reviews.[78]

Against these alternatives, he sensed that professional ambitions were pointless because war was coming. In Paris on 26 September 1938 he listened to Hitler's famous broadcast on the radio, and accepted the Munich agreement for what it seemed at the time, a last ignominious throw of the appeasement dice that was to buy 'peace for six months'.[79] He was in Oxford working for finals when the Danzig crisis began in early March of 1939, and when Madrid and the Spanish republic fell at the end of the month. He wondered whether he would even have time to sit Schools.

The certainty of war shaped his actions. Before it began he wanted to endorse his commitment to Winnie in marriage. They both wanted to have a child.[80] He was determined to finish at least his first novel. He was determined to get a First. These matters preoccupied him in his final year at Oxford. Gordie Craig had returned to the United States,[81] and Dan moved into lodgings with Guy Nunn at 14 Warnborough Road. Here he led a tranquil existence, reading and studying, dining with Guy, lunching in college, untroubled by university regulations.[82] At the end of their second term Dan and Guy had to seek new lodgings when their landlords were forced out of the house in Warnborough Road by debt. They found rooms, for their final term, at 100 Banbury Road,[83] though moving house was a solitary endeavour because Guy mysteriously disappeared for a while. When he came back, just in time for the new term, it turned out that he had been to Prague on a clandestine mission for an American refugee agency to help three dozen Jewish refugees escape to Britain.[84] The war was close now, and getting personal.

Dan was happier living in digs than he had been in college, partly because it made it so much easier for him to be with Winnie at weekends when she could escape from her teaching job in Surrey.[85] They met either in Oxford or in London, where they would take a room at the Sussex Hotel, in Sussex Gardens, near Paddington Station.[86] This was a difficult time for Winnie, who was occasionally unhappy about her circumstances. Early in 1938 she had been selected for a teaching position at a girls' school in Prague, Czechoslovakia, and had been very excited at the prospect. The job began in April, but the appointment fell through at the last minute. Given what then happened in Prague, she came to see that this was no bad thing, but at the time it had felt like an end to her ambitions for independence and adventure. The school at Effingham was not without its difficulties, and she felt isolated there, lonely, and sometimes miserable. She developed an infection that was a long time being cured. She missed all her friends in New Zealand. Dan's letters to her throughout this year are playful and tender. His new love-name for her was 'Frog', and his correspondence flows with love and concern. 'Do not squander your feelings in sorrow for your solitude,' he wrote to her, 'but dam them up and drown me in their tide when next we meet.'[87]

When she came up to Oxford they went to Rhodes House and other functions together, and became friendly with the Warden, C. K. Allen, and his wife. Dan called him C. K., which he seemed to like. They also made friends with a young Egyptian, Munir Sabry, who came up to Balliol in October 1938. He was the son of Hassan Sabry Pasha, briefly Prime Minister of Egypt. Munir was a man caught between the nationalist radicalism of his own generation and the Establishment to which his parents in Cairo belonged. To be caught between the pressures of age and institution was a condition with which Dan sympathized.

In the summer term, with Schools set to start on 1 June, Winnie visited hardly at all and Dan worked relentlessly, partly out of habit, but also this time goaded by the belief, a last vestige of the fading resentments still harboured towards his own country, that he had to get a First in order finally to prove himself in New Zealand. He had tutorials in philosophy from the Master of Balliol, 'Sandy' Lindsay, 'a philosopher of sorts' as Dan called him. Without believing that Dan was a great scholar, Lindsay nevertheless expected him to get a First. Dan's views about Lindsay were, if anything, slightly more equivocal, but he admired him for his principles and his courage, particularly during the famous Oxford by-election campaign of the autumn of 1938 when Lindsay stood against the Tory Quintin Hogg.[88] When exams were over Lindsay helped to get him a month tutoring in a Workers' Educational Association summer school in Oxford, which began on 5 July, a week before his viva voce examination. The work earned him £20.

His viva, on 12 July, went well, almost a formality. Ronald Syme, a young classical historian from New Zealand who was an examiner that year, did not even bother to ask a question. He told Dan some years later, when they had become friends and colleagues, that it had been unnecessary. D. M. Davin was awarded a first-class degree. It is a guide to his style at the time that so many contemporaries were surprised. He had worked long and hard, but they had not noticed. Kenneth Bell, the Moral Tutor at Balliol, sent him a note: 'I see you've got a First. Why don't I know you?'

Exams completed, students gone down, his Rhodes contemporaries scattered, Dan's world in Oxford was now dissolving. Lindsay suggested to him that from September he might have a WEA lectureship in North Staffordshire. The salary was £350 per year, which was less than he had been getting as a Rhodes Scholar, but in Bennett's 'five towns' it would be more than enough to live on, even married. On the strength of this possibility, the cheque for July teaching, and his last Rhodes stipend, Dan and Winnie were married in Oxford at the Catholic church of St Aloysius on Saturday, 22 July.[89]

The day began as a chapter of accidents. Winnie travelled down from London by car with Bob Cotterall, his younger brother Richard, and Mike Joseph. Traffic was slow, and they were running very late. As the four of them sped across the plain from the Chiltern Hills, and down from Headington, 'Winnie accomplishe[d] marvels by changing shoes, stockings, dress, hat and make-up in the car, Mike and I acting as dressers in the rear'.[90] Even so they were twenty minutes late at the church. Perhaps this was as well. Arthur Pyper had come back to Oxford from Donegal for his viva voce examination without subfusc, so at the last minute Dan lent him his suit. Pyper's interview was delayed, and Dan was suitless until almost zero hour.[91] Somehow, after all that they had been through, the idea of Dan and Winnie, separately, scrambling into their wedding clothes under odd circumstances and in the nick of time, seems appropriate.

The ceremony was Catholic, but no member of either family was present. Teddy McCullough, looking a cut above all the other men in a thrillingly well-made suit, acted as best man. He had known Winnie for ten years. Mike Joseph was a witness. Afterwards there was a small party in Balliol: a Commonwealth affair, with Elizabeth and Ian Mason, Bernard O'Brien, a Jesuit priest from Christchurch, and Hart Massey from Canada, who supplied beer and silver tankards to drink it from. When it was over Dan and Winnie had a few days in a hotel, and then went back to Paris, fearing that it would be their last opportunity for a long time.

They settled back into Guy Nunn's apartment in the Rue Delambre. In the mornings Dan worked on *The Mills of God*, now called *Cliffs of Fall* from the poem 'No worst, there is none' by Gerard Manley Hopkins. Under the influence of Dostoevsky, Lawrence, and the decadents of the 1890s, he mixed a peculiar brew of passionate madness and literary despair.

He and Winnie also re-established contact with Geoffrey Cox, not seen since the Students' Union at Otago in 1932. After his Rhodes Scholarship years in Oxford Cox joined the staff of the *News Chronicle*, and became a celebrated name as one of only two Fleet Street correspondents covering the siege of Madrid. He was now diplomatic correspondent for the *Daily Express*, and after covering the *Anschluss* from Vienna and the Munich crisis from Prague, had come to Paris for the last round. There was little doubt that war was close. On 23 August came the

Nazi–Soviet non-aggression pact, turning Communists and their sympathizers in the popular front head over heels. On 29 August Dan wrote a short story, never published, called 'Crise de Nerfs'. A title for its times. Three days later Germany invaded Poland.

Dan and Winnie were in bed in the Rue Delambre when the police beat on the door at 7.30 a.m. Dan opened it to find Guy Nunn and his Norwegian girlfriend Annie, laughing at their own joke. They had just arrived from Biarritz. It was Dan's twenty-sixth birthday. They went to Le Viking for a birthday breakfast, then to a café at the Madeleine, near the Norwegian Embassy, where Annie was to collect her mail. 'She returned, calling across the room to us, tears streaming down her face, "Hitler has invaded Poland . . . and I must return to Norway at once." '[92] Dan and Winnie saw the pair of them off at the Gare du Nord and then went looking for Geoffrey Cox at his office in the *France Soir* Building in the Rue du Louvre. When they had last seen him, the office was busy, Geoffrey constantly on the phone to Berlin, London, or Rome. When they came in this morning he was alone, his feet on a desk, the telephones silent. There was nothing more to say. Diplomacy was finished. Winnie recalled that Geoffrey's suitcase was in the corner of the room, packed and ready. Dan liked to say it contained evening dress for use in the bomb shelters.

The truth was more disheartening. Geoffrey Cox was giving up his flat at Saint-Cloud and shipping his possessions to England. He still had commitments in Europe, but he advised Dan and Winnie to return to England straight away. At the flat in the Rue Delambre the concierge was in tears, her husband already on his way to the Maginot Line. They caught a boat train, packed with voluntary refugees like themselves. On the Channel ferry they bumped into a Balliol man who had a decent position by some suitcases, and Winnie was able to rest for the uncomfortable overnight crossing. In London they found Mike Joseph and some of his relations. Wealthy investors, they had fled New Zealand in 1935 to escape the Labour Government, and settled in an hotel in Bloomsbury. Here, on the morning of 3 September, when the air raid warning sounded for the first time, they assembled with the residents and staff in the cellar to hear Chamberlain state that Britain's ultimatum to Germany had expired unanswered. The hotel maids were weeping. The war had begun.

7

FROM OXFORD TO CRETE

Stages in one's life should break off with a snap instead of
dribbling to their conclusions and merging in the next.

(WKDP: DMD to WKD, 'Tuesday' [13 June 1939?])

Aldershot . . . that uniquely detestable town.

(Anthony Powell, *The Kindly Ones*, 11)

From the sense that everything was happening to nothing happening at
all. The term 'phoney war' perhaps fails to capture the reality of individual
experience in the autumn of 1939. Dan and Winnie left the weeping
maids of Bloomsbury and took a train to Oxford. They had no other
home. They found rooms with a kitchen at 26 St John Street, a little up
from Wellington Square, behind the familiar territory of St Giles'. In
this, their first married 'home', Winnie tried to teach Dan the rudiments
of cooking, a skill for which his Irish, Catholic, male, New Zealand,
working-class origins had left him ill-prepared. Laboriously, he mastered
an omelette. Mysteriously, a few days later Arthur Prior and his wife
Claire appeared on this domestic scene and moved into the same house.
The world was out of joint, and Arthur and Claire wanted to discuss with
Dan the intimate details of their sexual lives. It would be hard to imagine
a man less appropriate for the role of sexual confidant. And in any event
Dan was preoccupied. He wanted war work, and to find a publisher for
his novel.

Oxford was full of young men waiting for the war to come to them. In
the glorious early autumn weather they gathered every day in Balliol
quad, lying around the lawn, talking, wondering, waiting. Lindsay, the
Master, and various other college heads, eventually got a government and
military recruitment board created for Oxford, and in due course, at the
beginning of October, Dan went before it. He had always assumed that
his fate would be military, and it was only in the last weeks of September
that he realized that there were alternatives for people like himself, people
with languages and a background of scholarship. Man after man, going
before the board, was recruited into supply, or intelligence, or economic

warfare. Dan, with no clear preference in his own mind, though vague hopes for something useful without being too dangerous, found himself before a committee on which an army brigadier gave every sign, after several days of yielding to one or other of his colleagues, of feeling frustrated. 'A New Zealander eh?' he said, perking up, leaning forward. 'Play any games?' 'Rugby', said Dan. 'Excellent. Infantry. Any objections?' The military man glared at his colleagues. Only Lindsay stirred, but ineffectively, and presumably on the well-known committee principle that every dog must have his day, Dan went to the infantry. This was his first taste of military decision-making.

In this way, after a physical in which he was found to be A-1 fit for service, Dan's papers eventually came, assigning him to the Royal Warwickshire regiment, and instructing him to report to the Budbrook Barracks, Warwick, in mid-November. On the appointed day, his train departing in the late afternoon, Dan and Winnie went for a last lunch together at the George in George Street. There, in the upstairs dining-room, every table was occupied by parties like themselves: young men setting off for basic training in the afternoon. Someone bought a bottle of wine for friends at another table. The idea was taken up; bottles passed overhead, hand to hand, in convivial finality.

The wonderful autumn turned to a foul winter. Warwick was cold and miserable; the Budbrook food inedible. Dan, as we know, had little patience with authority, and no natural tendency to obedience. The Royal Warwickshire regiment, known popularly by the sobriquet 'the fooking Warwicks', was one of those English regiments in which the social distance separating the barrack room from the officers' mess seemed expressly designed to alienate a New Zealander of Dan's background and temper. The barrack dormitory, and the wretchedness of living by the clock in a disciplined all-male environment, brought vague reminders of Sacred Heart College. He appealed for relief to Winnie, and she came to him in early December, a selfconfessed camp follower, taking a room in a Warwick lodging house.[1] In this way he staggered through the necessary tedium of drill, PT, and mindless exhortation, and escaped whenever possible to her company. Life was better than it might have been because Winnie discovered in late November that she was pregnant, so that one of their aims was on its way to realization. The secret pleasure of this, hugged to himself, was antidote to any drill sergeant.

This phase of life, quickly forgotten, came to an end after only two months, when Dan was posted to Aldershot for officer training.

He reported to 168 Officer Cadet Training Unit (OCTU), Ramillies Barracks, on Saturday, 13 January 1940, and was assigned to D Company. This was his home for the next four months and four days. The OCTU was under the command of Colonel Bingham, slightly notoriousas 'Bang-it-into' Bingham, an educational philosophy that did not appeal to Dan.[2] His immediate superiors, however, Sergeant Love and Corporal Nightingale, who had command of D Company, were much liked by the men. 'Corporal Nightingale, go and fetch me a red lamp from the stores. Say it's for Sergeant Love.' 'Sounds bad sergeant.'[3]

Among the cadets were a number of young Oxford graduates. Dan was already friendly with Heugh Drummond, a New Zealander, and like Dan from a big family, who had overlapped with him at Balliol. Peter Frankenburg, another of the Royal Warwicks who was also a Balliol contemporary, and Robert Rayner, a recent graduate from Oriel College, were other connections. Heugh and Dan would go in the evening to the Queen's Hotel, returning late to barracks where, after lights out, they would perform 'a spirited haka, rendered in army boots on the resounding floor boards'.[4] Drummond, who was short and stocky, naturally acquired the nickname 'Bulldog' after the fictional character by 'Sapper'.[5]

These were early days of the war. There were not yet 'Battle Schools', and OCTU instruction took the form of platoon and company tactics, weapons drill, the contents of King's Regulations, and occasional lectures by outsiders, some eminent, like Mountbatten. Everyone was amused, perhaps bemused, by the reputation left behind by a cadet on the immediately preceding OCTU called Enoch Powell. This young man was supposedly so brilliant that after a visiting lecturer's departure he could quote the entire lecture back verbatim. Dan had heard of this man already—he was another 'fooking Warwick'—and he formed the impression of an interesting personality.

They were similar in one regard. Like Powell, Dan's arms drill was reported as 'determined but inexpert',[6] which fitted with the overall impression that he made. He did not have a particularly military bearing, his cadet uniform could be awry, 'his side cap pulled down over his large face rather than cocked at the regulation angle'.[7] But, unlike Professor Powell, who was clumsy and not tough, he exuded an air of great pugnacity. Geoffrey Cox recalled how, when he first saw Dan march his platoon on parade in the summer of 1940, he realized, with great relief, what a profound error of judgement Hitler had made in going to war.[8] In this sense, Dan fitted well at the OCTU, where, though there wasn't much in the way of compulsion, the men were expected to be tough and to get tougher.

Cadet Davin's nerve may have been strengthened by his first real literary success. John Hackney had advised him to read the short stories that appeared regularly in the *Manchester Guardian* so as to get a feel for what was being published. He did, and decided on the strength of it to send the paper his short story 'Toby'. They published it on Monday, 22 January, and the fee of two guineas got him from Aldershot to Oxford for a weekend with Winnie.

'Toby' is the story of the efforts of four small boys to save their dog, Toby—under sentence of death for biting 'one of our own'. They hatch a scheme, and carry it through, but their father is as cunning as he is implacable. He shoots Toby, and jeers at the boys for their futile efforts to save the dog. 'They did not know the jeer came from a heart as sore as their own, but one which had been hardened by life and work until it was ashamed to admit emotion at a mere animal's death.'

Like his other early but unpublished stories 'Toby' is an exercise in almost drab realism. The death of the heart is mirrored in the coldness of the prose, and no effort is made to extract an enriched fiction from the events of experience. The girls in the story are Molly and Evelyn, the two boys who are named, Tom and Pat. The only concession to English publication is the location of the dog's hiding place, a 'cave on the moor', though it is also called 'Faraway Hill'. When they learn that Toby is dead, the boys go up to look at the grave. ' "Good-bye, Toby," they said. "We will never forget you." '

The little work rings like a promise kept, or a commitment honoured, but it is still incomplete. It would be another seven years before its underlying power would be fully exploited in the longer short story 'The Death of a Dog': the sensitive portrayal of one boy's mind, its growing awareness of his parents' motivations, and its penetration of the complexity of human action that signals the loss of innocence as eloquently as the death of the dog itself.

With a first publication to enhance his status and self-esteem, Dan's weeks of officer training passed in a congenial way, though other factors also made their contributions: recent release from basic training as a private soldier; the initial absence of any actual hostilities; the sense of preparation for a mission whose full brutality had not yet been, indeed could not be, revealed; and, towards the end of the course, in the first days of April and May, the sudden eruption of real war in Europe with the German invasions of Norway and Denmark, Belgium, Holland, and

France, that signalled to everyone that their training had been in the nick of time. On 10 May Chamberlain resigned, and Churchill became Prime Minister. 'At last', Dan wrote in his diary.

A week later, on 18 May, a fresh Aldershot graduate, Dan was by his own request commissioned as a second lieutenant into the Second New Zealand Expeditionary Force, the 2NZEF, the main fighting component of which, 2 NZ Division, was known as 'the Div.'[9] He was gazetted incorrectly as David Marcus Davin. His number was 978. The second echelon of troops from New Zealand, on its way to Egypt, was diverted to England on 15 May when it was three days out from Fremantle, in response to the rapidly worsening military situation in Western Europe. By the time it arrived on the Clyde on 16 June, the BEF had been evacuated from Dunkirk. On 20 June, two days after it went into billets and bivouac in and about Mytchett, just outside Aldershot, Pétain's government concluded an armistice with the Germans.[10] In the interim, Dan was attached to a British regiment, and sent to Hythe in Kent for small arms training. He arrived in Mytchett to take up his commission with 23 Battalion (Canterbury and Otago) under the command of Colonel Leckie, of Invercargill, on 20 July. On the day he arrived the Battalion was away on tactical exercises in the Ashdown Forest.[11] He dropped his kit and went straight back to London, anxious for Winnie. The same day, in Oxford, she gave birth to a daughter, whom they named Anna Deirdre, but he was not to learn the news until the next day, and it was almost another week before he could get leave to visit them.

The duties of a one-pip lieutenant were initially as perplexing and frustrating to Dan as to most others. At first he was attached to Battalion HQ, but within a month was appointed commander of 13 Platoon, C Company. The job of platoon commander required a combination of nanny, disciplinarian, imaginative leader, occasional lawyer, military tactician, friend, and boss. Not caring much for discipline himself, Dan found it difficult to inflict on others. Sometimes critical of his own bouts of laziness, he found it hard to criticize in those subordinate to him. He was constantly aware of the egalitarian heritage of his own New Zealand background, and sympathetic to the problems of his non-commissioned officers in trying to secure compliance from the men without resorting to discipline. On the other hand, he was conscious of the demands of war: the need for readiness, determination, and steadiness under stress.

Each of these conflicting attitudes was to find ample expression over the summer of 1940, when the sun shone down on southern England, and the Battle of Britain was waged in the skies above. At first Dan's unit was under canvas at Mytchett, on the edges of a field set among acres of pine trees. Every morning the band played reveille, walking round and performing in front of each group of tents. Dan found his compatriots, among whom he had not lived for four years, to be 'nice fellows' but inarticulate, though he was pleased to see Geoff Cox again, a new recruit after spending nine exciting months reporting the wars in Finland and Belgium, and the fall of France. Dan also began to make various casual friendships among the other junior officers. An occasional German air raid livened up proceedings without bringing serious harm.

The greatest enemy was boredom. Dan longed to be able to write, but detected in himself 'a hatred of writing which is the obverse of its love . . . My love of writing is somehow like my love of Winnie. Indispensable yet cruelly neglected. Perhaps it is the fear of failure, the thought of being committed wholly and then not being good enough.'[12] His natural curiosity remained intact, however, both about people and about literature. He managed to make a start with writing in the middle of August, reworking a short story, probably 'Cain as Abel'. And as usual, all the time, he read: Freyberg's *A Study of Unit Administration*; Somerset Maugham; *Madame Bovary*; Katherine Mansfield stories again; Melville's *Typee or a Peep at Polynesian Life* (which he found 'intolerable');[13] *Brief Light* by Jack Lindsay; Isherwood's *Mr Norris Changes Trains*; and Zernatto's *Die Wahrheit über Oesterreich*. Later in the autumn he read De Quincey's *Confessions*, Balzac's *Peau de chagrin*, and George Borrow's popular *Wild Wales*, (which had 'much charm'). He was 'pleasantly surprised' by Anthony Trollope's *Barchester Towers*, but left unrecorded what he thought of Konrad Heiden on *Hitler*.

It is tempting, but probably mistaken, to see a pattern in this nineteenth-century reading. In the army, Dan read what came to hand, whatever he could get hold of in bookshops and libraries, and the pattern emerged from the reading, not vice versa. He was, however, accumulating a prodigious knowledge of nineteenth-century literature. What must have struck his contemporaries in the blunt world of the army was not simply his ability to read fluently and to translate in and out of five languages, but rather more the pleasure he took in doing so. Geoffrey Cox summed it up many years later when he said that Dan was a 'natural scholar'—someone who not only did well at scholarly work and in examinations, but who took pleasure in learning.[14] This was where he felt at his natural best. Cultivated reading was never a pose with Dan—however peculiar his military comrades may have thought it. It was a pleasure, somewhere he went when he wanted to relax, to be happy or diverted. So too it was a necessity, a prerequisite of the balanced life.

At the end of August he found lodgings for Winnie and Anna at 67 Coleford Bridge Road in Mytchett, and was able to spend a week's leave with them prior to the Battalion's expected departure for Egypt in the middle of September. Winnie had spent the last two months of her pregnancy, and the first month on coming out of maternity hospital, staying with C. K. Allen and his wife Dorothy at Rhodes House in Oxford, a grand residence. Dorothy Allen was a famous housemother to Rhodes Scholar families, and C. K.'s reference to himself ever after as Winnie's accoucheur was a light-hearted arrogation of her role. Dan never forgot their kindness.

'In the army, anything that's not worth doing is worth doing well', Dan noted at his OCTU at the beginning of the year. The late summer and autumn of 1940, when the Battalion's move to Egypt was cancelled, and they hung on in southern England to defend against invasion, went past in fulfilment of this well-known military principle. There were route marches: 'Much disheartened by my men's performance. Definitely the worst in the battalion for falling out' (17 October); Divisional manœuvres: 'Exhilarating day charging through bush and hedges marred at end by muddle in embussment. Tempers running high in Coy HQ' (23 September); 'to the coast on manœuvres and had the usual comedy of errors, making on the whole a satisfactory day' (29 September); and even real operations when, with invasion threatened, the Battalion moved to the area between Dover and Deal charged with a counter-attack role in case of German seizure of the ports. They spent a 'tedious day as reserve battalion' and Dan was 'very angry this evening with the men for laziness in stand-to. They seem to have no gift of pretending or make-believe' (16 September).

He was having to acquire this skill himself because military arrangements ordained that the egalitarian Dan must nevertheless have a batman, a personal servant. He entered into the 'curious state of intimacy in an unintimate society'[15] that this relationship involved with Private 'Ginger' Evans, formerly a miner, whom he found 'a little raw' and 'sentimental' but 'even-tempered not a fool, willing, young, robust'.[16] Ginger was to work for Dan when he was on active service for the next three years. Winnie thought that Dan (and she too initially) were exploited by him rather, and she may have been right. Dan brought his washing home, though this was supposed to be one of Ginger's tasks, and before the Battalion left England at the turn of the year Dan even gave

Ginger the revolver that Marge Thompson had given to him for his eighteenth birthday nine years before. Winnie was particularly displeased by this. The gun had no particular sentimental value for her, but she did want it herself, as she planned to kill a German when the invasion came.

In addition to his platoon duties, Dan gave a number of lectures to the Company on topics of contemporary interest in political philosophy, such as the origins of totalitarianism, and also participated in debates, courts martial, and military courts of inquiry. These were of nothing more significant than the usual AWOL charges, or inquiries into the loss of military equipment, but Dan enjoyed them, rediscovering the pleasures of debating. A powerful memory helped him master King's Regulations, and a subtle mind enabled him to sway military judgement. He liked King's Regs., which he thought were funny. The term 'dumb insolence'—a well-known device in the ranks for expressing silent criticism—passed into his own small collection of favourite phrases. In this way he developed a reputation as the private's friend, and throughout the war past subordinates asked for him when they found themselves in military trouble.

Dan's own occasional military troubles, such as they were, might be said to have their origins here. Just as in social life he was a Janus figure, at once depressive and convivial, so too his attitude to authority was paradoxical. By inclination he was its opponent, but by ambition and talent he sought promotion in it. In some ways his experience of the army, as a talented but subversive officer, was parallel to his quest for a Rhodes Scholarship. The profound desire for escape was not there, but the idea of a bohemian and unconventional character gatecrashing a conservative Establishment is similar. It did not take him too long to discover, however, that by contrast with the British army, in which he had had a brief and largely unhappy experience, the Div. was a genuine citizens' army, capable, as it matured through battle experience, of absorbing difficult characters, employing and promoting their talents, tolerating their differences.

Dan's normal social preference was to go to the pub for a drink with whoever was the best and most interesting conversationalist, and, failing that, to get a period of peace and quiet as orderly officer so as to get some reading and writing done. At the same time, money and ambition pushed him both to want and to seek promotion. He understood this paradox himself. '[O]n the one hand I feel unfit for the job of commanding men since no-one is ever really fit for such a huge responsibility and on the other feel the job beneath some of my capacities.'[17]

These sentiments arose in connection with anxieties about Winnie and Anna as the invasion threat receded with the autumn, and the second echelon awaited its own expected embarkation to foreign service. Where should they live while he was away on active service? Geoff Cox and John Mulgan had arranged long since for their wives to go to New Zealand, a journey which had now become impossible. He toyed with the idea of Ireland. This anxiety was mixed up with another one about money. After three years of comparative affluence on a Rhodes Scholarship Dan was now a subaltern in the New Zealand army on pay of 16s. 6d. per day. This represented a reduction in income of 25 per cent, and he now had a wife and child to support. He did not bother to take his Oxford degree, saying it would just be a waste of money if he was killed.

Rumour suggested that departure would not long be delayed. At the end of November Dan went to Rochford and Southend for a last fling with Geoffrey Flavell, himself about to become an army surgeon. Then he moved Winnie and Anna into new digs at Camberley. In mid-December he managed a weekend in Oxford where he had lunch at Rhodes House with the Allens and where he found Lovelock, the great New Zealand middle-distance runner, recovering from concussion. He dined in Merton with Cobb, where they bemoaned the passage of old friends like Guy Nunn and Mike Joseph while condemning the juvenility of new undergraduates in hall.[18] He put his financial affairs in order, and then went back to Camberley, where he got breakfast in bed and an opportunity to play with Anna.

Two weeks later they were parted. He bought himself Italian and modern Greek grammars to study, and Winnie gave him a travelling chess set. He left her his short stories and the manuscript of *Cliffs of Fall*, and she promised to try to find them a publisher. 'Animated in company, gloomy alone'[19] he saw out the old year, and on 3 January the Battalion marched to the railhead at Farnborough for the night train ride to the coast.

I shall long remember that march out of Camberley, in the early night, the men too heavily loaded but glad to be again on the move, the anonymous goodbyes cried from the dark, the people at their doors, not framed in light as in peacetime but merely pale vague interruptions of the shadow. And the men called back to them and whistled as they marched through the night . . . The moon was new and high, the night clear and occasionally away to the flank we could hear the AA guns, or the reverberant boom of a bomb. So New Zealand said goodbye to Camberley and I passed for a while and perhaps for ever from the life of Winnie and Anna.[20]

They boarded the *Athlone Castle* in Newport docks at lunch-time on Saturday, 4 January 1941, sailed from there to join the rest of their convoy in Belfast Lough, and on 12 January set sail from there for Egypt via the Cape. With a five-day port call in Cape Town the voyage took a day over seven weeks. Also on board were the Maori Battalion, for whom Dan now formed a deep and enduring affection: 'their keen alive faces, their discipline, good humour and the poise that comes from their culture and their pride' made an instant and lasting impression.[21] It was one that he was later to generalize to the whole of the Division.

The voyage went relatively smoothly. Dan played chess with a Maori called Wattie McKay, talked dialectics with a Catholic padre Forsman, whom he already knew and liked, and attempted to steer clear of his old Otago University enemy Hawksworth, who had turned up on board as one of the medical officers. Dan had sworn never to speak to him again, and still harboured hopes of revenge. It was typical of Dan that he should have linked up with 2nd Lt. W. H. (Wattie) McKay and Father Edward (Ted) Forsman. McKay was a journalist in civilian life, and had a swift natural intelligence. In Crete he was appointed 28 (Maori) Battalion interpreter because he had learned Greek so rapidly. He was mortally wounded at Pirgos on 22 May rushing an enemy spandau post, and died a prisoner of war on 30 August.[22] Later in life, when Dan talked or wrote about the Div. with affectionate honour he was thinking about men like Wattie, the brief friendships that flowered and died, and the lesson of war: 'how sudden death is, how unjust in its election, how heedless of whether or not the lives it cuts off have been fulfilled.'[23] Ted Forsman was of mixed Irish and Swedish stock, a product of Auckland Grammar School, the Mosgiel seminary, and the Propaganda College in Rome. He was a great lover of opera and literature, wrote poetry, and was a resourceful debater. Dan adjudicated him winner of a mess debate on the topic 'Is man responsible for his actions?' during the Battalion's stay at Mytchett, and he and Dan became lifelong friends.[24]

Throughout the voyage he tried to work at his own writing and at his languages, though he was eventually to be hampered in Greek by the theft of his grammar. There was a widespread rumour that they were *en route* to Greece, on which the Italians had declared war in early November, and many of the men were trying to acquire suitable phrases for the usual social purposes. He did, however, make a good start on Italian because Forsman spoke it fluently, and agreed to practise conversation with him. Some contemporaries recalled that Dan came on board without speaking the language, and went ashore at Port Tewfik speaking it fluently (and there is enough truth in this story to bear repeating). He also made a start on a second novel which, though still without a title, was set amid the bohemian life of Montparnasse in the days before the war. Once again he gave a few lectures, participated in debates, did his periods as duty officer, wrote and helped to produce a shipboard magazine, and schemed among the senior officers, by being willing as well as principled and intellectual, to secure a more interesting job than that of platoon commander.

Dan liked to travel by sea. He was never seasick, and the pace of life, the opportunity to drink and talk in a handy bar, to smoke cheaply, to read, to reflect, and to write, was always welcome to him. The padre said he could see himself in Dan as he had once been 'before . . . abandon[ing] materialism'. Dan commented: 'he forgets that I have no ardour, am mystic without faith, interested in theories for the persons and style of their expounders, fundamentally unreligious, and a proteus of opinion.'[25] Much of the journey was spent in this sort of profitable reflection in his diary, and the only interruption to the tranquillity it implies was the port call in Cape Town from 8 to 12 February. Here the men were put through a route march every morning, but allowed shore leave thereafter. Dan spent his evenings in this *ville lumière* at the Ritz bar, finding local company, eating and drinking. He thought Cape Town

the most interesting place I have seen for a long time: the atmosphere is full of tension and stress. There is antipathy everywhere. Germans hate British, British hate Germans and dislike Dutch, Dutch hate English and all hate the natives with the fervour of potential fear. And the jews enjoy a common disfavour. The place is full of dynamite . . .

He was happy to escape, though some were less fortunate. On the last evening there was 'the second battle of Cape Town' so that when the ship left port the Battalion was twenty men short, and the colonel was 'not unnaturally furious'.[26]

The *Athlone Castle* docked at Port Tewfik on 3 March, and after a tedious train journey the next day, 5 Brigade went into camp at Helwan, a place of 'yellows and clay colours set against the desert hills'.[27] For the next three weeks they were engaged on route marches, kit inspections, and occasional forays into the 'tenacity and parable'[28] of Egyptian life. On a couple of visits to Cairo Dan contacted Munir Sabry, the Egyptian he had known in Balliol, went with him to the Egyptian Officers' Club, and to dinner at his home. But the Battalion knew that it was moving again, and everyone's thoughts were elsewhere: in the past with families left behind; or in a future which promised, though there was no official confirmation, action in the Balkans. On 17 March the Battalion moved by train to Alexandria, where it went into camp for another week, the route marches unabating. On the train Dan bumped into the brother of an old Dunedin flame who told him that she was married. His sudden appearance brought her back 'like a ghost, meagrely'.[29]

The incident emphasized a truth which was about to be endorsed in war. Without making the geographical journey, Dan had none the less returned to his homeland when he joined the Div., and it thrust him back into the world from which he had fled. He had become conscious of this by the time they sailed for Egypt, writing in his diary: 'In parts this battalion is a travelling Invercargill, a peregrinating small town . . . impregnable in the complacencies of its provinciality.'[30] With it came reminders of his childhood and youth, his days at Otago University: figures and faces, the friends of relations, people who were neighbours of acquaintances, the sudden appearance of men not thought of for years prompting reminders of incident and circumstance thought forgotten. This had two effects on Dan. One was stimulating, enabling him to write about the past with a freshness that might otherwise have faded. The other was more complex. It brought home to him the density of experience: the sense of the past not as a serial or sequence, but as an accretion of experience, layer upon layer, whose effect is to illuminate the present. For Dan, the perception was particularly fecund. Just as he believed that conversation was an end in itself, so his sense of the construction of experience, lying parallel to his view of conversation, enlarged and enriched it. Conversation, and the contribution brought to it by experience and the study of history, was a sort of performance art, a form of aesthetic creativity that lived in and for itself. Once spent or dissipated it could not be retrieved, though its influence lived on in the enrichment that it brought to recollected experience in others. In Dan's life, the Div. was at the heart of this because it bridged his worlds, linking his New Zealand past to the rest of his life.

They sailed from Alexandria eventually on 26 March, travelling on a Greek tub, the MV *Cameronia*, rusting and dirty, with too little room for the men, the mattresses filthy, and the boat lying so low in the water that the rough sea slopped in through open portholes. Despite the conditions Dan was able to write: long entries in his diary, and a short story about 'The Milk Round' he had had as a child, written in much the same style as 'Toby', but expanding the context, and introducing a family of boys he called the Connollys. He was able to write under the most difficult circumstances. Three days later they docked and disembarked at Piraeus, Dan's mind preoccupied as they sailed up the island-littered approaches with thoughts of the sea routes taken by 'the old Athenian fleets on blockade'[31] as also with the threats that lay ahead, threats of danger and of death.[32]

Eventually they got into Hymettus Camp in the early hours of the morning, fed up with Movement Control, and with nowhere to sleep. Dan immediately wangled a day's leave in Athens, but it was a Sunday, the city was dead, and he fell into depression. No time for self-pity, however. The next day, after packing up again, he was on the train north to Katarene via Larisa, and rejoined the battalion lines on Mount Olympus on Wednesday, 2 April. Dan's platoon was to hold one end of the line on a ridge running parallel to the main Olympus Range, and on a section that included the small village of Lokova. Their role was 'the breaking up [of] any attack before it reached the main positions of 14 and 15 Platoons'.[33] These positions had not been easy to reach. The engineers had built new tracks into the mountains, but rain and mud made them slippery, and the mountainous terrain added to the difficulties of movement. Against these detractions, for a scholar of the classics actually to be camped below the abode of the gods seemed a particular privilege. And it was spring, the woodlands were a mass of flowers, little green lizards darted among the rocks, and the '[t]inkling of cow-bells gave the whole place [the] air of Sabbath calm'.[34] Dan felt fit, was becoming proud of his men and their potential fighting qualities, and in the two weeks that he spent in this exposed forward position, while still reading, and writing in his diary, also began to learn some of the most difficult aspects of the soldier's art.

Physical discomfort was one thing. The spring was hesitant, and after a few days there was a heavy fall of snow.[35] It was Easter, 11 and 12 April, and there were blizzard conditions overnight, followed by sleet and cold rain. The mountains were shrouded in mist, the men wet; hot food and sound sleep were impossible. The exposure was not just physical, but mental. The whole of Lustre Force, which included the Div., under the command of General Sir Henry Maitland Wilson, occupied advanced positions on the eastern seaboard of the Greek peninsula just south of Salonika. In the west, the Greek forces, after first stubbornly defeating the Italian attempts at invasion, were now in disarray. To the north, the Germans were advancing rapidly across the plain of Salonika. In purely military terms, the Allied military presence in northern Greece disobeyed every principle of military strategy. It expected to fight on terrain it had not chosen, according to a hastily assembled plan, with forces that had not been trained for it, and under command structures that had not been tested. It had been assembled to defend the Aliakmon Line south of Salonika, which presumed German attack from Bulgaria and Romania, but which was open to outflanking manœuvres from Yugoslavia via the Monastir Gap and Kozani.

Within a few days of the arrival of the Division, attacks from both directions had been launched, and it was clear to senior officers that any German success in the assault from Yugoslavia must result in either withdrawal or catastrophic defeat. To add to this sense of insecurity and forward exposure, Rommel launched an attack in North Africa on 31 March, and within a fortnight had taken Benghazi and surrounded Tobruk. Forces that might have been in reserve for the defence of Cairo, Egypt, and the Suez Canal were strangely placed in northern Greece.[36]

Dan's own circumstances were a microcosm of this strategic muddle. He thought his own men dangerously exposed, their line too thin. He was worried about the possibility of infiltration by German infantry, and considered that his platoon risked being outflanked, a view which he persistently drew to the attention of his superiors. One section in particular, under Corporal Quinn, was the source of profound anxiety, as they were overlooked by an undefended spur. Nevertheless his men organized themselves as best they could, digging in in the rocky terrain, laying wire, clearing fields of fire in the undergrowth. Dan called for a volunteer to patrol the exposed spur 'to create the illusion of its being defended, and selected Corporal Campbell for this difficult and dangerous task'.[37] On 11 April, as accounts of the advancing Germans spread, many of the villagers of Lokova departed, and Dan moved his platoon HQ into an abandoned house. The place reminded him of Ireland. Despite being under cover neither he nor any of his men could get dry. The rain continued. He went on his rounds, the men lived in fox-holes and slit trenches, and stood to at 5.30 every morning. The tension mounted. 'We have probably the most dangerous position in the battalion. However even a peaceful man like myself can't be kept waiting 18 months for an enemy without achieving a certain anxiety to meet him.'[38]

They did not have long to wait. The next night, Tuesday, 15 April, Dan spent in the platoon battle HQ, a hole in a cliff-side, but machine-gun and artillery noise made sleep impossible. Early in the morning German troops from 2 Infantry Regiment began infiltrating, as he had feared, on the spur overlooking 3 Section. Dan called for assistance, and two patrols from HQ Company cleared the spur. The men settled in to await a bigger and more determined assault, which would not be long in coming because Dan could see a large party of Germans, estimated at a company strong, massing in the scrub near a cemetery some five hundred yards away. When he reported this, 5 Field Regiment shelled the area to good effect. In the afternoon the spur was once again infiltrated, and 3 Section cleared it themselves. Shortly after this 13 Platoon received orders from Company HQ to withdraw at 8.30 in the evening. Five minutes before they were due to leave, Private Inglis, one of Corporal Quinn's section, arrived to say that they had been overrun.

It was too late to commit the platoon to action which might have made disengagement impossible. Davin therefore decided to get the rest of the platoon out as quickly as possible.

'I and the sergeant drove and scolded the men until they were through 15 Platoon perimeter. Once they were through I handed them over to Sergeant Dutton and went back (followed against orders by Congo Smith, a fine, bold ruffian) to see if I could find any of the others. We hadn't gone far when we heard cries. Eventually we found Todd—almost exhausted, but still with his Bren. With him were three or four others, but missing were Quinn, Campbell, Martin, Fisher and Weir.'[39]

Martin was killed in action; Quinn died of his wounds the next day, 17 April; Campbell, Fisher, and Weir were all taken prisoner. Dan believed that their loss had been avoidable, and the bitterness he felt towards his superiors about this he also directed at himself.

There was no time for recrimination, however. He and the men he had found rejoined the rest of the platoon and in pitch darkness they climbed a steep mountain track to the pass which, belying the term, was almost impassable. When they had reached the top, the route out was a further seven miles. Mud was two feet deep in places, all the men soaked through and exhausted. It took them over eight hours, from 9.00 at night till 5.30 in the morning, and on arrival at their staging area in the small town of Kokkinoplos Dan found that another of his men, Dalton, had been lost en route. The men had to abandon much of their personal equipment, and Dan lost his valise, sleeping bag, and overcoat, as well as the sole of one boot. He had also begun to develop balanitis, but at the time it seemed to him less serious than the fact that, among the possessions he had had to abandon, was the manuscript of the first part of his novel about bohemian life in Paris.[40] Once lost, the projected book became, like those happy Parisian days and nights of the pre-war years, a part of his past that was never to be re-created.

The exhausted men tried to dry out in Kokkinoplos, but with little success. In the afternoon they formed the rearguard that fought a short engagement with advance parties of the approaching Germans. Then they withdrew on foot to the village of Pithion where the Battalion regrouped, had a hot meal, and was transported south in vehicles of 4 RMT to Larisa, then to Pharsala, and via Dhomokos and Lamia, to a bivouac area near the Pass of Thermopylae. The weather was grey and drizzling with rain, but low cloud shielded the convoy from attacks by the *Luftwaffe*, which now had control of the skies. All the way the roads teemed with civilian refugees, and the shattered remnants of the Central Macedonian Army, Greek divisions in full and undisciplined retreat. Every town and village through which the New Zealand trucks passed had been bombed, the streets littered with dead people and animals, wrecked and burning vehicles.[41] At the bivouac at Thermopylae Dan slept under his raincoat. It was terribly cold, but the men slept an exhausted sleep.

A fighting withdrawal is a defeat under conditions of orderly resistance. Its essence is dogged persistence made possible by the refusal to submit. The purpose is to deny the aggressor a victory, while declining to commit forces to a full-scale battle that would risk annihilation. In a fighting withdrawal, each unit or element of the army disengages, its formation and discipline maintained, and withdraws through the lines of another, already prepared to resist in its place. As it does so, sappers sabotage and destroy the route behind it. Weapons are brought out, though much in the way of supplies is usually lost. Service units operate round the clock to keep the men fed, prepare bivouac sites for rest, tend and evacuate the wounded, and stock temporary dumps along the line of withdrawal.

A fighting withdrawal is always complex. It requires initiative and flexibility in situations that may verge on the chaotic: military calm amid surrounding civilian panic; a high degree of co-operation among units; and innovation to overcome obstacles along the way. At the end of the exercise, if it is being fought in a foreign country, there has to be a planned evacuation. For the ordinary soldier caught in one of these exercises, the difficulties are immense. He can see none of the overall picture, and will have been told only a small part of the plan. Such part as he is told may be changed almost immediately to take account of some other development. So it was at Thermopylae for the four days that Dan was there from 18 to 22 April.[42]

On the evening of Saturday, 19 April C Company was trucked forward to within about a mile of the bridge towards Lamia. At first they thought it was to do immediate battle, but on arrival they were instead ordered to dig in and be wired before dawn. This was just about impossible to do as no orders were given about boundaries, officers had not been able to reconnoitre, and some platoons found themselves ordered to dig in in the swamp. 'We delayed till morning.'[43] At first light on Sunday the men dug in quickly, though there was a shortage of tools. As soon as this was done they were ordered to move to new positions on the mountain side, and to dig in once more. Departure was delayed, and the climb arduous, but eventually 13 Platoon took up positions on a little plateau on top of a spur, and spent the next day, Monday, 21 April, digging in once again.

The little plateau was wonderfully beautiful: wild mountain flowers grew everywhere among little dwarf oaks and the sage: purples and whites and delicate reds. Behind these were fields of wheat in irregular patterns leading up to the bold bluffs. And behind these was the splendid mountain barrier. Our position commanded a view of the great river flat several miles across by the straight white road which pointed to the heart of Lamia at the foot of its own great range. On the right the sea's arm long as the law, on the left the flat winding into the hills. The river languished in and out like Meander itself. But there was much to do and nothing to do it with.[44]

He spent the morning getting his men organized and fed, then attended a Battalion conference. They were to change position again.[45] This they accomplished in the evening, and were awoken the next morning by an artillery duel.

Dan's Greek war was over, however. The balanitis had turned suppurative, so that he could barely walk, and the pain and discomfort was disabling. A medical officer ordered his evacuation, and with premonitions of disaster for the Battalion (misplaced in the event: they were all evacuated to Crete from Porto Rafti on the night of 24–5 April), and in sorrow for his men and shame for himself, he bade farewell to his platoon and was driven to an ADS. Here he met Ralph Park, the poet of *Critic* days, now in the 2NZEF medical services. The next day, on a road packed with fleeing civilians and many desperately fearful soldiers, repeatedly strafed and bombed by planes of the *Luftwaffe*, he was driven by ambulance to Levadia and from there to Athens. In Levadia, in an 'amusing scene', he got a glimpse of Freyberg directing the traffic, 'raging'.[46] In Athens he was hospitalized, and had a bath followed by a long day of rest in a clean bed that he called 'ineffable'.[47] The following day he was driven to an olive grove near Megara where about a thousand wounded were gathered awaiting evacuation. Among them he found Nancarrow, a fellow officer from Mytchett, whom he had not seen since leaving England. Nancarrow had a leg wound from a bomb. They idled away that day and the next, Anzac Day, with talk, a few books from the hospital, and food from an abandoned truck, until at 1.30 in the morning of Saturday, 26 April they were taken off aboard the *Thurland Castle*. The vessel was repeatedly but inexpertly bombed, and shortly before midnight, in Suda Bay, the men disembarked into a 'Black Hole of a tender'[48] and were put ashore on the island of Crete.

8

FROM CRETE TO TUNIS

I think it is at the age of about thirty that one begins to envy the young and to wish one had a dozen lives with which to experience all that is. But in that very wish there is something wistful. One would perhaps not have it if it were not for the growth of one's own death wish, the decline in power.

(DMDP: Diary, 9 Jan. 1944)

in another sense, the whole world is the Acceptance World as one approaches thirty; at least some illusions discarded. The mere fact of still existing as a human being proved that.

(Anthony Powell, *The Acceptance World*, 178)

The army was in evacuation chaos in Crete when Dan arrived on the morning of 27 April 1941, but after hours of waiting and queueing and being moved apparently aimlessly, he eventually found blissful sleep in the wrong bed of the wrong ward of a hospital. On waking up he bullied his discharge from treatment, found out where 23 Battalion had been sent, and rejoined his Company. He was sick with a stomach ailment, but the Cretan spring was lovely, and the Battalion bivouacked in a cool olive grove with views of the Mediterranean. But for the absence of books, life was kind again.

Crete lies like a lizard 'on the confines of the three parts of the world, Africa, Asia and Europe'.[1] Once a temperate island of forests and rich valley soil—'fair and fertile', Homer called it—its cypress forests were logged by successive maritime invaders, the greatest depredations being committed by the Venetians. The destruction of its natural resources reduced the rainfall, and turned it into a dry and stony place of windswept uplands and high mountain ranges, sharp and dryly eroding. At the western end of the island the White Mountains, the Lefka Ori, are both landmark and barrier, but there are three other formidable mountain ranges, and ravines and steep valleys break up the landscape north to south. Crete has nurtured civilization probably for longer than anywhere else in Europe, its evidence scattered across the island in such places as Knossos, Mallia, Phaistos, and Zakros. It is the home of the legends of the birth of Zeus, of Minos, Rhadamanthys, Pasiphae and the Minotaur, of Daedalus and Icarus, Theseus and Ariadne. Its people are the inheritors of five thousand years of history, a history captured in palace murals, Byzantine churches and Venetian forts, as well as etched into the landscape of their vineyards and stony fields. They are an island people, maritime by instinct, proud, valiant, dogged; open-hearted and generous to friends; secretive, resolute, unforgiving to enemies. New Zealanders, who until this time knew nothing of Crete or its people, were welcomed as saviours by the Cretans, and in their straightforward way they responded as friends.

The Div. came ashore under aerial bombardment in Suda Bay, the deep-water port on the northern shore, and took up positions to the west. The south coast of Crete is impracticable for large-scale military manœuvres, and the principal towns lie along the northern coastline. The main town to the west of Suda Bay is Canea, a fishing port. Approximately fifteen miles further west, beyond the village of Pirgos, is Maleme, site of the only airstrip then capable of servicing military operations.

The four battalions of 5 Brigade, under Brigadier Hargest, had been allotted the task of defending the Maleme sector. Lt.-Gen. Freyberg was appointed GOC Creforce on 30 April, and three days later, after a general adjustment of positions, 23 Battalion moved to occupy an area round the village of Dhaskaliana, south-east of Maleme airfield, and a few miles east of the small town of Pirgos. The coastal road from Canea west to Platanias, Pirgos, and Maleme lay just to the north of them. Here Dan's platoon HQ was in another olive grove, and his bed scooped out in a field of barley. It was spring, and the weather warm and balmy. There was a deep creek where the men could wash and swim, and a gully running through the position that afforded excellent cover. 'The birds sing more sweetly than I have ever heard birds sing',[2] and in the creek the frogs were mating. He managed to scrounge a pair of Australian boots to replace the ones wrecked on Olympus Pass, but they were a little too small to be comfortable, and didn't match. His men nicknamed them 'black and tan'.

Like his men, Dan was not really sure why he was in Crete. Initially it appeared to be a temporary halt in a general evacuation from the Greek mainland back to Egypt. Then it was presented as a purely interim task, to defend the island from a possible airborne attack. Most of the men appear not to have really believed in this role, or expected it to last for long. Airborne assault was a concept never before tried, and anyway it was obvious to all that the Div. needed rest and new equipment. Dan thought that they would stay in Crete for a week or two, and then return to Egypt to reorganize before being sent to Libya or Iraq.[3] Such rumours, gossip, and reflection did little to disturb the immediate present.

We overlook . . . a beautiful valley, ineffably green and threaded by a snow river of the clearest and coldest water. Orange groves and lemon line its banks and their hard shiny green contrasts with the weary grey of the olives which look somehow as if the long passage of their centuries had coated them with fine dust. On the other side hills again, curious conical hills, reminiscent of Japanese prints . . . Beyond, mountains and the snow. The vines too look fresh and the young grapes are forming but I do not think we shall see their vintage . . . [T]he weather is as lovely as the land. When I read Greek again I shall read it with fresh pleasure from having seen Greece.[4]

He managed to cadge a lift into Canea one day and found a few odd books in French and Greek. But mainly the first two weeks of May went past in cultivating the military virtues of readiness and fitness: stand-to from 5.30 to 6.15 every morning, water and ration parties after breakfast, swimming in the sea in the afternoon, another battle-ready stand-to in the evening.

On 13 May, with a change in the command of the Battalion,[5] Dan was appointed Battalion Intelligence Officer, and moved from his platoon to Battalion HQ. He was greatly relieved at this. It got him away from 'the grinding boredom of the training syllabus'[6] and offered the possibility of learning to speak modern Greek fluently through contact with an interpreter. A Battalion Intelligence Officer's principal task was to gather intelligence about the enemy and the terrain for his commanding officer. This meant that Dan was in a position to familiarize himself with the wider disposition of troops and the local Cretan military scene. When the German invasion took place, his duties would expand to include the interrogation of prisoners of war, reporting from the field on enemy units and their locations, and supplying information about enemy weapons and ordinance, morale and fighting spirit. An interesting and useful job. For the first few days he was employed mainly on route reconnoitring: walking out in various directions through the beautiful spring country-side, to be ready with informed advice should an engagement become mobile. On the evening of the day he was appointed to this new job, Maleme was bombed for the first time.

For the whole of the following week air raids were frequent, though generally they occurred at the same times each day, and were of a regular duration. The *Luftwaffe* had uncontested control of the skies and could work to routine.[7] Suda Bay was bombed heavily every day, and was soon 'full of sunk vessels'.[8] On 15 May Maleme, where 22 Battalion was dug in, was subjected to a terrible pounding. Three days later, with intelligence forecasting an imminent invasion, 5 Brigade was issued Operational Instruction No. 4 which required it to maintain a defensive line running east–west from Platanias to the Tavronitis River (a mile or so west of Maleme airfield) with special regard to the defence of Maleme aerodrome; to counter-attack and destroy immediately any air- or seaborne attack; to maintain 'spirited defence'.

The attack came on the morning of Tuesday, 20 May, announcing itself by the unusually long aerial bombardment that interrupted breakfast. Dan wrote in his diary: 'A. P. [anti-personnel] bombs fell closer than usual, raid heavier. Also seemed to be longer. Shortly lookout from hill reported gliders over the drome. Very irritated at this departure from routine. Thought Jerry had more respect for schedule: and now he falsifies my prophesies and puts the intelligence report more or less in the right. Clearly the attack had come.'[9] The next hour seemed to compress a lifetime. After the bombing and strafing suddenly the air was thick with troop carriers and then the white mushrooms of parachutes. Men ran in all directions. Excitement and terror mixed with elation and confusion. 'Terrific uproar of small arms fire from our men, like the crackle of a great bush fire. My men [intelligence section] firing with great gusto.'[10]

This attack from the air was carried out by 3 Battalion, Assault Regiment, of the German 11 Air Corps. They were supposed to come down astride the length of the Platanias–Maleme Road, and, after assembly, attack Maleme aerodrome from the east. Instead they fell at right angles to their drop area, and more or less exactly on top of 23 Battalion. It was a catastrophe for them. '[T]here they were . . . unreal but very real, bouncing up and down on the parachutes, rather pretty but very terrible. There was nothing to do except shoot . . . I shot. They were like dolls, marionettes; as the bullets hit them they doubled up, knees came towards chins convulsively and down again. They were seconds only in the air.'[11] Most of the German Battalion's 9, 10, 11, and 12 Companies were cut to shreds. Two-thirds of the Battalion were killed, perhaps as many as 200 of them outright in these first minutes. The dead included every single officer. As a fighting unit they made no further contribution to the battle of Crete.

Dan got hold of the HQ bren carrier and did a swift tour of the Battalion's positions. There were dead men everywhere, all German, slung in the trees, twisted in gullies. An occasional sniper's bullet, badly aimed, indicated that a few of the parachutists had come down intact, but patrols were already out from each New Zealand company hunting them down. He reported back to HQ that all was well, and set off with a signaller, Sergeant Bertwhistle, for the Battalion lookout. To the side of a gully just in front of Battalion HQ, he spotted a parachute container and went to investigate, hoping he might find a pair of sun glasses. The first things he found inside were grenades, which he passed back to Bertwhistle. He had just turned his attention to the rest of the container, squatting on his haunches, when there was a burst of fire 'spreading out like a ripple in my fingers and left thigh below the groin'.[12] Dan had been hit by two bullets. One passed between the second and ring fingers of his left hand, scarring both but breaking neither. The other penetrated his left thigh and passed through into the buttock, where it broke up, the casing splintering into various fragments, the core coming to rest between the base of his spine and the prostate gland. No major artery was severed, and no bone broken, though he bled heavily from both wounds, and was soon in great pain.

Before I knew what I was doing I had leapt in the air and fallen flat on my face. From where I lay I could see the blood pouring from my fingers. Bullets were still zipping by but I couldn't see where they were coming from. I was in an open hillside olive grove towards the bottom. On my right a deep gully ran diagonally away. Behind me was the road. The gully was my only chance. Ten yards away. I called out to Bertwhistle I was hit and to fetch stretcher-bearers from the RAP about fifty yards away. Then I began to work my way along with my right elbow and leg. I could see some riflemen from the edge of the gully trying to spot the sniper and cover my return. Then I saw Bertwhistle climbing out of the gully. I called, Get back you silly young bugger, get under cover. I felt a furious rage against him and against the sniper. But in spite of bloodcurdling abjurations from me B. ran to me and began to help me along. Another burst from the sniper and we crouched flat. Reply from our riflemen. I tell B. to go back again. He refuses. Slowly we push to the right rear where there is a dip of about six inches in the ground. We make it. More bullets and we rest. Then I see the stretcherbearers come out of the gully. I roar with rage and my self-consciousness is so overlaid with action excitement that I barely notice this is the correct thing to say anyhow. They ignore me, walk out with their stretcher, put me on it and the two stretcherbearers and Bertwhistle carry me off not down the gully for fear of hurting me but in the open back to the road in full view and round over the bridge. By this time the sniper is fully engaged. My old platoon goes over and hunts him down. They come back later with his machine gun. The sniper stays behind.

As I am carried along I think any moment now we're for it. But I'm not very frightened, only very excited and very angry at being hit just when I was rather enjoying myself. Also I felt rather a fool. And you know how I hate that. At the same time reason which abides even in the intoxication of battle was saying These are lucky wounds. If only you can get evacuated now you are a lucky man.[13]

Dan was taken to the RAP, his wounds dressed, and as the excitement and adrenalin high receded given morphia for the pain, which now became intense. He was put in a dugout in the side of a gully where he stayed for the rest of the day with four other 23 Battalion wounded as well as a number of Germans, whom he was able to interrogate.[14] Early the following morning, under the cover of dark, he was moved from Dhaskaliana to Platanias, where 5 Field Ambulance was set up in a school. Here, amid many far worse cases than his own, his wounds were dressed, and he was able to chat for a while to Ralph Park. Here too there was a scene of high comedy when Hawksworth appeared. Dan, captive to his old enemy's attentions at last, found himself being shaken warmly by the uninjured hand, aware of 'the dramatic appropriateness of the situation but . . . too weak to resist its cogent sentimentality'.[15] He was kept here for forty-eight hours until early in the morning of Friday, 23 May while the fighting intensified and came closer. 22 Battalion had withdrawn from Maleme airfield, and the Germans were now able to pour in fresh troops and supplies. The Maori Battalion, fighting to hold a line at Pirgos, suffered terrible losses amid heroic deeds, the news of both filtering back with the wounded. It was impossible to move in daylight as the *Luftwaffe* kept up continuous strafing, on occasions so close to the dressing station that its occupants, vulnerable and immobile, expected catastrophe. An exploding artillery ammunition dump a few hundred yards away created an air of helpless expectancy.

At 2.00 in the morning on Friday, 23 May he was moved to Canea where the hospital was overflowing, so like others of the wounded he was put in the cathedral, where in the evening 'Greek girls came round gravely and gave us a flower each. I was lucky and got a rose and a carnation. I have always loved carnations, the first flower I can remember, growing in our garden in Gore.[16]

The bombing came closer, and the windows of the cathedral were blown in, the plaster in the great domed ceiling above them cracking. Dan read *L'Homme qui rit* by Victor Hugo, which he had found somewhere. The numbers of wounded swelled grotesquely: Shell-shock victims, their wits gone; an old Greek man, horribly smashed up, who died on a blanket on the floor beside him. After dark the walking wounded, who, *in extremis*, now included Dan, were loaded on to trucks and driven to Suda Bay through 'the havocked streets, the red fires burning across the bay'.[17] They boarded the destroyer *Abdiel*, the same vessel that had just delivered Evelyn Waugh and his party of commandos, and put to sea where for much of the next day they were bombed en route for Alexandria and the relative safety of Egypt.

I sat long awake smoking and thinking of Winnie and Oxford and good times gone and bad times just endured. Always too one asked oneself how are the others? I am usually a callous man but my heart went out to them. And the faces of the wounded I had seen came back and I thought what a blessing pity was because I had pitied so many lately that often I had forgotten myself. The largeness of calamity exacted a certain bigness of oneself, and it was a better me those last few days than I had often known.[18]

The *Abdiel* docked at Alexandria at 9.00 p.m. on Sunday, 25 May, and Dan was transferred to the military hospital at Helwan where he was operated on on 4 June. The casing fragments were removed, but the bullet was judged too close to major organs for extraction. He carried it for the rest of his days. The powerlessness he experienced in his legs after surgery filled him with remorse for the rabbits that he had shot in his youth. He vowed never to kill again, and he never did.

In hospital he had visits from Munir Sabry, who brought him books; various officers of 23 Battalion, including its commander Leckie, all wounded, and with stories to tell of the ten days of the battle for Crete; and from Colonel Quilliam in Army Intelligence, who asked him to write a report about the parachute assault as he remembered it.[19] He was stuck in the hospital until 20 June, for a few days in great pain from his operation. He had plenty to read because Munir kept him supplied, but he became miserable in reflecting on his career in the army. Given the time to think about it, ambition returned, and with it, fears that promotion might have little connection with either ability or talent. He sensed that professional soldiers of field rank, majors, colonels, brigadiers, did not like their intellectuals to be bohemians. Such men were generally conservatives, possibly reactionaries. Dan, like many others, was an anti-Fascist who had gone to war to fight against the politics of Hitler and Mussolini. If he was going to get on in a world run by officers whose intellectual powers were at best latent, a certain amount of dissembling was going to be required. Dan found this difficult to accept. He sensed, however, in his hospital bed in Helwan, that his future was compromised. Leckie did not seem to want him back as Battalion Intelligence Officer. Other alternatives slipped away as soon as mentioned. His promotion to full lieutenant was blocked for bureaucratic reasons. 'The mistake young officers make', he wrote in his diary, 'is to look for a job that suits their capacities. Their seniors never commit this error.'[20] Dan had no desire to return to being a platoon commander, and began to regret ever transferring to the Div.

Perhaps his pessimism was evidence of post-battle fatigue, post-operative depression, and further illness. He was discharged, and went to stay with Munir, but a day later was running a temperature of 103, and on being returned to hospital was diagnosed as suffering from hepatitis and acute infectious tonsilitis. For nearly three weeks he was very ill, at first running a high temperature, subsequently unable to eat. Worst deprivation of all, he was unable to read. When he surfaced from this at the end of the second week of July it was as a magnificently difficult patient, yellow all over, and with a deeply jaundiced view of the world to match. No aspect of the hospital, from doctors and nurses to orderlies, from food to clerical administration, was too obscure or unimportant for his critical condemnation. 'To be on a special diet is to be perched precariously between starvation and poisoning.'[21] He was 'much cast down with the reflection that the world will fall to NZers and people like them: the people who listen to commercial broadcasts, go three times to Gone With the Wind, argue about football matches and talk about motor-car gears.'[22]

Not all was hopeless, however. He had visits from Frank Guest and Eric McCormick, who had turned up in lowly military capacities, and happily knew nothing about Scarlet O'Hara, football, or differentials. Hepatitis gave him a lifelong joke he enjoyed telling at his own expense. 'Is life worth living?' 'It depends on the liver.' And Colonel Quilliam came back to tell him that he wanted Dan to join the Intelligence staff of Army HQ in Cairo. His report on the airborne assault in Crete had attracted attention, and the Div., for the moment at least, was prepared to let him go. Eventually he was released from hospital on 31 July and after sixteen days convalescence at Moascar in Ismailia, went up to Cairo, booked into the Hotel National, and began work at GHQ on 20 August. He was to hold this job for a little over 13 months, until the end of September 1942.

At the beginning, Dan was still lame and using a stick. He had lost weight, looked sallow, and was unwell. The least scratch or cut festered in the Egyptian climate. He was still in pain, and for the first month or so worked only in the mornings, while trying to retrieve his strength. But idleness and boredom bred depression, and he was happier working longer hours. His specific area of work at the beginning was the German battle order in the Balkans, so that he rapidly became an expert on the corps and divisional structure of the *Wehrmacht* from Trieste to the Crimea. There was an elaborate army intelligence network throughout the Middle East which filtered information from Romania and Bulgaria, and as Dan's year with Army Intelligence HQ went by, lines of communication from Cairo were established with partisans in Crete and mainland Greece that also supplied information. Great quantities of material came in from London. There was no shortage of data, and the days often seemed too short for the quantity of analysis that was required. Partly this was due to working hours. The heat of summer made the afternoons unbearable, so that office hours were morning and evenings, with the afternoons for siesta. Partly it was due to the other Intelligence staff, who were interesting men. Dan made friends with Bill Williams,[23] a young history don from Merton, Paul Rollo, another historian and contemporary from Balliol,[24] Joe Japolsky, known as Joe Jap, another Oxford contemporary whom he had known by sight, and John Willett, a modern languages graduate from Oxford, well read, intelligent, amusing, and critical, who became a particular friend.

After a couple of months Enoch Powell arrived, giving substance to the myth. For a while in 1942 he and Dan shared an office, though this was not a success. Powell turned out to be rather as Dan had imagined from his reputation: a rigid autodidact in whom logic and insensitivity were combined. He was famous, no matter how great the heat, for wearing full service dress with long trousers, collar and tie, tunic and Sam Browne, supposedly on the grounds that it 'kept up his morale'.[25] The reality seemed to Dan to be more that it enabled him to wear regimental insignia, thus preserving a distance between his own status and those who were merely Army, or, worse still, colonial. The other effect of this habit of dress was exacerbated by a reluctance for some health reason ever to take a bath. Dan summed him up in his diary after one particularly infuriating incident in the office, detecting the young Powell's ambition to be a philosopher-king: 'Erudite and incapable of humanity . . . A military martinet . . . A raging egotist with a bookish twist, whose jokes provoke painful silence among the intellectual and charitable tolerance from those with enough Greek to recognise a ponderous allusion . . . [E]xceptionally able, but . . . inhuman.'[26]

The interest in these encounters at the office was balanced by the greater world of Cairo. From 1940 to 1943 Cairo became, thanks to Hitler's war in Europe and Asia Minor, the cosmopolitan capital of the old world, everything that Paris and Berlin had been between the wars, but with the additional distinctive flavour of the Levant. Cairo, and to some degree Alexandria, had always been at the crossroads between the distinctive cultures of Europe, the Middle East, North Africa, and Asia, but now, for a brief few years, and under the additional pressures of wartime conditions, travellers did not move on. Many of them were refugees from the Balkans: Greeks, Romanians, Albanians, Serbs. There were Armenians and Palestinians, French North Africans, Russians via Paris and Algiers. Many were intellectuals, or at least competent to play at appearing intellectual. A polyglot but transient society flourished in the cafés and restaurants, bohemia in exile, flavoured with the excitement and intrigue of war.

Dan needed no invitation to become involved in bohemian life, but his passage from depressed and misanthropic isolation to integration in this new world was enormously aided by Geoff Cox. He and Dan ran into each other in the lobby of the Hotel National in late August. The hotel was a dreadful *pissoir* of a place which in the fortuitous circumstances of war was making a killing by overcharging. They agreed to rent a flat, and within a week had moved into a three-bedroomed apartment with a balcony on the seventh floor of a building in the Garden City, more or less next door to Army HQ, and close to the British Embassy. This was Dan's home for the next ten months, but Cox, as a Divisional Intelligence Officer for 2NZEF, stayed only briefly, and was replaced by a shifting population of other tenants.[27]

Geoff Cox also brought with him to life in Cairo the talents of the good foreign correspondent. He was experienced at finding his way about strange cities, and getting to know the people of interest. He introduced Dan to journalists like Keith Scott-Watson, Alan Moorehead, and Richard Hughes, and it was Geoff who brought Dan together with another young New Zealand subaltern, Paddy Costello.

Costello had already aquired such a reputation in the Div. that, though Dan was close to him on a couple of occasions, he resisted making contact. Perhaps, for the only time in his life, he was a little in awe of the intellectual reputation of another. Paddy was an Auckland Catholic of Irish extraction who, like Dan, came from a family of four boys and two girls. He studied classics at Auckland University College, and won an overseas postgraduate scholarship to Trinity College Cambridge in 1932, where he read the classical tripos and took a First. Here he made friends with John Cornford, the young poet whose life became legend after he was killed in Spain at the end of December 1936. Like Cornford he was a member of the Communist Party while he was at Cambridge, but he left it in August 1939 over the Nazi–Soviet Pact. He spent a year doing research in Athens, before being appointed to a lectureship in Classics at the University of Exeter in October 1936. He married, in September 1935, Bella Lerner, known as Bil, a young Englishwoman of Russian extraction from the East End of London. Paddy's Latin was as good as Dan's, his classical Greek rather better (he used to enjoy twitting Dan about the inadequacies of Oxford for Greek studies), and he spoke demotic Greek fluently. His talents were numerous, and at languages he had no peer. He spoke Greek, French, German, Italian, and Spanish without hint of being a foreigner. Indeed, in Spanish and Italian he was so skilled in dialect that he could pass for a local at the regional level. When Dan first met him in Cairo he had just started to learn Russian in his spare time from his mistress, a White Russian émigrée, and was already reading Tolstoy in the original. He rapidly became completely fluent. Later in life he taught himself Persian.

At the start Dan must have thought some of the similarities between them uncanny, but he knew from the beginning that there was a difference in ability. Everything that he thought of himself as doing well, from parsing a line of Greek verse to singing an Irish song, Paddy could do too, but better. They became friends instantly, and remained so for the rest of their lives, but it is probably true that Paddy meant more to Dan than Dan meant to Paddy. The reasons for this are complex, but chief among them was a fundamental disagreement about politics. Paddy, the brilliant logician, with a brush-stroke of romantic, Irish revolutionary fervour, was a Marxist of formidable intellectual powers, both analytical and rhetorical. Dan as we know, though radical and anti-Establishment, saw Marxist dogma as surrogate Catholicism,[28] and though interesting, possibly even correct in some parts of its analysis, nevertheless a prison for the intellect rather than a playground.

Disagreement about theory spilled over into practical life: the area known to Marxists as praxis. Though one of nature's aristocrats, Paddy was determined to be proletarian. He joined the New Zealand Army in London at the outbreak of war without revealing his background, and served initially as a private. Conscientious and effective, he was promoted lance-corporal in a signals unit of 21 Battalion, and served in this capacity through the Greek campaign, where his intimate knowledge of Greece and its language could hardly be kept a secret from his superiors. As a result of various mishaps he was left behind during the evacuation, but with a number of other men, mainly officers, he acquired a caique and sailed it, after a series of abortive landings on islands then also being occupied by the Germans, to Crete. Having brought himself to the attention of senior officers in this way Lance-Corporal Costello found it impossible to continue to hide in the trade union of the ranks. Before the battle of Crete began he was sent on by air to attend an OCTU at the military barracks in Cairo. This was where Dan found him, three months into his course, at the end of August.

Despite elevation to the officer class, Paddy had no intention of being an officer type. He regarded Geoff Cox, who though a keen anti-Fascist described himself in those days as a democratic socialist, as an exemplary bourgeois. He was the son of a bank manager from Invercargill, after all. The debates that Paddy had with him, and with Ted Forsman, Dan's Catholic padre friend, Marxist versus Catholic, for and against the existence of God or the necessity of revolution, were as famous for their intensity as for their dialectics. Dan loved this kind of thing. He was very good at getting other people to talk, discuss, disagree, and argue, and enjoyed sitting by and listening. When the conversation turned in his direction, friend or not, Paddy could be equally aggressive: Dan was a class traitor corrupted by brougeois literature, more interested in art than in the social and economic conditions that determine it.

Arguments of this type became staple in afternoon and late-night Cairo, just as they were to do later when Dan and Paddy briefly served together at Staff HQ. When drink was involved, the arguments grew heated. Paddy became aggressive under the influence of drink. At this time he believed Dan was wasting his time trying to be a writer, that it was a worthless bourgeois project of no importance to history, and irrelevant to progress. Dan, a wrestler and an Irishman after all, would give as good as he got. Paddy was a victim of his own intellect; he harboured romantic illusions about ordinary people that were merely disguised as science; in the names of freedom and equality he would imprison and discriminate. Eventually they would come to blows and bitter imprecations, though generally Paddy would pass out and have to be put to bed before matters reached this stage. The relationship between them was so intense that sometimes it had more the quality of affair than of friendship: similar but opposite, separate but inseparable.

There were interruptions to this long-running friendship. Paddy was posted to the Long Range Desert Group from the end of September 1941 to the early new year of 1942, when he was brought back to Cairo to work, like Dan, at Army GHQ. In May he was off again, posted back to the Div. as an Intelligence Officer on Freyberg's Staff.[29] During these early months of 1942 they saw a great deal of each other, and the strongest bonds were forged. For Dan the relationship was unique, and never supplanted. After Gordie Craig in pre-war Oxford, Paddy was probably the only other male friend in whom Dan confided. Similarly, it is doubtful that anyone understood Paddy better than Dan, who had the same intellectual grasp and curiosity. Unlike Paddy's other friends and relations, many of whom, like Henri Curiel, the Communist son of a French-Egyptian banker, were also Marxists, Dan saw in him and treasured the humanist and the raconteur, the singer and convivial companion who also saw the realm of the heart, its joys and deep discomforts.

And these matters were much on Dan's mind in Cairo. Like other soldiers, he longed for and missed his wife and child, and although by late September 1941, when he was fully established in his flat in Cairo, he had been gone from them for only nine months, with all that had happened in the interim their world seemed as distant as another life. Winnie had taken Anna to Scotland in early May to stay with Elizabeth and Ian Mason, themselves expecting a baby.[30] The Crete campaign, observed from a distant Scotland with only a poor supply of censored news, was an agonizing trial of the emotions. The New Zealand authorities successfully let Winnie know fairly soon after the event that Dan had been wounded, but with the subsequent collapse of communication during the retreat and evacuation, she spent ten days knowing nothing more: how badly (perhaps mortally?), where, whether taken prisoner or evacuated. It was not until Munir Sabry cabled her in early June with news of Dan's safe arrival at Helwan hospital that she learned anything more at all.

Winnie's powers as a correspondent were still ebbing, and did nothing to equal either her sympathy for Dan and his circumstances, or her love for him. But she knew now that the war was going to last a long time, and that Dan was gone from her and their child for as far forward as it was either possible or prudent to think. She became preoccupied with trying to find a useful life for herself in these new conditions, and eventually, in the autumn of 1941, found employment as a social worker at the University Settlement at Barton Hill in Bristol. The Settlement undertook family care work, infant welfare, the provision of clubs for young and old, and functioned as an extension of university social work training and education. Winnie was employed, amongst other things, to establish and maintain a hostel for mothers and their babies and small children—people who had been bombed out of their homes, widowed by the war, and so on. Her job involved fund-raising and finding staff and furniture, Citizens' Advice counselling and child care, indeed, just the sort of jack of all trades skills for which a Southland background had fitted her.[31] In due course the Settlement acquired a country house establishment a few miles south of Monmouth, where mothers and babies could go for holidays, and where Winnie herself sometimes filled in as resident warden. News of her working life in Bristol and South Wales eased some of Dan's anxieties, but her failure to write could also upset him deeply, just as the arrival of one of her occasional letters would cast him into fits of pleasure and happiness.

After Christmas 1941 and until the end of January 1942 Geoff Cox was in Cairo doing a job for Bill Williams at GHQ Intelligence. One weekend he took up an invitation to lunch at 19 Sharia Ibn Zanki, the home of Walter and Amy Smart at Zamalek, near Maadi, and took Dan with him. Smart, the Oriental Counsellor at the British Embassy, 'Smartie' to his friends, was a learned man, a scholar of Persian and Arabic, and a patron of the arts. Clever, amusing, and a good talker, he kept a salon in Cairo, and liked it to be a place where literary people came to talk.[32] His second wife, Amy, was the daughter of Dr Fares Nimr Pasha, the founder of the leading Arab newspaper *El Mokkatam*. She was a painter, interested in the arts and literature, and like her husband enjoyed entertaining, which she did well, without snobbery. This owed something to Amy's being Egyptian, and to the fact that Smartie, being divorced, expected to rise no further in the British diplomatic service. Dan became a popular and frequent visitor to their home. In their salon and around their dinner table he met people from all over the Middle East and Europe, from Romanian princesses to Palestinian doctors and Coptic lawyers. And writers were plentiful. Here he met Lawrence and Nancy Durrell,[33] the Greek poet Elie Papadimitriou, and the expatriate British poets Bernard Spencer, Robin Fedden, Terence Tiller, Roger Bowen, and G. S. Fraser.[34] And there must have been others, because one story—the battle of the poets—has Dan, challenged at Cumberland wrestling, defeating seven of them one after the other.[35]

From these contacts Dan met and made friends with a young English lecturer, Reggie Smith, 'a great, brown, black-browed man'.[36] The war had displaced Reggie from his British Council post in Bucharest and, together with his wife Olivia, and after many adventures, he had eventually wound up in Cairo. Here he had a difficult time. The British Council was slow in finding him local employment, and his wife, 'slim and tubular, with a face at once oval and birdlike',[37] whose carping and vindictive personality was quick to make enemies, did not make his situation any easier. Reggie, however, was a relaxed and cheerful personality, generous to a fault, a great talker and drinker, a Marxist who thought politics should be fun, like Terence Tiller and Dan himself a keen chess player, a raconteur and singer with a penchant for English and Irish folk-songs. He and Dan enjoyed each other's company, and any evening on which he might be brought together with Paddy offered the certainty of great talk and wondrous singing.

Such evenings were few, however. Olivia, whose health was poor, and who resented a social world which she was, by personality, incapable of sharing, would drag her long-suffering husband away, moaning about the company he kept, the lateness of the hour, the pointlessness of conversation. In apparent sympathy with her views, Lawrence Durrell is said to have remembered that Reggie 'always had a gaggle of disreputable people in tow',[38] but this is surely the pot of Alexandria calling the Cairo kettle black. In later life Olivia complained of being snubbed by Amy and Walter Smart, who invited her to dinner once, but never again. The apparent neglect was no mystery to others of their circle. Olivia was simply a disagreeable companion. Dan, according to his diary, took the trouble to tell her so:

. . . and no doubt once again [I will] shudder at his [i.e. Reggie's] shrewish wife. At our last encounter we conversed:
'I should think you must be one of the happiest of women.'
'Why?' Bridling.
'Because you do most successfully that which you set out to do.'
'And what is that?'
'Be as unpleasant as possible to as many people as possible.'[39]

At this remove, it is hard to understand why Reggie and Olivia were married at all. She was incurably middle class in the English manner, the daughter of a naval officer, narrow-minded, spiteful. He was a working-class intellectual, generous, amusing, and thoughtful. She was six years older than he was. Perhaps what they had in common was literature. Winnie thought, meeting them both after the war, that he cherished her for her literary talent, and seemed to like looking after her. Olivia was certainly not an incurious person. Indeed, she took an observant interest in others, and had an intuitive understanding of the sources of egotism. Her pessimism attributed all human action to wilful self-interest. With the addition of mathematics and a little theory she might have made a micro-economist.

At the end of her life she took revenge on the wartime Cairo that she felt had snubbed her in her famous novels known collectively as the

Levant Trilogy,[40] in which she took the truth as she wished it to have been, and reinvented herself as Harriet Pringle, a thoughtful, acute, and wronged woman whose husband, Guy, is indifferent to her, and, in his political views and social activities, a hypocrite. The books draw minutely on actual events in Cairo, including the death of Amy and Walter Smart's little boy Micky, and the suicide of the young English actor Stephen Haggard. By implication through her fiction, she makes Amy responsible for her own son's death, and Reggie for the suicide of Haggard. Like Reggie's many other friends, Dan was enraged by these literary acts of malice. He harboured few grudges against people, and was famously tolerant of human diversity, but when he heard of Olivia's death, in the year that her trilogy was complete, his first comment was: 'poisoned, no doubt, by her own venom.' Despite his affection for Reggie, and the wrong that had been done to him, Dan was nevertheless always ready to praise the imaginative transformation that Olivia had worked in her fiction, particularly in the treatment of the sympathetic Harriet. 'Good art nearly always forgives bad character', he would say.

In the Cairo autumn of 1941 the death of the Smarts' boy, Micky, lay in the future.[41] For the time being—he was 6 years old—it was his life that, indirectly, brought change to Dan. For it was in the garden of the Smarts' house, among the mango trees, that Dan first met a young Danish woman called Elizabeth Berndt who worked for Walter and Amy as nanny to the little boy.

At least Elizabeth said she was Danish. She was actually born Elizabeth Cornelia Johanna Reventlow on 2 March 1912 in the town of Sönderborg in the old province of Schleswig.[42] The family was effectively German. Her father is believed to have been a captain in the German navy, one of her uncles an active member of the Nazi Party, and the family's first language German. She grew up an attractive young woman of medium height and build, with rather beautiful fair hair. For reasons that will probably always be obscure, because not only did she resist talking about her past, but, in certain areas, told deliberate and misleading falsehoods about it, Elizabeth became a determined anti-Fascist. Perhaps it had something to do with her education, which may have been unconventional. Certainly she spent a happy period in her teens living with an aristocratic family in Eibesfeld, near Leibnitz, in the southern Austrian province of Styria.[43] Later she went to work as children's nanny for a Berlin family called Grünbaum.

Grünbaum was a Jewish paediatrician, a man of action who took Hitler at his word. When the Nazis came to power in 1933 he decided to leave, and took Elizabeth with the rest of his family to Italy, where they settled first in Capri. Elizabeth said that she took all their money for them, to avoid confiscation. She was just 21. They were in Italy for some years, where she appears to have lived a happy life of some freedom, travelling to Siena and to Rome. 'You could be free in Italy', she said, 'even though the times were so bad.'[44] She took up painting and studied art. The deteriorating situation in Europe in the mid-1930s, however, persuaded both her and the Grünbaums that Italy might not be safe either, and in 1937 they moved to Palestine.

Here, where she found work with the British Council in Nablus, she met and was befriended by George and Katy Antonius. George Antonius was a leading intellectual figure on the moderate wing of the Arab nationalist movement, and Katy (née Nimr) was the sister of Amy Smart.[45] It was at their villa outside Jerusalem that Elizabeth met Amy, and, with painting in common, they became friends. The timing of their meeting was propitious, as Walter and Amy were looking for someone who could speak several languages to come and be nanny for their son. Amy offered Elizabeth the job, and she moved to Cairo.[46]

She seems to have fallen in love with Dan almost at first sight. 'Amy said to me: "Leave your hands off him. He's a married man." And I replied: "I don't want to *marry* him." '[47] They became friends, then lovers. It is difficult to date exactly when this happened, or to trace the course of their love-affair. Dan avoids almost any mention of Elizabeth in his diary, and in the two periods when he surely saw the most of her, January to April 1942 and February to mid-May 1943, diary entries are missing.[48] An educated guess on tangential evidence is that they became lovers at the very end of 1941.[49] Late in life, in August 1986, Dan wrote a short poem for Elizabeth which he called 'December':

> The honey of that summer still
> Combs through our thinning minds.
> The bees, in their generations, now are dead.
> Their hives, like ours, are empty to the winds.
> The flowers sleep for ever in a frigid bed.
> Winter with its sheets of sleet unwinds,
> Whitening the stony quilts where sleep the dead.[50]

There can be little doubt that he was very much in love with her, at least for a time. Out of nowhere he suddenly comments in his diary:

Love as we grew up to imagine and expect it would have been too easy a solution. Monogamy would not then be a makeshift, a second best for want of a best, but an inevitable. But things are not so simple and to grow up is largely to learn this. As a universal illusion it was our worst legacy from the last century.

The problem of monogamy is partly a consequence of man's vanity. The endorsement of his self-esteem by his wife in the end becomes unquestioningly as accepted as his own endorsement. It requires fresh conquests as it first required hers.[51]

It is far from clear what this means, and far from obvious that Dan actually believed what it might intend. What it does do is to illustrate his own confusion and uncertainty about the situation that had arisen. His own love for Winnie continued, and, given what it had survived in the past, would endure. But his attachment to Elizabeth was real and profound. 'In the war, in Cairo, he was happy.' He was good and innocent, but also sharp, Elizabeth said. 'We were very much in love.'[52]

Every day in the late afternoon he would go to the garden bar at Groppi's, where other officers from GHQ Intelligence, or any of his friends from journalism, the Div., the British Council, or the universities would also drop by. Dan would go back to work around 6.00 p.m., and then go home at 9.00 p.m., by which time Elizabeth could slip away from the Smarts and join him for dinner. Sometimes Walter and Amy invited him to dinner with them. At weekends, if he had no extra work, he could go out to the house at Maadi, or down to Alexandria, where it was a little cooler, both the heat and the urban muddle less intense. Sometimes in the Cairo evening, along with the poets Bernard Spencer and Terence Tiller, and the journalists Keith Scott-Watson and Richard Hughes, they would go to the Big Ben, Lucky's, or the Crystale where one night Paddy sang them Sicilian songs 'with such fidelity of words and voice that the waiters stopped waiting and the host himself joined in with the refrains'.[53]

Thus despite the war, and the inherent insecurity of his situation, Dan led a settled and stable, though still bohemian existence in Cairo for the year that he was there. Life was hardly routine, however. His health was still poor, and he had to go back into hospital for ten days at the end of December 1941 to have his tonsils removed.[54] And no life could be either orderly or routine under wartime conditions made all the more unusual by the kinds of friends that Dan had collected over the years, and who were likely to be washed ashore on the shifting Cairo sands. As evidence of this, in mid-May 1942, just as Costello had gone back to join the Div., Dan got an urgent message to go to see Teddy McCullough, who was then employed as an anaesthetist in the British Royal Army Medical

Corps at a tented hospital fifty miles east of Alexandria. Dan found him in an army prison under close arrest, guarded by MPs dressed in what Teddy later called 'the most tempting shorts'. In truth his situation was far from funny. He had been accused by a medical orderly of sexual molestation actually during an operation: a dereliction of duty as well as a sexual offence, the two likely to produce, if he was convicted at the court martial, a severe prison sentence under the most vile conditions. Teddy was in a state, and needed a bit of strengthening. Drawing on his knowledge of King's Regulations, and his experience of courts martial, Dan realized instantly the gravity of Teddy's position. He got him paroled from prison and took him up to Cairo where he installed him in the flat for the next seven weeks, a fairly arduous test of nerves. Through his Cairo connections in social and political circles he found for Teddy exactly the kind of lawyer that he needed, and together they organized a defence.

The denouement, though it lacked the tragic irony of Wilde, seemed to satisfy Hegel's conviction about farce. Teddy came to trial in the Mustapha Barracks in Alexandria on Monday, 29 June. He was 'by this time pretty broken. Hair had begun to look like the underside of a ferret's belly when it has been sleeping in hot straw.'[55] But this was as nothing compared to the British Eighth Army, which was at that very same time being broken under the wheels of Rommel's swift advance on Alamein. The night of 27–8 June was the occasion of the Div.'s celebrated break-out from almost certain destruction at Minqua Qaim, and on 29 June its units were reforming on the Alamein line. Matruh fell on the night of 28 June, with the destruction of 10 Indian Division. And the 90 Light Division of the *Panzerarmee* resumed its advance along the coast road at 1.00 p.m. on 29 June, reaching the Alamein line the next day.[56] Teddy's trial took place to the distant sound of artillery bombardment, the panic of retreating troops, and the withdrawal of the British Navy from its base at Alexandria. At this distance there is something of rare symbolic value in this combination of events: five British brigadiers and colonels sitting in solemn judgement on Teddy McCullough's sexual preferences while Rommel pounded on the half-open door of their empire's last redoubt. Nor does the outcome disappoint our sense of the symmetry of things. Teddy's sharp Egyptian-Jewish lawyer ran rings round the prosecuting officer, and he was acquitted. True to some inscrutable logic perhaps not its own, the RAMC posted Teddy to a hospital in Cyprus, the Isle of Phallus.

The Cairo to which Dan returned that Monday evening, after a celebratory drink with Teddy at the Union Club in Alex., was a city in the grip of fear and excitement. Egypt was not at war with the Axis Powers, so that its status was curious, and many Egyptian nationalists would have welcomed an Afrika Corps victory. The authorities feared a fifth column. Some Egyptians who had worked with the British feared retribution, the Jewish community was in terror, there was a run on the banks. The British—civil authorities, the diplomatic community, the army Establishment—were planning a hasty withdrawal to Palestine. Army HQ went on twelve hours notice of evacuation the next day, Tuesday, 30 June, and the later days of the week were known as ash Wednesday and black Friday because of the huge quantities of official paper being burnt, and the pall of smoke that hung over the city.[57]

Dan went through all this with a certain sang-froid. He did not believe that Rommel, even with the *matériel* he may have captured at Matruh, could really take Cairo with such an extended rear line of supply. Dan had already been in two tighter corners, on Mount Olympus—for which he had been Mentioned in Despatches[58]—and in Dhaskaliana on Crete. He was a free man, alone, and as he wrote in his diary in reverse of the bourgeois assumption: 'it is easy to be dignified if you have no bank account.' Rather than make his own life impossibly difficult in the wake of an alarm that he thought misplaced, he burnt only the bare minimum of office paper, enough to indicate compliance. Also he was well connected. He went to see Amy Smart, and they drank champagne from the Counsellor's cellar on the grounds that it was preferable to leaving it for Rommel.

A few days later, having had to give up his flat, he moved in with the Smarts at Zamalek for a while. He found new accommodation eventually, a room in a flat on the eleventh floor of the building that also housed the New Zealand Club, with marvellous views over the city and the country beyond. A few weeks later he moved again, taking Bernard Spencer's room while he was away. But Dan's time in Cairo was coming to an end. With the stabilization of the front, changes were afoot. Montgomery arrived to command a re-equipped and revitalized Eighth Army. There was a shake-up at GHQ in Cairo, the Intelligence service reorganized. De Guingand, until then Director of Military Intelligence, went to be Chief of Montgomery's General Staff, and Bill Williams to be Intelligence Officer to Eighth Army. Initially Dan stayed on, but then just as suddenly he was ordered to rejoin an active unit. He left Cairo for the front on 30 September, three weeks before the battle of Alamein.

Elizabeth, after Dan had gone, found Cairo 'like a cemetery',[59] and decided to leave it too, returning to Palestine. She had been an almost symbolic inhabitant of wartime Cairo: a German Dane with an assumed name and no papers, a painter, speaking English, living and working for an Anglo-Egyptian family among New Zealand and British intellectuals who moved easily in the world of Coptic, Jewish, and *émigré* society. Her departure in a sense marked the end of cosmopolitan Cairo. Parting was wretched, but wartime was a sequence of these things, and Dan was as haunted by the imminence of death as by the living present.

He went not to the Div. but on secondment and on promotion (he was made captain on 26 October), to a new army unit called J Staff Information Service, also known as the J Squadron.[60] This seems to have been a bright idea of de Guingand.[61] It consisted of mobile units equipped with radio whose task it was to report directly from forward positions on the conduct of operations: in effect a network of observers listening in to their own troops' radio traffic, summarizing the situation on mapboards, and then reporting directly to Army HQ instead of passing the intelligence through divisional or corps structures. The faster reporting was intended to improve and accelerate calculated response, for instance with air support. It came into existence on 1 August,[62] and Dan went forward to join it on 6 October. The officer in charge of J Squadron was the aptly named Brigadier 'Crackers' May, and the other members of the original team, apart from Dan and the various drivers and signallers, were George O'Brien Power, Steve Morgan,[63] and somewhat later, Bryan Sell. Dan thought most of them 'very very British Army'[64] but they functioned well as a unit, and the bonds of comradeship that developed at Alamein all survived into old age.

This is hardly surprising in the context of what they went through together. They moved up into close formation with the advance armour of 10 Corps of Eighth Army on 20 October, camped on a mound between Alamein and the sea. They went for a swim, Dan's first time in the Mediterranean since Pirgos, 'again on the eve of a great battle'.[65] The following night, at 10.00 p.m., the now famous artillery bombardment began, and at 5.00 in the morning of 24 October J. Squadron moved forward in the tracks of the Australian tanks. The sound of huge formations of armour moving across rough terrain was to haunt him for years to come. From then until 6 November J Squadron saw continuous battle service, bombed and strafed from the air, shelled by German tanks and artillery, working twenty hours in twenty-four: 'one lives these days pent up in a workchair or sleeping in our holes—and v little of the latter', Dan scribbled in his diary.[66] Compared with the ordinary tank commander or infantry soldier, the members of J Squadron were pretty well informed about the battle, the phases that it passed through, the preliminary check, the renewed assault of Supercharge, and the eventual breakout. Listening to the radio traffic of their own Eighth Army tank crews gave them particularly good insights into the location and fortunes of individual units. On one occasion Dan was even able to identify Freyberg's voice. Even so, the fog of war was pretty impenetrable.[67] They did their job, exhausting and dangerous, unable to see a larger picture, uncertain of the fate of their friends and comrades elsewhere in the killing zone. This was hard, mechanized warfare, where death and dismemberment came in ugly jagged pieces of metal, unpredictable and vile. Unwashed and uncomfortable most of the time, the food bad and irregular (though he had Ginger back as his batman),[68] the water salty. They were plagued by flies until the atrocious downpours of rain in early November, after which the mosquitoes came. Dan wore his old battledress, with the bullet hole still in the trousers.

His own way of coping with the stress and terror of battle was, as one might guess, literary and classical. He went into battle reading Findlay's *Greece Under the Romans*, then read a short biography of Goethe—'reminds me too much of Middleton Murry',[69] and after that settled down to the *Aeneid*. On 3 November, when the battle of Alamein briefly was at a lull after the terrible fighting of the previous day, and when J Squadron had been shelled and bombed repeatedly, he read Book IV, the terrible and beautiful love-story of Dido and Aeneas, another sort of North African tragedy.

This was distraction, but not rest. Aided by the weather, Rommel and the Afrika Corps managed to disengage and embark on a fighting withdrawal. Dan was now a pursuer, and for the rest of the year and until 28 January 1943, when the New Zealand Division asked for him to be returned to them,[70] he lived the motorized advance with J Squadron: Daba, Fuka, Mersa Matruh, Sidi Barrani, Buq Buq, Tobruk, Derna, Barce, Benghazi, Agheila, Nofilia. A litany, almost poetic in its own way, of the life of North African soldiers from 1941 to 1943, now coming to an end, but always to be remembered by them. The going was no longer the terrible days and nights of Alamein, and Dan had time to drink whisky with Bill Williams in Montgomery's mess, and to seek out Paddy in the Div. HQ for an evening's argument and song. In this way, through danger, discomfort, and the friendships of the mess, the North Africa campaign finally moulded Dan into a New Zealand soldier, comrade of all the other New Zealand soldiers. At long last, in his thirtieth year, he actually felt he belonged. On 11 January he noted in his diary an idea for

a novel about the war, to be set in Cairo and North Africa: 'three themes
love, politics, time.'[71] This was the genesis of his war novel, which he gave
the provisional title *Alms for Oblivion*. Oddly, just as a new life, a fresh
outlook, opened up, an old one came to haunt him. Winnie wrote to say
that she had found an agent who was prepared to try to place *Cliffs of Fall*.[72]

Recall to the Division actually meant leaving it. He was being sent to
Staff College at Sarafand in Palestine, and on graduation would return to
active service as GSO 3 (I).[73] After the parade for Churchill in Tripoli on
4 February he packed and went by air—his first flight—to Cairo ('it is
grand to be here')[74] and then after a few days in Jerusalem to Tel Aviv and
Sarafand. Palestine brought a renewal with Elizabeth, and their love-
affair flowered again. It gave him a chance to see Reggie Smith and
Olivia, who had moved there, and he also made a new friend in Noel
Gardiner, known as Wig, who had been sent on the same course. They
shared a room, and Dan gave Wig advice on how to deal with the rather
less rough-edged junior British officers who made up the great majority
of their fellow students. Wig probably needed this advice. He was a brave
and sometimes irascible machine-gunner who as lieutenant in command
of 8 Platoon 27 Machine Gun Battalion had won a DSO on Miteiriya
Ridge under unusual circumstances during the battle of Alamein.[75] He
was a New Zealand original, another version of the New Zealand writer
and story-teller Jim Henderson, a talking, posturing, noisy version of the
fearless Charles Upham, a brilliant earthy raconteur, an egalitarian without side who spoke his own unconventional mind and never gave a damn
what anyone else thought. He was a bit in awe of Dan, the educated
much-travelled scholar, and they formed a rather peculiar team. But Wig
opened Dan's ear to the vernacular in New Zealand language, and taught
him how to hear it, copy it, use it in his fiction. Wig was unaware of this
contribution to New Zealand literature. He was hardly a reflective man.
He was a man for whom life was a route march, with much of interest to
be seen and done along the way, but for whom the march was definitely
the thing.

The Staff College course was not the stuff of intellectual challenge.
They had lectures on movement by road, and traffic control. But Dan
gave a lecture on J Squadron, and there were the inevitable TEWTs, and
a great deal of travel the length and breadth of Palestine. And there was
also time for recreation. It was spring, the almond and orange trees were
in blossom, and the war zone far away. Dan bought a Corona portable
typewriter and put his short stories in order, catching up on ideas that he
had jotted down in Cairo the year before. Ten of the stories subsequently

published in his first anthology were finished here, and when it was time to leave and return to the Div. he gave them all to Elizabeth for safe keeping. Shortly afterwards she sent them by post to Winnie in Bristol. Apart from the Staff course itself and his writing, he played chess with Reggie Smith, made love with Elizabeth. The appearance of tranquillity was deceptive, however, for Dan was in reality increasingly disturbed. He had started to have a repetitive nightmare, in which his heart was being forced up into his throat, and, on waking, he found his heart racing and his memory sometimes destroyed. He went to the Staff College Medical Officer, but the diagnosis of an anxiety syndrome did no more than give a name to what he already understood. Dan believed that 'what begins in the mind the mind should be able to conquer',[76] but the encroachment of this subconscious terror that only manifested itself in his sleep added to his fits of depression. These were doubtless made worse, as the end of April arrived, by his having to leave Palestine and Elizabeth, and return to the front.

As in the past, the crisis that this represented in his life came out in a sequence of ill-judged bouts of excess. At a party with Wig in Cairo on the night of 11 May he got horribly drunk, then involved in a wrestling match in which he fell badly against a table, so that he arrived back at Divisional HQ with a badly cut skull, and his head in a bandage. When he and Wig finally arrived on 13 May they found that the campaign was over, Tunis had fallen, the war in Africa was at an end. There were then more terrible celebrations that culminated in another set-to, and the recent graduate of Staff College found himself being reprimanded by Major Bill (later Lt.-Gen. Sir Leonard) Thornton, the G2.[77] Where had he been all day? Both he, Thornton, and Colonel Queree had been looking for him. The storm clouds eventually passed, and he took over as GSO 3 (1).

Two days later he set out with the rest of the Div. to drive to Egypt, sixteen days on the road back through so many places fought through. He and Paddy travelled together in, and sometimes on the top of, an LCV, 'talking books and singing Irish songs'.[78] Occasionally they slipped away from the column to visit the ruins of antiquity. They went to the magnificent site of Leptis Magna. In Cyrene they wandered among the ruins while a theatre group from the RAF rehearsed a performance of *A Midsummer Night's Dream*, and then they swam, 'forbidden but good',[79] in the temple baths. At Apollonia they risked the dangerous road down to visit the ruined temple, and on the beach at Daba, like children released from school, they swam and built sand castles.

Back in Maadi the news was that all married men who had served three years were entitled to three months home leave, but Freyberg would not be without both Costello and Davin. Though each qualified for leave, only one could go now. They were to draw lots to see who should go first. Dan won, or perhaps, given how guilty he felt about it on Paddy's behalf, and the conflicting sentiments that must have beset him about Elizabeth, he lost. Whichever, after a period of near intolerable waiting in Cairo, he boarded the *Dominion Monarch* at Port Tewfik, and on 16 June set sail for England.

9

THE TOILS OF WAR

Our passing interrupted the road crossing, and the crowds bunched on both sides waited for us to go by as we have all waited for the war to go by, thinking we can suspend or postpone living and not knowing that in war the heart grows older than it does in dreams.

(DMD, 'In Transit', *GBP*, 169)

It is not easy—perhaps not even desirable—to judge other people by a consistent standard. Conduct obnoxious, even unbearable, in one person may be readily tolerated in another; apparently indispensable principles of behaviour are in practice relaxed—not always with impunity—in the interests of those whose nature seems to demand an exceptional measure. That is one of the difficulties of committing human action to paper . . .

(Anthony Powell, *A Question of Upbringing*, 54)

The *Dominion Monarch* made its way down the Red Sea in sweltering heat. The vessel carried mainly British troops, and Dan shared a cabin with a bore, a major in the Sappers, whom he nicknamed Pig's Trotter. At first he was able to write, finishing two short stories,[1] and he made as good use as possible of the ship's limited library, diving in the deep water of T. S. Eliot's poetry before surfacing through Graves's *I, Claudius*, and a German grammar, into the popular shallows of J. B. Priestley and Galsworthy—'a refined Kipling . . . the Ramsay McDonald of literature'.[2] They put in at Colombo for a couple of days, he did his share of being duty officer, and he played chess. At Cape Town, where they arrived on 10 July, the ship needed repairs, so instead of a port call of a few days they ended up staying for three weeks.

Dan used to say that what you read was often determined by what happened to come your way, and this tedious voyage may be where he acquired the principle. He might equally well have quoted Aldous Huxley's dictum that the things that happen to people are basically like the people they happen to. In Cape Town he met a widow known as Dinks Williamson. She remained in the shadows of Dan's life because he never

169

drew her into the light, but he had a brief affair with her during this July interval. Her maiden name was Cato Ladan. She was a striking mature woman with long flaming red hair, great vivacity, and still remembered for her independent spirit, for her adventures with various male friends, and for the exotic jewellery which was a feature of her dress. Her husband, Bill Williamson, had been a pilot in the First World War, and she was believed to be the first woman in South Africa to obtain a private pilot's licence.³ After her husband's death she returned to live in the old Ladan family home, 'Schoon Zicht' (Fair View), which stands on prominent ground—it was once a whaling look-out—about half a kilometre from Kalk Bay Harbour, and overlooking the False Bay coast towards Fishhoek, Simonstown, and Cape Point. The lovely old house, with a cactus garden at the front, and spacious grounds on the seaward side, has a wide stoep, and in 1943 was one of only a handful of residences along this glorious stretch of coastline, with its connections to the history of whaling, and its intimate exposure to sky and southern ocean.⁴ Was there an echo here of a lost Southland? Of Colac Bay, or the wild exposed beaches of Te Waewae Bay north-west from Pahia Point? Dan left no trace of his own sentiments about this interlude, but he certainly spent some days living at 'Schoon Zicht'. It was winter, the weather cloudy and cool. They went for an occasional drive in the country, but generally they seem to have stayed indoors, where they built log fires, drank Advocaat, read together, and he talked to her about his writing, and about his wife and child in England. At night, the air silent, the barbarity of war far away, the warm rooms of the old house were flooded by the light of a full moon.⁵

Such of the idyll as this may imply—time out of time—was fractured by Dan's state of mind. The nightmare that had started in North Africa and gone with him to Palestine, in which his heart was bursting up into his throat, continued to haunt him here at the Cape. Dinks took him to see a clinical psychiatrist, but the diagnosis remained the same as it had been in Sarafand: an anxiety neurosis requiring complete rest, 'very little alcohol and no violent exercise'.⁶ Like uncertain travel, the brutalities of war, and his magnetic sexual charm, the nightmare of death by torture of the heart was becoming a set feature in the topography of his experience.

When the *Dominion Monarch* eventually got away from Cape Town on 4 August, its complement of irritated passengers having been aboard for three days before it set sail, Dan bumped into Bill Sitwell. He was a Royal Navy officer serving on Africa convoy duty, and was being sent home to take over another ship. They played chess and yarned while the 'most deadening'[7] voyage dragged itself out. They stopped at Freetown for a couple of days, put into Gibraltar on the eve of Dan's birthday—'800 miles closer to England than we were on 15 May'[8]—and out again the next morning, and as the ship ran out of cigarettes and lavatory paper—'All we need now is to run out of water and life will become completely spiritual'[9]—finally docked at Liverpool on 9 September.

Homecoming had an element of comedy, if not farce, reminding him, perhaps, of Winnie's arrival at Toulon aboard the *Ormonde*, or of frantic clothes-changing before their wedding. Dan had to see a draft safely dispatched from the Liverpool quay before he could depart himself. Winnie was at Caer Llan, the Settlement country house in Monmouth. He had been unable to tell her of his leave because reports of troop movements were not permitted in private correspondence. An evening train to Bristol took him as far as Hereford, but there was no connection to Monmouth till the morning. A friendly guard let him sleep in a railway carriage. A companion on the train who was going on to Bristol said he'd try to get a message to Winnie to let her know Dan was arriving in the morning. He succeeded, but only just, so that Dan was in a taxi heading for Caer Llan from one of the two Monmouth railway stations when he was overtaken by Winnie in perhaps the only other taxi in the whole county racing after him from the other station.[10] Both vehicles slewed to a halt, and reunion occurred in the no man's land between them, the middle of the road.

Dan had been away for a little more than two years and nine months. Their daughter Anna, still being breast-fed when he left, was now over 3 years old, a lively toddler with a pronounced Bristol accent. She might have been even more perplexed by his sudden irruption into life with mummy were she not already experienced at communal living. Anna's development was not the only surprise. Winnie had had much to cope with in the years of his absence, not least the demands of a complicated job that required a multitude of wartime talents, and at which she had now been employed for two years. She had become more practical, surprising Dan by knowing how to fix the Caer Llan water ram. She was more radical too: the poverty and deprivation that she encountered seeming to come from another age, not her own.

They spent two weeks together at Caer Llan, living in a little apartment above the stables, an interlude of bucolic tranquillity, in the serene beauty of the Usk Valley, with walks to Tintern Abbey, and pints in the local pub. It is cliché to say that Dan and Winnie, like the millions of others separated by the war, had a lot of catching up to do. And in any case this was hardly new to them. In the more than twelve years that they had known each other they had never lived a settled life together for more than a month or two at a time. But the absences of the war were both greater and darker, played out in ignorance of the other's whereabouts, and in fear for each other's safety and survival. And Dan had much on his conscience. He had gone into the war believing that he would be killed. He had gone through most of it on the presumption that each day might be his last. The principle was not a bad one. He had seen or heard of so many men killed, many of them in what seemed to be almost trivial ways, pointlessly, that fatalism and its moral consequences seemed a reasonable approach. In wartime, and not only for men trained in philosophy, the question was not 'How shall I live my life?' but rather 'How shall I encounter and endure my death?' This made matters of scruple in living less urgent, but it also had another and more corrosive effect.

Each returning soldier carried with him his own experiences of death, fear, and valour that would later become bar-room and dinner-table staples. Those who knew only the table and the bar were not to know that much of this was camouflage, hiding more painful truths. One story that Dan frequently told was apparently about Costello and Freyberg. The two of them had gone over to Australian HQ one morning during the Alamein offensive. Shortly after arrival they had been dive-bombed and one of the New Zealand party, a young officer called Colin Curry, had been killed outright by shrapnel.[11] On the way back, one seat in the staff car empty, Freyberg observed that it was a pity about Curry, he had been a promising young officer. 'And a courageous one', Paddy commented. Freyberg replied: 'Courage, my dear Costello, is a quality I take for granted in my officers.' Paddy said afterwards to Dan that it was all very well for Freyberg, who was notorious for never having experienced fear. *Real* courage was to be like him, Paddy, frightened witless in every attack, but still doing his job nevertheless.

The missing figure here is Curry himself, reduced to a death on which to hang a story that illustrates both Freyberg and Costello. The truth, however, is more dense. Curry was a virgin, so a man who had not yet entirely lived, and his unfulfilled anticipation of life, often discussed, joked about, advised on, was metaphor, perhaps even symbol. Dan used to call himself a callous man, but the reverse was true. He felt death and all the negation of life that it entails and implies, immediately, viscerally. Curry's death—the slaughter of an innocent—affected him deeply. The point can be laboured, but one more example from many endorses it. Dan's J Squadron truck came on a party of three signal linesmen outside

Nofilia on 18 December 1942. One of them had just trodden on an anti-personnel mine and was dead outright. A second 'with a bleeding artery to which Steve . . . applied tourniquet. Other bleeding severely with wounds in stomach and legs. Second one had both legs fractured, one in four places. Ambulance sent for; artery man ghastly pale. Other one crying "I can't breathe, can't breathe." "All right, chum, all right." Blood and pain. A grim spectacle.'[12]

This, surely, was the true terror of war, and it could only be broached as a topic of domestic conversation, if at all, by reformulation into something else. From this sprang the habit of camouflaging ugly truths that, even if expressed, were otherwise unlikely to be understood. Nevertheless, and behind the camouflage, such incidents remained the hard material of which the experience of the war was composed, and their presence, whether distorted in the recollection, or suppressed into tormented silence, was corrosive. They ate away at a soldier's sense of moral connection with others, promoting a degree of alienation that is easy to underestimate.

At the end of September Dan and Winnie moved back to the Settlement's premises in Bristol, left Anna with a friend, and went up to London via Oxford. At lunch with C. K. Allen and his wife at Rhodes House Geoffrey Dawson was also present: 'a pink, pursy old man whom I disliked immediately.'[13] And after that on to publishing business. During Dan's absence Winnie had sent Cliffs of Fall to various publishers without success, until Ursula Beck suggested that she send it to an acquaintance of hers who was partner in the literary agency of Pearn, Pollinger, and Higham.[14] In this way the manuscript went to Nancy Pearn, and she sent it to Walter Allen for a reader's opinion.[15] He liked it. The book had faults, but they were the faults of a creative mind that had not yet stabilized. The writing was powerful, inventive, and new. She should certainly try to place it. On the basis of this advice, she sent the book to various publishers, and eventually it was accepted by Nicholson and Watson, whose reader was Walter Allen, and he gave them the same advice he had given Nancy Pearn. She took Dan and Winnie to lunch at the Café Royal to give them the good news.

Nick and Wat were a firm to watch in the early and mid-1940s. They published Tambimuttu's Poetry (London) series,[16] and had their antennae tuned to the world of Fitzrovia, London's bohemian over-ground, where pub life, literature, and the new world of Film married Charlotte Street to Golden Square and Soho. As early as 1938, this had been part of Dan's chosen world away from Oxford. Nick and Wat were as subject to the difficulties of wartime publishing as anyone else, but by the luck of the arbitrary principles on which rationing was based, they had relatively good supplies of paper, a fact well known to literary agents. Because of it they prospered in the war when there was a widespread thirst for books. As Dan commented later:

While it [the war] went on there was a captive mass audience, mad for any distraction from the shabby daylight and the dismal dark, starved of theatre and sport and the hundred diversions which in peacetime enable the English to dispense with art.[17]

It has always been difficult for a beginner to have a first novel published, and to do so during the war was still difficult. If you could manage it, however, the outcome would be as Dan described. A few good reviews would ensure good sales, not because there was little new fiction available, but because serious fiction, and in particular established classics, were in short supply.[18] Something else also worked to Dan's advantage. In all circles, especially intellectual ones, the war against Fascism was popular, and Dan, as a soldier who had seen fighting and been wounded, was a figure to be admired. Popularity was not something that he sought, but it was a pleasant as well as a new experience not to have his credentials, either as person or writer, questioned.

Through Nancy Pearn he met John Lehmann, the editor of *New Writing*, who had agreed to publish some of Dan's work. It wasn't a comfortable encounter. Dan 'felt no great warming to him. The civilian gulf. And he's a sentimental fellow . . .'[19] And through Nicholson and Watson he was put in touch with Walter Allen, whom he went to visit in Exeter, and who became a lifelong friend. While in Exeter he also visited Paddy Costello's wife Bil, to deliver messages as well as his own regret at having won the ballot for leave. Bil did her best over the weekend of his visit to convert him to Communism, but where the Catholic Church had failed, her powers also proved nugatory.[20]

With these occasional sorties, and life *en famille* in Bristol and Monmouth, three months of leave soon disappeared. He tried to settle to writing, but found it almost impossible, partly because of the attentions of a small child. And there were other distractions, perhaps of maturity. He found that the desire to write poetry was almost completely gone, as though it had been a visitor who had suddenly left. Later in life, Dan ascribed his abandoning of poetry to the influence of Dylan Thomas and Louis MacNeice, whose talents were so prodigious they made his own far more limited ones seem futile. In fact he was already contemplating his

THE TOILS OF WAR

own withdrawal from the field of verse then, in the British autumn of 1943, over a year before his first encounters with Thomas, and five years before he met MacNeice.

The life of wartime movement had also made him restless. After meeting Dick Campbell at the New Zealand High Commission, he agreed to undertake a round of speaking engagements for the Ministry of Information.[21] In part he took this on for the money, which he badly needed. In the event, however, the series of factory meetings in various places in the London suburbs and the home counties, held in canteens at lunch-times, or between day and night shifts, proved interesting.[22] Factory owners and managers were the sort of people he had not met before, and the opportunity to talk directly to often large groups of workers, men and women, about the conduct of the war in the Middle East, the morale of the troops, and the nature of the fighting, was novel and stimulating. He was also unusually well informed, as a result of his year at GHQ Cairo Intelligence, and his friendship with Paddy, about the German Army and the situation that it faced in the East, so that he was able to respond to questions about the Russian front—a major topic of interest, and not solely to politicized trade union officials—from a position of some knowledge.

And his leave was also intruded upon by the world of his New Zealand family, now seven years left behind, and dwindling to an object of curiosity. His oldest sister Evelyn had had a nervous breakdown. His other sister Molly had, at long last, and after many hesitations on the brink, married. Like Evelyn, she married a widower, and was taking over a family with five children. Then at the end of November Winnie had news that her brother-in-law, Bill Baird, had died suddenly of a heart attack in September, leaving her sister Mollie pregnant with their fifth child. With Dan due to return to the front in ten days or so Winnie's thoughts were suddenly of Southland and her distant sister, and had there been any possibility of arranging transport she would certainly have gone home. There was none, however. In this way the war closed off paths that otherwise would have been taken. The randomness and pathetic quality of experience, summed up in Bill Baird's death, received shocking endorsement the very same day that they had news of it when, in the middle of Bristol, Dan and Winnie were witness to a fatal road accident in which a little girl was crushed under the wheel of a lorry trailer.[23]

At the end of his leave Dan was ordered to report to an assembly point in London on 6 December. Winnie went with him, once again via friends in Oxford, and they had a few last nights at their old haunt in Sussex Gardens. Winnie was pregnant again, probably from the very day of the double taxi episode in Monmouth, and they were both in sombre mood at his departure. However, Movement Control contributed its habitual few days' delay, so there was one last weekend together, on the Friday of which, in the Wheatsheaf, they met a writer called Julian Maclaren-Ross.[24] It was a whiff of things to come, but no more than that. The war still dominated everything, and even one of Julian's notorious monologues could not divert Dan and Winnie from the reality of his imminent departure.

He went on the Sunday, a bitter evening ride in an open lorry to the railway station, and thence to Liverpool and a cold and gloomy, storm-filled passage through the Bay of Biscay and up the Mediterranean to Port Said, where the ship docked on New Year's Eve and Dan briefly, and for no reason, was reunited with Crackers May of J Squadron days. Eventually he was permitted to disembark and travelled to Maadi, and from there he had a day or so in the once familiar world of Cairo, now grown dull and toothless with the passing of its cosmopolitan season.

Dan's destination was Italy, where the Div. was now serving on the eastern side of the peninsula, before Orsogna. Every travelling infantry officer had men to organize, and Dan had a draft of 110 soldiers to get on to another troopship at the end of the first week of the New Year, 1944, the year in which he, like almost everyone else outside of Germany, believed the war would end. They docked in Naples, and disembarked a week later. Naples had virtually ceased to exist as a city, bombed, shelled, and booby-trapped into ruins amongst which its inhabitants were starving. For three days Dan was in camp here, and then took a train from the shattered railway station for the small town of San Basilio near Bari. They travelled in wagons, lighting a fire on bricks on the floor, watching the American military police at each frequent halt beat civilians away from the doors. At one of these stops he gave a shirt to a little boy, ragged and thin in the freezing winter weather.

This frightful journey took two days, but was to no purpose. The Div., which had been fighting for Orsogna across the Sangro a hundred miles to the north, had been brought out of the line and relocated in the valley of the Volturno River, near the village of Alife, and only about twenty-five miles from Naples. Elaborate precautions had been taken to mislead the Germans of the whereabouts of the New Zealanders, who had been renamed Spadger Force, and had their insignia removed. These measures may not have had much success with the *Wehrmacht*, but they certainly appear to have bamboozled Eighth Army. After visiting the wrecked port of Bari on 21 January it took Dan three days of motoring to track down

Div. HQ.[25] Paddy was overjoyed to see him, Dan's arrival presaging his own departure. Freyberg was less sure. He had grown so attached to Paddy that he procrastinated, and the poor man was kept waiting almost another month before the precious leave pass was finally official.

Meanwhile, Dan took over the duties of Staff Intelligence Officer, answering direct to the GSO 1 for intelligence matters. The main daily task was the preparation of an Intelligence Summary, which generally had to be written at night in time for distribution first thing in the morning. Summaries typically contained an appreciation of enemy positions and strength of operational units—order of battle material of the sort that he had seen much of at Army HQ in Cairo, but here on the ground much more localized and specific—with additional comment on other matters of interest, such as enemy morale, and the design and function of new booby traps or anti-personnel weapons. The material was gleaned from the interrogation of newly taken prisoners of war; letters, diaries, and other materials retrieved from enemy casualties; intelligence assessments coming 'down' from Corps or Army HQs; intelligence reports coming 'up' from battalion level; and deduction from previous knowledge and experience. Each battalion had its field intelligence officer; Dan had an intelligence officer under his own command, Tony Cleghorn; and Div. HQ had a small staff of signallers and drivers for communication. But the GSO 3 (I) led largely an independent existence, 'a little off to one side'.[26]

What gave the position particular cachet at the Div. was the sequence of interesting and gifted young officers who held it in succession—Costello, Davin, and Cox—and the particular relationship that each of them held in turn with the GOC, Freyberg. The General, known affectionately to his friends—many of them in high places—as 'Tiny' because of his size, had what many of his staff officers considered a weakness for intellectual and artistic types. Though not an intellectual himself, he was undaunted by them, enjoyed their company, and listened to their opinions. Men like Queree, whom Dan used to call Sabretooth, and who was Chief of Freyberg's Staff when Dan arrived, and Thornton, who replaced Queree as G1 of 2NZEF from 3 February to the end of March, believed that their General's weakness for clever young men dated from his days in the Naval Division in the First World War, when he had been friends with a notable group of young aesthetes and intellectuals from Oxbridge, who had, perhaps, 'dazzled' the 'simple colonial boy'.[27]

By the start of the Second World War, however, it was his professionalism as a soldier that motivated him. One close observer of Freyberg throughout the war thought him unusual among divisional commanders in his desire to know 'the broad picture', and in the importance that he attached to Intelligence for field operations. Together, these matters more or less ensured a personal relationship with the GSO 3 (I).[28] Furthermore, Freyberg had to write appreciations of divisional activities for his government, which made top level intelligence information particularly important in his eyes. In this regard, he could make his Intelligence Officers, all bookish men, well read and skilled in composition, testing grounds for his ideas. Freyberg also took an intense interest in the Russian front, kept maps of the Eastern European campaigns in his caravan, and counted on his Intelligence Officer to keep him up to date with developments. And finally, Freyberg liked to be able to pull in his Intelligence Officer for an appreciation of the current situation at any time of day or night, especially if he had a visitor—a visiting general, or a politician—whom he wanted to inform or simply to impress. Each Intelligence Officer in his turn learned to be ready for any of these possibilities, and, performing well, to move up in Freyberg's estimation of the job he was doing.

The job got done in the I truck, a famously disreputable LCV, notorious for the fug of cigarette smoke and the litter of empty bottles, the mess of rolled-up maps endlessly escaping all attempts to hold them down, the piles of paper and pencils, drawing pins and paper clips, and a mass of things to read and learn.[29] Kippenberger, at this time Brigade Commander of 5 Brigade, was said to wipe his feet as he *left* the I truck—and this in the Italian winter of 1944 when the land, when it wasn't under snow or water, was a sea of mud. The I truck was known as the Café, whereas the Operations truck Dan and Paddy called the Chapel, because there you had to worship the Chief Staff Officer.

In the meantime the I truck continues to be the café, even the Saloon, of this HQ, where men in long black coats with derringers and aces in the sleeves sniff cambric handkerchiefs and others in check shirts finger greasy counters and call for madder music and stronger wine. Here we have dicing and debauchery, irreverence and lewd witticism. Fifty yards away devout men are bowed in prayer in the ACV where the waning sunlight strikes shafts of light through the long stained glass windows, motes dance in the incense thick air (but only ritual and reverent dance), G3 acolytes swing thuribles, G2 hands the book to G1, Monsignor Queree, who robed in purple of sacrifices stands before the altar and intones sonorous supplication to Lord Tiny. At other times of course the place is nothing but a corrugated iron chapel Presbyterian Sunday School where pious platitudes cow the venturesome sceptic.[30]

Once Paddy had finally departed, Dan ruled an empire in the Café that was at once squalid and miraculous. Squalid for its conditions of work, and miraculous for both the warmth and stimulation of its atmosphere, and for the intelligence of the appreciations and elegance of the prose which daily came out of it. Dan lived there a lot of the time, rolling himself in a blanket at night and sleeping on the bench. It was the place where he entertained, and a shelter for anyone in search of good conversation and a drink. Murray Sidey recalled the Café as a friendly place where the conversation, though it was never about the army, sizzled. 'HQ mess was only seven people. Mainly colonels. I was only a captain, and often with nothing to do in the evening, and used to wind up being entertained in the I Truck.'[31] He had this in common with Fred Kersh, a British officer who specialized in the new military science of aerial photographic reconnaissance interpretation. His military title was Mediterranean Air Interpretation Unit (West), so he was known as Mae West. After the war he chose to remain with his New Zealand comrades, and emigrated.[32]

Dan was not the tidiest of soldiers, and was not attracted by the logic of order and discipline by which armies are run. He was, however, skilled at keeping his professional and bohemian lives apart. Geoffrey Cox said: 'Whatever reservations he had about men like Queree or Thornton or Gilbert, Dan was punctiliously soldierly and correct in his dealings with them.'[33] He came, in due course, to hold great admiration for both Freyberg and Kippenberger. Thornton he admired for his ability as a professional soldier, which he detected from the beginning. In return, Thornton, with hindsight, was more critical. He thought Davin intellectually arrogant, lacking in tolerance, and with a macabre sense of humour, all of which made him 'difficult to deal with', though he 'did his job more than adequately'.[34]

Dan might not have disagreed with this assessment. From the time when he joined the British Army he found many senior officers dull, humourless, and unimaginative, and did not expect them to understand him, or his ideas and beliefs. In particular Dan never developed any respect for the man who succeeded Thornton as GSO 1 2NZEF at the beginning of May 1944, Brigadier Gilbert, who was keen on traditional military discipline, and held reactionary political opinions.[35] Inevitably, there was 'some friction in [their] relations'.[36] It is true also, however, that staff officers 'came to accept the I truck as functioning, once the I summary was sent out for the day, as an unofficial mess anteroom and bar *when the Div. was not in battle*'.[37]

In practical terms, though these matters are interesting for the light they shed on personalities, such differences counted for little. What mattered were the operations then about to begin. Staff officers were preoccupied with them, and Dan had very little time to learn the job. Perhaps the arrogance that Thornton noted was, as Dan himself was fond of saying, evidence of his own feelings of inadequacy.[38] Ten days after he arrived in Latife the Div. moved up to positions to the south of the Gustav line, the German winter system of fortifications that stretched from the Tyrrhenian to the Adriatic Seas, and that had its hinge at the little town of Cassino. The town stood at the confluence of the Gari and Rapido rivers, beneath the mountain fortress of the Benedictine monastery that 'hung like a hateful tapestry on the wall of the western sky'.[39] On 5 February, towards San Pietro, Div. HQ was in the lee of Monte Camino, an area of wrecked houses, shell-stunted trees, and water-logged bomb holes. Here they were shelled from time to time. At the end of the month they moved forward a couple of miles and into olive groves at San Pietro itself, where they were under a bit of cover and mercifully out of the mud. Here, on 1 March, Dan played a couple of games of chess with Howard Kippenberger. The next day Kip, 'our ablest soldier and nicest man',[40] stepped on a mine on Monte Trocchio and lost both his feet. 'Only yesterday in his caravan he commented on the waste and futility . . . He was always depressed before a battle, fearless himself but sensitive to the fear of others, brave and deploring the need to squander others' bravery.'[41]

Dan was depressed himself, not just by temperament but this time by the circumstances. Route Six came up from the south, skirted the base of Monastery Hill in a loop to the west through the centre of the town of Cassino, and then turned north into the broad Liri valley towards the Alban Hills and Rome. All military commanders, on both sides, agreed that this little town, and the road that twisted through it, held the key to the capture of Rome and the liberation of central Italy. The Germans, under Field Marshal Kesselring, believed that they needed to hold it at all costs: the allied commanders agreed with them. These commanders were a polyglot crowd. In addition to the British, New Zealanders, and Americans, there were division-size formations from India, Poland, France, and South Africa. Dan's job required co-operation with all of these at Army, Corps, and Division levels. In addition, the Div. Intelligence Officer was much sought after by the press. When operations were in progress, his telephones rarely stopped ringing, day and night. When formations were reorganized for operational purposes, as they were at Cassino with the creation of a New Zealand Corps (that came into existence for the period 3 February to 26 March), administrative complications were added to operational difficulties.[42] These matters were further complicated by the people attracted to the Café by its reputation as a place of intelligent and resourceful conversation, wit and conviviality.[43]

Dan quickly formed sharp and durable judgements about his colleagues in the other divisions. The Poles were loveable and impossible, 'the Irish of Europe'. The French he admired for their fighting qualities, which they demonstrated time and again on the Italian front. He also shared their judgement of the Americans, which was low to begin with and got lower with every week that passed. They seemed to have no appreciation of the quality and endurance of the German infantry, and to believe that equipment and intention—' "We gota get Cassino tomorrow" '[44]—could somehow substitute for battle experience, and the military virtues of courage and stoicism. Dan's affection for his Oxford American friends, Gordie, Guy, and Joel in particular, was never shaken by his working contact with their compatriots in Italy, but like many active soldiers in the field he had greater respect for the military prowess of the enemy than of some of his own allies.

Any cool strategic head could see that at Cassino the Germans had accomplished one of the most difficult of tactical manœuvres: to bring an enemy to battle on ground of their own choosing, that suited their own military capabilities, under climatic conditions that worked to their advantage. Dan, like his superiors in the Div., saw that this was true, as did the French and at least some of the British. Perhaps the US V Army under General Mark Clark, and the British Eighth Army now under Lt.-Gen. Sir Oliver Leese (of which 2 NZ Div. was one formation), could see that it was true as well, but if so they proposed no alternative to fighting the battle into which they were being drawn, and, at least as far as the Americans with whom Dan had to liaise were concerned, seemed to hold the view that it could be won quickly. Dan accepted his GOC's view, that there was no military merit in the assault, with only a poor chance of victory: worth taking, but a big risk.[45]

In their judgements, the military commanders of the various HQs were themselves the creatures of global strategy being made elsewhere. In Washington and London the Allies believed it essential to keep as many German divisions as possible tied down in widely dispersed operations, partly to placate the Soviet Union, partly to limit German responses at D-Day, now under preparation. Drawing German formations to southern Italy, holding them there, and forcing them to pay a heavy cost in men and war *matériel*, suited these objectives.[46] The New Zealand Division was to be a principal factor in this equation. What was depressing for so many New Zealand soldiers on the spot was precisely the sense of being a mere pawn in the larger game. By the middle of February, with the Americans demanding a fire that they had proved unable to ignite themselves, and with no room left in the field for either tactical manœuvre or diversionary operations, the New Zealand pawn was to be advanced.

When they arrived at the front, Cassino had been under siege for nearly two months. In all that time, despite atrocious casualties, the American 2 Corps had not succeeded in putting any men across the Rapido River, or in taking Monastery Hill from the rear.[47] Following the logic of the land and the German defences, however, the area of battle had closed to a narrow front concentrated on the town and the hill behind it. This was the time when the Div. 'took up a battle already half fought'[48] but with a tactical scheme of its own devising. There is insufficient space in a biography to rehearse in detail the two battles of Cassino in which New Zealanders fought, but for anyone who was there the experience was ineradicable from memory, often pivotal in experience. Dan was no different in this regard, though there were times in the course of these fearful six weeks when he was frustrated by feelings of irrelevance, the sense that he was making no contribution to the fighting, while being shielded from its dangers.

These feelings probably began on the very day that he officially took over as Intelligence Officer: 15 February. This was the day that, at Freyberg's insistence, and over Mark Clark's indifference, the Monastery was bombed to destruction.[49] The question of whether this should or should not have been done has been repeatedly analysed. Here we need only say that though Dan made no contribution to the decision, he believed it was right, and never changed his opinion.[50] Paddy thought the same, though as he took his leave of Dan, standing on Route Six waiting for transport, he also vouchsafed the view that when he returned in three months, Cassino would still be in German hands, and the Gustav line would still have to be broken.[51]

Of the two battles with which Freyberg hoped to prove him wrong, the first and shortest, *Avenger*, fought over twenty-four hours on 17 and 18 February, was by far the best adapted to New Zealand's military strengths. While 7 Indian Brigade attacked the monastery from the hills, a small formation of hardened New Zealand infantry troops—two companies of 28 (Maori) Battalion—crossed the Rapido south of the town at night, and despite the water-logged ground and intense enemy fire, seized the first of three objectives: the railway station round house. A feature called the hummock and a group of houses at a road junction on the southern edge of town proved too difficult to take, but the Maoris dug in, and behind them teams of engineers worked furiously in appalling winter weather conditions, in the dark, and under fire, to throw bridges across the river, to remove obstacles, and to repair German demolitions.[52] The plan was to get sufficient armour across the river by daylight to consolidate the infantry salient, and with the enemy pegged back in the town, to advance rapidly up the Liri valley. With a war of movement and pursuit, at which the Div. was skilled, substituted for a battle of attrition at the town of Cassino, Monastery Hill and its defenders, despite their position and their capacity to harass with shell-fire, would become irrelevant.

The plan came within an ace of success. By day-break, however, the engineering work was unfinished, the massed armour could not be put across, and the Maoris, dug in in full view of the German defenders, were condemned to endure a day of bitter exposed fighting. Efforts were made to lay a constant screen of smoke across their positions, and to bring accurate artillery fire to bear on their tormentors, but by evening they were threatened with extinction, and the survivors withdrew the way they had come. Of the 190 men who had gone in the night before, there were sixty-six survivors, 'a pitiful remnant'.[53]

The second plan was the child of the first. If small numbers working fast at night and with the element of surprise to the south of the town could not peg the German defenders inside it, then large numbers, operating from the north in combination with armour, and after a devastating aerial bombardment, would drive them out of it. The plan, code-named *Dickens*, was devised within days of the failure of *Avenger*, and set for 24 February.[54] The weather, already wet and cold, deteriorated further however, and with the rain and mud came delay. The Germans used this interregnum to put 1 Parachute Division, under Lt.-Gen. Richard Heidrich, into Cassino town.[55]

Nothing could be done until 15 March when, at long last, the weather had cleared sufficiently for Freyberg to call up his 'secret weapon'. This was the systematic destruction of the town of Cassino by heavy bombers, a softening-up exercise designed to enable the rapid deployment among the ruins of infantry, who, supported by armour, would dispose of such Germans as had survived the bombardment. The air attack in the morning achieved its purpose of destroying the town, but thereafter '[n]othing went according to plan'.[56] The weather deteriorated again, with heavy rain in the afternoon. The ruins and craters impeded the tanks of 19 Armoured Regiment as they tried to go forward. German units, having survived the bombing in their cellars and fortified dug-outs, appeared among the ruins to offer fierce resistance. The brisk mopping-up of demoralized defenders, which the New Zealand command had expected to be 25 Battalion's role, turned out to be a terrible battle of attrition fought from the rubble of one ruin to another. As it intensified into ever smaller areas, neighbourhood fighting of the cruellest kind, it sucked in more troops. The Germans put in reinforcements from 115 Panzer Grenadier Regiment on 18 March, when the New Zealanders committed 24 and 26 Battalions. The next day, 28 (Maori) Battalion was added, while an armoured 'hook' on the Monastery over the hills failed because the going was too difficult. On 19 and 20 March, with a general reorganization, and the fighting more intense than ever, New Zealand Corps committed 23 Battalion and units of 78 Division as well. Thus it was that Cassino acquired the reputation, probably deserved, of being a First World War battle fought with Second World War weapons.

After a week of this, when questions of morale as much as fighting efficiency were now to the fore, most military observers believed that the breaking-point was near. Certainly at NZ Corps HQ nerves were frayed and tempers short as senior commanders wrestled with the decision of whether to continue or to disengage. Alexander[57] came forward to see for himself. The next day Dan commented: 'Some big decisions being taken. Everyone feeling the strain. Generals beginning to behave more and more like children. It is now we feel the loss of Kip.'[58]

Dan was a cautious man when it came to the interpretation of intelligence. He had little confidence in the knowledge of even experienced private soldiers, and so tended to put little weight on accounts of military situations that were derived from POWs of junior rank. Alexander and Freyberg, naturally anxious to know as much as possible about the German position inside Cassino, expected the Intelligence Officer to have ready answers about the state of German morale. He declined to give it, privately criticizing their 'absolute failure to comprehend the limitations' of intelligence derived from prisoner of war sources. And in any event, he believed that the state of German morale was irrelevant. The paratroops would 'fight on [obstinately?] till they're finished and it doesn't matter then what their morale is'. The battle had become 'a killing match' and 'to pull out would be fatal'.[59]

Fatal or not, it was what happened. Failure was acknowledged and the battle lost. On the night of 24–5 March hillside outposts were withdrawn, forward units in the rubble of Cassino itself pulled back, and a new line stabilized under orders of active defence with vigorous patrolling.[60] The next day, 26 March, New Zealand Corps was disbanded. Between 1 February and 10 April New Zealand losses amounted to 1,596: 269 killed in action; 74 later died of wounds; 1,211 wounded; and 42 prisoners of war.[61] Though high strategists asserted otherwise, to the men on the ground it looked as though much had been lost for nothing gained.

Freyberg's HQ, and the Café with it, pulled back to Lignano, just off Route Six in the rear of Eighth Army, and stayed there ten days before moving to Montaquila, on the slopes above the Volturno River, about thirty miles to the north. After the cold of battle came the warmth of spring, the fields a mass of flowers, flies and lizards in the grass. Dan had a busy round of visits to make to Eighth Army, and to the Polish 5 Kresowa Division, which the Div. was replacing on this sector of the Apennine front.[62] A week later he was moved forward over the hills approximately ten miles to the village of Casale, half-way between the Volturno and Rapido valleys.

From the rubble of close urban fighting, the 5 and 6 Brigades of the Div. had now taken up positions in the upper reaches of these valleys. This part of the Apennines is on the edge of the Abruzzi National Park. It is glorious mountain country, wooded, slit with steep river valleys, winding roads, and rushing streams. In the spring of 1944, however, even areas well away from the front were not safe. North Road, on which Casale was located, and the aptly named Inferno Track, both of which linked the Divisional reserve area at Montaquila with the front, were within range of enemy guns, and could be the targets of accurate fire at short notice. A large supply dump called Hove near the junction of these two roads was completely destroyed by artillery fire on 7 May.[63] Furthermore, the road that went from there, across the floor of the valley, and then up the hairpin route to Terrelle, was even more exposed.

These were, however, and of necessity, the roads over which staff officers, engineers, supply columns, and messengers had routinely to travel. It could make for anxious journeys. On one of these, Brigadier Weir, Murray Sidey, Dan, and Freyberg's driver found themselves being put through one of the General's strange bouts of courageous excess. On a particularly exposed portion of road, known to be under observation and within range of enemy artillery, Freyberg suddenly told the driver to stop and turn off the engine. In the pastoral silence he drew everyone's attention to a bird-song, and asked whether they thought it might be a nightingale. They all listened, obedient to the principle that if a General tells you to do something, you do it. Eventually it sang, and Sidey said he thought it was a thrush. Freyberg thought not, so they all had to listen till it sang again. 'There, surely it's a nightingale?' he said. Weir elbowed Sidey in the ribs so hard that he was bruised for days afterwards, saying simultaneously: 'Of course it's a bloody nightingale. Let's get out of this.' And they drove on.[64]

Like the story of Curry and his death at Alamein, this glimpse of Freyberg at war became a matter of table-talk such that its point was somehow missed. Those with no experience of war took it to be an expression of Freyberg's extraordinary sang-froid, perhaps also his playfulness. His son said that it 'illustrated his occasional forgetfulness of his own safety'.[65] Others, loyal and so silent, saw in it a recklessness with life that might be admirable only in the way that some childish exploits are admirable: luck and innocence combining for magical effect. Dan's affection for Freyberg was deep, and became more so in the years after the war, but he was not blind to his vanity or the danger to which it exposed both himself and others. It was in incidents such as this one that he conceived the desire to write Freyberg's biography, and it was the ambiguities of Freyberg's character, mixed with his own, which kindled the desire still further.[66]

There was time to reflect on this sort of thing. The routines of front line duty on a relatively quiet sector—the rotations of the troops every ten days, and so on—meant a more settled existence. Dan had four days' leave in the first week of May and spent them visiting the cliff-side towns of the Amalfi coastline—Positano, Amalfi, Vietri—no doubt seeing them, at least in part, through the pre-war eyes of Compton Mackenzie. The Gulf of Salerno, where orange trees flower and fruit by the pavements of the seaside towns, was a reminder of a past that he had lived through books and the imagination, far away in Invercargill.

On his return to the front, the pace of work increased. The Div. was involved in various feints and manœuvres in the mountains, designed to ensure the Germans retained forces on the sector while the Allies launched another assault south of Cassino. At last, between 13 and 16 May, Eighth Army established a bridgehead across the Gari River, while the French forces in Clark's V Army made sweeping gains to the south, between the Liri River and the sea. On Montecassino, the Poles eventually succeeded where all others had failed, and the Monastery was taken. But the Germans had begun to withdraw on 16 May. A week later, when

Eric McCormick turned up, Dan took him to visit the ruins of Cassino town and its chilling mementos: 'a skull among the rubble, neutral now.'[67] Geoff Cox arrived back from Washington on 26 May, bringing with him news of American friends, Guy Nunn and Joel Carmichael. He and Dan talked late, and it takes little effort to imagine what they must have said of General Mark Clark's decision the day before, after his V Army had at last broken out of the Anzio beach-head, to turn north for Rome and the PR benefits of appearing the liberator, instead of east for Valmontone in fulfilment of the plan to bottle up and destroy the German X Army.

The Gustav line was broken, and the Germans were pulling back along its entire length: a fighting withdrawal of their own. For two weeks from 26 May, when the Germans on the New Zealand sector withdrew across the Melfa River, the Div. fought an engineers' war: their slow advance on Avezzano—finally occupied on 10 June—repeatedly broken at Sora, Atina, Balsorano, while the sappers threw bridges across rivers, bulldozed German demolitions, lifted mines, and dismantled booby traps. In the early summer orchards the Germans had even set booby traps on the cherry trees. Route 82, thirty miles long from Sora to Avezzano, follows the line of the upper Liri River through deep clefts in the mountains, the Serra Lunga to one side, the Monti Simbruini to the other. The weather was fine. The fields and hillsides were covered brilliant red in poppies.

Yet every step was dangerous, and the minefields and booby traps were not solely military. Prisoners of war were suddenly numerous, as were escaped prisoners from the allied side, crossing back. All these people needed to be processed through the Intelligence Officer's information filtering system. A war of movement meant more maps to mark up, and a fluid military situation constantly under analysis. Freyberg was notorious for demanding sudden intelligence assessment, and this duty fell, as it had to Costello before, and would to Cox after, on Dan's shoulders. This was routine, but the burdens were added to by a week-long visit from the New Zealand Prime Minister, Peter Fraser, accompanied by the Chief of the General Staff, Lt.-Gen. Puttick. Dan found himself taking the PM with him to interview a prisoner of war, putting the politician's questions to the surprised young man.[68]

With the taking of Avezzano on 10 June—undisputed, the Germans had withdrawn, and the Fucino Plain lay peaceful and beautiful at the feet of the New Zealand troops—Dan, like his comrades, could draw breath. But his feelings were mixed, perhaps even confused. Winnie, coming to term, was due to give birth to their second child on 5 June, and he was anxious for news. On 3 June he heard from his brother Tom that their mother had died. Tom's letter was not entirely direct, but Dan learned that Mary had died in Seacliff, the very same mental hospital that had been a terror to her when he was a child. There were mysteries as well as sadness in the symmetry of this, and they were not to be cleared away for another four years.

Mary Davin died on 10 May 1944 of a cerebral haemorrhage. She had been taken to Seacliff on 27 April suffering from delusions of persecution that took the form of violent outbursts against Patrick, her husband, and which he became progressively incapable of managing. She had been suffering for months. The causes of these things were doubtless complex, and little understood either by doctors or by other family members. On the day of her death she had apparently been visited by a doctor only an hour before her fatal collapse and he had detected no unusual symptoms. Her daughter Molly said that 'the arch of her mind collapsed'. Some features of the immediate landscape of her experience are worth identifying, however, because they were family matters, and so ones in which Dan was inevitably himself entangled, albeit at a distance. Mary Davin was known to hold deep anxieties for the welfare of her family. Dan's presence in the war zone troubled her. Her youngest child, Pat, had returned from military service with 3 Division in the Pacific Islands, to find his wife had been having an affair with an American serviceman. He was miserable and confused, not knowing whether to seek a divorce, under pressure to stay in the Catholic Church. The younger of her two daughters, Molly, who had married the widower Barry in 1943, had discovered within days that wedlock did not suit her, and had left him to return to live with her parents. In an Irish Catholic household of the 1910s—which was what Patrick and Mary Davin were still living in—this was a tragic scandal, both for them, and for Molly herself. Barry put his five children into an orphanage. In the middle of these catastrophes, Martin, Dan's immediately younger brother and childhood companion, planned to marry, and had set the date: 8 May. In the end he and his fiancée Rae decided to go ahead—wisely, they had a good marriage—but there was tut-tutting from the rear pews.[69] Unbeknown to Dan, his mother had taken in a young railway employee as a lodger when the last of her own children left home. She grew very attached to him. He volunteered for the New Zealand Army in 1942, as soon as he could, and was killed at Cassino. The news of his death, in the middle of all her other troubles, both real and imagined, must have been devastating.

Tom did not send Dan a telegram of the news of his mother's death, and in his letter and his diary makes no mention of Winnie, nor much of how Dan must be grieving for his mother. He bought a wreath for his mother's funeral, which was held on 16 May, 'on behalf of Adelina and myself'.[70] No one seems to have thought of doing the same for Dan and Winnie. A distant family member, still caught up in the old web, confided to me in 1991 that Mary Davin died from the pain of knowing that Dan had deserted the Church, his child left unchristened. Sticky terrain . . .

And as though this death, half the world away, was a passage in 'the music of men's lives',[71] so the great world of the war and the other world of the self now kept discordant harmony. The Allies were in Rome on 4 June, and two days later came the invasion of Normandy. Dan was touring Allied HQs, and dined that night at Eighth Army with Donald Prater and John Willett, old pals from Cairo, Alamein, and the days of J Squadron, with whom he could reminisce about the past, and talk knowledgeably about the progress of the war. Three days later, on 9 June, Dan and Winnie's second child was safely born in Bath.[72] They called her Helen initially, a name Dan liked, but she preferred Delia at the age of 7, and has been known so ever since.

While family matters preoccupied him, the Div. was enjoying a few days of cheerful brigandry on and about the Fucino Plain, and just for a day he joined in. Along with a friend, Dick White, he went off on 'one of the more surprising days of my life', to 'liberate' two small Italian towns, Castel d'Ieri and Goriano.[73] The Germans had withdrawn, the Partisans were out, the peasants and town dignitaries knew that there were Allied troops near by, and suddenly these two young men in their jeep arrived. It was time to celebrate. Old ladies kissed their hands, babies were brought for inspection, Dick White said Dan should make a speech. Before he knew it he was on a balcony praising the liberation, the resistance and freedom, condemning the Nazis, the Fascists, Il Duce. At Goriano they were carried shoulder high among cheering delirious crowds, and again he had to speak, from a balcony above the market-place—'this time taking the odd cut at the church and tricking them into a viva Stalin'.[74] The celebrations turned to dinner and free-flowing wine, and the conquering heroes, out of petrol in the dead of night, snored under the stars before creeping back to base 'half frozen and with monstrous hangovers'.[75]

For a month after this there was temporary peace and quiet. The Div. went into rest and training near Arce on the Liri River. Dan paid visits to Rome, where New Zealand troops had been allotted the Quirinale Hotel on the Via Nationale, and for the first time he was able to walk among the ruins of the civilization he had so long studied. After Cassino it was instinct to compare these ruins to his own, more recent ones. Once again there was a July moon, and once again he started a new relationship,[76] this time for a few days in an apartment on the Via Piave, a smart address overlooking the grounds of the Villa Bonaparte at the Porta Pia. There was an unmistakable mood of victory in the air now. A post-war world seemed not only possible, but certain. When he returned to HQ Freyberg chatted to him about the job of war historian. Was it something he would like to do? Eric McCormick, on an earlier visit, thought he should return to Otago as Professor of Classics.[77] These glimpses of a peaceful future mocked the danger of his immediate prospects. Cox's return meant that Major Davin would have to move on. Div. HQ was a world of colonels and captains where majors were out of place. GHQ captains who came into their majority went back to the Battalion for active duty as company commanders. There was still fighting to do before the histories could be written. Dan had been promoted to major on 4 April. He wrote to Geoff Cox: 'Uneasy lies the shoulder that wears a crown.'[78]

Nevertheless, during June, he was saved from the further excitement of front line fighting by Freyberg, who recommended him for a job at the War Office in London as a New Zealand representative on the Control Commission for Germany, a body set up to administer the dismantling of Nazi institutions, and the treatment of German officials, collaborators, and records in the formerly occupied areas of Europe, and, ultimately, in Germany itself. The job would take him away from the Div., but it would return him to a city he had learned to like, away from the front line killing and the killed, back to a life where he might be able to live with his family, and write the war novel that he had been incubating since January 1943. Freyberg encouraged him to take it, and he accepted the advice.[79]

Before he could leave, however, there was one last operation. The Div. was suddenly called 200 miles forward to Lake Trasimene to reinforce 13 Corps in an attack on German positions dominating the approach to Arezzo.[80] Once again there were the pre-battle procedures of intelligence gathering, analysis and dissemination. There were Staff meetings at which to give appreciations of enemy strength and position. This time he worked in tandem with Geoff Cox, and in the summer weather there were no delays. New Zealand troops took up their positions on the nights of 12–13 and 13–14 July. On 15 July 25 Battalion assaulted the German-controlled heights of Monte Lignano, and after a brisk battle in the dark, in which 12 New Zealanders were killed and 27 wounded, the high point was taken. Since Monte Lignano dominated the Arezzo theatre, the

German Army had little option but to withdraw. In this way, the city of Vasari and Petrarch, of the church of San Francesco with Piero della Francesca's Legend of the True Cross frescos, and of San Domenico with its crucifix by Cimabue, was liberated. This was Dan's last engagement in the war to end Fascism.

He had a few more days in Rome, and then was flown to England from a military airfield at Barat on the night of 28 July. He was not to serve with the New Zealand Division again, and his departure from it was an emigration, a second leaving of his home country for another land. The last images that he took with him, however, were the bitter fruits of discord at Cassino. The battle had brought out the best and the worst in the New Zealand male character. Thornton was right, the IO was a little 'off to one side', but this did not mean that he was unaware of what was going on in the counsels of the Ops. truck, or the General's caravan.[81] And from his position of informed detachment, Dan had the idea of writing a play based on what he had seen. He carried this idea inside him, in embryo, to the end of his life. Perhaps in preparation for it, he carried with him on the plane out of Italy an aerial reconnaissance photograph of Cassino, and copies of NZ Div. HQ Intelligence Summaries. In transit at RAF Station Rabat Sale, British Military Security confiscated them.[82]

After being reunited with Winnie, Anna, and the new baby in Bristol, he began work at the War Office on 9 August. Life in London was not easy. In the last year of the war the country was exhausted, rationing strict, train travel a nightmare. And the home front had its dangers too. He took a room in a house at 15 Vincent Square in Westminster, but had been there only a few days when a VI came down fifty yards away and blew in all the windows. He was in bed at the time, and unhurt by the flying glass, but in the absence of blackout he had to find somewhere else to live. Briefly he was at 9 Hasker Street, near Sloane Square in Chelsea, and then he and Winnie found a small corner house, 2 Jameson Street, in Notting Hill, where the family was reunited in September. The house, like much of the English housing stock by the last year of the war, was fairly dilapidated, the kitchen and bathroom primitive. London was black, weeds and rats in the bomb-sites, the beer watery, the weather in early autumn already coming on to be winter cold, and coal hard to get. A taste of things to come.

Worse than these deprivations, which were at least the common lot, Dan was in serious psychological and emotional difficulty. His recurrent nightmare increased in frequency, hardly a night going by without his waking in a sweat of deathly panic. And into this world of half-understood terrors came letters from Dinks Williamson in South Africa to say that she had had his baby. It was a boy, born on 28 March, and she had christened him Dan Bill. He talked of this with no one, and wrote none of it in his diary, though one enigmatic entry says: 'Dreams and the fear of madness. To go on in guilt or like a rabbit sit shivering in one's tracks?'[83] Dinks and the baby Dan began to appear in his dreams, and also, eventually, in his speech while asleep. Winnie was not to be misled, and under interrogation he told her the hurtful truth. It is difficult to know, at this remove, what must have passed between them. Dinks Williamson's letters express her astonishment that he should have told 'their secret'—as she seemed to want to keep it—to his wife. According to her few letters that survive, she went to Port Elizabeth to have the baby; only the doctor and nurse who delivered it knew that it was hers; and the baby was then looked after by a nurse while she, Dinks, tried to put into effect a scheme to 'adopt' a child, so that she could then bring up as her own child the baby who really was her own.

In the New Year of 1945 Dinks wrote of her anxiety for the child because there was so much illness about. She was particularly worried about an epidemic of poliomyelitis. Later in the year—dates are difficult because letters are missing—Dan Bill was dead.[84] No photographs of the child have survived, and the only documentary evidence, the few strangely stilted, artificial letters, themselves the remnants of a larger correspondence, provide little additional information.

Inquiries in South Africa suggest several possibilities. One is that the child never existed except in Mrs Williamson's imagination. A second is that Mrs Williamson had the baby, but invented its death to cover the fact of having it adopted by a third party. A third is that the cover was to conceal her own 'adoption' of the infant, in such a way as to keep Dan out of its life. A final possibility is that the child was born, and did indeed die.

These possibilities suggest themselves for various reasons. First, neither birth nor death certificates can be found in South Africa in the name of Dan Bill Williamson or Dan Bill Davin or Dan Bill Ladan. At least officially, the child does not appear to have been born.

Mrs Williamson died in 1990, but various residents of the Kalk Bay coast and neighbourhood, one of whom, aged 85, knew her all her life, asserted that she had never moved away from 'Schoon Zicht', had never had a child, and never been pregnant.

This empirical evidence supports another feature of this strange matter. Mrs Williamson's letters, in both their timing and their content, seem to me hollow, expressive of an inauthenticity that is troubling. One example: no sooner, apparently, has Dan written from London to tell her that he has explained about the child to Winnie, than Dinks begins to air her worries about the child being at risk of serious illness. It is almost as if ground is being prepared. Another example: although a letter with the particular news of Dan Bill's death is missing, references to his death in subsequent letters seem to be without sufficient distress. And the letters which contain some description of the infant do so in the sort of terms which might be relied upon by someone with general but unspecific experience of babies, unable to express the quirks, beauties, and individualism of even the youngest of infants. The absence of photographs—though at least one does appear to have been sent—is troubling.

My own view, at a remove of fifty years, without the benefit of discussion with Mrs Williamson herself, and on balance, is that Dan Bill never existed, and that his 'birth' was a hoax. Whether it was intended as preliminary to something worse we have no means of knowing. Dan's connections with Mrs Williamson came to an end in 1945.

Whatever the biographer might think, however, at the time Dan believed in this child, and Winnie did too, and they continued to do so for the rest of their lives. Even so, its impact on their relationship is obscure. Winnie took the view later that Mrs Williamson meant nothing to Dan. He had been lonely, and it was wartime. Death might come tomorrow night, or next week. Nobody crossed the North Atlantic in 1943 without living in fear of U-boats. These were the things that happened in the war, when much that was unwelcome had to be endured. Dan had survived, and come back to her, just as he always had in the past. Her own commitment had been made ten years before, and it was not to be shifted now.

Winnie was also sustained by her long-held belief in Dan as a writer, which she still thought among the most important things. And in the last year of the war, amid the emotional turmoil of his nightmares and his guilt, it was becoming a reality. On 16 September he began work on his war novel, at first called *Alms for Oblivion*.[85] In November, two of his short stories were published simultaneously, one of them in *Good Housekeeping*, a women's magazine with a large circulation, while a third was accepted for an important anthology.[86] The following year his short story 'In Transit' was published in *Life & Letters Today*,[87] and in April 1945, after numerous wartime delays, his first novel, *Cliffs of Fall*, was at long last published by Nicholson & Watson.[88] In the last year of the war, in the literary circles of London, Dan Davin was a coming man.

And Mark Burke, the young protagonist at the centre of his first novel, was widely thought to be the writer's *alter ego*. He is a young New Zealander from a Catholic family studying at university. His university and home towns are never named, nor is his subject. In embryo he is the *Übermensch*, committed to the triumph of the self through the will. Rebellious, he has rejected his family's religion and its petty working-class morality. At university he has met and befriended a young woman, Marta. She works in a shop, and has had a troubled past, including an abortion, a period of loose living in which she acquired a reputation for sexual promiscuity among medical students, and bad relations with her family. Mark has made her pregnant and is confronted with the problem of what to do: another abortion?—which she won't accept; simply abandon her?—which he shrinks from, though she appears to expect and accept it; marry her?—which she wants, but of which he is afraid; or kill her?—which he is drawn to as an exercise of the will, proof of his freedom and superiority. He chooses to kill her, but in this (he strangles her), and in the subsequent hunt for the killer, he discovers his own murderous self, and in trying to grapple with himself falls to his death in the sea.

The book was described as a brilliant failure:[89] brilliant in the way it conveys the character of the boy's home life, its futility and shallowness; the atmosphere of his university existence in the marginal world of bed-sitting-rooms, pubs, and streets; and the brisk portraits of his family and contemporaries, especially his father, his older brother Joe, his sisters, and Peter, his friend at university—a musical boy wasting his talents under the repressive ambition of a dominant mother. A failure because the central ambition of the work, to convey the pathology of the 'rational' killer as metaphor for the victimization of circumstance, is not sufficiently well realized in the protagonist. The novel invites speculation about existentialism, the role of Nietzschean heroes in both society and philosophy, and the concentration of social pathology in a single character. The speculations are valid, but the novel not strong enough to bear their weight, so that the answers—that egotism and excess lead to madness, despair, and death—seem too extreme for the problems as they are posed. To explain why a monster like Burke should kill, rather than simply reject, his chosen Marta, would require rather more evidence than Davin gives.

Nevertheless, the book deserved an audience. Despite occasional awkwardnesses, especially in dialogue, and an overly poetic density of description in places, the book goes swiftly and confidently about its business. It teems with ideas, suggestive of a young man anxious to say *everything* that he thinks before it is too late. In places it is very funny, a fact which seems to have been lost on a solemn audience. And it has telling criticisms of New Zealand society, particularly in the pub conversation between Mark and Peter,[90] in the painful depiction of the family table at home, in the irritable disharmony of Marta's family, and in the self-confident presumption of middle-class university types.

None of the book's weaknesses was lost on its critics, yet in general they applauded its daring.[91] Writing in the *New Statesman & Nation* Philip Toynbee, detecting the influence of Gide and Dostoevsky, said Davin's 'theme is titanic, and defeats him from the first page, but I doubt whether this will greatly disturb him'.[92] He catalogues the book's faults, but admires it nevertheless. 'The passion is in the writer, constantly breaking out into admirable, though incidental expression . . . Mr. Davin (I have warded it off as long as I could) will go far.' The anonymous reviewer in the *TLS* thought not.[93] He or she (one senses one of those refined Regent's Park sensibilities, more at ease with Elizabeth Bowen and drawing-rooms than with rebellious young colonials and public bars) read the novel as realism, and condemned it roundly, in particular the failure to introduce Mark Burke's 'tendency to schizophrenia' before the final few pages, the 'tedious and improbable conversations', and the 'strained' manner of the writing. John Hampson, in the *Spectator*, thought he saw the influence of Theodore Dreiser, drew comparison with Graham Greene, and shared Toynbee's perception that 'the author has passion, a quality which is more rare and more valuable than competence'.[94] The most thorough notice appeared in the weekly paper the *New Zealand Listener*, where Dan's old acquaitance Eric McCormick had space to review it at length. Its failure was, in his view 'worth a dozen timid successes'. True to their shared bohemianism of Dunedin a decade before, he suggested that the book would have benefited not from less of a breach with the conventional novel form, but from more. '[P]oetic drama might have provided greater scope for his talents . . . Perhaps . . . something like . . . the novel developed by Kafka.' Such initiative would have made 'the test of plausibility . . . irrelevant', making the work 'a study of diablerie and tragic conflict'.[95] Though he was far away from its country of publication, McCormick certainly caught the British perception: 'though I don't think its author has produced anything like a masterpiece, I feel that he might some day.'

By the time of its publication, Dan's own views about the novel were almost unspeakable. He had finished it six years before in a world that seemed now, at the end of Hitler's war, to have been swept away. Its origins lay even further back, in a student's bohemian world of Invercargill and Dunedin, dominated, in the absence of a varied and complex life as he now understood it, by literary substitutes: Dostoevsky, D. H. Lawrence, the poets of decadence. The events in the story were parallel both to his own gloomy jealousies and fears, but also to real events that, though true in their way, now appeared small and irrelevant in the devastated Europe of 1945. He had outgrown the work, which seemed, in its independent existence, not really a part of him. He was flattered, though surprised, by the book's relative success with the critics. Nick and Wat had no such misgivings. The book went into a second printing, and sold all ten thousand hardback copies. Dan received over £500 in royalties.[96]

Dan Davin was now a literary name, and whatever his misgivings about its editor might have been, his name belonged to the world of John Lehmann's *New Writing*, the quarterly paperback which, at the end of the war, was about to go into its twenty-fifth issue. Lehmann published poetry by Dan's Cairo friends Terence Tiller and Bernard Spencer, critical pieces by his mentor Walter Allen, short stories and reportage by New Zealanders Erik de Mauny (whom he had known in the Div.), Denis Glover, and Frank Sargeson. There were Julian Maclaren-Ross's stories, and pieces by Lawrence Durrell. Any issue of *New Writing* that Dan opened now contained only names that he knew, many of them friends, some of them intimates, most of them inhabitants of the same world as his.

The geographical centre of Dan's literary world was the region of London on either side of Oxford Street to the west of Tottenham Court Road, the district that came to be known as Fitzrovia, and in which social life was pub and restaurant life.[97] Dan had been an *habitué* of the Wheatsheaf and the Fitzroy before the war, occasionally eating at Bertorelli's, and it was the district of London that he naturally returned to in the autumn of 1944. Here he took up with Julian Maclaren-Ross, whom he had last seen—and first met—just before setting off to Italy a year before. They became friends, but no friendship with Julian could or should be thought of like any other friendship. For one thing, friendship was something that flowed towards Julian, a supreme egotist, rather than away. The poet Vernon Scannell called him 'the one-man cast of a continuous private movie, skilled with the pen but stupefying with the tongue'.[98] He expected, indeed demanded, attention both to what he said and to his immediate desires, of drink, or food, or comfort. Like all dandies he enjoyed his own fur-coated reflection, affected a terrific social pre-eminence, and became morose and truculent if unable to dominate any gathering fortunate enough to have acquired his presence. Rather like the hand in the Escher print that is drawing itself, Julian was a writer engaged on a writing project in which both the subject and the object of creativity were the self.[99] Even so, he lived a way of life hardly conducive to the hard work of creation, writing with his Parker fountain pen in his miniature italic hand only early in the morning and late at night, living the rest of the day in pubs, bookshops, and restaurants all within the small radius of Soho Square, camping rather than living in cheap hotel rooms, and always travelling by taxi. Unsurprisingly, and despite his success as a writer of short stories, documentary films, occasional pieces of criticism, and (later) treatments for feature films, he was always chronically short of money, and Dan, like Julian's publishers and occasional employers, was regularly tapped for his contributions.

Strange people gathered about Julian. Apart from his various 'girls'—at this time there was one called Monica—his friends included the painter Gerald Wilde, an alcoholic subject to occasional bouts of psychosis that could make him murderously unstable;[100] Tambimuttu, the notorious editor of the Poetry (London) series, whose idleness and administrative incompetence made him a byword for the bohemian;[101] Augustus John, Nina Hamnett, and Dylan Thomas. From August 1943 till the end of the war Maclaren-Ross and Thomas both worked for Strand Films, Donald Taylor's company that made documentaries. When they and their friends gathered there would be gossip, laughter, and stories, but the egos here were strong, making for weak bonds of friendship.[102]

Dan was such a punctilious man, always on time, ever determined to complete what he began, that he might be thought to fit awkwardly into this company. This is to accentuate one side of his personality against another. He admired structure in literature, knew that no great work was possible without it, and understood that structure was preceded by order and discipline. But he also loved the bohemian, the disorganized, the pleasure in the spirit of conversation and the fact of a life lived in it—transient but fulfilled. He was also a great observer. The talents he had brought to wild life and the countryside as a boy, and put to use as an intelligence officer in the army, he turned on his literary and artistic contemporaries at a time when he could still 'afford the unnatural concentration [their] egotism required'.[103]

In part this was made possible by the German Control Commission. Dan's part of it, in the War Office, was located in Norfolk House, where it wallowed in the doldrums of having to plan operations without execution. Dan was bored by a job that was ill-defined, and found his colleagues at the office for the most part tedious and uninteresting.[104] He did his job there well, and was warmly praised for his work,[105] but he felt himself side-lined from the serious business of war, and never became enthusiastic in his new administrative role. After work those 'who had actually heard shots fired' would have a drink in the Red Lion, off St James's Square. It was only later that Dan discovered that one of their number, Lt.-Col. W. S. (Fred) Friedrichsen, a linguist and author of a German dictionary of military terms, was a great Gothic scholar, and much admired by Kenneth Sisam.[106]

Daily life at this time did have a certain interest. The constant terror of V1s and their successors, the infinitely more surprising V2s, saw to that. Dan's work held out to him the brief distraction of a short visit to Brussels, and the repeated planning for a rather longer tour of Allied occupied Germany that never materialized. But despite these things, in the last wearisome year of the war, he could hardly ignore the fact that life lay elsewhere: in Fitzrovia, in Notting Hill with Winnie and his two small children, in the literary pages of the weeklies, and in the dark areas of his conscience and his recurrent nightmare.

These private complications were further disturbed by questions about the future. What should he do after the war? Paddy's departure for the USSR in the New Zealand diplomatic service, coupled with his own brief but satisfactory lecture tour for the Ministry of Information in the autumn of 1943, prompted Dan to inquire about the possibility of 'a senior post' at the British Embassy in Moscow.[107] Early in May, he applied for a position of talks producer with the Overseas Unit of the BBC.[108] Once more he got in touch with Lindsay at Balliol, and once again Lindsay, famous for his tenacity, brought up the idea of WEA lecturing in North Staffordshire. Lindsay also suggested that he write to Kenneth Sisam, Secretary to the Delegates of Oxford University Press, to inquire about a possible opening. Unlike many contemporaries who had risen in the war, Dan had no ambition to remain in the army. He joined it to fight and defeat Fascism, and endured it for that reason alone. More or less as soon as the Germans had surrendered unconditionally, he resigned his commission and left, substituting 'the civilian jungle for the military zoo'. He applied for his discharge on 11 June, and was released from military service on 31 July. He was Mentioned in Despatches again on 9 July, this time for 'gallant and distinguished services in Italy', and on 13 December he was awarded the MBE (Military Division) with the same citation, but he cared little for awards and decorations. The warrant of appointment

MBE came with a receipt and an envelope for its return to the Central Chancery of the Order of Knighthood at St James's Palace. He never bothered to return it. Nor did he bother to apply for any of the medals to which he was entitled.[109]

Sisam invited Dan to Oxford on 31 May, and he had the kind of informal interview to which one New Zealand Rhodes Scholar who had specialized in English and Classics might subject another. He was particularly glad to establish that Dan had played rugby, as he believed intimate experience of team-work essential to publishing. Dan probably had his mind on the fact that he would be stepping into the shoes of John Mulgan, who had recently committed suicide in Cairo, and that the man interviewing him was the author of the textbook on medieval English that he had studied as a student thirteen years ago in Dunedin. Sisam offered him a job on the spot, and wrote to confirm the offer the same afternoon.[110] The salary of £500 a year plus £25 per child was no more than he was paid as a major in the New Zealand Army, and only 25 per cent more than he had had as a Rhodes Scholar nine years before. But it offered a career in books in the familiar territory of Oxford, and Sisam's written assurance that 'I don't think you would have cause to regret taking the risk' was, from such a man, virtually a promise of prosperity.

Dan was free of the army by the end of June. He was owed a month's leave, which he had to take before his discharge, and he had enough money to stay on in London until the end of August while he worked at his novel, and looked for a house to rent in Oxford. This was not a carefree time, however. Winnie was pregnant again, and Dan was still wrestling with the painful private consequences of his wartime life. The complications, already great, kept growing.

PART III

WRITER AND PUBLISHER, OXFORD
1945–1978

10

EIGHT VIRTUOSO YEARS

Every publisher is an author's sepulchre.

(DMDP: DMD, 'Myself and the Oxford University Press: 1945—', uncompleted MS, [1978?])

Objectivity is not, of course, everything in writing; but if one has cast objectivity aside, the difficulties of presenting marriage are inordinate. Its forms are at once so varied, yet so constant, providing a kaleidoscope, the colours of which are always changing, always the same. The moods of a love affair, the contradictions of friendship, the jealousy of business partners, the fellow feeling of opposed commanders in total war, these are all in their way to be charted. Marriage, partaking of such—and a thousand more—dual antagonisms and participations, finally defies definition.

(Anthony Powell, *Casanova's Chinese Restaurant*, 96)

Dan and Winnie moved to Oxford on the last day of September 1945. On the way from Notting Hill to Paddington station Anna, lively in the back of the taxi, fell out on to the road. Remarkably, apart from bruises and grazes, she was unhurt. The life and death of little children was much on Dan's mind. Close upon the news of Dan Bill from South Africa had come word from the Middle East that Elizabeth Berndt had given birth to a daughter, and that she was his. Conceived during Dan's time at Staff College in Sarafand, she was born in Palestine on 1 December 1943, and christened Patricia Katarina after Elizabeth's mother. Everybody called her Patty.

It is not clear how Dan learned the news. No correspondence between him and Elizabeth has survived. One witness said that Elizabeth determined never to tell Dan about the baby, and only did so when her circumstances became difficult during 1945. One letter from Dinks Williamson implies that Dan had written to her asking for her advice, if not her help, in assisting Elizabeth and Patty to emigrate to South Africa.[1] Whatever the strict order of events, letters to Dan from Joe Japolsky, an old acquaintance in Cairo, written early in 1946, suggest that he had for some time been trying to find ways of helping her.[2] This was far from easy to do. Immediate post-war Europe was awash with refugees. Elizabeth had no papers or other evidence of nationality. Her origins, as well as her connections in the 1930s, had been German, a matter which she had wisely obscured during the war and which would hardly bring her sympathy in immediate post-war Britain. Her preferred nationality was Danish, but she could not establish Danish citizenship. She did not wish to return to her family, whom she had left many years before, and had no desire to see again. When she visited Cairo, Japolsky advised her to pull strings through the Smarts, but pride prevailed over material interest. Her hope lay in Dan, and the sense of obligation that she knew he would feel for his daughter. At first, Dan attempted to avoid having to tell Winnie the unwelcome news. But by the end of 1945 Elizabeth, who could be a forceful woman, was hammering on the door, Palestine becoming an uncomfortable place to be in, and he owned up. Winnie, who never lost her spirit, was furious, her anger made worse by the extent of her recent relief that Dan Bill and Dinks were not after all to become fixtures in her life. Her anger was not mitigated by the fact that she could see instantly that Dan's problem was also hers, that Patty and Elizabeth had to be looked after, and that the only course of action would be to bring them to England. John Street, another wartime acquaintance, kept Dan informed about changes to immigration regulations, and the revival of the system of pre-war Ministry of Labour entry permits.[3] When these came back into force Dan and Winnie lodged an application to bring Elizabeth, whom they characterized as a children's nurse, to work for them. They may not have intended that she should stay long. In New Zealand, Mike Joseph wrote on Dan's behalf to the Department of Internal Affairs inquiring about immigration regulations there.[4]

Meanwhile, in Oxford, Dan had found a furnished house to rent at 77 Rose Hill, east of the town, and they moved in on 30 September. It was a difficult transition from the bohemian London of the last year of the war to suburban Oxford in the first months of peace. Living with rationing involved developing a relationship with local retailers, and a house removal broke ties that had then to be re-created. Winnie was nearly eight months pregnant, Delia only 15 months old, Anna, who had had her fifth birthday in July, starting her first term of primary school. For the first time they employed a young woman, an *au pair* in today's terminology, to help with the children and the housework, a practice that they were to continue, off and on, for the next ten years. In November, Winnie returned to London for the birth of their third child. Another girl, she

was born on 19 November, and although they named her Katharine
Brigid, she has always been known as Brigid.

The Rose Hill house to which Winnie brought her new baby stood on
what was then a main road, and their nights were often disturbed by the
noise from lorries changing gear at the top of the hill. Dan's recurrent
nightmare intensified, sapping both his energy and his concentration,
and both he and Winnie were constantly distracted by the responsibility
of preserving the furniture and fittings of a rented property from the
depredations of young children. Almost from the beginning they hoped
to move closer to both the centre of town and Dan's work. A year later
the hope was fulfilled when a house owned by the Press became vacant.
It was situated at 103 Southmoor Road in North Oxford, and it became
their home for the rest of Dan's life.

Despite its being a Press house, competition for housing was so intense
that it might still have been a near thing. Dan rang Winnie from the
office to say that the house was available, and would she like to go to see
it with him. 'No', she replied. He was nonplussed. 'I don't want to see it,'
she continued, 'and neither do you. Just take it. It must be what we want.'
They moved in shortly before Christmas 1946, and briefly were in some
distress. The house was unfurnished. Delia was suffering from a terrible
cold. The bitter winter of 1946–7 had started early, and the place was
frozen solid. Winnie collected snow from the garden to make tea and
cook vegetables when they first arrived. Dan, completely unworldly about
such matters, would have found these problems intractable, but fortunately the Sisams paid the house a surprise visit one afternoon to see how
they were settling in, and were appalled by what they found. Press
handymen were quickly rounded up to get the water flowing, the pipes
lagged, and fires lit.

Problems of supply were renewed, but on this occasion Christmas cheer
was restored by Bernard Freyberg, now Governor-General of New Zealand. From the abundance of a New Zealand summer he sent them a
parcel which included a ham, bully beef, and a huge tin of spam, a
wartime addiction from which Dan, like many ex-servicemen, was never
free.[5]

Even so, life was spartan for a while. Apart from books and clothes Dan
was completely uninterested in possessions. As a young man, indeed far
into middle age, he regarded the ownership of property as a menace to
personal freedom. On his Press salary, and once the post-war house
building boom had developed, he might easily have secured a mortgage
and purchased a house in the conventional English middle-class way, but

he never sought to do this. His instinct was for rented accommodation, and his instincts were served in one pragmatic way by taking a Press house. Not only was the rent low, but house maintenance was the responsibility of the landlord, and the Press, with numerous properties to maintain, had the staff for the job. In this way Dan's natural inability at technical subjects, so amply illustrated in his university entrance examinations, was extended to the practical.

Winnie used to say of 103 that the 1 was her Dan, the 0 was herself, and the 3 was for their three girls. It was a four-bedroom semi-detached house (an 'end-terrace') with a basement and three upper floors, and a bathroom on a mezzanine floor half-way up the stairs. From the back door of the basement a long narrow garden ran down to the bank of the Oxford canal, where, once the greater tumult of childhood was over, and the girls were in their teens, a pair of swans nested every spring and raised their cygnets. A hundred yards beyond the canal was the railway line. Beyond that lay Port Meadow, the great area of Oxford common land that avoided enclosure, and on which any citizen has the right to graze animals. Horses, ponies, and cows have grazed on Port Meadow since at least the Domesday Book survey, and still do today. The boundary on the far side of Port Meadow was the River Thames, with its tow-path walks north to the lock at Godstow and the bridge at Wolvercote. To the west was the Perch, a thatched inn, and to the north the Trout, a stone riverside pub, both with gardens as well as cosy bars and pub food.

Dan did not choose this setting for his house. It was what was available, and he took it unseen. But if you had to find in Oxford a setting that most nearly conformed to that of his Invercargill childhood, you would look no further. The kitchen door on to garden, canal, and countryside; the common land with its animals; the waterways with their wild life; the railway trains moving north and south along the tracks, steam and smoke drifting across the back garden, the house itself shaking gently at night with the passage of the trains. The house was little heated. They had a coal fire in the living-room in winter, but otherwise it duplicated Southland in this regard too: it was almost always cold. Everything here was familiar, and his nightmare was finally laid to rest.

A larger house could not have come along at a better time. Elizabeth's circumstances had not improved, and in December 1946 Dan at last obtained a work permit for her. She and Patty departed from Tel Aviv in January 1947 and came by boat to Liverpool, then south to Oxford by train. Winnie paid their fares with the last little bit of money set aside from the insurance payment from the fire in Otautau, money with which she had intended to buy a washing machine. Patty was just 3 years old. Elizabeth had not been in Europe for a decade, and she had never been to England before. She found it very strange. All the way south on the train it snowed. It was early February 1947, and they were to live with the Davins in Oxford for almost four years.

Whatever social difficulties might have been posed by these additions to the Davin ménage appear to have been dispersed by Patty. When they arrived, Winnie took her downstairs to look at a doll's house so that Dan and Elizabeth could have a few minutes together. It was four years since they had seen each other. Patty looked at the little toy house and said: 'Oh, que c'est formidable!' She spoke only French. Winnie reported herself 'instantly captivated'. Patty rapidly became a companion for the Davin daughters, though they did not know that she was their half-sister for many years. The love-affair between Dan and Elizabeth had died, but in the trial of these new circumstances they had the good sense to get along in a companionable way. She still wanted to paint, as she had in Palestine and in Cairo, and Dan tried initially to have her commissioned to design the jacket for his collection of short stories, *The Gorse Blooms Pale*, published in the autumn of 1947. Her various design proposals did not appeal much to Nicholson and Watson, however.

On another front, she had slightly more success. Dan and Winnie introduced her to a young New Zealand woman, Wendy Campbell-Purdie, who had turned up and settled in Oxford. Campbell-Purdie came from a wealthy Auckland family, the Williams, and was a woman whose independence of ideas and spirit matched her independence of means. She purchased a large house at 86 Woodstock Road and ran it as a combination of boarding-house, bohemian salon, and residential home for artists. One day she and Winnie, talking to their friend Gerald Wilde, indigent in London, were alarmed at his state—no coat, his shoes stuffed with paper, coughing, and with nowhere to stay—and suggested that he come down to Oxford, where he might paint in peace, and perhaps find patrons. Dan was always generous with money when he had any, and for a number of years in the late 1940s he helped Gerald with introductions and occasional cash. Dan and Winnie also collected his paintings, including the remarkable 'The Monster' and (one of Winnie's) 'By Grand Central Station I Sat Down and Wept'.[6] Wilde moved into Campbell-Purdie's house, where he met Elizabeth, and they became friends. Some thought them to be lovers for a while, though if this was true it must have been a difficult if not dangerous liaison, because Gerald's tastes were perverse, and his mind psychotic under drink. On several occasions Dan was called out late at night to restrain and settle Gerald, grown menacing in his cups. Despite, perhaps even because of the *frisson* of excitement generated by such tensions, Elizabeth enjoyed his company. They painted together, and Dan believed that at least one of Wilde's larger canvasses was actually completed jointly with Elizabeth.[7]

Campbell-Purdie was not always an easy woman either. She had an explosive temper, and once threw a cup of coffee over Dan for uttering a 'mistimed sincerity'.[8] After her mother died in Oxford in October 1949, she decided to take the ashes home to New Zealand, and invited Winnie to accompany her there on a winter voyage. Dan ruefully encouraged Winnie to go, and she was away from 30 November 1949 to 24 March 1950. After Winnie's return Wendy announced that of course it had always been understood that Winnie must pay for her own passage, though this was not how Dan and Winnie had understood the original invitation. Dan had to find £250 at short notice. There was some bitterness about this. Paddy Costello, whom Wendy visited in Paris in the early 1950s, thought her 'a bitch: a cool exploiter of her friends' good nature'.[9] But it was typical of both Dan and Winnie that whatever bitterness they felt was set aside, and the friendship, though strained for a time, was never broken.

The most difficult aspect of Elizabeth's arrival in their household, as Dan and Winnie saw it, was the danger of gossip in the University, and the harm that it might do to Dan's prospects. Joyce Cary used to refer to Oxford as 'the hotbed of cold feet'. Dan saw the University as a small-town society: very similar in many ways to his native Invercargill, though with wholly different *raisons d'être*.

In a small town there is no anonymity to protect you. Hungry for a morsel they watch you. If it is raw and bleeding, so much the better. Carnivores walk the main streets of the world. The newspapers are the restaurants where their prey is cooked and served.[10]

Later he wrote to Frank Sargeson: 'There are times when one finds Oxford has too much in common with what one least liked about N.Z.'[11]

Between them, Dan, Winnie, and Elizabeth agreed on the plausible fiction that Elizabeth was a Danish refugee whose husband had been killed in the war, and who was employed as their housekeeper. Elizabeth obscured her German origins, even from Winnie, and Dan remained ambivalent about them. Obscuring Patty's paternity ensured the whole family's common survival in the notoriously dangerous waters of Oxford

Senior Common Rooms and North Oxford drawing-rooms. These compromises with the truth may seem odd today, but the climate of convention in immediate post-war Britain makes them understandable at the time. In any event, whatever moral scruple may be felt by those at some historical remove from Dan's circumstances, Winnie supported him in this course of action. Elizabeth never did anything to disturb it. And its primary objective, to accept responsibility for Patty, and to offer her the same opportunities as they were able to offer their own daughters, was fully realized.

In this new setting of Southmoor Road with a suddenly expanded 'family' to cater for as well, Dan and Winnie kept a house of open invitation. Friends were always welcome, as were strays, the friends of friends in need of a feed or a bed. And when close friends came to stay, when Paddy Costello or Reggie Smith or Geoffrey Flavell and his wife Fan, or Richard Cobb were there for the weekend, then the talk and singing went on late into the night, and the children would hide behind the chairs and settees to listen, while the grown-ups pretended not to notice.

After sixteen years of constant movement, the nomadic life of the student, scholar, and soldier, Dan became a creature of routine in this new setting. A pet cat called Big Cat became a fixture, and a favourite of family and visitors alike for sixteen years. They also, and at different times, had kittens in the house. From Joy Zangwill, the wife of Oliver, the theoretical psychologist, they bought a schnauzer puppy which they called Kate. Kate died young following a spectacular accident, when she fell from the parapet of the chapel tower at Rycote, the famous English country estate where Elizabeth had once been held prisoner by Mary Tudor. Dan was bitterly upset about this death of a dog, and though they had other schnauzers, the next called Ngaio, and after her Kate II, she was never really replaced in his affections.

In the mornings Dan was up early, and as often as possible went for a run on Port Meadow, or, in the summer, a swim in the River Thames at Medley. It was Winnie who taught the children to swim, and once they were proficient, by the age of 7 or 8, they would sometimes go with him. Afterwards, in the bath, he would sing the Irish songs of his childhood. In the days when the children still needed to be taken to school, up until about 1952, Winnie was up early as well, and made breakfast for the whole family, during which Dan made a start on *The Times* crossword, a habit he retained for the rest of his life. At the weekends, once rationing was finished, Dan made bacon and eggs.

He was at the office by 9.00 a.m. for a day of business that lasted until 5.30 p.m., but almost always in these early years at the Press, he came home for lunch, also prepared by Winnie. Dan was a busy man, with several careers, but with three daughters to care for, the house to maintain, and all Dan's needs to look after, Winnie's life was the full and busy round of a devoted wife and mother. In those days everyone at the Press worked on Saturday mornings as well. At home in the evening there would be family dinner, radio programmes (Dan was avid for the Third Programme, and cultural topics in the Home Service of the BBC) and then, after reading for an hour or so, or stories for the children, he would go to his study to work. If there were visitors there might be an outing to the nearby Victoria Arms, and, after closing time, they might bring beer home by the jug.

OUP was situated then, as it is now, in Walton Street, facing across the road to the back of the Radcliffe Infirmary. The Press building is in Greek Revival style, Corinthian Classical, with a 'handsome Graeco-Roman façade', and behind that a square of substantial buildings around a grassed quadrangle. Designed by Robertson and Blore, it was finished in 1830.[12] Above the entrance is a clock tower, and immediately below this the Secretary's office. To the extreme right, overlooking Walton Street, were three smaller offices, and it was here that Dan first took up residence. In 1948 he moved one door along, into a room that had previously been Sisam's. To the rear of these rooms, steps led down to the Printer's library, and thence into the printing works. To one side, and down another short flight of steps, was the finance office. In his early years at the Press Dan also imagined what he called his 'escalier d'esprit'—a claudestine route into the street, and freedom.

Sisam wanted a protégé, and Dan was quick to see him as patron. Sisam was a big man in every respect, physically and morally, but ascetic and a little withdrawn, though capable of great warmth and generosity. Those who did not know him well could think him remote and eccentric. Those who worked for and with him knew him to be shy, but deeply loyal and honest, and with a fine, sharp, scholarly intelligence. He never took lunch, preferring a large mug of tea and a few dry biscuits in his office, when he would always leave the door ajar, open to anyone who wished to discuss problems with him. Though a publisher, he took little personal interest in books. He had only one bookcase in his holiday home in the Scilly Isles, to which he planned to retire in 1948, and it contained only Middle English texts and various learned works of philology. At 'Gatsden', his home on Boars Hill, he kept a substantial garden, and was a keen amateur naturalist. He rarely read novels, and he never kept private correspondence. 'I keep tidy by destroying everything, knowing no better way', he wrote. 'The prospect of reading old letters gives me a feeling of desolation.'[13] Unlike most Oxford men—there were very few women, even in 1945—he was almost entirely free of vanity, so that when he argued on some matter it was reasonable to presume that the matter, in itself, was important. He generally prevailed too, a fact which made his relations with John Johnson, Dr Johnson, the University Printer, difficult.

There was little surprise in this, as Dr Johnson's relations with the Press on the whole were notoriously sticky. Johnson was a classics scholar with a formidable knowledge of the history and technology of printing, and he ran the empire of his printing works with 'capricious and paranoic tyranny'.[14] He had fought Chapman, Sisam's predecessor, to a standstill, and conducted relations with the London branch publisher, Sir Humphrey Milford, much as a border laird would have conducted a family feud: with unremitting ferocity.[15] It was said that when one of his assistant printers, Vivian Ridler, married Milford's niece, Johnson found reasons for requiring him to resign, which he did.[16] Johnson's relations with Sisam were cold rather than hot. This was because Sisam usually won any argument, while bringing to it an enthusiasm for battle equal to Johnson's own. They were also united in their hatred of the Nazis. Unlike most people, Dan had placid relations with Johnson during the three years in which their careers overlapped, a fact which he ascribed to the benign although wholly independent influence of Denis Glover, a New Zealand printer and poet, who became a friend and pupil of Johnson during his wartime leave from the Royal Navy. Somehow Glover seems to have convinced him, in advance of Dan's arrival, and despite the contrary evidence of Sisam, that New Zealanders were harmless.[17]

OUP was a department of the University, and its executives belonged to Senior Common Rooms, and kept University terms. The relative freedom that they enjoyed as a result was balanced by the fact that they received salaries on a par with the dons, far smaller than they would have received in commercial publishing. Technically, it is true, Dan had just four weeks holiday a year, and not the great expanses of the University vacations, but in practice he had plentiful opportunities to pursue research, and keep abreast of literature and scholarship. Dan was initially appointed as an editor. He had much, indeed everything, to learn: about the editing of manuscripts and relations with authors; about book production and design; about business methods; and about the ways of a scholarly publishing house. Sisam took his education personally in hand, setting him to read in the files, the great repository of the history and methods of the Press. He also enacted a ritual every morning when, in the mail room, after the morning's letters had been opened and laid out on a butler's tray, he looked through them, and as he distributed them to each pigeon-hole, picked on a topic or two that might illuminate a particular problem or general principle 'as a text for a brief and pungent tutorial'.[18] These 'morning prayers', as Dan liked to call them in echo of his military days, he was to continue for the rest of his career.[19] Later in the day Sisam would go through the letters Dan had himself written, and the tutorial would resume. Dan later passed on the two central pillars of his mastery of the business letter: 'the object of all correspondence, if possible, [is] to prevent a reply'; and 'Every letter you write you should write with the recollection that that letter may some day have to be looked at by the Delegates or by a lawyer or by some impartial person, and he has got to be able to say to himself, "Well, my God, what a patient fellow Davin was!" '[20]

Sisam also set Dan to look after the Press's relations with various refugee scholars whom Sisam and other Oxford dons had brought from Germany and Italy. In this way he was reunited with Arnaldo Momigliano, whom he had known in pre-war Oxford, and who went eventually to a chair at UCL. And he also came to know Jacobsthal, the historian of Celtic art; the Greek historian Jacoby; Fraenkel, then working on his edition of Aeschylus; Pfeiffer, at work on Callimachus; and Maas, a medievalist, world renowned for textual criticism, but equally at home in Greek metre, and a formidable linguist. Dan recalled that 'their perfectionism and prolixity were a great trial', but their skill and dedication in the arts of scholarly conflict were an education in themselves. Dan's later famous tolerance for the querulous academic author has its roots in this international soil. Paul Maas was particularly influential. He was a man of spartan habits who rode a bike but never wore an overcoat, was notorious for his brevity, and refused to accept a salary of more than £100 a year. In the summer Dan would come across him on his pre-breakfast swim in the Thames at Medley 'floating serenely on his back'.[21]

The Press that Dan came to in 1945 was very different from what it is today, and since much of the transformation occurred during his publishing career, its evolution is central to his own biography. OUP was not a single business, but more a holding company with various businesses in its possession. The Oxford publishing business comprised the Clarendon Press, the scholarly publishing imprint; educational publishing, under the imprint Oxford University Press—then devoted mainly to school texts;

dictionaries and reference books, including the *DNB* and *OED*; the Bible publishing division; and the cartographic department.[22]

The printing business, though its premises were contiguous with the Oxford publishing business, was conducted quite independently.[23] It fulfilled all the University's printing requirements—the *Calendar*, *Gazette*, examination papers, university diary, and so forth; printed all the Clarendon Press books, and a high proportion of works for other divisions of the Press; and also took in work from other commercial clients. Apart from university printing, which it performed at a discount, all OUP work was carried out at commercial rates. Under a succession of printers, of whom Johnson was simply the most dictatorial, it established and maintained a quality of production that was widely recognized as almost without peer. As an apprentice publisher, Dan paid close attention to this.

If Charles Taylor, for example, who had joined the Press as a boy, and been a CSM in the 1914–18 War, and was now head of production, held a manuscript in his hands as if weighing both it and its quality[,] and asked in neutral tones whether it had to have the Clarendon Press imprint, you would be wise to think again . . . He wouldn't have read it—couldn't have—but his intuitions were to be respected.[24]

Beyond the printing works was the Bindery, also part of the Printer's domain.

In the village of Wolvercote, on the river a few miles to the north, was the paper-mill, also then wholly owned by the Press. Paper has been manufactured at Wolvercote since 1674, and the mill had belonged to OUP since 1872. Under a Controller, it operated as a separate business, supplying paper of many different qualities to OUP, but also contracting with other commercial clients.

In addition to this cluster of businesses in and around Oxford, the Press also owned the London business, in those days housed in Amen House, Warwick Square, just below St Paul's, and under the direction of 'the Publisher', Geoffrey Cumberlege during Dan's first decade at the Press. Under the imprint 'Oxford University Press, London' it published works in all fields of general trade publishing with the exceptions of new fiction and prose drama. The underlying principle of selection was quality—a work had to be worthy of the title of Oxford book—but at the same time it had to make a profit, as its main role was to finance the Oxford academic business. Unlike the CP, whose purpose was to publish scholarly works that might not show a return on investment—at least for many years—OUP London operated wholly as a commercial publisher. Its list included many popular series, such as the World's Classics and Oxford Standard Authors, and it developed successful reference works such as the *Oxford Dictionary of Quotations*, a substantial list of technical and medical works, and an outstanding business in music publishing.[25] In the educational field it published numerous works for developing countries, and during the 1950s it expanded into the fields of English language teaching materials with great success, and turned its children's books department, founded in 1907, into a flourishing business. In addition to publishing new books, the London business was responsible for the distribution of all Oxford publications, including Clarendon Press books and the Bible and other religious books, and for the management of the OUP warehouse at Neasden, which had been opened in 1933. It was also responsible for the conduct of OUP branches in Canada, Australia, Africa, India, and Asia, and acted, quite profitably, as agent for a number of foreign university press imprints in Britain.[26]

Unlike the other branches, the largest of them, OUP Inc. New York, was a direct responsibility of the Oxford business. It acted as distributor of all Press books throughout the United States, and also published on its own account a substantial list of original works, both for the academic and the general trade markets. Unlike OUP operations in Britain, it had expanded into the field of college textbooks—a fact which reflected the growth and character of the tertiary education sector in the United States compared with Britain.

All of this amounted to big business. For the financial year ended 31 March 1946, the English businesses made a profit before taxation of £280,000 on sales of £1,725,000. The US business contributed a further $267,000 on sales of $2,458,000.[27] The result reflected great credit on Sisam, Milford, and Johnson since it came at the end of a long world war in which publishing had been extremely difficult. Shortages of every kind of material, but in particular paper; lack of stock; the absence of skilled labour: these difficulties, common to all producers, had been aggravated in the case of OUP by its position as an academic publisher. It had been accomplished, moreover, with the most frugal of staffing. When Dan joined the Press the editorial staff of the Oxford business consisted of the Secretary plus two Assistant Secretaries—Sisam, Norrington, and Dan (who was promoted to Junior Assistant Secretary in 1946)—a couple of editors for science and education, and 'about six people in finance, two in production, one on publicity and jackets, two looking after stock and two looking after illustrations'.[28] Even eight years later, in 1953, by which time the Press had expanded greatly, and taken on numerous new projects, the CP staff still numbered only thirty-six.

Dan fitted well into this world of great books and close intellectual companionship. Later in life he was to attribute this to his experience in the war, specifically in the New Zealand Army, from which he transferred his feelings of loyalty. He saw in Sisam an inspirational leader worthy of his own commitment. This, at any rate, was his later explanation:

And so I settled to two identities: the residual sceptical outsider and the member of an organisation to which I felt myself dedicated, devoted even, in the old Roman sense. For the Clarendon Press was a very special place. The quality of what one produced was the ultimate criterion for oneself as a publisher just as it was for oneself as a writer. In so far as money mattered it was only as a means to the end of quality: a profit had to be made, and reasonable economic efficiency regarded, so that the unprofitable could be given its proper due. We did not work for shareholders: our shareholders were the cause. For that cause one worked, and not for oneself, except in a transcended sense; just as in the war we had given everything, and been prepared to give life itself, for a cause that was above us.[29]

These feelings can hardly have been instantaneous. For one thing, and as we have seen, they romanticize his actual feelings, at the time, about much of his military service. Nevertheless it remains true that Dan grew into the Press during his first few years there under Sisam's tutoring, so that it became not simply a place of work, but his spiritual home. As his apprenticeship advanced, Sisam expanded the areas of his publishing responsibilities, so that by the end of the 1940s Dan was responsible for ancient and modern history and philosophy, English language and literature, modern languages and literature, dictionaries and reference books, and various occasional miscellaneous projects. By the time the post-war problems of rationing and shortages had been overcome, the CP was publishing about 200 books a year, and of these Dan was personally responsible for approximately half. Yet despite this heavy work-load he was always available to give advice about other projects, whether at Oxford or in the London business, and even, though rather more rarely, in any of the overseas branches. There are few files in the Press archives that are not adorned by his elegant and pithy internal memos, which, in echo of the undergraduate journalist in Dunedin, he wrote on green paper. He was promoted to Assistant Secretary in 1948, when Norrington succeeded Sisam as Secretary. He became a director of the New York business in 1949, by which time his salary was £1,150 per annum.

The business into which Dan grew was growing itself. The modest expansion undertaken in the late 1920s and early 1930s was resumed in the post-war climate. There was much ground to be made up: many titles had gone out of stock, and were once more in great demand. There were projects to retrieve from wartime suspension, and new projects to be launched. New equipment was needed, for printing, paper-making, and the warehouses. New staff had to be found, new offices opened abroad. All these policy matters were overseen by the Delegacy. As a department of the University, the Press was governed, in lieu of a Board of Directors, by fourteen Delegates, all members of Convocation appointed (or delegated) by the University. They included the Vice-Chancellor, the two Proctors,[30] and the Assessor, plus ten other Delegates. The Vice-Chancellor served for a term of two years, and proctorial appointments revolve in a similar way, so the heart of OUP's governance fell to the ten appointed Delegates, one of whom also served as chairman of its all-important Finance Committee. This committee, like the Delegacy itself, was serviced by the Secretary of OUP—hence, indeed, his title, which in any other major business concern would surely have been that of Chief Executive and Managing Director.

Of the ten Delegates, five 'ordinary Delegates' were appointed by the Vice-Chancellor and Proctors for periods of seven years, and five 'perpetual Delegates' were selected by the Delegates themselves from among the ordinary Delegates. Perpetual Delegates served until death, resignation, or the age of 75. Hardly surprisingly, the Delegacy on Dan's appointment reflected the pre-war world. Sandy Lindsay, still Master of Balliol, had been a Delegate since 1937. Another Balliol don, Cyril Bailey, a classical scholar, was a Delegate from 1920 to 1946. 'His life was devoted to his edition of Lucretius . . . one of the last of those works where a passionate and turbulent Roman emerges somehow as an upper-class Englishman who, in more favourable circumstances, might have been an anglican.'[31] Another Cyril (later Sir Cyril) Hinshelwood, scientist and linguist, with his 'inscrutable smile, faintly oriental,' had been appointed to the Delegacy in 1934, and served for thirty-three years, until 1967. W. D. (Sir David) Ross, a moral philosopher, and by this time Provost of Oriel, served almost as long as Hinshelwood, from 1922 to 1952. A humane man who had published a volume of moral philosophy called *The Right and the Good*, he was an 'indefatigable Aristotelian' though 'defective in humour'.[32] J. H. Wyllie, a Latin lexicographer at the Press, wrote in a satirical epic that once had some currency in Oxford circles: 'Sir David Ross can make a joke | And elephants can dance.' His solemn imperturbability was illustrated for Dan in tragic circumstances in 1948, when the Vice-Chancellor of the University, Stallybrass, fell from a London train and was killed.[33] The Press had for a long time planned to hold a dinner the following Monday to mark Sisam's retirement. Ross, chairman of the Finance Committee, host for the dinner in his own college, had surely to be consulted about the possibility of cancellation as a mark of respect. Norrington rang him, egged on by Dan, as they could not decide what to do, and asked whether he had heard the news. 'News? What news?' 'About Stallybrass. His accident.' 'Ah yes, that. Tragic business.' Pause. 'Davin and I wondered what we should do.' 'Do?' 'Yes. About the dinner.' There was another pause. 'Ah', said Ross at last. 'I see what you mean. An empty place at table: whom should we ask instead?'

The business and financial affairs of the Press were the province of its Finance Committee, then chaired by Ross. The principle task of the full Delegates' meetings, then as now, was to assess proposals for new CP books.[34] At their regular Friday afternoon meetings the Secretary and the Assistant Secretaries presented them with the pros and cons of any proposal, along with the substance of their advisers' reports, and an assessment of the investment required, likely size of the loss, if any, and such other matters of general principle as might be involved.[35] The Secretary had to avoid advocacy, though he might be called upon to give a personal opinion. Dan found that 'the Delegates were . . . the best committee with which I have ever had to deal—expeditious, each of them with a strong sense of relevance and concision, constructive in approach and admirably just'.[36]

This did not mean that there were no strains or tensions, however. Neither Ross nor Lindsay, for instance, had any time for new trends in philosophy, such as logical positivism, and their opposition made it difficult for the Press, at least for a while, to develop the philosophy list with new names and younger authors. This position was not improved by the fact that Sisam, brilliant and inexorable in argument, had often defeated such Oxford luminaries as Lindsay or Maurice Bowra. Victory is not easily forgiven among academics, least of all in Oxford Senior Common Rooms, so that Sisam had enemies as well as friends. In some quarters it did not do to be thought too closely associated with Sisam.

In this environment, Dan rapidly learned the etiquette of Oxford publishing politics. The commissioning editor, having taken advice on a proposal or a manuscript, could only advise an author of its likely fate, not offer or refuse a contract. Only the Delegates could do that. This was a useful device, not generally available to publishers. Over the years Dan became a master of both the gracious rejection letter, praising while regretting, and explaining the Delegates' view; and the acceptance letter, congratulating, referring to the concurrence of the Delegates with his own judgement of the book's merits, and all as though this had nothing whatsoever to do with his own powers of advocacy. More important than this, however, he learned the personal arts of the publishing impresario: to trawl extensively for contacts, to find ways of hearing academic gossip about who was doing what research, and how fruitfully. Gregarious and agreeable, Dan developed his friendships with academics in Oxford and then throughout the United Kingdom. Like Chapman before him— though not like Sisam, whose one weakness as a publisher was his retiring nature—Dan made a point of dining in colleges so that he could gather intelligence from the academic front of high table.

As his training advanced he visited universities more widely, first in London and Cambridge, then in Nottingham, Manchester, Leeds, Bristol, Exeter, and Edinburgh. At the beginning of June 1949, he made the first of many post-war visits to Ireland, going first to Queen's University in Belfast, then University and Trinity Colleges in Dublin.[37] Winnie went with him, and they travelled by car, driven by Wendy Campbell-Purdie, so that this was also partly holiday. From March to May 1952 Dan visited the New York business for the first time, travelling rather grandly, as Press Assistant Secretaries did, on the 'Queen Mary'.[38] In New York he learned about the business, met Press executives, and built contacts among east-coast academics. Here he was reunited with his old American friends, and went down to Princeton with Gordon Craig. 'A wonderful reunion which affected me with nostalgia for days.'[39] On these journeys, both in Britain and abroad, Dan laid the foundations of career-long relationships with many of the scholars of the age, relationships which were to foster many of the great works of scholarship published by the Press over the next half century. And on a more personal level, his relentless travelling also ensured that he became an archive, for the most part closed, of academic gossip, scandal, and intrigue.

When Dan came to Oxford he thought of himself as a writer going into publishing. Sisam recognized the importance of this self-image, and did everything he could to encourage it. Dan had put the summer of 1945 to good use, and when he arrived in Oxford his war novel was nearly finished. By the end of October he was typing it up, and before the end of the year David Higham, who had taken over from Nancy Pearn as Dan's agent, had shown the work to Nicholson and Watson. Early in the new year they offered him remarkably good terms: an advance of £150 on signing the contract, 15 per cent of the retail price on the first 5,000 and 20 per cent thereafter. Dan's editor at Nick and Wat was Dorothy Santer, and she originally intended that *For The Rest of Our Lives* should be published in November 1946. Post-war shortages, production difficulties and error slowed it down, however, and he did not have the galley proofs until late August, or the page proofs until mid-November.[40] In the end publication was delayed until Tuesday, 27 May 1947, when it appeared in an edition of 5,000 copies.

Dan had projected *For The Rest of Our Lives* as a novel of love, war, and ideas. In the event, he was deeply influenced during the period of its composition by his friendships with Julian Maclaren-Ross and Dylan Thomas, both then employed in the London film industry. For a while in 1945 Dan had hopes that *Cliffs of Fall* would be made into a film, and he had similar hopes for his war novel.[41] Its action follows the main current of his experience in Cairo and the western desert, though with important modifications and frequent diversions along tributaries of confluent events. The three main characters, Frank Fahey, Tony Brandon, and Tom O'Dwyer, are based heavily on Davin, Cox, and Costello, but with their features scrambled. Tom O'Dwyer, the Costello of the piece in his orthodox Marxism, has Davin's broken nose, and had worked, like Dan, on the wharf at Bluff. Tony Brandon, a Cox in his social democratic insistence on the importance of individual judgement, is a veteran of the Spanish Civil War—in which both Davin and Costello wished they had fought, and where Cox was actually a war correspondent—and has a streak of the impulsive heroism which all three hoped they would have if it ever came to the test. His mistress in Cairo is a Russian *émigrée*—which was Costello's fate, never Cox's.

Frank Fahey, the character most like Davin himself, is an intellectual and linguist. After being wounded in Crete he is now employed at GHQ Intelligence in Cairo, where he watches, with cynicism and sardonic humour, the foibles, weakness, and wickedness of a world on the brink of dissolution. He is drawn to the Communism of O'Dwyer, whom he admires deeply, but is saved from it by his sense of despair, of the constant presence of death in life, and of the futility (he is reading Gerhardi) of all belief. After various empty affairs, he falls in love with Lucile Scott, the daughter of a wealthy anti-Semitic capitalist and his painter wife Blanche—a pastiche of Amy Smart, with her hooded eyes and sharp intelligence. Lucile wants to break away from her parents' world, but her love for Frank is doomed by his cynicism, and his belief that love inevitably fades to habit. When he returns to the front as Divisional Intelligence Officer, she finds someone else, and their love is broken.

The novel has almost no beginning—' "And that is the end of the news" ' are its opening words—and no end either in the sense that the events described are cast on the final page, where the soldier dances with the prostitute, as the sum of experience to last a lifetime. In its appearance of shapelessness, in the episodic character of its seventy-six short chapters, or scenes, Dan sought to capture the essence of experience—the sense that there is a pattern to what happens in life that gives to experience its organized though directionless quality—and in doing so to marry the model of film to that of novel. Each brief episode is piled on the ones before much in the manner of a film 'treatment', and through the use of flashback, the roving eye or camera of internal monologue, brief, sharp descriptions of battle, love scenes, scenes of argument and disagreement, comradeship and humour, smut, bawdy and sentiment, the whole creation comes together like a feature film. Though long, it is best read at a sitting, and one still comes away from it, fifty years after it was written, as one might leave a cinema: the mind's eye full of images, the ear of snatches of dialogue, and the mind itself more alive to sensation. As with film, the best is in the scenes of action, whether on the battlefield or the bed. But like a film, some of the feelings of satisfaction that it evokes fade rapidly.

The three main characters are too alike. Even when they disagree and argue, there is little of substance between them. When each internalizes his view of the world, reflects on it, criticizes it, there is no difference in the voice that we hear: each is a Davin voice. They all struggle with commitment in love, they all hold that capitalism is defunct, they all admire Republican Spain and Communist Russia, they all propose a socialist analysis of the human predicament and the motions of history. Each is a hypercritical man, quick to condemn, wary of feeling lest it be inauthentic, hostile to sentiment as the enemy of analysis. When they discuss topics of weight, they lecture. When they are alone they are morose. Except for the battle scenes, in action and in the company of other men, each is the observant, detached eye, never the participant. Even in bed, making love, the mind is at work, critical, taking away from sensation its moment of passionate interdependence.

Despite these drawbacks, the book is absorbing and persuasive. The battle scenes at Bel Hamed, Minqar Qaim, Ruweisat, El Mreir, and Alamein, each based on accounts that Dan picked up soon after the event in mess bars and convoy rides, are brilliantly done, evoking the excitement and the terror of mechanized warfare, yet remaining truthful to what we know of the things that happen at the forward edge of battle areas. Since Dan participated in only the last of these engagements, and that in a capacity somewhat removed from the infantry action described in the novel, these passages are testimony to both the power of his imagination and his meticulous attention to detail.[42]

Similarly well done, though in another sphere, is the novel's humour. Gina, an aging courtesan, sits opposite Frank, so that 'when she bent forward to sip her coffee, she was best placed for him to glimpse the opulence with which time and pastry had compensated her for the slenderness they had taken'.[43] 'A poet came out on to the balcony with a pair of binoculars. He seemed tight. But the source of intoxication with poets is often difficult to detect.'[44] 'The human soul was the only Black Forest that remained and even here the analyst's axe was busy with the trees.'[45] In a hospital bed at the New Year, Frank dreams of a God cast as army officer and city gent, and the comic exchange between them has the rare quality of true satire.

As with *Cliffs of Fall*, Dan is not in awe of the task he had set himself. The prose is confident, and the author makes no concessions either to convention or to markets. Soldiers swear as soldiers will (though less, and less savagely than they actually did); men have mistresses and go to brothels—one whole scene, chapter 37, is set in a brothel, where Frank observes the recruitment of a new courtesan; and the soldiers drink and argue and fight in a way which, though perhaps common knowledge to an audience today, offended against the prim sense of wartime chivalry that had in some measure been preserved then, at least in the remote dominion of New Zealand, and among the officer class in Britain.

The novel's reception reflected these attitudes, though its structural origins in the world of film escaped detection. Pamela Hansford Johnson, writing in *John O'London's Weekly*, thought it a notable advance on *Cliffs of Fall*, but advised the author to plan his novels rather more. None the less, she thought the dialogue 'excellent. His ear is peculiarly sharp, and he records the casual speech of intimate life without exaggeration and without reducing it to boringness.'[46] L. P. Hartley, reviewing it on BBC Radio, described the ingredients—'Battle, sex, drink, argument, soldiers' "shop", reportage, sensations and impressions'—as making 'an unforgettable assault on the nerves of the mind . . . [T]o criticise the book . . . for incompleteness of vision is to criticise war itself.'[47] Walter Allen, writing in the *New Statesman & Nation* a week later, observed: 'One is aware in reading that one is in the presence of a new kind of mind, which fascinates and also repels; it is as though Macaulay's New Zealander has at last arrived, and his attitude to the ruins of London is ambivalent.'[48] In *Tribune* Erik de Mauny, a New Zealander who had served in the Div., described it as 'a long, sprawling narrative . . . part fiction . . . part history', and thought it captured in its language, 'the vitality of the New Zealand fighting man'.[49]

Reviewers in New Zealand were far less generous. Dan's home newspaper, the Southland *Times*, described his talent as still immature, and condemned the work as too detailed, its characters ill-defined, its profanity boring.[50] The reviewer for the New Zealand Returned Servicemen's Association roundly criticized the book's pro-Russian sympathies, the sex scenes—which he thought lowered the tone—and the intellectual discussions—which presumably raised it too high. He doubted whether Dan wrote the book 'to please his readers' and confessed that its 'all-pervading scepticism' left him 'with a slight hangover'.[51] Arthur Sewell contrived that most satisfactory of New Zealand responses: to condemn both the work and its countrymen simultaneously. He considered the epic scale of *For the Rest of Our Lives* too grand for its New Zealand characters. To capture the essence of the New Zealand voice 'we have to look at writing less wide in range and perhaps inferior in power'.[52] John Reece Cole, writing in the *Southern Cross*, though he praised the book in some specifics, thought it too hastily written, 'insensitive to language' with 'lazy verbal flourishes'. He thought the love scenes 'shabby nihilism' and compared Davin unfavourably with John Mulgan, who 'managed to subordinate his ego to the development of his craft'.[53] At greater length, and with a nicely modulated appearance of dispassionate judgement, Lawrence Baigent, a pacifist and a lecturer at Canterbury College, assassinated the author's intentions as well as his accomplishments in the review pages of the fledgling quarterly *Landfall*.[54] 'There is no plot; there is no tension, and in the absence of plot one is led to conclude that he intends the interest to centre round the presentation of three principal characters . . .' 'Philosophically the novel is curiously immature. There is an undergraduate flavour about the banal political and ethical discussions in which the book abounds.' Baigent quoted André Gide with approval as evidence of Davin's lack of aesthetic purpose.

This review aroused some controversy, with lines of New Zealand literary battle quickly drawn.[55] In general, it seemed that those who had served in the Middle East liked the book, while those who had not, did not. Certainly two military men gave it more generous reviews. In the *Otago Daily Times*, David Buchanan, though deploring some scenes, and the fact that many of the characters were identifiable, none the less found 'the characterisation . . . convincing, the descriptions vivid, the insight penetrating'. And this view was amplified by Howard Kippenberger's review of the novel in the *New Zealand Listener*.[56] Though he disapproved of some of the Cairo material Kippenberger still thought it 'most cleverly done', and his delight in the battle scenes was unrestrained: 'all are without fault . . . there is no mistake or slip in idiom or fault in atmosphere.'[57]

What Dan took from these reviews was that reviewers could be relied upon to be true to type. None more so than Olivia Manning, who reviewed it in acid for *Our Time*.[58] 'His novel reads like a conscientiously kept day-to-day diary', she wrote. The characters were 'crude, shadowy and seem to be seen, not with the dispassion of the artist, but in the light of an old grudge.'

On publication the book had a curious history. In New Zealand the Customs Department put it on their monthly list, which was circulated in confidence to the Library Association and the Booksellers' Association. The books and magazines listed were not prohibited from entry into the country, but might become the subject of prosecution for obscenity. Dan considered this 'a cowardly device designed to achieve the effect of censorship without incurring the odium and publicity that would be caused by it'.[59] He tried to mobilize opinion against this censorship, but got only a patchy response. Brasch at *Landfall* and Roy Parsons, then New Zealand's premier bookseller, both shared his anger, and tried to help.[60] So did Kippenberger, who urged him to take on the Minister, Walter Nash, who 'has already made himself silly' on censorship matters.[61] Curiously, however, both John Reece Cole, then a member of the Library Association, and Frank Sargeson, then establishing himself as New Zealand's leading writer, remained aloof, and counselled caution. 'Frankly I'm not surprised your book is on the customs list', Sargeson wrote. '[T]hese things have been going on for years . . . Unless there are copies available for importing I should be against making a stink . . . [M]y view is that raising a fuss only attracts more attention from more busybodies . . .'[62]

By the time these positions were taken the book had sold out. All 5,000 copies were gone within a year of publication, and Nicholson and Watson had no plans for a second printing.[63] Dan earned £300 in royalties, all paid in advance in 1946 and 1947, thus substantially increasing his income at a time of great domestic need—when his expanded family required furniture and clothes, and there were two extra mouths to feed. Those who accused him of writing too rapidly could know nothing of these pressures.

With his income from writing, Dan had had to get an accountant, and through the advice, astonishingly, of Julian Maclaren-Ross, and less surprisingly of David Higham, he went to the City firm of Charles Wakeling & Co., where a man called Gerard Kealey specialized in the tax problems of writers. He remained Dan's loyal and helpful accountant for the next thirty years.

In one other regard *For The Rest of Our Lives* was an indicator of things to come. In June 1947, on the strength of a review, the Swedish publishers Hoekerberg made an offer for a Swedish edition. Two months later, when they had read the book, they withdrew it on the grounds of the novel's pro-Communist sympathies.[64] Four months later the Czech publishing house Náše Vojsko made an offer for a Czech edition, but withdrew it in June 1949 because their government would not give them a permit to publish—presumably on the grounds that the novel was not sufficiently pro-Communist.[65] Dan's cynicism was endorsed, but these early cold-war clouds were warning of more serious storms of personal vendetta to come.

On a more personal level, the work brought endorsement from New Zealand that tied him more closely to his country. Both Freyberg and Kippenberger wrote privately to congratulate him,[66] and so too did Frank Sargeson. The scribe of Takapuna was brief but enthusiastic. He had become, he wrote, Davin's 'devoted reader',[67] and with this letter they started a correspondence that lasted for a quarter of a century. It is hard to think of two men more different. Sargeson was a homosexual and intensely private. He lived almost entirely for his writing, which he produced slowly. He rarely travelled, and devoted himself to the project of being above all a New Zealand writer. His influence on the literature of his own country was enormous, partly because of his work, but also because he cultivated younger writers, protected them, defended them, gave them his support and trust. Under his patronage many of them flourished. Writers such as Janet Frame, C. K. Stead, and Maurice Duggan owed him much. This was a deliberate part of his project. One senses from his correspondence with Davin (like many of Dan's Oxford contemporaries he preferred the surname) that he regretted Dan's distance and independence. The control he normally sought was out of his reach. Dan happily grasped at the compliment of Sargeson's opening a correspondence and unhesitatingly responded as an equal, which may not have been quite what Sargeson intended.

Nor was it really true, though 1947 was the year in which Dan's literary career showed its greatest promise. While he was still writing *For The*

Rest of Our Lives, and on the strength of the commercial success of *Cliffs of Fall*, Nicholson and Watson had agreed to publish a collection of his short stories, *The Gorse Blooms Pale*, with its title taken from his poem 'Knowledge'. The agreement was signed at the end of August 1945, and early in the new year of 1946 Dan settled, with Winnie's help, to the task of ordering and editing the material. Of the twenty-six stories that he selected for the book, three were written in 1939 before the war started, and four in 1946 after it had finished. The great majority were written in Cairo in 1942, or in Sarafand in the spring of 1943, or during his autumn leave in Britain the same year. Arranged in a chronological order that follows his own experience, the first eight stories deal with childhood and family life in Southland, the next seven with episodes from student life in Dunedin and Oxford, and the last eleven with wartime. Of the later ones, 'Mortal', 'The General and the Nightingale', and 'Not Substantial Things' show the influence of Maclaren-Ross, who persuaded Dan that many of his war anecdotes were almost perfect short stories, provided that he could find the appropriate authorial voice in which to tell them.[68] Dan's taste for experiment led him to attempt stories in the vernacular, aiming to capture the rhythms, cadence, syntax, and vocabulary of the ordinary New Zealander. In 'The General and the Nightingale'—the story of Freyberg's test of his subordinates' courage through attention to bird-song on the 'inferno track' near Cassino—the raconteur is the driver, a simple private soldier whose presence behind the wheel is almost invisible to his superiors, and whose subordinate rank enables a more vigorous criticism of the officer class to be heard.

Just as, in the stories of childhood, Dan captured the tone and cadence of Irish New Zealand voices in 1930s Southland, so in the later war stories he established himself as the voice of the ordinary New Zealand soldier in the Second World War. These were roles that he practised and relished for the rest of his writing career.

Despite the fact that some of the stories in this collection, particularly those dealing with student life, are unsuccessful, the book none the less has a unifying shape in the growth and development of the writer projected in the various voices. This unity is emphasized in the dominant theme, which is one of loss: the loss of an arcadian world of childhood, itself captured in the title of the collection and the poem from which it came; in the physical and emotional losses of death; and in the political and psychological losses that accompany a growing pessimism about human motivation, and a deepening depression about life and its purpose. There is a light touch to some of the stories, but overall the matter and the impression that they leave are sombre.

The final selection was complete by the end of September 1946, and the book published a little over a year later, at the end of November 1947, just six months after *For The Rest of Our Lives*. It was well received in Britain, where the 'shy, secret, pervasive tenderness'[69] of the early childhood stories was contrasted with the war tales, which 'are as good as anything the war has produced',[70] and secured for him another good notice from Pamela Hansford Johnson in *John O'London's Weekly*.[71] New Zealand remained harder to satisfy. The anonymous reviewer in the *New Zealand Listener* thought only 'about a dozen' of the stories to be 'stories in the accepted sense. The others are sketches and character studies with action, sometimes exciting and sometimes not, thrown in from the outside.'[72] The tone of superiority in matters technical (we know what a story is 'in the accepted sense') and the effect of the word 'thrown', with its implication of careless composition, capture very well the note of rejection that New Zealand practises on expatriate talent. It did much to endorse both Dan's sense of exile, and his preference for it. This was also endorsed by the letters of congratulation that came in, and by the additional money it brought. Of the edition of 3,000 copies, almost a half were sold by the end of the year, even before Australian and New Zealand orders had arrived.

With his war novel and his collection of stories finished towards the end of 1946, though before either had been published, Sisam suggested that Dan take up a pre-war project that had been left incomplete by John Mulgan, his predecessor at the Press: to produce a new and updated edition of Emile Legouis's *A Short History of English Literature*, a scholarly textbook survey designed for sixth-form use.[73] Dan suspected that Mulgan's effort at the chore was marred by boredom, and he rewrote substantial parts of what had been done.[74] He then added a whole new final chapter, 'From 1880 to the Present Day', which constitues a quarter of the complete book, appended a list of important dates, and prepared a new index. The work took up all his spare time in the winter of 1946–7, for well read as he already was, there was still much to cover. But by May 1947 he was able to write the new preface, in which he defended his selection of the novelists discussed in the final chapter as 'those who have influenced the novel towards change [rather] than those who have excelled in the form as already accepted'. He hoped for 'the indulgence of all those who realise that the discussion of contemporary literature is valuable rather for the criticism it challenges than for any dogmatic judgements it may try to impose.' True to his private perception of what Sisam had in mind with the book, Dan asserted that the work was really Mulgan's, and that he had merely put it into order for publication. John Mulgan and D. M. Davin, *An Introduction to English Literature*, was published by the Clarendon Press in October 1947.

Mulgan's ghost also appeared on another feature of the literary landscape. Shortly before his suicide in Cairo on 28 April 1945, he had sent a manuscript to his wife in New Zealand. She sent it in turn to Mulgan's old friend Jack Bennett, another New Zealand Rhodes scholar of the 1930s, and now a tutor in English at Oxford. Dan and Bennett were brought together by Sisam in 1946, and became good friends, a friendship that lasted until Bennett's sudden death in 1981. It began when they worked together to edit Mulgan's manuscript, which OUP published in 1947 under the title *Report on Experience*.

The work is unusual in the canon of English literature. The French would call it a *document*: a work of reflection and social criticism that is part autobiography, part political discourse. It established Mulgan's reputation as the Camus of New Zealand writing: trapped between the countries of his birth and adoption; between the worlds of action and reflection, the abstractions of philosophy and the realism of fiction; uneasy with his conscience; too conscious of human frailty for the comforts of belief. *Report on Experience* has 'the poetry of enigmatic passages in an unfinished or mutilated manuscript', which Powell attributed to 'the potential biographies of those who die young',[75] and it had a deep, though ill-defined impact on Dan, like walking in earnest conversation with someone whom you feel you know intimately, yet have no recollection of ever having met.

Once Mulgan's posthumous book was off his hands, Dan was at work in his spare time between May and July 1947 editing another, though very different, New Zealand book. This was *Infantry Brigadier*, the war memoirs of Howard Kippenberger, with whom Dan had played chess in the Café the night before Kip lost both his feet from an anti-personnel mine at Cassino.[76] Kippenberger recuperated from his wounds in England in 1944, and remained there in charge of the repatriation of New Zealand returned prisoners of war throughout 1945. Dan saw him occasionally during this time, encouraged him in the project of writing his war memoirs, and helped him, through Higham and, later, Cumberlege, to get them published. *Infantry Brigadier* is one of the very best books to come out of the war: it combines autobiography and reportage with deceptive simplicity, offering a portrait of men at war, their sympathies and sufferings, that is almost without parallel. Dan's work as its editor, unmentioned and unknown to all except themselves, Higham, and Cumberlege at OUP in London, is at least in part responsible for the book's considerable merits.[77] *Infantry Brigadier* went straight into a second printing in 1949, the year it was published.

This was an important time in Dan's life for another and more personal reason. In the late summer of 1947 his mentor Walter Allen introduced him to the novelist Joyce Cary.[78] Dan and Winnie knew a little of Cary's work already, having heard about him from C. K. Allen in 1940. (He and Cary were fellow air raid wardens for a time.) When they eventually met him at his house for dinner on 30 August it is not too extravagant to say that they fell under his spell, and for the next ten years he occupied a position of great importance in their lives. Cary lived at 12 Parks Road in Oxford, where he worked at his writing with a deliberate and professional dedication that Dan and Winnie much admired. He was a serious man, quiet in manner, very entertaining in conversation (always an important consideration with the Davins), widely experienced yet humble, modest, generous, and shy. In many ways he was not like Dan at all. He never went in pubs, for instance. He was gregarious, however, loving company and talk. Every Sunday night he gave a little party at his home, with good wine to drink. Twenty-five years older than Dan, he had trained as a painter and was an excellent draughtsman, a skill he brought to the design and execution of his novels. He had worked for many years in colonial administration in Africa, and had a keen understanding of both bureaucratic politics and political theory. When he and Dan first became friends Cary's work, though widely admired, had only recently started to enjoy commercial success. The popularity of his novel *The Horse's Mouth*, published in 1944, changed his circumstances though not his character.

Not very long after they had met, and while Winnie was away in New Zealand in the winter of 1949–50, Cary's wife Trudy died. Dan, lonely without Winnie, and Joyce, grieving for Trudy to whom he had been devoted, spent a lot of time together, and became close. When Winnie returned she entered into the friendship too, but on her own and independent terms, and in due course so did each of the children. Cary had four sons, all grown up by this time, but no daughters, and he 'adopted' Anna, Delia, and Brigid as additional 'honorary' godchildren. In this way began eight happy years of friendship with this remarkable man for each of the Davins. Like Dan and Winnie themselves he had an extraordinary capacity for friendship, and brought to each of them a sensitive awareness of their particular and individual needs. He became a frequent visitor to

Southmoor Road, often on a Wednesday after school, when he would have tea and tell the children another episode in the long serial story that he composed especially for them. As the children grew up he took them to the St Giles' fair every September, and included the Davins in his own family's Boxing Day outing to the pantomime. Afterwards they would go back to Parks Road for tea. Dan and Winnie always saw in the New Year with him at his home.[79] From 1950 onwards, to have a sense of the Davins' domestic life, the personality and lively grace of Joyce Cary must be imagined, ever-present, foreground and background, to their activities.

This friendship, and another with Enid Starkie, the French tutor and fellow of Somerville, illustrate different sides of Dan's character. If Cary was a father figure to him, Starkie was a reminder of the bohemian. 'In Oxford . . . she exemplified that local rule by which the eccentric if persisted in becomes licenced, and indeed accepted. Unlike most eccentrics, however, Enid Starkie could transcend the tolerance that attempts by assimilation to anaesthetise . . .'[80] She had a mercurial mind and temperament, and was as keen a drinker as Dan. For many years she presided over the Somerville cellar, and permitted Dan, in common with Joyce Cary, to purchase from its reserves. She also enjoyed pub life, and together with Dan instituted a regular gathering at lunchtime on Saturdays at the Lamb and Flag in St Giles'. Dan would go there from the Press and be joined by Winnie and Elizabeth, Enid, Gervase Mathew (Dan's Dominican friend from 1930s Oxford), Audrey Beecham, Gerald Wilde, Richard Cobb (now dividing his time between various archives in France, so only an occasional visitor to Oxford), and such other friends and acquaintances, old pals from the war, or visitors from New Zealand as might turn up. Audrey Beecham, who had been heiress to a pharmaceutical fortune until her father lost all the money, had studied in Paris in the 1930s (where she knew Lawrence Durell), and was herself a published poet. Rather surprisingly, she had been engaged for a while to Maurice Bowra, a liaison too difficult to sustain. For a while in the late 1940s and early 1950s she lived close to A. J. P. and Margaret Taylor, and was privy to some details of Margaret Taylor's awkward relationship with Dylan Thomas, whom she had known earlier, and independently. A big, robust woman, rather in the manner of a John Betjeman tennis player, she occasionally challenged Dan to a bout of Cumberland wrestling. The Lamb and Flag gathering was an institution, and ran well into the mid-1950s. It was of such importance in Enid Starkie's life that she would write Dan a note of regret if she was unable to attend.

Very occasionally, the gathering included Dan's older brother Tom. Deliberately and tirelessly he had climbed the bureaucratic ladder in the New Zealand capital, Wellington, then won a transfer in 1945 to the newly founded Department of External Affairs—which grew into the New Zealand diplomatic service. At the end of March 1947 he visited Southmoor Road for the weekend during a flying visit to a conference in London, and he returned to London a year later to serve at the New Zealand High Commission. He and his wife Adelina, and their only child Antonia, moved into a flat in Frognal, in Hampstead, where they stayed until Tom was posted to Paris in September 1949. The differences between him and Dan had not diminished in the separations of time, however. Delia recalled how, during one of his visits to Oxford, her Uncle Tom and Dan went into the garden together to re-hang the children's swing on the apple trees. Within minutes Tom was arguing about how it should be done. She had never seen anyone stand up to Dan before. Delia was a little in awe of her father, and this sight of stubborn Tom telling Dan how things should be done had the character of revelation.

Some of the old friends who turned up in Oxford could hardly have been more different. These were members of the infinitely amusing but disreputable crowd from Fitzrovia. Dylan Thomas and his wife Caitlin were frequent visitors. Winnie would install them in the front bedroom at the top of the house, where they wore Dan's old rugby jerseys to go to bed, and the morning air was thick with Dylan's terrible groans, only dispelled by large servings of Winnie's oyster fritters, a Southland speciality which he craved. In his diary Dan referred to the Thomases as 'the DTs'. Sometimes Julian Maclaren-Ross arrived, and Dan would join the line of those keeping him afloat with money. Sometimes it was John Davenport, a BBC producer and notorious Fitzrovian who had once been a professional wrestler in California, and was an excellent pianist. After a few drinks he could become irascible, and was sacked from the Garrick Club in London for hoisting an MP on to a very high mantelpiece from which he found it impossible to climb down. Davenport's rudeness in Oxford on one occasion made Dan fear that he was angling for a fight, but he was saved from this gruesome prospect by Winnie, who breezed into the pub, summed up the situation, and said 'John, why are you being so offensive to everyone?' which silenced him nicely. Friendship with these improbable but fascinating characters, as this anecdote implies, owed as much to Winnie's character as to Dan's.

The linkage between Oxford, Fitzrovia, and the BBC was important to Dan at this time. He was perennially hard up, and any extra money that he could persuade to come his way was more than welcome. The BBC had a strong commitment to cultural programming, and so was one place where writers, musicians, and artists could earn a little money.[81] Dan was no stranger to radio broadcasting. He had given a talk for the BBC Pacific service in September 1944 on 'New Zealanders in Italy'—a talk which had been keenly listened to, despite the atrocious reception, in his home country. And in the spring of 1946 he both wrote and performed in a 15-minute programme about New Zealand for the schools broadcasts of the BBC Home Service. Greater opportunities presented themselves a year later, however, through the historian Alan Bullock. Dan had come to know Bullock well through the Press, where in collaboration with F. W. Deakin they were preparing the series of the Oxford History of Modern Europe. Bullock, who was then a fellow of New College, was a forceful character. David Cecil, when asked one evening at Joyce Cary's dinner table what Bullock was like, replied: 'Oh he has so much energy. He does make one feel rather like china in a bull shop.' Bullock admired a similar energy and tirelessness in Davin. One day, at the BBC, he recommended Dan to a talks producer called Anna Kallin, and through her Dan began to contribute talks about books and literary topics to both the Third Programme and the Home Service. In the six years from 1947 to 1953 he contributed several items a year on such topics as James Joyce, Tolstoy, the Catholic novelists Evelyn Waugh and Graham Greene, and the novels of Joyce Cary. He also wrote for schools broadcasts, contributing on aspects of New Zealand life, such as sheep farming on the Canterbury Plains, though his account of it sounds like Southland to anyone who knows both. Hardly surprising, since Dan had then never been to Canterbury.

One circle of literary life is linked to another, and through his connections at the BBC Dan found himself sought after as a reviewer for the *New Statesman* and, in due course, the *Times Literary Supplement*. Two long pieces of his, surveys of new developments in New Zealand fiction, appeared in the *TLS* in the August of both 1951 and 1952. In 1951 he edited the New Zealand entries in Cassell's *New Encyclopaedia of World Literature*, and to do this he wrote to all New Zealand writers of any note to solicit biographical details. Frank Sargeson kept him up to date with occasional gifts of books and with letters full of literary gossip. In these various ways Dan stayed in touch with the personalities as well as the texts of contemporary New Zealand fiction. As a result of all these activities he established himself as the voice, in some spheres the representative, of New Zealand letters in Britain. This was how he was increasingly seen in New Zealand, from where he received a steady stream of requests to contribute to one or another of the little magazines.[82] In Britain it was a role that would eventually become more important in his life.

The BBC also brought Dan into contact with W. R. (Bertie) Rodgers and Louis MacNeice, both of whom worked there as producer-writers of features after the war. He first encountered them, separately, in the autumn of 1948 in the Stag, one of the BBC pubs 'where lunchtimes lasted through opening hours and where it was hard to distinguish poets from producers'.[83] His friendship with Rodgers flowered quickly, for Bertie was a great talker. Like Maclaren-Ross, he was addicted to monologue, but he moved in it through the device of anecdote rather than abstractions, and had a huge bag of waspish Irish stories on which to draw. A Protestant from the North, he had the tolerance and humour to move easily in the South, and was a source of innumerable introductions that Dan took up on his visit to Ireland in June 1949: 'I saw Belfast through his eyes and those of his friends . . . It was a more humane and friendly city than I would otherwise have seen . . . And in Dublin, too, I met his skein of friends . . . [T]he Dublin of Austin Clarke, Donagh MacDonagh, Paddy Kavanagh, Theo Moody, Ben Kiely, was a Dublin—or Dublins—it would have taken me a long time to find without Bertie's help . . .'[84]

Dan's friendship with MacNeice began more slowly, each a little suspicious, Dan conscious that among true writers publishers are the enemy, MacNeice (at least according to Bertie Rodgers) never able to give full friendship to anyone with whom he had not got drunk. He was not an easy man to know at first, his 'cagey leashing of words and feelings might have fooled those who did not know him that he was a cold man'.[85] Dan was trying to devise a book to be called *The Character of Ireland*, a collection of essays which, in homage to his own roots, would explain the Irish adequately to themselves, and perhaps to others. He filled out the project during his car trip to Ireland in June 1949, returning with the idea that Bertie Rodgers and Louis MacNeice should edit it jointly. Rodgers and MacNeice, already friends, readily agreed, and the saga of this book, its slow progress to non-completion, provided the context in which Dan's friendship with both of them slowly evolved.[86]

These friendships were mixed up too not just with his career as a publisher and broadcaster, but with his own evolution as a writer. Throughout 1947, as his books were being published, his home life passing through a phase of turbulence with the arrival of Elizabeth and

Patty, and his work as publisher becoming daily more onerous, he was at work in the evenings on another novel. Eventually he settled on the title *Roads from Home*, and after an autumn of continuous nightly labour, it was finished early in the new year of 1948. In this manuscript he was still experimenting, looking for a way of breaking the grip of mere narrative to achieve a greater realism both of effect and content. The device on which he fastened, interior voice, sometimes monologue, but generally simply a 'point of view', was hardly original, since the novels of Joyce and Woolf had exploited it fully. But it was rare in New Zealand fiction; it was also modern in that he was trying to capture a multiplicity of such inner voices, rather than simply one dominant one; and it was new in marrying the technique to the cadence of the Irish New Zealand idiom.

Roads from Home was published in April 1949 by Michael Joseph. Dan had become dissatisfied with Nicholson and Watson, whose production standards were low while his own, as a publisher himself, had risen sharply. When, in the spring of 1948, Nicholson and Watson hesitated briefly over whether or not to take *Roads from Home*, Dan had the opportunity to look elsewhere. Higham went straight to Michael Joseph, and once again Walter Allen was employed as their reader. Within weeks they offered him generous terms, with a £200 advance. This was a good career move for a still young writer publishing only his third novel. Michael Joseph's fiction list included Walter Allen himself, H. E. Bates, Joyce Cary, Monica Dickens, C. S. Forester, Pamela Hansford Johnson, and Gwyn Thomas. Dan's publisher there was Robert Lusty. He felt himself now to be well up the ladder.

In *Roads From Home* Dan turned to the Invercargill of his young manhood, to a 1930s Catholic, working-class family, the Hogans. Jack, a railwayman, his wife Norah, and their four children, John, Ned, Paddy, and Kate, are living on the cusp of some indefinable transformation in their lives. Part of it is simply the passing of an old world, the world of migrant Galway peasant farmers and their culture, summed up in the death and funeral of Larry O'Daly, an itinerant story-teller. Another part of it is the breaking of ties, as young men grow to maturity and confront the boundaries of family restriction. Yet another is the passing of religious sentiment, illuminated in Ned's disenchantment with the vocation of the priesthood, to which he had once been committed, but from which he is now fleeing after a nervous breakdown; in John's unsuccessful marriage to a Protestant girl, Elsie; and in the young adolescent Paddy's free-wheeling lack of interest in the old ways of religion. Above them all, their mother, devout, a matriarch with her brood, worries and frets about them, bosses and cajoles them, watches and loves them with a sort of burning intensity, a 'grave tenderness' 'in a prose that has its own personality and grace.'[87]

The main plot of the novel concerns the oldest son John, a railwayman like his father, who has discovered that his wife Elsie has never loved him, but had loved another called Andy Saunders. Elsie taunts her husband with the possibility that she had come to their marriage already pregnant with Andy's child. The child, Michael, is now a toddler. Andy returns, and Elsie is once more unable to resist him. Discovering this, John hesitates over whether to seek a divorce, but late at night, returning by car from the Gore races, Elsie and Andy are killed when their car is in collision with an express train at a railway crossing. One of the footplatemen on the train is John, who learns from Elsie, as she dies, that the little boy Michael is really his own son.

The central thread of the story, the possibility of a child born between rather than to partners, was somewhat more than incidental to Dan's own life at the time. The interest in the novel, however, lies as much in the treatment of ordinary Southland life, the descriptions of an auction and a rugby match, of Mass and a burial service, of ferreting and garden labour, of the social world of pubs and sly grog shops, dances, fist fights, and the domestic table. Within this small world, the central characters, Jack and Norah, John and Ned, observe and reflect each on the others. And, as Eric McCormick detected,[88] by far the most effective of them is the mother, Norah. *Roads From Home* might still best be read as a tribute by Dan to his own mother, Mary. In its pages she is captured with great fidelity, not just in manner and in appearance, but particularly in tone of voice, the rhythms of her speech.[89] And it is done with very great affection, all the bitterness and anger of the young rebel now set aside, propitiated in death.

But Dan had other intentions in the novel, weightier ones to do with the metaphysics of choice, the intellectual values of theological reasoning, the symbolic hinterland of the psychology of behaviour. The place of trains in the work, much taken by critics at the time at face value, deserved better analysis. In general, the book's reception was the reverse of Dan's previous experience: much criticized in Britain, and fairly well received in New Zealand. In the *Observer*, Lionel Hale disliked the melodramatic ending. In *Punch*, Helen Parry Eden faintly praised his 'infinite patience with his unprepossessing crowd' of characters. The *New Statesman* disliked the characters and the plot, and said the book was 'without distinction of style'. In *John O'London's Weekly* Pamela Hansford

Daniel and Nora Sullivan, Dan's grandparents, *c.*1916 '... the hard nose and the hard, undoubting eyes.' *RFH*, p. 193

Patrick Davin (r. rear) and Mary Sullivan (c.) on their wedding day, 28 January 1907

Five Davin children, l. to r., Dan, Martin, Molly, Evelyn and Tom, *c.*1917

Marist Brothers' High School, Invercargill, 'examination successes' 1929. Dan (c.) looks pleased enough

Otago University Latin picnic 1932. Dan extreme r., Angus Ross in front of him, and Frank Hall back l. Winnie McQuilkan is in front middle, Ida Lawson in the dark jacket behind her.

Dan as he left New Zealand, 1936

Winnie Gonley as provincial schoolteacher, c.1936

Peggy Spence-Sales, c.1934. 'For your lips my beloved I thirst'

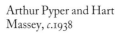
Dan in Balliol, 1937

Arthur Pyper and Hart
Massey, *c*.1938

Americans of 'the short
twentieth century':
Rhodes Scholars (l. to r.)
Walt Rostow, Philip
Kaiser and Gordon Craig,
Balliol, 1937

In the hills above
Florence, July 1937

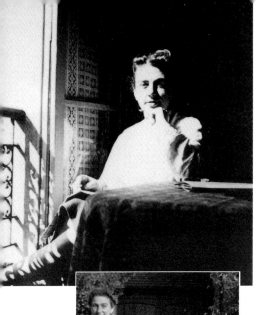

Winnie in the Rue Delambre,
summer 1938

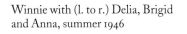

Winnie with (l. to r.) Delia, Brigid
and Anna, summer 1946

Dressed in the nick of time. Wedding day,
Balliol quad., July 1939

Paddy Costello,
intelligence officer,
(2nd from l.), 8 April
1943. General
Mannerini,
Commander of the
Italian Saharan
Group (c.) has just
surrendered

Johnson criticized its 'ramshackle construction' and confessed herself 'more deeply interested in the actual quality of [Davin's] prose, which is very strong, original and evocative, than in the people, or the philosophical content, of his tale; and this should not be'. The *Times Literary Supplement* shared a similar distaste for the characters. 'The fault lies somewhere, perhaps, in a kind of national egotism, an ingrained implication that there is something interesting in itself in being of Irish origin.'[90]

No one thought so in New Zealand, where the book's reception was respectful. In the Southland *Daily News* A. R. Dunlop called it 'another big step forward' in Davin's evolution as a writer, and in *Landfall* D. H. Monro called the background 'exceptionally interesting', 'the central themes . . . well handled'.[91]

The platitudes of foxed reviewers were without influence where it mattered. *Roads From Home* was commercially popular. The edition of 5,000 sold out in a month.[92] Dan had a mailbag of appreciative letters from those whose opinions mattered to him most: Paddy Costello in Moscow, Geoff Flavell in London, Kip in New Zealand, Joyce Cary in Oxford.[93]

Nevertheless, everyone missed the point. *Roads From Home* seemed to intelligent and well-educated people then, and still seems so to all readers today, to be a lively and affectionate portrait of a society about to disappear. The fact is, however, that the Catholic family portrayed in the novel was being shown in a shocking light. The boy destined for the priesthood has had a nervous breakdown, and surveys a godless world through the gloom of depressive illness, a taboo topic at the time. His older brother, married to a Protestant, imagines himself the 'father' of another man's child, and in response contemplates *both* divorce *and* keeping the infant. Such possibilities were a source of dread in Catholic families. Illegitimate children were put to adoption, and divorce meant a break with the Church and, as often as not, family too. Worse, if anything, John goes through the motions of his religion as though a hypocrite, for his mother's sake, and for peace and quiet. The father drinks and fights, and the youngest boy Paddy has his mind at the crossroads between the hunt for rabbits and the hunt for girls. Though Catholic families knew such things, it was a betrayal to air them in public.

The accurate social observation of the novel, its apparent affection for its characters, and the strong sense of place in which they are rooted, added to its subversive power. It all seemed so natural, so plausible. Some were not fooled, however. In Ireland the book was banned by the Irish Censorship of Publications Board in July 1949, where it appeared on the same list as George Orwell's 1984 and *She came to Stay* by Simone de Beauvoir. In Hollywood, Twentieth Century Fox added the judgement of the market to that of the moral authorities in Dublin. The admirably named Barbara Noble wrote that *Roads From Home*, 'being based very largely on doubts concerning the Catholic faith, seems to me to be over-controversial for the medium of the screen'.[94]

These reactions seem peculiar today largely because Dan's assessment, that this was a way of life about to disappear, was itself correct. Adjustment to social transformation takes time, however, and in the Catholic homes of Southland, particularly in the houses of his own relations and their friends in the community and the Church, the idea of Davin as apostate, and traitor to his home and people, lingered on for many years.

Paddy Costello's admiration for the novel came with a pressing invitation for Dan and Winnie to visit Moscow, where he had recently become New Zealand chargé d'affaires. He longed to show them 'the general movement of this working class city' and had plans for the Bolshoi and other outings. They were tempted, but declined because by this time, the summer of 1949, Dan was immersed both in the demands of his work at the Press, and in writing a history of the battle for Crete in the Second World War.

The opportunity to write this volume in the New Zealand Official War History series arose from his wartime connections: in particular with Howard Kippenberger, who, on his return to New Zealand in 1946, took up the appointment of Editor-in-Chief of the New Zealand war histories. He went with an oral commitment from Dan to write the volume on the Crete campaign, and in the interim between Kip's return to New Zealand and the official invitation being extended, Bernard Freyberg, who was still in London at this time prior to his departure to take up the post of Governor-General of New Zealand, gave Dan confidential access to his personal archives.[95]

Kip wrote to Dan, asking him to do the book, early in September, and by January of the new year 1947, his appointment approved, the wheels of official research had begun to turn. Official history of the wartime campaigns is a specialist form. Each writer was expected to bring something of his own analysis, style, character even, to the task, but the task itself was in some measure a group effort, since the quantity of material involved was immense. The finished product bore the author's name, but the name, though it appeared to stand alone, also stood for a considerable body of other historians, analysts, and archivists, as well as former commanders and other senior officers. It was one of Kip's great strengths as

Editor-in-Chief that he welded this body of sometimes difficult, vain, strong-minded, and irascible figures into a unit that facilitated, without dominating, the writing of each volume in the series. Kip was a commander who had led his men in war by example, reason, and persuasion, and he brought these same talents to the world of official history, though his office, the Official History Branch, was located in the New Zealand Department of Internal Affairs, a civilian, bureaucratic environment.

Kip expected his subordinates to do their duty. He was a man of great integrity and personal courage himself, but he also understood failure, and had learned forgiveness. Comparing the ancient Athenian expedition to Syracuse to the New Zealanders' experience in Crete, he wrote:

The end there was more disastrous . . . Our prisoners of war were not enslaved for the rest of their lives, and our leaders were not tortured and put to death. There have been times, particularly in the first few days of June 1941[,] when I would have been inclined to radical action of this sort against some of our leaders, but I am more charitably minded now. There is a certain amount of parallel between Nicias and Putt [Puttick], each of them made every decision that led to defeat, and no decisions that gave a chance of victory, and yet each was brave and devoted and technically competent.[96]

Kip's experience between the wars as a solicitor in a small South Island country town had doubtless yielded many opportunities to see and understand human motivations, how people responded to the pressures of small family affairs as well as the larger terrors of the depression and natural calamity. Already a kind and generous man, he added to these strengths an intuitive understanding of human frailty, and a deep, wide-ranging compassion. Since he was also free of the vanity of so many senior military commanders, he enjoyed the comradely respect of junior officers during the war, just as his wounds and the physical adversity that he surmounted with great fortitude, brought him respect, admiration, and affection from all those who worked for him after it.[97] Dan was no exception.

The feelings were returned. Kip's world had not previously been one of writers or intellectuals, but he valued their discovery, and appreciated Dan's friendship. He read and enjoyed his fiction, and wrote him letters of appreciation, as well as advice on how to improve his work for the ordinary reader. 'I believe that if I constantly rubbed my wits against yours I would eventually become quite intelligent.'[98]

Work on the *Crete* volume started in earnest in early 1947 with the preparation of a narrative of the battle. This was written in the first instance by W. G. McClymont (who later wrote the volume on the campaign in Greece) but was subsequently substantially amended and expanded by Walter (Spud) Murphy. Murphy was a young returned serviceman with an agile brain, quick to judgement, and opinionated, but remorselessly exact in the pursuit of detail. Kip relied on him and his personal, almost zealous hunt for the truth, but frequently had to temper his tendency to allocate blame. The narrative took a year to produce, and was eventually sent to Dan in Oxford in the spring of 1948. In addition he was sent a huge volume of material dealing with every aspect of the military situation in Crete, from the personal reminiscences and diaries of individual soldiers, to unit histories, war diaries, and the personal papers of commanders.

While all this material was being prepared, and in addition to all his other work at the Press, the publication of three books, and the writing of *Roads from Home*, Dan nevertheless found time to start work on Crete. Throughout the summer and autumn of 1947 he was involved in advising a *Daily Telegraph* journalist, Christopher Buckley, who had been appointed to write an official popular account of the British campaigns in Greece and Crete.[99] In October he took great pains correcting, editing, and advising Angus Ross on the draft chapter on the Greek campaign for his history of 23 Battalion, and he did the same a year later for the chapter on Crete.[100] In October 1949 Winston Churchill gave him permission to read in draft manuscript the chapters from Volume III of his war memoirs that dealt with the Crete campaign.[101]

Throughout this period he was also frequently in London to read in the Cabinet Office archives, where he was given access to Army and Navy sources, and to the Cabinet and Middle East files that dealt with Crete. It was on one of these research visits to London, on Friday, 21 May 1948, that he first met Martha McCulloch. Dan had got a lift to London with a character called Jack Diamond, a man once active in the Manchester Labour Party, and now living in Headington. On the way home in the evening Diamond also had Martha with him in the car, and along the way they stopped for drinks in West Wycombe, and then had supper together. Martha was nearly 44 years old, an educationalist in the field of children with special needs, but at that time working on a critique of children's films made by the Rank organization. Just prior to this she had been a secretary to Ellen Wilkinson, Minister of Education in Attlee's post-war government. Before the war she may have been one of Oliver St John Gogarty's lovers, but there is some obscurity here. Gogarty, the model for James Joyce's Buck Mulligan, was then a name to conjure with in Dan's imaginative world, and he later got to know him in New York.

Martha was short in stature, with dense, dark hair, strong features and a confident manner. She was proud of her culinary skills, and of her keen dress sense, and approved of people who were 'well turned out'. She made all her own clothes, and took trouble over things like matching accessories, or manicuring only with a file, never scissors.

No doubt she had been beautiful as a young woman, but she had been seriously injured by flying glass at Victoria station during a bombing raid in the war, and plastic surgery to the head (performed by the New Zealander Archie McIndoe) had left her not with visible scars, but with a faint air of inauthenticity. This was more than compensated for by strength of personality. She was a thorough organizer (some said bossy) with strong left-wing political opinions (dogmatic and authoritarian) with which she generally required agreement (intolerant and manipulative). She was a good talker (domineering and argumentative), and could be excellent company, but it clearly helped if you shared her views in the first place. Some of Dan's friends who knew her independently of him, like John and Anne Willett, and Teddy McCullough, who called her 'the girl with the Carmen eyes', liked and admired her. Others, who saw her only in Dan's company, like Geoffrey Cox and Geoffrey Flavell, found her trying.

Dan took to her instantly, admiring her intelligence, spirit, and style. He was not yet 35 when they met, liked women to dress well and wear make-up, and enjoyed critical people, people who sided against privilege. The day after their meeting, Wendy Campbell-Purdie had a party to which Martha also came. Dan wrote in his diary: 'Haven't enjoyed a party on this scale since old NZ days . . . the same gaiety, the same timelessness.'[102] From this time onwards, Dan and Martha became intimate friends. She lived in a top-floor apartment in Bloomsbury, at 41 Coram Street, close to all the restaurants and watering-holes of the old Fitzrovia to which Dan still gravitated whenever he was in London. Her home there, and later at 53 Gower Street, to which she moved in 1966, became his London base where, for the next twenty-five years or so, he usually stayed when he was in London. These addresses also became familiar to a generation of New Zealand writers and academics, to whom Dan introduced her, and for whom she performed countless deeds of hospitality over the years.

More important still, Dan introduced Martha into his home life in Oxford, where she established herself as a regular visitor, and a participant in family life. This development had a number of important effects, the main one deriving from her skill, which she had in common with

Enid Starkie, of getting people to share confidences with her. She knew, for example, from fairly early in her relationship with Dan that Patty was his daughter. Elizabeth and Patty were now living much of the time at Wendy Campbell-Purdie's establishment in Woodstock Road, but they returned to 103 Southmour Road for the winter months of 1949–50, when Winnie and Wendy were away in New Zealand, and Elizabeth really was working as housekeeper for the Davin family. Elizabeth, who certainly had little but Dan in common with Martha, believed (at least in later life) that Martha was jealous of her and her position. Her suspicions were surely misplaced. Martha, like many strong-willed people, certainly sought control in her relationships, but her self-assurance precluded jealously. What she sensed, rather, was that Dan and Elizabeth were getting on each other's nerves, that Dan needed tranquillity in which to work, and that his domestic arrangements needed taking in hand.

From her pre-war days in the Manchester Labour Party, Martha knew the Tylecote family, and in particular Mabel Tylecote, a historian, one time lecturer at Manchester University, and a prominent Labour Manchester City Councillor.[103] In 1932 she had married Frank Tylecote, a consultant physician and professor at Manchester University, and thus became stepmother to his 16-year-old son Ronnie. During these years Martha was an occasional visitor to Heaton Lodge, the old Tylecote family home, where she was known as 'Mac', and where Mabel used to hold left-wing beer evenings in what had been the Heaton Lodge billiard room.[104] Ronnie trained as a metallurgist, married, and had children, but by the late 1940s his marriage was in difficulties, and in the summer of 1950, when his wife left him, Ronnie moved to Barnes with two of his three children, and started divorce proceedings. Martha, who knew all this, saw an opening for her organizing talents, and acted as go-between in arranging for Elizabeth to move to Barnes as Ronnie's housekeeper. Thus it was that Elizabeth and Patty left Southmoor Road in the autumn of 1950.

This closed a chapter in Dan's life. Patty remained part of the family, but of necessity her relationship with Dan, whom she still did not know was her father, became more remote. She still visited occasionally, generally at Easter, and sometimes for a summer holiday with the Davins, but a certain distance was established that lasted for over a decade. Delia still recalls the profound disappointment she experienced at Patty's separation from her. The distancing intensified in 1953 when Ronnie took a position at King's College, Newcastle, and he and his family, including Elizabeth and Patty, moved north. As for Elizabeth, she dropped out of Dan's life more or less completely for the next nearly thirty years. For Elizabeth, the end of this chapter was the beginning of a new one. She and Ronnie got on well, and proximity turned eventually to friendship, affection, and intimacy. They married on 12 June 1958, thereby at last solving Elizabeth and Patty's documentation problems. A man of great charm, intelligence, and integrity, Ronnie drew Elizabeth into a partnership not only in their private lives, but also in the academic field of archaeometallurgy, of which he was an internationally respected pioneer.[105]

Despite domestic adjustments, and the firm foundation of affection that underpinned Dan and Winnie's marriage, Dan's relationship with Martha continued for a number of years, until eventually she became a part of the family circle, like a maiden aunt who visits a lot, and assumes particular rights when it comes to weddings or other family occasions. Also she was pubbable, as John Willett put it, a companion in London pubs in the 1950s and 1960s, where she became a member of Dan's circle of poets and radio producers. As before, Dan's way of life owed much to Winnie's tolerance. Her sense of his needs in their relationship, and her willingness to adjust to them, coupled with his unshaken desire for her companionship and intellectual strength, made their marriage imperishable. Dan's mistresses were always defeated by it in the end.

The complications of Dan's private life in the period from 1948 to 1952 were the backdrop against which he wrote his history of the Crete campaign. As if in echo of them, Kip wrote to him in December 1947: 'You are going to have a most delicate and difficult job in assessing responsibilities for Crete and may occasionally be glad to shelter behind the reticences proper to an Official Historian.' And again, a week later: 'we must not be tempted to hurry . . . [T]he Crete story . . . can be one of the heritages of our people.'[106]

Haste was hardly possible. Once he had mastered the background material, which was largely in his possession by June 1948, Dan was flown out to New Zealand for discussions. The New Zealand government, anxious to conserve valuable foreign exchange, questioned the necessity of this visit, but Kip prevailed, and Dan was set to travel by RNZAF some time in August. The Berlin crisis intervened, however, and instead of the discomfort of military transport, he flew on the new commercial service. He left Heathrow on 12 August, and flew via Heliopolis, Karachi, Calcutta, Singapore (where they stayed at Raffles), Port Darwin, and Sydney, arriving in Auckland by flying boat on Tuesday, 17 August.

This was the first time that Dan had been home to New Zealand in twelve years, and his feelings were muddled and confused. In Auckland there were old friends from SHC days to see—Cotterall, Zam, and Mike Joseph—as well as wartime friends—in particular Wig Gardiner—and new literary people whom he did not yet know, but whose names were familiar, and who later formed another circle of the penumbra of his wide-ranging friendships. He visited Frank Sargeson at his bach in Takapuna, where he also met the young Maurice Duggan, whom he instantly liked. Like Sargeson, Dan was convinced of the young Duggan's talent, of which he became a critical advocate.[107] Here he also met Helen Shaw (later Hella Hofmann) whose own short stories promised a writing career. At her request, a year later, he wrote a critical piece, 'The Narrative Technique of Frank Sargeson', for a collection of articles about Sargeson, *The Puritan and the Waif*, which she edited, and which was to have been published by Glover's Caxton Press.[108]

Further south, in waiting, lay Dan's family, and with them all the echoes and memories of Catholic Invercargill and bohemian Dunedin. There were shadows and ghosts here that might have made a melancholy man, given to drink, confused enough to lose his way. Happily the strict purpose of his visit—to work on the history of Crete—provided an organizing principle that kept him focused. After a few days in Auckland he went down to Wellington on 19 August where he was met by Kip, and installed in the Midland Hotel. That afternoon and the next morning were spent in the War History Branch, meeting the team and discussing problems. The Saturday morning he spent with Freyberg at Government House, and then had dinner and spent the evening talking history with Kip at his home. On the Sunday he was back at Government House, this time for dinner with the Freybergs, and further talk of Crete. 'An obsession with BF', Dan noted in his diary, 'no doubt because this was the critical battle of his career. Had we won the highest commands would have been open to him. (Of course he doesn't say this.)'[109] This round continued until 9 September, and included lengthy meetings with Puttick, who had commanded New Zealand troops in Crete, and whom he found 'talkative and open', and rather liked.[110] He lunched with Kip almost every day, either at the Wellington Club or at one of the city's hotels, and he met Blundell and McIntosh and many others from the thin higher echelons of New Zealand public life.

After this he went south for a week, first to Invercargill, where he was reunited with his father and his sister Molly. He went to visit his Aunty Annie and her husband Harry on their run-down farm at Oteramika, and in Invercargill he was treated to a mayoral civic morning tea—'a comic occasion'.[111] He went out to Woodlands to visit the Concannon farm, dropped round to see Winnie's sister Mollie, and paid a sad visit to his mother's grave in the East Road cemetery. He persuaded his father to travel with him by aeroplane to Dunedin. Twelve years had gone by since Dan last left Invercargill, yet:

In spite of the pubs, the town is in its spirit unchanged—jealous, strong, narrow, small, censorious, ignorant, intolerant, prosperous, conceited, generous and hospitable, mean and complacent. The world's worst small town . . . It is a town which strangles the heart and yet gives it intimations of a world beyond, escape and freedom. I owe much to it and can never forgive it for the time I spent there, caged.[112]

In Dunedin he and his father stayed at Ma Blaney's pub. He walked the town—'At every step a shade of the past'—and visited his old friends Paish and Frank Guest. Then he and his father travelled by bus to Roxburgh to visit his sister Evelyn at the Dunlay fruit farm at Cold Creek, and there were family photographs with the famous expatriate.

After Mary Davin's death Patrick had suddenly and unexpectedly married a wealthy publican widow. The marriage made him deeply unhappy, and he left it after a short while, eventually moving with his daughter Molly to Dunedin, where both he and she lived for the rest of their days.[113] Dan dutifully paid a visit to the stepmother, whom he had not known. Later these experiences were the basis of two short stories: 'A Return' and 'First Flight'.[114] 'Dunedin had stood up best to time,' he reckoned. 'The streets were the same length as they used to be, my friends here were the least change[d], the blue of the hills and the Scotch mist were more beautiful than I had remembered them. I shall regret not having come here sooner and stayed longer.'[115]

From Dunedin he paid an overnight visit to Christchurch where he stayed with Arthur Prior, visited Denis Glover at the Caxton Press, and met James K. Baxter the young poet, a prodigy already. Back in Wellington he opted out of the Midland, and went to stay instead with his younger brother Pat, then just starting what was to be a successful entrepreneurial career. They talked late, raking over the coals of family history. Dan was back in touch with Peggy Spence-Sales, then living in Wellington, though now in 'her first traumatic marriage'.[116] They went to the pictures together, and he visited her home several times. She drew his portrait, and talked about painting. 'Cold fires', he wrote in his diary,[117] but he sought her company just the same, and there was still an understanding there, however feeble. In Wellington he also met Oliver Duff, editor of the *New Zealand Listener*, his old undergraduate acquaintance

John Maconie, who now worked for Duff; Roy Parsons, the bookseller; and writers and critics like John Reece Cole and James Bertram. He made a number of radio programmes, on one discussing different approaches to literary life with Sargeson, on another taking part in a 'Brains Trust'. Dan brought to his friendships in literary circles in New Zealand the same instinct for companionship and pleasure in gossip that he brought to the world of publishing in Oxford. From it sprang many later opportunities as well as friendships.

For a man of Dan's temperament, this intense sequence of experiences, mixing a nostalgia and bitterness for the past with a constant but only surface-deep round of introductions and new faces, coupled with family reunions, and encounters with old army friends, was more than sufficient to induce dejection. The addition of drink, of which a great deal was consumed at every stage of the journey, gave him 'the BGs'—boozers' gloom, from which he suffered almost every day. Happily, there was still Crete to distract him, and on which to focus. He had further meetings in Wellington on Friday, 17 September, spent the Saturday evening with Kip at his home, and dined once more at Government House on the Sunday with Freyberg and Stewart. The next day he met Walter Nash at noon, and then Kip and Andrew 'the Maleme Colonel' in the afternoon.[118] He flew back to Auckland a day later, and left New Zealand at the end of the week on Friday, 24 September, getting back to Oxford five days later, 'exhausted'.[119]

After these exertions he began to write. The task posed enormous problems. The quantity of material was oppressive, demanding condensation without loss of content. The complexity was very great, for although the battle covered only ten days or so, the movements of units and even individual soldiers had to be accounted for hour by hour. Despite the quantity and complexity, crucial episodes, particularly those of critical decisions that influenced the evolution of the battle, were poorly documented and much of what documentation there was lacked consistency. Commanders were understandably reluctant to retrieve the whole truth from what were in any case possibly faulty memories. Both Dan and Kip were conscious that, the battle having been lost, and so many men killed, wounded, and taken prisoner, the book would be most closely scrutinized in their homeland. Many would want blame apportioned. Several senior officers stood in grave danger of losing reputation: Freyberg, for the initial disposition of troops and overall command; Colonel Andrew, commander of 20 Battalion, for his decision to retire from Maleme; Brigadier Hargest for deciding to confirm this withdrawal without going forward; Puttick for his decision not to make a second attempt to recover Maleme; Gentry and Kippenberger for their decision to give up Galatas against the view of Brigadier Inglis. Dan's task was made harder by the strength of some of these personalities. Hargest, who had subsequently been killed in Normandy, left behind a diary full of charges against other officers. Inglis, known as 'Whisky Bill' to the ordinary soldiers, was a lawyer by training, and by this time a member of the War Crimes Tribunal in occupied Germany. He had a 'habit of confusing after-knowledge with prescience' and 'remembers things very vividly but sometimes his recollections are startlingly different from those of anyone else'.[120] Puttick, who after Crete had been made Chief of the General Staff in New Zealand, was now in retirement, taken up with his pursuits of horse racing and fishing, and loath to rake over the ashes of a terrible experience. Andrew, who was a genuinely courageous man who had won the VC in the First World War, was enigmatic and remote, almost impossible to interpret. Somehow, out of this after-fog of war, Dan had to produce a work of scholarship, accurate as to fact, honest as to truth, realistic as to analysis, yet faithful to the realities of war in such a way as to recommend it even to those damaged by its findings.

Any writer would need persuasive reasons to undertake such a task. In Dan's case they were threefold. He had been trained as a historian, and wanted to put his training to use. The invitation came at a time when the connections, the money (he was paid a fee of £1,200 to write the book), and the opportunities it afforded him suited his needs. But above all it was an act of piety towards his countrymen, and in particular his comrades in the Div.

Dan was acutely conscious of how his 'lucky wound' had saved him from perhaps far worse, and of how others had lost far more. Of the 43 officers on the strength of 23 Battalion in July 1940 (when Dan joined it), 7 were killed and almost all the others wounded, some dreadfully, by the end of the war. In Crete, at the counter-attack on Galatas on 25 May 1941, all the officers and most of the NCOs of C Company (which was Dan's unit) were wounded, and only about 30 men of the entire company were left standing by the end of the day.[121] Almost all those wounded in this action were taken prisoner of war. When the remnants of 23 Battalion were evacuated from the beach at Sfakia, 'the only surviving officers left on the active list were subalterns'.[122] The Battalion suffered 299 casualties out of a total strength at the start of the battle of 571. Dan felt a deep sense of commitment to these men, regret and sorrow mixed with pride. He referred to it only rarely, but it is no exaggeration to say that he wrote the

Crete campaign for them. He believed that in books the collective memories of a civilization are preserved, and that in this way the missing comrades would not be forgotten. The strength of his feelings may be detected throughout the book, but it is particularly apparent in his description of the attack on Galatas: a sublime piece of historical narrative.[123]

Writing *Crete* took him the next two years, painfully at a few hundred words a night after work, each paragraph footnoted, each allusion justified. Later he said that the effort nearly killed him. Only by October 1950 was he in a position to start sending the first chapters of the nearly 700 pages of manuscript to New Zealand. Kip greeted them with acclaim. 'It is almost a relief to find a few points on which to disagree with you', he wrote.[124] 'This is a classic campaign and we will produce a classic history.'[125]

The complete draft of the book was finished by the end of January 1951. Kip circulated it to all the senior officers involved in the battle, and, along with his own criticisms, collated such criticisms and comments as came from them. Murphy, prolix and a terror for detail, wrote 104 foolscap pages of commentary of his own. On receipt of these, Dan was deeply disheartened at the quantity of work still to be done. Much of Murphy's response he thought jejune, but his earlier experience of the expatriate scholars in Oxford stood him in good stead, and he remained buoyant and cheerful in his correspondence about the final draft, which he was eventually in a position to send to Wellington in November 1951. Murphy apologized later, admitting that he had learned far more from Dan than he had been able to contribute, and regretting his own 'long-winded and often fatuous comments'. 'It was only on the reading of your final draft that I could see [its] shape and . . . merit.'[126]

This satisfaction apart, another benefit that Dan extracted from these final months of forced labour on the text was collaboration with the radio writer and producer Leonard Cottrell. Working from a draft by Dan, they jointly wrote the script of a one-hour radio drama about the fall of Crete. It was broadcast on the BBC Home Service on the evening of Sunday, 22 July, with Dan acting several of the parts, and earning almost £60 in fees for his efforts.

With appendices to be polished, photographs to select, and maps to draw, the book was a long time in production, but was eventually published on 12 August 1953 in an edition of 4,000 copies. It sold out at once, and soon established itself, as Kip had thought it would, as 'a classic'. Though New Zealanders were grudging in their praise,[127] it received good reviews in Britain, where *The Economist* called it an 'admirable account', 'exceptionally well-written' and a 'first class piece of military scholarship'.[128] In the *New Statesman* Nigel Nicolson called it 'bold' for its critical analysis of commanders' actions,[129] and in the *Spectator* G. M. O. Davy singled out the description of the counter-attack at Galatas as 'vivid and thrilling'.[130]

One aspect of the battle Dan could not have foreseen: the controversy about Enigma. Not until the Ultra source was declassified in 1974 did its existence, derived from the decrypting of German military communications by the team at Bletchley Park, come to public attention. It did not take military historians long to ask: had the British High Command derived advance intelligence of German intentions in Crete from the Ultra source? If so, was Freyberg privy to it? Was it perhaps possession of this intelligence which, in accordance with the highest policy priority (that the Germans should never even suspect that their encryptment codes had been broken), inhibited him from altering the disposition of his troops on the ground in the final critical few days before the airborne invasion occurred?

Freyberg died in 1963. Though Dan saw him on a number of occasions in the 1950s, and they certainly discussed Crete, Freyberg—as is only to be expected in an honourable former commander of great discretion—never mentioned Ultra. Paul Freyberg, in his biography of his father, states that shortly before he died, and in the greatest confidence, his father told him that he had had access to Ultra, and that this was indeed the reason for the general absence of tactical manœuvre either before or early in the battle.[131] Dan believed the younger Freyberg's account of his father's initiation into Ultra to be true, but urged him to find documentary evidence in the official record.[132] Despite his efforts, neither written reports, nor the identity of the Ultra liaison officer in Crete, could be located. Much material was burned in Cairo during the German summer offensive of 1942.

However, F. H. Hinsley, in the first volume of the official British history of wartime intelligence, is quite specific that 'General Freyberg received it [Ultra] . . . disguised as information supplied by an SIS agent in Athens'.[133] In other words, Freyberg was initiated in Ultra, and had a cover story to explain its source.[134]

Dan knew nothing of Freyberg's explanation to his son until Paul Freyberg wrote to him about it in November 1981, but he followed the publication of Ultra histories with great interest, and he certainly read the first two volumes of Hinsley *et al.* on wartime intelligence. These are explicit, and do little to support Freyberg's line that his father was inhibited from altering the disposition of troops in order to protect his intelligence source. On the contrary: 'it was the foreknowledge provided by the Enigma which gave the defenders the confidence and time to concentrate all their forces at these points'[135] and which resulted in Crete being such a pyrrhic victory for the German invaders. Argument about the minutiae of military decision-making during battle has, for the uninitiated, something of an angels-on-pinheads quality to it. In this instance, much turns on what instructions, if any, Freyberg gave to his commanders concerning the deployment of troops once the German invasion had begun. And these in turn raise issues of interpretation— what the instructions actually meant to individual commanders.[136] What is possibly the case in this instance is that Puttick, commander of the New Zealand Division in Crete, and not an Ultra initiate, may have discounted some of Freyberg's intelligence information derived from 'an SIS source in Athens', on the grounds, as experienced commanders well knew, that such intelligence was notoriously unreliable. His restraint in counter-attack, when the battle was in the balance, may support such a view. What is clear, however, is that there have been various claims since Enigma was declassified in 1974 that one or other disaster was caused by the need to conceal the Enigma source—most notoriously, the alleged failure to alert defences of Coventry before it was destroyed. Hinsley examined each such claim as he came to it, and found no evidence that it happened. Had Paul Freyberg's defence of his father on these same grounds appeared earlier, it seems unlikely Hinsley would have treated it any differently.

All the judgements of history are provisional. What makes Dan's history of the Crete campaign all the more remarkable is that the subsequent publication of intelligence secrets unknown to him have nevertheless made no difference either to the force or the direction of his analysis. It is an extraordinary achievement.

Writing *Crete* had a number of effects on Dan's life that he could not have foreseen. Perhaps the most important was that it made him aware of the difficulties, and the drudgery, as well as the intellectual satisfactions, of scholarship. Having finished it, he thought himself, surely correctly, far better placed to be a scholarly publisher. A second effect was social. The research drew Dan into the world of the New Zealand Establishment, which he belonged to for the rest of his life. Freyberg in particular valued his friendship, but he was also now on terms with most of the senior figures in the armed services, public administration, universities, and diplomacy. At the same time, he was *perceived* by his countrymen as belonging to this company, which—for a man who had valued his bohemianism—was certainly a change. A third effect was literary. The history of the Crete campaign loomed so large in the specialist world of official military history that no subsequent historian of either the Crete campaign specifically, or the Mediterranean theatre in the Second World War in general, could really proceed without consulting him. Over the next thirty-five years *Crete* brought Dan into contact with successive generations of historians, both professional and amateur, whose attentions, even when he found them perhaps ill-prepared, he enjoyed and reciprocated. Basil Liddell Hart became a friend and admired colleague, whose later work Dan read in draft, and he particularly valued the friendship also of Dr Ian Stewart to whose book *The Struggle for Crete: 20 May–1 June 1941*[137] he made a significant contribution, not least by lending him files of New Zealand material unobtainable anywhere else.

But *Crete* had one other effect that went deeper, and was more persistent. It exhausted him. The pace at which it was written, crawling forward at a few hundred words a night, week after week, month after month, was torture to a man adept at swift composition. 'Crete is a cross', he wrote to Sargeson.[138] It left him with no spare time for other writing, and his ambition for fiction lay completely neglected. It is astonishing that he still had so much time for his family and his friendships. When it was finally finished, he confided that writing *Crete* had changed his work habits. Writing had become 'a burden instead of a triumphant pleasure'.[139]

11

THE PLATEAU OF SUCCESS

My chief positive quality, stubborn, stealthy, tortuous subterranean tenacity, which wronged becomes vindictiveness, triumphant looks like luck, disappointed is not known because it has not shown itself.

(DMDP: Diary, 24 Sept. 1941)

So often one thinks that individuals and situations cannot be so extraordinary as they seem from outside, only to find that the truth is a thousand times odder.

(Anthony Powell, *At Lady Molly's*, 194)

The labour of *Crete* certainly inhibited Dan from writing, but the inhibition was not new. More than a decade earlier he had detected a 'dreadful reluctance to write warring with the hunger to'.[1] He knew that he had writer's block—'the most unpleasant part of writing occurs before you begin'[2]—and that where he had conquered it had been with the tactic of routine. Now there were social factors which made this more difficult. Family life, even after the departure of Elizabeth and Patty, grew more complicated. The children were growing up: Anna was 13 in 1953, Delia 9, and Brigid 7. They were all healthy, intelligent, lively girls, with a maze of friendships in North Oxford, and their home was a place of open invitation. Miriam Margolyes, later a distinguished actress, who was a near contemporary of Anna and Delia, recalled the pleasure of visits to the Davin house, a place of 'glamourous raffishness'.[3] It was also a very happy home, where the children grew up to feel secure because they knew they were loved unconditionally. Anna always sang as she went about the house. Brigid was funny and always smiling, popular with everybody. Delia was a serious little girl, still shy as she grew up, but like her sisters immensely inquisitive and thoughtful. Winnie was, as ever, the main provider at home, but Dan was fully present as a father and not unhappy to be distracted by Winnie and the children. His biggest problem was that if he wanted to write there was rarely any peace and quiet. In envy of Sargeson at home in the silence of his North Shore bach, Dan wrote to him: 'worst of all is not having solitude which provides a kind of fertile melancholy of tone which enables continuity'.[4] And sixteen months later: 'Easter is over thank God. I planned gigantic labours but we never sat down to a meal of less than 10 people and to get over my hunger for solitude I had either to stay in bed or go out and induce gregariousness by drinking beer. The office is a relief after these social exhaustions.'[5]

The tumult of a lively family was also occasionally fractured by discord. Anna recalled that as a child she was the most embattled with Dan. Dan wrote that 'Anna's disposition to argue with her Papa now makes me penitent for my disputes with my own parents'.[6] Like many children conceived at the beginning of the war, Anna as an infant had barely known her father. He returned once, when she was 3, an invader into her relationship with her mother. When he came home the following year, just after her fourth birthday, it was to establish himself as the figure of authority, strong-willed, occasionally short-tempered. Anna ate slowly and had little appetite for meat, both likely to attract Dan's disapproval. Her memories are of being unable to keep up with his expectations, of being corrected ('not to stride out like a bush-ranger') and having her attention drawn to some slip of speech ('couples, not pairs'). Anna had her mother's toughness, her father's determination, and their joint intelligence. It was a recipe for battle, rarely joined, but turbulent when it was. From the age of 10 or so, Anna would be left to look after the Saturday and Sunday lunch, which Winnie had already prepared, while her parents met their friends at the Lamb and Flag or the Perch. On their return, as often as not, they found her deep in a book, the vegetables burnt. Painful at the time, it became the stuff of family legend in due course.

Dan's struggles with Anna, ever determined to be different; his affection for all the children; Delia's shy and fearful respect for this tough, energetic, melancholy, brilliant but sometimes taciturn father, are examples of the complexities of family relationships that were themselves a distraction from work. Dan knew that it was an 'almost impossible job' to integrate his work at the Press and his desire for literary creativity into a happy domestic life.[7] For the ten years or so that spanned his daughters' adolescent development his ability to write declined. Like all parents he worried about his children, and the act of worrying reminded him of his mother, of the suffocations of his own childhood, and of his determination that his own children should not suffer as he had done. The problem was how to give effect to this laudable long-term ambition in the short term of today's tumult and disruption while also sustaining a time-consuming part-time career as a writer. He never found a satisfactory answer, but his habitual pessimism assured him that 'one's best years will be few—intentionally I waited a long time—and there is much to be done. In a millennium that will be too late for us I should have inverted God's role [?rule] and rested for six days, creating on the seventh.'[8] The fantasy is not entirely in jest. From about the age of 35 he took the view that his life had reached its summit, and was now in descent. As John, the principal figure in *Roads From Home*, and still a young man, reflected on his ruined marriage: 'he too had crossed the crown of his own life. This . . . was the sort of thing that happened when you were past your best years, moving on to the defensive.'[9]

Not all the distraction was unwelcome. Dan enjoyed his family, and was eager for the affection they gave him. And many of the interruptions were simply a product of Dan and Winnie's talent for friendship, and instinct for hospitality. In the early 1950s the stream of visitors from New Zealand was steady, and they were hosts to Maurice Duggan and his wife Barbara, to the poets Basil Dowling and Allen Curnow, the young academics Bill Pearson and Alan Horsman, Arthur Sewell (Mike Joseph's old mentor at Auckland), and the historians W. H. (Bill) Oliver and Keith Sinclair, and many others. One old friend never came back. Fred Petricevich told old schoolfriends in Auckland that he was dismayed by what he detected as a portrait of himself in *Cliffs of Fall*, and severed all connections with Dan. He never fulfilled the promise of his early brilliance, and remained in obscure exile for the rest of his life in London. Among old acquaintances, the passage of time did bring back Maggie Cotterill, Dan's colleague and sparring partner from their days editing the Otago *Review*. Married (now Margaret Black), she came as a visitor from Auckland in 1952, hesitant at first (it was sixteen years since they had met or corresponded), a down-to-earth, friendly guest, full of trepidation on her first trip abroad. Maggie, Dan, and Winnie became good friends, corresponded for the rest of their lives, and stayed with each other on their occasional long-distance visits. When her son Peter was involved in a horrific car accident in Britain in 1963, in which her daughter-in-law was killed, Dan and Winnie looked after Maggie, and stood by her in the innumerable ways necessary during the twelve months of her son's slow, painful recovery.[10]

The early 1950s were also notable for the friendship that perhaps made the deepest impression of all on Dan. In August 1950 he went as New Zealand delegate to the International PEN meeting in Edinburgh, where he met and befriended a thin, lonely, isolated man who said that he represented 'Yiddish', and whose name was Itzik Manger. His claim turned out to be true. Itzik was one of the lone survivors of the Nazi genocide that has stripped Central Europe of one of its greatest cultural heritages, the living literature of the Yiddish language. In his isolation at the conference, he seemed expressive of his culture, reduced to a solitary, roving minstrel of the emotions. Dan's sense of himself as outsider was instantly attracted to this curious, charming poet and story-teller, and they spent much of the six days of the conference talking to each other in one or other Edinburgh hostelry instead of sitting in their delegates' seats in George Heriot's School listening to the 'appalling oratory' of cold war literary rhetoric.[11] It was Itzik's intensity that first caught Dan's attention, then his frailty and loneliness, then—once they began to talk—his astonishing powers of conversation, story-telling, and invention. The nature of their first meeting and the course of their subsequent friendship tell us much about Dan. On the surface the two had nothing in common. Dan knew barely a word of Yiddish. Their upbringing, family experience, religious sense, everything about them was different. Yet there was an exchange of human sympathy that was somehow bed-rock. We can tell this by the fact that although Dan never kept a diary account of their first meeting, or many aspects of the subsequent course of their friendship, it remained—while so much else was forgotten—clear in his mind for the rest of his life.

On his return to Oxford from Edinburgh Dan invited Manger to stay, and he came up on the Sunday of 5 November, took part in the back garden ritual of bonfire and fireworks, and entertained all the family with his jokes, practical and verbal, and with his marvellous stories and anecdotes. He captivated Winnie, as he had done Dan, and she and Itzik became friends too. One of his poems is dedicated to them jointly. Itzik came again during the winter, and Dan saw him several times in London, but in the spring of 1951 he at last managed to get a visa to the United States, and left to live in New York. They had known each other for less than a year, yet it was the friendship of a lifetime, and Dan and Winnie carried Itzik with them in spirit wherever they went.

This was one friendship of companion spirits to set beside another, rather more difficult. With the dissolution of Fitzrovia, the evaporation of exhilarating wartime social anarchy, the collapse of many little magazines, and the bankruptcy of the British film industry, Julian Maclaren-Ross's career was on the skids. Perhaps it was to save money, or at any rate to be closer to a reliable source of the stuff, that he decided to abandon London, and go to live in Oxford. Suddenly he appeared in the autumn of 1954 occupying furnished rooms at 59 Southmoor Road. His monologues, famous for fantasy, had now acquired the disagreeable feature of self-pity, not all of it related to the slide in his literary fortunes. He had formed an obsession for Sonia Brownell Orwell, once an assistant to Cyril Connolly at *Horizon*, briefly wife and then the widow of George Orwell. He began writing anguished love-letters to her in his tiny italic script, fantasized about her, and poured out his hopes and sorrows to Dan at every opportunity, either in person or in ghastly begging letters, full of terrible tirades. Anthony Powell guessed that it must have been 'perfectly awful' to have 'MR' as a neighbour.[12] Gordon Craig, who visited the Davins from 20 to 23 November 1954, could hardly believe his eyes and ears: 'a writer named Julian McLaren-Ross [*sic*], who seems to live as much with the Davins as by himself and who talks about himself all the time . . . [He was] eating something called "green bombs" and going on for ever.'[13] Maclaren-Ross's powers of extracting money were legendary. Arthur Crook, editor of the *TLS*, described him as 'the only man I know who extracted two separate payments of £25 *in advance* from the *TLS* and never turned in the articles'.[14] The Davins gave him money too, and he still had his reviewing work for *Punch* and other magazines, but the time that Maclaren-Ross lingered in Southmoor Road, tormented and tormenting, was a trial. When he was unwell, which was often enough, Winnie cooked him hot meals, and delivered them down Southmoor Road on her bike. Later Dan comforted himself with a remark made to him by Jack Gallagher, Beit Professor of British Commonwealth History at Oxford: 'Everybody has an awful friend, and everybody is somebody's awful friend.'

One solution was to go elsewhere to work. After Sisam's retirement in 1948 he invited Dan to visit him at his house, Middle Carn, on the island of St Mary's, in the Scilly Isles. Dan and Winnie took the children there for a summer holiday, and from 1952 Dan went there on his own for the last fortnight of the summer vacation, before the start of the Oxford Michaelmas term. This became, over the years, an annual secular retreat, a time of complete quiet and almost total isolation in which he was able to concentrate on writing, and in which he replenished his resources before returning to the maelstrom of business and publishing commitments. It was a retreat that he continued to make almost until the time of Sisam's death in 1971.

New Zealanders like the Scilly Isles. Both coastline and climate remind them of their own country, and there are cabbage trees, flax and tough grasses, wild succulents and little flowering climbers. 'As Sisam . . . although absent most of his life from NZ has a very good memory for the

King Country[,] there are times when one is almost at home again.'[15] The Sisams had a launch for fishing and for expeditions to Tresco, with a boat-house for it, empty in the summer. This was Dan's den, where a bed, table, and chair kept company with ropes and anchors, gardening equipment, nets, lawnmowers, and tools. He ate at the house, and in the evenings sat on with Sisam to gossip about Oxford, publishing, and the world of letters. 'Sisam and I have scarcely stopped talking since I got here—mostly Sisam. It's like a refresher course in publishing and most heartening (as well as disconcerting at times).'[16] Dan turned to Sisam for advice with problems, and for guidance on the history of particular projects in the Press, for many years to come.

Apart from these evenings of conversation, Dan lived and slept in the boat-shed. Every morning and afternoon he wrote, setting himself a quota of words per day, breaking only at lunchtime for a brisk solitary walk to Hugh Town and a pint at the local pub, or to go foraging for mushrooms. These two weeks of literary solitude and intellectual companionship with Sisam wrought annual renewal, physical as well as intellectual. Sisam followed a healthy diet, rich in freshly caught fish, and they might have just one drink in the evening. Dan always came away feeling fit, and virtuous from both literary composition and abstinence.

When he could not be in the Scillies, Dan liked to escape to the Oxfordshire countryside. James Sutherland, the Professor of English at UCL, and his wife Helen, who worked for an advertising agency, had a Queen Anne house at Sutton Courtenay whose grounds abut the church-yard where George Orwell is buried. On a number of occasions they lent it to Dan for a week at a time. From spring to autumn they had family excursions at the weekends, on Port Meadow or to the surround-ing countryside, to Rycote, Bagley Woods, Wittenham Clumps, or Cotswold villages. Such places stirred dreams of having a cottage of their own where Dan could write, and they could all be away from the clamour of Oxford. The quest for the cottage 'seemed like a holy grail or a pie of youth at the time'.[17] Such trips were not always easy to arrange. Dan took no interest in cars and never learned to drive. The Press owned a number of vehicles for the use of senior executives, and although Dan was initially uncomfortable at being driven by a chauffeur, he adjusted to the advant-ages, and Murphy, his driver, was devoted to him. In later years, younger colleagues remembered Dan's generosity in allowing them to take what was really 'his' company car for their own use at weekends. He remained dependent all his life on the rural bus services, the local trains (which were withdrawn in the early 1960s), taxis, and the offer of lifts from friends.

To these brief interludes must be added the longer excursions of family summer holidays. After two holidays together in the Scilly Isles, they went to Barmoor Castle in Northumberland in both 1955, when Joyce Cary accompanied them, and 1956. This was Bill Sitwell's family pile, a stately, dilapidated, palatial residence from which they went on country walks. On various occasions in the 1950s they went to Normandy to stay at Le Thil-Manneville, where John and Anne Willett had a country house. Dan had known John Willett by sight in pre-war Oxford, but they got to know each other well during the advance from Alamein to Tunis in the autumn of 1942, when Dan was with J Squadron, and Willett was on Montgomery's GHQ Intelligence staff under Bill Williams. A German scholar, fluent in French, he went to work after the war in literary journalism, and in due course joined the *TLS*. He and Dan were alike in their talent for friendship, and his knowledge of literary London was unrivalled.[18] His wife Anne is half French, a war veteran of secret Allied operations with the French Resistance. Their house at Le Thil, which they bought in 1952, was a favourite in the summer with people as diverse as Richard Cobb, John Davenport, the painter Alan Lowndes, and Robert Conquest, historian, linguist, and iconoclast. Throughout what seemed in retrospect to have been endless days of summer sunshine, there were trips to the beach, long lazy kitchen table meals of Anne's memorable food, and generous, keen conversation.

Did all this country living signal the onset of middle-aged bourgeois respectability? Dan celebrated his fortieth birthday in 1953, when he was approaching the end of his eighth year at the Press. His apprenticeship as a publisher was finished. His history of the battle for Crete had just been published. In its wake he had assembled two books for the World's Classics series, one an edition of New Zealand short stories, the other a volume of short stories by Katherine Mansfield. Both were long in print, and sold well. The New Zealand short stories became the foundation of a series of later editions that were for many years the benchmark of excellence in the genre in his home country. To New Zealanders he was now a figure of considerable prestige; in literary circles in Britain, an established writer, though more of promise than achievement; in bohemian life, a good companion, generous patron, amusing raconteur; in academic circles, a publisher at the centre of learning and high culture.

Reputation may be important when you do not have it. For Dan, the status he had achieved so rapidly was, at least for a while, illusory. The reasons for this lay in his position at the Press. Dan had been an ambitious man, not in a conventional way, for honours or prestige, but for particular goals that he set himself, and in pursuit of objectives which he felt important. At every stage, university entrance, Rhodes Scholarship, promotion in the army, the hunt for literary recognition, he had never been thwarted. He prided himself on a certain political astuteness, the capacity to secure an objective despite resistance. In Walton Street he was defeated for the first time in his career.

When Sisam retired in August 1948, Dan succeeded to the position of Assistant Secretary. Sir Arthur Norrington, who became Secretary, had long experience in the Press, and had specialized more lately in education texts—the profitable line of schools publications—while Dan's responsibilities, in Sisam's footsteps, lay largely within the Clarendon Press. His relations with Cumberlege, the Publisher, and his staff in London were good. Vivian Ridler, who had taken over as Printer in 1948, he counted a friend as well as colleague. He understood the American business, which he had visited in the spring of 1952. In the eyes of much of the academic world, his name was synonymous with Oxford University Press, and it was certainly the case that the Delegates, with whom he had become a familiar and dependable colleague, appeared to treat him in this light. In 1952, when Norrington announced his intention to retire from publishing to take up the position of President of Trinity College, Dan was thought likely in some circles to succeed him as Secretary.

But this was not to be. In the autumn of 1952 Colin Roberts, a classical scholar and papyrologist, fellow of St John's College (always closely linked to the affairs of the Press), and an OUP Delegate since 1946, was nominated to succeed Norrington as Secretary in 1954.[19] Dan's immediate reactions to this are as obscure as the method by which the decision was reached.[20] Sisam, who had coached and supported him for the appointment, wrote: 'Your news is a personal disappointment to me as it is to you. My interest has always been in the welfare of the Office [of Secretary], which is the heart of the business.'[21] It is not clear why Dan did not get the appointment. Sisam was inclined to think that the reasons were twofold: that the Delegates were largely inexperienced—'there are very few "old hands" with long experience of their own ignorance; and that means oversimplification and a chance for bright thoughts to be put into practice'; and that perhaps they were looking for someone to be more the 'supra departmental general manager' and no longer, as he had liked to think of himself, 'the head of the C.P. department, mouthpiece of the Delegates, and their right-hand adviser'.[22] Others took the view that the decision had rather more to do with personalities. Dan was closely associated with Sisam, which would have been no recommendation to Bowra, then Vice-Chancellor of the University.

Winnie said in long retrospect that Dan had been 'quite passive' about his own application to be Secretary of OUP; that his main worry at the time was the possible appointees who were being discussed, or at any rate gossiped about, because there were some under whom he would not have been prepared to serve. She recalled that he went to discuss the problem with the historian G. N. (Sir George) Clark, Provost of Oriel, one of the editors of the Oxford History of England, and a power-broker in University affairs. Clark asked him whom he would prefer as Secretary. Dan told him Colin Roberts. His own preference thus coincided with the growing consensus. Nevertheless, Dan was looking elsewhere. He wrote to Kip asking for advice about possible positions in New Zealand, and Kip took soundings among eminent figures in diplomacy, the public service, and the university world.[23] Their responses were positive, but a month later Dan changed his mind, and the project was suspended.

If Dan did still have ambition at the Press, Roberts's age surely dispersed it. Only four years senior, his tenure could be expected to ensure Dan's career-long exclusion. Winnie, always sympathetically ambitious for Dan, was upset, and perhaps perplexed at first by the fact of Dan's adjustment to it. For his disappointment was very soon replaced by satisfaction. Dan did indeed work well with Roberts, and his confidence in him was reciprocated. They were both classicists, and had already worked together in revising and extending the Oxford Classical Texts series, for which Dan was responsible at the Press. They were both sticklers for the details of textual preparation, and enjoyed editing difficult manuscripts. They were both stylists in the use of language. They both had prodigious powers of work. Roberts had a close New Zealand connection through his long and intimate friendship with Charles Brasch.[24] Like Dan, Roberts had wartime experience of intelligence, though on the civilian side, first at Bletchley Park, and later in Whitehall, where he 'was deep in ULTRA, on the political side, from very early on'.[25]

In other ways they differed, however. Roberts was 'genuinely pious'[26] and socially stiff, a stiffness that hardened with the years. He would not have felt comfortable in a pub, any more than would Sisam. His father had been a builder, and Roberts and his wife Alison bought one and a half acres of land from St John's College on the south-west side of Cumnor village, where they built a new home, 'Appleton House', facing southward to the Downs, and north-west to the Cotswolds beyond Leafield and Chipping Norton. Here they entertained with dinner parties at which ladies and gentlemen wore evening dress—a source of embarrassment for any who arrived unprepared. '[A] tall spare straight figure who carried about with him a touch of English austerity', the style he brought to the Press seemed to look backwards, to a vanished age.[27]

It makes little sense to search for objective reasons in Roberts's appointment over Davin. Roberts, a senior classics scholar of St John's, with a brilliant First; a university lecturer and fellow; wartime Whitehall insider; pious and discreet: he was an Oxford man of his day, through and through. In the private world of Senior Common Rooms he was the sort of man other men like him would want at the Press. In this context, Dan was a parvenu. In the last analysis, there was no other reason for him not to be appointed than that he was who he was, and the Delegates—who constituted a self-appointing and exclusive club—did not prefer him. It was a decision that had profound consequences later for OUP.

As a result of his Whitehall war, Roberts had some experience of management in a more hierarchic and didactic style, and he set his mind to exercising close administrative control over the whole OUP enterprise, finding it difficult to delegate. The main effect of this on Dan was that, as the Press grew, Roberts was compelled to leave him greater and greater freedom to deal with the more purely literary side of the Clarendon Press business, taking more of the administrative, and all the financial burden on himself. This freed Dan from the aspect of publishing which he found irksome, and permitted him, over the next ten years, to establish himself as, in all but name, the Clarendon Press Publisher. Roberts, meanwhile, adopted increasingly the position of 'supra departmental general manager' that Sisam had foreseen. In this way, slowly at first, and without any clear plan ever being adopted, Dan came to have primary responsibility at Delegates' meetings for information about CP titles and projects on which the Delegates made decisions, while Roberts was the administrative force on the Finance Committee, where questions of management, administration, and investment were settled. It was a division of responsibilities which suited Dan's temperament. Failure to secure the position of Secretary brought him intellectual liberty.

In 1953 the burden of whatever personal disappointment he felt at the Press was exacerbated by bad health. He was progressively ill and in pain, his appetite poor, his digestion wretched. Paddy Costello wrote to hope 'it [sic] the sort of thing which can be eliminated without recourse either to surgery or to abstention from alcohol',[28] but neither hope was well-founded. Investigation showed an advanced case of gallstones, and he was advised to have surgery for the removal of his gall-bladder.

The operation was performed at Guy's Hospital in London on 29 January 1954 by Heneage Ogilvie, whose sister Gertrude—known to everyone as Trudy—had been Joyce Cary's wife. Dan met him at dinner at Cary's in the autumn of 1953, and when it came up in conversation that he was to have the operation Ogilvie offered to do it himself. Geoffrey Flavell greeted this news with gloom. He told Dan that it was unwise to be operated on by great surgeons at the height of reputation because they were always in decline. The man to choose was an up and coming fellow, someone still making his way. Perhaps with this in mind (Flavell was now a surgeon at several London hospitals, and had consulting rooms in Harley Street) he asked for permission, which was granted, to assist at the operation.

At this time a gall-bladder excision was serious surgery. Flavell made light of it: 'Dan's gall-bladder was a poor little shrivelled scrotum of a thing', he said. But Dan was very badly knocked. The wound took many weeks to heal.[29] He was in hospital for three weeks, and after two weeks at home went down to the Scilly Isles to convalesce at Sisam's house for another fortnight. 'I was an octogenarian when I came home', he wrote from there to Sargeson, 'but have now gone back to the middle sixties and look forward to being forty again very soon . . .'[30] Back in Southmoor Road, he kept the gallstones in a jar on top of his bedroom wardrobe, where they frightened the children.

Personal and professional troubles were compounded by more worldly events. From 1948 onwards, for thoughtful people who paid attention to world affairs, or who made a living from any of the intellectual professions, the cold war was not a distant, abstract concept, but a sequel to the hot war, in many ways equally uncomfortable, and constantly threatening to break into private life as much as public affairs. Dan's own brushes with it, in the peculiar reception accorded *For The Rest Of Our Lives* among European publishers, in the change of travel plans imposed on him in 1948 by the Berlin crisis, had been relatively benign, but he watched with distaste the rise of McCarthyism in the United States, and the election of Conservative governments in both Great Britain and New Zealand at mid-century. The growth of intolerance in the United States had a direct impact on both university and intellectual life more generally, fuelling suspicions and provoking resentments that soured relationships and damaged, sometimes wrecked, careers. Dan had first-hand experience of this working with Isaac Deutscher.

Donald Tyerman of *The Times* introduced Deutscher to the Press in January 1947 when Deutscher was contemplating writing a history of

Soviet Russia.[31] Simultaneously he had in mind writing a political biography of Stalin, and in the event this was the project on which he chose to concentrate. Dan met him on his first visit to Oxford on 6 February 1947, and subsequently introduced him to the London business. Over the next couple of years they became friends, and although OUP London published his books, it was Dan who acted as his editor, reading and commenting on the manuscripts, correcting solecisms, improving the style, and testing the judgements. They had occasional meetings for lunch or drinks, usually at Deutscher's home first at Haverstock Hill in north London, and subsequently, from the late 1950s, at Wokingham in Berkshire. Once his *Stalin* was finished, Deutscher set to work on a biography of Trotsky, and for this he needed to go to the United States to work in various archives. The timing for such a visit was ideal, since it could be coupled with the promotion of *Stalin*, which was to be published in America in September 1949. On the strength of this OUP agreed to pay his fare. At this point, however, the American authorities refused his application for a visa, because he had been a member of the Polish Communist Party in the 1930s.

As in much of the dialogue of cold war there was irony here. Deutscher was now a leading revisionist, author of a critical biography of the Communist leader whom, a mere five years earlier, American and British governments alike had lauded as partner in the alliance for freedom. Now Deutscher was too dangerous, a threat to democratic stability. Eventually, after many months of expensive legal representation at various hearings, and after a number of refusals, Deutscher and his wife were admitted to the United States under a waiver clause, and they sailed for New York on New Year's Day 1950. By this time his book had been published for over three months, and the controversy that it stirred had come and gone in his absence, so that whatever impact his presence might have had on sales was lost. There were those in OUP, at Amen House and on Walton Street, as well as in New York, who imagined that this had always been the purpose of American policy.

While Deutscher was at last enjoying the fruits of his first research trip to the United States, Ian Milner, the New Zealand Rhodes Scholar whom Dan last saw at Oxford before the war, was making up his mind that he had had enough of New York, where he was employed in the United Nations Secretariat. In the summer of 1950 he and his wife Margot, on holiday in Europe, decided to travel to Prague, and having arrived decided to stay. He acquired a lecturing position at Charles University, and made Czechoslovakia his home for the rest of his life.

Milner's Marxist radicalism, his wife's Communist Party membership, and his apparently sudden decision to abandon a lucrative post as international civil servant, were sufficient to earn him the title of defector. Four years later, during the Petrov affair in Australia, he was named as a spy. The truth or falsity of the accusations and counter-accusations that flew in the wake of Petrov are not the issue here. Dan had no more access to the truth—whatever that might have been—than any other spectator of events in the hall of mirrors where cold warriors seek security. His instinct was threefold: to put little trust in official accounts of 'secret' matters, which from his experience in wartime intelligence he knew to be subject to 'the necessary lie'; to expect men to act in the first instance in response to private moral (or indeed immoral) considerations, unconnected to public affairs or the motions of history; and to have confidence in the personal, not the public. This instinct made him sympathetic to Milner.[32]

This view was, like all opinion, folded into the fabric of the times. The Korean War divided the 'free' United Nations from the 'Communist' bloc; in South-East Asia 'republican' French battled against 'Communist' Vietnamese; in Berlin East and West glowered at each other across the ruins of a shattered civilization, each proposing an alternative account of how it should be rebuilt; in dozens of small nations, American and Russian 'advisers' installed puppet regimes of varying degrees of vileness in advertisement of their resolve. Quite apart from Korea, a more general war threatened constantly, and for a time in 1950 and 1951, like others of his generation, Dan expected that it would come, and that it would destroy his world.[33] Like most reasonable people, widely read in literature, trained in the classics and historical analysis, Dan detested the world that was being erected on the victory over Fascism, a victory which he felt belonged in part to people like himself and Geoff Cox, and Paddy Costello, and all their friends in the Div., men of good will who had done the fighting. In short, Dan experienced in the cold war of the early 1950s, and in all the personal tragedies that the war inflicted, both disappointment and disillusion. He felt that history had rolled over him, that the wave he thought to have been riding had broken, leaving him floundering.

The sensation was emphasized in his friendship with Paddy Costello. Paddy spent nearly six years in Moscow, from 1944 to 1950, when, after a brief return visit to New Zealand for consultations, he was posted to the New Zealand legation in Paris. Throughout this time he corresponded with Dan, leaving a partial record of his views about Soviet Russia and his life of diplomacy in Moscow.[34] He was particularly active in the artistic community, befriending writers, and making contact with composers and painters. He was friendly with Pasternak, whom he met through Dan and Winnie. They knew Pasternak's sister Lydia, who lived in the Oxford suburb of Park Town, and whose daughter Ann was one of Delia's best friends at school. On one occasion Paddy and Dan acted as go-betweens in smuggling Pasternak manuscript notes to Oxford. Dan persuaded Paddy to edit a volume of Russian poetry for the Press,[35] and he worked on various other literary projects for which Dan's correspondence was valuable.

Once Costello was installed with his family in Paris, Dan was able to visit, which he did on at least three occasions: in June 1951 *en route* to and from an international PEN meeting in Lausanne; at Easter 1953, when he took Anna with him; and again in August 1953, when he and Winnie went up to Paris for a few days from 'Le Thil'. Paddy's place in Dan's life was unchanged. Dan still rather envied him the strength which his firm convictions gave to his actions and thoughts.[36] Perhaps Paddy was now, in some slight degree, disenchanted with the Soviet Union, but his analytical Marxism was as resourceful as ever, his judgement of the United States contemptuous, and his view of international relations pessimistic. From Moscow he had written of the Americans' reinstating war criminals in positions of power in Germany and Japan, and the anger felt about it by the Russians.[37] In Paris, where he was learning Persian in his spare time, he watched the development of the arms race, and other features of the cold war, with dismay: 'the things I have to see and describe are so distasteful as to be nearly intolerable.'[38]

This comment was in the context of the Indo-China war, from which he feared a thermonuclear war might develop, and more specifically a first strike by the Americans against China.

Probably the greatest hope lies in the uncertainty about Russia's strength: has Russia got hydrogen bombs in quantity? Will she use them if China is attacked by the Americans? At the same time the very uncertainty is also a source of danger. There are lunatics who argue that the Russians will probably not react to a U.S. attack on China, and that the risk (termed, by antiphrasis, 'calculated') is worth taking.[39]

This letter was written under strain. Costello had known for a year that the New Zealand government was under pressure to remove him from the diplomatic service.[40] Since early 1953, though unaware of the threat to his career in diplomacy, Dan had been helping him to try to find an academic position in Britain. Matters were finally brought to a head in the second half of 1954 when Costello was required to resign from the service. His resignation took effect from January 1955.[41] No publicity was attached to the case, and no charges were ever laid against him. To Dan, Costello attributed his failure to his personal incompetence as a diplomatist. Six years before he had written from Moscow:

I should say that I was not cut out for a propagandist any more than for a diplomat. Most of the time I can conform to the regulations of this world . . . but there come moments when, usually under the influence of wine, I can hold out no longer . . . I don't often in public tell an American First Secretary that I think the President of his country is a bum. I have done so, nevertheless, and am revealed thereby as an indifferent diplomat.[42]

In 1954 he catalogued the issues on which he had argued to Wellington against American interpretations of events, and concluded: 'When all the major assumptions underlying a country's foreign policy are mistaken, it is folly on the part of an official to draw attention to the fact.'[43]

Costello believed, in tune with both his war experiences and his theoretical Marxism, that Americans were unreliable allies, incompetent analysts, bullying in victory, malicious in defeat. He thought New Zealand should have a foreign policy independent of the great powers. This was heresy during the height of the cold war, and a man raised in Catholicism must have known the penalties for staining the purity of dogma. It is hard to believe that he would not have expected the Americans and the British to be reading his correspondence, even harder to imagine that, in the wake of the Burgess and Maclean scandal, a Marxist with a pedigree of 1930s Cambridge, brilliant, argumentative, intolerant of fools, would not have fallen victim to counter-intelligence.

Costello looked for employment at UNESCO, but no international agency was now open to him. Through his many contacts in academic circles, and by the timely good fortune of the position coming vacant, Dan supported Paddy for the post of Professor of Russian at Manchester University. He was appointed, and took up his position in October 1955. His return to Britain brought great pleasure to Dan. He was soon active in the community of Russian scholars in Britain, particularly in Oxford, where Max Hayward, long known to Paddy, was also a friend of Dan's. Paddy became a frequent visitor at Southmoor Road, improving the quality of the conversation and the singing whenever he was there.

Through Dan Paddy also got to know Martha McCulloch, a fixture in the domestic life of the Davins in the 1950s. When Dan brought Delia a pinafore back from New York in 1952, it was Martha who finished it with cross-stitching. She knitted each of the girls a woollen hat (which they disliked and never wore). Winnie persevered through this sort of thing, quite admiring Martha's energy for handicraft tasks which she herself detested. Only once was she really upset by Dan's dependence on Martha for trivial matters. On one occasion when Dan was away on business, Winnie planned to take the family to Italy to stay with her friends Alessandro and Miti Galante Garrone, and for some reason, perhaps her reputation for efficiency, Dan asked Martha to make the travel arrangements. Winnie, a far more experienced traveller than Martha, was upset about this. In other ways, however, Martha seemed to fit into the family. Only Anna never liked her at all.

In any event, by the mid-1950s Dan's relationship with Martha was changing, as his circle of friends in Oxford expanded. In 1954 Dan and Winnie made friends with a young anthropologist in Oxford called Godfrey Lienhardt.[44] They met first in a pub, the Anchor, in Chalfont Road. Lienhardt recalled that he was sitting there, rather lonely, when this couple came in and got two pints of bitter. The man, sitting down with the *TLS*, said to the woman: 'Timor mortis conturbat te',[45] and Lienhardt was immediately engaged. They got into a conversation which lasted for thirty-six years.

Lienhardt was partially of Swiss extraction, but had grown up in Yorkshire, where he was an outstanding product of Batley Grammar School. He won an open scholarship to Cambridge in 1939, planning to read English under Leavis. When news of the scholarship arrived in the mail, his mother, unable to conceal her pride, told her neighbour of it over the fence. 'Aye,' this woman replied, in her broad Yorkshire tones. 'You can educate 'em till they're daft.' Another story that Lienhardt liked to tell of himself was of his returning late one night with his brother Peter to find their mother waiting up for them. 'Oh,' she said, 'so here you are at last. And all that worry wasted.' Lienhardt's ear for the telling phrase, the illustrative anecdote, delighted all who knew him, Dan in particular. His academic career was interrupted by the war. At first he was appointed instructor in Transport Command, until it was detected that he could not drive. He was sent to East Africa ('to inspect margarine'), and on the strength of his experiences there was drawn into the world of academic anthropology by Edward Evans-Pritchard when they met in Cambridge after the war. A year later he followed E-P to Oxford, though he spent the years 1947–50 and 1952–4 doing field work in the Sudan, where he lived among and studied the Dinka and the Anuak. Not long after he met the Davins he was off again, going to Baghdad for a year as Professor of Anthropology, but on his return he settled in Oxford, and remained there the rest of his life.

Lienhardt was small and thin, fragile in appearance, but of a physical and mental toughness that could surprise. He smoked continuously, apparently without discrimination, everything from pipes and cigars to cigarettes. Along with books and company his first love was conversation, to which he brought a mannered style, quick wit, and waspish tongue. He nicknamed a couple of young women who, in thrall to Dan, used at one time to hang around the pub, 'Grin and Bear it.' And he once displeased Dan somewhat by persuading him, in all seriousness, to attempt a translation of the inscription, 'Ore stabit, fortis arare placet ore stat'.[46] When he and his brother were absent from the pub one evening, Dan inquired, 'Where are the Lienhardts killing tonight?', a reference to their reputation for launching unprovoked and savage attacks on people who were invariably incapable of protecting themselves—something they would not do at the pub. Despite this occasional and inexplicable quirk, Godfrey's company was sought by a continually widening circle of friends, colleagues, and acquaintances from all over the world, all races and all walks of life. Dan, Winnie, and Godfrey took to going each evening to the Tudor Snug, a small front bar down a few steps in the Victoria Arms on Walton Street, close to Southmoor Road. Snug it was in those days, though there was nothing Tudor about it. It even had a couple of paintings by Gerald Wilde on the walls, though they were hard to see behind grilles more reminiscent of traditional divers' headgear than of art galleries. These were tribute for the fivers and free pints that George Clack, the landlord, had given Wilde over the years. After her husband's death Mrs Clack took over the licence, started to wear false eyelashes— they would occasionally fall into the beer as she pulled it—and hunted, unsuccessfully, for a replacement husband. When the local bookmaker got married to a woman of 60 or so Mrs Clack was heard to comment: 'Why can she get somebody and I can't get no bugger!'[47] An unusual woman, affectionately remembered by generations of regulars (she served a term as President of the Oxford Licensed Victuallers too), her presence added colour to the environment where a circle of friends developed. In due course it included Lienhardt's brother Peter, also an anthropologist, specialist in Asia Minor. Other regulars were John Veale, the composer, David Pocock, an anthropologist with special interest in India, Jonathan Price, and Peter Sutcliffe, two CP editors, Enid Starkie (though her attendance was occasional rather than regular), and such guests, visitors,

Elizabeth Berndt in Egypt, 1942. On the back she wrote 'Salùte and cheer up!'

Dan in Palestine, 1943

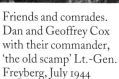

Friends and comrades. Dan and Geoffrey Cox with their commander, 'the old scamp' Lt.-Gen. Freyberg, July 1944

Dan with his sisters Molly and Evelyn (fruit boxes behind), September 1948

Family portrait with (l. to r.)
Brigid, Delia, Winnie and Anna,
c.1953

In New Zealand to give the Macmillan
Brown lectures, March 1959

Nuala O'Faolain, 1964

singly, the Vicky did not favour those for whom conversation
~~en~~. Dan still delighted, as he had in the 1930s, in setting other
~~ee~~, aiming to liberate conversation, not imprison it. '[H]e
~~as~~ other people talked more and the chief use he made of his
~~ries~~ and jokes was to start an atmosphere where other people
~~in~~ to feel at ease and let themselves go.'[50] Alan Horsman
~~ing~~ in the pub one evening with Keith Sinclair, then a rising
~~w~~ Zealand academic history. Sinclair, in whom talent and
~~mixed~~ in almost equal proportions, seized the floor and held
~~ng~~, talking, explaining, expounding, lecturing. Dan, while
~~clair~~ every impression of close attention, occasionally threw
~~a~~ little grin, 'not malicious, but amused and amusing', that
~~ged~~ Sinclair's egotism while tolerating it.[51] There were those
~~ved~~ that Dan was merely 'collecting copy' in the pub, by
~~n~~ exploiting friendship for literary purposes. This is a complete
~~tanding~~, possibly malicious. Dan's diary entries, even when he
~~eping~~ a continuous record again in 1964, contain nothing
~~out~~ his friends at the Victoria Arms. The occasional aphorism
~~vanted~~ to remember is all. The three novels that he wrote in
~~f~~ his public house tenure contain no reference to it, and the
~~ncluded~~ in *Closing Times* largely predate these experiences. It
~~ly~~ the absence of ulterior motives or secondary considerations
~~iendship~~ that made it special and memorable.

~~ndencies~~ in Dan were not new, but they did emphasize a
~~m~~ that had been rather more concealed in the days of his
His intolerance of incompetence, prominent in the war
~~d~~ disappeared. 'One must just accept the fact,' he wrote to

~~f~~ considerable energy but also of considerable limitations will
~~themselves~~ into positions of administrative power . . . This is just
~~circumstance~~ and to my thinking the artist must simply accept it
~~on~~ trying to contend with it[,] as he must reckon on having to
~~stupidity~~, apathy, poverty, and all the other things that drag at his
~~d~~ frustrate him.[52]

~~is~~ own recipe, he submerged the occasional brash arrogance of
~~nfident~~ young intellectual, and replaced it on the surface with
~~s~~ self-deprecation, ironic and amused, as though the youth he
~~vas~~ now someone else, quite entertaining to watch, but only
~~tance~~. It was this self-knowledge that made him wonderfully

Martha McCulloch, 1967

Dan on his
retirement,
summer 1978

Dan and Anna, *c.*1983

Delia, 1984

Dan and Brigid, 1982

Patty and Philip Watson, c.1980

At the cottage in
Dorchester, c.1988

Pencil drawings by
Laura Buxton, March
1990

or occasional participants as might
might be invited. This last was im
standing that members would not c
guest meant reflecting on whether
enjoyed.[48] It also meant sharing in the
newcomer in half-pints approximate
over on a tray, and then poured into
This required a steady hand, not a
occupied the same corner, which w
worn threadbare and sunken where
window, he had a good view of the
his place tended to be left vacant,
ignorant of protocol, could generate
round tables, lower than the settle an
to sociability. A newcomer who knew
and empties from the tables on arriv
the group's corner, home in her ter
'high table'. She would cash cheques
the days before bank cards, and right
regard. For the group, the Tudor S
ground.

Dan had taken to using a cigarette-
like a literary FDR or Trevor Howa
occasionally the same jauntiness of sty
This sometimes persuaded visitors, pa
him as presiding over a court. This imp
were not courtiers, and Dan was never
the only way to be certain of giving
remarked of a New Zealand visitor tha
conversation the man had no idea wh
criticism. Then he brightened. 'Still,'
Joseph, he picks it up, puts it in his po

The anecdote had point. Public h
does not suit all tastes, and Dan's pre
in this way closed some avenues. Mik
example. On his sabbatical visits to
uncomfortable in the pub, and prefer
Bertram, the patrician of New Zeala
referred to 'Dan and his cronies'.[49]
think of a more inappropriate word t

Unsurp
was a bur
tongues
talked les
fund of st
would be
recalled b
star of N
vanity we
it all eve
giving Si
Horsman
acknowle
who belie
implicatio
misunder
took to
intimate
which he
the years
memoirs
was preci
in Dan's

These
side of h
ambition.
diaries, h
Sargeson:

that men
always pu
a universa
and recko
encounter
energies a

True to
the self-c
a humoro
had been
from a di

26

receptive to younger writers, especially from New Zealand, in whom he detected the same features that he had himself once had.

This did not happen overnight. Rupert Hart-Davis, who sat next to him at a Johnson Club dinner in Worcester College on 20 July 1957, found him 'aggressive but intelligent and incisive'.[53] There would have been high table defences at work here. Elsewhere, the aggression was giving ground. Some of the tolerance was spawned at home, where first Anna, and then both Delia and Brigid, brought boyfriends. Open invitation was extended for supper on Sunday evenings, and they would sit down, with other friends and visitors, twelve to twenty at the table. These were not always easy occasions. Dan was ambitious for his daughters, and quick to detect inadequacy in their boyfriends. Brigid thought that he probably 'loathed all the boys we brought home. He would pretend to be kind and polite but was really being a bit cruel.' One poor boy used to get so nervous he had to rush upstairs to be sick. Delia remembers, however, that Dan was not a 'jealous guard' of his daughters, though he worried about them, and would never go to bed before they were home at night. Even so, none of the daughters had any recollection of receiving sex education at home. Brigid said Dan once asked her, when she was 14, if she knew about sex 'and so on'. 'Oh yes, Dadda, really, absolutely everything.' They both knew it was not true, but embarrassment impeded further progress.

Nevertheless, young adolescents in the house strengthened his tolerance, while his discovery of the role of mature man prepared to listen brought him a popularity which he did not seek, but which he enjoyed, particularly among the graduate students whom Godfrey occasionally brought to the pub. Several generations of young anthropologists carried memories of Dan's wit, charm, and friendship away to some of the obscurest places in the world, as well as the most famous universities. And since Dan was so well-connected in intellectual and university life, on any evening a young scholar might find him- or herself, in the quiet atmosphere of the Tudor Snug, on temporary equal terms with the great and famous: Conor Cruise O'Brien or Richard Ellmann; Richard Cobb or Evans-Pritchard; Helen Gardner, Theo Moody, Neville Rogers, or Gordon Craig.

Ambition is trimmed by success as well as by defeat. In a way, and without realizing it consciously, Dan had found the social milieu towards which his struggles in Otago and Southland a quarter of a century before had been aimed. He now lived at the centre of the world of intellect and literature of which he had once only dreamed. He and Winnie were invited to Compton Mackenzie's house at Denchworth, near Wantage.[54] At Joyce Cary's dinner table they met Middleton Murry: a legend to Dan and Winnie, someone who had been intimate with Katherine, satirized by Aldous, friends with DHL.[55] In Dublin they met the former National Librarian, Richard Best, who appears in James Joyce's *Ulysses* under his own name. When Dan took part in a writers' forum at a British Council summer school in Oxford in August 1956, other speakers with whom he shared the platform were C. P. Snow and Pamela Hansford Johnson.

But the eminence of his position was not just by association. He was much sought after as speaker and writer. When the New Zealand High Commission in London mounted an exhibition of New Zealand books in co-operation with the British National Book League, they turned to Dan to give a lecture on 'New Writing in New Zealand'.[56] He was in demand to speak to the Booksellers Association, along with men like Basil Blackwell and Philip Unwin. He was invited to write about the Commonwealth for the Central Office of Information. He continued to contribute talks to the BBC on literary and historical topics. In 1957 he collaborated with Paddy Costello and General von Senger (a former Rhodes Scholar himself) in a radio discussion about the battle of Cassino.[57] This was the life of a successful man of letters, and in itself the partial fulfilment of his early ambition.

Those who paid only flying visits to Oxford might believe that Dan's life was pub life alone. It was certainly important, but his days were too full for it to dominate. He still tried to keep fit, and continued the games of squash that he had been encouraged to take up in order to lose weight before his operation. He played either with Peter Frankenberg, or with his Somerville friend Jean Banister. He still ran on Port Meadow occasionally and, when time permitted, went swimming. And he still played chess. In 1957 and 1958 Robert Walmesley came to live at 103. He was the son of an American actress, Dorothea Biddle, whom Dan had first met in England in the summer of 1948 through Joel Carmichael.[58] Robert was preparing for university entrance in Britain, and, briefly, was for Dan and Winnie like a son. While he and Dan played chess, Brigid and Delia took Robert cheese, food for the brain. Dan also played chess with H. W. Garrod in Merton, who, if Dan had won on the previous occasion, gave him port to drink, 'the effect of which impaired my game'.[59] His main partner, however, was Winnie, with whom he played chess a lot, generally on Sunday afternoons, and always so if the weather was bad. Chess battles are rightly metaphor for intellectual companionship.

A full life, and less enthusiasm for writing, did not terminate literary ambition. When he finished *Roads From Home* Dan had two ideas for novels in mind: one set among expatriate New Zealanders in London at the end of the war; the other about an expatriate Protestant Englishman in Catholic Southland before it. They were to be part of a pattern of novels that summed up his homeland. Robert Lusty encouraged him to write the London one first, and with *Crete* behind him he tried to settle to the task first in July and then at Christmas 1952, and again the following Easter. Progress was negligible, however. By the autumn of 1953, with Press work, illness, and his operation hanging over him, he was badly stalled, and it was not until his convalescence at Middle Carn in March 1954 that he began to make rapid progress. Once launched, composition was quick, and back in the Scilly Isles in the early autumn he finished a complete draft. In succession to *Roads From Home* he began with the working title *Home From Home*, but by 1954 the novel was called *The Death of the Dead*, an echo of a novel by Elizabeth Bowen, *The Death of the Heart*, which Dan admired.[60]

The strength of the working title was its expression of the central theme of the work: the idea now generally associated with Sartre's *Huis Clos*, that the dead live on as long as they are remembered by the living. True death, in Sartre's terms liberation into the infinity of nothingness, but in Davin's the final loss of existence in the preoccupations of the living, is thus something that comes after the event itself.[61] The weakness of the title was precisely its negative force, and Robert Lusty encouraged him to change it. The title on which he eventually fixed, *The Sullen Bell*, is taken from Shakespeare's 71st sonnet—'No longer mourn for me when I am dead'—a favourite poem of Dan's. The title, though not precisely faithful to the book's theme, certainly captured its tone. He adopted it in late August 1955, when the book was already accepted for publication.[62] Michael Joseph were efficient at their work. Dan had the proofs in early January, and *The Sullen Bell* was published on Monday, 14 May 1956, a week earlier than Lusty had provisionally proposed.[63]

In this novel Dan persisted with the experiment he had launched in *Roads From Home*, adopting a narrative technique of multiple internal 'points of view', each one character-specific, so that we read as though hearing a diversity of perceptions. The characters are numerous, a large cast appropriate to the novel's big city setting, but similar in that they are all New Zealanders, and all are suffering from the loss of family or friends in the war that has just finished. Sally McGovern, a young woman who has come on to London from wartime service in Italy, is still mourning the death in a London hospital of her friend Bill, an Alpha figure from Otago university days, who haunts her memory, in part for the fact that they were never lovers. Hugh Egan, the protagonist, is a former wartime battalion commander and university historian, now engaged on a volume of war history, and living for a year in a small Bloomsbury flat to work in the archives. He is also escaping from Otago, where his wife Alison, depressed from the death of their baby, has recently drowned herself in 'the swift, green Taieri'.[64] Hugh and Sally become lovers at the end of the novel, and in doing so 'bury their dead' in a new start of springtime affection.

Between them and the mutual recognition of their love both for each other, and for life over death, lies a winter of darkness and cold conflict filled with the squabbles, passions, fights, parties, and politics of mid-1940s London. The cold war is beginning, an era of spy trials and mistrust. Former soldiers, released on to the civvy streets of London from the Div. and the POW camps, find it hard to adjust to a peacetime world of routines in work and leisure. Bob Ritchie finds secure but uncomfortable employment in an advertising agency while writing 'romances' for the trash literature market; his brother Alec passively goes where the rising and falling tides of change occasionally deposit him; Dave Macnamara drifts from job to job, in and out of the black market, and from mistress to mistress.

As in Dan's previous fiction the characters are drawn from his experience, but mixed together in different compounds. A Knightsbridge photographer, Mercia Firth, bears a resemblance to Eileen Deste, the photographer in Dunedin and then Wellington whom Dan had known through Peggy Spence-Sales, and who did indeed have a studio in London during and after the war.[65] Hugh Egan, whom the *Landfall* reviewer, R. A. Copland,[66] found too unnecessarily like Dan himself, actually contains a lot of Kippenberger, both in having been a battalion commander, and in his automatic assumption of the obligation to advise and to lead. Men in trouble, who knew Hugh in the Div., go to him when they are in a fix, just as men in the war used to go to Kip. He is their father figure. Similarly, Dave Macnamara, another who is apparently partly Davin in style, contains some of Angus Ross (including his two Military Crosses), and some of Wig Gardiner in his direct no-nonsense approach. Bob Ritchie bears similarities to both Dan's younger brother Pat and to a former New Zealand serviceman called Jack Gillies, who successfully converted his writing skills into a considerable commercial fortune in the ten years after the war, and went to live in Ireland where the tax regime was more friendly. Gillies was a great fund of immediate post-war stories, including one in which he and a friend 'liberated' a huge Mercedes coupé, once the property of the Munich *Gauleiter*, and after various adventures (since it had no licence plates) managed to get it to England. They kept it in a barn in Surrey, and occasionally took it for a spin, especially to the yard of the Wheatsheaf in Fitzrovia. Maclaren-Ross, who called it 'Black Beauty', adored being driven about in it. Dan had known similar types in immediate post-war Oxford, including a small group of former commandos who came up to Keble. One of them had been Evelyn Waugh's runner, and told stories of his former commander that showed him in a decent and humane light. Dan was surprised but also convinced by these revelations. The tedium of post-war life was a torment for such men.

As with the real lives of people such as these, there is much entertainment to be had in *The Sullen Bell*, including the characters' occasional and unintentional pomposity, but once again the dominant tone is sombre. Death, though apparently defeated at the end, dominates the work. There is little conviction in the notion that Sally will dispel Hugh's morbid sense, at the age of 40, that 'the ground in front grew smaller and only his possessions in the rear enlarged'.[67] The war has made these men feel that the best is behind them now, that the future holds nothing but boredom and death, and they see its shadow in everything.

This was the frame of mind that Dan brought to the novel in 1954. The death of Dylan Thomas the previous autumn 'was a very hard blow' that left him 'quite downhearted for a week or more: which is more, I'm ashamed to say, than I would feel for most people'.[68] Dan said later that he regarded Dylan Thomas as one of only three geniuses that he had known (the others were Gerald Wilde and Joyce Cary), though he had often found him difficult. At the New Year of 1950 he had written to Winnie:

I confess I find a little of both [Dylan and Caitlin] goes a long way—not that I tire of Dylan's company but I tire of its consequences. And also his mode of argument—emotional and assertive—gets on my nerves a bit. For he hasn't a first class brain, or at least a trained one, and a good deal of noise is spent on propositions which are either obvious or absurd.[69]

It was DT's command of language, the speed of his wit, his powers of mimicry and pastiche, the heady mixture of fast talk, great humour, and swift repartee, that Dan loved and admired. Though he said it was a blow he felt for a week, in fact Dylan's death was a loss for which there was never compensation. Understandably, and in view of the fact that it was sudden and unexpected, Dan mixed it with fears about his own surgery, pending in the new year.

Dylan was only the most recent of many deaths, however. The war had brought a stream of them on the battlefield. His mother had died without his seeing her again. His first literary agent, Nancy Pearn, died in 1950, still a comparatively young woman. Dan Bill, his never seen son, he thought dead in South Africa. Keith Scott-Watson, a journalist friend from Cairo days, died suddenly in Italy at the beginning of 1951. All these deaths are present in *The Sullen Bell*. Gus Hayward, a returned prisoner of war, even has a schnauzer bitch called Kate.

Neither the theme of the novel nor its treatment was likely to appeal to reviewers, and the reception the novel received was poor. In Britain, the *TLS* detected 'death reluctantly weakening its hold over life', but felt the novel nondescript.[70] The *Manchester Guardian* thought there were too many characters in danger of becoming mere 'case histories' but that with his ability Davin could 'fine it down into something very good, if he chose',[71] which might have done for a reader's report rather than a review. In *Time and Tide* Fred Urquhart argued that Dan's talent was 'not seen to its best advantage; it demands a sturdier vehicle'.[72] Copland, in New Zealand *Landfall*, found himself 'obliged to acknowledge that [Davin] writes an inferior form of fiction', fulminated against the novel's documented, factual detail, and yearned for more art, 'not the facts . . . the author's synthesis of them'.[73]

In sum, however, the reviews were not so much hostile as neutral. There was a lack of interest. As before, the novel sold out rapidly—it was gone by September 1956, and was never reissued—but it was little noticed. Dan and Winnie believed that the fault lay with Michael Joseph, who advertised it little, and then ineptly, and it is true that the firm was distracted in the summer of 1956. Robert Lusty was preparing to leave to be Managing Director of Hutchinson's. Roland Gant, who replaced him, was new in the job, and still trying to be a novelist himself. These changes probably contributed little to the book's invisibility, however, which was more the product of other social and cultural factors.

Dan had not published a novel for seven years. He had always been an outsider in literary matters, going his own way, not genuflecting to the altar of popular taste. But this had mattered little while he was in tune with the dominant themes, political and literary, of his age and generation. By the mid-1950s, this was no longer the case. One pointer is the company involuntarily kept by *The Sullen Bell*, which was published at the same time as Angus Wilson's *Anglo-Saxon Attitudes*, a novel which, more perhaps than any other, defined the literary temper of mid-1950s Britain.[74] *The Sullen Bell* was unsympathetic to such an audience. Though set in London, it was not about British society (though it contained a catalogue of the expatriate New Zealanders' complaints about it). Such social criticism as it contained, about rationing, the black market, bad restaurant food, and so on, was fair for 1946 and 1947, but the novel was published a decade later, when the British, in common with the rest of Western Europe, were putting the immediate aftermath of the war behind them. Grumpy pessimism and cold despair were no longer welcome.

Literary revolt was in the air, but its mood and tone were different, a tone set by Kingsley Amis's *Lucky Jim* (1954), and by Iris Murdoch's *Under the Net*. Like *Anglo-Saxon Attitudes*, these were novels about *British* society, introspective, funny, claustrophobic. He wrote to Sargeson: 'I feel no wish to write about anything but NZers—indeed don't feel or don't feel in the same way about anyone else—and all the time the old navel-cord is getting more shrivelled. The Press Assoc. cable is no substitute.'[75]

In 1956 it was twenty years since Dan had left New Zealand. Joining the Div. in 1940 had returned him to his homeland in a way, and writing the Crete campaign volume had prolonged the renewal of relations. By the time *The Sullen Bell* was published, however, the fact of his permanent exile was increasingly apparent. Within it he sensed a double exile. For was not he also Irish, and in exile from there too? This growing sense of an identity in isolation worked with his instinct for the bohemian to attract him to the new experimentalism in fiction, an experimentation which he deeply admired but could not emulate. It was already detectable in the works of Samuel Beckett and Patrick White, and was soon to attract popular acclaim in Lawrence Durrell's *Alexandria Quartet* (*Justine* was published in 1957). Dan wrote about all these writers with great critical sympathy.[76] He knew that in their company his own work was unfashionable, limited in interest as well as in power, and stood for an immediate post-war realism which, though it still had an audience, no longer attracted critical attention. A sensitive critic, he understood this, and tacitly began to organize his withdrawal. He was encouraged in it by a wickedly clever letter from Flavell. In response to *The Sullen Bell* he wrote Dan a pastiche called 'Nells of Doom' which, after the first wry smile of recognition and amusement, left behind the uncomfortable sensation of being too close to a painful mark.[77]

Nevertheless, once *The Sullen Bell* was published Dan was keen to return to the other New Zealand novel which he had had in mind for almost a decade. Circumstances made this difficult, however. With the Press continuing to expand, and the extent of his obligations with it, he found that he was now not even a weekend writer. All his working time was consumed by publishing business, and much of his home life too. There were education costs to pay, though Anna had a scholarship at Oxford High School. He and Winnie were still hoping to find a country cottage for weekend escape. Winnie, who had taken on various free-lance jobs over the years, increased this work as the children grew up, and in due course took an editing job at OUP. Here she worked on the Oxford Junior Encyclopaedia, an enormous reference work that occupied her professional energies for many years to come.

So it was that the pattern of working on a long manuscript only in the peace of the Scillies was set. When Dan went back there on 28 September 1956, he began work on *Without Remittance*. A week later, by which time he had finished Part II (about a quarter of the whole book) it was called *No Remittance*. The story was an imagined version of the life of his uncle Harry Doley, the friendly, disorganized, incompetent, and occasionally dissolute uncle at Oteramika, a man of English origins, a Protestant 'homey' who had somehow married Annie Sullivan, Dan's mother's sister, and so become an unsuitable member of an Irish Catholic clan. A man with no knowledge of farming somehow settled on a small farm in Southland. A weak man, out of place and a failure, paralysed by vacil- lation, and crippled by idleness, yet with an endearing honesty that made him his own first critic. His life was a comic tragedy, but one for which Dan had deep sympathy. He visited the Doleys during his visit to New Zealand in 1948, and brought away with him a sense of Harry's courage and endurance, sad and obscure, yet admirable.

Back In Oxford Dan managed only a very little more work on it. In addition to the normal distractions of term time, family, Press, and pub, there was the 'desperate slow tragedy' of Joyce Cary's illness. He had contracted amyotrophic lateral sclerosis, known more commonly today as motor neurone disease, and by the autumn of 1956 was entering the last stages of decline. 'The development of this', Dan wrote in one of his rare diary entries, 'will overcast our whole winter and I fear he will not live much beyond that.'[78] The whole family was involved in Cary's last months of life, his inexorable wasting and progressive paralysis, his good humour and courage in managing it, the 'ritual celebrations' of Christmas and the New Year which, despite Cary's now desperate condition, were 'a success against the odds, something not macabre'.[79] He died, as Dan had feared, at the end of the winter, on 29 March 1957. Compound with his own grief was that of his family, for all of whom the loss was traumatic. Dan and Winnie had each other for support in sadness, and they needed it to help the children. Dan spent several days at home to be with them, and they walked on Port Meadow, and talked about Joycey and all the happiness that he had brought into their lives. Dan felt a deep respect for Winnie's friendship with Joyce, and realized that in the intensity of her grief she needed help with the children. Delia remembers Winnie rallying in time to take them all shopping for their first suits to wear at the funeral. The friendship and then the loss of Joyce, a man so respected as well as loved, stayed with each of them. Winnie performed the duties of literary executor for over thirty years, editing *The Captive and the Free*, seeing other unpublished works through the press, and finding a willing donor in their friend James Osborn of Yale University, a wealthy bibliophile and scholar, who purchased Joyce Cary's papers, and presented them as a gift to the Bodleian Library. And Anna, Delia, and Brigid recalled him ever afterwards as a part of the most intensely happy memories of childhood.

Cary's influence abounds in *No Remittance*, in which some critics were quick to detect his 'histrionic method'.[80] But his influence was not unique. The tenderness and sympathy, the general air of forgiveness that is worked into the book, also reflect the influence exerted over Dan by Howard Kippenberger. Kippenberger died shortly after Cary, on 5 May, so that two of the older figures of influence in Dan's life were dead within weeks of each other. Never slow to sense intimations of mortality, readily depressed by experience, already given to pessimism about his own age, and the passing of his youth and vigour, Dan felt these losses sorely. But he had learned from them too. He wrote much later of Cary: 'he accepted . . . that grief is the price of happiness'.[81] So for once loss surfaced in his work not in gloom, but in a life-asserting refusal to be crushed, whose origins lay in the genius for living, despite adversity, of Joyce Cary and Howard Kippenberger.[82]

Dan returned to the Scillies on 26 September 1957, and a week later he had finished the first draft of the book. *No Remittance* is written in the first person as if by Richard Kane, an Englishman born in 1880, but now aged 70, and looking back on a life of misadventure, occasional criminality, moral and personal weakness that has brought him to his old age on a run-down farm in an out-of-the-way corner of what had once been empire. Dan plundered his family memory for this book. The O'Connors, the fictional family into which Kane marries, are the Sullivans of his mother's youth. His own parents are present in the minor role of the

Hogans. Richard and Norah Kane's children have much of his own siblings in them, including the oldest, John, a serious and stubborn boy, who by becoming a priest precipitates the deepest and most prolonged estrangement between his parents.

No Remittance is fictional autobiography. Its strength derives first, from the great labour that Dan invested in ensuring that the historical facts were right, and second, from the intimacy that he achieved with his fictional narrator. For the first he ransacked his own and others' libraries, turning over old copies of newspapers and magazines, early colonial histories, general history books, stock agents' catalogues, price lists for corn and seed potatoes, almost anything that he could bring to hand. An old wartime acquaintance, John Robertson, who had gone back to Southland to work on the Southland *Times*, answered his queries and supplied him with much of this background. One senses here the artist's rejection of the criticism that *The Sullen Bell* had attracted in *Landfall*. Dan's view of art in literature was grounded in realism. The imagination might supply character, but time and place exerted a discipline that the artist should accept.

For the second, the voice in monologue of his central character Dick Kane, Dan turned in small part to his Uncle Harry—the exterior portrait is certainly him—and in large part to himself.[83] The seamlessness of the perceptions, the way they fit together, accumulate, explain the choices and the compromises made in a long life, all speak for the degree to which Dan had internalized his character. So too does the speed of composition. The novel was written, in large measure, at two sittings of about a week each, though a year apart. It flowed from the pen, and was barely corrected. The tone of the book is quite new. The sentiments are kinder, irony replacing the savagery of satire. No gloomy Davins shed metaphysical pessimism. Where there is criticism of social behaviour, it crops up either in gentle humour, or in a resigned recognition on the part of the narrator that, well, 'fair enough', he may have been wrong about this or that. Dick Kane is a reprobate and a fraud, when young a scoundrel, when older a coward and a cheat. Morally, he is hardly admirable. Even so, and even though he does all the talking himself, he is hard to condemn. When he does wrong he knows it, and the voice we hear is that of a man who knows enough both to feel and to admit remorse. But he is also blinkered enough not fully to understand why he is a figure of fun and derision to the other members of the clan around him. And when his perceptions fail him, we hear and know enough to feel sorrow on his behalf, even as we laugh with the rest of them.

Dan took the manuscript of *No Remittance* back to Oxford from the Scilly Isles on 4 October 1957, and over the next three months gave it a final polish, and had it typed. It was homage both to Cary and to Kippenberger, a last affectionate portrait of his childhood and of the world in which he had himself grown up to be an outsider. Just as it was finished, on 3 January 1958, news came that his father had died. Patrick was 80, and had continued to live in Dunedin with his daughter Molly. Despite his age, the stroke which caused his death came as a surprise, as he had continued to be strong and robust through his seventies. Dan had not seen him since his visit to New Zealand in 1948, and the week that they had spent together then had been the first since 1936. In spirit, Dan had left home in 1931. In all the many years that he had been away his father almost never wrote to him because writing letters was, in Patrick's view, a mother's job. Dan used to say that he only had one letter from his father: a letter of disgust in 1939 that any son of his should have joined a British regiment. And although this was not strictly true—-Dan preserved one long letter from his father about his mother, written after her death in 1944—it is certainly the case that they had long since ceased to communicate about anything outside the formalities of family and calendar. But although his father was a figure grown distant by almost thirty years of estrangement, Winnie believed that Dan always felt quite near to him because he thought his father never changed. Brigid recalled that when her Uncle Tom telephoned with the news, Dan wept, and went to his study to be alone. The separation and the silence of those nearly thirty years suggest, however, that the tears may have been more for the final passing of that unchanging Southland of Dan's youth, and that his specific feelings for his father were ones common in cases of long separation: the baffling inability to mourn, coupled with the realization that he had been cheated of it in the past.

Dan sent the manuscript of *No Remittance* to David Higham in late January, and Michael Joseph accepted it for publication a few weeks later. There were delays in the spring because Michael Joseph himself died in March, and the firm went through a reorganization. David Higham was equally distracted. Laurence and Gerald Pollinger, his associates, left Pearn, Pollinger Higham to set up their own agency, and Dan's agents were restructured as David Higham Associates.[84] Despite these distractions, production went ahead reasonably quickly. Dan corrected the proofs in the last week of October, and the book was published on 19 January 1959.

The book had mixed reviews. John Betjeman found it 'readable',[85] and Pamela Hansford Johnson praised its 'life-giving element'.[86] Julian Maclaren-Ross, in *Punch*, called it Davin's 'best novel to date', particularly admiring the first person narrative, 'easy and colloquial, with much discreetly-conveyed period-detail but no crypto-sentimentality'.[87] This was precisely what J. D. Scott, in the *Sunday Times*, disliked about the book: 'in place of a hero destroyed by his weakness in heroism, we might have had a rascal destroyed by his weakness in rascality.'[88] Norman Shrapnel, now launched on his career of incendiary polemicist at the *Manchester Guardian*, rejected the whole work as 'backdated' and its theme as 'plainly impossible to flog' in Britain. B. Evan Owen, in the *Oxford Mail*, thought it written with 'a beautifully controlled fluency' to provide 'an absorbing view' of New Zealand.[89] The reviewer in the *TLS* attempted high theory. As 'an essay in psychological irony' the novel was poorly served by characters too 'typical' of their origins. 'Only the odd is ever truly and creatively alive; therefore the centre of Mr. Davin's book is empty and the flaw in his hero's character works in the void'[90]—a criticism which, thought about briefly, is indeed meaningless.

The luck of the draw is paramount in reviews. Four months after *No Remittance* was published, the *Listener* ran one by Goronwy Rees. He called it a 'sad' and 'not very interesting' story, and confessed himself puzzled as to why Davin should have written it, though he admired the 'deceptively modest and unpretentious style', and thought that if Davin 'had a story worth telling, he would tell it extremely well'.[91] One advantage of being a publisher himself was that even when subjected to the *ad hominem*, Dan retained his balance about reviews, their worth and function.

And in any event, in early 1959 his mind was on family matters. For four years or so Anna had been friendly with the Hodgkin family, Thomas (Dan's old friend) and Dorothy, the brilliant biochemist, fellow and tutor in Somerville College, and their children. They lived at 94 Woodstock Road, a big house with two families, the Hodgkins and the Paines, eight children, and a noisy world of lively intellectual fun. The oldest of the Hodgkin children was Luke, who was 18 in 1956, the year he went up to Balliol from Eton. He was clever, and good company, and he and Anna became friends. After school Anna was a frequent visitor to the Hodgkin house, more so after Joyce Cary died in 1957. These were very happy years for her: there were Shakespeare play readings, riotous performances of Luke's own surrealist plays, and occasional help with her homework from a young man who had a good command of both Latin and Greek. She and Luke formed a strong bond. Dan and Winnie were very fond of him too. In the summer of 1958 Anna went on holiday to Austria with the Hodgkin family, and on their return she began her final year at school, Luke his final undergraduate year at Balliol. At the end of October she discovered that she was pregnant, and she and Luke decided that they wanted to get married. In those days the decision meant that Anna would have to leave school, where she had been a brilliant pupil, a star performer on the radio programme 'Top of the Form', and generally expected to win a scholarship to Oxford. Now she was their first schoolgirl pregnancy. No North Oxford gossip could have wished for better material. Dan, who had a strong grounding in gossip 'in an inbred and highly uncharitable community like a university',[92] was mainly saddened at what he saw as the lost educational opportunity. Silently, and to himself, he could see in what was happening to his daughter, some sort of possible alternative of his own past.

The wedding took place on 20 December 1958 at the registry office in St Giles'. Some of this was bizarre. Martha, determined that Anna should look the part on her wedding day, towed her round London for silk and accessories, and then sewed a smart dress for her, all of which she detested. At the ceremony, the address was given by Gervase Mathew, untidy as ever, his dog collar concealed behind the familiar stained polo-necked sweater, his theme a sort of secular piety, religion without God. During the ceremony Anna, though happy with Luke, was feeling a little tearful, but afterwards there was a wonderful, happy party at 103.

Anna and Luke went to live in 'the cottage', a little house in the garden of 94 Woodstock Road ('the compound' Thomas Hodgkin called it) where they became 'Lukeanna', celebrities of radical Oxford undergraduate life. At home in nearby 103 Southmoor Road, the atmosphere changed. Now that she had gone, Dan missed Anna's voice, singing as she went about the house. At supper on Sunday evenings she was no longer a resident inviting guests, but a guest herself. Dan felt like John Mulgan's dons of the 1930s, who had 'succumbed in part to the cloistered and interior politics of a university world, and to brick houses and rebellious children in North Oxford'.[93] The sense of loss was multiplied by Patty. Elizabeth and Ronnie Tylecote, who had married in 1958, wished to settle Patty's nationality and status as a British citizen. Dan was asked to complete various formalities affirming his paternity, and agreeing to Patty's adoption by Ronnie. The formalities did nothing to alter circumstance, but in affirming a loss already conceded they returned it to him to experience again, so that within the space of months it seemed as though he had 'lost' two daughters to unimagined futures.

These family developments, heavy with sentimental and emotional content, were an impediment to work and thought. During 1958 Ian Gordon, Professor of English at Victoria University College in Wellington, had pressed Dan to visit New Zealand to give the Macmillan Brown lectures, a series of distinction named after a once prominent academic. Detailed arrangements were some time in the making, but the Press was happy that he should combine the trip with visits to various OUP branch offices along the way. Dan eventually agreed, and proposed to lecture on Joyce Cary. He was away from England for nine weeks from 17 February to 23 April 1959, visiting Karachi, Calcutta, Kuala Lumpur, Singapore, and Melbourne *en route* to Auckland, where he arrived on 5 March to spend three days before heading south. Dan kept no diary record of this trip, and it generated no subsequent fiction (partly because of that, no doubt). His route through New Zealand was much as it had been eleven years before, and combined a mixture of family and friends, academic contacts, wartime associates, and literary and publishing colleagues. It was a solitary journey through wet autumnal weather, and was not entirely successful. Loneliness and nostalgia bred melancholy, which led to brooding and to drink. Reunions meant talk about the past, late nights, and more drink. Behind the conviviality lay the complex antagonisms and jealousies of the New Zealand character which Dan well understood, and could detect in a glance or a turn of speech. The familiar resentment of expatriate success carped maliciously behind his back. Maurice Duggan, with whom he stayed in Auckland on 7 March, called his lectures 'a bit of academic spivvery to pay costs. Who cares?'[94] And Charles Brasch described him 'spinning round the country at high speed, throwing off a few lectures between parties—it sounds rather a prima donna tour, which is a pity.'[95]

Such criticism, sensed not heard, was more hurtful for having point. Normally he was punctilious in preparation, but the distractions of life in Oxford over the previous few months meant that he was less well prepared than usual. He gave three lectures each at Otago, Victoria (in Wellington), and Auckland on the topics of Joyce Cary, his life and character; his theory and early novels; and the middle and final novels. For some reason he was not invited to lecture at Canterbury.[96] Though he was to speak three times, he had only one lecture completely prepared in advance, and the other two remained a source of anxiety throughout the visit. He managed to ad lib successfully on each occasion, but the nervous apprehension that preceded each performance was great, and the subsequent relief too generously celebrated, the more particularly in Auckland where he gave his last two lectures on the same day, 2 April. These experiences formed a switchback of depression and exuberance that was ill-suited to some of his other obligations. In Invercargill he visited his father's grave, alongside that of his mother. Not one of his own immediate family now lived in Invercargill, a place of cemeteries, and of memories going stale. He stayed only overnight to pay his respects to Winnie's sister Mollie. Back in Wellington for Easter he devoted time to the OUP office, gave an interview for the *New Zealand Listener*, went to PEN and publishers' parties, signed copies of *No Remittance* at Parson's Bookshop, made some radio broadcasts, and visited his brothers Martin and Pat. By the end of these few days he was sick and depressed, his appetite for food too small and for strong drink too great. He had pain in his lower back, making him dread the prospect of the long flight home. He viewed his return to Auckland, where he was to spend the final week of his visit, and to give his last lectures, with foreboding and misery. He was saved from the worst by Maggie Black, who sent a telegram of invitation to him in Wellington to stay with her and her husband at their home in Remuera. When he arrived she looked after him, driving and delivering, getting him to his lectures on time, collecting him from social engagements. She took him out to visit Frank Sargeson at Takapuna, invited the Duggans round, and got him on to his flight for Los Angeles on 7 April.

In the United States his visit was all business, with three days in California devoted to meetings with academics. Then on to New York for ten days, a visit to the new OUP warehouse and accounting facility at Fair Lawn, New Jersey; a reunion with Itzik Manger; and meetings with authors. He was worn out by the time he reached London on 23 April, and confessed later to Frank Sargeson that it took him more than a year to recover.[97] The reasons were both physical and emotional. Physically, the pain in his back, first diagnosed to be in the sacroiliac, was the first apprehension of what was to become a chronic problem. Emotionally, he was unbalanced by his return to New Zealand. The country had changed little, but he had changed a lot, and the sense of his exile took deeper root. When he visited Sargeson at the end of his tour there was some sort of exchange of unpleasantness, Dan said of no consequence,[98] though Sargeson apologized for it later.[99] Sargeson was under strain at the time, suffering from his 'nervous complaint', which could make him irritable. Also he had a poor opinion of *No Remittance*, which he may have expressed.[100] Shortly after Dan's return to England Anna and Luke made him a grandfather with the birth of a son, Dominic, on 28 June: a matter for rejoicing, though it whispered his mortality too. Almost simultaneously, he was wounded by B. M. O'Dowd's review of *No Remittance* in *Landfall*, where she called the early chapters 'novelettish in their smooth, glib failure to actualize either character or situation' and praised the later chapters faintly as having 'smooth proficiency . . . [and] an easy ironical control, which is due probably to the decision to handle more tractable material rather than to genuine development'.[101]

The exhaustion from travel to his homeland translated into an exasperation with his own fiction. In the Scilly Isles in the autumn he attempted to start a new manuscript, but managed only five thousand words—normally a day's work. Eleven years were to pass before he published another novel. He located his disillusion in his way of life, the 'conditioning to academic and administrative and logical modes of thought'[102] inimical to imaginative creativity. Wrestling with this, he was tempted to return to history, this time marrying historical fact to the demands of characterization in biography. Freyberg's was the life he wanted to write. He was still in touch with the General, now Deputy Constable and Lieutenant-Governor of Windsor Castle, and in early February 1960 Freyberg invited Dan and Paddy Costello to visit him for dinner, and to stay overnight. It was a merry occasion, and gave birth to a famous story in which Davin and Costello, heading for drink after the rest of the household had retired to bed, found themselves in Lord and Lady Freyberg's bedroom, and were then discovered (much to the amusement of their host) trying to make good their retreat on hands and knees.

Despite conviviality, the aspirant biographer was rebuffed. Briefly, Dan had cause to hope that Freyberg might agree to the proposal, but eventually he said that he was not ready.[103] Dan tried again four years later, after Freyberg's death, when he talked with Paul Freyberg, who now had control of his father's papers. 'I told him the next move was for him and he seems anxious to have [another] meeting.'[104] But nothing came of this either. And he tried again in 1969, before his next visit to New Zealand, when he asked Paul Freyberg what he had decided because the visit offered an opportunity to interview the General's now ageing former military colleagues. Once again the answer was negative. The reasons for Paul Freyberg's reluctance became obvious only later when he revealed his father's knowledge of Ultra, something he could not even contemplate doing before the Enigma was declassified in 1974. Dan continued to collect material on Freyberg's life, but more in frustration than in hope. It would have made a man of smaller sympathies grow bitter. The beginnings of this frustration were allied to another, more specific. Close to Southmoor Road, also backing on to the canal, was an engineering firm, Lucy's. Here, even into the twentieth century, there had also been a foundry. In many ways, the factory had become an anomaly: a noisy industrial site left over from an earlier age, and now located in a residential neighbourhood close to the centre of town. There it was, however, and in the post-war economic climate of the late 1950s its directors planned expansion, and had acquired land for the purpose. Expansion would bring congestion to narrow streets, the contraction of amenities on open land abutting Port Meadow, and further increases in visual and atmospheric pollution, and noise. Like his neighbours, Dan resented all this, and joined with other residents of Southmoor Road to fight the proposals. They formed a committee, of which he became chairman; presented evidence at the hearings of planning bodies; and represented residents' views in newspapers and on the radio. In this way, some concessions were won.[105] Lucy's was, however, both determined and well connected. In the following years the company put up a steady stream of new proposals, each one requiring local residents' attention, sometimes legal representation. And despite assurances, the noise level from what was a busy industrial plant continued to rise. Dan found it impossibly intrusive, reviving the spectre of his nightmare. The impulse, other than for collective action, was for flight. Dan and Winnie now began to look seriously for a country retreat, and in the spring of 1960 they found what they had been searching for.

The cottage stood in grounds adjacent to the Norman Abbey in the village of Dorchester-on-Thames, overlooking leaning gravestones in the long grass. It was a half-timbered fifteenth-century dwelling of three ground-floor rooms with low beamed ceilings, and three small bedrooms above, reached by a narrow Y staircase so low that some best negotiated it on hands and knees. When they bought it from the Parish Council the cottage was dilapidated. The thatch roof needed renewal. The ground floor had to be lowered eight inches to meet building regulations. Modern plumbing was thought advisable. These complications preoccupied Dan and Winnie for two years until, in the late summer of 1962, the Dorchester cottage at 4 High Street, with its black-earth garden, at last became theirs to use.

In this setting, and for the first time (significant in the wake of his father's death) Dan became a gardener, though of the Southland Irish rather than the English type, with beds of potatoes, onions, and radishes, and rows of beans and tomatoes. The Lienhardt brothers contributed flowers and shrubs, Paul and Ivry Freyberg donated old English rose trees from Munstead House garden (Gertrude Jekyll, who created the garden, was Bernard Freyberg's aunt by marriage). In the spring the boundary ditch, reached by a path made from broken gravestone fragments, would flood, leaving silt in the beds to mingle with the rich organic material washed down from the sloping graveyard. Their pleasure in the garden was only partly derived from its products. Dan also took pleasure from the annual cycle of the gardener's life, the thrush that nested in the honeysuckle by the back door, the physical activity allied to the changing seasons, and the opportunity to immerse himself in its tasks (which would not wait) as release from the escalating pressures of his life as a publisher.

In addition to a peaceful environment in which to work—he turned the smallest upstairs room into a study—the cottage was a place of escape for them all. On a Sunday afternoon from early spring to late autumn, Dan and Winnie, and such visitors who might call, would walk across the fields to Warborough, collecting mushrooms, watching the birds. The Abbey provided a backdrop of visual and historical associations of which they never tired. The village had four good pubs: the Chequers, the Fleur, the George, and the White Hart: the first two with beer on wood; the other two with good kitchens and cellars which visitors, especially from overseas, enjoyed.

This closed a circle. His life as a publisher involved constant meetings and entertainment. In Oxford, Dan had always been able to take guests to the Senior Common Room in Balliol. In 1959, when he was elected a member of the Travellers' Club in Pall Mall, he at last had a base for entertainment on his frequent visits to London.[106] With the addition of Dorchester for weekends and occasional weeks at Easter and in the summer, he was now never without a place to invite friends, colleagues, or business associates. To them, he seemed now an Establishment figure, with his Oxford college, London club, and country cottage. Early in 1960 he even applied to the New Zealand military authorities for his war medals and insignia.[107] With the miniatures in line on his evening dress jacket he cut a distinguished as well as handsome figure.

These were real changes to a style that had seemed set, to his intimate friends and family, long ago. At the personal level, together with the regular hours that he spent among his friends at the Victoria Arms, they signalled the decline, after fifteen years or so, of open invitation at 103.

Occasionally friends still came. Paddy would never stay anywhere else, and friends from London such as Elizabeth Knight, a colleague in the London business, would always be welcome when work brought them to Oxford for a day or two.[108] But with these developments in Dan's life, and Anna's happy marriage to Luke (they had a second child, Kathy, in October 1961), there was no concealing that home and family were in transition.

In the summer of 1961 Delia, just 17 years old, decided that she too wanted to marry her boyfriend Bill Jenner, a student at Wadham College. He was about to start his final undergraduate year, she was still in High School. Jenner's parents were opposed, but neither Dan nor Winnie had any inclination to oppose their own children, and gave their permission, a legal necessity. The wedding took place on the morning of Saturday, 2 December, once more in the registry office in St Giles'. This time there was some social discomfort because Jenner *père*, not a man to change his mind, refused to attend, though Bill's mother and grandmother were both present. The atmosphere was subsequently transformed at a delightful party at 103, an occasion still remembered by Brigid as the time when she too began that re-formation of the past which is a part of growing up, and which brings in its train the reordering of family relations.

There was more reordering too in the return of Patty. In 1962 she started a three-year course of teacher training in Reading, and so became a frequent visitor to her old home in Southmoor Road, and also to the cottage at Dorchester, just coming into use. Her return served as a reminder that the past could not be remade, only glimpsed in the haphazard gifts of inheritance. Tall, slim, amusing, beautiful, a good painter with a strong sense of design and colour, intuitive in manner, her reappearance in Oxford at weekends briefly attracted a new swarm of young men to the house, reminding Dan of Zamalek.

Within months of this development, in December 1962, Brigid found that she was pregnant. Dan wrote to Martha: 'Calamity has struck again . . . The culprits, as usual, have difficulty in concealing their satisfaction.'[109] The wedding of Brigid and Andrew Sandford Smith, an undergraduate at Corpus Christi College, was held in the now familiar location on 6 April 1963. Anna's third child, Mick, was born on 30 June, and Brigid's first son Dan on 11 September. Dan and Winnie now had four grandchildren. In July, Delia and Bill Jenner set off for China, where they lived and worked for the next two years. In September, just after Brigid's son was born, Anna and Luke Hodgkin left for Princeton, the first of two moves that took them away from Britain for most of the next two years as well.

In late August, in the middle of this sequence of births and departures, Dan discovered, on his usual Thursday visit to London, that Louis MacNeice was ill in hospital. The next day, 30 August, he went with Martha to visit, and found him dying. On the way back to Oxford by train Dan was in a state of shock, remembering 'all those times at the George, the efforts to break away from the excitement of friends, and Louis, the centre of a little world of poets, a world that would die with him'.[110]

Two days later, a Sunday, Dan celebrated his fiftieth birthday, oppressed by sorrow and by reflections on the past: 'that past which like all our pasts had seemed never so full that it could not take another draught of time and living and love.'[111]

12

A LIFE IN PUBLISHING

[I]t is the irony of publishing that, though it is a man's interest in literature that usually brings him into the profession, it is the literary side of his temperament that lives nearest to starvation.

(DMD, 'Editor and Author in a University Press', *TLS*, 7 Dec. 1967)

'You can't close your ears to gossip in this University, however much you try,' said Sillery. 'It's rampant, I regret to say. Even at High Table in this very college. Besides, it's always wise to know what's being bruited about, even if untrue.'

(Anthony Powell, *Books Do Furnish a Room*, 19)

At OUP DMD lived in the same room for thirty years, from 1948 until his retirement. Lived is the appropriate word not because he ate and slept there (though he certainly worked long hours) but because by use he and it seemed inseparable. It was a tiny room, a burrow where the kippered atmosphere of constantly replenished cigarette smoke mingled with the scent of books, bindings, paper, and glue. The walls were covered with books, not according to Powell's satire—to furnish a room—but scholarly works that DMD had commissioned, edited, and published. Each held its place on his shelves because it was in some sense, however uncertain, in use, and might be required. A smaller bookcase by the door contained recent publications from which he might pick a volume for a departing guest.

He never used an executive desk, but worked at a writing-table, like an intelligence officer set down in the field. Almost every available inch of surface was loaded with manuscripts, coming or going. The telephone was an alien object. Since the turmoil of Cassino he hated telephones. The mere ring generated a maddening sense of frustration.

In the mornings, office life followed a strict routine. From 9.00 to 9.30, morning prayers in the mail room; 9.30 to 10.00, appointments diary and arrangements; 10.00 to 11.30, dictation; 11.30 to 12.30, editorial work. His focus was famously intense. At a sitting he could dictate dozens (the record was reckoned to be eighty) of witty, charming, businesslike, direct, or evasive letters, as the occasion demanded. And when, as a result of travel, or brief illness, he got into what he called his 'arrears', then the pace, already fast, quickened. He generally took visiting academics, authors, or friends to lunch in Balliol, where he was a member of the SCR through the 1950s, and was elected a Professional Fellow in February 1965. Afternoons were less intense and more diverse, with manuscripts to read, authors to meet, details of printing or of contracts to oversee. He developed, with the years, a 'formidable reputation' as an editor,[1] and never read anything, from newspapers to dictionaries, without a pencil between his fingers to jot corrections or to note errors in the margin. Once a week, generally Thursday, he went to London to meet authors, discuss contracts, visit the London offices, or call on academic advisers and friends at the various colleges of London University. When he joined OUP, business conferences were rare: Delegates met only four times a term, and once in the long vacation. By the early 1960s, however, committees of various kinds were becoming more frequent, and by 1970 they had taken over most of his post-dictation time. The *escalier d'esprit* stood neglected with the years.

The comparison of army intelligence to life in Dan's room is not confined to the writing-table. He took with him to OUP the language of the front, and for the ten years or so after the war his memos employed advances, foraging, assaults, lines of communication, Huns, and interrogations. The military expressions became less bellicose with time, but the intelligence officer's style remained. DMD believed in judgement, and in arriving at it quickly. You analysed and assessed, and then you judged, and you backed your judgement with your reputation, even though you knew that much hung on the outcome. This approach never faltered. Kathleen Tillotson and Alan Bell, both authors whom DMD encouraged to publish with the Press (though nearly thirty years apart), recalled their surprise as well as pleasure at DMD's decisiveness. And Robert Burchfield remembered the same brisk and straightforward mastery over matters like appointments, promotions, or business decisions of various kinds. Once he judged someone competent to write a particular book, or to carry out a particular task, that person had his wholehearted support, though he also knew how to manage troublesome authors.[2]

His support might last a lifetime, a principle illustrated in the case of the *Complete Works* of John Locke. The Lovelace collection of Locke Papers was deposited in the Bodleian Library initially for a period of five years in 1942. During the war, Sisam employed one of his war refugees, W. von Leyden, philosopher, historian, and linguist, to examine the collection and to prepare a report. Sisam's aim was the production of a

Collected Works, and he saw the Lovelace collection as a cornerstone of the undertaking.[3] In 1947 Bodley purchased the collection for £7,900, the Pilgrim Trust contributing almost half this sum, and OUP some of the rest. From 1947, for almost ten years, the project was stalled for want of a suitable editor. Various names were canvassed. The distinguished Cambridge historian, Peter Laslett, gave advice. Eventually, in early 1956, DMD put up the name of Esmond de Beer.[4]

His timing was excellent. After twenty years' work, interrupted by the war, de Beer's great scholarly edition of Evelyn's Diary was published by the CP in six volumes in 1955. Esmond de Beer was an independent scholar of the seventeenth century, bibliophile, collector, and philanthropist of private means, known in scholarly circles to be meticulous as well as diligent, and completely disinterested. For Locke, DMD wooed him like a lover. On his return from six weeks in Italy in early 1956, de Beer found waiting for him a copy of Walcott's *English Politics in the Early 18th Century*—exactly the sort of gift he treasured. It came from the Assistant Secretary of OUP. When de Beer wrote to express thanks, DMD replied that there was 'another matter about which I should like to have a talk to you when you have cleared up your arrears a little', and suggested lunch. Eventually, they dined together at the Atheneum on Friday, 20 April. The following week DMD sent him von Leyden's wartime report, promising to 'prepare you a memorandum about the plan for an edition' and hoping that his interest would not flag. From the questions that de Beer raised in subsequent correspondence it was clear that there was no danger of that: he was hooked. Just three weeks after they had dined together DMD took to the Delegates the proposal that de Beer should edit the Locke correspondence. He drew their attention to de Beer's own reservations about his qualifications in 'philosophy and latinity. They refused to be distressed by these . . .'[5]

While de Beer prepared himself for the task of transcription, DMD took care of the administrative side. There were many questions still to be answered about the shape and size of the edition, publicity that it was under way, co-ordination with other libraries and institutions that held Locke material, provision of help with transcription and typing, and the elaboration of editorial principles. DMD brought de Beer together with Jacob Viner, a Princeton scholar and great Locke expert. For the rest of his career at OUP, during the whole of which time de Beer was at work on the CP Locke edition,[6] he solved problems, smoothed away difficulties, and opened doors. The correspondence was eventually published in seven volumes between 1976 and 1982.

The story of the publication of the Locke manuscripts is indicative of the life of an academic publisher. The length of the project, which began three years before DMD joined OUP, and was completed years after he left it, is far longer than almost anything in the world of commercial publishing, and illustrates some fundamental principles. If the commissioning editor is midwife, then it is an odd sort of midwifery: one where the infant is defined in advance, a search is mounted for the parent capable of bringing it to term, and the length of gestation almost a matter of indifference so long as the product, on delivery, is immaculate. DMD had the right combination of qualities for this unusual profession: perseverance, energy, the judgement to seek advice in the right quarters and the grace to accept it, an understanding of the nature of scholarship, and a great love of learning. In de Beer, with whom he formed a profound and reciprocal affection, he found the ideal scholar and author. That de Beer was also a man from Dunedin gave DMD additional pleasure.

Similar strengths were at work in the classical history field, where Ronald Syme, a near-contemporary from Auckland who had sat on Dan's Greats examination board in 1939, dominated scholarship for almost half a century. As early as 1946, at Sisam's suggestion, he had drawn up a list of 'desirable books on Greek and Roman history', and from time to time over the next twenty years he and DMD and Roberts would get together to review progress, adding titles and possible authors. DMD then wrote to the people suggested by Syme, soliciting their views and perhaps the outline of a proposal which could be presented to the Delegates. Syme would comment on the proposal, correspond with the author, and read the completed manuscript when it eventually arrived. As Dan observed in a memo of 16 June 1955 after lunch with Syme and a visiting author: 'As usual, Syme displayed so much knowledge and enthusiasm that he became the obvious author for this book as for many others.'[7]

This was team work of a voluntary kind, impossible without the disinterested commitment of scholars to the development of their discipline. Dan believed that it was possible because OUP was, and was understood to be, an integral part of the University.

DMD's work with Syme, with Jack Bennett, and also with Norman Davis, his near-contemporary at Otago, now a fellow of Merton and readily available to advise on literary and classical topics, implied to some the existence of an Oxford New Zealand scholarly 'Mafia'. Certainly they were linked by nationality, and some believed that DMD felt more at ease with New Zealanders. Perhaps it was more that they felt so with him. But it would be wrong to detect in their co-operation a Camorra intent on mutual self-advancement. The adhesive was not self-interest, but disinterest.[8] In any event, as we have seen, by the mid-1950s Dan was becoming detached from his New Zealand roots. Exile made him a particularly good academic publisher, happiest at the level of international scholarly exchange. On occasions he was able to bring scholarship, academic publishing, and friendship together, as for instance when he published Gordon Craig's first book, and then introduced him to Alan Bullock in November 1954, a meeting at which Craig was invited to contribute the volume on Germany to the Oxford History of Modern Europe.[9] Both books won prizes. DMD regarded this as part of the job. '[O]f course, you must exploit every friend and acquaintance you might possibly have in this perfectly respectable and honourable way.'[10]

Publishers are generally in a hurry, but DMD knew that scholarship sets its own pace. Some of his authors, like A. J. P. Taylor, were 'performers' who could be relied upon to produce rapidly once a commitment had been made. DMD saw both his *The Struggle for Mastery in Europe*, and *English History 1914–1945*, through the Press, and then looked after them through various reprintings and editions.[11] This did not mean that, as an author, Taylor was trouble-free. Like many Oxford dons he was opinionated, and capable of astonishing but calculated rudeness intended to unbalance opponents. In his dealings with the Press some of this was defensive, because he suspected DMD of siding with men whom he thought opposed to him, his views and his historical methods. He should have known better. DMD was as much, if not more of an outsider than he was himself. Of course, DMD knew all the gossip, indeed his knowledge of Oxford gossip was unrivalled, but so was his discretion.[12] Another of his contemporaries was notorious for a reckless disregard of the truth (in itself interesting in a historian), and a penchant for spreading false rumour. Such scholars are trouble requiring treatment:

All the editor can do is to preserve a meek and civil front, give the truth such chance to prevail as may be compatible with discretion, and choke down whatever talents and taste he may himself have by temperament for controversy. The effort will sometimes be great and he will often lie awake at night writing in his mind the letters he would like to send but may not; and, dealing with men whose energies often delight in polemic, try to reserve his own as best he may for getting on with the routine work that is at least in the end more productive, murmuring perhaps 'I do not like thee, Dr. Fell, especially as I cannot tell'.[13]

Troubles there will always be, but not always with authors, a fact illuminated in the history of the Pilgrim edition of the letters of Charles

Dickens. The critic and scholar Humphry House began collecting the letters in 1949, a task continued after his death in 1955 by his widow Madeline House, together with Graham Storey, a fellow of Trinity Hall Cambridge. Their intention was to publish with Rupert Hart-Davis, and Volume I was scheduled for 1957. In the event 'this proved hopelessly optimistic',[14] as the quantity of letters swelled to a flood, and the problems of textual accuracy and commentary proliferated. At first, the Pilgrim Trust adopted financial responsibility for the edition through a series of grants, but the cost spiralled, and in 1964 OUP took over publication. The Pilgrim Trust made a once-only gift of £20,000 to cover administrative and production costs—the sum to be administered by OUP—and Volume I was at long last published in February 1965. Since then a further six volumes have appeared,[15] progress so slow that the enterprise has been in danger of failing because of escalating costs. In the early 1980s, some years after DMD had retired, OUP (though it would continue to publish the work) declared itself unable to support the project financially, and the British Academy stepped in, first with grants, and then in 1984 by adopting it as an official research project.

DMD's role in the publication of Dickens's letters was pervasive. His own broad knowledge of nineteenth-century literature inclined him to expand OUP's commitment to it, and he began by initiating the CP edition of Dickens's novels, first discussed in 1955 with the scholars John Butt, then at King's College, Newcastle, and Kathleen Tillotson in London. Tillotson he already knew and trusted from publishing her influential first book *English Novels of the 1840s*.[16] The respect was reciprocated. They began editorial work on *Oliver Twist, Martin Chuzzlewit,* and *David Copperfield* in 1958, and over the next twenty years came not only volumes in the complete edition of Dickens's works in the uniform CP edition, but also CP editions of the works of Anne and Charlotte Brontë, George Eliot, and Thomas Hardy. With the *Letters* there were unquestionably frustrations. Procrastination, costs, disruptions owing to political circumstance (the winters of 1971–2 and 1973–4, when the government was in dispute with the National Union of Miners, were a nightmare for OUP), illness and indisposition of the editors: all these matters required frequent attention, the good-humoured smoothing of irregularities, the maintenance of a steady course. DMD used to comment wryly that he expected the final volume of the Dickens letters to appear in 2014, fifty years after OUP took them on, 'about as long to publish as it took Dickens to write them'. The forecast may be rare evidence of his optimism.

Academic publishing is not a science. Scholars can be brilliant but unproductive, inventive but eccentric, dynamic but careless. To find the right author on a topic, or to assess the quality of an author trawled at a conference, or met across a college dinner table, is a difficult and delicate art. In the case of error, resources may be committed for years without return other than hope. In his thirty-three years of publishing DMD made surprisingly few errors, but as he knew from chess, one learns more from defeat than from victory. One such checkmate occurred with the work of the great phoenix of English poetry, Percy Bysshe Shelley. The Delegates had long wanted to publish a new and authoritative text of the *Complete Poems* in their Oxford English Texts series, to replace the Hutchinson edition of 1904. A post-war stimulus renewed the desire: the gift to the Bodleian in 1946 by Sir John Shelley-Rolls of a number of Shelley manuscripts to add to the substantial collection donated to the library by Lady Shelley in 1893.

Sisam invited John Wain, then a lecturer in English at Reading University, to examine the papers. His report of February 1947 was generally negative, arguing that all the Shelley manuscript sources, both in Bodley and elsewhere, had been fully exploited, and would add nothing by being published except to 'demonstrate the haste with which Shelley wrote his first drafts'.[17]

There matters lay for four years until in the summer of 1951 the *TLS* ran a series of three articles by Neville Rogers in which he described and analysed the contents of the Shelley-Rolls manuscripts in a fresh and invigorating light.[18] In September Rogers wrote to OUP in London inquiring about the possibility of a book along the lines of his articles, and Cumberlege passed the letter on to the Oxford business. DMD wrote for advice to Edmund Blunden at the *TLS*—a Shelley enthusiast—and to both Garrod and Nichol Smith in Oxford. Neither of the Oxford advisers was completely convinced. Nichol Smith thought the *TLS* articles had a 'slightly overconfident tone'.[19] DMD and Rogers then corresponded, and Rogers came up to visit DMD at the Press on Saturday, 1 December.

Rogers was a London schoolmaster, with some background in the classics and Italian, and with a tenacious, obsessive interest in Shelley studies, to which he devoted his life. DMD detected an outsider, and warmed to him. Also he talked well and freely, enjoyed gossip, and liked to drink beer. DMD was not alone in forming a favourable impression. By the time of their first meeting, the Delegates had already agreed to the proposal that Rogers should write a short book on the Shelley-Rolls manuscripts, and this grew eventually into his book *Shelley at Work*.[20]

Apart from a year on a Leverhulme Fellowship in 1952–3, Rogers wrote this book under difficult circumstances, labouring at night and at weekends, and only able to put in longer stints with the co-operation of his headmaster. DMD liked him the more for working in. these circumstances, ones which he knew only too well himself.

Rogers finished the manuscript in October 1955, and CP published it in September the following year. Shortly before this, and with the support of a warm and not entirely candid reference signed by Roberts but drafted by DMD, Rogers at last secured an academic post—a two-year research fellowship at the University of Birmingham. The Delegates agreed to the proposal that he should be contracted to produce a new Oxford English Texts edition of *The Complete Works of Shelley* in five volumes, the first an edition of the *Esdaile Notebooks*, plus four volumes for the poems. Then the fun began.

Shelley at Work received some good reviews, but DMD had a letter from John Wain (a not wholly disinterested observer, since Rogers's book could be construed as a rejection, if not refutation, of the scholarly advice he had tendered to the Delegates ten years before) pointing out errors in a quotation in the book from a newspaper article that he had written. 'I am not being ironic when I say that I hope, for all our sakes, that he had better luck when transcribing the material he was working on than when copying out of a newspaper.'[21] In confirmation of this bow shot came a broadside by John Buxton, tutor in English at New College, in the *Oxford Magazine* of May 1957 in which he condemned the book for frequent errors of transcription as well as interpretation. Buxton gave DMD a copy of the book with many of the errors marked, and DMD forwarded it to Rogers with a letter that is an early masterpiece of his publisher's style. 'There are some unlucky mistakes on pages 119, 128 and 153, and in the circumstances your irony about Shelley's punctuation on page 135 is a little unhappy.' The Press would 'have to be particularly careful about your citations' in future.[22] The damage was done, however. The Delegates had already paid Rogers an advance for the *Complete Poems*, and DMD had gone out of his way to secure him rare editions of Shelley books, and photocopies of manuscripts in other libraries.

In the face of criticisms levelled at *Shelley at Work*, Rogers emerged as a difficult character, quick to detect academic intrigue. His letters to DMD at the Press came marked 'Personal', though like many who are secretive in manner he was unable to keep a confidence. Eventually, he secured a professorship in the United States from where he waged a lifelong war with other Shelley scholars and librarians. His feud with the Pforzheimer

Library in New York might make a book in itself. In the spring of 1966 the CP brought out his volume of *The Esdaile Notebooks*, and Volumes I and II of the poetry eventually followed in 1972 and 1975, but at every step there was controversy. His weakness for errors of transcription, some comic, was never cured. No doubt, had he been able to work faster and with greater precision, his five-volume edition would have been published in its entirety. DMD was constantly urging him to get a move on, though his loyalty to him and to the project never faltered in public. Rogers failed however, even after twenty-five years, and with a change in OUP's fortunes in the 1970s, his inability to treat effectively with new personnel at the Press, and his progressive isolation on scholarly matters (largely perhaps a matter of temperament), Rogers's edition of Shelley was terminated. His pleas for help to DMD, now retired and unable to offer any practical assistance, mark the end of an unhappy episode.[23] Its progress may perhaps be detected in DMD's speech to an OUP training conference in 1966, when, in an amusing description of the varieties of difficulty with which an editor might have to contend, he warned against such authors with a typically ironic self-reference: 'usually you only come into contact with them because you spent a long time growing with them into their second childhood, and by that time it is too late to retreat.'[24] Of the thousands of projects that passed across DMD's desk, many were dropped before going to the Delegates, some, through death or other of life's misfortunes, were dropped after contract, but only Rogers—a distinction of a sort—was terminated when three of five volumes in a set had already been published. The losses incurred by an incompletion of this sort are heavy, both in material and in reputation. It was a sorry story, and would be quarried for stones to throw in due course. Dan was sufficiently troubled by the controversy to set down his impressions of, and frustrations with, Neville Rogers, though it was years later, and he was himself ill and infirm by then.[25]

The dangers of faulty judgement are illustrated in this isolated case. DMD learned from the mistake, largely one of seeing himself in others. To balance it we might turn to a jewel in the crown of OUP, the *Oxford English Dictionary*. *OED*, in ten volumes, was the parent from which a family of dictionaries was descended, the most important of them at that time being the *Shorter*, or *SOED*. The most pressing problem of the ten years after the war was to supply sufficient stock to meet demand. The second problem was to maintain demand by improving the product, ensuring its authority. In the years immediately after the war, C. T. Onions produced new 'Addenda' for a reprinting. In 1954 the Finance

Committee agreed to investment in the paper-mill at Wolvercote. As a result of improved technology the mill manufactured a paper which, while still being opaque, was half the weight of its predecessor. With this, *SOED* was produced in a single volume, instead of the previous two, and this new version was published, with Onions's revisions, in 1957. The book was very profitable, and generated a lot of new business, including deals for marketing it through *Encyclopaedia Britannica* and through *Reader's Digest*, both of which brought great financial reward.

Meanwhile, the Delegates had decided that, good as Onions's revisions were, the *OED* required a supplement, to bring it up to date by incorporating all the new words, meanings, and derivations that had come into usage since the *OED* was finished in 1928. They first appointed to this job in 1956, Alan Horsman, a young New Zealand English scholar from Durham University. Horsman, however, was poached to a chair at Otago University a year later, and in his place Robert Burchfield was appointed. Burchfield was also a New Zealander, a Rhodes Scholar at Magdalen College (1949–53) where he was known to both C. T. Onions and Jack Bennett (both men whose judgement DMD respected), lecturer in English at Christ Church (1953–7) and fellow of St Peter's (1955–63). Initially he was given a secretary, two assistants, and seven years in which to produce the *Supplement*. From this beginning, and partly in response to the demands of scholarship, partly in response to competition from other publishers, the project grew and multiplied. With steady support from DMD through all the inevitable vicissitudes, the *Supplement* was eventually published in four volumes over twenty-eight years, while Burchfield's office grew to a staff of eighteen, with substantial premises at 37A St Giles', a large reference library, and a huge file of illustrative quotations.[26] Many believed that it was the appointment of Burchfield, and the revival of *OED* and its various progeny, such as the *Concise Oxford Dictionary*, that saved the Press when its financial fortunes were dramatically reversed in the 1970s. By the time DMD retired in 1978 the Press had 'met and overcome the severe competition from Longmans, Collins and Chambers'.[27] Speaking in a BBC Radio 4 'Profile' programme on 8 April 1983 DMD described Burchfield as 'emperor and architect' of *OED*, terms which Burchfield wrote really belonged to DMD himself.[28] The truth lies between. Lexicography at the very end of the pre-computer age required co-operative enterprise: Burchfield and DMD were Directorate rather than emperors, and the comparative ease with which *OED* has made the transition to a CD-ROM version says much both for the appointments, and for the principles that, though first laid down in the

1880s, were built on after 1956. The lexicographers honoured DMD as lexicographers can, inserting in the *Supplement* to *OED* 165 quotations from his work.

If the *OED* may be said to crown the CP as an enterprise, then it was the *New History of Ireland*, uniting DMD's love of Ireland, scholarship, history, good books, and friendship, which may be said to have crowned his own career within it. The idea germinated in the 1950s when, on one of his occasional visits to Ireland, he discussed Irish historiography with Theo Moody, a historian at Trinity College Dublin.[29] Nothing happened for a number of years, but then his memory was jogged in the spring of 1963 after talking to staff in the London business about their efforts to get a short history of Ireland for the Home University Library—one of their popular series. He wrote to Moody in March, and found that simultaneously Moody had himself been actively pursuing similar ideas with colleagues. DMD went to Ireland in the summer, and he and Moody met to talk on 13 August. Various proposals were developed, including one for a three-volume history to be published by 1970, itself to be a pilot for a longer work in multiple volumes. The Delegates were in favour of this idea, but Moody encountered difficulties of various kinds, and the project was stalled until 1968 when it was revived under the auspices of the Royal Irish Academy.[30] An editorial committee was established, and three editors appointed: Moody himself, plus Professors F. X. Martin and F. J. Byrne, both of University College Dublin. The Irish Government instituted a series of annual grants, the Royal Irish Academy provided facilities and other assistance, and an American benefactor contributed money for help with primary research. More than sixty scholars were involved in the collaboration that went into devising and writing the work.

With the enthusiasm of this new departure, the scheme grew from three to five volumes, then six, then seven, six of text and one of reference material. DMD went to Dublin on 16 April 1969 to discuss the latest developments, and as a result it was this larger project that the Delegates subsequently agreed to in May. By the end of the year, however, when Moody visited DMD in Oxford, the editors had added a second volume of reference material, making eight in total. The next three years were arduous on both sides: in Dublin to prepare the manuscripts, in Oxford to persuade the editors of financial prudence. The complexities were enormous. Private skirmishing among academics, vanity of patrons, too little appreciation of publishing constraints, the pressure of the general business climate. The project involved considerable capital outlay, and cash-flow considerations were to become increasingly important in the inflationary 1970s. At the end of 1970, the proposal grew to nine volumes. In the summer of 1971 Dan and Winnie took their holiday in the west of Ireland, and DMD and Moody had a meeting at Westport. Moody and his colleagues clung tenaciously to simultaneous publication of all nine volumes, and although Vivian Ridler, the printer, pronounced it feasible, DMD's analysis of the capital outlay made him pessimistic. In any event, fish can be allowed to run. '[I]n spite of the extraordinary gifts you have shown for bringing recalcitrant authors up to scratch,' he wrote to Moody, 'I shall still be surprised if you in fact manage to have all the volumes ready at the time stipulated.'[31] DMD went to Dublin and met the editors on 7 January 1972, and after long discussions got them to agree to publication in series, three volumes at a time. When he met them in Dublin again at the end of July 1973, they still stuck to their programme, which envisaged submission of manuscripts for the first three volumes in the spring of 1974, but privately he expected that 'the programme will be thrown out'.[32] In the event his pessimism was justified only nine months later when Moody had the unhappy task of confessing that two of his authors had defaulted. DMD replied: 'Your account of the difficulties that have led to the delay . . . does not altogether astound an experienced publisher, maddening though it must be for you all.' And he lost no time in pressing what was now his advantage: 'But I wonder whether we are right to think still of publishing three volumes in the first batch.'[33]

In the event, difficulties on both sides slowed the project to a manageable timetable. The first volume to appear was Volume III, *Early Modern Ireland 1534–1691*, edited by Moody, Martin, and Byrne, and published in 1976. It was the only volume to appear before DMD's retirement from the Press in 1978.[34] When Volume VIII appeared in 1980 (and because DMD had now retired) the editors were free to add what many hundreds of scholars must have wanted to write in the prefaces to their books, recording their gratitude to 'this large-minded and stout-hearted Irish New Zealander'.[35] Four more volumes of *The New History of Ireland* were to appear before DMD's death. He kept them at 103, not in his study or his bedroom, but in a bookcase in the living-room that held only items that were precious to him.

When DMD was close to retirement, and handing over various projects to his successors in the Press, he wrote to Moody that the newcomers would give 'prompter dealing than I have been able to offer in recent years, alas, because of my many other (and on the whole less interesting) preoccupations'.[36] By this he meant the accumulation of administrative and financial responsibilities which had altered his position at the Press, steadily eroding the editorial and literary freedom that he had enjoyed for most of his first twenty years in publishing. The change in circumstances was given official title in 1970, when his designation changed from Assistant Secretary to Deputy Secretary and Academic Publisher. The new title was much more than just a name, and reflected changing pressures on the Press.

Much of the pleasure that DMD was able to take in his publishing life derived from the fact that OUP was not a normal publishing house. As its initiates and insiders were fond of saying, it was 'a little peculiar'. Though the parts of it in London and New York may have given the impression of an international corporation, its offices and administrative machinery in Oxford really were run for the most part like the university department it was. The University of Oxford owned OUP, but no shares existed, and by the 1960s it was a century since the University had actually invested any money in the Press. It had no debt, and financed all its capital expenditure out of income. Though it made occasional donations to the University, generally in the form of support for Bodley collections, and in tendering university printing at a discount, it had never formally paid a dividend. The various branches of the Press, in London and overseas, and including the printing works and paper mill, were run as commercial operations; but largely unbeknown to the rest of the world, and probably to most Oxford dons themselves, the Press also had a long-established obligation—advanced as justification for its many peculiarities—to publish academic texts and scholarly works at affordable prices. To achieve this, the Clarendon Press divided its publications into various kinds, identified as Green, Red, and Amber. Green books were titles that were expected to show a profit in the normal way. Red books were those scholarly works which were likely to show a loss, or break even only after a period of time that would, under normal costing, have been thought unacceptably long. Amber were worrisome cases between. How judgements on these matters were reached was obscured by the fact that, though the OUP accounts were audited correctly, some of the financial accounts were unorthodox, and the detailed accounts along with the auditors' report were seen by only a tiny handful of university officials.

From the end of the war until well into the 1960s, the structure and methods of the Press attracted little attention. For one thing, it was apparently financially successful. In the March years from 1946 to 1965 the Clarendon Press made a net profit on sales of less than 10 per cent only three times,[37] and this was the imprint charged with the responsibility to make 'the necessary loss' where appropriate. Similarly the printing works, which printed for the University (though not the Press) at a discount, made an *average* net profit on sales of 13.83 per cent in the years from 1952 to 1970. The London business also averaged almost a 10 per cent net profit on sales from the end of the war until 1959, and since its sales were from three to four times greater than those of the CP, it constituted, along with the New York branch, the main source of investment funds for the enterprise as a whole.

Various major investment projects were undertaken in the 1950s and 1960s. In addition to the renovation of the paper-mill, the printing works were expanded with a new 100,000 square foot factory and the modernization of equipment, including, by the time of Ridler's retirement in 1978, web-fed presses, fine screen litho printing, and new composing techniques. The warehouse and accounting facility at Neasden was computerized ahead of most competition, and in 1965 the London business moved from Amen House to new premises at Ely House, off Piccadilly. A big new distribution warehouse and accounting centre, costing $500,000, was opened in 1955 on a greenfield site at Fair Lawn, New Jersey, for the New York business. In addition, commitments totaling £360,000 were made for particular publishing projects in Oxford in the ten years to 1968, a third of it for the *OED Supplement*, and most of the rest for other dictionaries, including the Gesenius *Hebrew Lexicon*, a Liddell and Scott *Supplement*, and the *Oxford Latin Dictionary*. From 1964 the Delegates made efforts to improve the range and quality of their science publishing.

Profits and investments together implied growth, and certainly when measured in terms of books produced and people employed, the growth of OUP was remarkable. In 1973, the last full year when Roberts was Secretary, the OUP general catalogue listed 16,000 titles in print, with between 1,300 and 1,400 new titles being added to the list every year, and books leaving the Neasden warehouse at the rate of a million a month. By this time the CP employed ninety-six people on its editorial and administrative staff, and sales representatives for OUP operations in the UK alone had more than doubled in the 1960s from thirty-eight in 1958.

Some would later argue, not without point, that this growth was a product not of business skill, but of circumstance. In the immediate post-war period there was a phenomenal demand for books, paper, and printing services, which the husbandry of Sisam and Johnson enabled the Press to serve despite the continuation of austerity measures. Thereafter, education in general, and higher education in particular, expanded greatly in the 1950s and 1960s, bringing sustained demand for OUP products. It was a sellers' market, and OUP grew fat on its sales. The apparent success disguised weaknesses, however. Despite modernization the paper-mill was a disappointment. After making net profits of almost 25 per cent on sales in the years from 1948 to 1952—a performance which persuaded the Finance Committee that substantial investment made sense—the mill never really paid its way again. Under the unanticipated impact of competition from EFTA countries, it made only losses or very small profits from 1958 right through the 1960s. And while the profits of the London business, on which the stability of the whole enterprise really depended, appeared to be in line with other commercial publishers, they were artificially inflated after 1959 by an accounting procedure which included in them the profits, but not the sales, of the overseas branches (excluding New York). Yet even with this sleight of the accounting hand, the profit of the London business stagnated at an average of only just above 7.0 per cent throughout the 1960s, and when the accounts were more properly drawn up in 1971 with the reinsertion of branch sales as well as profits, overall profit performance was shown to be very poor.

In due course, figures such as these became weapons on the battleground of restructuring. Defenders of the old ways pointed out that because the Press had no shareholders, and no commercial debt, it stood in a difficult position with regard to the Inland Revenue and had evolved various accounting devices to protect itself. For instance, capital depreciation of the paper-mill was accounted at 7.0 per cent per annum, twice the rate normal in commercial enterprises, in order to protect cash flow which was required for future capital investment. The appearance of depressed profits was a mere accountant's trick. There was some truth in these claims, but the truth tended to be outweighed by other developments that were too long unremarked by the Delegates and their senior advisers in Walton Street.

Two changes in particular were fundamental. The first was in the composition of the University. It grew dramatically in the 1950s and 1960s, and the great bulk of the growth was in the natural and applied sciences. By the mid-1960s, a majority of dons were scientists. They came to believe that the Press Establishment reflected the world of classical scholarship, history, theology, literature, and languages, which were no longer dominant in the University. In the language of the decade, they were not relevant. Many scientists believed that the Press took too little interest in their scholarship, neglected to publish adequately in their subjects, and was deaf to criticism. To their voice was added that of other new branches of university learning in the social sciences, which detected in the Press a comfortable private club of privilege. These changes in the demography of the University coincided with a change in social conditions generally: the coming of age of a post-war generation demanding a greater say in the governance of institutions, responding to the slogans of politicians and entertainers alike to apply 'the white heat of technology' and to expect greater participation.

Discontent sought an outlet in self-analysis, which in the case of Oxford University as a whole was summed up in the Report of its own Commission of Inquiry under the chairmanship of Lord Franks. The Commission held that OUP lay outside its remit, but in its Report, published in May 1966, it recommended that the University carry out an inquiry into the status, functions, and workings of the Press.[38] In this unobtrusive way was set in motion a process of restructuring that was to continue for twenty-three years, and change OUP out of almost all recognition from the University publishing department that DMD had joined in 1945. He noted that the paragraph in Franks 'fills me with fury',[39] but if so he never showed it. His commitment to both Press and University were to be sorely tried over the next twelve years, but he never faltered in his loyalty to either, though the personal costs were to be very great.

The first of these was measured in time. Efforts already made to try to improve science publishing were now redoubled. Active administrative measures had already also been taken to bring the operations of the various far-flung businesses under a common strategy with the creation of a Joint Management Committee, which brought together the heads of the London, Neasden, and Oxford operations in a regular monthly meeting. A London Management Committee and a CP Management Committee were established, the former meeting weekly, the latter monthly. Some repairs were, therefore, already in hand when, on 18 May 1967, the Hebdomadal Council announced the creation of a Committee on the University Press under the chairmanship of Sir Humphrey Waldock, Professor of International Law. From then until the publication of the Waldock Report three years later, much of DMD's time was taken up in supporting Colin Roberts in the preparation of material for the Committee: answering its inquiries when not anticipating its demands.

The Committee was small, only five members. Waldock was a lawyer, and a fellow of All Souls, where most of the Committee's deliberations took place. Two of the other members were from outside Oxford, R. J. L.

Martha McCulloch, 1967

Dan on his
retirement,
summer 1978

Dan and Anna, *c.*1983

Delia, 1984

Dan and Brigid, 1982

Patty and Philip Watson, *c.*1980

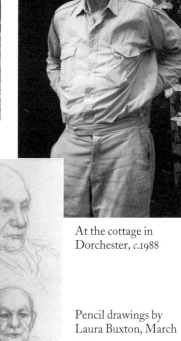

At the cottage in
Dorchester, *c.*1988

Pencil drawings by
Laura Buxton, March
1990

or occasional participants as might come along, or more generally as might be invited. This last was important. There was a tacit under-standing that members would not crowd the group, and that to take a guest meant reflecting on whether he or she would enjoy it *and be enjoyed*.[48] It also meant sharing in the rituals. Beer was purchased by any newcomer in half-pints approximate to the number in the group, brought over on a tray, and then poured into pint glasses retained by each drinker. This required a steady hand, not always available. The group always occupied the same corner, which was furnished with a padded settle, worn threadbare and sunken where Dan sat. Here, back to the wall and window, he had a good view of the room and the door. If he was away, his place tended to be left vacant, and any interloper who sat in it, ignorant of protocol, could generate a feeling of profound disquiet. Two round tables, lower than the settle and stools, meant there was no barrier to sociability. A newcomer who knew the ropes would always clear trays and empties from the tables on arrival. Mrs Clack never had to clear up the group's corner, home in her terminology to 'the Professor' and his 'high table'. She would cash cheques for Dan and Winnie, significant in the days before bank cards, and rightly interpreted as a mark of trust and regard. For the group, the Tudor Snug was a living-room on neutral ground.

Dan had taken to using a cigarette-holder, which made him look rather like a literary FDR or Trevor Howard, with the same mannerisms, and occasionally the same jauntiness of style which a cigarette-holder enhances. This sometimes persuaded visitors, particularly from New Zealand, to see him as presiding over a court. This impression was quite false. The company were not courtiers, and Dan was never regal. It was a society of equals where the only way to be certain of giving offence was to be dull. Dan once remarked of a New Zealand visitor that every time he passed him the ball of conversation the man had no idea what to do with it, and this was harsh criticism. Then he brightened. 'Still,' he added, 'when you pass it to Mike Joseph, he picks it up, puts it in his pocket and takes it home.'

The anecdote had point. Public house life, even as organized as this, does not suit all tastes, and Dan's preference for conducting his social life in this way closed some avenues. Mike Joseph and his wife Molly were an example. On his sabbatical visits to Oxford from Auckland they felt uncomfortable in the pub, and preferred not to go there. Likewise James Bertram, the patrician of New Zealand letters, who in a letter to Milner referred to 'Dan and his cronies'.[49] Coming from Bertram, it is hard to think of a more inappropriate word than 'cronies'.

Unsurprisingly, the Vicky did not favour those for whom conversation was a burden. Dan still delighted, as he had in the 1930s, in setting other tongues free, aiming to liberate conversation, not imprison it. '[H]e talked less as other people talked more and the chief use he made of his fund of stories and jokes was to start an atmosphere where other people would begin to feel at ease and let themselves go.'[50] Alan Horsman recalled being in the pub one evening with Keith Sinclair, then a rising star of New Zealand academic history. Sinclair, in whom talent and vanity were mixed in almost equal proportions, seized the floor and held it all evening, talking, explaining, expounding, lecturing. Dan, while giving Sinclair every impression of close attention, occasionally threw Horsman a little grin, 'not malicious, but amused and amusing', that acknowledged Sinclair's egotism while tolerating it.[51] There were those who believed that Dan was merely 'collecting copy' in the pub, by implication exploiting friendship for literary purposes. This is a complete misunderstanding, possibly malicious. Dan's diary entries, even when he took to keeping a continuous record again in 1964, contain nothing intimate about his friends at the Victoria Arms. The occasional aphorism which he wanted to remember is all. The three novels that he wrote in the years of his public house tenure contain no reference to it, and the memoirs included in *Closing Times* largely predate these experiences. It was precisely the absence of ulterior motives or secondary considerations in Dan's friendship that made it special and memorable.

These tendencies in Dan were not new, but they did emphasize a side of him that had been rather more concealed in the days of his ambition. His intolerance of incompetence, prominent in the war diaries, had disappeared. 'One must just accept the fact,' he wrote to Sargeson:

that men of considerable energy but also of considerable limitations will always push themselves into positions of administrative power . . . This is just a universal circumstance and to my thinking the artist must simply accept it and reckon on trying to contend with it[,] as he must reckon on having to encounter stupidity, apathy, poverty, and all the other things that drag at his energies and frustrate him.[52]

True to his own recipe, he submerged the occasional brash arrogance of the self-confident young intellectual, and replaced it on the surface with a humorous self-deprecation, ironic and amused, as though the youth he had been was now someone else, quite entertaining to watch, but only from a distance. It was this self-knowledge that made him wonderfully invited to Compton Mackenzie's house at Denchworth, near Wantage.[54] At Joyce Cary's dinner table they met Middleton Murry: a legend to Dan and Winnie, someone who had been intimate with Katherine, satirized by Aldous, friends with DHL.[55] In Dublin they met the former National Librarian, Richard Best, who appears in James Joyce's *Ulysses* under his own name. When Dan took part in a writers' forum at a British Council summer school in Oxford in August 1956, other speakers with whom he shared the platform were C. P. Snow and Pamela Hansford Johnson.

But the eminence of his position was not just by association. He was much sought after as speaker and writer. When the New Zealand High Commission in London mounted an exhibition of New Zealand books in co-operation with the British National Book League, they turned to Dan to give a lecture on 'New Writing in New Zealand'.[56] He was in demand to speak to the Booksellers Association, along with men like Basil Blackwell and Philip Unwin. He was invited to write about the Commonwealth for the Central Office of Information. He continued to contribute talks to the BBC on literary and historical topics. In 1957 he collaborated with Paddy Costello and General von Senger (a former Rhodes Scholar himself) in a radio discussion about the battle of Cassino.[57] This was the life of a successful man of letters, and in itself the partial fulfilment of his early ambition.

Those who paid only flying visits to Oxford might believe that Dan's life was pub life alone. It was certainly important, but his days were too full for it to dominate. He still tried to keep fit, and continued the games of squash that he had been encouraged to take up in order to lose weight before his operation. He played either with Peter Frankenberg, or with his Somerville friend Jean Banister. He still ran on Port Meadow occasionally and, when time permitted, went swimming. And he still played chess. In 1957 and 1958 Robert Walmesley came to live at 103. He was the son of an American actress, Dorothea Biddle, whom Dan had first met in England in the summer of 1948 through Joel Carmichael.[58] Robert was preparing for university entrance in Britain, and, briefly, was for Dan and Winnie like a son. While he and Dan played chess, Brigid and Delia took Robert cheese, food for the brain. Dan also played chess with H. W. Garrod in Merton, who, if Dan had won on the previous occasion, gave him port to drink, 'the effect of which impaired my game'.[59] His main partner, however, was Winnie, with whom he played chess a lot, generally on Sunday afternoons, and always so if the weather was bad. Chess battles are rightly metaphor for intellectual companionship.

receptive to younger writers, especially from New Zealand, in whom he detected the same features that he had himself once had. This did not happen overnight. Rupert Hart-Davis, who sat next to him at a Johnson Club dinner in Worcester College on 20 July 1957, found him 'aggressive but intelligent and incisive'.[53] There would have been high table defences at work here. Elsewhere, the aggression was giving ground. Some of the tolerance was spawned at home, where first Anna, and then both Delia and Brigid, brought boyfriends. Open invitation was extended for supper on Sunday evenings, and they would sit down, with other friends and visitors, twelve to twenty at the table. These were not always easy occasions. Dan was ambitious for his daughters, and quick to detect inadequacy in their boyfriends. Brigid thought that he probably 'loathed all the boys we brought home. He would pretend to be kind and polite but was really being a bit cruel.' One poor boy used to get so nervous he had to rush upstairs to be sick. Delia remembers, however, that Dan was not a 'jealous guard' of his daughters, though he worried about them, and would never go to bed before they were home at night. Even so, none of the daughters had any recollection of receiving sex education at home. Brigid said Dan once asked her, when she was 14, if she knew about sex 'and so on'. 'Oh yes, Dadda, really, absolutely everything.' They both knew it was not true, but embarrassment impeded further progress.

Nevertheless, young adolescents in the house strengthened his tolerance, while his discovery of the role of mature man prepared to listen brought him a popularity which he did not seek, but which he enjoyed, particularly among the graduate students whom Godfrey occasionally brought to the pub. Several generations of young anthropologists carried memories of Dan's wit, charm, and friendship away to some of the obscurest places in the world, as well as the most famous universities. And since Dan was so well-connected in intellectual and university life, on any evening a young scholar might find him- or herself, in the quiet atmosphere of the Tudor Snug, on temporary equal terms with the great and famous: Conor Cruise O'Brien or Richard Ellmann; Richard Cobb or Evans-Pritchard; Helen Gardner, Theo Moody, Neville Rogers, or Gordon Craig.

Ambition is trimmed by success as well as by defeat. In a way, and without realizing it consciously, Dan had found the social milieu towards which his struggles in Otago and Southland a quarter of a century before had been aimed. He now lived at the centre of the world of intellect and literature of which he had once only dreamed. He and Winnie were

Kingsford, who was a former Secretary to the Syndics of Cambridge University Press and a fellow of Clare College Cambridge; and a banker, A. D. Marris, the Senior Managing Director of Lazard Brothers. The two insiders were J. B. Bamborough, Principal of Linacre College, one of the new post-war Oxford Societies; and Professor Rex Richards, a brilliant scientist who was then Dr Lee's Professor of Chemistry and a fellow of Exeter College. Davin and Roberts regarded them all with foreboding. The only one with any experience of publishing came from The Other Place, where publishing operations were quite different. In due course these anxieties were in large measure allayed. DMD quickly found Richards impressive, and Marris's frequent absence from meetings did not, in his view, diminish their utility.

The Committee was time-consuming, however. Most of its members knew little of publishing, and next to nothing of the Press, and so had to learn. Roberts and DMD were greatly taken up with the preparation of documents for the Delegates to provide in evidence. There were also bush fires to fight. Some of the submissions forwarded to the Committee from members of the University were sharply partisan,[40] or ill-informed, but each had to be dealt with at painstaking length that took DMD away from the business of books. His worries about this were intensified by a memorandum prepared in March 1968 by Roberts in which he discussed the role of the Secretaries, and from which DMD feared that 'my job will have to become less directly with books and more with figures'.[41] The anxiety seemed justified when he gave his own formal evidence to the Committee at a meeting in All Souls at noon on Friday, 29 November.[42] In their report the Committee observed: 'The present Deputy Secretary—who also has general and administrative functions—told us that he was editorially responsible for some sixty-five of the CP titles currently in all stages of production and pointed out the difficulty of finding time to train additional editorial staff if these were available.'[43]

The Committee had unearthed a truth, that DMD was overworked, and that he concealed the fact only by the speed and determination with which he dispatched a quantity of work that might have fully occupied three other people. Another man of less conviction might have seen, in the Committee's willingness to understand his problems, an opportunity for constructive reform, but instead he felt himself under siege, caught in an 'us and them' mentality. In the spring of 1969 he wrote to Sisam:

The members of the Committee keep travelling in various directions and on various missions unconnected with the Inquiry itself. The longer it takes the better, I now think, since it will give us time to civilise our new

Vice-Chancellor, Alan Bullock, who takes over in the spring. The better he is acquainted with the way we work, the more likely he is to be on our side when the time comes.[44]

The reasons for this had to do with the position of the Press as a department of the University. DMD took this to be axiomatic, a guarantee of its scholarly credentials. He regarded the commercial London and New York businesses as the necessary source of essential investment capital. The Oxford business was different, and its difference needed to be preserved. It was also dominant in the whole structure of the businesses, and its dominance had to be assured. He feared that the Committee would either treat Oxford publishing as a commercial venture, proposing to turn it into a firm that could no longer command the disinterested allegiance of its authors and advisers; or compel it to move too quickly into fields for which it was not yet prepared. And his defensiveness was not ill-informed. He went about a lot in the University, dining at different high tables two or three times a week during term, and he knew the criticisms that were being made, both of the Press in general, and of its officers, including himself, in particular: Davin is an extraordinary man, but his allegiance is to classical and historical learning, he is overwhelmed with work but cannot delegate, and is defensive of the Sisam traditions out of loyalty and piety when modern business requires modern methods. A colleague confided in him about 'Trevor-Roper's attempt to get a History Faculty Committee to submit a savage, even mad, letter of attack on the Press which T.-R. had drafted—all about those "power-mad" bureaucrats Roberts, Davin and Sutcliffe.'[45]

DMD himself was due for some sabbatical leave, and was away from Oxford for three months in the summer of 1969. In his absence, his staff seized the opportunity to redecorate his office, and everything was removed into storage while the work was done. The story later circulated that on his return at the beginning of October everything had been restored to its rightful, though chaotic position with such precision that he failed to notice any difference. The truth is both less and more than the anecdote. He actually returned to Oxford in early September (when many of the staff, including Roberts, were away on holiday), found his room still being decorated, and worked for a morning in the tower instead.[46] Loyalty to the subsequent myth would not permit him to betray his knowledge.

The Waldock Committee eventually completed a draft report over the Christmas vacation, and it was forwarded to the Delegates in January 1970. DMD foresaw that 'the damned thing will be a plague on us for months to come,'[47] pessimism reinforced by the Delegates' view that it was a poor report. The revised version was at last published in May 1970, and although it is true that it is badly written, in the lumpy prose much favoured by English great and good reporters, it had a number of strengths which the Delegates themselves could not have been expected to applaud. After a fair review of the 'peculiar' history and structure of the Press, and a very great deal of generous, accurate praise for the remarkable work that OUP had accomplished since the war, it focused its analysis on governance. Waldock did not like the size of the Delegacy, or the way Delegates were appointed, or the length of time they served in the post. The Committee detected, though it did not express it so bluntly, that the Delegates constituted a self-appointed, exclusive club, and that this was a form of governing body inappropriate for what had become an international business organization.

To a degree, the Delegacy was a victim of its own success. Under the guidance of its Finance Committee the Press had become a big industrial undertaking, but its relationship to the University remained pre-industrial. What Waldock did not state—prudence forbade—was the legal reality, that OUP was an entity wholly owned by the University *with no limitation of liability*, and operating in a variety of countries in which political, tax, and legal regimes differed (Nigeria, Pakistan, the United States, for instance) any one of which might spell disaster. Oxford University itself has few assets, since these largely belong to the colleges and other independent societies, and there was a fear, much discussed in a few Senior Common Rooms though never advertised more publicly, that should OUP get into serious difficulties, the security and independence of the University could be threatened. Most of the Waldock reform proposals, whether having to do with appointments to the Delegacy itself, or the conduct and membership of Finance Committee, or the relations between the various composite businesses, were really directed at this fact. With hindsight it is hard not to agree with the need for reform.

In two other matters, however, the Committee may have been mistaken. On the one hand they failed to detect the crisis that was brewing in the London business. By urging a more commercial approach on the Oxford operations they appeared to be holding up Ely House as an example to be emulated, when the Secretaries in Oxford were only too conscious of the real position. The net profit of the London business of less than 7 per cent on sales for the year to 31 March 1970 was again too low, and its effects were already being felt throughout the whole of OUP as Waldock's report was being published. The proposal therefore appeared quixotic. The other matter had to do with science publishing. The Committee simply accepted scientists' criticisms, and recommended that science publishing be further expanded as a matter of priority, and without delay. Coming at the precise moment when the CP's own profit had fallen sharply to only 6.1 per cent, and was still falling in part because it had recently doubled the number of science editors, and was far advanced on a programme of publications from which cash returns were small and would remain so for some years to come, this proposal struck the Secretaries as reckless.[48]

DMD in particular deeply disagreed with this proposal. He was acutely conscious of the length of time that it took to train good academic publishers, to identify areas suitable for academic publishing, to find competent academic authors, and to bring academic projects to fruition. As we have seen, he had projects of his own that had been running since before he had joined the Press, and although he knew that the essence of scholarly publishing in the sciences involved a speed that was impractical for the arts and classics, nevertheless he held that the same skills of wide-ranging intellect, sureness of judgement, and ability to listen and to sift evidence, were necessary in the commissioning editor of science just as of arts. Under the impetus of the Waldock Report, OUP was now required to embark on a programme of expansion so rapid that he believed it would deprive him, as principal of the CP, of the opportunity to train the new intake.

In retrospect, the full effects of Roberts's appointment in 1952 are brought into focus by the issue of science publishing. In 1948 DMD had assumed responsibility at the CP for the fields of classics, history, literature, and reference books, fields in which he was trained and knowledgeable. Nothing in the twenty years after that had been suggested to change these responsibilities. The problem was that Roberts was himself a classicist, so that his appointment to the Secretaryship duplicated instead of diversifying areas of speciality at the top of the Press. In this context, science publishing, relative to other projects, was neglected. Whether DMD was conscious of the neglect throughout the 1950s is uncertain. What can be said is that, since it was not his field, and since he was not Secretary, it was not his fault. In his own fields, however, he was a superlative publisher, so that the books he and his people produced set the tone for the Press as a whole. Colin Roberts was also active in college and University affairs, but it is probably true to say that he was less readily identified with the Press, especially in the wider world of scholarship.

One senior academic, some years in retirement, told me that for many years he had had no idea that DMD was not head of the Press. In this way DMD later attracted blame for matters that were not his doing, while loyalty precluded criticism of others, even in private. Here the comparison with the Div. is at its most poignant. It was not for a junior officer

to imply or express judgement of the actions of men immeasurably my betters in . . . experience: among them men under whose command I had served and whose personal friendliness to me . . . reinforced the loyalty a junior officer owes to his commanders . . . [M]uch now clear was then hidden . . . the time to ponder the facts which is the privilege of the historian and his readers was not theirs; and . . . consequences which seem to us inevitable because we know they took place were . . . uncertainties of an inscrutable future.[49]

One other apparently small proposal in the Waldock Report also depressed him. Given the size and prestige of the business, Waldock proposed that the Secretary to the Delegates should be paid a salary of £7,500 to £8,000 per annum at 1968 values.[50] The proposal was couched in the language of 'commercial considerations'. What few people noticed, since it set a salary well above that then paid to University professors, was that it spelt the end of OUP as a University department. The Waldock Report is supportive throughout of the principle that OUP was special, did work that was not always to be judged by commercial criteria, and needed to be protected from the dangers of commercialization. But DMD saw in this one apparently minor proposal a wedge that made all the other sentiments nugatory.

The combination of recommendations depressed him profoundly. His own development in scholarly publishing had taken place in the light and shade of Sisam's training and example. He thought it the heart of what he believed to be the finest scholarly publishing house in the world. His own best contributions to the list of CP publications were made in the tradition and spirit that Sisam had passed on to him, and which he had continued to renew every year in his pilgrimage to Middle Carn. He believed the Waldock proposals would destroy the central features of the Press, and he brooded through the summer on resignation.[51]

He went to visit Sisam early this particular year, taking the train and helicopter to the Scillies at the end of the first week of August. He found his old mentor much reduced. Sisam would be 83 years old in a couple of weeks. He had lived virtually alone for more than twelve years since the death of his wife in March 1958, and although he enjoyed the long vacation visits of his daughter Celia, the visits of DMD and other friends, and the companionship of various island residents, his retreat into a world of separation and solitude was almost complete. They talked again about the Press, and DMD explained the Waldock proposals. He thought it possible that Congregation might not support the amendments to the University Statutes which gave effect to the Waldock reforms, but he felt little optimism in the thought. There were no boat outings this year because Sisam was too infirm. He 'carries his hands in front of him just below the horizontal, like forepaws, as if he was afraid of falling'.[52] And when DMD left on 20 August he wondered whether he would ever see Sisam again.[53]

The reforms did go through the University Congregation that autumn, and Kenneth Sisam died the following August, just a year after DMD had said his farewells. He took the night train and the boat back to Middle Carn for the funeral on 4 September 1971. After the service in the little local church,

the family group went to the ready-made hole in the 'Garden of Remembrance,' a lately recovered corner, where dandelions and blackberries still flourished. The casket was lowered on pieces of white string, rather like a child's parody of a coffin being buried. The thistledown and the shepherds' clocks of dandelion confirmed that all flesh was grass.[54]

Dan left the churchyard with tears in his eyes. His father in publishing was dead, and the son had lived only to see his house in disarray.

As DMD well knew, Waldock was not to be the end of reform, rather the beginning. And as he had feared the timing was bad. Increased expenditure on editorial staff, with no prospect of returns from sales perhaps for years to come, meant that the Clarendon Press made a loss in both 1971 and 1972. And this downturn in its fortunes coincided with the start of a period of sky-rocketing inflation, adverse trading conditions, the collapse of sterling, and intermittently disruptive political conditions. Labour relations in both the printing works and the Neasden warehouse deteriorated sharply. In Oxford, skilled labour proved hard to hold against competition from higher-paying car manufacturers. Profitable trading was just about impossible in these conditions. In the year ended March 1971, when the CP and the Wolvercote paper-mill both made a loss, and the profits from London and New York were tiny (1.7 per cent and 2.9 per cent respectively), only the printing business turned in a reasonable performance. That year group profits fell by 75 per cent. Even so, the appearance was stronger than the reality, for printing was struggling, and by 1974, the year of the three-day week, was itself in deficit.

In these new and unwelcome circumstances DMD became the businessman he had never wanted to be. From the London business he acquired Jon Stallworthy to take over English language and literature and Art books on the editorial side. This was a great pleasure to him. Jon was the son of Dr John Stallworthy, the great gynaecologist at the Radcliffe Infirmary, who in 1931, when Dan was a freshman, was President of the Otago University Union. The younger Stallworthy was also, by a quirk of fate, Sir Humphrey Waldock's son-in-law, a fact which was completely without significance as far as OUP was concerned, but to those given to conspiracy theory, appeared not to be. He had joined the Press in 1959, and served it in Pakistan, London, and South Africa, but he came to Oxford also known as a poet. DMD grew to have much the same regard for him as Sisam had had for himself, and he felt that the future of the Press as an academic house of scholarly standards would be assured in a succession that brought Stallworthy to the position of Academic Publisher. Stallworthy's great friend in OUP was Nicolas Barker, who joined the London business in 1971, and who was an expert on bibliography, and on the history and technology of printing, with long publishing experience with Rupert Hart-Davis, and Macmillan. Together they used to joke, half in earnest some thought, that they planned one day to be Secretary and Printer respectively at OUP. DMD, who liked and admired them both, would have been only too pleased. One day, coming out of the Travellers' Club after lunch with Barker, DMD spotted, chained to the railings of Pall Mall, a huge bicycle with a motor-cycle seat bolted on the vast iron frame. 'Good God,' he said, 'there's my father's bike.' 'No no,' Barker replied, 'it was *my* father's bike.' And he got on it and rode away.[55]

With the implementation of reform, the Delegacy was expanded to fifteen, none to serve (other than in exceptional circumstances) for more than two five-year terms. The changes were staggered, but even so six new Delegates joined in 1971: the largest single influx since the foundation of the Press. Hinshelwood had died in 1967, and when K. C. Wheare, who stood down in 1969, G. E. Blackman and Ronald Syme (1970), and Maurice Bowra and J. R. Hicks (1971) also went, the heart of the old Delegacy was gone. Between them these six had a combined total of 117 years of service: an average of nineteen and a half years each. With the retirement of three other long-serving members, H. L. A. Hart in 1974, and J. H. C. Thompson and Helen Gardner in 1975, the Delegacy that had directed the affairs of OUP through the 1950s and 1960s, and with whom DMD had been so closely associated, disappeared completely. In its place was a larger body of figures whom DMD knew more by repute than in person. The science members formed a caucus, with common views and a determined programme, and one of their number, Roger (later Sir Roger) Elliott, a physicist who was first appointed a Delegate in 1969, the last of the old dispensation, would in 1988 ascend himself to the post of Secretary of the Press.

The enlarged Finance Committee, of which DMD was now a full member, and to which he was responsible for the CP accounts (and which also now included outside advice), became far more active as a board of directors. The overseas branches were formed into a separate Division, and the first Branch Managers' conference was held in 1971. The firm's accountants were changed in 1970, and the accounts established on a new and more transparent basis.

Partly as a result of the poor results in the financial years 1971 and 1972, management consultants were brought in to prepare a corporate plan for the whole business. The three consultants from Cooper Brothers were *in situ* in Walton Street for nearly a year from the summer of 1972, men almost custom-designed to madden DMD. He thought their presumption that making books was a business just like any other, and so should be organized just like any other business, a low-level banality that was as useless as it was repugnant. Nevertheless, he spent many hours attending meetings of the joint management steering committee that worked with the consultants to devise a corporate plan, and outline the administrative machinery that could implement it. He opposed it to the last, questioning the utility of spending £20,000 a year on something of dubious intellectual value, but it came into being in June 1973, and he loyally worked through it to ensure its successful adoption. The consultants had some other interesting effects. By requiring everyone to compose a job description explaining what they did and why, they unearthed confusions long buried. By probing at methods of administrative control, they revealed that many junior staff in the Oxford business felt neglected. Roberts was remote and unapproachable; DMD too busy to be disturbed and with a reputation for brilliance and decisiveness that intimidated without his knowing it. The Press had no system of annual reviews for assessing and promoting its editorial staff. Many were uncertain what constituted a full and responsible work load. DMD could see that systematic management had to replace the vague pattern of traditional methods, and laboured hard to ensure that these concerns were met, but as he did so he found himself cast ever more into a role that he did not want, of businessman who was now unable to do what he loved, talk to authors, stimulate books, read manuscripts. He hated committees, which might take hours to resolve issues he would have decided in minutes. 'There is nothing worse than a Wykehamist socialist', he remarked to Bob Burchfield.[56] In compensation for the deprivation he worked ever harder, faster, and longer, hoping to do both. His diary records him all too frequently, in the years from the late 1960s until his retirement, getting to the cottage in Dorchester on a Friday evening, and immediately falling exhausted into bed. He might recover his energies by Sunday afternoon, barely in time to return to the fray on Monday morning.

In the middle of the corporate planning exercise, Roberts's retirement—he was due to leave at the end of September 1974—loomed on the horizon. The last thing that DMD wanted at this stage in his career (he was 60 himself in 1973) was to be appointed Secretary, but the Delegates asked him to allow his name to go forward, and in response to a personal appeal from Alan Bullock he agreed.[57] His forebodings became more profound when the advertisement for the post appeared in the national press in the middle of April 1973. Instead of referring to scholarly publishing and the need for a figure who combined a sympathetic understanding of scholarship with business methods, it stressed 'commercial and managerial ability' and envisaged the appointment of someone from industry or commerce. DMD was appalled. The advertisement seemed to him to signal the death of academic publishing at Oxford. In response, he wrote a devastating paper, 'The Secretary to the Delegates', in which he drew on the history of the Press, its growth and accomplishments, its recent difficulties and problems, to argue the case for the appointment of a scholar/administrator in the tradition of Cannan, Chapman, Sisam, Norrington, and Roberts. If there was a need for business and financial advice, then an Assistant Secretary (Finance) could be appointed—as had, indeed, been suggested by the Waldock Report. No mere businessman, DMD thought, could command the respect of the experienced publishing staff, the scholars who wrote Press books, or the other members of the University. Morale would be undermined. The appointee would be likely 'to blow cold' on unprofitable books, favour profit-making in every 'tussle for priorities', and make decisions 'prejudicial to the long-term interests of the Press' at all 'the really critical moments'. He sent this paper to Roberts with a covering letter expressive of his gloom and rancour.

We live, of course, in a time when experience almost disqualifies one from having a view at all, especially if it is accompanied by a certain scepticism of current vogues and fashionable catchwords. On the other hand, I think that the Press has a past to be proud of, one that contains lessons for a future of which I am very anxious that our successors can also be proud.[58]

This rearguard action met with some success when it was coupled with personal intervention. In response to Alan Bullock's personal request to him to be a candidate for the post, he went to see the Vice-Chancellor, and explained to him, as Winnie recalled that he had explained to Sir George Clark in 1952, that he would be unable to remain at the Press if an appointment was made of the kind envisaged in the advertisement.

Applications for the post closed at the end of May, and short-listed candidates were interviewed in the third week of July. DMD's case rested simply on his record, and at the interview he explained that he had no desire for the post, but was willing to serve if called on to do so. In the event he was saved by the appointment of George Richardson: an economist with interests in economic theory and industrial economics; a fellow of St John's College; himself a Delegate in the new intake of 1971.[59] The appointment was a bridge between those who wanted a businessman, and those who, following DMD, wanted a scholar with some knowledge of and background in scholarly publishing. Richardson was ten years DMD's junior, and with a background in social science that was modern. It was a long time since the Secretary of OUP had not been fluent in Latin. Later it was said that Dan now assumed a position at the centre of the Press 'comparable with that attributed to Leibnitz in the development of western culture: he was the last man to whom all knowledge had seemed available'.[60]

Even so, there were still things to learn. The commitment to a commercial approach, coupled with the poor financial situation in which the Press as a whole now found itself, meant further radical reform: to achieve economies; to reorient the direction of the business; to rationalize management. Early in 1974 the Delegates took the joint advice of the Waldock Report and DMD, and appointed an Assistant Secretary (Finance).[61] The man they selected, David Mitchell, was an inspired choice. An English-born Scot who had trained in business economics with W. R. Grace & Co., New York, and its subsidiaries, he had risen to senior management levels in both the United States and in Europe. He spoke various modern languages, had wide experience of the problems of running an international company, and was, without being a scholar himself, sympathetic to the objectives of scholarship. He was widely read as well as experienced, and, like Dan's friends Gordie Craig and David Pocock, wrote marvellous verse, moving and funny, clever in metre as well as wit. By some agency of the chemistry of human affections, he and DMD took to each other straight away, during Mitchell's interview for the job—a fairly grand affair with the full Finance Committee in subfusc, including Dame Helen Gardner unaware, no doubt, of the hard time she had given a rather younger David Mitchell at his viva voce examination in the 1950s.

On appointment it was Mitchell who carried OUP into the world of modern business, implementing one-year budgeting and three-year operating plans, creating management information systems, and installing cash flow and capital control, cost, price, and transfer-price monitoring. It is not fanciful to say that OUP might not have survived without him, and in this large thing he accomplished another: he convinced all the men who really mattered, principally DMD, Vivian Ridler, and Jon Stallworthy, not simply that these things were necessary and appropriate if OUP was to survive, but that they were essential if it was to prosper as a great scholarly publishing house. 'They—and pre-eminently DMD— had recognised that we were on the same side, and that of those to whom much is given, much is required . . .'[62]

George Richardson, of course, did not need convincing, but now he was not alone. Very quickly they were able to start pulling together. This was just as well because by the time Roberts handed over to Richardson, the position of the Press (as of the British economy generally) was dire. The price of paper trebled between December 1973 and June 1975, but under government price controls the price of books could not be increased. The brand new *Concise Oxford Dictionary*, launched at a party in London on 21 July 1976, was already being printed at a loss. And rapid inflation made it progressively more difficult to find capital from taxed profits (themselves depressed) to maintain, let alone increase, the volume of stock on which the welfare of the enterprise depended.

The Delegates rationalized OUP into a British Publishing business and an Overseas Publishing business. The Ely House premises in London were given up when the lease expired in 1976, and the whole of UK publishing activities concentrated in Oxford. DMD became the director of the Academic Publishing division of OUP, an outfit with ninety-six employees now to be joined in Oxford by the commercial forces of the former London business. But for his loyalty to the institution, and David Mitchell to assure him of the wisdom of this move, DMD might well have retired now, for though it had been on the cards for some years, and he had long since agreed to it, he feared that academic publishing might be swallowed in the amalgamation. His reluctance was grounded in the fact that Waldock had specifically rejected such a merger, saying it was likely to blur the useful distinction between an Oxford and a London book.

A year before the move, an old colleague from London, John Bell, gave up his job there as Deputy Head of the General Publishing Division, and came to Oxford to take more of the editorial strain from DMD's shoulder. Together with Jon Stallworthy he divided the labour that DMD had previously invested in texts. Even so, the man who trained in Sisam's shadow could not bring himself to abandon altogether the real business of publishing as he understood it. David Mitchell, in response to a request, offered him fifteen pieces of advice on what he should be doing. All of it was good, some exemplary. He should delegate most of what he was doing, cease all editorial involvement, take firm control of the CP list, and stand up for the unprofitable scholarly works that were the true heart of OUP.[63]

Good as the advice was, DMD could not bring himself to take all of it. In particular he found it impossible to stop being involved with the books and authors, such as his friends in Dublin working on the history of Ireland, with whom he had been so enjoyably involved for so long. And the fact is that the books were a necessary escape from the painful reality of his last few years at OUP.

The arrival in Oxford of the staff from the London business was an administrative nightmare, one made worse by a clash of cultures. The commercial world of London publishing was different in style from the scholarly world of Walton Street. London employees were paid higher salaries, and were used to some perks of London publishing life and rather shorter working hours. Oxford editorial staff had different values altogether, but were jealous of salary differences, which were obviously unsustainable under the new corporate structure. A number of the CP secretarial staff decamped to the newcomers almost on their arrival. Labour relations deteriorated for the first time in the history of the Press, and staff instituted first a work-to-rule and then a one-day strike, which was supported by a third of the Oxford publishing staff. The Secretary's observation that 'the dispute took up a great deal of time, caused emotional wear and tear, and engendered some distrust and misunderstanding'[64] seems in retrospect to be admirable understatement. David Mitchell saw it with perhaps greater clarity than most:

All the initial problems came from the second-raters, in London mainly, who had largely contributed to the troubles, by arrogating to themselves the privileges of the 'Oxford' name without really accepting either the academic or the commercial disciplines; who seemed to think that OUP could be run more sloppily than a 'commercial' publisher because it was part of the university—whereas, of course, it must be run as well as possible, for that very reason . . . Every unsuccessful editor and ineffective manager pleaded service to scholarship, when he was merely feather-bedding himself, or simply incompetent. I came to despise the 'Bookmen' . . . [and] soon found that OUP's financial problems were not caused by the genuine academic publishing, but by the list intended to make money.[65]

DMD was, more than ever, prone to bouts of depression. Disheartened by the constant disruptions, he drifted towards despair. The old OUP, which he compared in his mind to the Div., had gone, in part destroyed by the clever London people. To add irony to injury, the very people whose incompetence, as he saw it, had brought about the financial woes of the business were now installed at its heart, and presuming to set its standards. It was helpful of David Mitchell to explain to him that this was a temporary phenomenon, a product of restructuring, and that whereas formerly the Press had been an international business run like a university department, now it was being turned into a university department run like an international business, but it was hard for him to believe that scholarly publishing could survive in this new environment. His despair was deepened by Jon Stallworthy's decision in 1976, made partly for family reasons, to resign, and take a chair in English in the United States. Nicolas Barker went as well, going to the British Library. The search for a replacement for himself, when in his heart he could not bring himself to believe that anyone could do the job as he had hoped Stallworthy would do it, was resolved by the appointment of Robin Denniston, who also came from the world of London commercial publishing. He arrived early in 1978 to shadow DMD in his work for his final months at OUP.

This was the context in which DMD fought his last OUP battle. He was, in a sense, looking for a good crisp action against a worthy opponent of good books and serious ideas, and he found one in somebody he had long detested, Robert Maxwell. On 28 September 1977 Maxwell's Pergamon Press planned to publish something called *The Pergamon Oxford Dictionary of Perfect Spelling*, edited by one of his children. OUP took the view that the use of the words *Oxford* and *Dictionary* as part of the title of a work coming from another publisher was tantamount to seizure of their own territory. As publisher responsible for OUP reference works DMD led the fight, briefing solicitors and barristers, preparing documents. The first application to the High Court for an injunction to prevent publication was refused, but on appeal on 18 October 1977 before Lord Denning, Master of the Rolls, and two other Appeal judges, the application was granted and OUP awarded costs. Maxwell asked for leave to appeal to the House of Lords, but Denning would not permit it.

DMD was delighted with this engagement. At 103 he had kept a file of newspaper cuttings about Maxwell ever since the man first drew himself to national attention. He was of interest both as a fellow publisher in Oxford—Pergamon Press headquarters were in Headington—and as a former army officer. DMD thought he was a fraud, and occasionally talked about him in these terms. The opportunity to deal with him now in the interests of the Press was gratefully received. It was rare to hear DMD express pleasure in something he had himself done, but he was pleased with this, and he said so.

The year 1978 was the 500th anniversary of printing in Oxford, an occasion for substance to give way to public relations. 'A slightly spurious anniversary' as DMD called it, since the modern company, OUP, really only dated from the early 1860s, and book publishing in Oxford had been, to say the least, intermittent from the fifteenth to the eighteenth centuries. Nevertheless it was considered an occasion to celebrate, and for four years a planning committee had been at work organizing various functions. DMD proposed a Festschrift for which various Press authors would write about their relations with OUP, but the suggestion found little support. The BBC made a television documentary which included film of 'morning prayers'. On the day it was broadcast, 23 March, Foyles gave a literary lunch for the Press at which A. J. P. Taylor and Michael Foot were the speakers. Simultaneously OUP published two books about its own history, one of them by Peter Sutcliffe, DMD's colleague at the Press, once his protégé in the late 1950s, often a companion at the Tudor Snug. Peter had had a confused and difficult life with various personal disasters, and was in danger of becoming an alcoholic. It was typical of DMD that he should have seen that Sutcliffe was the ideal man to write a really good middleweight history of the Press, and that in doing it he might save his health and sanity, which he did.[66] Exhibitions were mounted at the Pierpont Morgan Library in New York, at the Bodleian, and at the Victoria and Albert Museum in London. On 5 April a great luncheon was served in the Codrington Library in All Souls, at which the Prime Minister, James Callaghan, was speaker.

DMD dutifully made his way through the celebrations, which coincided with his own retirement. In June, July, and August he travelled with Winnie, visiting OUP branches throughout the world to say his farewells. In Baltimore, at a meeting of the American Association of Academic Publishers, he was guest of honour, and principal speaker at a dinner on 12 June. It was a sparkling occasion—also the centenary of the Johns Hopkins University Press—and DMD made a gracious and witty speech which his audience greeted with acclaim. Back in Oxford, the Academic Publishing Division celebrated the quincentenary with a lunch in Merton on the very day, 29 September, that DMD retired. It was followed by a reception for him at the Press. The very last manuscript that he worked on in the morning before walking to Merton was Charles Brasch's memoirs, *Indirections*, with their accounts of Colin Roberts as a young man, life in Oxford in the late 1920s, Esmond de Beer as scholar and antiquarian, and a wartime of intelligence work far from home in Dunedin. At the afternoon reception DMD was presented with a painting of his cottage at Dorchester by the artist David Gentleman, which the Press had commissioned.

Dan—he would never again be DMD—had played a crucial role at the Press in his final years with it, but, like others of what was now considered to be the old guard, he was seen by the new young bloods not as a great academic publisher who, late in his career, and against many of his own preferences, had played a noble part in holding things together at a critical time, but as faintly dubious evidence of a past which the new men were keen to disown. George Richardson, who carried the burden of restructuring on into the 1980s, said later that DMD's support 'was crucial to me. I could depend on it when the going was very rough, whether or not it was deserved. He was naturally exceedingly loyal . . . I trusted him completely. . . . He was also shrewd, stylish and immensely honourable.'[67] David Mitchell recognized the truth too. 'Dan was . . . the symbol and embodiment of what the OUP, even Oxford itself, was—or should be—all about.'[68] Despite his despair, and his fear that the Press, Sisam's Press, might have been betrayed, Dan gave no signal of it to the outside world. Apart from Winnie and a few close friends, he kept his opinions strictly private.

At the start of 1978, OUP sold the Wovercote paper-mill.[69] The Press no longer made its own paper for its own scholarly books, and it had been common ground for some years that the Mill would be sold when a suitable buyer could be found. Dan's fear was that one day the Press might not bother to print, or then to publish, scholarly books either.

13

CRITIC AND FRIEND

The first requisite [of good criticism] is some modesty on the part of the critic; the second the sense to see that a good writer doesn't adopt a style, a theme, or a solution without having good reasons; the third, the patience and penetration to find it out.

(ATL: MS-Papers-0432-155, DMD to Frank Sargeson, 7 Dec. 1949)

The quinquagenarian may not be master of himself, he is, notwithstanding, master of a passable miscellany of experience on which to draw when forming opinions, distorted or the reverse, at least up to a point his own. After passing the half century, one unavoidable conclusion is that many things seeming incredible on starting out, are, in fact, by no means to be located in an area beyond belief.

(Anthony Powell, *Temporary Kings*, 229)

The death of Louis MacNeice in 1963 was followed six months later by another. On Sunday, 23 February 1964 Paddy Costello died suddenly of a heart attack. A newspaper rang to ask if Dan would be willing to write an obituary. Winnie said that she was sure he would, but there was no hurry obviously since Paddy was only 53 and in good health, and anyway Dan was out at the moment, playing squash with a friend. The reporter broke the news. When Winnie got the news to him, Dan came home, went into his study, shut the door, and was alone and silent for three hours, when he phoned the obituary through to the paper.

The disappearance of Costello robbed Dan of the brightest star in his universe: the man whose intellect and integrity he most admired, and in whose company he had enjoyed the keenest experience. Dan had a number of friends, like Gordie Craig, Geoffrey Cox, and Geoffrey Flavell, who knew him well. He had colleagues and acquaintances too numerous to count who considered him a friend. But Costello was the only man with whom Dan had enjoyed the deepest intimacies of intellectual exchange. When he lost him, he became, for all the conviviality of his later years, a solitary. In solitude lay the temptations of nostalgia, melancholy, and the danger of depression.

For the moment, these possibilities were obscured by more urgent considerations: principally the feeling that he ought to do something for the Costello family. Bil and her five children were not poor: they had a substantial house in Manchester, she had some insurance income, and was able to continue her job teaching Russian. Three of the children were quite grown up by this time, and either in or beyond university. Nevertheless, Bil was anxious about public school fees for the two youngest children. Dan and Winnie visited Manchester early in May 1964, and afterwards Dan wrote to various of Costello's friends in academic, diplomatic, and political life, soliciting gifts for a trust fund to help with school fees. In this way he collected over £1,200, and for the next six years or so he acted, in concert with the Registrar of Manchester University, as administrator of the fund.

In the course of these years Dan's interest in Paddy deepened. He wanted to explain and describe his own relationship with him: its intensity and purity. It was something on which he brooded. One immediate effect of this was that he started to keep a diary again, and continued to do so fairly faithfully from 1964 until shortly before his own death. This was a different sort of diary from the one he had kept before, however. He described it as a 'rather pointless journal',[1] by which he meant I think that the role of analyst was deliberately excluded from what was now a formal account of his daily life. He did not keep it every day, but wrote it up a week at a time, generally at Dorchester on a Saturday. From its contents, it is apparent that he sat down with his pocket diary, in which he would jot his appointments in a tiny illegible hand, and wrote out an account of the week that listed people, meetings, lunches and dinners, parties, weddings, feasts and travel: the weekly round of an always busy executive life that often enough became impossibly packed with commitments. Reading it, it is impossible not to feel sorrow for a life consumed by so much social toing and froing, the more so when one knows the world of knowledge, intellect, and human sympathy that lay behind it, unstated, as well as the quantity of 'hepatic ailment' so often referred to. It is also difficult not to feel exasperation at the handwriting. It was from this time that Dan's script deteriorated from the merely eccentric until, near his death, it approached the illegible. To receive one of his letters from now on was to have spirits raised in proportion to patience tested. Brigid Brophy spoke for Dan's many correspondents when she expressed 'Very many thanks for the extreme generosity and kindness of the two thirds of your letter that I could read'.[2]

Paddy's death also brought into sharp relief the odd events of the summer, one of those rolls of the cold war dice, trivial in itself, that so characterized the age. In 1963 a Russian-language collection of New Zealand short stories was published in Moscow.[3] Two of the fifty stories that it contained were by Dan, 'Milk Round' and 'In Transit', both taken from *The Gorse Blooms Pale*. The Russian collection is, now, a period piece, expressive of the then official Communist line on literary matters. For instance, although it contained four stories by Mansfield, and five by Sargeson, as well as a number by other established figures, it also contained what were presumably then regarded as correct, or at any rate progressive, stories by generally unknown authors, most of whom were associated with *Fernfire*, a dreary cyclostyled 'magazine' produced by fellow-travellers in Auckland, and certainly not representative of contemporary New Zealand writing. The book gave little indication of who might have advised on the selection of stories, and Winston Rhodes, an academic at Canterbury University who was for many years associated with the New Zealand–USSR Friendship Society, did not help to clarify matters in a 'disingenuous' article about the book in *Landfall*.[4] As usual with such Russian publications, its contents were stolen, for although fees were paid, copyright was expropriated.

Dan was not sent a copy of the book and was never at any time consulted about it. It was Bill Pearson, a young New Zealand academic whom Dan had first met in the early 1950s, and who was, in 1964, on sabbatical leave in London, who first brought it to his attention. He also kept him abreast of developments in New Zealand where *Truth*, the weekly tabloid that Dan had so long despised, published an article about it on 9 June. The piece was the customary mixture of cold war extremism, innuendo, and malice, and its principal effect on Dan was to make it difficult for him to register his own complaints without appearing 'to be associated with the[se] more intemperate views'.[5] Eventually, however, and on the advice of Max Hayward, he wrote to Moscow to protest, and while hoping that his letter 'will not be regarded as in any way an anti-Soviet gesture' he threatened to publicize the matter in writers' organizations in Britain.[6]

Eventually he received a reply containing various bromides, but since the Russian authorities had no intention of recognizing Western copyright law, the issue could only fizzle till it died.[7] It left a nasty taste, however; a sour residue, left and right, Moscow and *Truth*, the artist trapped between two falsehoods. Coming so soon after Paddy's death, it was like a tawdry footnote to the brilliance of his life. Dan was also disillusioned about Winston Rhodes who, he believed, had had more of a hand in the preparation of the book than he had implied in *Landfall*, but who had neglected to give any advance notice of it.[8] The affair did have one happy outcome, however. *Truth* was sued for libel by O. E. (Ted) Middleton, a writer whose work Dan admired, and one of whose stories had been included in the World's Classics volume of 1953. Middleton was awarded a considerable sum in damages, and in 1966 he spent some of it on a long visit to Europe, where he visited Oxford. He and the Davins became friends.[9]

One learns little about literary controversy of this kind from Dan's diary, where almost all that is visible among the thickets of social and professional obligation is the sheer density of his daily life. This left him little time for writing, certainly no opportunity for anything longer than a review or a short story. Nevertheless, after the publication of *No Remittance* in 1959, though only during his annual retreat at Middle Carn every autumn, he drafted a long episodic novel that was eventually published as *Not Here, Not Now*. The draft was ready in the spring of 1966. Although it took seven years to finish, it was not seven years in the writing, but rather composed in fragments over a period in which his own life went through many changes, including the deaths of friends, the marriages of children, and his own passage into his fifties. In all the seven years of its composition he probably worked at it for no more than a total of six months. He complained throughout these years that his creative literary imagination was moribund.

Some part of this complaint he attributed to his work at the Press, though characteristically it was the quality of the work, and not its quantity, that was the problem.

An exacting professional life develops a logic of brevity in writing which is disastrous to the logic of association on which the creative writer depends. Being continually exposed to the vanity of authors, one loses the confidence of one's own. Along with a scepticism about facts, there develops an excessive respect for those that can be established and this happens at the expense of the power to create fiction. As one grows older one becomes more interested in what is the same in people and sees the repetitions in their behaviour at the expense of delight in their variety. The philosopher overcomes the gossip, and thought kills life.[10]

The problem, and its analysis, led him to thoughts of retirement from the Press, and a life of full-time writing.[11] But it is only half the story, for there were other reasons to explain the drought. Partly it was loss of confidence. From the high point of his post-war success, and life in the literary milieu of Fitzrovia, Dan's literary career had been in decline. His 1950s novels were of no great interest in Britain. The disagreeable aggressiveness of reviews in New Zealand, an extension of what in local rugby football parlance would be called playing the man rather than the ball, were cause for chagrin, part of it stimulated by the unwelcome reflection that there might be some truth in what was written. 'It would be wonderful', he wrote to Sargeson, 'some day to produce a book of which one wasn't ashamed before the printer's ink was dry.'[12]

These reflections were entrenched by having to reread and edit *For The Rest Of Our Lives* for a new edition which Blackwood Paul published in New Zealand in 1965, but mainly they were generated by *Not Here, Not Now*. The novel was not published until 1970, but its place in his biography belongs rather earlier, to the period of its composition in the first half of the 1960s. The story of the novel needs no rehearsal, since it follows the course of his own career at Otago University in the 1930s. It is a 'rites of passage' novel in which the central adolescent figure, Martin Cody (M. C., like Mick Connolly in the sequence of childhood short stories, detected by one historian of the Irish as code for Michael Collins, revolutionary Irish martyr),[13] eventually, and ruthlessly, achieves his ambition of a Rhodes Scholarship despite the impediments placed in his way by his enemies.

Not Here, Not Now was the novel that Dan had wanted to write for twenty-five years. Throughout all that time he had continued to reflect on the drama of his first love-affair, the ambitions that Winnie had kindled in his heart, the excitement of his first publications, scholarly success, scandal, and intrigue. In his mind he relived it as the story of a young man from an exploited and repressed minority who had the nerve and talent to challenge the institutions of the Establishment and wrest from them, by their own methods, one of their glittering prizes. It was a good story, and the love-affair at its heart, with the tragedy of a young woman bent to his will, had a power which, distilled, might have brought literary success.

There were various reasons to explain his failure to write the story for so long. One was the fear of legal action. The Macdonalds were still alive, and the role played by Mrs Macdonald in wrecking his first attempt for the Rhodes was the stuff of which libel suits are stitched in New Zealand. In any event, Geoffrey Flavell was wary too. He did not want the story of his eviction from Medical School told until *he* was ready, and he was quick to extinguish whatever fires of gossip he encountered during his rise to medical eminence in London in the 1950s. Another reason was auto-biographical. Dan knew that in some regards he had behaved badly. 'I had married in 1939 a fellow New Zealander whose own, and greater, literary gifts I have to reproach myself for cannibalising', he wrote in 1965.[14] Severe as this judgement was, it was itself reference to a larger theme: his inability to write about his 'arrogant youth' or 'my life and crimes' as he liked to refer to it, without hurting people whom he now saw to have been innocent, yet wounded by his self-willed pursuit of success: scholarly, sexual, literary. For a writer of the realist method, one for whom the facts of the past were sacred, this impediment was almost insuperable. Since it also combined with remorse for many of the things he had done and said, it might seem odd that even so, he persevered in writing the novel.

Here we see his old stubbornness at work. He was still the boy who could never be deterred from a course of action on which he had set his mind. To put aside the story that had for so long been at the centre of his ambition would have been an act of surrender, and a negation of the self. He had set himself a programme, and *Not Here, Not Now* was to be its crowning work. To stop now would be to stop altogether.

It is hard to think of forces less suitable for literary composition. Trapped between a reluctance to tell the truth and a determination to do so, Dan found himself writing a novel that is almost the exact antithesis of his first book *Cliffs of Fall*. Martin Cody, the young hero of *Nor Here, Not Now* is a new monster of egotism and ambition, but this time unredeemed by the quest for authenticity. His struggles are for mere worldly success: almost a definition of *mauvaise foi*. The bad faith of the novel is betrayed in its language, which is sometimes awkward and stilted, though redeemed by occasional passages that recapture youth and the freshness of experience. The novel also lacks the sound structural principles essential to the success of any fiction perhaps because it emerged from the imagination of a writer deeply divided in himself about whether he should write it, and if so how. Its flaws are the fissures in his own intentions.

Dan sent the manuscript to David Higham at the end of April 1966. Its subsequent history was not happy. Michael Joseph, Dan's publishers, did not want it. Roland Gant, who had been Dan's editor at Joseph, and was now editorial director at William Heinemann Ltd., also turned it down. So did Cape, who saw it next; and Constable, who did not report until January 1967, but certainly spoke directly when they did: 'The general feeling was one of surprise that such an experienced editor . . . should have written something which seems curiously immature in its treatment of the theme—something which reads almost like a first novel by a recent graduate . . .'[15]

The criticism gave Higham pause, and he sought Dan's agreement to get another opinion on the manuscript. Dan suggested his old friend John Willett, who turned out to be someone well known to David Higham. Willett, a literary figure, experienced editor, familiar with contemporary fiction and publishers, was an excellent choice, but it set him a near impossible task. Any friend would find it hard to perform such a service objectively, the more so with a work replete with undigested experience. Given the difficulties, Willett performed his role well. He thought the novel good enough, and that Michael Joseph, as Dan's publishers, should have had confidence in it. Even so, the long last third of the book was poor. Apart from the hero's final triumph in securing his Rhodes Scholarship at the second attempt, nothing got settled. Perhaps what was really wanted was 'a blazing public scandal' over the deceits that had betrayed him at his first attempt.[16]

This was good advice, gently expressed, but it was not advice that Dan could take. For him, one of the most significant aspects of his experience of scandal at Otago was precisely that the lid stayed on the cauldron. The camouflage was preserved. All the deceits were in a fine balance, so that none could be expressed. There had been no public scandal, and its absence was climactic proof of the suffocations of his youth. It was a hypocritical world where what was known was said only behind hands, with malice. He could not possibly change this. So it was that his 'excessive respect for those [facts] that can be established' was 'at the expense of the power to create fiction'.[17]

Willett's letter persuaded Higham that it was worth persevering. He sent the manuscript to Bob Lusty at Hutchinson's. He did not want it, and neither did Cassell, nor Methuen. All young writers have to learn how to cope with rejection, but it is given to few to have to relive the experience in their middle fifties. Dan was stoically silent about it, but it is indicative of how keenly he wanted the book published in some form or another that when Martin Green at MacGibbon & Kee said that they might be interested if the author pulled the work into shape by making substantial cuts, he agreed to undertake the task.[18] Back in the Scillies in the autumn of 1967 he cut 20,000 words. Even so, and after further long delay, the novel was declined.[19]

The manuscript was then sent to Robert Hale Ltd., and this unfashionable house, though with connections to New Zealand, agreed to take the book provided further cuts were made. Dan agreed to this, but he was distanced from the work by this time, bored and embittered, and he proposed that Hale make the cuts for him to approve.[20] Even when this distasteful task was done the book's future was jeopardized. Hale wanted to publish it jointly with Whitcombe & Tombs, and somewhere between their London and New Zealand offices, Whitcombe & Tombs lost the revised manuscript. This turned out to be the only copy with the agreed revisions, both Hale's cuts and Dan's treatment of them. A second copy of the original had now to be cut more or less as the first, and Dan had then to agree it again, a 'maddening' task which interrupted his intense schedule of work at the Press, and his preparations for the sabbatical leave which he planned to take in New Zealand. Eventually the work was done by the end of the third week of May 1969, and the book was at long last published eight months later on 16 January 1970.

The history of the manuscript is one more explanation for the disjointed nature of the work. It had been doctored by several hands. This was unique in Dan's life. A few years later, when an editor at OUP suggested numerous alterations to the manuscript of his volume of memoirs *Closing Times*, Dan was ruthless and determined in rejecting almost all of them out of hand.[21] Why the difference with *Not Here, Not Now*?

In *Not Here, Not Now* Dan was still struggling to shed his past by speaking of it, and the death of his father in 1958 gave him some freedom to speak more plainly. He hoped, by getting it out of his literary system, to free himself to write about other topics and in a new way. *Not Here, Not Now* was a last compulsory rendering of the account of youth. This was how he started off, but by the time he was half-way through, he had lost interest. Why was this? One reason was that the subject had gone stale. It was all a long time ago. The world had changed, and so had he. A second was the discovery that the task was beyond him. He talked of having planned a sequence or cycle of novels about New Zealand, of which presumably *Cliffs of Fall* was a precursor, and the stories about the Connolly family from *The Gorse Blooms Pale; Roads From Home; No Remittance*, and *Not Here, Not Now* were the sum. If so, neither sequential nor cyclical relationship is readily detectable. Pattern, if such there be, might be thought superimposed by an older man, looking back. The probability is that the idea occurred to him in the mid-1950s, when half the work was done, and it was too late to devise it again as a fresh, more complex project. He could not refuse to write *Not Here, Not Now* because the work was central to his conception of himself. But he could not now write it as he wanted to, because his earlier work, as well as the need to avoid damage to reputations, had closed the options. In correspondence he defended the work bravely, but he knew that it was flawed, a novel whose only real interest lay in the light that it shed on a particular place and historical period: Otago University in the 1930s.[22] When it was published it enjoyed a certain *succès d'estime* among Otago undergraduates, for whom it was evidence that there had possibly been interesting life forms in Dunedin before themselves.

Dan's progressive detachment from *Not Here, Not Now* was intensified by his admiration for the work of Anthony Powell. He read each of the novels of Powell's *A Dance to the Music of Time* sequence as it was published, and saw in them the *roman-fleuve* that he would have liked to compose himself. Its intricacy and density, some characters carried forward from schooldays, others breaking in along the way, matched experience: Petricevich as a Stringham figure, Drummond killed in the war just like Barnby, Jenkins a lieutenant, then an intelligence officer like Dan himself, and so on. Comparison with and interest in *The Music of Time* was a preoccupation of Dan's in the 1960s and 1970s, bringing literature into experience itself, where it added its emphasis to the personal and private origins of his *malaise* with *Not Here, Not Now*.

It was coupled with other features of his world that were of more immediate interest to him. Patty's return to family life brought him pleasure which he was reluctant to give up for the necessary solitude of composition. He found great happiness in gardening, and expanded his activites, running gardens at both houses. He became a faithful correspondent with his three daughters by Winnie: Anna, first in the United States, then in Algeria; Delia, in China; and Brigid, who went with her husband Andy to what was then Southern Rhodesia, and then on to Northern Rhodesia (Zambia) in January 1965. He kept them abreast of family life by trying to write to each of them once a week, usually on Sunday mornings from the cottage. When he failed in the task—hardly surprising in a busy life—he was irritated by guilt. To Brigid he also sent money, so that she could have a separate bank account. She thought it was 'running-away money'. 'Dadda was very good at empathy, putting himself in other's shoes.'

Family correspondence in the Davin family was not a consistently simple matter. Each of the daughters had a fine sense of style and a surfeit of energy, and their letters brought him great pleasure, demanding response. Delia's letters from Beijing, where she and her husband lived through the onset of the Cultural Revolution, were so rich in observation that, barely edited, they were eventually published by OUP.[23] With her daughters all abroad, Winnie seized the opportunity to travel. In the autumn of 1964 she went to Beijing, and was gone for six weeks, returning to Europe on the trans-Siberia railway.[24] Five months later she went to Algiers to babysit for Anna and Luke, who were going to Italy. Wendy Campbell-Purdie took Winnie and her grandchildren to her villa in the oasis town of Bou Saada, on the edge of the Sahara, where she had established herself, and was busy with a project to plant trees.[25]

Increasingly, the place of creativity in Dan's life was taken by criticism. Oscar Wilde said that criticism is the only civilized form of autobiography. In his lecture to the Royal Society of Arts in 1962 Dan spoke of himself and other expatriate New Zealand writers as 'early settlers who by pioneering in this country have made it possible for our countrymen to stay at home. We may be regarded before long as extinct like the moa, but on an alien soil.' A reporter for the *TLS* thought this a 'remarkably modest argument' but agreed that in New Zealand 'the ground . . . has been cleared for a genuine national literature'.[26]

The meaning of these arguments may be obscure to modern readers. Until the 1960s, and with the significant exception of Katherine Mansfield, New Zealand literature had almost no existence outside its own shores, and only a tenuous presence within them. The local culture was not literary, which is why so many of its literary intellectuals fled. Censorship, both official and unofficial, was endemic and repressive, sometimes weirdly so. When a film version of Joyce's *Ulysses* came to New Zealand in 1967 it was shown only to segregated audiences, male and female. Charles Brasch's quarterly *Landfall* ploughed a solitary furrow for almost a quarter of a century, ever on the brink of financial failure. Paul's Book Arcade, the publishing child of Blackwood and Janet Paul that sought to bring out work of a consistent literary standard specifically for a New Zealand audience, was equally hard to sustain, and went into liquidation a few years after Blackwood Paul's early death in 1965. A few small enclaves of literary endeavour, such as the one grouped around Sargeson in Auckland, or those associated with the Caxton Press, and Ngaio Marsh and her theatrical productions in Christchurch, attempted to liberate the country from an insufferable cultural mediocrity. But it was always tenuous. The small circle that included Maurice Shadbolt, Kevin Ireland, and Maurice Gee in the mid- to late 1950s collapsed when Shadbolt and Ireland went abroad, and Gee withdrew to a life of literary isolation and solitude.

Like all colonial societies, the people of New Zealand then needed the endorsement of the outside world before they would recognize merit. This accounted for the recognition bestowed on Katherine Mansfield in New Zealand by those who, had they had any real understanding of what she was saying, and how she was living her life in order to say it, would have condemned her, and banned her books. In short, the country lacked cultural self-confidence.

In the years after the war a number of people attempted to rectify this state of affairs. Dan's part in it was central, however, because he occupied two seats at the very centre of British literary culture, and used them to advance the cause of New Zealand letters. One of these, at OUP, resulted in the World's Classics series of short stories, and in a general attention to New Zealand writers that would not otherwise have happened. DMD played his part, for instance, in ensuring that James K. Baxter was published by OUP, and that C. K. Stead was invited to edit the second series of New Zealand short stories in the World's Classics series.[27]

Dan's other seat was at the *Times Literary Supplement*. Between 1961 and 1974, when the then editor Arthur Crook retired, Dan wrote something in excess of a hundred articles for the *TLS*. It is difficult to be precise about the number because *TLS* reviews were not signed in those days, and the accounting procedures of the paper (which might have enabled a biographer to track dates of publication) were arcane. It is reasonably safe to assume, however, that if the *TLS* carried a review of a New Zealand book (other than one of his own) then the review had been written by Dan.

He had a distinctive style of reviewing, as well as the distinctive approach summed up in the quotation at the head of this chapter. It was an approach and style that marked it out from anything then practised in his homeland. A good example is the treatment accorded Bill Pearson's novel *Coal Flat*, which was published in 1963. Dan found it 'an impressive piece of work and an unusually full and convincing picture of New Zealand life', not one without faults or weaknesses, which he alludes to, but with undeniable qualities. Mrs Palmer, 'the part-Maori wife of a publican, is something of a minor masterpiece, a real *Urweiss*, comic and formidable in her pathos and power. She is perhaps as convincing a secondary character as any New Zealand novel can show.'[28]

By contrast, the novel's reception in New Zealand was bitchy. Louis Johnson, a poet, did a hatchet job on it in the *New Zealand Listener*, at which Vincent O'Sullivan, a young writer, attempted to protest, but was put down firmly, and rudely, by the paper's editor. Conrad Bollinger, a radical social critic, and Maurice Shadbolt, the rising novelist, then joined in, but the quality of argument never rose above burlesque. It surely had nothing to do with *Coal Flat*, or with literature in general.[29] In this context, Dan's review stood as example, both accusation and corrective. From exile he might show the way, albeit anonymously. He played this role for the rest of his life, setting a standard that, in due course, New Zealand critics themselves were compelled to acknowledge, even when they could not emulate it.

This was some part of what he had had in mind when he spoke at the Royal Society of Arts of his role as an expatriate New Zealand writer: to make it possible for others to stay at home. It was also a response to his own treatment at the hands of New Zealand critics, generally (and with the significant exception of Eric McCormick) people with little modesty, too little sense to see that a writer has some deliberate intentions, and too little patience or penetration to find it out.

Dan took his book reviewing extremely seriously. He read widely and constantly in the new literature of his own country, collecting a substantial library of New Zealand books. He greatly admired the work of Janet Frame, which he helped to draw to the attention of a wider audience. He was generous in praise of Maurice Shadbolt and Maurice Duggan, both of whom he tried to help in numerous personal ways, as well as through his criticism. Sargeson he championed as the founding father of a distinctive modern New Zealand literary identity. When he read Witi Ihimaera's *Pounamu, Pounamu* in late 1972, he immediately wrote to Arthur Crook at the *TLS* urging him to have the book reviewed. 'It is the best new stuff to come out of New Zealand for a long time and nothing like it has ever been written by a Maori.'[30] And he said as much again when his review of it appeared in the *TLS* six weeks later. The emergence of a new literary voice, distinctively New Zealand in character, the voice of Frame and Ihimaera, of Gee and Shadbolt, Stead and O'Sullivan, of Cowley, Kidman, and Adcock, McNeish and Tuwhare, was detected and encouraged in Dan's contributions in the *TLS*: consistent, reasonable, objective and humane criticism, detached and impartial with respect to merit, but passionately engaged with respect to the necessity of a vibrant literature.

This service to New Zealand was primary. Secondary, but only to that, was the service to English readers. Among his papers Dan preserved a copy of a British trade journal which included an item on immigrant writers in England.[31] 'New Zealand writers are a small group,' it says. 'The presiding figure is the fine novelist and short-story writer Dan Davin. Their novelists include John Mulgan, John Courage; their poets Fleure

Adcock and David Whebbil.' Dan would have taken no pleasure in praise from a critic unaware that Mulgan had been dead for twenty-four years, Courage was James, Adcock Fleur, and Whebbil possibly imaginary. The piece was symptomatic. If New Zealand letters were to make a mark abroad, clearly much still needed to be done.

Dan's role as *TLS* reviewer of New Zealand books was known among New Zealand writers, which is one major reason for his influence among them. He was a man to respect, and if possible to know. Given his gregarious nature, and his fondness for the pub as meeting-place, this was not hard to do. Throughout the 1960s and 1970s his circle of New Zealand literary friends and acquaintances expanded to include almost every writer of any note. He felt a particular friendship for Bill Pearson, who was a welcome visitor whenever he returned to England, and became something of a confidant for Winnie, and a lifelong correspondent of Dan's. The cottage at Dorchester was a near-perfect means of literary encouragement, and Dan was generous in lending it to New Zealand writers.

This New Zealand side to Dan's life in the 1960s and 1970s left his visitors with the sense of a man still bound to his country by ties of literature, personality, and affection. The impression was somewhat partial. For a start, New Zealand books were not his only area of critical work for the *TLS*, where he also reviewed the novels of Patrick White, and any new books on Joyce Cary and Louis MacNeice. White's novels were a particular enthusiasm. He saw White as one of, if not the, pre-eminent writer of the age, championed his work in the *TLS*, and was personally delighted by his Nobel Prize in 1973. Dan found White's autobiographical work, *Flaws in the Glass*, which came out in 1981, astonishingly sympathetic: intuitively he felt himself bound up with White, and said that he apprehended the world in similar ways, felt divided within himself like White, and fully understood how White might feel himself invested in each of his characters as he created them on the page. He and Winnie knew the artist Peggy Garland, Patrick White's cousin and correspondent.[32] She was herself connected with the literary world of 1930s England as well as post-war New Zealand, where she had lived in Wellington for a number of years. She now lived at Eynsham, just outside Oxford, and was an occasional visitor to 103. The worlds of their connections and common friends was as dense as the Southland bush.

In addition to these broader literary interests, Dan was also being drawn back towards Ireland. He had, in 1963, started work on what was to become OUP's *New History of Ireland*. Almost simultaneously, in the autumn of the same year, he met and befriended a young Irish student called Nuala O'Faolain.

Miss O'Faolain was a Dubliner from a big family who had studied English at University College Dublin, where she came under the influence of Father Tom Dunning, a famously generous Professor of Old and Middle English who had himself studied at Oxford, and was an old friend of Dan and Winnie's. In Oxford in the 1950s he had taught Gaelic to the Davin children. Nuala was also a friend of Harden Rodgers, Bertie Rodgers's daughter, and so, at one generation removed, already a part of that wider circle of friendship integral to Dan's life. She was a postgraduate student at St Anne's College Oxford, from the Michaelmas term of 1963, studying for the B.Phil. in English. By December Dan had already written to Dunning of their having met.

Both Dan and Winnie were interested in her and her background, which had been difficult: there were many siblings, a father who was much absent, and a mother who drank. Dan always encouraged young people to talk about themselves. His interest turned to sympathy, then to affection and infatuation. Thirty years after these events, Nuala would imply that Dan was a father-figure to her,[33] but though obviously true in one sense this may be to misrepresent their relationship a little, at any rate at the time. Certainly, he was of her own father's generation. She was an exact contemporary of Anna's, after all. But age never mattered in Dan's friendships. Conversation and human interest overruled other considerations. And he was very deeply attracted to her as well. They were to go on seeing each other for the next twelve years, though the circumstances of their relationship had changed by the end of the 1960s. In 1964 she moved out of her lodgings and went to live at 103 for a time. In the summer of 1965 Dan and Winnie lent her the cottage at Dorchester to work on her thesis.

A few years later, in his last novel, *Brides of Price*, Dan wrote of just such a relationship, and of the confusions that it may bring to the life of a man even when free of domestic constraint. Nor does the subterfuge which he planted in his diary do more than incite interest. In the same entry as his reference to it as a 'pointless journal'—itself an indicator of a sort—he wrote: 'Disappointed in my hopes of getting work done or much solitude while W. was away. Instead, was constantly out to lunch and dinner and practically never alone except when in bed.'[34] There were his dreams too: ever a tell-tale sign for Winnie, and reminiscent of the bad news of 1944 and 1945. 'W. . . . woke me from some unfortunate dream in which at first I thought I was talking to Nuala. Yesterday morning therefore in dog-house.'[35]

Whatever complexities of the personal kind these matters provoked, three other aspects loom larger in Dan's biography. Nuala made Dan happy, and his very deep affection for her was reciprocated. Whether or not he was the father she had never had, she loved him, and her love, though it changed with the years, never ebbed. Dan's capacity to evoke affection is at its most stark, almost primitive, here, but illustrates a general quality. In the twenty years or so from the mid-1960s to the mid-1980s, Dan's appeal was magnetic. Time after time, in interview and correspondence, interesting and intelligent people, women *and* men, often thirty years or so his juniors, and from every conceivable background, say quite simply that they loved him. He was a resident in that area of the territory of human sympathy where people find generous disinterested affection, and give themselves freely to it. It was an extraordinary quality.

Secondly, his relationship with Nuala helped to change the direction of his literary endeavours. The stream of New Zealand had, in *Not Here, Not Now*, finally run if not dry, then certainly underground, and he was in need of new sources. Nuala did not determine its course, but she certainly helped to channel it, in part because she came into his life when he was ready to start reanalysing his past. She was, so to speak, present at the death of Paddy, when Dan's mind was returning to the years from 1941, and reminiscence and nostalgia mixed with uncertainty and perplexity about experience.

Thirdly, she was another, possibly paramount, of the various influences that brought him back to Ireland. For the next fifteen years or so, the country of his family inheritance was to assume at least as large a position in his life as New Zealand. Larger, indeed, if visits, friendship, and familiarity are the test. Clarendon Press business now took him there frequently, and there were also social occasions associated with the cultural calendar. He and Winnie were, for instance, in Dublin in April 1967 for the Swift celebrations; back there in August 1968 when they stayed with Conor Cruise and Moira O'Brien; in Belfast and Dublin in April 1969; in County Mayo for a summer holiday in 1971 that included Brigid and her family; and so on. Whereas in the 1950s summer holidays had meant the Scillies, Northumberland, or France, in the 1960s and 1970s, they were more likely to mean Ireland.

The importance of Ireland in this phase of Dan's life was unquestionable to all those who knew him. Because he barely wrote about it, however (and not one of his novels, nor any of his short stories, has even an episode set in Ireland), its significance in his life was unknown in his native New Zealand. The 'obsessional commitment to all that is best and worst in a specifically New Zealand environment and heritage' which James Bertram detected in Davin's writing in the early 1970s was by then, if not dead, certainly in abeyance. For a decade it survived only in his reading and his critical pieces for the *TLS*.[36] Although he never wrote about it directly, however, the essay that Dan intended to contribute to MacNeice and Rodgers's 'book that never was' on *The Character of Ireland* is a pointer. It is a short piece on 'The Irish in New Zealand', written in 1957, in which he describes the cultural world of his childhood, its distinctively Irish qualities and features: the Gaelic language, the itinerant story-teller, the dense integration of home, family, school, church, and community, each inseparable from the others. But this was all in the past, now only a matter for recollection. Assimilation has worked its effects, and the specifically Irish quality is submerged. 'The fire of the Irishman may remain, the charm, the sentiment, the religion and the name, but the Irish in New Zealand are a part of history.'[37] It is almost as if he is writing about himself, a common thread after all. In it we hear the sense of his own diminishing New Zealandness.

There was to be a little more New Zealand work in the 1960s: three short stories that were published three years running in *Landfall*. But the two extended works that preoccupied him for the eight years from 1967 to 1975, the novel *Brides of Price*, and the collection of memoirs, *Closing Times*, had little to do with his homeland, and much to do with Oxford and exile. Ten years earlier he had only wanted to write about New Zealanders, but now he was ready to try his hand at writing about the British. He had no illusions about its difficulty. The characteristics of class, irony, and understatement, the meaning of silence in English conversation, the barriers to freedom of social movement: he understood these empirically from twenty years in Oxford, and he understood the difficulty of capturing them in literature from the novels of Anthony Powell.

The novel *Brides of Price* was the first fruit of this new departure. Its publishing history was as straightforward as that of *Not Here, Not Now* was convoluted. Dan began work on it in the Scilly Isles in the autumn of 1967, continued it there in 1968, and in Dorchester after his return from New Zealand in September 1969, when he had a 'taste of freedom and living the way I like best, for all its anguish'.[38] He completed the second draft at this time, and gave it to both Godfrey Lienhardt and Nuala to read,[39] but although it required perhaps only a week or two of further work, another whole year elapsed before he could finish the third draft and have it typed. It went to Bruce Hunter at Higham's in the new year of 1971. Robert Hale wanted it without hesitation, and it was published a year later.

The novel, set in Dan's present world, is his only work that does not look wholly backwards. The narrator, Adam Mahon, is a Reader in Anthropology at Oxford, implying Godfrey Leinhardt, though it is his 'dilemma . . . not his character'[40] that we find in the novel. The character is Dan. Indeed, it is such a good self-portrait that it may stand as the best description of him in the years from Paddy's death in 1964 to his own retirement from the Press in 1978. In his fifties, slowing down, no longer the trim figure he once was; still drinking and smoking more than he ought, but carrying it well; at home in pubs as well as at high tables; a lover of gossip as well as philosophy; shrewd observer, amusing raconteur, and good listener; occasional swift satirist, and huge storehouse of literary knowledge; a man impossible to pigeon-hole in the British class system because of his New Zealand origins, his war experience, and his instinct for individuals over types.

He has an inner life: 'Cheerful in company, melancholy alone. Reticent about . . . real purposes, and very obstinate',[41] but the narrator is a mask. The first person of the novel is not conducting an interior monologue of psychological or linguistic significance, but speaking his lines to an audience. We learn what we are told, and one of the things we are told is that there is much that cannot be learned, even about ourselves. '[I]t's impossible, looking back, to explain one's younger self. One has to admit that one's memory is reasonably accurate in recalling the outrageous things one did but one cannot reconstruct the mesh of circumstance and rationalization which enabled them to seem not just pardonable, but natural, inevitable.'[42] Adam listens

to the resonance of the past, with its counterpoint of what happened and what might have happened. I felt remorse and the folly of remorse. It is partial amnesia that prevents us forgiving ourselves. We cannot recall the extenuating circumstances. We are like archaeologists looking at the fossilized tracks of trilobites. We can follow our path in the past but not re-live the force that drove us.[43]

What preoccupies Adam Mahon is death. His field in anthropology is funerary rites, and he is at work on a synthesis of material that he hopes may yield a theory to account for the variety of ways in which human societies encounter and accommodate death in the midst of life. He is defeated by it in the end, the quest for high theory a mere circular argument, 'mirrors which gave you back nothing that wasn't already contained in you'.[44] Nihilism nurtured in the ego. But death is not only his academic subject: it is his current preoccupation as well. The novel opens with the death of his old friend Mary Grant, brilliant biochemist and crystallographer, communist in her politics, the first love of his youth in pre-war Oxford, but later crippled by polio. Adam lives alone because his wife Amy, tired of his failure to become the famous and powerful academic that she wanted him to be, has recently left him and gone to London to pursue a career as a commercial publisher in the world of smart bookmen. Her place in his sexual life has been taken by Ruth, a Liverpool Irish graduate student, thirty years his junior, who comes to him in his bereavement, and comforts him with her love.

The theme of death entwined with love is endemic in the novel, hinting as it had in *Cliffs of Fall*, *Roads From Home*, and *The Sullen Bell* at the 'poisoned embrace' of later commentary.[45] There is barely a page that does not contain reference to both. Yet unlike the earlier novels, *Brides of Price* is neither sombre nor solemn. It is told in the language of a comic tale, and carries the weight of its deadly topic without effort. The technical skill to bring this off is considerable, and depends on an adaptation of Anthony Powell's technique of exterior assertion, something about which Dan had thought a great deal since *A Dance to the Music of Time* began to appear in 1951, and about which he was to write in due course:

In Poussin's picture the dancers face outwards. And this is true of the characters of Powell's novel . . . Powell has made a complete break with the technique that James Joyce imposed on a whole succeeding generation of novelists, the technique of the interior monologue, of the stream of consciousness. It is part of what Powell is trying to tell us in his novel: that we live in a world of uncertain knowledge, whether of ourselves or of others. The interior monologue implies a knowledge of what is going on in at least one mind, it implies empathy. But for Powell empathy does not exist. Sympathy is all we have, sympathy and what we observe, from outside, in others. We have to make do with what our five senses tell us for the evidence with which we construct our understanding of ourselves and others. Neither Jenkins nor the people whose lives he narrates ever explain to us how people feel. We are told what they do and say; or rather what Jenkins observes or hears of what they are doing and saying—Jenkins, an Odysseus, eyes and ears open, tied to the mast of his own enclosed personality.[46]

The summary is Dan's own account of Anthony Powell's narrator, but it will do perfectly well to describe Adam Mahon and the technique of *Brides of Price*. Despite the severe constraint imposed by the method, Dan achieves in Adam Mahon's narration a plot of great complexity, with a big cast and a lot of movement. He avoids bathos by making his narrator a witty man with a light touch and a tolerant manner, as well as an anthropologist's observant eye for ritual, tribal conduct, and convention. He is particularly good at dissecting the behaviour of those who believe themselves liberated, a popular term of 1960s Oxford. The result is a small comic *tour de force*, in which Adam discovers a grown-up son he never knew he had, and rediscovers the love for the boy's mother that he thought he had lost twenty years before. Some passages, such as the description of a lunch party in Cambridge where Adam and Amy meet their daughter's lover for the first time, are simply very funny, bravura stuff. Adam is no curmudgeon, but he has antennae vibrant for the deceptions of youth, and knows how to expose hypocrisy with laughter, especially in the treatment of the wars between the sexes and the generations. But even when the narrator is taking himself and his audience seriously, we know he is listening to his own words, and already undercutting them with doubt, self-criticism, and humorous self-deprecation.

The novel had an interesting reception, both publicly and privately. John Sparrow, the Warden of All Souls, told Godfrey Lienhardt (at least according to Godfrey he did) that he had had no idea 'there was so much wenching in anthropology'. The *Daily Telegraph* thought it 'succeeds splendidly',[47] as did the *TLS*. 'The comedy is serious, amounting to a demonstration of the gulf between the tidiness of theory and the messiness of practice.'[48] Higham Associates sold the book to Coward McCann & Geoghegan in New York, the first novel of Dan's to be published in the United States. He received an advance of $3,000, and the book was published there in February 1973. It was not widely reviewed, but where it got a notice, the notice was good. The *New Yorker* said it was 'impossible to stop reading',[49] and the Philadelphia *Inquirer* called it 'mostly pure gold'.[50] Even in New Zealand Dan got a complimentary review, albeit back-handed, out of Denis Glover in the *New Zealand Listener*. 'It is a surprise to find that this personal friend has a depth of insight and subtlety that I had not suspected. He makes our struggling novelists look a bit silly.'[51]

Brides of Price was a literary departure, in terms of both style and technique. For once Dan allowed his wit, his skill for aphorism and comic juxtaposition, to be felt to full effect. The result did not appeal to the earnest. The novel's story of comic misadventure, and the unlikely tidy ending in which relationships are confirmed in happy marriage and amiable divorce, conceal the complexity of its structure, and the intelligence of its argument. High-minded intellectual readers, who nowadays expect to encounter literary art in post-modernist packages of elaborate and explicit self-reference, think *Brides of Price* trivial, perhaps contemptible.[52] The joke may be on them.

The joke was not on Winnie, however. The strains of Dan's relationship with Nuala were severe, and continued into the late 1960s, though by then they saw each other only intermittently. Nuala moved away from Oxford in 1966, and meetings were confined for the next few years to occasional visits. She lived in London throughout the early 1970s, and their love changed in due course to a platonic affection more like that of father and much-loved daughter, one in which he took her to good restaurants for the pleasure of giving a treat, and bought her small trinkets and gifts. Nevertheless it distressed Winnie, whose life with Dan was changed for a while, visibly so to friends.

Other features changed simply with time. Mrs Clack retired from her tenure of the Victoria Arms in 1967. The regulars clubbed together to make a presentation, and 'Professor Davin' made a speech. 'We had often known the ham rolls run out, the cheese rolls, the sherry run out, even the beer, but we had never expected Mrs. Clack herself to run out.'[53] There were sad echoes in the humour. This was also the year Dan and Winnie bought a television. Now Dan could indulge his love of rugby, though it was a sore trial of loyalties whenever Ireland played the All Blacks.

Teddy McCullough was more frequently in their lives again. He had found happy employment since the early 1950s as ship's medical officer on cruise liners serving the South Atlantic from England to Rio and Montevideo: the perfect life, with a splendid uniform, ladies to escort in the first class lounge, and welcome company below decks. When his ship was in port he came over to Oxford and took Winnie to the races, Cheltenham for the Gold Cup, Ascot in the summer, and—best adventure of all—the Grand National in the spring. In due course he bought a flat in New Brighton, across the water from Liverpool, and settled there. Winnie had known him for forty years.

Along with television, Dan and Winnie became householders. The passage of legislation in 1966 made it possible for long-term sitting tenants to purchase their rented accommodation, by compulsion if necessary. OUP had no inclination to resist, of course, and after a series of complicated legal manœuvres—St John's College owned the ground, which the Press had first to purchase before it could sell the freehold to the Davins—they became the owners of 103 in 1969, after twenty-three years of tenancy. It was a lucky purchase. House prices were about to rise sharply, and they got it for less than £3,800, and with a mortgage from OUP at 5.5 per cent.

It seemed to Dan like an island in a pretty rough sea, though not for the obvious reasons. Though it was true that Nuala had changed his life in some ways, and that he had become a member of the club of IBPs—Impossibly Busy People—with affairs at the Press increasingly demanding, books to review at the weekends, an expanding family, visitors and a ceaseless stream of old friends to shepherd and entertain, these were not cause for gloom. The problem was, as Adam Mahon so eloquently expressed it, the presence of death in life. Bernard Freyberg had died two months before Louis MacNeice. After Paddy Costello died, Archie Colquhoun went too: Dan's acquaintance from wartime Italy, and the man who had sponsored his membership of the Travellers'. He was an exact contemporary, just 51. And Julian Maclaren-Ross also died in 1964, on 3 November, another heart attack. Geoff. Flavell claimed that he caused it because he always gave Julian the fat from his roast beef whenever they ate together in Soho. Julian was addicted to beef fat. Maclaren-Ross was a very strange man altogether, but Dan had been his friend, and his death was a loss. It coincided with the presence in London of Blackwood Paul, the New Zealand publisher. Dan saw something of both him and his wife Janet, because Paul was arranging a contract with Michael Joseph for a new, joint edition of *For The Rest of Our Lives*. He was also seeing a specialist, who diagnosed incurable cancer. He died in New Zealand early in the new year, 1965. John Robertson died at the same time: another friend from the war, and, since the early 1950s, from his lair at the Southland *Times*, where he had kept Dan supplied with the local history and documents that he needed for his novels. His was a war death really, after twenty years of pain and disability borne in stoic regret. From opposite ends of Dan's life, both John Davenport and Bill Hawksworth died in the middle of 1966. Hawksworth, his old enemy from Otago, died in the Radcliffe Infirmary in Oxford, without ever reading *Not Here, Not Now*. This breach with the past was then reinforced in the death of Dan's sister Evelyn, without warning, on 10 December 1966. Their brother Tom rang with the news early in the morning. Dan had never been close to his sister, and the deep wound of his dead pet dog never healed, leaving him unreconciled with the 'Bane' of his childhood, which is how he always thought of her. She had grown up and matured of course, had children of her own, made a success of her life at Roxburgh: but Dan knew little of it, and had never shared in it. Brother and sister could hardly have been further apart, and now she was dead. Isaac

Deutscher died suddenly in Rome in the summer of 1967, the same year as Paddy Kavanagh, Irish writer, and a particular favourite of Dan's. Bernard Spencer, Cairo friend and expatriate poet, was killed in an accident in Vienna in September of the same year. At the other end of the world, Frank Guest died suddenly in Dunedin on 28 November. Like Hawksworth, though in a different sphere of the heart, Frank was one of the handful of people who defined Dan's undergraduate years at Otago, and he had retained a deep admiration for his acute mind and unique character. He was another of those good men in Dan's Div., the men who had done the spade work to destroy Fascism: wounded in Libya and four years a POW. Ursula Joachim, with her links to life in 1930s Oxford and Winnie's years as a war widow, followed in 1968. Then, hardest of all, both Bertie Rodgers and Itzik Manger within four weeks of each other at the beginning and end of February 1969. Dan had not seen Itzik since 1959, but the intimacy and enjoyment of each other that they had known at the first, in 1950 and 1951, had never faded. Arthur Prior, the philosopher whom Dan had known at Otago, then strangely in St John's Street during the phoney war, and who had eventually turned up again in a fellowship at Balliol, died the same year, the year in which Enid Starkie wasted away with cancer. She died at her home in Walton Street of a heart attack on 22 April 1970.

Dan walked in life through this expanding graveyard as all those with the talent for friendship must do. Certainly as Adam Mahon does in *Brides of Price*. To any observer he was on top of his work at the Press, vital and witty among his friends, a man like any other in the street. Dan could imply that there was no sting. Alone, however, the pain of death preoccupied him more and more. He began to collect obituaries from *The Times*. He toyed with the idea of writing a novel about an obituary writer, perhaps even about a man who kept the morgue at a great daily newspaper. Death was his subject.

It was this, though they could not name it, that people noticed when he was silent, or at rest for a moment: a shadow of melancholy that deepened in the years that were otherwise marked by so much friendship, work, and stimulation. Things that he had previously enjoyed he took less pleasure in. It found expression in an accumulating dissatisfaction with travel. In addition to the frequent trips to Ireland, of which he tired last, he travelled continually between 1964 and 1978. He was in New York on business for the month of September 1965, reunited with Joel Carmichael, and working at the Press offices. Here he had a comic late night adventure over a lost key and the breakdown of his watch: the watch his mother had given him on his twenty-first birthday amid the struggles over Winnie and Peggy Spence-Sales. The adventures were further evidence to him of the possibilities of a new literary style, already in embryo in his mind for *Brides of Price*, and he later wrote them up as a long short story, 'The Locksmith Laughs Last'.[54]

In the last week of March 1966 he and Winnie were in Paris, where he gave a lecture on Katherine Mansfield to mark the opening of a joint French/New Zealand exhibition. This was a diplomatic as well as scholarly and public occasion. He lectured in the Descartes Theatre at the Sorbonne, and there was a black-tie dinner the next day. He and Winnie stayed in a hotel on the Quai d'Anjou on the Île Saint-Louis, facing across the Seine to the Marais. It was to be their last visit together to the city of light, the home of their pre-war lives, a place also for ever associated for Dan with Paddy in the early 1950s, a storehouse of memory untouched since the manuscript lost in Greece.

And Greece was on his mind, because in the first week of August, he went to Crete to take part in a military tour and memorial celebrations of the battle in which he had fought and been wounded, and of which he was the official historian. The four-day excursion was run with military precision. They flew in planes of the Royal Air Force, and the historians among them, Dan included, gave talks and lectures along the way. After Heraklion, they visited Canea, and Dan went back to the site of 23 Battalion HQ, and the olive grove where he had been wounded. He visited the Tavronitis bridge, and point 107 overlooking Maleme. The party laid a wreath at the memorial in Galatas. At the military cemetery at Suda Bay, he found himself in tears. They were a tough touring party with some exacting celebration, and on the first leg of the flight home, from Suda Bay to Malta, he confessed in his diary to 'a vile headache, sinusitis, constipation, heartburn, alcoholic gastritis, boozer's gloom [a term he hadn't used for twenty years], death wish etc. etc.'. These were surface manifestations. Ten days later he confessed that 'The whole tragedy of time and lost life and youth was there and is working in me still'.[55]

The long-awaited visit to New Zealand in 1969 was partly sabbatical leave, partly Press business, and partly literary tourism and holiday. Dan wanted to be present for the centennial celebrations at Otago University, and although he was not the official Oxford representative at these festivites from 8 to 11 August—a role played by Sir Robert Aitken—it was Dan, ever the Intelligence Officer, who supplied information about Otago to Colin Hardie in Magdalen College, Oxford orator, and responsible for writing the official message of congratulations. The two-month journey began on 7 July and was conducted at a punishing pace. The first three weeks, *en route* to Auckland, were filled with Press business. They went first to Tokyo, flying straight through via Tel Aviv, Tehran, Delhi, Bangkok, and Hong Kong, 'a fiendish journey' during which he read Michael Frayn's comic satire *Towards the End of the Morning*, and revelled in its treatment of airports, which he now detested.[56] A few days there, then back to Hong Kong where he was reunited with Dick Hughes, the journalist and old friend from Cairo days, and now at the height of his notoriety. The same business of only a few days, then on to Kuala Lumpur, and then the same again to Singapore, and then once more to Melbourne. On 22 July, their thirtieth wedding anniversary, they flew to Sydney, and were reunited with Peter Concannon, Dan's cousin from the farm at Woodlands, childhood ferreting companion, versed in the same secrets of a now dispersed Southland clan. There was a side trip to Canberra to see Torrance Doig, the robust outsider from the time of Dan's struggle for a Rhodes, long since reformed as a diplomat in the Australian government service. Back in Sydney the Concannons took Dan and Winnie to an evening at the Eastern Suburbs Rugby League Football Club, an unlikely venue for Dan, and deeply troublesome the next morning when he felt rotten. They were to go to the Concannons again that evening, Winnie's sixtieth birthday. Dan commented dryly in his diary: 'Have taken the precaution of eating some sandwiches. You never know when you're a Concannon prisoner what might happen.'[57]

The next day they were in Auckland, staying with Maggie Black in Remuera. There was the usual relentless round of reunions, dinners, meetings, and parties: many old friends, and one or two new ones. Dan first met the poet Kendrick Smithyman at this time—he drove Dan to see Keith Sinclair, convalescing from Asian flu—and also Tony Stones, the sculptor. Stones's work was greatly admired by Eric McCormick, on whose advice Dan agreed to sit for him. On his first visit to the makeshift studio in a converted butcher's shop in Wellington Street, he had no sooner settled in a chair on the little platform than the room was invaded by James K. Baxter, the poet. Baxter, who was in full bohemian flood at this stage of his life, plumped himself down on the concrete floor, and delivered his 'regulation tirade about cops drugs and so on'.[58] Later the captive audience was threatened with a Baxter fraternal embrace, which he was barely able to avoid. Dan returned twice to sit for Stones during August, on the last occasion taking Winnie with him. They both liked the head, which was subsequently exhibited in an Auckland Festival

Exhibition at Moller's Gallery in 1970, and Winnie bought a bronze cast of it. They both admired Stones's work as much as Eric McCormick expected they would, and they were keen patrons as well as good friends in years to come.

The pace could not slacken, however. On 3 August they flew down to Wellington, where they stayed with Dan's younger brother Pat, and there were reunions with Martin, who was temporarily in hospital, and with Tom and his now quite strange wife Adelina. She had suffered from a rare form of emotional instability for fifteen years past, and Tom had cut short a diplomatic posting in New York to bring her home to New Zealand. During Dan and Winnie's visit to the house she went into the kitchen, and refused to come out. Their daughter Antonia, brilliant at French, had gone in the 1960s to study for a doctorate at the University of Louvain in Belgium, from where she was for some time a regular visitor to both 103 and Dorchester, so that Dan and Winnie brought news of her. In Wellington there was also work at the OUP offices, and another round of receptions and dinners.

And so it went on: in Dunedin the next weekend for the Otago University centenary and reunions with friends; in Invercargill, Bluff and Otautau, Queenstown and Roxburgh, on family visits. 'Winnie is having a great time', Dan wrote to Brigid. 'Southland is full of babies and their photographs.'[59] There were interviews for the press almost everywhere he went, old wartime colleagues and acquaintances, school-friends, academics, authors and writers. From the kaleidoscope of impressions one particular epiphany clung to him for the rest of his life. On the evening of Sunday, 17 August, in Dunedin, Hone Tuwhare, the poet, gave a party where there was masses to eat, including mutton birds—a childhood favourite dish. Dan and Winnie stayed late, though they had much to do the next day, which was to begin with an interview for the Otago *Daily Times*. At length they dragged themselves away, but on the stairs they met various people, including Charles Brasch, just arriving, and bringing another keg of beer. This fragment of recollection, of leaving the party behind him just as fresh reinforcements arrived, clung like a garment for the rest of his life. In the recollection it had pictorial force, a self-portrait in the very act of loss, being deprived of the desirable by obligation; another source of his sense of nostalgia, made all the more poignant in due course by the fact that it was the last time he would see Charles Brasch.

They were back in Wellington on 19 August, and four days later flew north to Auckland. 'Homing instinct v. strong today', he noted in his diary,[60] in endorsement of what some had noticed: that New Zealand was indeed no longer his home. Still, there was a whole week more of Auckland to negotiate, and although they failed to get to Northland, where Dan had hoped to find a location for events in *Brides of Price*, the Blacks took them instead to the resort of Piha, where they had a house on the beach.[61] Then they were *en route* for Honolulu and the west coast of the United States, to a reunion with Gordon Craig in San Francisco. At dinner on 29 August, Craig had 'to sing all the songs Walt Rostow and I wrote at Oxford thirty-three years ago while [Winnie] supplied the words I forgot. We were best on "Booted and Spurred." '[62] Despite the conviviality Dan was by this time feeling low, wishing that he could 'fly straight from here to Dorchester', and not even revived by news in the paper of Robert Maxwell's near disastrous difficulties with Pergamon, then in financial crisis.[63] In this mood he celebrated his fifty-sixth birth-day—'Alas'[64]—and then pressed on to New York, where they stayed at the Algonquin, and he worked for four days at the New York office. The city was 'unbearably hot' and humid, with record rainfalls. He could not eat, and could not sleep. Grumble, grumble, grumble. By the time they reached Heathrow on an overnight flight on the morning of 6 September, he was on the edge of depression. The demands of an arduous journey had killed all pleasure in travel, which from now on he detested. Airports were 'the gateways to hell'.

Pleasure at being home, and at having a full month of writing in store at Dorchester, was crisply dispersed. Delia brought her baby Lucy to meet them at Heathrow—she had been born on 30 June, a week before their departure—but also had to tell them the news that her husband Bill Jenner had left her for another woman almost as the baby was born. Dan was utterly confounded by this news, deeply angry as well as bitter, his outrage amplified by his surprise. Only ten months before, at the start of what was to be a difficult pregnancy for Delia, he had written to Anna: 'Bill is being a saint. (You children are lucky in your husbands. Think if you'd been married to someone like *me*!)'[65] In addition to worry about Delia and his new grand-daughter, he was anxious for Winnie, whose sadness was palpable. Delia had kept the news from her parents at the beginning of July in order not to spoil their long-awaited trip: Winnie had not been to New Zealand for twenty years, and had been very happy at the prospect. Her silence notwithstanding, Delia was traumatized, and some years in recovery: years which, astonishingly, she spent living with her baby first in Japan, then in Paris and China. She became a fluent Chinese speaker, and in due course an academic in Chinese studies.

This domestic upheaval matched another. Not all the details were available to Dan, but he knew that his oldest daughter Anna had had an unusual career once she returned to England from Algeria with her husband and children. Dan and Winnie were very pleased that she took a degree in history at Warwick University, where Luke was lecturing. She became a professional historian, was active in the History Workshop group of young academics from 1969, and in the mid-1970s played a part in founding the *History Workshop* journal. Her politics were reflected in the radicalism of the time, the style of which did not appeal to Dan. On issues he may have shared her views, but on tactics they disagreed. The end of her marriage to Luke Hodgkin caused him concern, anxieties made all the more sombre perhaps by his sense that, unbeknown to her, they looked very much like a repetition of himself at exactly that age. Political discord with Anna, particularly over Vietnam, was expressive of the war between the generations, since his view of the issue itself was much the same as hers: he had simply grown pessimistic about the possibility of individuals making a difference. It troubled him because he had opportunities of his own. His old American friend Philip Kaiser, a man of great personal charm, had risen in American politics, and was appointed Minister, Deputy Chief of Mission, in the US Embassy in London for five years from October 1964.[66] Dan and Winnie were occasionally his guests, and sat down to dinner with American senators and British politicians, including Denis Healey, not seen since Balliol in the 1930s, but now Minister of Defence in Harold Wilson's cabinet. The younger Dan, urgent in opinion as well as conversation, would surely have seized the moment for controversy. The older Dan, now in his fifties, 'master of a passable miscellany of experience', held his peace. How well, he came to see, Anthony Powell expressed exactly these experiences. He felt it again every time he watched Enoch on television, dealing the race card, or later polishing the Loyalist chestnut, and dwelt on how he had evolved since OCTU days, and the offices of GHQ Intelligence in Cairo. The penumbra of associations, growing denser with the years, was brought into sharp focus in his relations with Anna: pride and disapproval together. The underlying pull of his paternal affection for her at this time is expressed in the relationship between Adam Mahon and his daughter Isabel in *Brides of Price*.

In this way the secrets of Dan's past life imprisoned him in the present, a fact brought home with almost tangible force within two weeks of their return from New Zealand in 1969, when Patty was married. Her bridegroom was Philip Watson, the son of an academic. Patty had met him in Oxford, where he was an undergraduate at Christ Church, at the time when she was herself studying at Reading. They had first met at 103, where Watson had visited with a friend. Winnie and the Davin daughters liked him, but Dan was wary now of daughters' husbands. They married a few months before Patty's twenty-sixth birthday, on 19 September 1969, in the cathedral at Christ Church, and there was a reception afterwards in the college. Ronnie Tylecote, as her father, gave her away. The Davins were there in force, since Patty was family, though Anna arrived only at the last moment. She had been in Helsinki with her companion. They had rowed bitterly, indeed terminally, and she had walked out on him, though without much money. She hitch-hiked from Helsinki to Turku, then spent all her remaining money on a train ticket so that she arrived at the cathedral in the nick of time but very hungry. A family of secrets and surprises, everyone else assumed the Davins were present simply as old friends. Dan was understandably unhappy in the role of deceiver. It was one he had selected long ago, and it was not done punishing him yet. The element of charade was endorsed at the reception, where Elizabeth strolled among the guests stripping the ostrich feathers from her enormous hat, and scattering them among the perplexed celebrants. For reasons that were never clear to anybody, Elizabeth disapproved of her son-in-law, and it was a long time before she was reconciled to him.

After a last two weeks of happy composition of *Brides of Price* at Dorchester, Dan was plunged back into the affairs of the Press at the end of the first week of October. Much of his desire to get 'home' had been anxiety about the Waldock Report, so long delayed, and from the time of its first circulation in draft early in 1970 onwards his life was dominated by OUP. Time for writing was in short supply, and there was never again to be a fortnight of autumnal isolation at Middle Carn for work of a sustained kind. He had to snatch the opportunities of weekends and occasional summer weeks at Dorchester to keep up his reviewing for the *TLS*, and to write the small number of short stories that he produced in these years.[67]

His mind was now fixed, however, not on these more ephemeral activities, but on his own past, the role that friendship had played, and the dread presence in it of death. He had, between the summers of 1967 and 1968, already drafted an essay about Julian Maclaren-Ross. The decision of the OUP London business to publish the *Collected Poems* of W. R. Rodgers then offered him an opportunity to contribute a preface about Bertie in the form of a memoir, which he drafted at Easter 1970, finishing

347

it by the end of May.[68] A year later, once again starting at Easter, he wrote 'In a Green Grave' about Louis MacNeice, and the following year memoirs of Enid Starkie and Joyce Cary. Dylan Thomas followed in the summer of 1973, when Dan also made a start on his recollections of Itzik Manger.

This last posed larger problems than the others. Dan had failed to keep diary entries about Itzik, and after Manger's departure for New York in the spring of 1951, he had seen little of him. They had been reunited in 1952 and 1959 during Dan's visits to the United States, but they did not meet again after that, and correspondence had dried up. 'I saw these particular friends of mine at intervals only, and for long periods some of them I scarcely saw at all.'[69] In search of more information he contacted various Jewish acquaintances, including his old friend Joel Carmichael in New York, and through Joel he was eventually brought into contact with Meyer Weisgal, Chancellor of the Weizmann Institute of Science at Rehovot, in Israel. Weisgal was a dynamic Israeli intellectual and academic entrepreneur, eclectic and vibrant. When he read a draft of 'A Dream Takes Wing' he was in raptures, wrote to Dan to say so, and then invited him to visit Israel in June 1974 to present the Itzik Manger Prize, an annual award that he had instituted.[70] Manger's return to Israel, though haltingly at first because of the strong local prejudice for Hebrew over Yiddish, had brought him back into prominence as an important voice of Jewish culture. In Israel, Manger was a cultural hero, and Dan's knowledge of him during a period of his life that was little documented, a matter of some interest. For a few days from 23 to 28 June 1974 Dan was lionized in the Palestine that he had not seen for thirty-one years, among the survivors of the cultures of Central Europe on whose behalf, as he liked to think, he and so many like him had gone to war, and in the place where his own daughter Patty had been conceived.

On his return he was able to finish the draft of the memoir about Manger, and then to write an introduction for the collection which was published a year later as *Closing Times*. The title, with its reference to pubs and to death, gave him trouble, and it came to him only after about thirty alternatives had been canvassed. It did not, however, give him as much trouble as Catharine Carver, the editor at OUP in London whom John Bell put to work on the text. Catharine Carver was American in origin, a friend of Lionel Trilling and others of the circle of New York intellectuals for whom the doctrinaire right in American politics had made life so uncomfortable in the 1950s. She had left and gone to England. An exile herself, persecuted by cold war ideologues, she and

Dan might have been thought to have much in common. She may have liked the topic of Dan's manuscript, but she did not much like the form, which she found repetitious, or the language, which she found overly dense and ornate in places. 'Cant' was one word she employed to describe some of it. Of course, she came out of the completely different tradition of New York editing (though she had been gone from it for twenty years): one in which an editor works to improve a writer's style. She put in long hours on *Closing Times*, and then sent Dan many pages of suggested improvements.[71] She knew that DMD was himself perhaps the most experienced publisher's editor in Britain. She could not have known that these particular essays were the touchstone by which he expected to be judged by such of posterity as might care to look, or that they were infused with his own *amour propre*. Whatever the causes, she found a key to unlock his vanity: 'so carefully camouflaged and surrounded by such defences in depth that even I sometimes lose sight of it or forget the way in.'[72]

Incensed may be too weak a word to describe his anger about her editorial proposals. He wrote her a note thanking her for the work and urging her not to 'worry' about it—a nice conceit in its way—and then later wrote a brisk letter rejecting most of her recommendations. 'Sometimes you and I simply differ in our literary taste: yours is more severe and metropolitan than mine. This what you call "canting" (perhaps a less offensive word in American than in English) I consider to be nothing of the kind, or at any rate not what I understand by the word.' He congratulated her on a 'courageous job acutely and thoroughly done'[73] but his manuscript went to press virtually unchanged.

Closing Times was published by OUP in April 1975, at a time when Dan was back in New York for three weeks on business. His second collection of short stories, *Breathing Spaces*, was brought out by Robert Hale six months later, on 2 October. Godfrey Lienhardt said, in his sharp voice and precise enunciation: 'How clever of you Dan, to publish two different books in the same year with the same title.' Both volumes were well received, and *Closing Times* quickly recognized among literary people as a minor masterpiece. Its style, which is deliberately fragmentary to match both the nature of the recollections and the different qualities of each portrait, certainly did it no harm in the United States. It went through a second printing, and was subsequently published in paperback. The money that he earned from it Dan thought of as reward for the many subventions paid out to Maclaren-Ross at a time when he could little afford them.

The essays in *Closing Times* echo in many different ways, not least because they are a form of camouflaged autobiography. The scale of the literary figures is great, casting shadows in the path of unwary readers who might fail to notice that the central figure throughout is really Davin himself. Despite this fact, and because of the disjointed narrative, we get only a partial view of selected aspects of his life from 1944 to 1957, with a few fragments thereafter. Dan does nothing to disguise his presence, it is simply that the presence, though essential, is partial. Each essay opens with himself in the foreground to bring a moment or a location into focus before the lens of recollection passes to his companion, and description turns to anecdote. There is a sharp visual quality to each memoir, recalling Dan's 1940s interest in the cinema, and the nostalgia for time lost is intense: a nostalgia that is entirely Davin's, since there is little evidence to show that his friends had felt it with such intensity. One critic, seizing eagerly on Dan's identification of Manger with the tradition of the itinerant Irish story-teller, a *seanchai*, makes much both of that in Dan's fiction, and of the fact that each memoir in *Closing Times* is itself about a wanderer, exile described by an exile.[74] The truth of this insight is less compelling than it might at first appear. Dan wrote of these people because he was a professional writer, and their names would appeal to the editors of magazines where he hoped first to publish them. The linking theme to his mind was not that they were expatriate: 'My chief parameter . . . is that of art, since it is writers who most concern me now.' His intention was to extend the series.

There were others from the past, soldiers and scholars, whom I might some day wish to try and celebrate also; but I mention them now only to indicate that there are parameters to these recollections which may not be immediately apparent: the world of learning with the piety towards the past which it teaches one to cherish; and the war which taught my generation and the one before us how sudden death is, how unjust in its election, how heedless of whether or not the lives it cuts off have been fulfilled.[75]

When he wrote these words he was already at work on a biographical essay of Bernard Freyberg, which was also published in 1975 in a collection edited by Field-Marshal Lord Carver.[76] And a year later, in July 1975, he wrote another Freyberg portrait, this time for the *DNB*. Both of these were more strictly factual pieces—though he allowed himself some rhetoric of nostalgia in the final lines of the first of them. He planned a quite different memoir of Freyberg, in the style of *Closing Times*, to follow them. Others that he also planned included Kenneth Sisam, Paddy Costello, and Howard Kippenberger, along with such possibles as L. F.

Powell, the great Johnson scholar, Ronald Syme, the classical historian nonpareil, Gervase Mathew, a true polymath,[77] Gerald Wilde, the painter, and Christopher Hill, the historian and Master of Balliol in whose life Dan and Winnie had both played parts.[78] No particular importance attached to exile in Dan's choice of these subjects. It is in the nature of art, warfare, and scholarship to make expatriates and exiles of their devotees. He wrote about the men and women who had come the way of a man with a great capacity for friendship. As he remarked once to a friend, emphasizing the role of accident in life: 'without collisions there would be no meetings.'

The true source of inspiration for *Closing Times* is Dr Johnson, and in particular his *Life of Richard Savage*. Dan was so clear about this that he put it in the opening lines of his introduction to the memoirs. He disguised it slightly, instantly shifting the focus to Maclaren-Ross, whom we can almost see, now cast as Savage, alongside Dan with a pint of bitter in the Turl bar. But the reference, as with all of *Closing Times*, is to do not so much with Maclaren-Ross as with Dan himself: he is telling us how he has written these pieces, and, by implication, how we should read them.

The biographer Richard Holmes has explained how to read Johnson's *Life of Savage*,[79] and in so doing has made it easier to understand Dan's intentions, for when he mentions Johnson's name at the very beginning of *Closing Times*, he is not doing it as a dilettante might. Dan was a considerable Johnsonian, widely read in the literature of the eighteenth century, familiar with the Johnsonians of his own and the immediately preceding generation of scholarship. Since the mid-1950s he had been an occasional guest at dinners of the Johnson Club, and from the early 1970s he became a full member. The Club, which was founded in the Old Cock Tavern in Fleet Street on 13 December 1884, the centenary of Dr Johnson's death, met four times a year: in March, October, and December for a dinner—usually then still at the Old Cock Tavern, though it moved to the Savile Club in 1980—and for a weekend excursion in July. Its purpose was 'fellowship and free exchange of mind', and the only qualification for membership, a true interest in the eighteenth century. Generally, before each dinner, a member read a paper on some aspect of Johnson studies.[80] Dan loved the Johnson Club, enjoyed attendance at its meetings, and served as its President from 1979 to 1981. It brought him together regularly with other Johnsonians, including his old friend Esmond de Beer, and it linked him, through shared interest, with the American eighteenth-century scholars whose company he always enjoyed on his occasional visits to the United States, or on their more frequent visits to Britain: Mary Hyde (Lady Eccles), one of the truly great twentieth-century American patrons of scholarship, Jim Clifford,[81] and Louis Landa.[82] The Club occupied a central position in Dan's conception of himself. When he took a guest to one of its meetings, as for instance when he invited Jon Stallworthy to the dinner in March 1974, and George Richardson to the July outing to Basil Barlow's country house at Stancombe Park the following July, he was expressing both friendship and admiration.

There is no question that Dan identified with Johnson: the outsider who went to the centre and succeeded there, the man too poor to finish his degree, the lover of scholarship as well as gossip, of tap room and high table, of the classics in the service of the present, of the bohemian turned apparently Establishment. And he understood what Savage must have meant to the young Johnson when he first arrived in the metropolis in the 1730s, and of how he employed that meaning in the treatment of the poet's biography, sometimes ignoring fact in order to sustain a portrait that has a higher truth, albeit unsupported by footnote. No one who approaches *Closing Times* with this as background can fail to understand either Davin's objective, or how close he came to realizing it. It is assuredly not history, nor biography, but such invention as it contains is insufficient to qualify as fiction. It is simply memoir: an art form, and one that is little practised, not simply because the scholars and editors of the modern world—the Akensons and Carvers, if you will—may not sympathize with the form, but because it is extremely difficult to do.[83]

The introduction to *Closing Times* repays close textual analysis in the light of Dan's biography: in it he contrived both summary and exposition in a shorthand that is difficult to interpret without the context of his life. 'No-one really had a past for you, in any but an obituary sense, unless you were contemporary with that past.'[84] In this context, the emphasis that he places on gossip as one source of inspiration for the memoirs is particularly interesting, since he makes so much of what is normally thought so trivial.

Through gossip we acquire the sense of others without which we fail as social beings and which is the *sine qua non* of charity. Gossip is the currency of the existence beyond ourselves which delivers us from narcissism and without which love is vain, no better than adolescent fantasy, where the love's object is not objective, does not exist except as our own projection, and the lover does not accept, does not even know, that all human beings are imperfect and that love or friendship which do not see and acknowledge and accept imperfection in others with the same large tolerance we reserve for our own defects do not deserve their names.[85]

The passage is a bridge both to Invercargill and Dunedin, to the worlds of gossip that nearly wrecked his early opportunities, and also to early post-war Oxford, when fear of the same small-mindedness led him to hide Patty's paternity. He will take the sword of gossip and turn it into the pen, disarming detractors. He bows to Horace (*aere perennius*) but only to make a partial defence of the pursuit of immortality: 'though we know that bronze itself is not immemorial but only a little less quickly perishable than flesh and that fame is less immemorial than bronze, we nonetheless strive for life after death'.[86] It is the paradox of art: the pursuit of immortality in the certain knowledge that it is unattainable. And it is assuredly not Cary or Thomas, or any of the others, whose immortality he is seeking.

The publication of *Closing Times* brought various consequences. The University College of Swansea wrote to ask him to give their Professor W. D. Thomas Memorial Lecture for 1976.[87] He agreed, and offered to speak on the *Music of Time* novels of Anthony Powell. His lecture, given on 16 November, and subsequently published as *Snow Upon Fire*, took up much of his spare time that year, but it was a project he had long contemplated. There is deep sympathy for Powell in Davin, the similarities of their experience, his recognition of a talent and an artistic commitment that he can admire intellectually as well as understand empirically. Powell's work is, like the origins of *Closing Times* in Samuel Johnson, the second key to understanding Davin's view of life residing in death, and both coexisting in a godless universe.

The missing dimension in this [Powell's] world is faith, faith as a passion. And this is what makes the sequence, however amusing on its surface, so ultimately bleak. Underneath the comic world—so often reminiscent of Wycherley and Congreve—there is a tragic negation. True, there is a residual moral code . . . But the real religion, however reticent . . . is absent.[88]

The bleakness was precisely what Dan approved of. Tragic negation summed up his view of experience.

As if in resistance to this, *Closing Times* brought him into correspondence with Bill Naughton, the famous author of *Alfie*. Naughton, in tax exile on the Isle of Man, had known Bertie Rodgers well in London in the 1950s, and he wrote to congratulate Dan on the portrait of him in 'At the End of his Whether'. He also wanted to recount various items from his own extensive journals of the period. In this way they got into a correspondence that continued for a decade. They never met because neither of them would travel, but they became good friends—an eighteenth-century relationship. Twice, in 1980 and again in 1981, Bill sent Dan a gift of £500, sensing, by some turbulence of the literary ether, that his Oxford friend could use a draught. Dan accepted the money gracefully. It was exactly the kind of unexpected generosity that he had himself long extended to others.

Closing Times also brought an invitation to return to Jerusalem. 'A Dream Takes Wing' was translated into Hebrew, published and widely read in Israel. In May 1976 the Mayor of Jerusalem, Teddy Kollek, invited Dan to spend up to three months at Mishkenot Sha'ananim ('Peaceful dwellings'), a small residential settlement of modern apartments, initially built in 1860 on the initiative of Sir Moses Montefiore, which the city of Jerusalem made available to artists and scholars. The guest list since it had been opened in 1973 was very distinguished, and Dan was pleased with the invitation, which, however, he felt able to accept for only three weeks. He and Winnie were in residence there from 17 August to 9 September 1977. Mishkenot is just outside the Old City walls of Jerusalem, with a beautiful loggia and terrace, and has picturesque views of Mount Zion. Dan planned to start work on a new book that he had been thinking about for two years. The working title, *The House of Fame*, suggests a novel about a publishing business. He had overestimated his stamina, however. He had his sixty-fourth birthday at Mishkenot: he was ageing, tiring more easily, his back giving him trouble, struggling to give up smoking, still working hard at the Press but requiring longer periods in which to recover his forces. In the event, the weeks at Mishkenot with Winnie passed quietly as holiday, with visits to the Old City, and outings to tourist sites.

On their return from Israel he began his last year at the Press. Winnie had retired in July 1974, on her sixty-fifth birthday. Everyone who knew Dan at this time knew how keen he was to retire, to take up his other life as a writer. Already, for over a year, he had been counting down the number of Delegates' meetings still to be negotiated.[89] He had one or two health problems: three upper teeth that had to be extracted in February 1978, the usual anxieties of the liver, and a great deal of pain in his lower back, a constant source of at best irritation, at worst near immobility. Despite these signs of wear and tear he still felt himself to be young, and looked forward to a creative retirement. The disappointments of his last three years in Walton Street, from the departure of Jon Stallworthy through the merger of the Oxford and London businesses, from the distancing of true editorial work to the rise of what he thought of increasingly as ill-prepared and poorly trained staff, made the prospect of departure more attractive than it would otherwise have been. None the less he enjoyed much of the festivity of the 500th anniversary celebrations of printing in Oxford, and he played his part in them with aplomb. He even had the stamina to go with Winnie once more round the world of OUP offices between 26 July and 17 September 1978 to say their farewells. In Kuala Lumpur, over the last three days of July, they stayed with Patty and her husband Philip Watson, now pursuing a successful career in the British diplomatic service. In Wellington he had the energy to take part in a seminar on 'The New Zealand Short Story'.⁹⁰

This visit to the land of his birth, the fourth in forty years, promised to be the last. For four weeks they travelled the now familiar route among the thinning ranks of old friends (Charles Brasch had died in 1973), as well as among family circles growing larger with new generations, and a literary scene peopled with new characters met for the first time, such as Patrick Evans and Patricia Grace. The journey was tiresome. From Dunedin he wrote to Brigid: 'Dying (living?) to get home.'⁹¹ In Wellington he gave a long radio interview to the historian Michael King, the continuation of a friendship that began in England in 1975. After visiting family in the South Island they returned to Auckland for a final week. While they were there, Martha McCulloch, who had grown increasingly irascible with the years, harder and harder to converse with, had a mild stroke in London, and went into Queen Square Hospital. It was a pointer to the terrain of old age ahead.

The incident that best illustrates Dan at this time occurred not in literary or university circles, but among wartime comrades. His old friend from the Div., Wig Gardiner, organized a little get-together at the Auckland RSA in High Street. Dan was accompanied by Tony Stones. Gardiner knew Stones: he had been instrumental in Stones being awarded a commission to make a sculpture of Freyberg, and he suggested that he come along as well. The eight or so survivors stood around the RSA bar and drank whisky while they reminisced. After about an hour of this, Stones recalled:

Wig suddenly turned formal and said: 'Brothers before we break up I'd like to ask Dan to say a few words about our mates who didn't make it back to be here tonight.' They were standing in a ragged line with Dan in the centre. He stood like an old boxer, a fist gripped round his whisky, looking bulky in his Donegal tweed suit, and he extemporised a short speech of grace and elegance on the theme that Wig had suggested. It was just as in his stories, he gave their memories and sentiments a form of which they were incapable. He spoke for the men there and the men who weren't there. It was a privileged thing to have seen and heard . . .[92]

They were ten days getting back to England via the United States, and as before Dan was exhausted by the travel. He expected to have no further taste for it. He wanted Dorchester, and the pub, and the life of the writer. In Baltimore at the American Academic Publishers' Association conference in June, he had lost both his glasses and his pen, and despite the efforts of the conference organizers, they were never found. Ominously, when he left Auckland on 6 September, *en route* for retirement, he had lost a second pair of glasses.

PART IV

OLD AGE, HONOURS, AND DEATH
1978–1990

14

A FIGHTING WITHDRAWAL

Life always carries out its threats but seldom fulfils its promises.
(DMD in 'I sing to you Strangers', BBC2 television
documentary about Dylan Thomas, 5 Nov. 1983)

But, in a sense, nothing in life is planned—or everything is—
because in the dance every step is ultimately the corollary of the
step before; the consequence of being the kind of person one
chances to be.

(Anthony Powell, *The Acceptance World*, 70)

Withdrawal from OUP was carried out in good order. Almost the last
item on the programme was a radio documentary for the BBC: 'The
Character of Ireland: the book that never was.' Dan worked on the script
with the producer John Scotney in the late summer of 1977, and rehearsed
and recorded it in November. Dan was the narrator, speaking for himself,
and Denis Hawthorn read the poetry. The programme was broadcast on
18 July 1978. The text is ironic and detached, in a tone of disengagement,
and the story captures the wraith-like quality of the two recalcitrant
authors, MacNeice and Rodgers, as they repeatedly fail to meet their
deadlines and obligations. The piece is witty and urbane, full of the
sympathy and the durable generosity of Dan's later years. But behind
the light touch there is no mistaking his true subject: the defeat of
the publisher by his two archenemies, the bohemian tendency in art,
anddeath. Dan might have written about thousands of publishing
triumphs: instead, as he left the Press, he wrote and performed a piece
about defeat.

The significance of this fact is related to another. Dan had been
contemplating autobiography for almost forty years. Long before, during
the war, it had seemed a grey though inviting prospect. 'I recall my
childhood', he wrote in his diary, 'by certain incidents and as I remember
them I can feel the same emotions I felt then. And none or scarcely any
of these are happy memories. My memory has a gift for retaining the
unhappy. Only the happy man perhaps has no autobiography.'[1] The
thought is kin to Esmond de Beer's perception that 'The annals of

happiness are apt to be monotonous; while there is much to remember there is little to record.[2] In Davin's case, however, though the perception is logical, it is paradoxical, because more or less everything he wrote was about himself and his experiences, and yet much of the best of it—in particular the short stories of childhood, and the memoirs in *Closing Times*—is coloured not by unhappiness, but by a sad nostalgia for times and occasions which, though lost, were treasured.

Dan was capable of projecting this paradox not only into the past, but into his own imagined future as well. In another wartime diary entry, we again find him contemplating autobiography while reflecting on Homer's Ulysses:

he led the life all men secretly desire: wide travels with great adventures and many women and at home always waiting, a loyal wife, a growing son, a faithful retainer and a dog that loved him. . . . [I]t is a parable of masculine fulfilment, the perfect life. . . . How often Ulysses must have sworn and believed that such and such a night or hour was unforgettable and how he must have fumbled through the past in old age on Ithaca trying to recall the unforgettable . . .[3]

The thought is parent to Adam Mahon's belief, thirty-five years later in *Brides of Price*, that though we can remember, generally with remorse, the things we have done, we can no longer recall the original motivations for them, 'the mesh of circumstance and rationalization which enabled them to seem not just pardonable, but natural, inevitable'.[4]

Dan toyed with the idea of autobiography all his life. The written record of his musings on the subject runs dry in the 1950s, when he ceased keeping a diary, but it flows once more in the 1960s, and is in flood by the time of his retirement. Numerous little essays spell out incident and atmosphere: the item he wrote for *Midcentury Authors* in 1965; his piece for the *Round Table* of 1976 on 'My Language and Myself'; the item on 'Early Reading' published in New Zealand in the same year; the introductions to his *Selected Stories* (1981) and his collected war stories (1986); various unpublished essays such as 'Myself and OUP' and 'Galway 1936'; and some recollections of Lewis Namier, whom he had known at the very beginning of his publishing career, and whose influence on others of his contemporaries, in particular A. J. P. Taylor, had been so great. In many of these pieces he revisited scenes of his childhood and adolescence, dwelling on particular incidents—finding *The Rime of the Ancient Mariner* on a rubbish tip, the four books that were the sum of his family's home reading matter, and so on—though viewed a little differently each time, first from one angle, then from another. In others he began to put into order the jumble of his recollections about young manhood. He worried, however, about his memory. Before going to New Zealand in July 1969, he wrote to the borough librarian of Gore seeking information about the town in the years from 1914 to 1920, when his family lived there. She put a letter in the *Ensign*, the local paper, asking for help. He particularly wanted information about a classmate, Tommy Breen, who drowned in the flooded Mataura River, aged only 4 or 5. Back came the news that the boy's name was Tommy Bates. Similarly the parish priest, not Father O'Neill but Father O'Donnell. The realist in Dan took these lapses as serious warnings.

This was one impediment to autobiography. Another was distaste for writing about matters for which he now felt remorse. A third was his more general literary ambition, long nurtured with retirement in mind. In early November 1978 he had a meeting with two OUP executives to discuss books that he might like to publish with them. He was thinking of a second volume of memoirs, *Soldiers and Scholars*, and two collections of war stories. And in addition to these, before he could get to autobiography, was the novel so long planned, *The House of Fame*.

At first, however, he was tired, and there was clearing up to do, both at his office in Walton Street, and in his study at 103. Added to this was the unusual experience of being free all day, which stimulated pleasurable idleness. Kevin Ireland, the New Zealand poet, dropped in to see the Davins at Dorchester one Sunday in December 1978, and reported: 'Dan finding it hard to organise himself into the routine of writing full-time. Alarmed at how time skips away when you've suddenly got so much of it.'[5] Dan's powers of work were not like other people's, however. He believed himself lazy, and felt frustrated by it, but this was also the time when he drafted and rewrote his long critical essay on Maurice Duggan's *Summer in the Gravel Pit*, a collection of short stories that he read repeatedly. Speculative criticism was reinforced with a close reading of Duggan's correspondence, as well as his own intuitive understanding of Duggan's complex personality—in some respects so like his own. The result, published eventually in 1982, remains a key to the difficult world of Duggan's fiction.

And there were other sources of inertia which reticence concealed. His back was badly damaged, causing him terrible disabling pain. In February 1979 he went into hospital for a laminectomy. He faced this with some dread. A laminectomy is an operation on the spinal column, typically of the lower back in which a prolapsed disc (broken, or displaced, bone or ligament tissue) has resulted in nerve compression, causing pain. The defective tissue is removed from one or more adjacent vertebrae, which may then be fused together, to seal them. As with all surgical intervention there are risks of collateral damage, likely to be catastrophic if the spinal cord, or associated parts of the nervous system, are seriously affected. In Dan's case the operation was apparently a success, but its effects, even so, were close to intolerable. He made light of them in a letter to Mary Hyde:

All went very well, it seems, but my mobility and power to dig the garden are still somewhat restricted. So is my figure: I'm condemned to wear a corset for some time to come. It's only now that I realise what my poor mother felt like all those years ago, when she came in from some social occasions. 'For the love of God, Mollie, help me off with these stays. They're killing me altogether.'

He said he had been unable to write anything until then, but '[e]ver since the operation . . . I've had a sense of returning creative energy and I hope to come into full spate soon.'[6]

In the circumstances this was more defiance than truth. The wound was a long time healing, the pain acute, and the success of the operation limited. Thirty months later it needed doing again. In the circumstances it was difficult to work, and difficult to find alternatives to work that were not physically diminishing. Nevertheless, he managed a few pieces of composition, including a riposte to an article on 'New Zealand Literature' by Keith Sinclair that had appeared in the April 1978 issue of the *New Zealand Journal of History*.[7] Lightly, he panned Sinclair's 'misleading or even mischievous' speculations and ridiculed his 'observations about a catholic mafia and a homosexual mafia'. The humour of Dan's reply helps to conceal his testiness about Sinclair's original squib. Dan was rarely a man to write to the papers, but his distaste for this was real.

Despite the distraction of his physical woes, Dan took on various obligations. In January 1979, on the death of Professor E. R. Dodds, he agreed to act as literary executor for the estate of Louis MacNeice. He became President of the Johnson Club, and served with great pride for two years from August 1979. During his presidency he tried to nudge his fellow Johnsonians towards the admission of women: still a difficult task, though opposition was dying down. He also helped to guide the expansion of the Club, and was instrumental in bringing into membership his old friend Geoffrey Flavell, a considerable (though amateur) student of the eighteenth century. He also brought in Alan Bell, librarian and biographer. 'I should perhaps confess', he wrote to Bell, 'that the guilt of the actual nomination was mine but Robert Shackleton was an enthusiastic accessory after the fact and the subsequent collusion was universal.'[8] The liveliness of Dan's correspondence belied his physical pain and emotional frailty.

During these years he was also involved with the Salamander Oasis Trust, a charitable body established to publish the work of servicemen from the North Africa campaigns of 1940 to 1943. Dan 'had the misfortune to become chairman'[9] in November 1980, and continued in this capacity until September 1983. During his chairmanship the second anthology, *From Oasis Into Italy*, was published, and Dan devoted much time to giving advice, offering editorial guidance, and in one instance rewriting an important contribution. There were some personality difficulties that needed defusing, and many letters to be written. Dan was repeatedly amazed at, and occasionally confounded by, the energy of Victor Selwyn, a retired (though still free-lance) journalist, who lived in Brighton, and was the driving force in the Trust. From the autumn of 1981 until his retirement as Chairman, Dan's association with Salamander Oasis was overshadowed by illness, so that his experience of it—which touched on an aspect of his past that might, under different circumstances, have perhaps been relived with relish—was ashes. It was an indicator of a sort. So was the brevity of his involvement with a committee of worthies put together by Wendy Campbell-Purdie for a new scheme to plant a forest in North Africa, this one to spread west from Alamein. In due course the grandiose project was trimmed to a plantation at the Alamein war memorial and cemetery, but Dan's contribution was truncated by illness.

One side of his literary work never declined, however. No matter what his complaints (and they were many) in the six years or so from 1978 to the end of 1984, his generosity as friend, counsellor, guide, and critic never flagged. He was always prepared to write a testimonial, draft a letter, write touching but unsentimental letters of condolence and regret, read and comment on manuscripts, advise younger writers, entertain visitors—often people whom he barely knew, or who were the friends of his children, or the children of his friends. He devoted a great deal of time to editing his old friend Wig Gardiner's war book, *Freyberg's Circus*, including suggesting the title. And away from literature, though his friends were mainly literary people, he was sensitive friend and wise counsellor, and always courteous to a fault. The New Zealand writer Elspeth Sandys, whom he had encouraged with advice and criticism of her early manuscripts in 1973 and 1974, and who was then married to the actor Bruce Purchase, recalled that they came to live in Oxford in 1983. Dan liked and enjoyed the company of both Bruce and Elspeth, and when their marriage broke up with some acrimony it was a source of sorrow to him. He was one of the few, however, who remained on close terms with them both, and for whom—as he showed in this instance as in many others—friendship was not divisible by marriage or divorce, by the imposition of distance, or by the passage of time.[10]

By the autumn of 1979, after a full year of retirement that had included an August holiday in the Scilly Isles, once a second autumn home, now full of nostalgic memories, Dan was still suffering from his old enemy, writer's block. He wrote to Maurice Shadbolt on 1 September, as he entered his sixty-seventh year: 'Old age is unmanning, if only because of its contradictions: I feel 40 in some parts, 100 in others, and 67 in none.'[11] He was planning to go to Dorchester the next day to be alone and write for a week: 'Trouble is I'm still feebly fluttering, like an autumn blowfly, between various possibilities, a safe way of getting to grips w. nothing.'[12] Which is a good enough description of what happened. At Dorchester he was happy with the garden, the pub at lunch and in the evening, the literary periodicals to read, a little correspondence to keep up, and the friends who dropped by. When Shadbolt visited him in the autumn, he later reported to Eric McCormick that 'Dan . . . is still dismayed by a writer's block. I'm sure it won't last: it's just the first shock of freedom.'[13] Visiting friends tended to be more worried by Winnie's state of health, which was alarming, particularly to Dan. She had managed to give up smoking in November 1978, but had developed such bad asthma that it was, initially, barely controllable, and she seemed sometimes to perch on the very edge of extinction. During these years her health marched unsteadily out of step with his: when he was well she was ill; when his health declined, hers improved. The cycle, noticeable to their friends, was not hidden from Dan. 'She [Winnie] fortunately, is always rather better when I'm a bit low . . .'[14]

Briefly, with Christmas and the new year, Shadbolt's analysis came true. Dan sat down to work on his memoir of Paddy Costello. He had many purposes in starting to write this piece, but principal among them was to justify Costello, to clear him of the charge laid secretly and anonymously thirty years before. He also wanted to understand and to explain the unity of the man, how loyalty and integrity made treachery impossible. Quite when Dan conceived the idea of writing a memoir about Costello is unclear, but the probability is that it dates from the late 1960s, when he was beginning to write about his *Closing Times* friends, and that the project intensified with the years without ever fully crystallizing. The causes lay in the shadowlands of counter-espionage. According to the stories of journalists to whom members of the security services leaked partial accounts of their suspicions, Anthony Blunt identified Costello, once he was dead, as a spy; another of the Cambridge circle of 1930s KGB recruits.[15] The accusation added another mirror to an already confusing hall. Blunt was a consummate liar. Costello could not answer the accusation. The security service already believed him a Soviet agent. Writers vary in their motivations. Everybody knows that it is easiest to protect the living by blaming the dead.

Dan had always thought the accusation against Paddy absurd, and often said so. But as the 1960s and 1970s unfolded, and the stories of Burgess and Maclean were amplified; as the details of Philby's existence as the 'third man' and of his escape from Beirut to Moscow in 1963 came to light; as the journalists' hunt for Blunt and Cairncross slowly evolved; and as fanatics of various sorts set about exposing innocent people as 'deep moles' even within the fabric of the counter-espionage service itself, uncertainty replaced confidence. Difficulty was compounded by motive. If Costello was not the victim of calumny, then those who trusted him were deceived. Dan was an expert in deception. In some personal matters he had grown up in it. He had worked in military intelligence, where it is routinely practised. It was discomforting to think of it, but what had Patty's disguise in Oxford been, but an elaborate deception? It was impossible not to fear that with Paddy he might himself have been, like a deceived lover, the victim.

Dan never did finish a memoir of Paddy. The draft which he began at the new year of 1980 is an account of their first meeting, and of the time that they spent together in the war. He reworked this draft in 1982, and again in 1984, without getting it beyond military recollections, in which two young men fight the war, argue, and drink. The emphasis on drink in this manuscript is intense and alarming: bottles of brandy and Scotch consumed at a sitting, night after night, while the conversations flow. Dan seems bent on negative proof: Costello was so often in his cups with me, and so often out of control when he was, that certainly he would have betrayed himself. I would have known. Possibly true, but beyond this plausible but inconclusive point, he found himself unable to go. He asked Bella, Paddy Costello's widow (she reverted from being called Bil in the 1980s) for access to Paddy's papers on various occasions throughout the 1970s and 1980s. She always assured him that they were available any time he wanted, but at a time when he was still willing to travel it proved inconvenient to her. Because of his work commitments before retirement, and his ill health after it, it never proved possible to go for more than one lunch-time visit. Eventually he hated to be away from home too much to stir, and the project lay on his hands, unfinished, at his death.

These facts pose problems. Dan did not really need to read in Paddy's archives to write a memoir of him. He had his own diary for the war years; his collection of Paddy's Moscow letters; and his own recollections of the Paris years, and of Costello's life in England thereafter. None of the other memoirs that Dan wrote involved archive research. Each was written from memory and the imagination, with a little reminiscence from friends, and a dip or two into his diary or his files of correspondence. Writing about Paddy was different because the externally imposed need for evidence displaced in importance every other consideration about him. Dan needed archive research because he needed proof. Eventually he despaired of finding it, and this wrecked his confidence. 'Not everything, though everyone, is untrue', he wrote in his notebook. And a few pages later: 'It is not that old age has nothing more to say: it just sees no point in saying it.'

So it was that Dan's sorrow at Paddy's death turned, very slowly with the years, into the worst kind of tragedy: one from which there is no redeeming catharsis. Dan lived with it continuously, sometimes at the forefront, always in the background to the rest of his life. When he noted in his diary, as in April 1968, that he had spent an evening talking to Isaiah Berlin about spies, we know that even if the name never came up in the conversation, it is Costello whose ghost was at his elbow.[16] Costello did not dominate everything else in his full and varied life before retirement, but after 1978 the problem of Paddy became almost obsessional, disabling him in the very region of his writing that was central to his own self-esteem: his past, and its justification. He never believed that Paddy was a spy, and this was evident to all his friends. He never spoke of Paddy except in terms of admiration and respect. Dan was a loyal friend in death as he had been in life. But loyalty, as we know, was one of Dan's strongest features: to the Div., to his commanders in war, to his artist friends, to the many women he had loved, to the University Press: at every turn of his adult life he had remained true if not to the truth of things, at any rate to an idealized version of them. His marriage was still a central point of reference in his self-image, and he had remained loyal, if not faithful, to that too. He knew that his 'excessive respect for those [facts] that can be established' was 'at the expense of the power to create',[17] yet he was unable to do anything about it. It was a curious impediment, but it loomed ever larger in his retirement as one principal cause of his writer's block and the depressive illness which developed in its wake.

Briefly, however, in the late winter and spring of 1980, once he had at last got something down on paper about Paddy, he did have a revival of energy. He set to work editing a volume of selections from his short stories, for which he drafted a short autobiographical introduction. He wrote a new short story, 'The Dog and the Dead', which the *New Zealand Listener* published in August. This brought him into correspondence with Andrew Mason, the literary editor of the periodical, a young man who recognized in Davin an important New Zealand talent, too little acknowledged in recent years in his own country. He began sending Dan books for review, and the great bulk of Dan's occasional criticism, and short fiction of the 1980s, was thereafter published in the *New Zealand Listener*, rather than in journals in Britain. In this way, in his old age, he had a homecoming of sorts. It was endorsed by his giving an extended radio interview in 1980 to James NcNeish, the New Zealand novelist, for broadcast in his home country. And four years later a television documentary about his life and work was made by Gordon MacLaughlan, a New Zealand television personality, who came to Oxford for the purpose, and included in his film scenes of Dan at home and at the pub. Though these acts of publicity brought him closer to New Zealanders, he confessed himself a stranger to the land of his birth: 'an intimate stranger, but a stranger nonetheless.'[18]

This revival of energy and productivity augured well throughout 1980 when Dan was, perhaps for the last time, settled and content. He still dreamed of his new novel *The House of Fame*, and also of a full-length autobiography, and the collection of memoirs, *Soldiers and Scholars*, and he started to keep notes and jottings for all of them. His way of life was now inimical to sustained composition, however. He had always been a creature of habit, mastering his early writer's block by routine in 1940s Oxford. This had given way eventually to a pattern in which Middle Carn was central. After Sisam's death, when Dan's retreats to the Scilly Isles came to an end, he was robbed of it, and never found an alternative. Everything composed after 1969 was short story, brief memoir, or literary essay.

The new routine established at 103 and Dorchester after retirement simply did not allow for the solitary life of writing. Dan took to getting up later, pottering in the garden or study, and going to the pub for a pint and talk with friends. After a late lunch he might snooze, then read for a while, and write a few letters before setting off back to the pub. The old routine of work had gone, and with it all the other fixtures of days so long lived according to the demands of punctuality. Even the Tudor Snug at the Victoria Arms had gone from the daily agenda. It had become progressively uncongenial to the group after Mrs Clack's retirement, the wooden kegs displaced by metal, among other derelictions, and in 1974 they moved a hundred yards or so to the Gardeners Arms in Plantation Road. In this way time came full circle in forty years, for this was the pub which Dan had frequented as a student in the 1930s, where Walt Rostow had played the piano while the friends sang the Craig–Rostow songbook. In the mid-1970s the piano had gone. Dan and Winnie installed themselves at a square table in the window, where there was a good view of the approaches, and reasonable sight-lines to door and bar. This was to be, with occasional interludes elsewhere, their home away from home in Oxford henceforth.

A similar pattern established itself at Dorchester, even when, as he now tried frequently enough to do, Dan went out there for a week at a time on his own with the intention of working. The days simply turned out to be too short. One tactic for dealing with this will be instantly recognizable to all practitioners of procrastination: he discovered a routine task that was a persuasively essential preliminary to the real work. He needed to type up his diary, a major exercise. He began in 1980, and continued thereafter, off and on, for the next three years, covering the period from 1940 to 1944. He made no attempt to edit the diary as he went along, though some passages caused him deep discomfort. Occasionally, here and there in the margin, he inserted a comment, the older man looking back at the younger with a mixture of disapproval and resignation. He catches his younger self, for instance, on the edge of Cassino on 11 March 1944, feeling inert and unable to act: 'Shouldn't be writing this if I could be doing any of the things I ought', says the diary. 'Ditto today. DMD 7 March 1982', Dan comments in the margin.

Apart from diversion, this effort with the war diary had three purposes. Stalled in his effort to write about Costello, he went back in search of the evidence, both of him and of Freyberg, for the memoirs he planned to write. In similar vein, he wanted to recapture his experiences on Crete for a project that had taken root in his mind. Thirdly, he wanted to find a way, perhaps he might locate it embedded in the diary, of writing his autobiography in a new, possibly experimental way, 'to avoid that clamancy of self which would make it impossible for the reader's identity to merge in his'.[19]

All these activities—the little bits of writing that he accomplished in 1980, the laying of plans for larger works, the typing of his war diaries— were brought more or less to a complete halt at the beginning of 1981 when he contracted shingles. Herpes zoster is a viral infection of the nervous system caused by the same virus that produces chicken-pox. Generally, in people over 60, it is exactly the same virus, which has lain dormant in the nerve cells since childhood. The characteristic belt of skin rash and blisters was over in the usual three weeks or so, but the pain, post-herpetic neuralgia, 'that scoffs at analgesics',[20] was intense, and lingered in Dan's case for a year. The distraction was disabling, but the reasons for this were a warning. Shingles may happen to anyone over 60 who has had chicken-pox earlier in life. The duration of the subsequent neuralgia frequently depends on the effectiveness of the patient's immune system. People whose immune system is impaired, for instance through taking drugs for other conditions, may suffer acutely. Dan's case was a first suggestion that his own system was endangered.

In May 1981, still in pain though apparently cured, he was invited to go with Winnie to Crete for the fortieth anniversary celebrations of the battle. They both hoped that this excursion might free him from the depression that illness had brought in its wake, and accordingly they decided to have an extra ten days' holiday after the celebrations, 22 to 25 May, were over. An official party of New Zealanders attended the events, including the Minister of Defence, David Thompson, and the Secretary of Defence, Denis McLean, as well as various senior military officers and celebrities. Charles Upham was in the party: a happy reunion. Dan and Winnie stayed for the first three days at a hotel in Canea and were looked after by a Greek army officer, who devoted himself to their welfare, discussing the battle, and helping them to visit the various battlefields. Much had changed in the fifteen years since Dan had last been there, and he had difficulty locating the spot where he had been shot.[21] Dan was, however, deeply moved by this last return to Crete. In church with the delegation on the Sunday morning he wrote on his order of service: 'wounded now by time.' He began to speculate on the peculiar shape of the events that had linked his own life to this Mediterranean island. On a bit of paper he noted 'Crete ? Echoes of Life and Battle' and followed it with a list of jottings each oddly connected to the next, beginning in the Royal Albert pub in Dunedin in 1948, and moving backwards and for- wards through the people, places, times, and events by which Crete had crossed and followed the tracks of his own life. Later he began writing something titled 'Crete in the Royal Albert' in which the opening phrase—'I have escaped'—referred to evading his sister, and the rest listed the pubs among which he hesitated to make a choice. The piece, put aside, was never taken up again, though he went on thinking about it, and mentioned it to Paul Freyberg later that year as 'a long article or short, rather personal book on Crete 1941–1981'.[22]

After the official celebrations Dan and Winnie went to the eastern end of the island and stayed on for their holiday. Here they made two new friends: Margot McLean and Margaret Maehy, two young New Zealand medical students taking a year off from their studies to travel in Europe. Margot was the daughter of Denis McLean, who was attending the ceremonies in official capacity, and his wife Anne. The two young women drove a rental car that Dan and Winnie hired, and together the four of them toured places of interest. Dan recalled, in later years, the refreshing company of two unaffected young people, steady with that peculiar maturity that young New Zealanders bring to their travels. It was both relief and distraction. He was still suffering from the neuralgia of shingles, and his back was again in agony. He had developed arthritis in his right hip. Set down in a strange place, with no routine to guide and plan the day, his tendency to drink accelerated. At home in Oxford and Dorchester he was relatively safe from hepatic attack because he drank English beer. Once abroad, deprived of it, his taste went back to whisky and brandy. The effects now, given the quantities consumed over the years, were more or less instant, and the anaesthetic effect particularly welcome.

Back in England the summer went by in slow composition, the tedious complications of the Salamander Oasis Trust, and thoughts of mortality. He had agreed to edit a volume of short stories from the Second World War for OUP, and he managed to work on this sufficiently well to get the manuscript off his hands before returning to the Nuffield Orthopaedic Hospital on 20 October for further back surgery. This time the offending vertebrae in his lower back were scraped and he had a spinal decompression, in which fluid is drained away and the damaged vertebrae fused together. The effects of this ordeal on his general health were lamentable. He was weak and in pain for months, condemned to a life of little movement and, so it seemed to him, less pleasure. He was limited in how far he could walk (never again further than a quarter of a mile), and for any major expedition he had to wear a corset. Worst of all, however, he found himself to be impotent. Whether a consequence of the operation itself, or of depressive illness in combination with alcohol, or of a lifetime of heavy smoking (a common cause, little known, of impotence in men), or some combination of all these influences, its effect on him was tragic. Self-knowledge, image, presentation, all were intimately a part of the same Homeric conception of the self: a virile, active man, tough, independent, and loving. It was a terrible wound, lowering him in his vanity, his self-esteem, and his self-confidence.

Initially, in the November when he came out of hospital, he gave every sign of fighting back. Paul Freyberg had at long last started to write his father's biography, and he and Dan corresponded at some length about the General; in particular, the issue of Enigma.[23] Three months later Paul and Ivry Freyberg visited Dorchester, and together with the Davins had lunch at the George. There was much talk of Freyberg both then, and afterwards at the cottage. Crete was in the forefront of Dan's mind anyway. His old friend Ian Stewart, whose book on Crete he had so much admired in the 1960s, visited him in January, and they talked at length of Dan's developing plan for an autobiography, one in which he himself, as narrator, would be largely absent.[24] The inspiration for this interesting experimental idea was Nick Jenkins, the narrator of Powell's *Music of Time*, where he exists

in a way that makes him almost a vacuum. He is, as it were, in one of those chambers from which it is possible to see outwards but not in; and what knowledge we gain of him is mainly by inference from what he reports himself as seeing. It becomes quickly clear that the novel is not, at least directly, about Jenkins.[25]

These further thoughts of autobiography were linked to another development. James Bertram, away in New Zealand, had decided to write a short book about Davin for an Auckland OUP series which he edited on 'New Zealand Writers and their Work', and he wrote to Dan for information about his childhood and university days. Dan's letters to him are small masterpieces of compression, giving some of the truth through allusion and evasion.[26] One of the truths, that amused him right until his death, was how certain people seemed to arrogate to themselves the touch and smell of history; to appear somehow to have been present among the great events and people. Bertram was one of these. He gave the effortless impression, without ever actually laying the claim, of being one of Dan's oldest friends, someone who had known him since their days as Rhodes Scholars, and who had special, private access to wisdom about both him and his writing. This was quite untrue. They were never at Oxford at the same time, and did not meet until Dan's visit to Wellington in 1948. They barely corresponded thereafter—perhaps four letters in thirty years before

1982—and although Dan saw a little of him in Oxford on his sabbatical visits, and always felt warmly towards him if only for the fact of his lifelong friendships with Jack Bennett, Charles Brasch, and Ian Milner— they could hardly be called friends. Theirs was a New Zealand literary acquaintance, tied into the web of associations of a small country. For all its apparent subtle claims to omniscience, and Dan was wry in his smile of recognition, Bertram's little book came at a good time for Dan. It was well reviewed in New Zealand, and together with his contributions to the *New Zealand Listener*, and his media appearances, reminded New Zealanders of his importance to their culture at a time when failure to write in England was making him progressively invisible in the land of his exile.

Physically, Dan appeared to be recovering by the spring of 1982. His orthopaedic surgeon, Robert Duthie, advised him to go somewhere warm for a holiday, and he and Winnie talked of Greece. But Dan had no intention of travelling again: the business of airports, taxis, and hotels was repugnant. Secretly he was fearful of the effects of disrupting his routines. A year later, in May 1983, he was persuaded to adopt a plan to go to France, to see Erik de Mauny in Brittany, and to visit Paris, where he and Winnie could enjoy a secure base with friends only yards from the Rue Vavin and the old haunts of 1930s Montparnasse. At the last moment before they were due to leave, however, he was too depressed, and the trip was cancelled. Dan was deeply relieved: 'I secretly did not want to go anyway because I hate travel.'[27] The friends were disappointed but not surprised, receiving intelligence by telephone from Caroline Lewis. Caroline was a New Zealand businesswoman who had settled in Oxford, and was befriended by the Davins at the pub. She could be wildly amusing in the outrageous stories that she told, and Dan in particular enjoyed the vivacity and occasional hilarity of her conversation. She was smart in the clothes she wore, and he still liked women to wear make-up and perfume. Visiting the pub one evening in 1981 she met Tony Stones, Dan and Winnie's sculptor friend from Auckland, then on a visit to Britain, and they became friends. Later, in 1983 and after some intercontinental manœuvring, they married and returned to live in Oxford. The Davins welcomed Tony with introductions, and both agreed to sit for him. The portrait head of Winnie was Dan's gift to her on their forty-fourth wedding anniversary on 22 July 1983.

The deep affection of their relationship of more than fifty years had long since been renewed. When OUP published Dan's edition of *Short Stories from the Second World War* in 1982, he wrote in his copy to her: 'To my dear and only wife, Winnie, with inexpressible gratitude for years of patience and selflessness from her ever-loving Dan.'

Dan struggled on through 1982, feeling the blows of mortality. Mike Joseph had died in Auckland on 4 October 1981, and Dan contributed an obituary to *The Times*.[28] Frank Sargeson died on 2 March 1982, and once again Dan was the obituarist in *The Times*: 'the unquestioned doyen of New Zealand letters.'[29] Norrington died two months later, on 25 May, and Dan wrote his obituary notice in the *Bookseller*.[30] The influence of these deaths, and his natural preoccupation with them, can be found in the short story that he wrote at this time, 'When Mum Died'. In it an ordinary soldier at Cassino recounts a story about his commanding officer, and the death of his mother, and of how the two are bent together, like twine, on the stem of shared recollections of a lost past. The story was torture for him to write, and took five months of laborious effort before it was done in early August. Sheer guilt then drove him on to write his *DNB* entry on Air Marshall Sir Keith Park, long commissioned, and due in September. It was done on 25 August, but by then he was in serious decline, taking anti-depressants, and painkillers for back and hip. He had periods of giddiness, was developing a tremor in his right hand, and showed symptoms that suggested liver disease. He went into the Radcliffe Hospital for a liver biopsy on 30 September, and while he was there resolved, successfully, to stop smoking.

By now, however, he had entered the cycle of dependence so destructive of creative power: depression leading to drink, drink entrenching depression, anti-depressant drugs mixing badly with drink. And all further complicated by an increasing dependence on painkillers. For a year from the summer of 1982, he suffered the most unpleasant side-effects from this combination: in particular horrific hallucinations, quite real to him, in which the most gruesome and bloody scenes would be, to his eye, acted out in bedroom or kitchen, and he would need Winnie to come and clear the spectres away. Later he tried to recapture some of these draining scenes in a short story, 'The Battle of Dorchester', never published, in which he probed for the odd reality of hallucinatory experience. In addition to this weird and frightening development, he would lose his sense of balance, so that he repeatedly fell down, and would turn up at the pub or the dinner table with the most remarkable bruises which, in the ageing man, were slow to heal. Fearful of Winnie's anxiety, he sought to conceal them by various strategies, largely ineffective. He had to give up riding his bike.

Diminished by drugs, paralysed by the length of the list of possible books that he might like to write, shocked by the state of his health, and deeply depressed by the effects of time, age, weariness, and the loss of powers, he slumped into an intolerable quiescence. Whole mornings drifted by as he lay listless in bed, 'staring at the wall and sometimes being granted the brief oblivion of a doze'.[31] He ate less and more hurriedly. His powers of conversation declined. The man once so vigorous and strong had vanished into the figure of an old man. To those who visited only occasionally, it seemed to have happened overnight. He was no longer so tall. His figure had gone, slumped into bulk, carried badly; the hair, once thick and dark, thinned away to almost nothing; the eyes, once so sparklingly blue, now paler and leaking water. The tweed suits, long a part of his style, hung on him shapeless and baggy.

Nevertheless, he could still perform. The Rhodes Scholarship eightieth anniversary reunion in June 1983 included a gaudy (a college feast) in Balliol, at which Dan gave the speech in reply to the toast. Somehow he managed to husband his resources and turn in one of those public platform performances that persuaded people that the old lustre was still there, the sparkle and pleasure in life undiminished. It was pure thespianism now, made at enormous cost. However, at another event connected with these celebrations, Dan happened to sit next to an American doctor, Tina Chidson. He confided in her, describing his difficulties. She was horrified. He absolutely had to stop taking the anti-depressants while looking for something more suitable. He should see a clinical psychiatrist. To suffer from these things was dreadful when there were measures that might be taken. Dan did as she suggested, and went to see a psychologist at the Warneford, the Oxford hospital where Janet Frame had been for a while in the late 1950s. The psychologist 'considered me to be at least as sane as he was and the standard did not seem to me to be too low'.[32] He was taken off the anti-depressants. Shortly afterwards he became a patient of John Ledingham, the Nuffield Professor of Medicine at Oxford. After the summer he was prescribed a new anti-depressant called Mianserin, which gave him none of the side-effects he had so painfully suffered. He was very strongly advised by Ledingham to stop drinking.

These improvements revived him. In July 1983 he started to employ a secretary for a few hours several days a week, and made an assault on his arrears of correspondence. He took part in a television documentary for BBC2 on the life and poetry of Dylan Thomas. He began writing poetry again himself, and also wrote several longer reviews and short stories. As his health returned, so did his vigour. He was 70 on 1 September 1983, a day for family. Anna had successfully resisted any threat of simpler circumstances throughout the 1970s, though she had formed a long-lasting relationship in 1975 with Walter Easey, a Chinese-speaking former Hong Kong policeman and self-defence expert. He was ebullient, tough, and fun to be with, and called Dan and Winnie his 'out-laws'. Anna and he had a daughter, Sally, in February 1977. Delia had also remarried. As a lecturer in Chinese studies at York and later Leeds, she married Andy Morgan, an economist, on 12 June 1976. Their two children, Gareth, born in May 1977, and Sian, born in June 1980, brought the total of Dan's grandchildren to eleven, Patty and Philip Watson also having two, Petica and Nicholas. On Dan's seventieth birthday they ranged in age from 24 to 3. Winnie took more joy in them than Dan, who kept a certain distance, partly the demands of work before retirement, partly the gap of ages after that. The war, and his immediate post-war life, had shielded him from child care, behaviour that neither his upbringing nor the climate of the times had modified. Babies, and probably their photographs too, were women's work.

Dan was, however, immensely proud of his daughters, each of whom had accomplished much, and most of it in the world of books: Anna as historian in London; Delia as Sinologist and demographer at York; Brigid as a businesswoman—she was, from 1984, manager of the Economist Bookshop near the London School of Economics, and went into partnership to open her own specialist bookshop in London in due course. Dan still worried about them all, but in a general way, rarely precise enough to remember a birthday in time for the actual day, but always sufficiently broad enough to make the cheque and the amusing letter of good wishes welcome when it came. In the things that mattered, however, he was an excellent father: he never interfered; he always allowed his children to make their own decisions and live their lives as they wished; and he always supported them in whatever they decided to do even when, privately, he disagreed. They had all made successes of their lives in interesting ways, and though circumstance had made them sometimes physically distant, and they were all very busy with young children, they remained close to Dan and Winnie. In this way, they together managed one of the hardest transitions of all, from child and parent to friendship.

As his health very slowly improved in the autumn of 1983 he wrote two more short stories about Italy during the war, 'Cassino Casualty' and 'North of the Sangro'. And in 1984 he followed these with a third, 'The

Albatross', set in his childhood New Zealand. Expectantly, hopefully, the possibility of renewed creative vitality began to grow not only in Dan, but also in his friends and admirers. Winnie, caring and cooking, and always his loving companion, yearned for him to settle to the work again, aware that he was happy only when writing. Oddly, most of what he now did write, however, was poetry. 'I had a very severe attack of persecution by poetry during the autumn and this has produced a very large corpus of unrevised verse. . . . I can reassure you, however, I think I have made a complete recovery . . .'[33] There were two main causes of this 'attack'. One was very simply that verse was a form amenable to composition in bed, where it might be revised in the mind and then scribbled down, though often hard to decipher later. The other was a young American friend Beth Darlington. She was a Professor of English at Vassar College in New York who had been introduced to Dan in the early 1970s by friends they had in common in Oxford. She was a scholar of Romanticism. She brought Dan American academic gossip of which he had once known much. She returned to England for the academic year 1982–3, when she was a visitor both to the Gardeners Arms and to the cottage at Dorchester. Poetry was her main literary interest, and if it was her influence that led him back to poetry, then it was largely benign. Much of his poetry from this time, though only a little was ever sufficiently polished for publication, was interesting: witty, clever in both construction and drama, and above all almost completely devoid of the dull metaphysics that had marred his poetic debut as a student, and during the war. Most of the poems are about death and sterility:

> On reflection, if one cares to look at it,
> How terrifying is one's doom?
> The mirror of the infinite
> Is the looking-glass of whom?

from a poem written on 18 and 19 August 1983. And this, from a longer piece written a month later:

> He lies there, idle, except he's conducting
> The orchestra of his aches and pains and sorrows
> And the pros and quos and quiddities
> Of ending more tomorrows.

There is a lot of this poetry, almost all incomplete, unrevised, extremely difficult to assemble from his jottings and crossings-out. It offers repeated insights into his state of mind, the cloak of depression lifting and falling, the sense of guilt, the steady war of attrition with the idea of God.

God is the very devil
Have no truck with him
He is the death watch beetle of the soul.
He's in the timber of your temple
And ghosts will spring from every whole.[34]

The poems did not appeal to everyone he showed them to. Gordon Craig, when he visited in 1984 and read a sheaf of them at Dan's request, felt that they were too clever in language, and insufficiently rich in feeling, though he liked one 'Belated Love Poem' addressed to Winnie, that begins 'She has brought my loving death-bed | Who loved to lie with me.' Winnie confided in Gordon that Dan's poetry frightened her.[35] Dan did not, as he had confidently expected, recover from his poetic affliction. He continued to write verse for the last six years of his life, some of it scatological, all of it interesting, a few fragments of it deeply troubling and moving, both in intensity and as witness to his pain.

Recovery to good health and writing vigour in 1984 was dispersed by success, or more correctly, by honour. On 2 April 1984 Dr Robin Irvine, Vice-Chancellor of Otago University, wrote to invite him to accept an honorary Doctorate of Literature, an honour that he was 'proud and pleased to accept'.[36] 'So many people have died,' he wrote to Walter Allen, 'and so much time has elapsed that they have forgotten, even if they would not have forgiven my various crimes.'[37] The degree ceremony was scheduled for 8 December, and they flew directly from Heathrow to Auckland on 22 November. For the first time since 1936 Dan was to spend a summer in New Zealand. Afterwards, on the way home, they planned to visit Guy Nunn on his Hawaiian island, and then to stop in San Francisco to see Gordon Craig, and New York to see Joel Carmichael. This was a journey Dan had never expected to take again, and one that he most assuredly would not have taken but for the bait of an hon. D.Litt. from Otago.

In anticipation of it, and for money to help pay for the trip, various matters were put in order. Dan had already agreed to sell his papers to the Alexander Turnbull Library in Wellington, and a first consignment (mainly draft manuscripts) was parcelled and sent off in mid-November. He also agreed to sell his entire collection of New Zealand books, plus 150 Irish books, to the Library at Exeter University, and a deal was struck in October whereby he received payment, but kept possession of the books for as long as he wished. For a man of Dan's literary preoccupations, these moves were a clear surrender of territory.

Matters went wrong even before they left England. Guy Nunn, brave anti-Fascist and trade unionist with whom Dan had shared digs in Oxford before the war, and who had been a companion Colditz prisoner with Charles Upham, died suddenly at his home on 14 October. Dan had not seen Guy since 1978, when they called on their way home from the retirement trip. His death now was a gloomy preliminary to departure.

On arrival in Auckland once more they stayed first with Maggie Black before heading south to brothers Tom, Martin, and Pat in Wellington. Here the city was in its summer best, and on 30 November Dan and Winnie were invited to lunch by the Governor-General Sir David and Lady Beattie. By some turn of the dance, it was exactly fifty years to the day since Dan's first and unsuccessful Rhodes Scholarship interview, when Bledisloe asked him about cattle breeds, and he had been fed sandwiches in a scullery while Mrs Macdonald's influence worked insidiously on the selection committee. Afterwards, pride and vanity wounded, had been a crisis in his young life. The last time he had been here, thirty-six years before, Freyberg was in residence, and the talk was of war and the history of war.

In Dunedin a few days later, the burden of the past was, if anything, heavier. Of all the cities of New Zealand, Dunedin had changed the least over the years. The footprints of the younger man were still visible, at least to his eye, in every street, under every lamp-post, in every pub. The University put them up in a motel in Duke Street for their first four days. Rodney Kennedy, Charles Brasch's friend and companion, detailed Peter Leach, an art historian with particular interests in Italian art as well as an encyclopaedic knowledge of the New Zealand art scene, to look after them. Kennedy was good at that sort of thing. If he asked a favour for someone, it became a mission. Peter Leach, who had never met the Davins before, squired them from motel to lunch engagement, to pub and to dinner appointment, for a week. He had expected the Establishment figure that every honorary degree ceremony threatens. Instead he found a bohemian: 1930s version, but still working at it; alive to friendship, urgent in conversation, and astonishingly knowledgeable.

Of course, a very great deal was drunk. Far too much had been drunk even before they arrived in Dunedin. Winnie complained that it was always the same when you went home. People had not seen you for years, so when you came through the door they opened a bottle of whisky and threw the cork in the fire. You knew you were in trouble. The trouble deepened with every port of call, and Dan slid ever deeper into depression, 'the black cloud' he called it. He seemed in quite good shape on

Degree Day itself, and got through the ceremony with éclat: appropriate gravity and chuckles for the manner in which Professor Gibson, introducing the honorary graduand, glossed his career. The evening reception was rather harder, his stamina being tested. The next day he was front page news in the Otago *Daily Times*, and the subject of an editorial. Civic pride in a local boy.

After this they went south for ten days or so to stay with Mollie Baird, Winnie's sister. Winnie's brother Jack was also there, and there were outings to the old haunts—truly haunted now—at Bluff, Otautau, and Queenstown. The weather was glorious, even the cabbage trees were in flower, and at every place Dan's unhappiness deepened. However, he still managed to perform in company, a performance in tune with his anticipation of events. When the Invercargill public librarian wrote to tell him that the mayor wished to give him a civic tea on 11 December he had replied:

I have a great horror of public occasions but I would not wish to be discourteous and, little as I like afternoon tea, and little as I like Mayors, I feel that I cannot be so ungracious as to refuse an occasion so graciously prepared. I ought to mention anyway, although I am not subject to the vice of gratitude, how Invercargill Public Library helped me when I was what now seems to be a child, although at the time I seemed to be a monster.[38]

In this style and spirit he left his mark once more on the city of his birth and childhood.

A few days before Christmas they returned to Dunedin, and stayed for three weeks in the home of Stephen and Margaret Baird on Maori Hill, above the Town Belt. Stephen Baird, a lawyer at the University, was Winnie's nephew, the youngest son of her sister Mollie; Margaret, his wife, a research scientist. They were away, and pleased to let Dan and Winnie have the house. Winnie settled in happily, and spent her time writing the first draft of an essay about her life during the war.[39] But Dan had now arrived at a crisis. The combined effects of Guy Nunn's death, the loss of routine to the life of travel, pain from his physical ailments, constant reunions with old friends, a succession of public occasions and entertainments, and everywhere the reminders of his youth and escapades, now stale in the impotence of illness and old age: all brought him to the most impenetrable area of depression. The old bohemian instinct revived. Despite, indeed in the face of, Professor Ledingham's warnings, he returned to drinking liquor in quantities that recalled the war, or the occasional post-war London binge. There is a scene in *For The Rest Of*

Our Lives in which three or four soldiers, with a weekend pass from the desert, rent a Cairo hotel room, buy a case of Scotch, and drink it. One is reminded of Jake Donaghue in Iris Murdoch's *Under the Net* trying to purchase a bottle of brandy over the counter at closing time in the Skinners' Arms. He is going to stay up all night, drink it, and go for a swim in the Thames. Some instinct, some reminder of the hard man now lost, like his youth, returned him to this point, and he embarked on a swift course of self-destruction.

Somehow he struggled through these weeks, including a Christmas lunch with Ted Middleton at his home in Clifford Street, but by the time they returned to Wellington on 11 January he was immobilized by despair. His brother Pat, who had himself been through depressive illness a few years before, got him to a doctor, and the doctor prescribed an anti-depressant and an embargo on alcohol. With this assistance he survived a few days with friends in the Wairarapa, and then another week in Wellington, where Pat drove them hither and yon like a benign guardian uncle. Perhaps the catastrophic combination of illness, drugs, and drink could have been avoided by an extension of this, but Dan and Winnie were committed to a holiday in the Bay of Islands, a glorious area of water, beaches, islands, and magical skies in Northland, where neither of them had ever been before. For two weeks in early February they stayed in an old wooden house with a verandah, close to beach and pub, in the historic township of Russell. In this isolated paradise of lonely beauty Dan confronted himself once more, alone and bleak. He was merely drinking now, unable to eat, and Winnie distracted with alternate bouts of dread, anxiety, and misery for Dan. They made it back to Auckland on Thursday, 21 February, where the figure of Wig Gardiner, old mate from the desert, hard drinker and convivial prankster, lay in wait. They went to stay, and in the early hours of Saturday, in atrocious pain and vomiting blood, Dan was rushed to Auckland hospital with a perforated stomach ulcer.

He was safe in hospital, at least for the moment, but something had changed, or at least intensified. He no longer really wanted to live. Some surmized that the cause was simply a sense of finality. The honorary degree had cleared the troubled ground of the past, and he was free to go now. Others put it down to the loss of routine. Still others presumed the underlying force of depressive illness robbing him of the stoicism to confront the pains of the last years of life. Each was right in a way, though one larger part, his impotence, was concealed. But a deeper truth lay, perhaps, in an even remoter area than this, a region of doubt: that at some point, some day, some crisis in his past, he had selected the wrong path, and an alternative life, a life altogether different if not richer, more varied, more creative, had been lost. His topic for many years had been death. Now, in the land of his birth, he became its subject as well.

He was in hospital a week, put on a proper diet, fed vitamins, encouraged to start treating his body with more respect. He enjoyed being looked after. One of the nurses turned out to be a great-granddaugter of Mrs Keith, years before licensee of the Otautau Hotel. Illness also saved him from the dreaded prospect of American travel. They changed their tickets, and flew home directly, arriving in London on 12 March. Various friends came to see them off at Auckland airport. Dan was in a wheelchair pushed by Zam, his old friend from Sacred Heart College and Otago days.

Back in Oxford, Dan was on a knife-edge. When he had recovered from the exhaustion of travel he took up the threads of his previous existence, but under the covers of an occasional pint he was once more drinking heavily. He kept bottles in his bedroom. Going to the bar for a round of pints for the group he would surreptitiously sink a double vodka, odourless on the breath. He became an adept at the alcoholic's deceptions, talking of restraint but consuming ever more. His old sense of timing and of propriety never deserted him, or almost never. Only once, at a public lecture by Alan Bell in the Sheldonian to commemorate the centenary of the *DNB*, was he actually seen the worse for drink. At home, as he struggled from one day to the next, he took ever larger quantities of pills: painkillers, vitamins, anti-depressants, antacids, emollients for incipient ulcers. His bedside table was a pharmacist's Christmas. He lay in bed all morning, unable to stir, terrified of himself. Winnie grew ever more alarmed and despondent simultaneously: he was impossible to help but impossible to neglect. It seemed unendurable after a love that had endured so much. He did not want this life, that had grown intolerable.

At Whitsun Winnie went away for a long weekend to visit Teddy McCullough in Liverpool, and Dan stayed on at 103 on his own. On the Friday night his failure to answer the telephone alerted Delia and Brigid. They asked friends in Oxford to see if he was well, and in the absence of a persuasive answer Brigid raced from London to investigate. She found Dan in acute distress, but got him to hospital, and waited with him through the harrowing hours of uncertainty.

He was diagnosed with pancreatitis, of which there are two principal causes: gallstones and alcoholic poisoning. The scar across his thorax was evidence enough that Dan's problem was not in the gall-bladder. Delia, meanwhile, had driven Winnie down to Oxford, where they learned that if Dan lived through the night in intensive care then he would probably survive, but that his way of life would have to change. Medical care and a remarkably strong constitution pulled him through, and after ten days he was conscious enough to begin once more taking an interest in the ward around him. He started keeping notes about the other patients, as if planning to write about this experience. Also in these notes, his gratitude to Delia, who repeatedly drove from Leeds to be with her mother and to visit her father, is touching in its affection.

The stern medical warnings against drink should have carried greater weight this time, and when he came out of hospital in the third week of June he seemed a reformed man. Winnie's life had long since resolved itself into one of continuous care for Dan, and she redoubled her efforts. He started to have acupuncture treatment for his back. Very slowly he began to write again. This was the final phase, and it lasted until the autumn of 1986. To all appearances he led an ordered and settled existence, anathema to the bohemian still struggling for release, and made dismal by alcohol-free beer, a ridiculous concept. There were still the passages of visitors, enjoyed at least in the appearance. And pleasure to be taken in the gossip of friends and his ever expanding family, grandchildren growing into adulthood, having children of their own.

At this time Dan was contacted by Dave Arthur, a young writer from Tunbridge Wells, who did occasional free-lance work for radio and in various magazines, as well as folk-singing and television script-writing: a multimedia performer. He wrote to ask if he could interview Dan, and they agreed to meet in the Horse and Jockey at lunchtime on 12 November 1985. He arrived to find Dan deep in conversation with Iris Murdoch and the brothers Lienhardt, but Dan steered him to another table where they could talk apart. '[T]he friendships of later life, in contrast with those negotiated before thirty, are apt to be burdened with reservations, constraints, inhibitions.'[40]

Dave Arthur had various plans to make radio programmes both with and about Dan, and over the next few years or so he made a number of tape recordings in which Dan reminisced about various aspects of his life. Arthur was a charming and generous man. He never did make a programme about Dan, though he wrote a sketch portrait of him, 'Dan Davin, a Sombre Beast?', that was never published, but which Dan corrected for him, and rather liked.[41] Arthur also became a faithful and reliable driver, offering to transport Dan to and from hospital when one or other of Dan's daughters was unable to do so. Dan became very fond of him. His was a new ear, knowing nothing at first of Dan's past or his remorse about some of it, and offering an opportunity for him, in conversation with a willing listener, to reinvent himself a little. Not only was this a late friendship, it was also an uncharacteristic one: one in which Dan, often with a tape recorder running, did most of the talking.

What seemed like the placid days of 1985–6 brought occasional social events, such as the reception in Lady Margaret Hall for His Grace Sir Paul Reeves in November 1985. Reeves was nominated to be Governor-General of New Zealand, the first Maori to hold the position, having also been the first Maori to become the Anglican Primate. He was visiting Oxford to receive an honorary degree from his old university. Duncan Stewart, himself once a New Zealand Rhodes Scholar, and Principal of LMH, made a speech in which he referred to the Oxford Mafia, but spelt it out M.A.W.H.I.A. Dan winced visibly. A glimpse of Sir Paul suggested that he was not alone. The days of New Zealand intellectual pre-eminence in Oxford were over.

The appearance of a placid and agreeable existence in a shady evening-time of life belied reality. Shortly after he came out of the Radcliffe from his brush with pancreatitis, Delia came to see her parents. It was Wednesday, 3 July 1985. She brought with her a letter to Dan and Winnie from Patty in which Patty explained that she had, a year ago, been diagnosed as suffering from a rare form of leukaemia. She had not told them because she had not wanted to burden them, and in any event she expected to be cured. Perhaps she only told them now because she was having chemotherapy, and had lost her hair. Delia's role in this (she, Brigid, and Anna had all known since the summer of 1984) was to emphasize Patty's determination, and the optimism of her therapists at University College Hospital in London. Delia played her part courageously, but Dan was not fooled. He turned white, and was speechless at the news. Despair, already deeply entrenched, was frozen into place.

For the next year or so Dan still managed to write. In August he 'fiddled with'[42] his piece on 'Galway 1936'. He had agreed to collect his short stories about the war for OUP, and he set about this in the summer of 1985, reviewing each one, deciding on a method of presentation. It was slow work as he had little energy and failing enthusiasm, but over the Christmas and New Year period of 1986 he eventually managed to write an introductory preface and append a glossary of military terms. He chose to order the stories according to the shape of his own experience: Greece, Crete, Cairo, North Africa, Palestine, Italy. This is far from the order in which the stories were written, but the effect is to bring greater unity to the collection. Referring to his 1947 novel *For The Rest of Our Lives*, he reflected: 'I doubt if I realized then . . . just how deep go the experiences which one has in one's twenties and how, because they are the years when we are at the summit of our powers, we tend in retrospect to remember what was good and forget what was bad.'[43] Glimpsing his own bohemian, radical self in the same heat that had warmed the soldier, he dedicated the collection 'To those who, out of principle, refused to fight, and suffered for it. And to those who fought so that, among much else, that principle should be safeguarded.' *The Salamander and the Fire* was published in 1986 as an OUP paperback, well received when reviewed, though that was little. It was his last book.

Somehow he continued to work, even seemed at times to be staging a return to good health. He wrote a few reviews, and settled to a few more short stories, all about his childhood. In 'The Unjust and the Loving', an old man recalls, through the troubled haze of a kindergarten child's understanding, the death of a relative in the great flu epidemic, and the first stirring of love for a little girl classmate, someone who, 'if we hadn't moved and I'd kept on seeing her, I wouldn't remember . . . so clearly'. In August 1986 he wrote the delightful little poem 'December' which he sent to Elizabeth.[44] These pieces of work about his now remote past were almost the last. Patty's illness carried him to the darkest regions of isolation, where the old man understood what the schoolboy had discovered at the tip: 'A wicked whisper came, and made | My heart as dry as dust.'

He was drinking heavily again, and by October 1986 was so unwell that he went once more to see Ledingham at the Radcliffe. No advice could stop him, however. In December he collapsed, and was readmitted suffering from hepatic encephalopathy, delirious, and with paranoid delusions. The nurses were plotting against him, people on the ward carrying guns. Once more he was brought back from the brink, but on his return to 103 in January the life he resumed was barely animated. He found it impossible to concentrate for longer than an hour. The tremor in his hand made it virtually impossible to write. Handwriting already bad degenerated into hieroglyphics, and his correspondents were relieved to receive his letters dictated and typed. He lost all interest in reading, and found even the favourite books of his past unpalatable.

In this state, on New Year's Day 1987, he was appointed CBE in the New Zealand list. Letters of congratulation flowed in, and, without disguising his physical circumstances, he managed to reply to them all with some of his customary wit. He determined to accept the honour in person at a Buckingham Palace investiture, and eventually was well enough, correctly attired in morning suit, to present himself to the Queen on Tuesday, 28 July. The day before was Winnie's birthday, and there was a dinner party at Brigid and Andy's home in north London. Both Brigid and Winnie went with him to the Palace the next day. Simultaneously, in Moscow, Dorothy Hodgkin, his fellow grandparent, was awarded the Order of Lenin for her services to science and medicine.

Dan's own need of medicine was now constant. Ledingham said he was absolutely not to drink, that another episode would kill him. And he did try, one more time, in the dark English winter and early spring of 1987. He was suffering too for Patty, now nearly three years into her own illness and struggling from one crisis to another. No one knew better than Dan how to read his own condition. The intelligence officer could still draft a report from the front: his gall-bladder was gone long since; the pancreas damaged; the stomach wounded; the liver close to failure; the mind in torment. Dan had written, in September 1984, in a clever but devastating squib 'On retirement': 'the artist cannot retire, he can only surrender: what he has been doing all his life is inescapable and, as senility overtakes and unmans him, he has to accept that for him there is no escape through the imagination from the ultimate impotence of life and art.'[45] In May 1987, after another brief brush with whisky, he was persuaded to go as a patient to St Andrew's Hospital.

St Andrew's is a private residential psychiatric hospital on a substantial estate just outside Northampton, with a department, Spencer House, that specializes in drug and alcohol addiction. Dan was admitted for the first time on 20 May 1987, and came under the care of Dr Tim Kidger. For the next three years he was in constant touch with the hospital and its staff. He went there to stay on eight separate occasions, sometimes for as long as a month, and he also had a number of out-patient consultations and numerous telephone talks. From the beginning Dr Kidger developed a particular liking for Dan, and it was reciprocated. He was almost the last friend that Dan made: a friendship founded at first on dire necessity, but one which grew rapidly into an understanding founded on the truth. Kidger had no illusions, after all. Simple blood tests on admission revealed a body, and specifically a liver, in crisis.[46] Dr Kidger recognized alcoholism when he saw it, and understood the worlds of pain and distress that lay behind it. Dan was nearly 74 years old, and his physical condition very poor, so that the idea of a cure had a certain irrelevance. Kidger sought to limit the amount of damage that Dan was doing to himself, to help him to stop drinking, and to lift his depression, which he quickly detected as principal cause.

Whenever Dan was in the safety of the hospital, these objectives seemed plausible. The depression never cleared, but there were some days better than others. As he stopped drinking altogether when he was there, and the staff always got him quickly on to big doses of vitamins, so his physical condition would improve enough for him to participate in the life of Spencer House. This included regular blood tests, with explanations of what the results meant, and of the physical and mental damage that alcohol causes; individual therapy with Dr Kidger; lectures, films, and talks of various kinds about addiction and how to deal with it; aversion therapy; and group therapy with other residents. In group therapy each patient had to introduce a session with a prepared talk, laying out the duration and features of the experience of addiction. In this way, and in a forum that he could never have anticipated, Dan told those parts of his life story that, suitably edited, could be shared. He was still capable of telling a story, the ghost of Larry Hynes at his shoulder. He began: 'I have a very long past and a very short future.' It was like revisiting his childhood, and relearning the magic of itinerant fiction, a magic re-kindled on the car journeys back and forth to Oxford in his conversations with Dave Arthur.

St Andrew's Hospital became his last redoubt, and it was from there, in mid-March 1988, that he wrote to Patty in University College Hospital, to tell her how he wanted to write a poem for her, and how he went to sleep at night holding her hand. She wrote back on St Patrick's Day. 'Well what a pair we make you and me, you in your hospital and me in mine.'

I can't think of anything nicer at this moment which I would rather do than be sitting beside you holding your hand and supporting each other[.] Mostly I feel quite strong mentally and can cope and feel determined to beat this beastly disease really hard. *Everybody* has a hard life and I'll eventually beat it and be wiser . . . Darling Dan I don't want you to worry about me please, I am very happy very lucky in all my 4 parents (yes I've never told you how I've always considered myself quite the luckiest person on earth) . . . I have such a lot to say to you . . . Oh how we're both going to win our battles, and oh how I would like to be with you.[47]

In reality she was failing, her illness entering its final phase, her resistance and the powers of medicine both exhausted. Delia drove Dan from Northampton to London to see her for the last time before she died on 12 April. In the death notices she was the daughter of Professor and

Mrs Tylecote. The Davins went to her funeral in Hampstead parish church on the afternoon of 19 April, and afterwards to Philip Watson's mother's home nearby. Dan was embarrassed at being asked what his relationship to Patty had been, and could not reply. Later, in a letter to Paul Freyberg he described himself in 'great grief about a kind of goddaughter of mine who died last week'.[48] Elizabeth, unable to confront the occasion at all, stayed away, and lit candles in another church. Dan, still trying to be the company commander that his major's crown had made him, advised Philip to find another wife.

Patty's death was the last devastating bombardment. All his defences were gone now, and he bowed his head. He wrote a long poem in May and June called 'Waiting, Snookered', a poem about his youth and desire, girls and women on the corners, Dee and Tay, of Invercargill streets. It finishes:

I wait now, still. No corners. No misleading streets, or smiles.
A road. A straight road. She is not there.
Nor am I. We have reached the uncovenanted, mourning, uncornered street,
Where we die.

The body still had a surprising toughness, and he lived on for more than two years, but with ever more frequent visits to St Andrew's. Even so, he could still respond to the gestures of interest in others. In the pub one evening in January 1990 he noticed a young woman making a sketch of him, and they got into conversation. She was Laura Buxton, Scottish by origin, though resident in Paris; a professional artist visiting Oxford for a few months for portrait commissions. She had an attractive and straightforward dedication to her art, became friends with Dan and Winnie, and did a number of notable pencil drawings of Dan.

Old friends still visited. Gordie Craig, still incredibly vital, came for the last time in March 1990. But their generation was thinning out now, and it was the newer, younger friends who were most likely to call. Family came too, and he was particularly glad of the company of Kate Hodgkin, Anna and Luke's daughter, who worked from time to time for several years on the ordering of his collection of papers, destined for the Turnbull Library.

Dan still had plans to work, and even wrote of assembling the material for another volume of short stories.[49] By the end of the summer of 1989, however, he had stopped writing anything extended, and took to jotting comments and aphorisms in a notebook, or on scraps of paper that he left around the house, under tables and down the backs of chairs. 'In a marriage of trust guilt is the only thing one has of one's own.' 'It is not the things we are ashamed of that cause us shame, but the things that we ought to be ashamed of.' 'Sleight of mind.' When, on 2 May 1989, the OUP Printing House was closed, one of Dan's darkest fears from the now distant days of early restructuring was fully realized. He had managed to detach himself from the Press, and most of the people he had trained or worked with had retired or moved on. But the end of printing at Oxford University meant, to Dan, the closing of a chapter not of his own life, or of his generation, but of scholarship itself.

Retreat became rout. Martha McCullough died on 4 February 1990, irrascible to the last. Her behaviour had grown so reprehensible that Dan had broken off relations with her in 1984, and at the end only Anne Willett and Gordon Gardiner, a dentist and caring friend, still occasionally saw her. At her own request, her cremation was attended by no one. Colin Roberts died exactly a week later, a last link with the Press broken, though Dan believed that the Press had died first. Ronnie Tylecote died on 17 June. After retirement in 1981, he and Elizabeth had moved permanently to their house at East Hanney, in the country a few miles southwest of Oxford. The move had brought them back into Dan and Winnie's life as occasional visitors, both to 103 and at Dorchester.

Dan was backwards and forwards to St Andrew's throughout 1990, but when he returned for five days in mid-August there was little that could be done for him. He was in such pain that he was taking large doses of paracetamol, which he believed less harmful to his stomach than aspirin. They could have done his liver no good. In the second week of September he was readmitted to the Radcliffe where he had two ultrasound examinations of his liver. '[T]he liver was so sick that the clinicians were looking for anything they could reverse.'[50] There was nothing. Dan was buoyed slightly by the news that he might have been suffering from a malignancy rather than cirrhosis, but 'the diagnosis was by that time academic since whatever the pathological process the liver was non-functioning'.[51]

He was taken home to 103 where a bed was prepared for him in the bow window of the living-room, looking out on to Southmoor Road: the road where his children had grown up, where Julian Maclaren-Ross had come to live, where he had waited for the lively step of Paddy or Gordie on the footpath, of Bertie Rodgers or Gerald Wilde hunting for drink and conversation forty long years ago. 'Thank God', Dan said, 'for a room where there's something to look at.'[52] Anna, Delia, and Brigid all came to stay, sharing the burden of care with Winnie. Delia looked after the last fragments of necessary correspondence. He died at seven o'clock on the morning of 28 September, the four strongest women in his life all beside him. He was reconciled and willing to go. No priest was summoned at the last minute. Dan was defeated but he was not broken.

Far away in Australia, Patrick White died on the same day, and he and Dan shared the London newspaper obituary columns. John Willett wrote about Dan shrewdly in the *Guardian*, along with John Wain; Alan Bell, Vincent O'Sullivan, and Richard Charkin—once one of his editors at the Press, and another resident of Southmoor Road—in the *Independent*. *The Times* dealt backhandedly, and made much of his 'essential modesty', but the effect was unintended. Peter Sutcliffe wrote it with great affection, but all the personal detail was cut by the anonymous sub. An editor's revenge.

The funeral was held at the Oxford crematorium in Headington at 11.30 a.m. on Monday, 1 October. Bruce Purchase was MC to the gathering of family, friends, and academic Oxford who packed into the little chapel. John Willett came from Le Thil and spoke of Dan in humour and warm-hearted friendship. Fleur Adcock read two poems, one of them Dan's own 'The Gorse Blooms Pale', the other Donne's 'Death be not proud', one of Dan's favourites. Bryce Harland, the New Zealand High Commissioner in London, spoke about 'Dan the soldier and the chronicler of the New Zealand soldier in action in World War II'.[53] As the curtains closed on the coffin a solo violin played a Gaelic lament. Winnie's tribute, read by Purchase, was an epigram by Martial:

> In all thy humours, whether grave or mellow,
> Thou'rt such a touchy, testy, pleasant fellow,
> Hast so much wit, and mirth and spleen about thee,
> There is no living with thee, nor without thee.

The balance of literary friends, warfare, New Zealand, Ireland, and the classics emphasized Dan's wide-ranging experience; the diversity of people his talent for friendship. 'Most funerals incline, through general atmosphere, to suggest the presence, or at least the most salient characteristics of the deceased.'[54] Afterwards there was a gathering at 103 where a large crowd paid their respects, much was had by way of food and drink, and each lived up to the expectations of reputation.

Dan's little scraps of paper kept turning up at 103 for a year or so after he died. One of them had on it a line from the *Aeneid*, written in the shaky hand of his final days: 'forsan et haec olim meminisse iuvabit'—perhaps even these things, some day, will bring joy to remember.

NOTES

Chapter 1: *Origins*

1. There are authorities for both, though our Davins were brought up on 'poet' as the origin. However, Edward MacLysaght, *The Surnames of Ireland* (Dublin, 3rd rev. edn., 1978), 75, specifically warns against confusion with *dámh*. Cognate surnames are Devin and Devine.
2. DMDP: DMD, 'Galway 1936', p. 15.
3. Dave Arthur, tape recording in conversation with DMD, 3 Dec. 1985; DMD, 'Bluff Retrospect', *BS*, p. 86.
4. Charlotte Macdonald, *The Dictionary of New Zealand National Biography* (Wellington, NZ, 1990), i. 96–7.
5. Patrick O'Farrell, *Vanished Kingdoms: Irish in Australia and New Zealand. A Personal Excursion* (Kensington, NSW, 1990), 187.
6. Ibid. 179–239.
7. Donald Harman Akenson, *Half The World From Home: Perspectives on the Irish in New Zealand, 1860–1950* (Wellington, 1990), esp. pp. 65–85.
8. New Zealand National Archives, file R AAEB 587 No. 8, p. 157, record no. 168019. The entry is dated 25 Nov. 1904. Patrick Davin, 'Labourer', is 'Appointed'.
9. This is DMD's account of their first meeting: DMD with Dave Arthur, tape recording, 3 Dec. 1985. Martin Davin believed their parents met in Wellington, where Mary was barmaid for a while at the Metropolitan Hotel in Molesworth Street. Martin Davin, interview, 11 Aug. 1991. Pat Davin believed the Wellington pub she worked at was the Britannic. Pat Davin, interview, 22 Aug. 1991.
10. Her birth-date was recorded as 1 Aug., but her oldest son Thomas recalled her as believing that she was actually born on 27 July.
11. Ruth Dallas, 'Bird and Flower', in *Landfall*, vol. 2, no. 4, Dec. 1948, 248–9. The poem is reprinted in her autobiography, *Curved Horizon* (Dunedin, 1991), 106.
12. *RFH*, p. 193.
13. DMD with Dave Arthur, tape recording, 3 Dec. 1985.
14. M. H. Holcroft, *Old Invercargill* (Dunedin, 1976), 83.
15. DMD with Dave Arthur, tape recording, 3 Dec. 1985.
16. DMD with Dave Arthur, tape recording, 1 Feb. 1990.
17. Father Pound, interview, 16 Aug. 1991.
18. Herries Beattie, *A History of Gore and Surrounding Districts 1862–1962* (Gore, n.d. [1962?]), 20–36.
19. *NR*, p. 110.
20. Beattie, *History of Gore*, 78.
21. *RFH*, pp. 214–18.
22. Ibid. 89.

23. DMD with Dave Arthur, tape recording, 1 Feb. 1990. See also *SS*, p. 10, and DMDP: DMD, Diary, 5 May 1941, in an olive grove near Maleme aerodrome on the island of Crete, when he fell to thinking about the first books he had read.
24. Pat Davin, interview, 22 Aug. 1991.
25. DMD with Dave Arthur, tape recording, 1 Feb. 1990.
26. *RFH*, p. 244.

Chapter 2: *A Catholic Childhood*

1. Martin Davin, interview, 11 Aug. 1991.
2. Pat Davin, interview, 22 Aug. 1991.
3. DMD, 'The Basket', *GBP*, p. 47.
4. *NR*, pp. 91–2.
5. Pat Davin, interview.
6. Specifically in New Zealand and Australia a term denoting any uncultivated area covered with trees or shrubs, which can vary from open scrubby country to dense rain forest.
7. Crawlies are fresh-water crayfish. The boys would find peat fires, and boil the crawlies in a billy. DMD, 'Early Reading: The Rime of the Ancient Mariner', in *Education*, 5 (1976), 27.
8. WKDP: DMD to WKD, 4 Sept. 1933.
9. Pat Davin, interview.
10. Father Pound, interview, 16 Aug. 1991.
11. *NR*, p. 184.
12. *RFH*, p. 134.
13. In Australia and New Zealand a term for a catapult. DMD spells it 'shangeye'. See *RFH*, p. 135.
14. Carbide was readily available for acetylene bicycle lamps, also employed as night fishing equipment.
15. DMD, 'Late Snow', *GBP*, p. 33.
16. Ibid. 30.
17. M. H. Holcroft, *Old Invercargill* (Dunedin, 1976), 112–14.
18. DMD, 'Growing Up', *GBP*, pp. 50–5.
19. DMD, 'The Apostate', ibid. 8.
20. DMD, 'Milk Round', ibid. 27.
21. DMD, 'Death of a Dog', ibid. 38.
22. Father Pound, interview.
23. DMDP: 'Mss scraps' file.
24. Southland sunsets are rightly famous. The Maori name for Stewart Island, *Rakiura*, means 'land of the glowing skies'.
25. DMD with Dave Arthur, tape recording, 3 Dec. 1985.
26. Janet Frame, *An Angel At My Table: An Autobiography. Volume Two* (Auckland, 1984), 72–6; Ruth Dallas, *Curved Horizon* (Dunedin, 1991), 73.
27. Martin Davin, interview.

28. DMD, with Dave Arthur, tape recording, 3 Dec. 1985.
29. Father Pound, interview; letter from Sally Savage, n.d. [Feb. 1992].
30. DMD, 'Bluff Retrospect', *BS*, p. 86.
31. *NR*, pp. 173–81; K. C. McDonald, *City of Dunedin: A Century of Civic Enterprise* (Dunedin, 1965), 322–4.
32. Ibid. 324.
33. *RFH*, pp. 108, 149–53, 182; DMDP: DMD, 'The Irish in New Zealand', unpub. MS, 1957.
34. Patrick O'Farrell, *The Tablet*, centennial edition, 3 May 1973, p. 55.
35. Martin Davin, interview.
36. *SS*, 'Introduction', p. 10; *RFH*, p. 117. There was also a Victorian *History of the World*, which, in its biblical section, contained 'a seductive picture of Rebecca'. WKDP: DMD to WKD, 30 Aug. 1933, a fact which he may have forgotten.
37. DMD with Dave Arthur, tape recording, 3 Dec. 1985.
38. Letter from Delia Davin, 10 Mar. 1995.
39. *FTROOL*, p. 183.
40. Ibid.
41. DMD with Dave Arthur, tape recording, 3 Dec. 1985.
42. Sally Savage, letter.
43. DMDP: DMD to Leslie Hannon, 29 Feb. 1984.
44. Pat Gallagher, *The Marist Brothers in New Zealand, Fiji and Samoa, 1876–1976* (Tuakau, 1976), 69–71.
45. J. O. B. Watt, *Invercargill Marist 75th Jubilee 1897–1972 Magazine*, p. 12.
46. Gallagher, *Marist Brothers*, 107–16.
47. DMD, with Dave Arthur, tape recording, 3 Dec. 1985.
48. Gallagher, *Marist Brothers*, 109.
49. DMD, 'Early Reading', 27. See also 'Late Snow', *GBP*, pp. 28–36; and *NHNN*, p. 93.
50. DMD, 'Early Reading', 27.
51. Brother Gerald Murphy to Bob Cotterall, 3 Nov. 1992.
52. Gallagher, *Marist Brothers*, 111.
53. DMD with Dave Arthur, tape recording, 3 Dec. 1985.
54. Ibid.
55. Martin Davin, interview.
56. Patrick O'Farrell, *The Tablet*, 3 May 1973, p. 55; and *Vanished Kingdoms: Irish in Australia and New Zealand. A Personal Excursion* (Kensington, NSW, 1990), 205–23.
57. Pat Davin, interview, See also DMD, *SS*, 'Introduction', p. 11.
58. DMD, 'Saturday Night', *GBP*, pp. 56–60. John Meredith Smith, *Southlanders at Heart* (Invercargill, 1988), 144, has a photograph of the Brown Owl.
59. Father Pound, interview.
60. Letter from Gerard Hall-Jones, 25 Aug. 1991, with a photocopy of his father's diary entry.

61. Martin Davin, interview.
62. DMD, 'Three Encounters Thirty Years Ago', *Islands*, vol. 6, no. 3, Mar. 1978, p. 306.
63. *The Tablet*, 3 May 1973, p. 56.
64. DMDP: Brother Egbert testimonial, 2 Aug. 1933.
65. Brother Gerald Murphy to Bob Cotterall, 3 Nov. 1992.
66. This story, which DMD believed himself, comes down by word of mouth. Sacred Heart College apparently had no records. See n. 2 to Ch. 3, below.
67. DMD with Dave Arthur, tape recording, 3 Dec. 1985.

Chapter 3: *Auckland Interlude*

1. WKDP: DMD to WKD, 28 Aug. 1934.
2. The school moved to its present site in the Auckland suburb of Glen Innes in 1955. Any records that the school may have had of its earlier history were reportedly lost or destroyed during this move. It is perhaps worth stressing, however, that members of the Marist Order take a particularist view of their obligations, and that this does not coincide with the interests of the biographer. As one Brother said to me by way of explanation: 'In success we rejoice with members of our community, and in failure we weep with them. You must write as you think fit, for I cannot tell you more.'
3. M. K. Joseph, 'A Private Movie', unpub. memoir, p. 30.
4. Gallagher, *The Marist Brothers in New Zealand, Fiji and Samoa, 1876–1976* (Tuakau, 1976), 112.
5. *The Gloomy Form*, 'A Dropsical comedy in four Acts and two Silhouettes', *Sacred Heart College Magazine* (1930), 94–6.
6. Brother Maurice Russell, a former Director, though after DMD's time. He took the directorship in 1936. Interview, 6 Nov. 1992.
7. Bob Cotterall, interview, 15 Nov. 1992.
8. Terence Thomas to Bob Cotterall, n.d. [Mar. 1994?].
9. DMDP: Vince McGovern to DMD, 15 Oct. 1931; Charles Zambucka, interview, 7 Nov. 1992.
10. Joseph, 'A Private Movie'.
11. Brother Maurice Russell, interview.
12. Terence Thomas to Bob Cotterall.
13. Letter from Bob Cotterall, 16 Apr. 1994.
14. Ibid.
15. Ibid.
16. Terence Thomas to Bob Cotterall.
17. SS, p. 11. Quoted in James Bertram, *Dan Davin* (Auckland, 1983), 6.
18. Brother Maurice Russell, interview.
19. SHC *Magazine*, 1930, p. 14.
20. Charles Zambucka, interview.
21. Tim Radford, *Guardian*, 9 Aug. 1988.

22. 31 Mar. 1930. SHC *Magazine*, 1930, p. 35.
23. Joseph, 'A Private Movie', 33.
24. Charles Zambucka, interview.
25. Joseph, 'A Private Movie', 47.
26. Ibid. 33.
27. Ibid. 44.
28. Ibid. 35.
29. Both Martin and Patrick Davin reported this, separately, but in exactly the same terms, and with the same emphasis.
30. DMDP: Vince McGovern to DMD.
31. The school holidays were 9–27 May, and 22 Aug.–16 Sept.
32. Letter from WKD, 10 Mar. 1995.
33. DMD to Anna Davin, 3 Aug. 1984.
34. DMD with Dave Arthur, tape recording, 3 Dec. 1985.
35. Joseph, 'A Private Movie', 35.
36. Ibid.
37. DMDP: Brother Borgia to DMD, 25 Feb. 1931.

Chapter 4: *Love and Books*

1. J. C. Beaglehole, *The University of New Zealand: An Historical Study* (Auckland, 1937), 44.
2. Under the University of New Zealand Acts of 1870 and 1874. Beaglehole, ibid. 14–108.
3. The census of 1921 gave 72,255; and 1936, 81,961.
4. W. P. Morrell, *The University of Otago: A Centennial History* (Dunedin, 1969), ch. 6, 'The Dominance of the Special Schools, 1914–1945', pp. 117–62, 244.
5. Ida Logan (née Lawson), interview, 21 July 1993. Her father was Professor of Education at Otago from 1923 to 1945. Janet Maconie (née MacBride), interview, 11 Aug. 1993.
6. A unit is a full year's course in a subject, and may consist of a number of papers, generally two or three at that time. Nine complete units over three years were required for a BA course, and students could take them, within limits set out in the university regulations, in different combinations.
7. DMD with Dave Arthur, tape recording.
8. His fees, five guineas per course per year, plus two guineas college and union dues, were paid by his scholarship, which also contributed most of his board and lodging. The cost of everything else—books and stationery, transport, pocket money (which had to pay for heating: the hated gas and electricity meters)—came from private funds, which at the depths of the Depression, when there were few jobs available, meant his parents. Patrick Davin's decision in 1905 to pursue security on the railways found its reward between 1929 and 1935. He was never unemployed. In an undated letter—WKDP: DMD to WKD [June 1932?]—Dan says that it had cost his mother £22. 10*s*. to keep him in 1931. 'That's too hard on

her. I wish I could knock off being kept . . .' The attribution is interesting: it was the woman who managed the household budget.

9. Winnie McQuilkan (1914–91) and Frank Hall (1914–79) were married in 1949. She was headmistress of Columba College, a Presbyterian boarding-school for girls in Dunedin, 1942–8; a gifted pianist; and, as Clare Mallory, author of the *Merry* series of stories for girls, *Merry Begins, Leith & Friends, The Pen & Pencil Girls*, etc. Frank Hall became a physician, having read Medicine after his Arts degree. A heart specialist, he was for many years the senior consulting physician at Wellington Hospital and the Home of Compassion.

10. Fred Petricevich to Bob Cotterall, 28 June 1931. 'Hell of a place too . . . It has about three streets, four suburbs and sixteen trams . . . We managed to drag out an existence there somehow.'

11. Martin Davin, interview.

12. The youngest child, Maurice, died when he was a boy. The others were Mary, known as Mollie, the oldest, then John (Jack), then Winifred, and lastly Michael (Mick).

13. Charlotte Macdonald, *A Woman of Good Character: Single Women as Immigrant Settlers in Nineteenth-century New Zealand* (Wellington, 1990), 66. Ellen Crowe must have been tough just to survive her first year. Few Irish peasant children born in 1846 lived to see 1847.

14. Charlotte Macdonald, *Dictionary of New Zealand National Biography* (Wellington, 1990), i. 96.

15. WKDP: DMD to WKD, [late Aug. 1932?].

16. WKDP: DMD to WKD, 30 May 1931. Emphases in the original.

17. WKDP: WKD to DMD, n.d. [2 June 1931?]; 'mo vohileen bawn' is a phonetic rendering of 'mo bhuacaillin ban' meaning 'my fair young lad'.

18. Elizabeth Mason, unpub. Memoir, ch. 13, 'Ten Stone Club'. This contains, p. 105, a description of Toni's state of knowledge about sexual matters such that, even if only 50 per cent of it were true, she was surely alarmingly badly prepared for life. Mrs Mason's entertaining recollections unfortunately contain various errors of fact.

19. Hypatia presumably after Charles Bradlaugh's daughter, herself named after the first pagan martyr.

20. Like Barbara Goring on Kenneth Widmerpool in Anthony Powell, *A Buyer's Market* (1952), 73–80, though in Mabel's case the offence seems to have been throwing jelly.

21. He became a distinguished endocrinologist.

22. FRS, 1936. He later became famous as the author of *Gallipoli to the Somme* (1963), reminiscences of the First World War, which he wrote as a student at Otago in the early 1920s, but published only 40 years later.

23. WKDP: DMD to WKD, n.d. [5 June 1931?].

24. WKDP: WKD to DMD, n.d. [May? 1932]: 'Marcus is a name I like greatly. It is a name like Stephen Dedalus. I am glad I read James Joyce's books so that I could know you.'

25. WKDP: WKD to DMD, 24 Nov. 1931.
26. WKDP: WKD to DMD, 30 Dec. 1931.
27. Sir Geoffrey Cox, interview, 13 Dec. 1991.
28. Mabel McIndoe seemed to be under the impression that the Club *really* *was* for slimming, and remembered proudly how she lost a stone. 'I'm not sure that the others tried very hard; their shapes didn't change' (Elizabeth Mason, 'Memoir', 106). The laughter of the Ten Stone Club echoes down the decades.
29. WKDP: WKD to DMD, 3 Dec. 1931.
30. This incident became enshrined in their memories as Dan's first contact with the Gonley family. The record is slightly different, though it does nothing to spoil the memory. Winnie's mother had been in hospital in Invercargill for an operation in late August 1931, and Dan, on Winnie's behalf, and at her behest, had visited her there. On this occasion he met Winnie's sister Mollie for the first time. Mrs Gonley gave him various messages for Winnie, and suggested that he might like to visit them in Otautau in the summer vacation. No doubt she may have neglected to tell her husband of this casual invitation, but the fact is that in December Dan's existence was already well known to both Mrs Gonley and Mollie (WKDP: DMD to WKD, 'Wednesday' [2 Sep. 1931?]).
31. Janet Maconie, interview, 11 Aug. 1993.
32. WKDP: DMD to WKD, 10 Dec. 1931.
33. WKDP: DMD to WKD, 18 Dec. 1931. Apuleius' *The Golden Ass*, also known as *Metamorphoses*, is the only Roman novel to have been preserved in its entirety. Compton Mackenzie's *Vestal Fire* (1927) is a sexual and social satire set on the island of Sirene in the Gulf of Naples. Its sequel, equally explicit, *Extraordinary Women* (1928), which Dan also read—though later—nearly brought Mackenzie a prosecution. One can only reflect on the liberating effect of these wonderfully entertaining novels for a young man in a Catholic working-class family in south-east Invercargill in 1931.
34. WKDP: DMD to WKD, 25 Dec. 1931.
35. WKDP: DMD to WKD, 5 Jan. 1932.
36. WKDP: DMD to WKD, [16?] Jan. 1932. Which of George Moore's numerous works he read at this time I have been unable to establish. It would be nice to think it was *A Modern Lover* (1883), a realist work of bohemian life: two major themes in Dan's own emerging consciousness. Moore, Irish, socially embattled, in revolt against prudishness and convention, and deeply influenced by Balzac and Zola, Turgenev and Dostoevsky, was surely one of his spiritual uncles.
37. WKDP: DMD to WKD, [30 Jan.?] 1932. Walter Pater's *Marius the Epicurean* (1885) is a fictional biography set in the Rome of Marcus Aurelius, so drew together two of Dan's immediate interests, literature and classical antiquity. Pater was still a popular critic in the late 1920s and early 1930s, and his invocation of the 'hard gem-like flame' still lit

intellectual fires. *Du côté de chez Swann* (1913) is vol. i of Marcel Proust's celebrated masterpiece, the *roman-fleuve*, *A la recherche du temps perdu*, which became a favourite with Dan, and which he read repeatedly, this first time in French.

38. WKDP: DMD to WKD, 18 Feb. 1932.
39. WKDP: DMD to WKD, 5 Jan. 1932.
40. WKDP: WKD to DMD, 6 Jan. 1932.
41. WKDP: DMD to WKD, 22 Jan. 1932.
42. WKDP: WKD to DMD, 24 Jan. 1932.
43. WKDP: DMD to WKD, 26 Jan. 1932.
44. WKDP: DMD to WKD, 18 Feb. 1932.
45. WKDP: DMD to WKD, [30 Jan.?] 1932.
46. WKDP: DMD to WKD, 15 Feb. 1932.
47. WKDP: WKD to DMD, 19–25 Feb. 1932.
48. 78 BC to AD 68.
49. WKDP: DMD to WKD, [June 1932?].
50. These comments are distilled from WKDP. See esp. DMD's letters of: 'Wednesday' [2 Sept. 1931?]; 'Saturday 15 January' [16 Jan. 1932?]; 1 and 2 Feb. 1932; 'Sunday 29th August' [28 Aug. 1932?]; 21 Nov. 1932; 'Sunday 11.30 a.m.' [4 Dec. 1932?]; [25–8 Nov. 1932?]; 21 Jan. 1933; 14 Feb. 1933; 24 Nov. 1933; 20 Dec. 1933; 23 May 1934; 28 Aug. 1934.
51. Capping Week—the last week of the first term, approximately 15–20 May—consisted of the degree ceremony on the Tuesday afternoon, followed by the Capping Ball at night, usually in the Town Hall and Concert Chamber; a procession on the Wednesday; four performances of a theatrical concert or 'review'; and various private functions, including dances at Cargill's Castle, a popular cliff-top seaside venue. The Students' Association published a Capping magazine of a humorous kind. The events had some similarity with 'Rag Week' at provincial British universities after the Second World War.
52. Founded in 1925, fortnightly during term: 12 issues a year. Part newspaper, part magazine, part forum of opinion, it adopted a newspaper format in 1932, when it was largely written by medical students, and sold for 3*d*.
53. Cunctator: one who acts tardily, a delayer.
54. *The Critic*, vol. viii, no. 3, 29 April 1932, p. 3.
55. It was held on 26 May, and, given the climate of opinion at the time, was a huge success.
56. Mr Small's punishment was eventually commuted to rustication first, then banishment. He had to finish his hospital training in Auckland. New university regulations for the conduct and control of student functions were introduced during the winter term. The new editors of *The Critic*, G. L. McLeod and A. L. Wilson, both medical students, produced an edition of the paper, vol. viii, no. 5, 1 July 1932, dripping with sarcastic obedience to, appreciation of, and pleasure in the Council, the

Professorial Board, and N. S. Woods, MA, OUSA President, who was held to have sided with the wrong lot during the 'crisis'. This issue also carried, without comment, H. A. Small's curriculum vitae, which was impressive.

57. WKDP: WKD to DMD, 6 and 7 June 1932. In this letter she also writes: 'Tu m'engage, m'occupe sans cesse jusqu'à ce qu'il soit nécessaire que je te réprimande. Je te demande: alors, veux-tu me tuer? Sans doute, je meurs en pensant trop à toi. Je m'évanouis de ton douceur ravissant.'
58. Charles Zambucka, interview, 7 Nov. 1992.
59. WKDP: WKD to DMD, 'Wednesday night by the fire' [8 June 1932?].
60. Professor of Ophthalmology, and Dean of the Faculty of Medicine at Otago University, 1914–36.
61. Letter from Geoffrey Flavell, 22 Dec. 1993.
62. WKDP: DMD to WKD, [28 and 29 Aug.?] 1932.
63. Ibid.
64. WKDP: WKD to DMD, 2 Sept. 1932.
65. WKDP: DMD to WKD, 5 Sept. 1932.
66. The poem was certainly written in 1932. In the letter in which it occurs she refers to her mother being in hospital in Invercargill, so it almost certainly dates from late May, only days before she learned that her mother was dying. In it she also writes: 'Harry is like a ghost now. Terrific influence he had over me, but unreal. Only you and he ever affected me: and you are real.'
67. WKDP: DMD to WKD, 10 Dec. 1932.
68. WKDP: e.g. WKD to DMD, 28 Nov. 1932 [26 Nov.? 1932].
69. There were also surface similarities, probably not lost on either Dan or Winnie, between Lawrence's background and his own. They are summarized in F. R. Leavis, 'The Wild, Untutored Phoenix', *The Common Pursuit* (1952), 233–5.
70. WKDP: WKD to DMD, 29 Nov. 1932.
71. WKDP: WKD to DMD, [early Feb. 1933?].
72. WKDP: DMD to WKD, 22 Nov. 1932.
73. WKDP: DMD to WKD, 'Thursday night 11.30' [22 Dec. 1932?].
74. *Brave New World* had only just been published. Winnie reviewed it in *The Critic*, vol. ix, no. 3, 13 Apr. 1933, p. 2. WKDP: WKD to DMD, 'Thursday night' [9 Jan. 1933?], 'Isn't the detail wonderful? Every single feature of the age, that you've privately rebelled at, damned utterly.'
75. WKDP: DMD to WKD, 24 and 25 Jan. 1933.
76. WKDP: DMD to WKD, 7, 8, and 9 Feb. 1933.
77. WKDP: DMD to WKD, 14 and 15 Feb. 1933.
78. Ibid.
79. That year edited by Frank Guest, with J. C. Mowat and John Maconie as associate editors, and Norman Davis as circulation manager. Hocken: MS 641/4 OUSA Executive Minutes 1933–36.
80. Ibid. His co-associate editor was Margaret Cotterill.

81. *The Critic*, vol. ix, no. 2, 30 Mar. 1933, 'Modernism in Art: 1—Clearing the Air'; no. 3, 13 Apr., '2—Antikodak'; no. 4, 27 Apr., '3—Upsidedown'; no. 5, 11 May, '4—Sex Appeal Versus Sculpture'.
82. Ibid., vol. ix, no. 5, 11 May 1933, 'The Art of the Motion Picture'.
83. Ibid., vol. ix, no. 6, 8 June 1933, 'Simple Susie Smites Her Sex'.
84. See the chronology of DMD's principal publications, pp. 448–57.
85. Swift's 'Modest Proposal' was to alleviate the suffering of Ireland by introducing a trade in fattened Irish babies for English dinner tables. DMD is lame in this context.
86. And became Arts Faculty representative for inter-faculty sports.
87. Vol. ix, no. 7, 29 June 1933, p. 8. DMD may have written this report himself! By this stage of the season they had won two, lost two, and drawn one.
88. WKDP: DMD to WKD, 1 June 1933.
89. Janet Frame, *An Angel at my Table: An Autobiography: Volume Two* (Auckland, 1983), 64. Twenty-five years before it had been a street of grand houses and big gardens owned by the Fels, Hallensteins, Todds, de Beers, and Braschs (Charles Brasch, *Indirections: A Memoir 1909–1947* (Wellington, 1980), 6–7).
90. Letter from James Raeside, 5 Apr. 1994.
91. Marion Steven was appointed temporary lecturer in anatomy at the Medical School for the academic years 1935 and 1936, and then awarded a scholarship to further her study of anatomy at the Middlesex Hospital in London. When the Middlesex discovered that she was a woman the scholarship was withdrawn on the grounds that they had no facilities for women. She abandoned medicine, and later took up the classics, graduating in Latin and Greek from Canterbury College. She became Reader in Classics at Canterbury University, retiring in 1975, perhaps the only MB, Ch.B. to have held a senior university post in Latin and Greek. James Raeside worked for many years for the NZ Department of Scientific and Industrial Research, and then as a consultant, living abroad for much of his life. He won the Wattie Award for Literature in 1978 for his biography of Baron de Thierry, *Sovereign Chief*. Unusual and gifted people.
92. In May 1933, much to their delight, she was appointed to a temporary teaching post at the Dunedin Technical Institute, a secondary school for young people pursuing trade or clerical qualifications. She taught there for the whole of the winter term, and was paid £14 a month (WKDP: WKD to DMD, 26 May 1933; DMD to WKD, 1 June 1933).
93. DMDP: DMD, Diary, 26 Aug. 1943. He is on a troopship between Freetown and Gibraltar: 'Port ran out yesterday. Now only liqueurs left and those South African. Drank a creme de menthe yesterday for the first time in years. Shades of the lounge in the City [a hotel] in Dunedin, with the horrible marble woman holding a torch, the uneasy Birmingham brassware, the deep chairs and the good fires and the Indian waiters bringing liqueurs to Winnie and me at a bob a time.'

94. *The Critic*, vol. ix, no. 10, 17 Aug. 1933, p. 5.
95. DMDP: Egbert to DMD, 2 Aug. 1933; Benignus to DMD, 3 Aug. 1933.
96. WKDP: DMD to WKD, 4 Sept. 1933.

Chapter 5: *Dominance & Escape*

1. *ODT*, 14 Aug. 1933, p. 8.
2. *ODT*, 19 Aug. 1933, p. 12.
3. In a controversial decision, Dr D. W. Carmalt Jones, from Britain, was appointed instead (W. P. Morrell, *The University of Otago: A Centennial History* (Dunedin, 1969), 124).
4. *ODT*, 14 Aug. 1933, p. 8.
5. Geoffrey Flavell, interview, 12 Dec. 1991; letter from Geoffrey Flavell, 22 Dec. 1993.
6. These are country towns in the south of the North Island of New Zealand, c.500 miles away from Dunedin.
7. *ODT*, 16 Sept. 1933, p. 13.
8. To the best of my knowledge these letters have not survived. However, there is an amusing example of Flavell's epistolary style, 'Reminiscence of a simple student', in *The Critic*, vol. ix, no. 2, 30 Mar. 1933, p. 10. It purports to be an account of a Friday night Bob Hop in Allen Hall, but is a vivid satire on the boredom, vulgarity, drunkenness, and vice of undergraduate life. Very funny, and surely quite untrue. It concludes with his meeting 'the most charming lady that I had so far encountered' whom he compares, in a brilliantly dense simile, with Walter Pater's encomium on the *Mona Lisa*, after which: 'Just then she saw me, smiled, and putting her arms about my unworthy neck, whispered in my ear, "Duckie, 'v'ya got enny mor gin?" And so to bed.'
9. 6 Oct. 1933. Hocken, MS 641/4.
10. Letters of 21 Aug. and 20 Sept. 1991. She asked to remain anonymous.
11. Though a survey of OUSA rankings and Prof. Board nominations suggests that, in practice, it did not carry much weight.
12. WKDP: DMD to WKD, 20 Dec. 1933.
13. WKDP: WKD to DMD, 28 Aug. 1933.
14. William (Bill) Hawksworth, 1912–66, consultant obstetrician and gynaecologist, United Oxford Hospitals, 1947–66. He served in the NZ Army Medical Corps, 1940–5.
15. *The Critic*, vol. ix, no. 11, 21 Sept. 1933.
16. e.g. WKDP: DMD to WKD, 24 Nov. 1933, where he describes the times as 'the age of Crusade. One vast Crusade against the individual; society is one God damned accursed conspiracy for the destruction of self-contained entity . . . Damn them, damn them, damn them.' He called this, his own letter, 'incoherent raving'.
17. WKDP: DMD to WKD, fragment only, 19 Feb. 1935.
18. Dan's father had a radio set, for the first time, at Christmas 1937, after Dan had left the country. A few of his friends at university had phono-

graphs, but they were expensive—by Davin family standards—and the music they played on them all came from abroad.

19. For those imperfectly acquainted with Curial casuistry on such matters of canon law, proof that Annette and Ronnie had not engaged in sexual union *after* the marriage ceremony would mean it was not consummated before God, and so therefore might be annulled.

20. WKDP: DMD to WKD, 24 Nov. 1933.

21. Ibid.

22. WKDP: DMD to WKD, 29 Dec. 1933.

23. Sigrid Undset, *Kristin Lavransdatter* (1923). Undset, a Norwegian, was Nobel laureate in 1928. The work is a trilogy consisting of *The Bridal Wreath* (1920), *The Mistress of Husaby* (1921), and *The Cross* (1922). Dan and Winnie probably read the Knopf American translation of 1927. The work has some properties of the epic, but it is a bleak and melancholy story set in medieval Norway in the first half of the 14th century in which sin, guilt, and the difficulties of securing redemption outweigh whatever happiness or joy life might bring. It is still read today, promoted as a 'historical' novel, but I doubt that either Dan or Winnie read it in that spirit.

24. WKDP: WKD to DMD, 17, 25, and 26 Feb. and 7 Mar. 1933.

25. WKDP: WKD to DMD, 7 Mar. 1933.

26. WKDP: DMD to WKD, [10 Aug. 1934?].

27. 26 Apr., at the Grand Hotel: tickets 5s. 6d.

28. Which was divided in 1934 between those whose primary interest was drama and dramatic productions, and those whose interests were, like Dan's, primarily literary. After some controversy the Society split in two at the end of the first term, and Dan and Frank Guest organized a new Literary Society that turned out to be much smaller and, one imagines, more intellectual than its predecessor.

29. *The Critic*, vol. x, no. 5, 7 June 1934, p. 1.

30. WKDP: DMD to WKD, 28 Mar. 1934.

31. There is one entry for 20 June, then a few pages more at the beginning of Sept. After that, nothing until Oct. 1936 in Oxford.

32. Older brother of Muff, Dan's friend in Invercargill. Earl was a train driver in Dunedin, earning a reasonable wage, and he was often generous to Dan, taking him out for a drink, or to dinner at a smart spot like Cargill's.

33. WKDP: DMD to WKD, 30 Apr. 1934.

34. WKDP: DMD to WKD, 23 May 1934.

35. Ibid.

36. WKDP: DMD to WKD, 28 May 1934.

37. WKDP: WKD to DMD, 29 May 1934.

38. WKDP: DMD to WKD, 1 June 1934.

39. Where they visited Dan's younger brother Pat, who at the age of 16 had left school and gone to work on a sheep station.

40. The paper has not survived, but DMD's 'Remarks on the Decadence in English Poetry of the 1890s', Otago University *Review*, 1934, pp. 22–5, is presumably a condensed version of his main arguments. It was awarded the Literary Society's essay prize jointly with an essay on 'Theology and Art' by Arthur Prior. The judge, Professor Ramsay, damned both with faint praise (ibid., 29–31). A. N. Prior was a student in Knox College, memorable to Dan and Winnie then because along with Divinity he was also reading Dante: unusual at the time, perhaps still. He became a philosopher, and, from 1966, fellow and tutor in Philosophy in Balliol College Oxford.
41. Mick had been a popular young man in Southland, bright and happy, a keen sportsman, a good organizer of Southland boxing tournaments. The local people planted a tree to his memory. It is still there, broad and strong, on the hill behind the Otautau recreation ground.
42. WKDP: WKD to DMD, 16 July 1934.
43. WKDP: DMD to WKD, 17 Aug. 1934. 'It seems ages since I have had a letter from you. You never write at all to me nowadays. I know nothing of what you do or think or say or feel.'
44. Ibid.
45. WKDP: DMD to WKD, [25 July 1934?].
46. WKDP: DMD to WKD, 16 July 1934. Her father was on the Professorial Board.
47. WKDP: DMD to WKD, 29 July 1934.
48. WKDP: DMD to WKD, 'Friday' [10 Aug. 1934?].
49. Behind L. F. (Lester) Moller, a lawyer and sportsman, and later a Judge of the Supreme Court; Cuddon, his old companion from SHC; and G. S. (Torrance) Doig, his new friend.
50. WKDP: DMD to WKD, 28 Aug. 1934. A quotation from it heads this chapter.
51. WKDP: WKD to DMD, 30 Aug. 1934.
52. DMDP: notebook. The pages are unnumbered.
53. DMDP: Peggy Spence-Sales to DMD, 2 Sept. 1934.
54. They thought they had found a buyer in late July, but the deal fell through.
55. It must be said that this is Winnie's version. Peggy Spence-Sales died in Aug. 1993, at her home near Grasse in the south of France, without my being able to talk to her.
56. The other was Lester Moller.
57. WKDP: DMD to WKD: n.d. [22 Oct. 1934?].
58. National Archives, Rhodes Scholarship Selection Committee. AAMJ Acc W3119 479. Minutes.
59. Miles had recently been appointed to the Chair of Mathematics at Victoria University College.
60. In New Zealand, a second home or cottage, generally at the seaside. Dan would have called it a crib, the term employed in Otago and Southland.

61. Eileen Deste, 1909–86. English in origin, she was born Eileen Leach, but left home, which she hated, in 1928, and set up as a photographer. She went to New Zealand in the early 1930s and had a studio first in Dunedin, and subsequently in Wellington, for a number of years at 101 Willis Street. She lived in a flat at 223 The Terrace, where Peggy shared a room with her. '[F]or me she was a kind of family I had adopted in preference to my own' (DMDP: Peggy Spence-Sales to DMD, 14 Mar. 1986).

62. Even though his disappearance was partially planned. He had written to Peggy during November, encouraging her to find somewhere for them to be together. Perhaps his original intention had been to stay only a day or two, but the Rhodes failure led him to change his mind. See DMDP: Peggy Spence-Sales to DMD, 19 Nov. 1934.

63. WKDP: WKD to DMD, 5 Dec. 1934. This beautiful and powerful letter, written when Dan was 'missing' in Wellington, establishes the tone of her feelings: generosity and sadness together. She decided not to send it, but after they had rowed she changed her mind. His reply of 8 Jan. 1935 is in quite a different manner.

64. She signed her letter of thanks 'Twinkleberry' (DMDP: Peggy Spence-Sales to DMD, [21 Dec. 1934?]). In her letter of 19 Nov. she had written him a poem of her own:

> Soft is this grass that I touch,
> Warm this brown earth and strong,
> For your lips my beloved I thirst,
> On your breast will I greet the fair Dawn.

65. WKDP: DMD to WKD, 8 Jan. 1935.

66. Otago University *Review*, 1935, p. 62.

67. There were only three places allocated in 1935 for students from Southland. Dan may have been overqualified, or qualified in the wrong subjects if they were looking for future maths or science teachers. He could be excused, however, for sensing discrimination once again.

68. Later a barrister and politician, Minister of Justice in the NZ Labour Government 1972–5.

69. The editor in 1935 was E. M. Elder, a medical student.

70. *The Critic*, vol. xi, no. 3, 19 Apr. 1935, p. 11.

71. Ibid., no. 2, 5 Apr. 1935, p. 9.

72. Cecil John Morkane, a secular priest, originally from Dunedin, who trained at St Patrick's College, Manly (Sydney, Australia), and the Irish College, Rome. He was professor 1904–20, and Rector 1920–34 of Holy Cross Seminary, Mosgiel, and had the reputation of an approachable, paternal figure. Students from Holy Cross followed courses at Otago University, and Dr Morkane would have been well known to the university faculty.

73. First appointed a part-time lecturer in 1916, he became Dean in 1935, and remained so until 1961 when he was succeeded by Frank Guest, who had himself been appointed Professor of Law at Otago in 1959.

74. The admiration was not reciprocated. 'Aubrey and she are I think the type who make love to other wives and husbands and then go to bed to compare notes' (WKDP: DMD to WKD, 21 June 1935).
75. WKDP: WKD to DMD, 27 May 1935.
76. Alice McKenzie, *Pioneers of Martin's Bay* (1947).
77. WKDP: WKD to DMD, 11 July 1935.
78. WKDP: WKD to DMD, 16 June 1935.
79. WKDP: WKD to DMD, 27/28 June 1935. Perhaps we can also detect here the influence of Sigrid Undset: 'this wild heart of yours will yet bring more sorrow over you and yours. You tug and strain like a young horse when 'tis first tied up to the stake, wherever you are tied by your heart-strings' (*The Mistress of Husaby*, 219).
80. Margaret Agnes Peacock, 1913–85. She married in 1939 and had five children, but after 1937 had passed completely out of DMD's life.
81. DMDP: letters from Peggy Peacock.
82. Morrell, *University of Otago*, 124.
83. WKDP: DMD to WKD, 8 July 1935.
84. Hocken: MS 641/4 OUSA Executive Minutes 1933–36, 22 Aug. 1935.
85. Ibid., University file no. 238. June 1935–Sept. 1936.
86. He was so poor that when the *Review* eventually came out he could not afford to send copies to Winnie.
87. DMDP: Peggy Spence-Sales to DMD, 4 Nov. 1935.
88. WKDP: DMD to WKD, [5 Dec. 1935?].
89. He was appointed a Justice of the NZ Supreme Court in 1957.
90. Much of this account rests on the testimony of DMD and WKD. DMD certainly sought out gossip about the incident throughout his life. The minutes of the Rhodes Selection Committee contain no account of it. The papers of Sir Michael Myers have been dispersed, and for the most part lost. There is no reference to any correspondence between Myers and members of the Professorial Board at Otago University among either the University holdings, or, in so far as I was able to establish, in the Hocken. Various people in the New Zealand legal community who knew both Myers and Haslam, though later in life, say that the roles I attribute to them here sound entirely in character. The main point, however, whatever the detail, is that DMD was discriminated against in 1934, but not in 1935. Something had changed. Crucial in this was surely the Otago University Professorial Board's decision to nominate him again, a move that they would no doubt have co-ordinated with informal approaches.
91. WKDP: DMD to WKD, [5 Dec. 1935?].
92. Where Mike Joseph went to teach English in 1936. Dan declined the SHC invitation because he wanted to stay near Winnie.
93. WKDP: WKD to DMD, 18 Mar. 1936.
94. Otago University MS 641/13, OUSA Capping Ball Reports, 1929–1941. Martyn Finlay was the Ball convenor. Newspapers used to carry attendance lists for the Ball. The *Evening Star* had Mr D. M. Davin there

unaccompanied, as also a Miss P. Spence-Sales. The *ODT* had neither of them. Winnie's dance card for the occasion shows that Dan filled in his own name for every dance, though Winnie recalled being more sociable.
95. WKDP: DMD to WKD, n.d. [15 July 1936?].
96. WKDP: DMD to WKD, 20 Feb. 1936.
97. The Rhodes Scholarship was worth £400 a year in England, but you had to get there to collect it. It did not pay fares.
98. WKDP: DMD to WKD, [25 May 1933?].
99. 'To shout' in Australia and New Zealand, to treat, or pay for someone.
100. M. K. Joseph, 'A Private Movie', unpub. memoir, p. 48.

Chapter 6: *Rhodes Scholar*

1. WKDP: DMD to WKD, 11 Oct. 1936.
2. *GBP*, p. 101. DMD began writing this story in Cairo in Aug. 1942 and finished it in Palestine the following Feb., so he must have had it on his mind for five years.
3. Dan's old friend Frank Hall was the editor.
4. DMDP: Joan McGrath to DMD, 30 Nov. 1936. Tom and Adelina were married on 2 Feb. 1939, after Tom had qualified LL B at Victoria University College through evening classes. He was awarded his LL M a year later.
5. DMDP: Marge Thompson to WKD and DMD, 14 Feb. 1939.
6. Father Basil Blake, Society of Mary: 1904–61. Priest and schoolteacher; MA Victoria University College, and in Oxford 1936–8 for further study.
7. A lecture 'which appears to have had very little effect' (DMD in a recorded interview with James McNeish for the NZBC, 'Intimate Strangers', 1980).
8. DMDP: 'DMD's first years in Oxford', n.d., a short manuscript that may be a transcript of an informal talk. See also notebook, Tuesday 10 Nov.
9. DMDP: 'DMD's first years in Oxford', p. 1.
10. WKDP: DMD to WKD, 11 Nov. 1936.
11. WKDP: DMD to WKD, 28 Oct. 1936.
12. Ibid.
13. WKDP: DMD to WKD, 21 May 1937.
14. Otago University *Review*, 1938, 'Exiled', p. 20.
15. WKDP: DMD to WKD, 23 Jan. 1937.
16. Ibid.
17. DMDP: notebook, 6 Nov. 1936. They had been listening to 'Strauss on Russia'.
18. Ian Milner, *Intersecting Lines: The Memoirs of Ian Milner*, ed. and introd. Vincent O'Sullivan (Wellington, 1993), 134.
19. See Ian Milner, *Milner of Waitaki* (Dunedin, 1983), *passim*.
20. As were his contemporaries James Bertram and Charles Brasch, who both played parts in Dan's later literary life.

21. So much so that he had actually mentioned it as one career objective in his second Rhodes application.
22. WKDP: DMD to WKD, 11 Nov. 1936.
23. DMDP: notebook, 14 Nov. 1936. 'DMD's first years in Oxford', p. 2. In his state of first-term misanthropy, however, Dan was still critical: 'Afternoon went to pretty bloody picture with Sitwell. Talked to him on return but he is pretty heavy going and I can't stand his pals' (notebook, 26 Nov.).
24. DMDP: Gordon Craig, 'Balliol, 1935–1939', a memoir, p. 26.
25. Arthur Pyper, interview, 22 Aug. 1992.
26. Balliol College archives: Arthur Pyper, 'Balliol 1935–1939', a memoir, p. 3.
27. Letter from WKD, 26 Apr. 1994.
28. Letter from Hart Massey, 21 June 1994.
29. Gordon Craig, 'Balliol, 1935–1939', p. 39.
30. Denis Healey, *The Time of My Life* (1989), 30.
31. Craig Papers, Diary, 26 Jan. 1938.
32. Pyper's speech-notes are among his papers in the Balliol archives. Davin's are in DMDP. DMD's gift for aphorism and the focused barb is much in evidence, e.g.: 'England's only gift to Ireland was the gift of political martyrdom which she bestowed with a generosity and discrimination conspicuously lacking in her other dealings with that country.' And: 'When free speech is completely suppressed and impartial justice unobtainable the treachery of a persecuted minority is on any fair judgement the sign of praiseworthy tenacity.'
33. WKDP: DMD to WKD, 21 Dec. 1936.
34. DMDP: 'DMD's first years at Oxford', p. 2.
35. WKDP: DMD to WKD, 12 Feb. 1937.
36. In Australia and New Zealand, to be drunk.
37. The 25 American Rhodes scholars of 1936 were 'Brothers' as a result of sharing the experience of a dangerous storm crossing the Atlantic on the *Laconia*.
38. Gordon Craig, 'Balliol, 1935–1939', 26–8.
39. He was originally Joel Lipsky, which he changed to Carmichael. He came from New York, where his father was a founder of the American Zionist movement.
40. Philip Kaiser, 'Guy Nunn, 1914–1984', in *The American Oxonian*, vol. lxxii, no. 2, Spring 1985, pp. 146–9. See also his *Journeying Far and Wide: A Political and Diplomatic Memoir* (New York, 1992), 45–103.
41. Gordon Craig, 'Balliol, 1935–1939'. The songs quoted here are at pp. 31 and 35–6. There is also a tape recording, Rostow on piano, vocals by Craig, recorded at the LBJ Library in Austin, Texas.
42. Gordon Craig, interviews, 19 and 21 May 1994.
43. There are two Gardeners Arms in North Oxford, and both eventually became important in Dan's life. The other one is in North Parade. Neither of them has an apostrophe.

44. Craig Papers, Diary, 13 May 1937; 23 Jan., 5 Feb., 14 Mar., 16 Mar., 21 Mar., 7 Apr., 29 May 1938.
45. At his first meeting with her, Gordon Craig immediately detected her power over DMD, particularly in alleviating his depressions: 'Davin's *fiancée* is charming. She told us stories all afternoon. Dan, for the first time since I have known him, was good-natured while silent' (Craig Papers, Diary, 4 Dec. 1937).
46. In the autumn and winter of 1937–8 he had an affair with a New Zealand student, Helen Coates. She subsequently married John Garrett, 1913–93, a Canadian Rhodes Scholar in Merton, and an occasional member of DMD's pub circle. He was Professor of English at Canterbury University, New Zealand, 1949–78. Letter from Helen Garrett, 27 Feb. 1995.
47. DMD reported going into Craig's rooms late at night and setting fire to one of his socks 'before his astonished eyes' (DMDP: DMD to Paish Johnson, 2 Nov. 1937). Fred Petricevich described Dan in London 'tearing down grills and removing any fixtures he takes fancy to' (Petricevich to Bob Cotterall, 1 Dec. 1936). The tone and bizarre nature of Petricevich's letters makes him an unreliable witness, however.
48. RTA: DMD file, confidential report to the New Zealand selection committee. Allen, in turn, is here quoting reports from Lindsay in Balliol.
49. DMDP: Diary, 29 Dec. 1940 and 24 June 1943.
50. WKDP: DMD to WKD, 21 Dec. 1936.
51. Ibid.
52. Ibid.
53. Ibid.
54. Patrick O'Farrell, *Vanished Empires: Irish in Australia and New Zealand: A Personal Excursion* (Kensington, NSW, 1990), 183.
55. WKDP: DMD to WKD, 21 Dec. 1936.
56. 'Galway, 1936', Otago University *Review*, 1938, p. 20.
57. WKDP: DMD to WKD, 21 Dec. 1936.
58. WKDP: DMD to WKD, 23 Jan. 1937.
59. Ibid.
60. DMDP: Diary, 8 July 1942.
61. Craig Papers, Diary, 21 Mar. 1938.
62. RTA: Lindsay's reports on DMD, Trinity and Michaelmas terms 1937.
63. WKDP: DMD to WKD, 28 Mar. 1937.
64. DMDP: Hannah Kahn to DMD, 11 June 1937. In his notebook, 10 Apr. 1937, reading Dostoevsky was 'like a new discovery'.
65. DMDP: notebook, 14 Apr. 1937.
66. The neighbourhood has been redeveloped somewhat since the 1930s, though the prison is still there. The Square de Port-Royal is now a development of modern apartments.
67. There were 132 francs to the pound sterling in 1937, and a good dinner at L'Alsacienne cost 10 francs or so. There is still a restaurant at 64

Boulevard de Port-Royal, but it has changed regions, and is now Le Languedoc.

68. DMDP: 'DMD's first years in Oxford', p. 4.
69. Ibid.
70. DMDP: DMD to Paish Johnson, 2 Nov. 1937.
71. DMDP: 'DMD's first years at Oxford', p. 6. Interesting things always happened in Flavell's company. He spent a long weekend in Oxford with Dan at the end of Oct. 1937, a lot of the time looking at pictures. Walking up the High they ran into Winnie McQuilkan, who reacted as though 'unexpectedly confronted by Lucifer and Beelzebub' (DMDP: DMD to Paish Johnson, 2 Nov. 1937).
72. DMDP: DMD to Mary Davin, 6 Sept. 1937.
73. At the end of Trinity term 1938 Dan spent a month from mid-June to mid-July in lodgings in the nearby village of Great Bookham so as to be close to Winnie till the end of her term (DMDP: DMD to Mary Davin, 21 June 1938).
74. DMDP: DMD to John Ayre, 24 Dec. 1979.
75. WKD to Marge Thompson, 13 Jan. 1939.
76. The stories were 'In Hell's Despite', 'Abel as Cain', 'Summer Storm', 'Boarding House Episode', 'Late Snow', 'The Vigil', and 'Toby'. The first three have never been published. The other four, much reworked, are in GBP, where 'Toby' is retitled 'Death of a Dog'.
77. DMDP: John Hackney to Elspeth Lloyd, 30 Jan. 1939.
78. DMDP: DMD to Mary Davin, 21 June 1938; Frank Hall to DMD, 18 Sept. 1938. WKD to Marge Thompson, 13 Jan. 1939. WKDP: DMD to WKD, 'Tuesday 13 Feb.' [14 Feb. 1938?].
79. A. J. P. Taylor's term to describe the diplomatic interlude between the Munich and Polish crises, a hollow echo of Chamberlain's 'peace for our time', captures well the feelings and expectations of this generation in the year that preceded war (A. J. P. Taylor, The Origins of the Second World War (London, 1961), 187–214).
80. WKDP: DMD to WKD, 22 Nov. 1938.
81. They said their farewells on 18 June 1938, and did not meet again for 14 years, the continuity of their friendship, like so many others, a casualty of the war.
82. Though not the by-laws. He was arrested one night, walking home from the pub, for urinating in the street. The overtones of the juvenile—a slightly more adult version of the childhood shanghai incident—did nothing to improve his opinion of authority.
83. WKDP: DMD to WKD, 'Tuesday' [14 Mar. 1939?].
84. Philip Kaiser, 'Guy Nunn, 1914–1984', 146–9.
85. WKDP: DMD to WKD, 18 Oct. 1938.
86. DMDP: Diary, 17 Oct. 1943, where he calls it 'the old haunt'. Later, he surely came to see its similarities to the occasional residences of Uncle Giles, Nick Jenkins's relative in The Music of Time. 1 Sept., DMD's birthday, is St Giles's day.

87. WKDP: DMD to WKD, 18 May 1939.
88. Lindsay stood as an independent candidate in opposition to appeasement, and had help from Liberal, Conservative, and Labour supporters. Quintin Hogg was 'the champion of Munich' (A. J. P. Taylor, *English History 1914–1945* (London, 1965), p. 436). Lindsay lost, even though Oxford was 'an untypical constituency' (Maurice Cowling, *The Impact of Hitler: British Politics and British Policy 1933–1940* (Cambridge, 1975), p. 218).
89. Geoffrey Flavell liked to say that actually *he* was responsible. Giving Winnie a lift to London from Oxford in his 'little Ford' one Sunday night, they were involved in an accident near Thame caused by a 'young blood' speeding in an Aston Martin. Winnie was flung out of the car, but landed unhurt on a grass bank. Flavell played his doctor card handily, and later in court asserted that Winnie had suffered from shock. She was awarded £30 in damages. 'This enabled them to marry, so it was entirely my doing' (Geoffrey Flavell, interview, 12 Dec. 1991). This is a typical Flavell story. Winnie had actually hurt her back quite badly, her dress was torn and ruined, her handbag lost. £30 seems little enough compensation.
90. Bob Cotterall, private diary entry.
91. Arthur Pyper, 'Balliol 1935–1939', 5–6. Interview, 22 Aug. 1992.
92. W. K. Davin, 'A Soldier's Wife', in Lauris Edmond (ed.), *Women in Wartime: New Zealand Women Tell Their Story* (Wellington, 1986), 65.

Chapter 7: *From Oxford to Crete*

1. W. K. Davin, 'A Soldier's Wife', in Lauris Edmond (ed.), *Women in Wartime: New Zealand Women Tell Their Story* (Wellington, 1986), 66.
2. Geoffrey Cox, *A Tale of Two Battles* (London, 1987), 21–3, records others of Colonel Bingham's eccentricities.
3. DMDP: Diary, 17 Jan. 1940.
4. Letter from Hugh Lee, 6 Apr. 1992. A haka is a Maori war chant accompanied by expressive gestures.
5. Dan's friendship with Heugh was deep but short. Drummond wanted to join the Black Watch, but they would not have him. He got a transfer to the Royal Air Force, and after flight training in Canada served in aerial reconnaissance. He went missing, believed killed in action, towards the end of the war.
6. Letter from Hugh Lee.
7. Ibid.
8. Geoffrey Cox, interview, 13 Dec. 1991.
9. DMD's personal military file, held at New Zealand Defence Force HQ records, contains the correspondence relating to his transfer, as well as copies of his various awards, honours and appointments, wartime gratuities and history sheet. DMDP contains a number of documents and military memorabilia, including his pay books. Where administrative

NOTES

details of his military career are given here, and in Chs. 8 and 9, these two archives are, unless otherwise stated, the source.

10. Details are in W. G. McClymont, *To Greece* (Wellington, 1959), 25–42. See also Cox, *A Tale of Two Battles*, 18–26.
11. Angus Ross, *23 Battalion* (Wellington, 1959), 15.
12. DMDP: Diary, 23 July 1940.
13. Ibid., 19 Aug. 1940. 'I had too much home-cured bacon as a child not to find it tiresome.'
14. Geoffrey Cox, Interview.
15. Anthony Powell, *The Kindly Ones* (1962), 76.
16. DMDP: Diary, 12 Sept. 1940.
17. Ibid., 27 Nov. 1940.
18. Ibid., 16 Dec. 1940.
19. Ibid., 29 Dec. 1940.
20. Ibid., 9 Jan. 1941.
21. Ibid.
22. J. F. Cody, *28 (Maori) Battalion* (Wellington, 1959), 88 and 104.
23. *CT*, p. xviii.
24. *E. A. Forsman: Priest, Padre, Poet 1909–1976* (Auckland: private circulation, 1992). 'He liked the company and the banter of those caught up in the publishing process', p. 15. When he stayed with the Davins in Oxford after the war he used to sing opera about the house, mainly Mozart.
25. DMDP: Diary, 9 Jan. 1941.
26. The official history reports only 'five delightful days in Cape Town' (McClymont, *To Greece*, 42). The quotations are from DMDP: Diary, 13 Feb. 1941. Lessons of the New Zealand visit were learnt promptly. Guy Crouchback, commenting on the efforts of reception committees in Cape Town later in Feb. 1941, reported them as 'partly to keep the soldiery out of mischief. I gather they had trouble with the last Trooper' (Evelyn Waugh, *Officers and Gentlemen* (1955), 107).
27. DMDP: Diary, 18 Mar. 1941.
28. Ibid., 23 Mar. 1941.
29. Ibid., 18 Mar. 1941.
30. Ibid., 29 Dec. 1940.
31. Ibid., 29 Mar. 1941.
32. At Piraeus he wrote a poem, 'Night Before Athens'. It is characteristic of the 30 or so poems that Dan wrote between 1936 and 1943, and thus perhaps deserving of a little commentary:

> Pack up the baggage once again,
> Again dissolve our world, create anew
> A universe, perfect and impermanent
> As ripple-pattern; let the new life
> Break the old as dawn the dream,
> And out of the chrysalis of this self

411

Soon dead come forth next
Weaving itself a fresh complex
And forging the chains of yet another tyranny.
Bonding habits must be broken and new bound
Until the last of all our worlds
Is ours, that habit of eternal stillness,
Our last chrysalis, the grave.

The tone of the 'poet's voice' is stereotype, a sinking into convention, and creates the impression (perhaps not entirely valid) of sterile metaphysics couched in images that are forced when they are not clichés. Dan was a perceptive and supple critic, and came to see, by the time he was 30 or so, that such poetic talent as he then had was in conflict with his intellectual habits of analysis. Of the few poems that he published, two might repay close attention, 'Galway, 1936' and 'The Gorse Blooms Pale', which he also called 'Knowledge' and 'Perspective'. In old age (see below, Ch. 14) he had what he called another 'attack of poetry' and produced enough for a slim volume. These are far better, witty, playful, occasionally intense: evidence of a poetic sensibility.

33. Ross, *23 Battalion*, 36.
34. DMDP: Diary, 3 Apr. 1941.
35. McClymont, *To Greece*, 117–314.
36. The higher strategic reasons for Lustre Force and the Greek campaign, largely irrelevant to a biography of one subaltern, are summarized in Charles Cruickshank, *Greece, 1940–1941* (London, 1976), 105–17. Dan's own view mirrored the official Allied position. 'Have grave doubts as to the expediency, though none as to the obligation, of trying to hold Greece' (Diary, 6 Apr. 1941). The confusions of strategic and military intelligence in this campaign are summarized in F. H. Hinsley *et al.*, *British Intelligence in the Second World War*, i (London, 1979), 360–73. And its effects are emphasized in Correlli Barnett, *The Desert Generals*, 2nd edn. (London, 1983), 46, where he asserts that intervention in Greece 'prolonged the war in Africa by two years'.
37. Ross, *23 Battalion*, 36.
38. DMDP: Diary, 14 Apr. 1941.
39. Ross, *23 Battalion*, 40. The account in McClymont, *To Greece*, 263, is slightly different. DMD read and commented on Ross's manuscript.
40. Balanitis, of which there are various kinds, is inflammation of the glans, or head of the penis, almost certainly caused in Dan's case by rubbing from wet and unclean clothing. This is a painful ailment, not uncommon among infantrymen. Once infected it becomes not only more painful but, untreated, dangerous.
41. Ross, *23 Battalion*, 45–7.
42. Ibid. 47–8.
43. DMDP: Diary, 25 Apr. 1941.
44. Ibid. The river was the Sperkhios.

45. McClymont, *To Greece*, 355, calls this sequence of exhausting and irritating changes 'laborious adjustments'.
46. DMDP: Diary, 25 Apr. 1941.
47. Ibid.
48. Ibid., 30 Apr. 1941.

Chapter 8: *From Crete to Tunis*

1. Francesco Basilicata in 1612, quoted in John Hale, *The Civilization of Europe in the Renaissance* (New York, 1994), 15.
2. DMDP: Diary, 5 May 1941.
3. Ibid.
4. Ibid., 30 Apr. 1941.
5. Leckie, who had been replaced as CO of 23 Battalion by Falconer for the Greek campaign, once again took command. He was CO 23 Battalion, Aug. 1940–Mar. 1941 and May 1941–June 1942. Brig. A. S. Falconer was CO 23 Battalion May–Aug. 1940 and Mar.–May 1941. He was a tobacconist from Dunedin turned regular soldier. His background and outlook were quite different from Dan's, who mistrusted him, especially after the Mt. Olympus incident (DMDP: Diary, 17 May 1941).
6. Ibid., 13 May 1941.
7. *Crete*, pp. 46–51, esp. p. 51 n. 2.
8. Ibid. 86.
9. DMDP: Diary, 'Morning of 20th' written 3 June 1941.
10. Ibid.
11. Ibid.
12. Ibid.
13. From an undated letter, DMD to WKD, copied and sent to Arthur Pyper by WKD, 7 Aug. 1941. She called it 'his melodramatic rescue'. For the record, the sniper seems actually to have been killed by men from another platoon.
14. 23 Battalion's losses on this first day of the battle of Crete were 7 dead and 30 wounded.
15. DMDP: Diary, 21 May, written 3 June 1941.
16. Ibid., 23 May 1941.
17. Ibid., 24 May 1941.
18. Ibid.
19. He did this straight away. The hand-written draft is in DMDP.
20. DMDP: Diary, 15 June 1941.
21. Ibid., 13 July 1941.
22. Ibid.
23. Edgar (Sir Edgar) (Bill) Williams, Chief of Intelligence on Montgomery's staff at Eighth Army HQ 1942–5; UN Security Council Secretariat, 1946–7; fellow of Balliol College, 1945–80; Warden, Rhodes House, 1952–80; Secretary of the Rhodes Trust, 1959–80; editor, *DNB*, 1949–80.

24. Another of Lindsay's young men, after the war he went to lecture in history at the University College of North Staffordshire, later Keele University.
25. Artemis Cooper, *Cairo in the War 1939–1945* (London, 1989), 148.
26. DMDP: Diary, 19 July 1942. Another interesting contrast between these two young officers: after the war DMD gave up shooting. Powell took up fox-hunting. Cooper, *Cairo in the War*, 148.
27. DMD moved in on 30 Aug. Cox initially put up most of the money, which DMD had to repay. He was anxious about money for most of his stay in Cairo. His allowances were only slightly more than half those of British officers of comparable rank. Price inflation in Cairo made life expensive, so sharing accommodation was essential. One letter in DMDP (DMD to I(a) Colonel [Quilliam?] but n.d. so perhaps never sent) indicates that he contemplated a transfer from 2NZEF to the British Army Intelligence Corps because of financial hardship.
28. A commonplace now. e.g. Leszek Kolakowski's 3-vol. history of Marxist thought (1978), in which the comparison of religious faith with Marxist dogma is drawn throughout.
29. Geoffrey Cox went, on secondment, to the New Zealand mission to the United States, the forerunner of the New Zealand Embassy in Washington, where he served as a diplomat under Walter Nash.
30. Winnie and Anna stayed with them from 10 May to 13 Oct. Ian Mason, a scientist, was working as supervisor in an explosives factory in Renfrewshire. The Masons' baby was born on 22 July.
31. WKD, 'A Soldier's Wife', in Lauris Edmond (ed.), *Women in Wartime: New Zealand Women Tell Their Story* (Wellington, 1986), 68–9.
32. See *Walter Smart by Some of his Friends* (London, 1963), which includes Lawrence Durrell, 'Thinking About Smartie', also published in Durrell's *Spirit of Place: Letters and Essays on Travel*, ed. Alan G. Thomas (London, 1969), 71–6. The Smarts' intellectual and social role in wartime Cairo is glossed in Artemis Cooper, *Cairo in the War*, 149–50.
33. Lawrence Durrell, English novelist, essayist, and poet. Most famous for his *Alexandria Quartet* (*Justine*, 1957; *Balthazar* and *Mountolive*, 1958; *Clea*, 1960). A small, aggressive man, he and Dan did not always get on.
34. Fedden and Spencer were lecturers at Fuad el Awal university. Together with Durrell they edited *Personal Landscape*, a literary journal that survived for eight issues between 1942 and 1945. Fraser worked for *Parade* magazine. See G. S. Fraser, *A Stranger and Afraid* (1983).
35. John Willett thought the others were probably two of Larry Durrell, John Waller, and David Hicks (interview, 13 Mar. 1993).
36. Fraser, *A Stranger and Afraid*, 124. Fraser's account of his own Cairo years is at pp. 120–70. See also Anna Davin, 'R. D. Smith', *History Workshop Journal*, 21, spring 1986, pp. 227–8.
37. Fraser, *A Stranger and Afraid*, 125.
38. Cooper, *Cairo in the War*, 155.

39. DMDP: Diary, 23 May 1942.
40. Olivia Manning, 1908–80. The novels are *The Danger Tree* (1977), *The Battle Lost and Won* (1978), and *The Sum of Things* (1980).
41. He died on 17 Jan. 1943. On a picnic expedition with his parents he picked up a stick bomb, and it blew up in his hands.
42. This is on the northern coast of the Flensburg Fiord, approximately 40 kilometres from the German frontier town of Flensburg. At the time of Elizabeth's birth this was part of Imperial Germany, but on the basis of a plebiscite after the First World War the disputed territory was divided, and her home was thenceforward the Danish town of Sønderborg.
43. Much of this information comes from Elizabeth Tylecote (née Reventlow, alias Berndt) herself (interview, 25 May 1992), but I am grateful to Delia Davin, and to John Tylecote—letters of 17 Dec. 1993 and 11 Feb. 1994—for additional material.
44. Elizabeth Tylecote, interview.
45. Geoffrey Cox, *A Tale of Two Battles* (London, 1987), 121–2.
46. Elizabeth was not a particularly good linguist, certainly not in the Smart, Costello, or Davin league. German was clearly her first language. Danish, which she professed to be her native tongue, she rarely if ever spoke, even with Danes whom she met later in life. Her Italian was eccentric, and even after many years' living in England her English remained idiosyncratic. However, she brought a dynamism and enthusiasm to speech which made much forgivable.
47. Elizabeth Tylecote, interview. The emphasis was in her voice.
48. The volume for the first months of 1942 was apparently lost. Entries in early 1943 are simply thin, four pages covering 15 weeks.
49. Elizabeth Tylecote, though she told me much that was of great interest, did not wish to discuss the details of this period, which in any event I do not think she could recall with precision, or perhaps which she preferred not to, having let them lie for so long.
50. *New Zealand Listener*, 20 Dec. 1986. DMD sent this poem to Elizabeth on 3 Aug. 1986 'with love'. Even allowing for the sentimental nostalgia of a now old and sick man, the implications reverberate. 'December' and 'summer' as a reversal of the European (though not the New Zealand, one must tread carefully) seasons, and the sense of an old man brooding on how youth, sweetness, and all its sources have been swept away, tempts one to retitle it 'December 1941'.
51. DMDP: Diary, 11 Jan. 1943.
52. Elizabeth Tylecote, interview.
53. DMDP: DMD, 'Paddy Costello', second draft of a manuscript memoir.
54. The operation, more severe for an adult in those days, was successfully performed on 17 Dec.
55. DMDP: Diary, 3 July 1942.
56. J. L. Scoullar, *Battle for Egypt: The Summer of 1942* (Wellington, 1955), 103–35.

57. There is a stiff upper lip account of these days in F. de Guingand, *Operation Victory* (London, 1947), 125–7. De Guingand was then Director of Military Intelligence.
58. The news was gazetted on 10 Jan. 1942, just as he finished ten days' convalescent leave after his tonsillectomy.
59. Elizabeth Tylecote, interview.
60. Not to be confused with J Force, the name given to New Zealand troops who participated in the occupation of Japan in 1945.
61. Though he gives the credit to Mainwaring, the GSO 1 Operations. See de Guingand, *Operation Victory*, 144–6.
62. F. H. Hinsley *et al.*, *British Intelligence in the Second World War*, ii (London, 1981), 410.
63. Who later changed his name to Darlot.
64. DMDP: Diary, 26 Oct. 1942.
65. Ibid., 22 Oct. 1942.
66. Ibid., 28 Oct. 1942.
67. Michael Carver, *El Alamein* (London, 1962), is a condensed account of the battle. It contains a chronology at pp. 206–7.
68. He had distinguished himself in Crete, after Dan was wounded, by acting as a stretcher-bearer, and was himself wounded and evacuated on 26 May.
69. DMDP: Diary, 29 Oct. 1942.
70. He had a brief interview with Freyberg on 24 Nov., always a sign that something was in the offing.
71. DMDP: Diary, 12 Jan. 1943.
72. Ibid., 26 Jan. 1943.
73. General Staff Officer, Grade 3, Intelligence—the officer responsible for military intelligence information at Divisional level.
74. DMDP: Diary, 11 Feb. 1943.
75. Noel Gardiner, *Freyberg's Circus: Reminiscences of a Kiwi Soldier in the North African Campaign of World War II* (Auckland, 1981), 79–100, 122–3, 134–6; and *Bringing Up The Rear: The Sequel to Frayberg's Circus* (Auckland, 1983), 61–4, 81.
76. DMDP: Diary, 11 June 1943.
77. Gardiner, *Freyberg's Circus*, 129. Sir Leonard Thornton, interview, 13 Aug. 1993, had no recollection of this incident, which DMD does not mention in his diary. However, DMD read and gave editorial advice on Gardiner's manuscript before publication.
78. DMDP: Diary, 21 May 1943.
79. Ibid., 25 May 1943.

Chapter 9: *The Toils of War*

1. They were 'A War Effort' and 'Bourbons'.
2. DMDP: Diary, 9 July 1943.
3. I am indebted to Richard and Pauline Austin, letters of 21 May 1994 and 16 Feb. 1995, for these details.

4. 'Schoon Zicht' is registered as a national monument for its connection with the history of whaling. In recent years it has served as an 'informal' museum, but is now owned by a Wesleyan Bible Society.

5. These details are reconstructed from DMDP: Mrs Williamson to DMD, ten letters from 7 Aug. 1943 to 13 Sept. 1945. DMD's Diary, 17 July 1943, mentions Mrs Williamson's sending a parcel to Winnie: 'that extraordinary hospitality with which the whites balance their deeds against the blacks'; but this is almost the only mention of her.

6. DMDP: Diary, 21 July 1943. His appointment was on 19 July. It was WKD who said that Mrs Williamson set it up.

7. Ibid., 19 Aug. 1943.

8. Ibid., 31 Aug. 1943.

9. Ibid., 26 Aug. 1943.

10. WKD, 'A Soldier's Wife', in Lauris Edmond (ed.), *Women in Wartime: New Zealand Women Tell Their Story* (Wellington, 1986), 71–2.

11. This happened on 29 Oct. 1942.

12. DMDP: Diary, 18 Dec. 1942.

13. Ibid., 17 Oct. 1943. Geoffrey Dawson 1874–1944, editor of *The Times* 1912–19 and 1923–41; a Rhodes Trustee from 1925. He had been a leading advocate of appeasement.

14. Ursula Joachim Beck, known as Ursy, a friend of Winnie's from the 1930s, was granddaughter of Joachim, the great violinist. A delightful and popular Oxford hostess for many years, she inherited Clara Schumann's pearls.

15. Walter Allen, novelist and critic. See W. E. Allen, *As I Walked Down New Grub Street: Memories of a Writing Life* (London, 1981). DMD reviewed it in the *New Statesman*, 4 Dec. 1981.

16. Robert Hewison, *Under Siege: Literary Life in London 1939–1945* (London, 1977), 99. Julian Maclaren-Ross, *Memoirs of the Forties*, introd. Alan Ross (Harmondsworth, 1984), 137–8, 141.

17. *CT*, p. 9.

18. And from 1940 books were exempt from purchase tax (Angus Calder, *The People's War: Britain 1939–45* (London, 1969), 508–23). The hunger for books was also created, like English town planning, by Hitler's bombers. Over 400 libraries were destroyed in the blitz, and five million books in publishers' stock were destroyed in the 1940 fire-bombing of London (Norman Longmate, *How We Lived Then: A History of Everyday Life during the Second World War* (London, 1971), 440–53. Oddly, one of the few publishing houses to avoid destruction on this occasion was OUP, whose premises in Amen Court, with a huge stock of Bibles, alone survived.

19. DMDP: Diary, 23 Nov. 1943. Their meeting was on Monday, 16 Nov. See also John Lehmann, *I am my Brother: Autobiography II* (London, 1960), 164.

20. Though, at least briefly, it was a close thing. 'An interesting weekend, leaving me shaken a bit. It's time I made up my mind. But I feel that the

sympathy I have for them would disappear if I became of them' (DMDP: Diary, 4 Nov. 1943). His weekend in Exeter was 29–31 Oct.

21. R. M. (Dick) Campbell, Economic Adviser at the New Zealand High Commission, London, from 1935. He served there almost continuously until his retirement as Deputy High Commissioner in 1958. His obituary in *The Times*, 4 Dec. 1974, called him 'a one man overseas diplomatic service for New Zealand'.

22. This was in the week 15–19 Nov. A plan for him to give a similar series of talks in Wales was dropped for shortage of time.

23. It was 26 Nov. Description is in DMDP: Diary, 27 Nov. 1943.

24. Julian Maclaren-Ross, 1912–64, a writer best remembered today as the original for X. Trapnel in Anthony Powell's *A Dance to the Music of Time*. In his memoir, 'Good Night, Julian, Everywhere' DMD dates their first meeting a year later, in the autumn of 1944, but this, like many of the detailed 'facts' in *Closing Times*, was not strictly true, but altered for reasons of literary effect. In the memoir, DMD also has a Welsh poet called Keidrych Rhys present at the first meeting, and, in the atmosphere of violent tension that pervades the opening exchanges of their conversation, Dan prepares to 'upset the table against his thighs and get my blow in before he recover[s] his balance', p. 4. This may not be true either. Rhys, whom DMD did know quite well (he was a regular at the Wheatsheaf), is not mentioned in the Diary, either for 1943 or 1944. The historian of wartime literary London, Robert Hewison, implies that this incident was between Dan and Julian, with Rhys not mentioned. See *Under Siege*, 66.

25. 2 NZ Div. was relieved at Orsogna by 4 Indian Division between 13 and 17 Jan. Details are in N. C. Phillips, *Italy*, i, *The Sangro to Cassino* (Wellington, 1957), 178–80.

26. Lt.-Gen. Sir Leonard Thornton, interview, 13 Aug. 1993.

27. Ibid. Paul Freyberg, *Bernard Freyberg, VC: Soldier of Two Nations* (London, 1991), 35–52, has the story in some detail. Freyberg was in the Hood Battalion of 2 Naval Brigade, and the clever young men were known as the 'Argonauts'. They included Arthur Asquith, son of the Prime Minister, Rupert Brooke, the poet and two Balliol men, Cleg Kelly, a music scholar, and Charles Lister, a classicist. Timmy, the younger brother of Freyberg's wife, Barbara Jekyll, won an Exhibition to Balliol at the turn of the century. Freyberg was supposedly in awe of Balliol men. One would have thought that by the time Dan arrived at the Italian front, Paddy would have done his best to put him right about this.

28. Sir John White, interview, 19 Nov. 1992. Sir John, who was the very last recruit to the first echelon of troops when it left New Zealand in Jan. 1940, served as Freyberg's personal assistant throughout the war.

29. DMDP: DMD, 'Paddy Costello', 33, contains some description. Also Sir Geoffrey Cox, interview, 13 Dec. 1991; and his *The Race For Trieste* (London, 1977), 64–8.

30. DMD to Geoffrey Cox, 17 Apr. 1944.
31. Murray Sidey, interview, 14 July 1993. Captain Sidey, from the prominent Dunedin family well known to Dan by reputation, was Intelligence
Officer to Divisional Artillery, Brigadier Weir's command. He served as
Freyberg's aide-de-camp for seven months from Dec. 1943 to July 1944.
32. Fred Kersh, interview, 20 July 1993. There is a portrait of Kersh at work
in Cox, *The Race for Trieste*, 64–5.
33. Letter from Sir Geoffrey Cox, 4 July 1994.
34. Sir Leonard Thornton, interview.
35. Brigadier H. E. (Bill) Gilbert, DSO, OBE, 1916–87, served as GSO 1
2NZEF from May 1944 to June 1945. After the war he became Director
of the New Zealand Security Intelligence Service.
36. Sir Leonard Thornton, interview.
37. Letter from Sir Geoffrey Cox. Emphasis in the original.
38. He referred to this, with respect to his student days at Oxford, in
interview with James McNeish for the NZBC, 'Intimate Strangers',
1980. In respect of his HQ war service in Italy: 'Bewildered and bemused
by . . . the immense amount of work before me. Incapable of grasping
very much so far' (Diary, 26 Jan. 1944). He was not helped by a hangover
from the previous night's reunion with Paddy Costello.
39. Phillips, *Italy*, i. 196.
40. DMDP: Diary, 2 Mar. 1944.
41. Ibid.
42. NZ Corps consisted of 2 NZ Div., 4 Indian Division, various US
Army armour, artillery, and anti-aircraft units, and, from 17 Feb., 78
British infantry division. Freyberg was GOC NZ Corps, and under
him Kippenberger became, 9 Feb. to 2 Mar. GOC 2NZ Div. These
were the tips of a general administrative reorganization in which
Dan, promoted temporary major, was involved. The Corps IO was
now the centre of attention from other Divisional IOs, as also from
an increased corps of press correspondents. Telephones became a
bugbear to him at this time, an experience from which he never really
recovered.
43. 'Press correpondents, LO's [Liaison Officers], Americans, Peter of
Greece, idlers and gossips, a continual stream . . . Interpreters and inter-
rogators also torment me. And the phones are abominable' (DMDP:
Diary, 18 Feb. 1944). Peter of Greece was Prince Peter of the Hellenes.
DMD called him 'The Hellenes Hamlet . . . Princes now are like tonsils,
even if they're any good, not much use' (Diary, 13 Feb. 1944).
44. DMDP: Diary, 9 Feb. 1944.
45. Paul Freyberg, *Bernard Freyberg, VC*, 457–67.
46. Allied disagreement on operational priorities, and the difficulties that
immediately preceded the battle at Cassino, are dealt with briefly in John
Ellis, *Cassino: The Hollow Victory: The Battle for Rome January–June 1944*
(London, 1984), 1–37.

47. Though the French had fought well in the mountainous terrain to the north-west, and captured notorious topographical landmarks—point 470, point 700, Colle Abate—in an attempt to turn the German defensive position. General Juin's comments on the 34 US Division's contribution to this offensive would have got no dissent from DMD. See Ellis, *Cassino*, 153–6.
48. Phillips, *Italy*, i. 217.
49. Mark Clark, true to his own reputation, later claimed to have opposed the bombing, and laid the blame on Freyberg. In this, as in other matters, the record does little to support his memory. See Freyberg, *Bernard Freyberg, VC*, 535–7.
50. The best exposition of the arguments is still in Phillips, *Italy*, i. 211–22.
51. DMDP: DMD, 'Paddy Costello', 35. Paddy did not return. He was invited to join the fledgling New Zealand diplomatic service, and was posted to Moscow.
52. This account is based on Phillips, *Italy*, i. 232–40. Howard Kippenberger, *Infantry Brigadier* (London, 1949), 348–60, is the commanding officer's view of this operation. He also includes some comments about British and US systems of command.
53. J. F. Cody, *28 (Maori) Battalion* (Wellington, 1959) 362. There were 20 killed, 80 wounded, 24 POWs.
54. Charles Dickens visited the Monastery at Montecassino in 1845.
55. New Zealanders had already encountered him in Crete, where he commanded 3 Parachute Regiment.
56. Phillips, *Italy*, i. 270.
57. General the Hon. Sir Harold Alexander, from 9 Mar. 1944, Commander-in-Chief Allied Armies in Italy.
58. DMDP: Diary, 23 Mar. 1944.
59. Ibid.
60. Phillips, *Italy*, i. 331. Many units were extremely difficult to extricate, and were not out of the line until the night of 8–9 Apr. See Robin Kay, *Italy*, ii, *From Cassino to Trieste* (Wellington, 1967), 11.
61. Phillips, *Italy*, i. table at p. 356.
62. 2 NZ Div. was now part of Eighth Army's X Corps. On 15 Apr. it assumed command of the southern sector of X Corp's Apennine position.
63. Kay, *Italy*, ii. 19.
64. Murray Sidey, interview. This incident, recast to be told from the point of view of the General's driver, formed the kernel of DMD's story 'The General and the Nightingale', *GBP*, pp. 190–8.
65. Freyberg, *Bernard Freyberg, VC*, 465.
66. Paul Freyberg's assessment of what we might call his father's generosity with others' courage is one extreme of a spectrum of perceptions. At the other, equally untrue one imagines, is a postcard, obtainable at Maadi camp during the North African campaigns, that showed Freyberg dressed as a butcher in front of rows of garrotted kiwis.

67. DMDP: Diary, 23 May 1944.
68. Kay, *Italy*, ii. 62–3; DMDP: Diary, 30 May 1944.
69. All these matters are mentioned in Tom Davin's Diary for 1944, private collection.
70. Ibid., 15 May 1944.
71. 'How sour sweet music is | When time is broke, and no proportion kept! | So it is in the music of men's lives' (*Richard II*, v. v. 40–2). DMD went back to reading Shakespeare after Cassino.
72. Though Dan did not learn of this until 18 June. Winnie suffered a post-natal haemorrhage.
73. This was on 12 June. The account is in DMDP: Diary, 15 June 1944. The fictional version is 'Not Substantial Things' in *GBP*, pp. 203–16.
74. DMDP: Diary, 15 June 1944.
75. Ibid. 'Now I know', DMD comments, 'the intoxication of oratory, the temptation of a spellbound and easily moved audience, what it was like to be Mussolini.'
76. DMDP: Ida Storch to DMD, 26 Oct. [1944?], 13 Feb. 1945, 26 May [1945?]. She appears to have been employed at the Red Cross in Rome, and she certainly wrote fluent English. DMD sent her photographs, and was still corresponding with her a year later.
77. 'On the Caesar principle of better to be first man in a village than second in Rome, no doubt' (DMD to Geoffrey Cox, 17 Apr. 1944).
78. Ibid. With promotion, the pips on the shoulder of a lieutenant and captain were replaced, for a major, with the insignia of a crown. The Shakespearian allusion is to *2 Henry IV*, III. i. 30.
79. In the same playful letter to Geoff Cox in which he painted his word portrait of the café and the chapel, 17 Apr. 1944, DMD also wrote: 'And of course the war has only postponed the choice between the single domestic hearth and discriminating promiscuity.' This seems to me an expression of the reputation that DMD had cultivated in the Div. rather than of a choice seriously confronted.
80. Kay, *Italy*, ii. 98–100 has a good description of the journey forward. The engagements are at pp. 106–12.
81. See Cox, *The Race for Trieste*, 66, where he points out that although the Café was 'unorthodox by army standards' its open-door hospitality meant that its occupants were unusually well-informed.
82. DMDP: memo from S/L J. D. C. Curtis to M.I. 12, 9 Aug. 1944. The Summaries were nos. 1, 22/6/42 to 295, 18/7/44. DMDP contains a number of Intelligence Summaries, dated between 16 Jan. 1943 and 2 Jan. 1944. The later ones were written by Costello. None of them is by DMD.
83. DMDP: Diary, 3 Aug. 1944. DMD stopped keeping his diary at the end of Aug. 1944. Though there are brief entries for 17 Sept. 1944, 16 and 30 Apr., and 21 May 1945, he did not start again until Sept. 1945.
84. Her letters are dated 7 Aug. 1943, 16 Nov. 1944, 13 Dec. 1944, 14 Jan. 1945, 26 Jan. 1945, 7 Feb. 1945 (which apparently included a photograph of the

baby, now missing), 13 Mar. 1945, 13 Apr. 1945, 27 July 1945, 13 Sept. 1945. Dan Bill supposedly died some time between 13 Apr. and 27 July.

85. See *Troilus and Cressida*, III. iii. 140–5:

> Time hath, my lord, a wallet at his back,
> Wherein he puts alms for oblivion,
> A great-siz'd monster of ingratitude:
> Those scraps are good deeds past; which are devour'd
> As fast as they are made, forgot as soon
> As done.

The idea of forgetting the war was actually the opposite of what he intended, and *Alms for Oblivion* was in due course rejected at WKD's suggestion. DMD replaced it with *For The Rest Of Our Lives*.

86. 'The Vigil' (*Good Housekeeping*); 'Danger's Flower' (*Selected Writing*); 'Bourbons' (*Bugle Blast*, no. 3, 1945).
87. *Life & Letters Today*, Aug. 1945.
88. On 24 Apr. 1945.
89. Stanley Unwin, the publisher, had described it thus when declining it in 1942. John Hampson, in the *Spectator*, 1 June 1945, employed the same expression.
90. *CoF*, pp. 107–17; e.g. 'there's no tradition of doing nothing here. People who want to do nothing go abroad and call it travelling.'
91. Nick and Wat even gave them a pointer. The book 'has faults' they wrote on the cover fly, 'but in our opinion it is—faults and all—a remarkable first novel'.
92. *New Statesmen & Nation*, 19 May 1945.
93. *TLS*, 19 May 1945.
94. *Spectator*, 1 June 1945.
95. *New Zealand Listener*, 28 Sept. 1945.
96. Not far short of £10,000, or $NZ24,000 at 1995 prices.
97. Hewison, *Under Siege*, has a map at p. 59.
98. Vernon Scannell, *A Proper Gentleman* (London, 1977), 39.
99. I am indebted to John Ridge for this image.
100. Gerald Wilde, 1905–86. He is often thought, erroneously, to be the original for Joyce Cary's Gulley Jimson in *The Horse's Mouth*. As Maclaren-Ross points out, *Memoirs of the Forties*, 191–3, Wilde and Cary did not meet until after the war—DMD introduced them—while *The Horse's Mouth* was published in 1944. In any event, Wilde's rebelliousness was far less rational than Gulley's.
101. Tambi, like Keidrych Rhys, lost Dan's poems when they were sent to him by Nancy Pearn (DMDP: Nancy Pearn to WKD, 15 Mar. 1944).
102. Paul Ferris, *Dylan Thomas* (London, 1977), 189–215.
103. *CT*, p. 21.
104. His official title was: GSO 2, Documentation Section, Intelligence Sub Branch, National HQ, Army Division, Control Commission for Germany (BE).

105. DMDP: Maj.-Gen. West to Brig. A. S. Park, 25 June 1945.
106. DMDP: DMD to Bob Burchfield, 26 Mar. 1979.
107. DMDP: H. P. Smollett, Director, Soviet Relations Division, Ministry of Information to DMD, 8 Jan. 1945.
108. DMDP: DMD to Lindsay, 11 May 1945.
109. They were: 1939/45 Star; Africa Star; Italy Star; Defence Medal; War Medal; NZ War Service Medal; Oak Leaf Emblem.
110. DMDP: Sisam to DMD, 31 May 1945; DMD, 'Myself and the Oxford University Press: 1945—', p. 3.

Chapter 10: *Eight Virtuoso Years*

1. DMDP: Williamson to DMD, 27 July 1945.
2. DMDP: Joe Japolsky to DMD, 21 Feb. and 22 Mar. 1946.
3. DMDP: John Street to DMD, 17 Mar. 1946.
4. Michael Joseph to NZ Dept. of Internal Affairs, 4 Feb. 1947; DMD to Michael Joseph, 30 Apr. 1947.
5. Michael Joseph's father also sent them food parcels in the winter of 1946–7. And Freyberg later repeated his generosity by sending 15 lbs. of sweets and chocolates in Aug. 1949 when the sugar ration was cut and sweets put back on the points system. In Apr. 1950 he sent them a side of bacon (DMDP: Freyberg to DMD, 15 Aug. 1949 and 5 Apr. 1950).
6. The Davins owned three other Wilde Paintings: 'Stage Design', 'Sunlight', and 'Woman and Bird', and also a couple of drawings.
7. DMDP: DMD, 'Gerald Wilde', unfinished MS [1982?]. But WKD said this was not true.
8. DMDP: Diary, 1 Nov. 1949.
9. DMDP: Costello to DMD, 10 Mar. 1955.
10. *RFH*, p. 47.
11. ATL: MS-Papers-0432-155, DMD to Sargeson, 7 Mar. 1954.
12. D. Yarwood, *Architecture of England* (London, 1963) 439, H. M. Colvin, *Biographical Dictionary of British Architects* (London, 1978), 116. The name Clarendon, which was applied to the imprint for scholarly publications—'Oxford: at the Clarendon Press'—comes from the historian whose *History of the Great Rebellion* generated the profits from which the first Press office, the Clarendon Building, was erected in 1711–15. The interior buildings, behind the frontage on Walton Street, have been greatly modified over the years, most recently with a major rebuilding programme in the early 1990s.
13. OUPA: Sisam to Norrington, 4 Mar. and 18 Feb. 1952. There is a portrait of Kenneth Sisam, partially dependent on advice and information from DMD, in Peter J. Sisam, *Roots and Branches: The Story of the Sisam Family* (Stroud, 1993), 186–98. The fine, and rare, photograph of Sisam at p. 195 was taken by DMD. The best account of Sisam is still Neil Ker, 'Kenneth Sisam 1887–1971', in *Proceedings of the British Academy* (1972), 3–22.

14. DMDP: 'Myself and the Oxford University Press: 1945—' , uncompleted MS [1978?], 8.
15. Milford was publisher from 1913 to 1945, and Cumberlege from 1946 to 1956.
16. He subsequently returned as Printer himself, 1958–78. His wife, Anne Ridler, is a distinguished poet.
17. D. F. McKenzie, 'Letters from Denis Glover to John Johnson', in *Stuttgarter Arbeiten Zur Germanistik*, 189 (1987), 25–54. See p. 51 n.
18. DMDP: 'Myself and OUP', p. 9.
19. Bickham Sweet-Escott, *Baker Street Irregular* (London; 1965), 250: ' "Morning prayers" . . . the daily briefing of the staff . . .'.
20. DMDP: 'The Editor and the World', lecture to an OUP staff training conference, 1966.
21. DMDP: 'Myself and OUP', 14.
22. OUP was, and still is, an organization of acronyms. Dan, after a brief flirtation with DD, became DMD, and was to remain so to his colleagues at the Press for the rest of his life. The right to publish the Bible, which is held in common with Cambridge University Press and the Queen's Printer, derives from a Royal Charter of 1636. The cartographic department was, like DMD, new: established in 1946.
23. It also owned and operated a warehouse at Jordan Hill, just outside Oxford.
24. DMDP: 'Myself and OUP', 11.
25. Founded in 1923 and located, during Dan's career with OUP, in Conduit Street, just off New Bond Street.
26. A New Zealand subsidiary was opened in 1946. Many of the contracts to distribute books for foreign academic presses were entered into in the late 1940s and mid-1950s.
27. Equivalent to a profit—British and American activities combined—of approximately £8 million at 1995 prices.
28. DMDP: 'Myself and OUP', 6.
29. Ibid. 5.
30. University officials, elected annually, with disciplinary and administrative functions.
31. DMDP: 'Myself and OUP', 11.
32. Ibid. 12.
33. 27 Oct. 1948. Sisam's dinner was held on Monday, 1 Nov.
34. The London business submitted lists of planned new titles or series, but these were questioned only in unusual circumstances. For education books from the Oxford business, the Delegates took an interest in new series proposals, but individual titles for series already approved were agreed to *pro forma*.
35. There were thirteen meetings a year, four in each term, and one in the summer vacation. Meetings were changed to Thursdays on 26 Oct. 1967. 'Very unnatural . . . after all these years' (DMDP: Diary, 26 Oct. 1967).

36. DMDP: 'Myself and OUP', 13.
37. DMDP: Diary, 15 June 1949. The dates of this trip were 28 May–8 June.
38. He sailed on 22 Mar. 1952 (WKDP: DMD to WKD, 24, 25, and 26 Mar. 1952).
39. Craig Papers: Diary, 29 Mar.–1 Apr. 1952.
40. The printers first set it in the wrong fount (DMDP: Santer to DMD, 10 July 1946); then they were slow in printing and binding (Santer to DMD, 9 Oct. and 5 Nov. 1946).
41. DMDP: Stewart Scott to DMD, 28 July 1945; David Higham to DMD, 20 June 1947.
42. As soon as the typescript was finished he sent it to Geoff Cox for his opinion, and for his knowledge of the battle settings, and he took Cox's advice into account for the published version. Geoff Cox was now working as Parliamentary Lobby correspondent for the *News Chronicle* (DMDP: Geoffrey Cox to DMD, 29 Oct. [1945?]).
43. *FTROOL*, p. 135.
44. Ibid. 143.
45. Ibid. 204.
46. *John O'London's Weekly*, 13 June 1947.
47. BBC Home Service, 'Book Talk', Friday, 22 Aug. 1947.
48. *New Statesman & Nation*, 30 Aug. 1947.
49. *Tribune*, 15 Aug. 1947.
50. Southland *Times*, an anonymous review, 3 Sept. 1947. Kippenberger told Dan it was written by Monte Holcroft—'a pitiful effort' (DMDP: Kippenberger to DMD, 16 Dec. 1947).
51. *RSA Review*, Sept. 1947, signed E. G. W. Presumably E. G. (Ted) Webber, a former New Zealand serviceman then employed by the New Zealand Press Association in London.
52. DMDP: Arthur Sewell, script for a BBC radio talk broadcast on 26 Aug. 1947.
53. *Southern Cross*, 27 Sept. 1947.
54. *Landfall*, vol. 1, no. 4, Dec. 1947, pp. 325–8.
55. DMDP: Charles Brasch to DMD, 24 Mar. 1948.
56. *ODT*, 13 Sept. 1947; *New Zealand Listener*, 12 Sept. 1947.
57. Later Kippenberger wrote to DMD that he had met three old soldiers on a train journey and they had discussed *For The Rest of Our Lives*, in particular the scenes in Cairo. 'In the finish they all agreed it was right, one said his mother and wife were very upset' (DMDP: Kippenberger to DMD, 1 Apr. 1948).
58. *Our Time*, July 1947.
59. DMDP: draft letter, n.d. [Nov. 1948?], to Walter Nash, New Zealand Minister of Customs.
60. DMDP: letters from Brasch to DMD, 5 Mar. and 6 Apr. 1949; letters from Parsons to DMD, 23 and 27 Dec. 1948 and 16 Feb. 1949.
61. DMDP: Kippenberger to DMD, 15 Feb. 1949.

62. DMDP: Sargeson to DMD, 24 Jan. 1949. John Cole to DMD, 11 Jan. 1949, took much the same line.

63. Blackwood Paul, a New Zealand publisher, showed an interest in publishing a second edition in Oct. 1951, but decided it was uneconomic (DMDP: Blackwood Paul to DMD, 19 Oct. 1951, 18 Apr. 1952). He revived the idea during a visit to London in the autumn of 1964, and organized joint publication with Michael Joseph, with support from the New Zealand literary fund. The second edition of *FTROOL* was published in Britain on 11 Nov. 1965, and in New Zealand, one month later.

64. DMDP: Higham to DMD, 17 June and 22 Aug. 1947.

65. DMDP: Higham to DMD, 1 Dec. 1947 and 9 June 1949.

66. DMDP: Freyberg to DMD, 10 Sept. 1947; Kippenberger to DMD, 4 Aug. 1947.

67. DMDP: Sargeson to DMD, 24 Nov. 1947.

68. 'I learnt a lot from him, almost without knowing it. My own weakness in those days was the grand style. His company was therapeutic. It was he who pointed out to me that anecdotes of the war, which I used to tell and which I took to be no more than anecdotes, intent as I was on Tolstoy, were really short stories which needed writing. If it hadn't been for this I might never have written "The General and the Nightingale" ' (*CT*, p. 6).

69. K. John in *Illustrated London News*, 31 Jan. 1948.

70. Walter Allen in *The New Statesman & Nation*, 7 Feb. 1948.

71. *John O'London's Weekly*, 20 Feb. 1948. She called DMD 'among the most interesting of the younger writers, his style and outlook fresh and exhilarating'.

72. *New Zealand Listener*, 12 Mar. 1948. It was probably Oliver Duff, then the editor. Sargeson thought so. See DMDP: Sargeson to DMD, 13 June 1948.

73. (Clarendon Press, 1934).

74. DMDP: 'Myself and OUP', 3.

75. Anthony Powell, *The Valley of Bones* (1964), 206.

76. DMDP: Kippenberger to DMD, 14 May and 23 July 1947.

77. DMDP: Kippenberger to DMD, 1 Nov. 1948: 'You have enormously improved the book by your amendments'; and 30 Nov. 1948, in which he gave Dan 25 guineas' worth of books in gratitude.

78. Walter Allen was a great Cary advocate. See his 'The Future of Fiction' in *New Writing*, no. 36, 1949, pp. 102–7.

79. *CT*, pp. 93–120; Barbara Fisher (ed.) *Joyce Cary Remembered* (Gerrards Cross, 1988), esp. the contributions of Walter Allen, pp. 124–8; Enid Starkie, 135–7; Tristram Cary, 163–8; Delia Davin, 233–40; and Winifred and Dan Davin, 264–73.

80. DMD, *The Times*, 23 Apr. 1970.

81. Kate Whitehead, *The Third Programme: A Literary History* (Oxford, 1989), 67–105.

NOTES

82. He wrote for *Parson's Packet*, a sheet published in Wellington by the
bookseller Roy Parsons; *Here and Now*, a short-lived Auckland journal
with which Mike Joseph was associated; and *Landfall*, Charles Brasch's
progeny in Dunedin.
83. *CT*, p. 27. Jon Stallworthy, *Louis MacNeice* (London, 1995), 392–3.
84. *CT*, p. 28.
85. Vernon Scannell, *A Proper Gentleman* (1977), 39.
86. *CT*, pp. 45–61.
87. Cyril Ray in the *Sunday Chronicle*, Manchester, 17 Apr. 1949.
88. *Education*, vol. 2, no. 5, Nov. 1949, pp. 63–6.
89. *RFH*. See esp. pp. 123–8.
90. *Observer*, 10 Apr. 1949; *Punch*, 4 May 1949; *New Statesman*, review by J.
D. Scott, 21 May 1949; *John O'London's Weekly*, 29 Apr. 1949 (Pamela
Hansford Johnson expressed similar views in a review in *Tribune*, 15
Apr. 1949, though in each case the overall tone of her reviews was
warm); *TLS* 23 Apr. 1949.
91. Southland *Daily News*, 25 June 1949; *Landfall*, vol. 3, no. 3, Sept. 1949,
pp. 290–2.
92. DMDP: Robert Lusty to DMD, 4 May 1949.
93. DMDP: letters of 13 June, 26 and 27 Apr., and 26 July 1949.
94. DMDP: Higham to DMD, 3 Mar. 1949.
95. DMDP: Freyberg to DMD, 11 Mar. and 17 Apr. 1946.
96. DMDP: Kippenberger to DMD, 3 Oct. 1951.
97. Bryce Harland, later a distinguished New Zealand diplomat, recalled
encountering him in 1944, laboriously climbing the stairs (rather than
use the lift) of the New Zealand High Commission in Halifax House
in the Strand. Questioned about this, Kip replied that the Italian terrain
was difficult, and if he was to return to the Div. he must master the use
of his prosthetic limbs. He did return, but only as a visitor. There is a
vignette of him in this role in Geoffrey Cox, *The Race for Trieste*
(London, 1977), 24–5.
98. DMDP: Kippenberger to DMD, 30 Nov. 1948.
99. Christopher Buckley, *Greece and Crete* (London, 1952).
100. Angus Ross, DMD's contemporary at Otago in the early 1930s, had also
risen to the rank of major in the Div. A historian by training, he was a
man of great military daring, and was twice awarded the MC. After the
war he had two years as a research student at King's College Cambridge,
during which time he visited Dan and Winnie in Oxford.
101. DMDP: General H. R. Pownall to DMD, 26 Sept., 8 and 16 Oct.
1949.
102. DMDP: Diary, 26 May 1948.
103. Mabel (Dame Mabel: DBE, 1966) Tylecote: 1896–1987.
104. Letter from John Tylecote, 11 Feb. 1994.
105. *Historical Metallurgy*, vol. 25, no. 1, 1991. This issue of a journal which
Ronnie Tylecote helped to found, and of which he was for many years

editor, contains obituaries, appreciations, and a full bibliography of his numerous contributions to scholarship. See also *The Times*, 27 June and 11 July 1990. The Tylecote Research Fellowship in archaeometallurgy at University College London, to which he also bequeathed his personal library, was endowed by, and named after him.

106. DMDP: Kippenberger to DMD, 16 and 24 Dec. 1947.
107. DMD, 'Three Encounters Thirty Years Ago', in *Islands*, vol. 6, no. 3, Mar. 1978, pp. 302–6.
108. Glover backed out, and despite DMD's efforts to interest Cumberlege in London, it remained without a publisher. Eventually Helen Shaw produced 50 copies of the 'book' on a Gestetner machine. A copy of *The Puritan and the Waif*, now a collector's item, is in DMDP. Details are in ATL: MS-Papers-0432-113, letters to Frank Sargeson from Helen Shaw.
109. DMDP: Diary, 22 Aug. 1948.
110. Ibid., 27 Aug. 1948.
111. Ibid., 10 Sept. 1948.
112. Ibid., 11 Sept. 1948.
113. Initially at 91 Riselaw Street, Carlton Hill.
114. *BS*, pp. 57–85.
115. DMDP: Diary, 15 Sept. 1948.
116. Letter from Dr Christabel Wallace, Jan. 1995.
117. DMDP: Diary, 25 Aug. 1948.
118. Ibid., 20 Sept. 1948.
119. Ibid., 29 Sept. 1948.
120. DMDP: Kippenberger to DMD, 28 Mar. 1951, 30 Nov. 1948.
121. *Crete*, p. 80.
122. Angus Ross, *23 Battalion* (Wellington, 1959), 93.
123. *Crete*, pp. 309–16.
124. DMDP: Kippenberger to DMD, 9 Nov. 1950.
125. DMDP: Kippenberger to DMD, 20 Dec. 1950.
126. DMDP: Murphy to DMD, 31 May 1952.
127. See, for instance, the review by L. R. H. in the Christchurch *Press*, 8 Aug. 1953. John Robertson gave it a strong, positive review in the Southland *Times*, 24 Aug. 1953.
128. *The Economist*, 23 Jan. 1954. The review was probably written, at Geoff Cox's instigation, by Bill Williams. See DMDP: Cox to DMD, 28 Sept. 1953. Williams also reviewed *Crete* in the *Oxford Mail*, 18 Jan. 1954.
129. *New Statesman*, 29 Jan. 1954. Nicolson liked the maps, which almost everyone else condemned as inadequate. A writer might guess that Nicolson had not read the entire book.
130. *Spectator*, 12 Mar. 1954.
131. Paul Freyberg, *Bernard Freyberg, VC: Soldier of Two Nations* (London, 1991), 2–4, 268–9. General Wavell was said to have initiated Freyberg

into Ultra in the garden of a small villa between Maleme and Canea on 30 Apr. 1941. There is a description of the villa, and of Wavell's visit, in Geoffrey Cox, *A Tale of Two Battles* (London, 1987), 51.

132. DMDP: DMD to Paul Freyberg, 16 Nov. 1981.
133. F. H. Hinsley *et al.*, *British Intelligence in the Second World War*, i (London, 1979), 417.
134. The cover story is confirmed in Cox, *A Tale of Two Battles*, 108.
135. Hinsley, *British Intelligence*, i. 418.
136. See e.g. DMDP: correspondence between DMD and Dr I. McD. G. Stewart, 15 Jan. and 11 Feb. 1982.
137. (London, 1966).
138. ATL: MS-Papers-0432-113, DMD to Sargeson, 15 Aug. 1951.
139. DMDP: Diary, 28 July 1952.

Chapter 11: *The Plateau of Success*

1. DMDP: Diary, 3 Dec. 1940.
2. Ibid., 25 Aug. 1942.
3. Letter from Miriam Margolyes, 12 Nov. 1992.
4. ATL: MS-Papers-0432-155, DMD to Sargeson, 29 Dec. 1952.
5. Ibid., 20 Apr. 1954.
6. DMD to Michael Joseph, private collection, 11 [21?] Jan. 1954.
7. ATL: MS-Papers-0432-155, DMD to Sargeson, 29 Apr. 1948: 'I have taken on the almost impossible job of being publisher by day and author by night—not to mention father and husband all the time . . .'
8. Ibid.
9. *RFH*, p. 213.
10. Margaret Black, interview, 8 Nov. 1992.
11. Twenty-Second International Congress of PEN, 18–25 Aug. 1950. The quotation is in DMDP: John Willett to DMD, 30 Aug. 1973.
12. DMDP: Powell to DMD, 16 May 1975.
13. Craig Papers: Diary, 20 Nov. 1954. The 'bombs' were believed to be amphetamines.
14. DMDP: ATL: MS-Papers-40304, 85-092-1/01, Arthur Crook to DMD, 11 July 1968.
15. ATL: MS-Papers-0432-155, DMD to Sargeson, 7 Mar. 1954.
16. WKDP: DMD to WKD, 21 Sept. 1952.
17. Letter from Delia Davin, 13 Mar. 1995.
18. He is, among many other accomplishments, editor, translator, and critic of the work of Bertolt Brecht.
19. C. H. Roberts, 1909–90. There is an appreciation by George Richardson in the OUP *Record*, no. 35, Dec. 1990.
20. DMD's personal file at OUP could not be located. The papers of the then Vice-Chancellor, C. M. (Maurice) Bowra, contain no reference to the incident.
21. DMDP: Sisam to DMD, 7 Nov. 1952.

22. Ibid.
23. DMDP: Kippenberger to DMD, 30 Oct., 12 and 18 Nov. 1952.
24. Charles Brasch, *Indirections: A Memoir 1909–1947* (Wellington, 1980) Brasch and Roberts met when they were undergraduates at St John's in the late 1920s. 'Partly in temperament, more in our thinking, and in a common love of poetry and all that is beautiful, we were as close as friends can be', p. 379. See also the dedicatory poem 'To C. H. Roberts', in Charles Brasch, *Disputed Ground* (1948).
25. DMDP: DMD to Paul Freyberg, 26 Nov. 1981.
26. Richardson, OUP *Record*.
27. Brasch, *Indirections*, 139. DMD and WKD went to Appleton House for sherry on May Day 1956. 'New house v. nice with superb view of Cotswolds etc. . . . W. and I fortunately not envious souls or we might have grieved over our own shabby circumstances' (DMDP: Diary, 3 May 1956).
28. DMDP: Costello to DMD, 8 Sept. 1953.
29. WKDP: DMD to WKD, 14 Mar. 1954. 'The wound has now scabbed up and I have ceased to use dressings for the last 48 hours. I no longer come back from walks in a shaky state . . .'
30. ATL: MS-Papers-0432-155, DMD to Sargeson, 7 Mar. 1954.
31. OUPA: BP 5064, and Pkt. 312.
32. Richard Manne, *The Petrov Affair: Politics and Espionage* (1987), and Harvey Barnett, *Tale of the Scorpion* (1988), both repeat that Milner was a spy, but unfortunately without analysing evidence. Richard Hall, *The Rhodes Scholar Spy* (1991), is peppered with errors of fact. The only systematic analysis of the two episodes in Milner's life—his decision to live in Prague, and his treatment at the hands of the Petrov Commission—is in Ian Milner, *Intersecting Lines: The Memoirs of Ian Milner*, ed. and introd. Vincent O'Sullivan (Wellington, 1993), 20–35, where the case against Milner, as currently documented, collapses.
33. DMDP: Diary, 30 Dec. 1950.
34. Ibid. Unfortunately, DMD's many letters to Costello have apparently not survived. Mrs Costello, interview, 26 Mar. 1993, assured me that her husband never kept letters.
35. P. D. Costello (ed.), *The Oxford Book of Russian Verse* (London, 1949). There was a 'captious review'—DMDP: Diary, 2 Apr. 1949—in the *TLS*, 1 Apr. 1949.
36. Letter from Sir Geoffrey Cox, 4 July 1994.
37. DMDP: Costello to DMD, 22 Mar. 1948.
38. DMDP: Costello to DMD, 22 Apr. 1954.
39. Ibid. WKD recalled Paddy 'one night when some debater expected him to sneer at the U.S.' praising it for resisting the threat or use of nuclear weapons against the Soviet Union after VJ Day.
40. Malcolm Templeton, *Top Hats Are Not Being Taken: A Short History of the New Zealand Legation in Moscow, 1944–1950* (Wellington, 1988), 22.

Costello believed that the pressure was being exerted mainly by the British: cf. DMDP: Costello to DMD, 27 Dec. 1954. There seems to be little truth in James Bertram's assertion, *Capes of China Slide Away* (1993), 294, that Costello had 'no defence from his permanent head'. Templeton says that McIntosh did everything in his power to keep him.

41. Chapman Pincher, *Too Secret Too Long* (1984), 255, 268, and 387, says that Blunt fingered Costello as a spy to his MI5 handlers, though only after Costello's death. Both British and American authorities are said to suspect Costello of having made New Zealand passports available for the Krogers (Morris and Lena Cohen) who were convicted as members of the Portland spy ring. John Costello (no relation), *Mask of Treachery* (1988), 7–9, condemns him for this, and also asserts that Costello was named a spy by the Soviet defector Golitsyn, but the few pages he devotes to the task are unpersuasive. They include the surprising assertion that Costello's 'importance to the Soviets [during the war] was his direct access to Ultra'. Among those singled out for 'special thanks' in the acknoweldgements to his book Costello names 'Professor Dan Devin' [*sic*]. DMD's indignation about this book was great, but he was old and sick by this time.

42. DMDP: Costello to DMD, 22 Mar. 1948.

43. Ibid., 27 Dec. 1954.

44. Godfrey Lienhardt, 1921–93. Lecturer in African Sociology at Oxford 1949–72, and Reader in Social Anthropology 1972–88; fellow of Wolfson College, 1967–88. Author of *Divinity and Experience: The Religion of the Dinka* (1961) and *Social Anthropology* (1964).

45. A deliberately amusing corruption of 'Timor mortis conturbat me' (literally, 'The fear of death troubles me'), the refrain from Dunbar's 'Lament for the Makaris'.

46. On a park bench in Mesopotamia. It was recently recut. If stuck try reading it in English!

47. DMDP: DMD, 'Gerald Wilde', unfinished MS [1982?], pp. 6, 8–9.

48. I am grateful to David Pocock for these reminiscences. Interview, 21 Aug. 1992.

49. ATL: MS-Papers-4567-004, James Bertram to Ian Milner, 20 Feb. 1961.

50. *NR*, p. 35, part of the description of Bob Poulter, surely DMD in brief, partial self-portrait.

51. Alan Horsman, interview, 14 July 1993.

52. ATL: MS-Papers-0432-155, DMD to Sargeson, 6 Oct. 1954. The remark was apropos of Ian A. Gordon, an academic entrepreneur at Victoria University College (later the Victoria University of Wellington) in New Zealand.

53. Rupert Hart-Davis (ed.), *The Lyttelton Hart-Davis Letters*, ii, *1956–1957* (London, 1979), 130.

54. ATL: MS-Papers-0432-155, DMD to Sargeson, 5 June 1953. The visit was on 31 May. In this letter DMD called Mackenzie 'old

scamp' which was a term he, Cox, and Costello normally reserved for Freyberg.

55. Early June [12?] 1954. ATL: ibid., DMD to Sargeson, 24 June 1954: 'I was not as surprised as I would have been a few years ago to find that I liked him.'

56. 13 May 1954 at the NBL premises in Albemarle Street, London, Hector Bolitho in the chair. Bolitho was one of Dan's pet hatreds. (He only had three, one of the others being Hawksworth.) Afterwards Muriel Harris, publications and exhibitions officer of the NBL, wrote to thank him: 'I hope the audience was not too large for you—or too small for Mr. Bolitho!' (DMDP: Muriel Harris to DMD, n.d. [14 May 1954?]).

57. A half-hour programme recorded on 11 Oct. 1957, and broadcast on the BBC Home Service on 31 Oct. It was broadcast in New Zealand on Sunday, 23 Feb. 1958.

58. DMDP: Carmichael to DMD, 4 July 1948. After the war Carmichael lived in Paris for a few years.

59. DMDP: 'Myself and the Oxford University Press: 1945—', uncompleted MS [1978?], 14.

60. The discarded titles survived as the names given to the first and third parts of *TSB*.

61. DMD's interest in Sartre was deepened by reading Iris Murdoch, *Sartre: Romantic Rationalist* (1953), during his convalescence on Middle Carn in Mar. 1954. See DMDP: Iris Murdoch to DMD, 11 Apr. 1954. DMD seems to me to have been greatly influenced by Murdoch's treatment of Sartre's account of interior monologue, the problem of voice, or point of view, in fiction.

62. DMDP: Robert Lusty to DMD, 24 Aug. and 17 Sept. 1955.

63. Ibid., 4 Jan. 1956.

64. *TSB*, p. 47.

65. At first, from 1942, opposite Claridge's. Later, in Seymour Place. She took the photographs for the dust-jackets of DMD's novels.

66. *Landfall*, vol. 10, no. 3, Sept. 1956, pp. 253–5.

67. *TSB*, p. 111.

68. ATL: MS-Papers-0432-155, DMD to Sargeson, 8 Dec. 1953. Dylan Thomas died in New York early in the morning of 5 Nov.

69. WKDP: DMD to WKD, 3 Jan. 1949 [1950?].

70. *TLS*, 25 May, 1956.

71. *Manchester Guardian*, 29 May 1956, review by Anne Duchene.

72. *Time and Tide*, 26 May 1956.

73. *Landfall*, vol. 10, no. 3, Sept. 1956, p. 255.

74. In *The Times*, 17 May 1956, they were reviewed together, to DMD's disadvantage.

75. ATL: MS-Papers-0432-155, DMD to Sargeson, 25 Sept. 1955.

76. 'Mr. Beckett's Everyman', *Irish Writing*, no. 34, Spring 1956, pp. 36–9; 'Attempting the Infinite', a *TLS* 'front' on Patrick White, 15 Dec. 1961;

'The Alexandria Quartet', a lecture to the International Graduate Summer School, Oxford, 11 Aug. 1966, ATL: 40304: 85-092-4/03.
77. DMDP: Flavell to DMD, 17 May 1956.
78. DMDP: Diary, 13 Oct. 1956.
79. *CT*, p. 119.
80. Pamela Hansford Johnson, in the *New Statesman*, 24 Jan. 1959.
81. *CT*, p. 120.
82. DMD describes him, under the attack of his illness, reorganizing his life 'like a commander preparing for a long series of withdrawals under enemy pressure' (*CT*, p. 114).
83. Harry Doley was still alive when *No Remittance* was published, though a widower by then, and living with a daughter in Hawkes Bay. He told a niece that he thought the novel was very amusing, and an excellent portrait.
84. Roland Gant, Dan's editor, became Editorial Director at Michael Joseph. The restructuring of David Higham Associates was completed in July 1958, though it had been on the cards since March.
85. *Daily Telegraph*, 23 Jan. 1959.
86. *New Statesman*, 24 Jan. 1959.
87. *Punch*, 11 Feb. 1959.
88. *Sunday Times*, 18 Jan. 1959.
89. *Manchester Guardian*, 30 Jan. 1959; *Oxford Mail*, 22 Jan. 1959.
90. *TLS*, 30 Jan. 1959.
91. *Listener*, 5 May 1959.
92. DMDP: 'The Editor and the World', lecture to an OUP staff training conference, 1966, p. 3.
93. John Mulgan, *Report on Experience* (1947), 28.
94. ATL: MS-Papers-91-047-16/2, Duggan to Maurice Shadbolt, n.d. [17 Mar. 1959?].
95. Ibid., 16/3.
96. DMDP: Renée Stockwell to DMD, n.d., but postmarked 24 Nov. 1959, contains some of the detail. Helen Garrett (formerly Helen Coates), then married to the Professor of English, John Garrett, whom Dan had known at Oxford in the 1930s, wrote that she 'never heard that any "omission" on the part of Canterbury University to invite him to visit ever aroused any comment' (Letter from Helen Garrett, 27 Feb. 1995).
97. ATL: MS-Papers-0432-155, DMD to Sargeson, 27 Sept. 1960.
98. Ibid.
99. In a letter that is missing from DMDP.
100. Letter from Michael King, 26 Dec. 1994, quoting Sargeson to Karl Stead, 15 Mar. 1959.
101. *Landfall*, vol. 13, no. 2, June 1959, pp. 180–1. Miss O'Dowd was a university lecturer in History.
102. ATL: MS-Papers-0432-155, DMD to Sargeson, 28 Sept. 1964.

103. DMDP: Higham to DMD, 14 Jan., 4 Feb., and 10 Mar. 1960.
104. DMDP: DMD to Higham, 9 July 1964.
105. See e.g. the *Oxford Mail*, 16 Oct. 1958.
106. He was sponsored for membership by Archie Colquhoun, a keen advocate of the Travellers' and a considerable Italian scholar. DMD had known him during the Italian campaign, when he was staff officer on X Corps GHQ responsible for liaison with the Partisans. The Travellers' was founded in 1819, and had 900 members when DMD joined. It was an odd choice of club, traditionally a Foreign Office enclave, favoured by members of MI5 and MI6, and a notably staid Establishment institution.
107. NZ Army, DMDPF, ML595, messages dated 10 and 11 Feb., 31 Mar., and 8 Apr. 1960.
108. Letter from Elizabeth Knight, 4 Mar. 1995.
109. DMDP: DMD to Martha McCulloch, 5 Mar. 1963.
110. *CT*, p. 61. Louis McNeice died the following Tuesday, 3 Sept. 1963.
111. Ibid.

Chapter 12: *A Life in Publishing*

1. Obituary in *PN Review* 77, vol. 17, no. 3, Jan/Feb. 1991, p. 4.
2. Interviews with Kathleen Tillotson, 11 May 1992, and Alan Bell, 27 May 1992. Letter from Robert Burchfield, 4 Mar. 1995.
3. Details are in OUPA: BP 5670, Collected Works of John Locke 1942–57. The files were central to DMD's idea of the Press. For an example of why and how, see *TLS*, 10 Feb. 1978, where DMD wrote to correct inaccuracies in Kathleen Coburn's book *In Pursuit of Coleridge* (1977). She had criticized OUP and in particular Sisam over the treatment of her proposal for a complete edition of Coleridge's notebooks. This had been rejected by the Delegates in Nov. 1938, but the file preserved in case she cared to return with a reformulated proposal. DMD was able to quote details from the file both to correct her errors, and to defend Sisam's reputation. DMD's first lesson from Sisam was to master the files. It was a principle that, in his turn, he instilled in all those who worked with him.
4. Esmond de Beer, 1895–1990. He was born in Dunedin, New Zealand, a member of the Hallenstein department store family, from whom he inherited his fortune. Charles Brasch was a cousin. See Charles Brasch, *Indirections: A Memoir 1909–1947* (Wellington, 1980), 147–51.
5. OUPA: BP 5670, DMD to de Beer, 14 May 1956.
6. Some further details are in OUPA: BP 824396, Locke Correspondence: Nov. 1950–Dec. 1973.
7. OUPA: Pkt. 76, Ancient History, 1925–69.
8. Letter from Robert Burchfield, 4 Mar. 1995. The flowering of New Zealand talent in post-war Oxford, a theme in itself, was expressive of two forces: the absence of opportunity for scholars in New Zealand,

which drove them abroad; and the continuing attraction to them of Britain, the 'home' country. Local university expansion, and the attraction of alternative foreign destinations, itself a feature of the decline in importance of Britain to New Zealand as a whole, have since made it a thing of the past.

9. Gordon A. Craig, *The Politics of the Prussian Army, 1640–1945* (Oxford, 1955); and *Germany 1866–1945* (Oxford, 1978).
10. DMDP: DMD, 'The Editor and the World', lecture to an OUP staff training conference, 1966, p. 4.
11. A. J. P. Taylor, *The Struggle for Mastery in Europe 1848–1914* (Oxford, 1954); and *English History 1914–1945* (Oxford, 1965). Details are in OUPA: BP 822101 and BP 372017.
12. Adam Sisman, *A. J. P. Taylor: A Biography* (London, 1994), esp. pp. 218–21, 224–5, 241–2, and 303–4. Sisman's occasional details about DMD (he says, e.g., that he was unpunctual) seem to me untrue, and to give the wrong impression both of him, and of his relations with Alan Taylor. Taylor was one of those academics of whom it is sometimes not wholly improperly said that their conduct of university politics is so brutal because the stakes are so low. He was a controversialist with polemical skills, and could be deliberately provocative. Any publisher would have had to keep a close eye on whatever he wrote. In this regard DMD did his job. He was, however, sympathetic to Taylor's intellectual beliefs, and to his situation at Oxford as an outsider, and while having to serve the Delegates (some of whom were not Taylor admirers) he did much to help him. One gets a better glimpse of the true relations between them in Sisman at p. 348.
13. DMD, 'Editor and author in a University Press', *TLS*, 7 Dec. 1967.
14. *The Times*, 28 Dec. 1964.
15. Vol. i, 1820–39, 1965; vol. ii, 1840–1, 1969; vol. iii, 1842–3, 1974; vol. iv, 1844–6, 1978; vol. v, 1847–9, 1981; vol. vi, 1850–2, 1988; vol. vii, 1853–5, 1993.
16. Kathleen Tillotson, *English Novels of the 1840s* (Oxford, 1954). OUPA: BP 811582.
17. OUPA: BP 5484, DMD's summary of adviser's report of Feb. 1947, 6 Dec. 1951.
18. *TLS*, 20 and 27 July, 3 Aug. 1951.
19. OUPA: BP 5484, memo by Spicer, 21 Sept. 1951.
20. OUPA: BP 811570, Neville Rogers, *Shelley at Work*.
21. OUPA: John Wain to DMD, 27 Dec. 1956.
22. OUPA: DMD to Rogers, 12 Mar. 1957.
23. DMDP: Rogers to DMD, 10 June [July?] 1983; DMD to Rogers, 29 July 1983.
24. DMDP: 'The Editor and the World', p. 8.
25. DMD, 'Neville Rogers', *Keats–Shelley Review*, 1987, no. 2, pp. viii–x.
26. He was Chief Editor, Oxford English Dictionaries, 1971–84. See his *The English Language* (1985). Also, E. G. Stanley and T. F.

Hoad (eds.), *Words for Robert Burchfield's 65th Birthday* (Cambridge, 1988).

27. Letter from Robert Burchfield, 4 Mar. 1995. Specifically on *COD*, however, see below, p. 315.

28. DMDP: Burchfield, to DMD, 10 Apr. 1983.

29. Theodore Moody, 1907–84. There is a brief biography by F. S. L. Lyons in F. S. L. Lyons and R. A. J. Hawkins (eds.), *Ireland Under the Union: Varieties of Tension. Essays in Honour of T. W. Moody* (1980), 1–33.

30. 'The Royal Irish Academy is a venerable institution founded in 1786, which seeks to combine mathematics and the natural sciences with what it calls "polite literature" and antiquities. It is one of those institutions in Ireland that, despite the "Royal", divides us least' (Moody to DMD, 17 Sept. 1968). Correspondence about the *New History of Ireland* is contained in OUPA: PP 11986 and 821737; and BP 6895. All subsequent reference in the text is to these sources.

31. OUPA: ibid., DMD to Moody, 9 Dec. 1971.

32. OUPA: memo of 3 Aug. 1973.

33. OUPA: DMD to Moody, 23 Apr. 1974.

34. It has since been reprinted twice, 1978 and 1991.

35. T. W. Moody, F. X. Martin, and F. J. Byrne, *A Chronology of Irish History to 1976: A Companion to Irish History Part I* (Oxford, 1982), p. v.

36. OUPA: DMD to Moody, 20 Jan. 1978.

37. 1947: 9.3%; 1954: 8.4%; 1955: 8.2%. Its average annual net profit on sales for these twenty years was 16.12%.

38. Franks Commission Report, 1966, para. 632 and recommendation 149.

39. DMDP: Diary, 14 May 1966.

40. See for instance the submission by Professor Hugh Trevor-Roper. One of his assertions, that the Press employed 'learned advisers' who were incompetent, is particularly unhappy in the subsequent light of his own contribution to the Hitler Diaries forgery, in which he played the role of learned adviser.

41. DMDP: Diary, 30 Mar. 1968.

42. Ibid., 30 Nov. 1968.

43. University of Oxford, *Report of the Committee on the University Press*, Supplement no. 7 to the University *Gazette*, vol. c, May 1970 (hereafter *Waldock*), para. 101, pp. 48–9.

44. DMDP: DMD to Sisam, 5 May 1969.

45. DMDP: Diary, 28 Oct. 1967.

46. Ibid., 8 Sept. 1969.

47. Ibid., 30 [31?] Jan. 1970.

48. The CP was effectively operating at a loss by the summer of 1970, and continued to do so for the next 24 months, the first time it had done so in all of DMD's career. Thirteen science series had already been started before *Waldock* was published, each of which had its scientific editors and advisory committees.

49. *Crete*, pp. vii–viii.
50. *Waldock*, paras. 217 and 218, pp. 106–7; and recommendation 16.
51. See e.g. DMDP: Diary, 8 Aug. 1970.
52. Ibid., 15 Aug. 1970.
53. Ibid., 23 Aug. 1970.
54. Ibid., 4 Sept. 1971 ['. . . that all flesh was grist'?].
55. Nicolas Barker's father was Sir Ernest Barker, the distinguished Cambridge Professor of Political Thought, a classicist and historian.
56. Letter from Robert Burchfield.
57. DMDP: Alan Bullock to DMD, 23 Oct. 1972 and 22 Mar. 1973.
58. DMDP: DMD to Colin Roberts, 20 Apr. 1973.
59. George Barclay Richardson, b. 1924. He was Reader in Economics at Oxford, 1959–74; chief executive and Secretary to the Delegates of OUP, 1974–88; and Warden of Keble College, 1989–94. His publications include *Information and Investment* (1960, 2nd edn. 1991); and *Economic Theory* (1964).
60. Peter Sutcliffe writing in the OUP *Record*, no. 23, Dec. 1978.
61. Now the Finance Director.
62. Letter from David Mitchell, 3 Nov. 1994.
63. DMDP: David Mitchell to DMD, 20 Nov. 1975.
64. George Richardson, OUP *Record*, no. 22, Dec. 1977.
65. Letter from David Mitchell.
66. Peter Sutcliffe, *The Oxford University Press: An Informal History* (Oxford, 1978). It got good reviews, and soon sold out. The other work was Nicolas Barker, *The Oxford University Press and the Spread of Learning 1478–1978: An Illustrated History* (Oxford, 1978), which was catalogue and commentary for the exhibition at the Pierpont Morgan Library.
67. Letter from George Richardson, 3 Oct. 1994.
68. Letter from David Mitchell.
69. It became a wholly owned subsidiary of Brittains Ltd. OUP continued as landlords, and also as shareholders in Brittains with a seat on their board.

Chapter 13. *Critic and Friend*

1. DMDP: Diary, 22 May 1965.
2. DMDP: Brigid Brophy to DMD, 1 Nov. 1983.
3. *New Zealand Short Stories*, selected by E. Dombrovskaya, with an introduction by V. Rubina (Moscow, 1963). WKD bought a copy in Moscow in 1964 on her way home from visiting Delia in Beijing.
4. *Landfall*, vol. 18, no. 2, June 1964, pp. 158–60. 'Disingenuous' was DMD's word for it (DMDP: DMD to Rhodes, 22 Sept. 1964).
5. DMDP: DMD to Moscow Publishing House of Belles Lettres, 30 July 1964.
6. Ibid.
7. DMDP: A. Puzikov to DMD, 31 Aug. 1964.

8. DMDP: DMD to Rhodes, 22 Sept. 1964; Rhodes to DMD, 29 Sept. 1964.
9. Fuller details of the affair are in ATL: Winston Rhodes papers, MS-424-25.
10. DMD in John Wakeman (ed.), *World Authors 1950–1970* (New York, 1975), 362–3.
11. ATL: MS-Papers-0432-155, DMD to Sargeson, 28 Sept. 1964.
12. Ibid.
13. Donald Harman Akenson, *Half the World from Home: Perspectives on the Irish in New Zealand 1860–1950* (Wellington, 1990), 97.
14. DMD in Wakeman (ed.), *World Authors*.
15. DMDP: Ben Glazebrook to David Higham, 11 Jan. 1967.
16. DMDP: John Willett to DMD, 14 Apr. 1967.
17. DMD in Wakeman, *World Authors*, quoted above, p. 323.
18. DMDP: Martin Green to Bruce Hunter, 22 Aug. 1967. Bruce Hunter became DMD's agent at Higham's from this time.
19. DMDP: Martin Green to Bruce Hunter, 24 Apr. 1968.
20. DMDP: DMD to Bruce Hunter, 11 June and 1 Oct. 1968.
21. DMDP: DMD to Catherine Carver, 22 July 1974.
22. DMDP: DMD to Janet Paul, 10 Aug. 1967: 'In my belief it's as good a novel as ever came out of NZ—and it gives a unique picture of university and domestic life at an interesting period. It also does, in my view, what it sets out to do in other ways—in particular, to form a *bildungsroman*, a developing portrait of an ambitious young man who gets what he wants, at the expense of losing a good deal of what was worth while in him.' The choice here of the active voice for the novel, in place of the writer's intentions in it, is interesting. Janet Paul had thought of publishing the book until she saw the manuscript, but then her firm went out of business anyway.
23. Delia Jenner, *Letters from Peking* (London, 1967).
24. She departed from Oxford on 24 Sept., when DMD went to Middle Carn for a fortnight.
25. See Wendy Campbell-Purdie and Fenner Brockway, *Woman Against the Desert* (London, 1967). The autobiography of Fenner Brockway, *Towards Tomorrow* (1977), 257–8 contains a description of her work at Bou Saada, as well as an interesting insight into her contrary character. See also Maurice Shadbolt, 'Wendy's War Against the Desert,' in *Love and Legend* (1976), 91–100.
26. *TLS*, 2 Mar. 1962.
27. Details are in OUPA: Pkt. 87, World's Classics 1960– . Stead was a controversial choice in some New Zealand quarters at the time, but DMD was steadfast in his support for him at OUP.
28. *TLS*, 5 July 1963.
29. Details are in ATL: Pearson Papers, MSZ-0455.
30. DMDP: DMD to Arthur Crook, 1 Jan. 1973.

31. *Journal of the National Book League*, Autumn 1968.
32. David Marr, *Patrick White: A Life* (1991), 484, 647.
33. Letter from Nuala O'Faolain, 7 Oct. 1994.
34. DMDP: DMD Diary, 22 May 1965.
35. Ibid., 31 July 1967.
36. James Bertram, 'Dan Davin: Novelist of Exile', *Meanjin*, vol. 32, June 1973, p. 149. Akenson, *Half the World from Home*, 94 ff., makes much of DMD's Irish, as opposed to New Zealand, literary heritage.
37. DMDP: 'The Irish in New Zealand', unpublished MS, 20 May 1957.
38. DMDP: DMD Diary, 6 Oct. 1969.
39. Ibid., 7 and 27 Oct. 1969.
40. Douglas H. Johnson, *The Independent*, 17 Nov. 1993.
41. *BP*, p. 147.
42. Ibid., 134–5.
43. Ibid., 153.
44. Ibid., 240.
45. Lawrence Osborne, *The Poisoned Embrace: A Brief History of Sexual Pessimism* (New York, 1993).
46. DMD, 'Snow Upon Fire: A Dance to the Music of Time: Anthony Powell', W. D. Thomas Memorial Lecture (Swansea, 1977), 7.
47. *Daily Telegraph*, 13 July 1972.
48. *TLS*, 15 Sept. 1972.
49. *New Yorker*, 2 Mar. 1973.
50. Philadelphia *Inquirer*, 18 Mar. 1973.
51. *New Zealand Listener*, 26 Mar. 1973.
52. See e.g. Akenson, *Half the World from Home*, 235 n. 33, where he ridicules it.
53. DMDP: DMD, Diary, 28 Oct. 1967.
54. In *BS*, pp. 171–94.
55. DMDP: DMD Diary. The entry for the trip to Crete, 4 to 8 Aug. was written on 17 Aug. 1966.
56. Ibid., 7 July 1969.
57. Ibid., 27 July 1969.
58. Letter from Tony Stones, n.d. [14?] Mar. 1994.
59. DMD to Brigid Sandford Smith, 14 Aug. 1969.
60. DMDP: DMD, Diary, 23 Aug. 1969.
61. *BP*, pp. 165–78.
62. Craig Papers: Diary, 30 Aug. 1969.
63. DMDP: DMD, Diary, 31 Aug. 1969.
64. Ibid., 1 Sept. 1969.
65. DMD to Anna Davin, 18 Nov. 1968.
66. Philip Kaiser, *Journeying Far and Wide: A Political and Diplomatic Memoir* (New York, 1992), 207–64.
67. 'The Locksmith Laughs Last', started just after Christmas 1968, was finished at Dorchester in the summer of 1972. This was a good summer,

when he also wrote 'Psychological Warfare at Cassino' and the first draft of 'The Wall of Doors': all in *BS*.

68. W. R. Rodgers, *Collected Poems* (London, 1971), pp. ix–xxv.

69. *CT*, p. xv.

70. DMDP: Weisgal to DMD, 25 Sept. 1973.

71. OUPA: BP 212197, Carver to DMD, 9 June 1974.

72. *CT*, p. 170.

73. OUPA: BP 212197, DMD to Carver, 22 July 1974. He was surely right about 'cant'. Whatever deficiencies *Closing Times* may have, insincerity is not one of them. Carver may perhaps have meant that she feared nostalgia coloured his recollections—a view that was certainly held by John Willett; cf. his letter to Carver in ibid., 9 May 1975—but it was no defence with DMD, of all people, to have used the wrong term inadvertently.

74. Akenson, *Half the World from Home*, 90, 93–4, and 118–22. To avoid argument: Akenson writes *seanchai*; *CT*, p. 173, *seanachair*; in Gaelic it is written *seanachaidhe*, but became *seanchai* with spelling simplification in the 1950s. It is sometimes Anglicized as *shanachie*. *OED* gives *sennachie*.

75. *CT*, p. xviii.

76. The first draft of this was finished on 12 Aug. 1974.

77. He died on 4 Apr. 1976.

78. DMD made the speech at the wedding of Christopher's daughter Fanny. His diary contains various references to Hill, and jottings made late in his life suggest that DMD planned a piece about the many sadnesses that Hill endured.

79. Richard Holmes, *Dr. Johnson and Mr. Savage* (London, 1993).

80. DMD's contribution was his essay on Chapman, 'The Devil Answers Even in Engines' (1976), which brought together his love of Johnson, OUP, history, and the role of fiction in understanding the past. A *tour de force* of critical insight.

81. Jim Clifford, 1901–78, author of *Hester Lynch Piozzi (Mrs. Thrale)* (1941); *Young Sam Johnson* (1955); and *Dictionary Johnson* (1981), among many other works of scholarship.

82. Author of *Swift and the Church of Ireland* (1954).

83. To be fair, Akenson, *Half the World from Home*, 93, does call it 'Davin at his best' and the book of his most likely 'still [to] be read with pleasure in the middle of the next century'.

84. *BP*, pp. 29–30.

85. *CT*, p. xiii.

86. Ibid.

87. DMDP: Aneurin Davies to DMD, 17 Nov. 1975.

88. DMD, 'Snow Upon Fire', 10.

89. DMD to Anna Davin, 30 Aug. 1976; to Brigid Sandford Smith, 14 May 1977.

90. 25–7 Aug. 1978.

91. DMD to Brigid Sandford Smith, 18 Aug. 1978.

92. Letter from Tony Stones.

NOTES

Chapter 14: *A Fighting Withdrawal*

1. DMDP: Diary, 24 Sept. 1941.
2. Esmond de Beer, 'On Raasay: An appreciation of L. F. Powell' (Oxford: privately printed, 1976).
3. DMDP: Diary, 5 and 12 Aug. 1940.
4. *BP*, pp. 134–5, quoted above, Ch. 13, p. 336.
5. ATL: MS-Papers-91-047-17/2, Kevin Ireland to Maurice Shadbolt, 14 Dec. 1978.
6. DMDP: DMD to Mary Hyde, 24 Mar. 1979.
7. Written on 30 Jan. 1979.
8. DMD to Alan Bell, 5 Mar. 1980. Shackleton was Bodley's Librarian.
9. DMDP: DMD to Noel Gardiner, 14 Apr. 1981.
10. Letter from Elspeth Sandys, 1 Apr. 1994.
11. ATL: MS-Papers-91-047-17/04, DMD to Maurice Shadbolt, 1 Sept. 1979.
12. Ibid.
13. Ibid., Maurice Shadbolt to Eric McCormick, 19 Dec. 1979.
14. ATL: MS-Papers-4567-11, DMD to Ian Milner, 18 Aug. 1982.
15. John Costello, *Mask of Treachery* (1988), 8. Chapman Pincher, *Their Trade is Treachery* (1981), was the main conduit for security service leaks. Nigel West, *Molehunt* (1987), catalogues various derelictions. Chapman Pincher, *Traitors* (1987), and Peter Wright with Paul Greengrass, *Spycatcher* (1987), illustrate, possibly unintentionally, the obsessional qualities of finger pointing.
16. DMDP: Diary, 1 Apr. 1968. DMD does not give the background, but the conversation was probably stimulated by Hugh Trevor-Roper's book *The Philby Affair* (1968).
17. DMD in John Wakeman (ed.), *World Authors 1950–1970* (New York, 1975), quoted above, p. 323.
18. DMD in a recorded interview with James McNeish for the NZBC, 1980. DMD's remark became the title for the series in which his interview was one: 'Intimate Strangers'.
19. DMD, 'John Mulgan', *Landfall*, vol. 2, no. 1, 1948, p. 52.
20. DMDP: DMD to Vincent O'Sullivan, 12 Mar. 1981.
21. DMDP: DMD to Robert Rutherford-Dyer, 29 Aug. 1982.
22. DMDP: DMD to Paul Freyberg, 16 Nov. 1981.
23. DMDP: DMD to Paul Freyberg, 16 and 26 Nov. 1981; 2 Jan. and 10 Feb. 1982; 22 June and 7 Oct. 1983.
24. DMDP: I. M. G. Stewart to DMD, 15 Jan. 1982.
25. DMD, 'Snow Upon Fire', 4.
26. DMDP: DMD to James Bertram, 9 Jan. and 6 Mar. 1982. See James Bertram, *Dan Davin* (Auckland, 1983), *passim*.
27. DMDP: DMD to Mywa Zielinski, 15 July 1983.
28. *The Times*, 23 Oct. 1981.
29. Ibid., 8 Mar. 1982.
30. *Bookseller*, 5 June 1982.

31. DMDP: DMD to Victor Selwyn, 20 Nov. 1983.
32. DMDP: DMD to Dr Tina Chidson, 15 July 1983.
33. DMDP: DMD to Margery Walton, 30 Jan. 1984.
34. Dated 19 June 1984.
35. Craig Papers: Diary, 1 Oct. 1984.
36. DMDP: DMD to R. O. H. Irvine, 10 Apr. 1984.
37. DMDP: DMD to Walter Allen, 17 Sept. 1984.
38. DMDP: DMD to Rosemary Boyd, 21 Nov. 1984.
39. 'A Soldier's Wife', in Lauris Edmond (ed.), *Women in Wartime: New Zealand Women Tell Their Story* (Wellington, 1986).
40. Anthony Powell, *Hearing Secret Harmonies* (1975), 76.
41. A copy, with corrections, is in DMDP.
42. DMDP: 'fiddled with' is written on the MS.
43. *TSF*, p. x.
44. See above, p. 160.
45. DMDP: DMD, 'On Retirement', p. 1.
46. For instance, the level of gamma glutamyl transferase (GGT), a sensitive measure of liver inflammation which detects the liver 'weeping' part of itself into the bloodstream, should have a normal value of 15 to 50. Dan's measure on 20 May was 1,360.
47. DMDP: Patty Watson to DMD, 17 Mar. 1988.
48. DMDP: DMD to Paul Freyberg, 22 Apr. 1988.
49. DMD to Gordon Craig, 4 Mar. 1989.
50. Professor J. G. G. Ledingham to Delia Davin, 3 June 1991.
51. Ibid.
52. Letter from WKD, 9 Oct. 1990.
53. Anthony Stones to Noel Gardiner, 3 Oct. 1990.
54. Anthony Powell, *A Buyer's Market* (1952), 261.

SELECT BIBLIOGRAPHY

1. *Primary sources.*

The Davin papers are the principal source. They went to the Alexander Turnbull Library in Wellington, New Zealand, in May 1994. By the generosity of Davin's literary executor, Mrs Brigid Sandford Smith, and his widow Mrs W. K. Davin, I was given first access to them in Oxford. They had not at that time been catalogued, and although some considerable work had been done to put them in order, they had not been filed systematically throughout. I took it as a part of my obligation to disturb them as little as possible. The problem is that, for reference purposes, no notation then existed. I have dealt with this by keeping footnote references as simple as possible, identifying individual documents by name, or by name of correspondent.

Mrs Winnie Davin's papers are still held privately. She kindly gave me access to a considerable collection of correspondence bridging the years from 1931 to the 1960s. Without the letters from the 1930s the biographer's task would have been greatly complicated. In particular, the letters she exchanged with Dan Davin between 1931 and 1936 constitute a remarkable record of intellectual and personal life in New Zealand of the period. These letters were not arranged chronologically, and frequently lacked both dates and addresses. In some cases where a letter was dated, the date was wrong. In others, only fragments survived. In places there are important gaps in the sequence. In footnoting this source for reference I have given the date as it appears on the letter if it had one, followed by an emendation, queried, in parentheses if it is incomplete or I believe it to be incorrect. In every case where the dating is mine it appears thus, e.g. [2 September 1933?] even in those cases where I am certain, from the internal evidence, that my date is correct. In those cases where a letter was dated, and the date is clearly correct, it appears without either brackets or query.

Records of Otago University, and of the Students' Union, are held in the Otago University Library. Other records of student life at Otago, including back numbers of periodicals and newspapers, are held by the Hocken Library in Dunedin. The records of the Rhodes Scholarship Selection Committee for the 1930s are held in the New Zealand National Archives in Wellington, as are the records of the 2NZEF, and of the War Histories Branch of the Department of Internal Affairs. The Alexander Turnbull Library in Wellington holds the private papers of M. H. Holcroft, Ian Milner, Bill Pearson, H. Winston Rhodes, Frank Sargeson, and Maurice Shadbolt, all of which I consulted for this work.

Records of Davin's period as a Rhodes Scholar at Oxford, though thin, are in the Balliol College Library and in the Rhodes Trust Archives. The diary of Professor Gordon Craig, from its beginnings in 1930s Oxford up to the 1970s, is on microfilm in the archives of the Cecil H. Green Library, Stanford

University. More recent volumes, as well as the original manuscripts for the whole, are in his private possession.

The records of Davin's service with the 2NZEF from June 1940 to July 1945 were kindly made available to me by the archivist of the New Zealand Defence Force.

The archives of Oxford University Press, a private collection, are housed at the Press offices in Walton Street, Oxford.

Other private correspondence, where cited in the footnotes, belongs to the correspondent named. Where a citation reads 'Letter from [name]' followed by a date, it is addressed to the author. Details of interviews, tape recordings, and radio and television programmes appear in the notes.

2. *Secondary sources.*

The life of literary intellectuals is the life of books, and to understand someone who lives such a life means immersing oneself in the same books. In Davin's case the problems of immersion are multiplied by his leading a professional life of books as publisher as well as a private life of books as reader, writer, critic, reviewer, adviser, lecturer, and friend. I have tried to read what Davin read, at least in the broad outlines, and in some areas I have read deeply as well as widely. I hope that this is detectable in the structure as well as the content of the biography.

A chronology of Dan Davin's principal publications is at pp. 448–57.

The notes contain specific titles relating to individuals, particular events, or controversies. In addition, the following texts were of general importance:

Akenson, Donald Harman, *Half the World from Home: Perspectives on the Irish in New Zealand 1860–1950* (Wellington: Victoria University Press, 1990).

Allen, Walter, *As I Walked Down New Grub Street: Memories of a Writing Life* (London: Heinemann, 1981).

Barker, Nicolas, *The Oxford University Press and the Spread of Learning 1478–1978: An Illustrated History* (Oxford: Clarendon Press, 1978).

Barnett, Correlli, *The Desert Generals*, 2nd edn. (London: George Allen & Unwin, 1983).

Beaglehole, J. C., *The University of New Zealand: An Historical Study* (Auckland: Whitcombe & Tombs Ltd.; London: OUP, for the New Zealand Council for Educational Research, 1937).

Beattie, Herries, *A History of Gore and Surrounding Districts 1862–1962* (Gore: Gore Publishing Co. Ltd., n.d. [1962?]).

Bertram, James, *Dan Davin* (Auckland: OUP, 1983).

Brasch, Charles, *Indirections: A Memoir 1909–1947* (Wellington: OUP, 1980).

Calder, Angus, *The People's War: Britain 1939–45* (London: Jonathan Cape Ltd., 1969).

Carver, Michael, *El Alamein* (London: B. T. Batsford Ltd., 1962).

Cody, J. F., *28 (Maori) Battalion* (Wellington: War History Branch, Department of Internal Affairs, 1959).

Cooper, Artemis, *Cairo in the War 1939–1945* (London: Hamish Hamilton Ltd., 1989).

Cox, Geoffrey, *The Race for Trieste* (London: William Kimber & Co. Ltd., 1977).

—— *A Tale of Two Battles* (London: William Kimber & Co. Ltd., 1987).

Cruickshank, Charles, *Greece 1940–1941* (London: Davis-Poynter Ltd., 1976).

Dallas, Ruth, *Curved Horizon: An Autobiography* (Dunedin: University of Otago Press, 1991).

Davin, W. K., 'A Soldier's Wife', in Lauris Edmond (ed.), with Carolyn Milward, *Women in Wartime: New Zealand Women Tell Their Story* (Wellington: Government Printing Office, 1986), 65–76.

De Guingand, Major-General Sir Francis, *Operation Victory* (London: Hodder & Stoughton, 1947).

Ellis, John, *Cassino: The Hollow Victory: The Battle for Rome January–June 1944* (London: André Deutsch Ltd., 1984).

Ferris, Paul, *Dylan Thomas* (London: Hodder & Stoughton, 1977).

—— *Caitlin: The Life of Caitlin Thomas* (London: Hutchinson, 1993).

Fisher, Barbara, *Joyce Cary Remembered*, compiled and edited by Barbara Fisher, Ulster Editions and Monographs I (Gerrards Cross: Colin Smythe; Totowa, NJ: Barnes & Noble Books, sponsored by the University of Ulster, 1988).

Frame, Janet, *To the Is-Land: An Autobiography* (London: The Women's Press Ltd. in association with Hutchinson Group (NZ) Ltd., 1983).

—— *An Angel at my Table: An Autobiography: Volume Two* (Auckland: Hutchinson Group (NZ) Ltd., 1984).

Fraser, G. S., *A Stranger and Afraid* (Manchester: Carcanet New Press, 1983).

Freyberg, Paul, *Bernard Freyberg, VC: Soldier of Two Nations* (London: Hodder and Stoughton, 1991).

Gallagher, Pat, *The Marist Brothers in New Zealand, Fiji and Samoa, 1876–1976* (Tuakau: New Zealand Marist Brothers' Trust Board, 1976).

Gardiner, Noel 'Wig', *Freyberg's Circus: Reminiscences of a Kiwi Soldier in the North African Campaign of World War II* (Auckland: Ray Richards Publisher in association with William Collins Publisher, 1981).

—— *Bringing Up The Rear: The Sequel to Freyberg's Circus. Further Reminiscences of a Kiwi Soldier* (Auckland: Ray Richards Publisher, 1983).

Hennessy, Peter, *Never Again: Britain, 1945–1951* (London: Jonathan Cape Ltd., 1993).

Hewison, Robert, *Under Siege: Literary Life in London 1939–1945* (London: Weidenfeld & Nicolson, 1977).

Hinsley, F. H., with Thomas, E. E., Ransom, C. F. G., and Knight, R. C., *British Intelligence in the Second World War: Its Influence on Strategy and Operations*, vols. i and ii, and vol. iii, part i (London: HMSO, 1979, 1981, and 1984); vol. iii, part ii, by Hinsley, Thomas, C. A. G. Simkins, and Ransom (1988).

Holcroft, M. H., *Old Invercargill* (Dunedin: John McIndoe, 1976).

Kay, Robin, *Italy*, ii, *From Cassino to Trieste* (Wellington: Historical Publications Branch, Department of Internal Affairs, 1967).

Ker, Neil, 'Kenneth Sisam, 1887–1971', in *Proceedings of the British Academy*, lviii (1972), 3–22.

Kippenberger, Major-General Sir Howard, *Infantry Brigadier* (London: OUP, 1949).

Longmate, Norman, *How We Lived Then: A History of Everyday Life during the Second World War* (London: Hutchinson & Co. Ltd., 1971).

McClymont, W. G., *To Greece* (Wellington: War History Branch, Department of Internal Affairs, 1959).

Macdonald, Charlotte, *A Woman of Good Character: Single Women as Immigrant Settlers in Nineteenth-century New Zealand* (Wellington: Allen & Unwin New Zealand Ltd. and Historical Branch, Department of Internal Affairs, 1990).

McDonald, K. C., *City of Dunedin: A Century of Civic Enterprise* (Dunedin: Dunedin City Corporation, 1965).

Maclaren-Ross, Julian, *Memoirs of the Forties*, with an Introduction by Alan Ross (Harmondsworth: Penguin Books Ltd., 1984).

Milner, Ian, *Intersecting Lines. The Memoirs of Ian Milner*, edited and introduced by Vincent O'Sullivan (Wellington: Victoria University Press, 1993).

Morrell, W. P., *The University of Otago: A Centennial History* (Dunedin: University of Otago Press, 1969).

O'Connor, Ulick, *Biographers and the Art of Biography* (Dublin: Wolfhound Press, 1991).

O'Farrell, Patrick, *Vanished Kingdoms: Irish in Australia and New Zealand: A Personal Excursion* (Kensington, NSW: New South Wales University Press, 1990).

Phillips, N. C., *Italy*, i, *The Sangro to Cassino* (Wellington: War History Branch, Department of Internal Affairs, 1957).

Piekalkiewicz, Janusz, *Cassino: Anatomy of the Battle* (London: Orbis Publishing Ltd., 1980).

Ross, Angus, *23 Battalion* (Wellington: War History Branch, Department of Internal Affairs, 1959).

Scoullar, Lieutenant-Colonel J. L., *Battle for Egypt. The Summer of 1942* (Wellington: War History Branch, Department of Internal Affairs, 1955).

Smith, John Meredith, *Southlanders at Heart* (Invercargill: Craig Printing Co. Ltd., 1988).

Stallworthy, Jon, *Louis MacNeice* (London: Faber and Faber Ltd., 1995).

Sutcliffe, Peter, *The Oxford University Press: An Informal History* (Oxford: OUP, 1978).

Templeton, Malcolm, *Top Hats Are Not Being Taken: A Short History of the New Zealand Legation in Moscow, 1944–1950* (Wellington: New Zealand Institute of International Affairs, in conjunction with the Ministry of External Relations and Trade, 1988).

University of Oxford, *Report of the Committee on the University Press* [the Waldock Report] (Oxford: Supplement no. 7 to the University *Gazette*, vol. c, May 1970).

Whitehead, Kate, *The Third Programme: A Literary History* (Oxford: Clarendon Press, 1989).

CHRONOLOGY OF DAN DAVIN'S
PRINCIPAL PUBLICATIONS

For written material, dates are those of first publication. Republications have been included only for books. Dates for radio and television material are of first transmission. Periodical reviews have been limited to those mentioned in the text. Dates and details of books are in bold.

October 1932	'Francis Thompson's Prose': Otago University *Review*, vol. xlv, pp. 39–41.
11 May 1993	'A Modest Proposal': as Jonathan Sloe, *The Critic*, Otago University, p. 6.
22 June 1933	'A Serious and Useful Scheme for the Benefit of Scholars': ibid. 5.
27 July 1933	'The Aposanctosis': ibid. 7.
5 October 1933	'Some Considerations of the Present Universal Distress, Together with a Simple and Ready Scheme for the Alleviation Thereof': ibid. 8.
October 1933	'Morpheus in mentem': poem in translation, Otago University *Review*, vol. xlvi, p. 28.
17 May 1934	'A Modest Preface': as Simon Bedlam, *The Critic*, p. 4.
7 June 1934	'Graduation Ceremony: Professor Hunter's Address': unsigned lead story, ibid. 1–2.
11 October 1934	'An Apologia for Politics': as Jonathan Sloe, ibid. 6.
October 1934	'Apathy': editorial, Otago University *Review*, vol. xlvii, pp. 3–5.
	'Decadence in English Poetry of the 1890s': ibid. 22–5.
	'A Sweet and Gentle Ballad of Youth': poem, ibid. 38.
19 April 1935	'The compleynt of football': poem, *The Critic*, p. 11.
September 1935	'Prometheus': short story, Otago University *Review*, vol. xlviii, pp. 26–9.
	'Deity'; 'There is about your silence'; 'Sunday'; and 'Standstill': four poems, ibid. 5, 6, and 43.
September 1938	'Exiled'; 'Galway, 1936'; 'The Far-Away Hill'; 'Knowledge'; and 'Harmony': five poems, ibid., vol. li, pp. 20–1.
22 January 1941	'Toby': short story, *Manchester Guardian*.
June 1942	'Under the Bridge': short story, *Penguin New Writing*, no. 13, pp. 30–4.

June 1943	'Night Before Battle': poem, *New Writing & Daylight*, no. 3, p. 163.
September 1943	'Jaundiced': short story, *Life & Letters Today*, vol. 38, no. 72, pp. 132–5.
February 1944	'Hope Against Hope': poem, ibid., vol. 40, no. 78, p. 85.
5 September 1944	'New Zealanders in Italy': radio talk for the BBC Pacific Service.
November 1944	'Danger's Flower': short story, *Selected Writing*, winter, pp. 37–47.
November 1944	'The Vigil': short story, *Good Housekeeping*.
1945	'Bourbons': short story, in Jack Aistrop and Reginald Moore (eds.), *Bugle Blast: An Anthology from the Services*, no. 3, London: George Allen & Unwin, pp. 120–6.
24 April 1945	***Cliffs of Fall*, novel: London: Nicholson & Watson, pp. 188.**
October 1945	'In Transit': short story, *Life & Letters Today*, no. 47, pp. 43–51.
21 June 1946	'Ao Tea Roa: the Long White Cloud': dramatic commentary for BBC radio Home Service for Schools.
1947	***An Introduction to English Literature*, with John Mulgan, Oxford: Clarendon Press. Reprinted 1950, 1952, 1957, 1961, 1964, and 1969.**
27 May 1947	***For The Rest of Our Lives*, novel: London: Nicholson & Watson, pp. 397. Second edition, London: Michael Joseph; Auckland: Blackwood & Janet Paul Ltd., 1965, pp. 416.**
11 June 1947	'From Cartoon to Portrait: James Joyce's *Stephen Hero*': BBC radio review.
7 October 1947	'Tolstoy's *Resurrection*: Ethics and the exploitation of Art': BBC radio review.
November 1947	***The Gorse Blooms Pale*, short story collection: London: Nicholson & Watson, pp. 216.**
March 1948	Review of John Mulgan, *Report on Experience*, in *Landfall*, vol. 2, no. 1, pp. 51–5.
27 April 1948	'Two Catholic Novelists: Evelyn Waugh and Graham Greene': BBC radio review.
27 September 1948	'The New Zealand Writer and his Craft': New Zealand Radio discussion with Frank Sargeson.
[December 1948?]	'A Return': short story, *Arena*, vol. 1, no. 4, n.d., pp. 72–8.
February/March 1949	Review of James Courage, *The Fifth Child*, in *Parson's Packet*, p. 3.

April 1949	*Roads From Home,* novel: London: Michael Joseph. pp. 254. Second edition, edited with an introduction, maps, notes and biographical sketch by Lawrence Jones, in the New Zealand fiction series, Auckland: Auckland University Press and OUP, 1976, pp. 250 + xxxiv.
July 1949	Review of James L. Clifford, Rudolph Kirk, and David Allan Robertson Jr. (eds.), *English Institute Essays 1946,* in the *Review of English Studies,* vol. 25, pp. 281–2.
September 1949	'The Quiet One': short story, *Landfall,* vol. 3, no. 3, pp. 228–40.
October 1949	'Mood Subjective': essay, in *Here and Now,* vol. 1, no. 1, pp. 6–7.
November 1949	Review of Frank Sargeson, *I Saw in my Dream,* in *Here and Now,* vol. 1, no. 2, pp. 29–30.
11 February 1950	Review of Desmond Young, *Rommel,* in *The Economist,* vol. clviii, no. 5555, pp. 314–15.
18 July 1950	'The Contemporary English Novel (7): The Work of Joyce Cary': BBC radio review.
16 February 1951	'Travel Talks. Round the Pacific. No. 5: Sheep Farming on the Plains of Canterbury': dramatic commentary for BBC radio Home Service for Schools.
22 July 1951	With Leonard Cottrell, 'The Battle of Crete': BBC radio documentary drama.
24 August 1951	*TLS,* 'New Zealand Survey'.
29 August 1952	*TLS,* 'The New Zealand Quality': survey article.
September 1952	Review of W. B. Thomas, *Dare to be Free,* in *Landfall,* vol. 6, no. 3, p. 249.
March 1953	With others, 'A Letter to Frank Sargeson', *Landfall,* vol. 7, no. 1, p. 5.
March 1953	'Presents': short story, ibid, 19–25.
1953	'New Zealand Literature': essay in S. H. Steinberg (ed.), *Cassell's Encyclopaedia of Literature,* London: Cassell & Co., p. 380. DMD also collected and edited short biographies of 35 New Zealand writers for inclusion in this work.
1953	*New Zealand Short Stories,* **selected and with an introduction, London: OUP World's Classics series. Reprinted 1954, 1955, 1957, 1961, 1966, and 1970. Reissued as *The Making of a New Zealander,* Short Stories I, Oxford: OUP paperback, 1976; reprinted 1989.** *Katherine Mansfield: Selected Stories,* **selected and with an introduction, London: OUP World's**

	Classics series. Reprinted in 1954, 1955, 1957, 1959, 1961, and 1964. Reissued with chronology and bibliography, World's Classics paperback, 1981.
August 1953	*Crete,* Official History of New Zealand in the Second World War 1939–45, Wellington: War History Branch, Department of Internal Affairs, pp. 547 + xvii.
13 May 1954	'New Writing in New Zealand': lecture at the National Book League.
30 May 1954	'Katherine Mansfield: Expatriate': book review of Anthony Alpers, *Katherine Mansfield*: BBC radio review.
December 1954	'The narrative technique of Frank Sargeson' in Helen Shaw (ed.), *The Puritan and the Waif. A symposium of Critical Essays on the Work of Frank Sargeson,* mimeo, Auckland: H. L. Hofmann, pp. 56–71.
July 1955	'Cultural developments in the Commonwealth': review article for the Central Office of Information.
1956	*The New Zealand Novel,* parts one and two, with W. K. Davin, Wellington: Department of Education, Post-Primary School Bulletin, n.d., vol. 10, nos. 1 and 2, pp. 65.
March 1956	'Winter Galway': poem in *Landfall,* vol. 10, no. 1, p. 11.
March 1956	'Mr. Beckett's Everyman': review in *Irish Writing,* no. 34, pp. 36–9.
14 May 1956	*The Sullen Bell:* novel, London: Michael Joseph, pp. 287.
12 September 1957	'The Time of My Life (5): the Fifties': BBC radio talk.
13 September 1957	With others, 'Tribute to New Zealand': BBC radio programme on 50 years of Dominion status for New Zealand.
31 October 1957	'Cassino': BBC radio forum with General von Senger and D. P. Costello. Broadcast in New Zealand, 23 February 1958.
1958	*English Short Stories of Today,* edited with an introduction, London: OUP for the English Association. Reprinted in 1959, 1961, 1964, 1966, 1969, 1972, 1975, and 1978. Reissued as *The Killing Bottle: Classic English Short Stories,* Oxford: OUP paperback, 1988.
25 April 1958	'Katherine Mansfield in Her Letters': lecture for the New Zealand High Commission at the Royal Empire Society.

5 November 1958	With others, 'Only Yesterday': ATV television programme.
19 January 1959	***No Remittance:* novel, London: Michael Joseph, pp. 224.**
6 February 1959	'New Zealand Day': unscripted interview for BBC radio Pacific service.
[February?] 1959	*Katherine Mansfield in her Letters*, Wellington: Department of Education, Post-Primary School Bulletin no. 20, pp. 24. (Slightly expanded version of the lecture of 25 April 1958.)
March 1959	'Joyce Cary': The Macmillan Brown lecture series given at Otago, Victoria, and Auckland University Colleges.
21 February 1960	With others, 'London Forum—Commonwealth forum—A Brains Trust on the Commonwealth': question and answer BBC radio programme in the General Overseas service.
1961	'New Zealand': essay in Kenneth Bradley (ed.), *The Living Commonwealth*, London: Hutchinson, pp. 185–201.
1961	Review of Thomas Flanagan, *The Irish Novelists 1800–1850* in *The Review of English Studies*, new series, vol. 12, p. 330.
15 December 1961	*TLS* front: 'Attempting the Infinite.' Analysis of the novels of Patrick White on publication of *Riders in the Chariot*.
19 January 1962	*TLS*, review of Janet Frame, *Faces in the Water*, and Pat Booth, *Long Night Among the Stars*.
22 February 1962	'The New Zealand Novel': Lecture to the Royal Society of Arts. *Journal of the Royal Society of Arts*, July 1962, pp. 586–98.
1962	Review of A. L. McLeod, *The Commonwealth Pen: An Introduction to the Literature of the British Commonwealth*, in *The Review of English Studies*, vol. 13, pp. 220–1.
6 March 1962	'Samuel Butler in New Zealand': radio talk for the BBC. Also published in the *Listener*, 22 March 1962.
23 August 1962	'New Zealand and the Common Market': *Time and Tide*.
9 November 1962	*TLS*, review of Patrick White, *The Living and the Dead*.
23 November 1962	*TLS*, review of Janet Frame, *The Edge of the Alphabet*.
5 July 1963	*TLS*, review of Bill Pearson, *Coal Flat*.

2 August 1963	*TLS*, review of Janet Frame, *Scented Gardens for the Blind*.
23 August 1963	*TLS*, review of Maurice Shadbolt, *Summer Fires and Winter Country*, and David Ballantyne, *And the Glory*.
25 February 1964	Obituary of Paddy Costello, *The Times*.
10 August 1964	With others, including Winnie and Brigid Davin, 'The Masters: Joyce Cary': BBC radio portrait.
2 October 1964	*TLS*, review of Patrick White, *The Burnt Ones*.
23 April 1965	*TLS*, review of Maurice Shadbold, *Among the Cinders*, and Maurice Duggan, *Summer in the Gravel Pit*.
18 June 1965	*TLS*, 'A sad and savage world': article on Frank Sargeson.
December 1965	'Autobiographical sketch': in John Wakeman (ed.), *Midcentury Authors*. Republished in John Wakeman (ed.), *World Authors 1950–1970*, New York: the H. W. Wilson Company, 1975, pp. 362–3. (version sighted.)
9 June 1966	*TLS*, review of Patrick White, *The Solid Mandala*.
September 1966	'New Zealand Literature': survey in the National Book League *Journal*, no. 367, pp. 161–3.
June 1967	'Bluff Retrospect': short story in *Landfall*, vol. 21, no. 2, pp. 163–7.
7 December 1967	*TLS*, 'Editor and Author in a University Press': feature article.
April 1968	'Roof of the World': short story, *Malahat Review*, no. 10, pp. 89–95.
December 1968	'Goosey's Gallic War': short story in *Landfall*, vol. 22, no. 4, pp. 387–96.
December 1968	'Goodnight, Julian, Everywhere': memoir in the *London Magazine*, vol. 9, no. 4, pp. 30–48.
March 1969	'First Flight': short story in *Landfall*, vol. 23, no. 1, pp. 12–33.
20 May 1969	With others, 'Battle for Cassino': television documentary for BBC1.
1969	'The Battle for Crete' in A. J. P. Taylor and J. M. Roberts (eds.), *History of the 20th Century* (in 96 weekly parts), London: BPC Publishing Ltd., vol. 4, ch. 64, pp. 1771–3.
16 January 1970	***Not Here, Not Now:* novel, London: Robert Hale & Co.; New Zealand: Whitcombe & Tombs Ltd., pp. 350.**
23 April 1970	Obituary of Enid Starkie, *The Times*.
April/May 1971	'Spoilt [also Spoiled] Priest': memoir in the *London Magazine*, vol. 11, no. 1, pp. 112–29. (Published in

	Closing Times, April 1975, as 'At the end of his Whether'.)
1972	'Preface' in W. R. Rodgers, *Collected Poems*, London: OUP, pp. ix–xxv. A memoir variant of 'Spoilt Priest'.
30 June 1972	**Brides of Price: novel, London: Robert Hale & Co., pp. 254.**
August 1972	'In a Green Grave: Louis MacNeice (1907–1963)': memoir in *Encounter*, pp. 42–9.
5 November 1972	Review of Maurice Shadbolt, *Strangers and Journeys* in the *Observer*.
January 1973	'The Chinese Box: Enid Starkie (1897–1970)': memoir in the *Cornhill Magazine*, no. 1074, pp. 361–84.
9 February 1973	*TLS*, review of Witi Ihimaera, *Pounamu, Pounamu*, and Paula Fox, *The Western Coast*.
June 1973	'Psychological Warfare at Cassino': short story in *Meanjin Quarterly*, vol. 32, no. 2, pp. 133–47.
24 August 1973	*TLS*, review of Michael J. C. Echerno, *Joyce Cary and the Novel of Africa*, and R. W. Noble, *Joyce Cary*.
3 January 1975	*TLS*, review of Maurice Shadbolt, *A Touch of Clay*.
April 1975	**Closing Times, memoirs: London: OUP, pp. 189 + xxii.**
June 1975	'Five Windows Darken: recollections of Joyce Cary': memoir in *Encounter*, pp. 24–33.
25 July 1975	*TLS*, review of Frank Sargeson, *More Than Enough*.
2 October 1975	**Breathing Spaces: short story collection, London: Robert Hale & Co.; New Zealand: Whitcoulls; pp. 221.**
January 1976	'My Language and Myself. English as Creative Power', *The Round Table: The Commonwealth Journal of International Affairs*, no. 261, pp. 19–25.
1976	'The Devil Answers Even in Engines: R. W. Chapman and the Fettercairn Papers': paper read to the Johnson Club.
6 April 1976	With others, 'The Book Programme': BBC2 television.
1976	'Early Reading: The Rime of the Ancient Mariner', in *Education*, Wellington: Department of Education, no. 5, p. 27.
1976	'Freyberg', in Field Marshall Sir Michael Carver (ed.), *The War Lords. Military Commanders of the Twentieth Century*, London: Weidenfeld & Nicolson, pp. 582–95.
16 November 1976	'Snow Upon Fire: A Dance to the Music of Time: Anthony Powell': W. D. Thomas Memorial Lec-

	ture, University College of Swansea. Published, Swansea: University College of Swansea, 1977.
27 June 1977	With others, 'Joyce Cary and his Vision of Life': BBC radio portrait.
October 1977	'Home and Colonial': review of M. M. Mahood, *The Colonial Encounter: A Reading of Six Novels*, in *Essays in Criticism*, vol. xxvii, no. 4, pp. 364–7.
March 1978	'Three Encounters Thirty Years Ago': memoir of Frank Sargeson, *Islands*, vol. 6, no. 3, pp. 302–6.
28 June 1978	After-dinner speech to the Annual Conference of the American Association of University Presses, Baltimore.
18 July 1978	'The Character of Ireland: the book that never was': radio documentary for the BBC. Rebroadcast on 5 June 1979.
1980	'Foreword', in Noel Gardiner, *Freyberg's Circus*, Auckland: Ray Richards with William Collins, pp. 7–8.
1980	'Cairo Cleopatra'; 'Egyptian Madonna'; 'Elegy I'; 'Elegy II'; and 'Grave near Sirte': five poems in Victor Selwyn, Erik de Mauny, Ian Fletcher, G. S. Fraser, and John Waller (eds.), *Return to Oasis*, London: Shepheard-Walwyn with Editions Poetry London for the Salamander Trust, pp. 153–5.
23 August 1980	'The Dog and the Dead': short story, the *New Zealand Listener*.
17 September 1980	'Intimate Strangers': radio interview with James McNeish for Radio New Zealand.
1981	'Freyberg, Bernard Cyril': in *DNB 1961–1970*, edited by E. T. Williams and C. S. Nicholls, Oxford: OUP, pp. 401–5.
1981	'MacNeice (Frederick) Louis': ibid. 709–12.
11 July 1981	'Finders and Losers': short story, the *New Zealand Listener*.
1981	'The Learned Adviser': in P. L. Heyworth (ed.), *Medieval Studies for J. A. W. Bennett, Aetatis Suae LXX*, Oxford: Clarendon Press, pp. 13–19.
1981	Review of Matthew Hodgart, *James Joyce: A Student's Guide*, and Hugh Kenner, *Joyce's Voices*, in *The Review of English Studies*, vol. 32, pp. 479–83.
1981	**Selected Stories, with an introduction, Wellington: VUW Press with Price Milburn & Co.; London: Robert Hale, pp. 319.**
23 October 1981	Obituary of Michael Joseph, *The Times*.
20 November 1981	*TLS*, review of Patrick White, *Flaws in the Glass: a Self Portrait*.

4 December 1981	Review of Walter Allen, *As I Walked Down New Grub Street: Memories of a Writing Life*, in the *New Statesman*.
1982	'Maurice Duggan's *Summer in the Gravel Pit* ' , in Cherry Hankin (ed.), *Critical Essays on the New Zealand Short Story*, Auckland: Heinemann, pp. 150–65.
1982	'When Mum Died': short story in *The Summer Book*, compiled by Bridget Williams and Roy Parsons, Wellington: Port Nicholson Press, pp. 42–56.
6 March 1982	'Coming and Going': short story produced as a play in the Television New Zealand 'loose Enz' series: dramatized by Bill Baer, produced by Tony Isaacs, directed by Murray Reece, and starring David McPhail and Kevin Wilson.
11 March 1982	Obituary of Frank Sargeson, *The Times*.
5 June 1982	Obituary of Sir Arthur Norrington, the *Bookseller*.
9 September 1982	***Night Attack: Short Stories From the Second World War*, edited with an introduction, Oxford: OUP, 1982. Issued as an OUP Paperback, 1984; reprinted 1989.**
1983	Editor, with Victor Selwyn, Erik de Mauny, and Ian Fletcher, *From Oasis Into Italy*, London: Shepheard-Walwyn for the Salamander Oasis Trust. The book includes DMD's 'Eavesdropping at Alamein': a diary extract; and 'Lybian Epitaph': a poem.
8 April 1983	*TLS*, review of Robert Bloom, *The Indeterminate World: A Study of the Novels of Joyce Cary*.
8 April 1983	With others, 'Profile: Dr. Robert Burchfield': BBC radio portrait.
1983	'Norman Davis: The Growth of a Scholar', in Douglas Gray and E. G. Stanley (eds.), *Middle English Studies*, Presented to Norman Davis in Honour of his Seventieth Birthday, Oxford: Clarendon Press, pp. 1–15.
5 November 1983	With others, 'I sing to you Strangers': a television portrait of Dylan Thomas, BBC2.
January 1984	'Cassino Casualty': short story, *Stand Magazine*, vol. 26, no. 1, pp. 8–19; also published in *Islands*, new series, vol. 1, no. 2, November 1984, pp. 105–18.
1984	Review of C. K. Stead, *In the Glass Case: Essays on New Zealand Literature*, in *The Review of English Studies*, vol. 35, pp. 109–12.

22 June 1984	'Dan Davin—a fond estrangement': *Kaleidoscope*. Television New Zealand portrait of DMD, produced by Gillian Ewart, presented by Gordon McLaughlan.
7 December 1984	Radio New Zealand interview by Jan Sinclair.
2 March 1985	'The Albatross': short story in the *New Zealand Listener*.
December 1985	'North of the Sangro': short story, *Stand Magazine*, vol. 26, no. 4, pp. 42–54.
1986	***The Salamander and the Fire. Collected War Stories, with an introduction and glossary, Oxford: OUP paperback, pp. 208 + xx.***
1986	'Park, Sir Keith Rodney' in *DNB 1971–1980*, edited by Lord Blake and C. S. Nicholls, Oxford: OUP, pp. 654–5.
1986	Review of A. Alpers (ed.), *The Stories of Katherine Mansfield*, in *The Review of English Studies*, vol. 37, pp. 595–6.
May 1986	Review of Clement Semmler (ed.), *The War Diaries of Kenneth Slessor*, in *PN Review* 53, vol. 13, no. 3, p.73.
December 1986	'Fancy Dress': short story: the *London Magazine*, vol. 26, nos. 9 and 10, December 1986/January 1987, pp. 22–31.
20 December 1986	'December': a poem in the *New Zealand Listener*.
1987	'Neville Rogers': a note, in *Keats–Shelley Review*, no. 2, pp. viii–x.
29 August 1987	'The Black Stranger': short story in the *New Zealand Listener*.
1988	'The Irish'; 'Infernal Idyll'; 'Day's End': three poems in Robert Welch & Suheil Badi Bushrui (eds.), *Literature and the Art of Creation: Essays and Poems in Honour of A. Norman Jeffares*, Gerrards Cross, Bucks.: Colin Smyth; Totowa, NJ: Barnes & Noble Books, p. 241.
7 January 1989	'Gardens of Exile': short story in the *New Zealand Listener*.

INDEX

Works of literature listed are by Davin unless otherwise indicated.

Cape Town 136, 169–70
Carmichael, Joel 112, 116, 117, 187, 270, 341, 348, 377
Carver, Catharine 348–9
Carver, Field Marshal Lord 350
Cary, Joyce 208, 228–9, 235, 256, 260, 270, 273, 276–7, 282, 348
Cassino 180–5, 191
'Cassino Casualty', short story 375
Cecil, David 231
Charkin, Richard 389
Chidson, Tina 374
Churchill, Sir Winston 238
Clack, Mrs George 266, 339
Clarendon Press 212, 213, 214, 215, 227, 259, 294, 301–2, 308, 310
Clark, G. N. (Sir George) 258, 314
Clark, Les 97
Clark, General Mark 181, 182, 187
Clayton family 46–7, 59
Cleghorn, Tony 177
Clifford, Jim 352
Cliffs of Fall, novel 124, 173, 193–6, 221, 252
Closing Times, memoirs 327, 335, 348–51, 352–4, 360
Coates, Helen 105, 113 n.
Cobb, Richard 116, 134, 229, 256
Cole, John Reece 222, 223, 244
Collins, Michael 324
Colquhoun, Archie 340
Concannon, Ellen and Michael (DMD's aunt and uncle) 8, 13, 24
Concannon, Pat (DMD's cousin) 13, 22
Concannon, Peter (DMD's cousin) 13, 22, 343
Connolly, Cyril 254
Conquest, Robert 256
Copland, R. A. 272, 274
Cornford, John 153
Costello, Bella ('Bil') 154, 174, 321, 365
Costello, Paddy 153–6, 165, 167–8, 172, 177, 182, 198, 208, 219, 235, 236, 259, 262–4, 270, 284, 320–1, 388
    DMD's memoir of 364–7
Cotterall, Bob 39, 104, 124, 242
Cotterall, Richard 104, 124
Cotterill, Maggie, *see* Black, Maggie
Cottrell, Leonard 246
Cox, Geoffrey 52, 54, 124, 125, 128, 131, 134, 153, 155, 157, 179, 187, 190, 219, 239

Craig, Gordon 111–13, 116, 119, 122, 218, 254, 293, 314, 345, 377, 387, 388
Crete 144–50, 342, 369–70, 371
Crete, campaign history 237–8, 241, 244–9
'Crise de Nerfs', short story 125
Crook, Arthur 254, 330, 331
Cuddon(-Large), Rupert 39, 42, 43, 49, 70
Cumberlege, Geoffrey 213, 227–8, 257, 295
Curiel, Henri 156
Curnow, Allen 252
Curry, Colin 172

Darlington, Beth 376
Davenport, John 230, 256, 340
Davin (family name) 3
Davin, Adelina (née McGrath) 53, 104, 230, 344
Davin, Anna (DMD's daughter) 130, 134, 171, 203, 204, 250, 251, 263, 265, 269, 276, 277, 280–1, 284, 287–8, 328, 346, 347, 375, 388–9
Davin, Antonia (DMD's niece) 344
Davin, Brigid, *see* Sandford Smith, Brigid

DAVIN, DANIEL MARCUS
    CAREER/MAIN EVENTS: birth, family background 3–9; childhood 9–34; education 26–44; falls in love with Winnie 49–69; Otago University 45–97; Rhodes Scholar 101–23; marriage 123–4; birth of children 130, 189, 203, 204–5; army 126–98; injuries 148–51, 167; decorations and honours 198–9, 377, 384–5; publisher 18, 204, 210, 257–9, 289–319; retirement 318–19, 359–68; illness and death 373–89; *see also* WRITING *below*
    CHARACTER AND OPINIONS: animals 17–19, 20–1, 129, 209; army officer 130, 132–3, 139–40, 146, 179; autobiography, plans to write 359–61, 371; bohemianism 61–2, 65–6, 71–2, 78–80, 83–6, 89, 153, 179, 196–7, 208–9; 'cold war' 262–3, 322; death, attitude towards 172, 336–7, 376; death of family and

friends 188–9, 192–3, 273–9, 288, 310, 320, 340–1, 373, 378, 386–8; depression 32, 113–14, 117–18, 151, 167, 191–2, 244, 317, 373–4, 378–81; gossip 71, 75, 95, 352–3; holidays 24, 254–6, 300; home ownership 191, 204–6, 285–6, 339–40; hospitality 207–9, 230, 252, 287; illness and injuries 62, 148–51, 161, 259–60, 361–2, 369–73, 380–9; intelligence work 146–7, 152, 163, 164–5, 177–80, 187; Ireland 25, 114–16, 334–5; literary reputation 196, 231–2, 256, 324; NZ literature 224, 231–2, 256, 329–32, 367; OUP career 211–12, 215, 218, 257–9, 301, 305–9, 313–19; OUP projects 226–8, 256, 261, 290–301; outbreak of war 121–7; plants 11–12, 285–6; politics 101–2, 108; pub life 113, 133, 229, 251, 266–9, 339, 368; reading 13, 28, 30, 41, 54, 57, 63, 65–9, 81, 83, 86, 116–17, 131–2, 149, 165, 169, 343; religion 8, 26, 32, 38, 102–5; Rhodes Scholarship candidacy 67, 69, 76, 79, 87, 88–9, 91, 94–6, school 27–9, 39–43; sexuality 31–2, 65–6, 86; sport 116, 127, 199, 270
RELATIONSHIPS: army friends 128, 135, 152–7, 177–80; in Cairo 153–60; with his children 171, 250–1, 269, 280–2, 287–8, 328–9, 345–7, 375, 383, 386–7; at Otago University 48–9, 63, 70–1, 93–4, 252; other women 86–8, 159–61, 169–70, 192–3, 203–4, 206–9, 243, 333–4, 339; at Oxford University 104–13, 116; at Oxford University Press 210–11, 311; with his parents and siblings 12–13, 18–21, 60–1, 103–4, 188–9, 230, 279; schoolfriends 31, 39–40, 104; see also individuals by name
TRAVELS: Australia 343; Cape Town 136, 169–70; Crete 144–50, 342, 369; Egypt 136–7, 150–63, 167–8; Greece 138–43; Ireland 110, 114–16, 232, 300, 334; Israel 348, 354; Italy 117, 118, 176–91; New Zealand 241–4, 282–3, 342–5, 355–6, 377–81; North Africa 164–6; Palestine 166–7; Paris

118–21, 124–5, 342; as undergraduate 113–21; USA 218, 283, 318, 341–2, 345, 356
WRITING: 109, 120–1, 124, 129, 131, 166–7, 193–6, 249–50, 254, 271, 274–5, 323–4, 360–1, 364, 367–9; broadcasting 231, 244, 246, 298, 355, 359, 367, 374; criticism/reviewing 231–2, 242, 329, 330–2, 362, 367; DMD's books reviewed 195–6, 221–3, 226, 234–5, 246–7, 274, 280, 284, 338; DMD's work published 129, 173–4, 193, 218–19, 225, 233, 274, 279, 324–7; editing 226–8, 256, 261, 330, 363, 370; history 232, 237–8, 241, 244–9; lecturing 270, 282–3, 331, 342, 353; letters 64, 65, 67–8, 83, 107, 113–14, 117, 122, 321–2, 328; memoirs 327, 335, 347–54, 359–60, 364–7; novels 24, 109, 173, 193–6, 219, 221, 233–6, 252, 260, 271–80, 283–4, 323–8, 333, 334, 335–9, 346, 360, 379–80; poetry 103–4, 120, 160, 174, 225, 376–7, 383, 384, 387; short stories 102, 125, 129, 137, 193, 207, 225–6, 243, 322, 342, 349, 367, 373, 375–6, 383–4; undergraduate articles 69–70, 82, 91, 103–4; war diaries 136, 137, 142, 144, 147, 148–50, 160–1, 169, 178, 368–9; see also individual titles of published works; Chronology of Publications

Davin, Delia (DMD's daughter) 189, 204, 205, 230, 240, 250, 251, 263, 264, 269, 277, 287, 328–9, 345, 375, 381–2, 383, 386, 388–9
Davin, Evelyn, see Dunlay, Evelyn
Davin, John (DMD's great-uncle) 4
Davin, Julia (DMD's great-aunt) 4, 23
Davin, Martin ('Matt', DMD's brother) 12, 13, 16, 18–19, 21, 25, 68, 188, 283, 344
Davin, Mary (DMD's mother) 6–8, 12, 17, 21, 22–3, 33–4, 58, 188–9, 234
Davin, Mary ('Molly', DMD's sister) 9, 12–13, 19, 129, 175, 188, 242
Davin, Michael (DMD's uncle) 115
Davin, Patrick (DMD's father) 3–11, 17, 20–1, 25–6, 97, 242–3, 279